AMERICAN ISSUES

THIRD EDITION

AMERICAN ISSUES

*A Primary Source Reader
in United States History*

Volume I: To 1877

Edited by

Irwin Unger

New York University

and

Robert R. Tomes

St. John's University

Upper Saddle River, New Jersey 07458

Library of Congress Cataloging-in-Publication Data
American issues : a primary source reader in United States history / edited by Irwin
Unger and Robert R. Tomes.—3rd ed.
   p. cm.
   Contents: v. 1. To 1877—v. 2. Since 1865.
   ISBN 0–13–094017–8 (v. 1).—ISBN 0–13–094018–6 (v. 2)
   1. United States—History—Sources. I. Unger, Irwin. II. Tomes, Robert R.

E173.A745 2002
973—dc21   2001021560

Editor in Chief: Charlyce Jones-Owen
Senior Acquisitions Editor: Charles Cavaliere
Associate Editor: Emsal Hasan
Senior Managing Editor: Jan Stephan
Production Liaison: Fran Russello
Project Manager: Russell Jones (Pine Tree Composition)
Prepress and Manufacturing Buyer: Tricia Kenny
Art Director: Jayne Conte
Cover designer: Bruce Kenselaar
Cover Image: The Library of Congress

This book was set in 10/12 Times Roman by Pine Tree Composition
and was printed and bound by RR Donnelley & Sons Company
The cover was printed by The Lehigh Press, Inc.

 © 2002, 1999, 1994 by Pearson Education, Inc.
Upper Saddle River, New Jersey 07458

Printed in the United States of America

10 9 8 7 6 5 4 3 2

ISBN 0-13-094017-8

Pearson Education Limited, *London*
Pearson Education Australia, Pte. Limited, *Sydney*
Pearson Education Singapore, Pte. Ltd.
Pearson Education North Asia Ltd., *Hong Kong*
Pearson Education Canada, Ltd., *Toronto*
Pearson Educación de Mexico, S.A. de C.V.
Pearson Education—Japan, *Tokyo*
Pearson Education Malaysia, Pte. Ltd.
Pearson Education, Upper Saddle River, *New Jersey*

Brief Contents

Contents

Preface

Americans worry about the state of education in the United States today. Recently we have been told how little students know about science, geography, mathematics, and history; we fear that our country will be unprepared to compete against the other advanced industrial societies in years to come. We are also concerned that the new generation will lack the shared civic knowledge essential for a functioning democratic system.

There is indeed reason to be dismayed by how small a stock of historical information young Americans possess. But it is important also to realize that education is not just transmission of data. It is also the fostering of critical thinking. The most encyclopedic knowledge does students little good if they cannot use it to reach valid and useful conclusions. It is this belief that has inspired *American Issues*. This two-volume work will stimulate critical thinking and active learning about U.S. history—leading students to reject received ideas when appropriate, relate the past to their own experience, and reach conclusions on the basis of evidence. At times, no doubt, students will have to do additional reading beyond this textbook; that, of course, is all to the good.

American Issues is not a compendium of scholars' views. It is constructed out of *primary documents,* the raw material of history. In its pages participants and contemporary observers express their opinions, make their observations, and reach their conclusions about events and issues of their own day that affected the nation and American society. The selections do not point in one direction on any given issue. On the contrary, they were chosen to raise questions and force the student to confront disparity, complexity, and apparent contradiction. *American Issues* avoids giving students the "simple bottom line." Rather, it compels them to grapple with the same ambiguous raw materials that historians process to reach their conclusions. To further the engagement process, each selection asks specific questions of the student. The approach resembles that of the 1950 Japanese movie *Rashomon,* in which an event was depicted from the perspectives of several participants and viewers were expected to reach their own conclusions. That approach, we believe, is an incomparable way to enlighten students about the rich complexity and fullness of historical reality.

We would like to acknowledge the following reviewers of this text: Stephen H. Coe, Eastern Kentucky University; Samuel Crompton, Holyoke Community College; Anthony O. Edmonds, Ball State University; John A. Hall, Albion College; Edward L. Schapsmeier, Illinois State University; Rebecca S. Shoemaker, Indiana State University; and Donald G. Sofchalk, Mankato State University.

The selections in Volume I and Volume II range widely in subject matter across the American past. Besides the key political questions, they deal with the social, cultural, economic, and gender problems our predecessors faced. *American Issues* is guided by the sense that America has always been a heterogeneous society whose inhabitants led their lives in many ways. Yet it does not abandon the view that all of our forebears were also part of the same American experience and shared many concerns of their era.

What can we expect from conscientious use of *American Issues*? No single text can turn a passive human sponge into an active seeker and thinker. But *American Issues* can, we believe, engage college students' natural curiosity and tendency to differ and encourage the habit of critical appraisal. Instructors and students alike will find *American Issues* a stimulating and challenging introduction to informed and discriminating thinking about the American past.

Irwin Unger
Robert R. Tomes

1

The Settlement Enterprise

No one today has to encourage people from other lands to invest their money or their lives in America. Indeed, judging by current immigration pressures, half the world seems eager to share in the "American dream," and some Americans worry that the nation may lose control of its borders and its cultural future under the pressure of newcomers.

But this was not always so. At the very beginning the risks to life and fortune of settlement in North America seemed daunting. And even the supposed advantages often turned out to be false. Europeans were initially ignorant of the climate, resources, and human environment of the New World, and often miscalculated the pros and cons of settlement. And yet somehow the necessary personnel and capital required for successful colonization were forthcoming. How was this result accomplished? What moved people, both literally and figuratively? In any enterprise that involved so many human beings over so long a stretch of time, individual motives were inevitably widely diverse. Still, can you identify the most important factors behind the transfer of capital and people from the Old World to the New?

The documents that follow describe some of the forces that induced people to take their chances on America. Which of the forces depicted, would you suppose, were the most powerful overall? Is it likely that the primary forces varied from colony to colony? Is it possible that they changed over time?

1.1: Richard Hakluyt on the Colonizing of North America (1584)

Richard Hakluyt, a young Anglican minister, was one of many well educated Englishmen who caught "plantation fever" during the reign of

Good Queen Bess (1558–1603). In 1584 he wrote a report, "Discourse of Western Planting," urging Queen Elizabeth to place the human and financial resources of the English nation behind the settlement and exploitation of North America.

It is not easy to penetrate the sixteenth-century English that Hakluyt, like Shakespeare, used. Yet if read carefully, the meaning of the "Discourse" comes through. How would you classify Hakluyt's inducements to establishing colonies? Are they primarily economic? Are the economic motives themselves varied? How important to Hakluyt are the political considerations? What European rival of England does Hakluyt target? Does he play on additional themes besides the political and the economic? Do you know if Hakluyt represents any school of thought during this period regarding the role of the state in economic life?

Why England Should Settle North America

RICHARD HAKLUYT

A brefe collection of certaine reasons to induce her Majestie and the state to take in hande the westerne voyadge and the plantinge there.—Chapter XX. of Hakluyt's Discourse.

1. The soyle yeldeth, and may be made to yelde, all the severall comodities of Europe, and of all kingdomes, domynions, and territories that England tradeth withe, that by trade of marchandize cometh into this realme.

2. The passage thither and home is neither to longe nor to shorte, but easie, and to be made twise in the yere.

3. The passage cutteth not nere the trade of any prince, nor nere any of their contries or territories, and is a safe passage, and not easie to be annoyed by prince or potentate whatsoever.

4. The passage is to be perfourmed at all times of the yere, and in that respecte passeth our trades in the Levant Seas within the Straites of Juberalter, and the trades in the seas within the Kinge of Denmarkes Straite, and the trades to the portes of Norwey and of Russia, &c.; for as in the south weste Straite there is no passage in somer by lacke of windes, so within the other places there is no passage in winter by yse and extreme colde.

5. And where England nowe for certen hundreth yeres last passed, by the peculiar comoditie of wolles, and of later yeres by clothinge of the same, hath raised it selfe from meaner state to greater wealthe and moche higher honour, mighte, and power then before, to the equallinge of the princes of the same to the greatest potentates of this parte of the worlde; it cometh nowe so to passe, that by the great

"England's Title to North America," *Old South Leaflets* (Boston: Directors of the Old South Work, 1902), vol. 5, pp. 444–449.

endevour of the increase of the trade of wolles in Spaine and in the West Indies, nowe daily more and more multiplienge, that the wolles of England, and the clothe made of the same, . . .

6. This enterprise may staye the Spanishe Kinge from flowinge over all the face of that waste firme of America, yf wee seate and plante there in time. . . . And England possessinge the purposed place of plantinge, her Majestie may, by the benefete of the seate, havinge wonne goodd and royall havens, have plentie of excellent trees for mastes, of goodly timber to builde shippes and to make greate navies, of pitche, tarr, hempe, and all thinges incident for a navie royall, and that for no price, and withoute money or request. Howe easie a matter may yt be to this realme, swarminge at this day with valiant youthes, rustinge and hurtfull by lacke of employment, and havinge goodd makers of cable and of all sortes of cordage, and the best and moste connynge shipwrights of the worlde, to be lordes of all those sees, and to spoile Phillipps Indian navye, and to deprive him of yerely passage of his treasure into Europe, and consequently to abate the pride of Spaine and of the supporter of the greate Antechriste of Rome, and to pull him downe in equallitie to his neighbour princes, and consequently to cutt of the common mischefes that come to all Europe by the peculiar aboundaunce of his Indian treasure, and thiss withoute difficultie.

7. This voyadge, albeit it may be accomplished by barke or smallest pynnesse for advise or for a necessitie, yet for the distaunce, for burden and gaine in trade, the marchant will not for profitts sake use it but by shippes of greate burden; so as this realme shall have by that meane shippes of greate burden and of greate strengthe for the defence of this realme, and for the defence of that newe seate, as nede shall require, and withall great increase of perfecte seamen, which great princes in time of warres wante, and which kinde of men are neither nourished in fewe daies nor in fewe yeres.

8. This newe navie of mightie newe stronge shippes, so in trade to that Norumbega and to the coastes there, shall never be subjecte to arreste of any prince or potentate, . . . but shall be alwayes free from that bitter mischeefe, withoute grefe or hazarde to the marchaunte or to the state, and so alwaies readie at the comaundement of the prince with mariners, artillory, armor, and munition, ready to offende and defende as shalbe required.

9. The greate masse of wealthe of the realme imbarqued in the marchantes shippes, caried oute in this newe course, shall not lightly, in so farr distant a course from the coaste of Europe, be driven by windes and tempestes into portes of any forren princes, as the Spanishe shippes of late yeres have bene into our portes of the West Contries, &c.; and so our marchantes in respecte of private state, and of the realme in respecte of a generall safetie from venture of losse, are by this voyadge oute of one greate mischefe.

10. No forren commoditie that comes into England comes withoute payment of custome once, twise, or thrise, before it come into the realme, and so all forren comodities become derer to the subjectes of this realme; and by this course to Norumbega forren princes customes are avoided; and the forren comodities cheapely purchased, they become cheape to the subjectes of England, to the common benefite

of the people, and to the savinge of greate treasure in the realme; whereas nowe the realme becomethe poore by the purchasinge of forreine comodities in so greate a masse at so excessive prices.

11. At the firste traficque with the people of those partes, the subjectes of this realme for many yeres shall chaunge many cheape comodities of these partes for thinges of highe valor there not estemed; and this to the greate inrichinge of the realme, if common use faile not.

12. By the greate plentie of thos regions the marchantes and their factors shall lye there cheape, buye and repaire their shippes cheape, and shall returne at pleasure without staye or restrainte of forreine prince; whereas upon staies and restraintes the marchaunte raiseth his chardge in sale over of his ware; and, buyenge his wares cheape, he may mainteine trade with smalle stocke, and withoute takinge upp money upon interest; and so he shalbe riche and not subjecte to many hazardes, but shalbe able to afforde the comodities for cheape prices to all subjectes of the realme.

13. By makinge of shippes and by preparinge of thinges for the same, by makinge of cables and cordage, by plantinge of vines and olive trees, and by makinge of wyne and oyle, by husbandrie, and by thousandes of thinges there to be done, infinite nombers of the Englishe nation may be set on worke, to the unburdenynge of the realme with many that nowe lyve chardgeable to the state at home.

14. If the sea coste serve for makinge of salte, and the inland for wine, oiles, oranges, lymons, figges, &c., and for makinge of yron, all which with moche more is hoped, withoute sworde drawen, wee shall cutt the combe of the Frenche, of the Spanishe, of the Portingale, and of enemies, and of doubtfull frendes, to the abatinge of their wealthe and force, and to the greater savinge of the wealthe of the realme.

15. The substaunces servinge, wee may oute of those partes receave the masse of wrought wares that nowe wee receave out of Fraunce, Flaunders, Germanye, &c.; and so wee may daunte the pride of some enemies of this realme, or at the leaste in parte purchase those wares, that nowe wee buye derely of the Frenche and Flemynge, better cheap; and in the ende, for the parte that this realme was wonte to receave, dryve them oute of trade to idlenes for the settinge of our people on worke.

16. Wee shall by plantinge there inlarge the glory of the gospell, and from England plante sincere relligion, and provide a safe and a sure place to receave people from all partes of the worlde that are forced to flee for the truthe of Gods worde.

17. If frontier warres there chaunce to aryse, and if thereupon wee shall fortifie, yt will occasion the trayninge upp of our youthe in the discipline of warr, and make a nomber fitt for the service of the warres and for the defence of our people there and at home.

18. The Spaniardes governe in the Indies with all pride and tyranie; and like as when people of contrarie nature at the sea enter into gallies, where men are tied as slaves, all yell and crye with one voice, *Liberta, liberta,* as desirous of libertie and freedome, so no doubte whensoever the Queene of England, a prince of such clemencie, shall seate upon that firme of America, and shalbe reported throughe oute all that tracte to use the naturall people there with all humanitie, curtesie, and

freedome, they will yelde themselves to her governement, and revolte cleane from the Spaniarde, . . . [H]er Majestie and her subjectes may bothe enjoye the treasure of the mynes of golde and silver, and the whole trade and all the gaine of the trade of marchandize, that nowe passeth thither by the Spaniardes onely hande, of all the comodities of Europe; which trade of marchandize onely were of it selfe suffycient (withoute the benefite of the riche myne) to inriche the subjectes, and by customes to fill her Majesties coffers to the full. And if it be highe pollicie to mayneteyne the poore people of this realme in worke, I dare affirme that if the poore people of England were five times so many as they be, yet all mighte by sett on worke in and by workinge lynnen, and suche other thinges of marchandize as the trade into the Indies dothe require.

19. The present shorte trades causeth the maryner to be cast of, and ofte to be idle, and so by povertie to fall to piracie. But this course to Norumbega beinge longer, and . . . so it cutteth of the principal actions of piracie. . . .

20. Many men of excellent wittes and of divers singuler giftes, overthrowen by suertishippe, by sea, or by some folly of youthe, that are not able to live in England, may there be raised againe, and doe their contrie goodd service; and many nedefull uses there may (to greate purpose) require the savinge of greate numbers, that for trifles may otherwise be devoured by the gallowes.

21. Many souldiers and servitours, in the ende of the warres, that mighte be hurt-full to this realme, may there be undladen, to the common profite and quiet of this realme, and to our forreine benefite there, as they may be employed.

22. The frye of the wandringe beggars of England, that growe upp ydly, and hurtefull and burdenous to this realme, may there be unladen, better bredd upp, and may people waste contries to the home and forreine benefite, and to their owne more happy state.

23. If Englande crie oute and affirme, that there is so many in all trades that one cannot live for another, as in all places they doe, this Norumbega (if it be thoughte so goodd) offreth the remedie.

1.2:   John Winthrop Advises Puritans to Emigrate (1629)

John Winthrop was a gentleman of Suffolk in East Anglia, a corner of England where, in the early seventeenth century, many of the people, including Winthrop, were Puritan dissenters against the established Church of England. In 1629 Winthrop and a group of fellow Puritans concluded that the England of Charles I was an inhospitable place for people of their views and circumstances and resolved to emigrate to a portion of North America for which they had secured a royal charter. That year Winthrop circulated the letter below among influential Puritans, explaining why the time to leave England had arrived.

Winthrop was a lawyer, not a clergyman, yet like most Puritans he was intensely devout, a man for whom religion was virtually the core of existence. Does his argument for leaving England emphasize religious reasons? Why should people like him have found the English religious scene so deplorable in 1629? What other arguments for a Puritan exodus does Winthrop make? How do you explain these other arguments?

(In 1630 Winthrop followed his own advice and led the first Puritan contingent to Massachusetts Bay. For the next nineteen years, until his death in 1649, he served the colony successfully as governor and deputy governor.)

Why We Should Leave England

JOHN WINTHROP

Reasons to be considered for justifying the undertakers of the intended plantation in New England and for encouraging such whose hearts God shall move to join with them in it.

1. First, it will be a service to the church of great consequence to carry the gospel into those parts of the world, to help on the coming in of fullness of the Gentiles, and to raise a bulwark against the kingdom of anti-Christ which the Jesuits labor to rear up in those parts.

2. All other churches of Europe are brought to desolation, and our sins, for which the Lord begins already to frown upon us, do threaten us fearfully, and who knows but that God hath provided this place to be a refuge for many whom he means to save out of the general calamity. And seeing the church hath no place left to fly into but the wilderness, what better work can there be than to go before and provide tabernacles and food for her, against she cometh thither?

3. This land grows weary of her inhabitants, so as man who is the most precious of all creatures is here more vile and base than the earth we tread upon, and of less price among us than a horse or a sheep; masters are forced by authority to entertain servants, parents to maintain their own children. All towns complain of the burthen of their poor, though we have taken up many unnecessary, yea unlawful, trades to maintain them. And we use the authority of the law to hinder the increase of people, as urging the execution of the state against cottages and inmates, and thus it is come to pass that children, servants, and neighbors (especially if the[y] be poor) are counted the greatest burthen, which if things were right it would be the chiefest earthly blessing.

4. The whole earth is the Lord's garden, and He hath given it to the sons of men with a general condition, Gen. 1:28, "Increase and multiply, replenish the earth and subdue it," which was again renewed to Noah. The end is double moral and natural: that man might enjoy the fruits of the earth, and God might have his due glory from

Massachusetts Historical Society Proceedings, vol. 8 (1864–65), pp. 420–427.

the creature. Why then should we stand here striving for places of habitation (many men spending as much labor and cost to recover or keep sometimes an acre or two of land as would procure them many hundred as good or better in an other country) and in the meantime suffer a whole continent as fruitful and convenient for the use of man to lie waste without any improvement?

5. We are grown to that height of intemperance in all excess of riot, as no man's estate almost will suffice to keep sail with his equals, and he who fails herein must live in scorn and contempt. Hence it comes that all arts and trades are carried in that deceitful and unrighteous course, as it is almost impossible for a good and upright man to maintain his charge and live comfortably in any of them.

6. The fountains of learning and religion are so corrupted (as beside the unsupportable charge of the education) most children (even the best wits and fairest hopes) are perverted, corrupted, and utterly overthrown by the multitude of evil examples and the licentious government of those seminaries, where men strain at gnats and swallow camels, use all severity for maintenance of capes and other complements, but suffer all ruffian-like fashion and disorder in manners to pass uncontrolled.

7. What can be a better work and more honorable and worthy a Christian than to help raise and support a particular church while it is in the infancy, and to join his forces with such a company of faithful people as by a timely assistance may grow strong and prosper, and for want of it may be put to great hazard, if not wholly ruined.

8. If any such who are known to be godly, and live in wealth and prosperity here, shall forsake all this to join themselves to this church, and to run a hazard with them of a hard and mean condition, it will be an example of great use both for removing the scandal of worldly and sinister respects which is cast upon the adventurers, to give more life to the faith of God's people in their prayers for the plantation, and to encourage others to join the more willingly in it.

9. It appears to be a work of God for the good of His church, in that He hath disposed the hearts of so many of His wise and faithful servants (both ministers and others) not only to approve of the enterprise but to interest themselves in it, some in their persons and estates, others by their serious advice and help otherwise. And all by their prayers for the welfare of it, Amos 3. The Lord revealeth His secrets to His servants the prophets; it is likely He hath some great work in hand which He hath revealed to His prophets among us, whom He hath stirred up to encourage His servants to this plantation, for He doth not use to seduce His people by His own prophets but commits that office to the ministry of false prophets and lying spirits.

Divers objections which have been made against this plantation with their answers and resolutions.

Objection 1:   We have no warrant to enter upon that land which hath been so long possessed by others.

Answer 1:   That which lies common and hath never been replenished or subdued is free to any that will possess and improve it, for God hath given to the sons of men a double right to the earth: there is a natural right and a civil right. The first right was natural when men held the earth in common, every man sowing and feeding where he pleased, and then as men and the cattle increased they appropriated certain parcels of ground by enclosing and peculiar manurance, and this in time gave them a civil right. Such was the right which Ephron the Hittite had in the field of Machpelah, wherein Abraham could not bury a dead corpse without leave, though for the out parts of the country which lay common he dwelt upon them and took the fruit of them at his pleasure. The like did Jacob, which fed his cattle as bold in Hamor's land (for he is said to be the lord of the country) and other places where he came as the native inhabitants themselves. And that in those times and places men accounted nothing their own but that which they had appropriated by their own industry appears plainly by this: that Abimelech's servants in their own country, when they oft contended with Isaac's servants about wells which they had digged, yet never strove for the land wherein they were. So likewise between Jacob and Laban: he would not take a kid of Laban's without his special contract, but he makes no bargain with him for the land where they feed, and it is very probable if the country had not been as free for Jacob as for Laban, that covetous wretch would have made his advantage of it and have upbraided Jacob with it, as he did with his cattle. And for the natives in New England, they enclose no land, neither have any settled habitation, nor any tame cattle to improve the land by, and so have no other but a natural right to those countries. So as if we leave them sufficient for their use, we may lawfully take the rest, there being more than enough for them and us.

Secondly, we shall come in with the good leave of the Natives, who find benefit already by our neighborhood and learn of us to improve part to more use than before they could do the whole. And by this means we come in by valuable purchase, for they have of us that which will yield them more benefit than all the land which we have from them.

Thirdly, God hath consumed the Natives with a great plague in those parts so as there be few inhabitants left.

1.3:   A Cavalier Goes into Exile (1649)

Twenty years after Winthrop and his fellow Puritans first made plans to leave the realm of England, their royalist-Anglican opponents found reasons themselves to consider America a refuge. Between 1629 and 1649 the Roundheads, Puritan followers of parliamentary leader Oliver Cromwell, had defeated the king and his supporters in a bloody civil war and imposed their own political and religious regime on England. In January 1649 the victors tried Charles I for high treason and soon after beheaded him. With the Roundheads in control of England, many royalists, often called Cavaliers, sought a safe haven elsewhere for themselves and their families.

The following document is by a Colonel Norwood who chose Virginia as his refuge. Why did Norwood choose Virginia? Do you know if the Cavalier emigration to that colony had an effect on its social structure or values? Was Virginia settled predominantly by Cavaliers?

A Voyage to Virginia

COLONEL NORWOOD

Time of Setting Out

The month of *August, Anno* 1649, being the time I engag'd to meet my two comrades, Major *Francis Morrison,* and Major *Richard Fox,* at *London,* in order to a full accomplishment of our purpose to seek our fortunes in *Virginia,* (pursuant to our agreement the year before in *Holland*) all parties very punctually appear'd at the time and place assign'd, and were all still in the same mind, fully bent to put in practice what we had so solemnly agreed upon, our inclinations that way being nothing abated, but were rather quicken'd, by the new changes that we saw in the state of things, and that very much for the worse: For if our spirits were somewhat depress'd in contemplation of a barbarous restraint upon the person of our king in the *Isle of Wight;* to what horrors and despairs must our minds be reduc'd at the bloody and bitter stroke of his assassination, at his palace of *Whitehall?*

This unparallel'd butchery made the rebels cast away the scabbards of their swords with both their hands, in full resolution never to let them meet again, either by submission or capitulation; so that the sad prospect of affairs in this juncture, gave such a damp to all the royal party who had resolved to persevere in the principle which engaged them in the war, that a very considerable number of nobility, clergy, and gentry, so circumstanc'd, did fly from their native country, as from a place infected with the plague, and did betake themselves to travel any where to shun so hot a contagion, there being no point on the compass that would not suit with some of our tempers and circumstances, for transportation into foreign lands.

Of the number who chose to steer their course for *America,* such of them as inclin'd to try their fortunes at *Surinam, Barbados, Antigua,* and the *Leeward Islands,* were to be men of the first rate, who wanted not money or credit to balance the expence necessary to the carrying on the sugar works: And this consideration alone was enough to determine our choice for *Virginia,* had we wanted other arguments to engage us in the voyage. The honour I had of being nearly related to Sir *William Barkeley* the governor, was no small incitation to encourage me with a little stock to this adventure: Major *Morrison* had the king's commission to be captain of the fort; and Mr. *Fox* was to share in our good or bad success: But my best cargaroon[1] was his majesty's gracious letter in my favour, which took effect beyond my expectation, because it recommended me (above whatever I had or could deserve) to the governor's particular care.

"A Voyage to Virginia," in Peter Force, ed., vol. 3, no. 10, *Tracts and Other Papers Relating Principally to the Origin, Settlement and Progress of the Colonies in North America,* p. 1844.

[1] A passport, in effect; actually, a sort of bill of lending—ED.

1.4: The Common Folk Come to America (1683)

Both Richard Hakluyt and John Winthrop were promoters of colonies, although Winthrop also emigrated to America himself. But what brought ordinary men and women to the new European settlements? We can assume that the religious factor was important in the founding of some colonies, especially in New England. Obviously politics could also be important, witness Colonel Norwood and Virginia. But were there other motives, especially in the case of the "common sort"?

The following document is an excerpt from a letter of 1683 written by William Penn, the founder of Pennsylvania, to a group of business people interested in trading with his new colony and speculating in its land. Penn had just returned from his first visit to Pennsylvania, and the inducements offered to prospective settlers that he describes were based on his recent experiences.

Penn obviously emphasizes the attractive economic environment for men and women of the laboring class, but he also talks about "younger Brothers of small Inheritances." What is he referring to here? And what sort of people were "Men of universal Spirits"? Why might the American colonies provide the common people with superior economic advantages compared to their native land?

Who Should Go to Pennsylvania?

WILLIAM PENN

IV. These persons that providence seems to have most fitted for Plantations are,

1st. Industrious Husbandmen and Day-Labourers, that are hardly able (with extreme Labour) to maintain their Families and portion their Children.

2dly. Laborious Handicrafts, especially Carpenters, Masons, Smiths, Weavers, Taylors, Tanners, Shoemakers, Shipwrights, etc. where they may be spared or are low in the World: And as they shall want no encouragement, so their Labour is worth more there than here, and there provision cheaper.

3dly. A Plantation seems a fit place for those Ingenious Spirits that being low in the World, are much clogg'd and oppress'd about a Livelihood, for the means of subsisting being easie there, they may have time and opportunity to gratify their inclinations, and thereby improve Science and help Nurseries of people.

4thly. A fourth sort of men to whom a Plantation would be proper, takes in those that are younger Brothers of small Inheritances; yet because they would live in sight of their

Albert Cook Myers, ed., *Narratives of Early Pennsylvania, West Jersey, and Delaware* (New York: Charles Scribner's Sons, 1912), pp. 209–210.

Kindred in some proportion to their Quality, and can't do it without a labour that looks like Farming, their condition is too strait for them; and if married, their Children are often too numerous for the Estate, and are frequently bred up to no Trades, but are a kind of Hangers on or Retainers to the elder Brothers Table and Charity: which is a mischief, as in it self to be lamented, so here to be remedied; For Land they have for next to nothing, which with moderate Labour produces plenty of all things necessary for Life, and such an increase as by Traffique may supply them with all conveniences.

Lastly, There are another sort of persons, not only fit for, but necessary in Plantations, and that is, Men of universal Spirits, that have an eye to the Good of Posterity, and that both understand and delight to promote good Discipline and just Government among a plain and well intending people; such persons may find Room in Colonies for their good Counsel and Contrivance, who are shut out from being of much use or service to great Nations under settl'd Customs: These men deserve much esteem, and would be harken'd to. Doubtless 'twas this (as I observ'd before) that put some of the famous Greeks and Romans upon Transplanting and Regulating Colonies of People in divers parts of the World; whose Names, for giving so great proof of their Wisdom, Virtue, Labour and Constancy, are with Justice honourably delivered down by story to the praise of our own times; though the World, after all its higher pretences of Religion, barbarously errs from their excellent Example.

1.5:   Indentured Servants: Upward Mobility or Deeper Bondage (1622)

Many poor people came to America as "indentured servants." "Indenture" referred to the terms and conditions of service to which they agreed in exchange for transportation to the New World. Situations varied, but harsh conditions usually preceded later manumission. Some servants found themselves in deep bondage, while others ran away to the backwoods or found refuge in Indian lands.

Do the terms of this agreement seem fair or demanding? If the contract was violated, what risks were involved? What forces do you think pushed or pulled people to enter into such arrangements? On which side of the Atlantic did people expect to find greater opportunity?

Servant's Indenture for Transportation to Virginia (September 25, 1622)

To All to Whom these Presents Shall Come Greeting in our Lord God Everlasting.

Know you that I, Wessell Webling, son of Nicholas Webling of London, brewer, for and in consideration that I have been furnished and set out and am to be transported unto Virginia at the costs and charges of Edward Bennett of London, merchant, and

H. R. McIlwaine, ed. *Minutes of the Council and General Court of Colonial Virginia*, pp. 124–125.

his associates, and for and in consideration that they have promised and covenanted to maintain me with sufficient meat, drink, and apparel, do, by these presents, bind myself an apprentice unto the said Edward Bennett for the full term of three years to begin the feast of St. Michael the Archangel next after the date of these presents. And I do promise and bind myself to do and to perform all the said term of my apprenticeship true and faithful service in all such labors and business as the said Edward Bennett or his assigns shall employ me in and to be tractable and obedient as a good servant ought to be in all such things as shall be commanded me by the said Edward Bennett or his assigns in Virginia. And at the end of the said term of three years the said Edward Bennett do promise to give unto the said apprentice a house and 50 acres of land in Virginia to hold to me, my heirs, and assigns forever, according to the custom of land there holden and also shall give to the said apprentice necessary and good apparel and the said apprentice shall inhabit and dwell upon the said land and shall pay yearly for the said fifty acres of land from and after that he shall thereof be possessed unto the said Edward Bennett the yearly rent of 50 shillings sterling forever and two days work yearly and to all and singular the covenants aforesaid on behalf of the said apprentice to be performed and kept in manner and form as aforesaid. The said apprentice binds himself to his said master by these presents. In witness whereof the parties aforesaid to these present indentures have set their hands and seals the 25th of September 1622.

Signet   *Ed. Bennett*

1.6:   Coercion: The West African Slave (1729)

Thousands of the men and women who crossed the Atlantic during the colonial period came to America against their will. Some of these coerced immigrants were from the British Isles: youths kidnapped by unscrupulous ship captains, convicted felons "transported" as seven-year indentured servants, Irish rebels exiled for defying English rule in Ireland. The largest group of these unwilling newcomers by far, however, consisted of men and women plucked by slavers from their homes along the Atlantic coast of the African continent.

The abduction of human beings from Africa for inclusion in the slave trade constitutes one of the darkest chapters in human history. The methods by which individuals were delivered into European custody often pitted African against African, thus plunging the continent into a vicious cycle of intertribal wars, causing divisions that some historians argue have not been healed to this day. Just as slavery transformed the history of the Americas, it also transformed the history of Africa.

Venture Smith, *A Narrative of the Life and Adventures of Venture, A Native of Africa, But Resident Above Sixty Years in the United States of America* (Middletown, CT: J. S. Stewart, 1897), pp. 5–22.

Many thousands of West Africans were brought as slaves to the Western Hemisphere in the sixteenth, seventeenth, and eighteenth centuries. Most were put to work on the sugar plantations of the Caribbean and South America. Relatively few came directly to the British mainland colonies. One who did was Venture Smith, a young man from Guinea who was seized by slavers in 1735 and brought to Connecticut to work as a house servant and farm hand.

Do you think Venture Smith's experiences, as described in the document below, were typical? What was the typical experience of the transplanted African in mainland British North America? Where did most go? What did most do? Do you know if the treatment of slaves on the mainland colonies was more humane than on the Caribbean sugar plantations?

An Eighteenth-Century African Describes His Enslavement

VENTURE SMITH

Chapter I. Containing an Account of His Life, From His Birth to the Time of His Leaving His Native Country.

I was born at Dukandarra, in Guinea, about the year 1729. My father's name was Saungm Furro, Prince of the tribe of Dukandarra. My father had three wives. Polygamy was not uncommon in that country, especially among the rich, as every man was allowed to keep as many wives as he could maintain. By his first wife he had three children. The eldest of them was myself, named by my father, Broteer. The other two were named Cundazo and Soozaduka. My father had two children by his second wife, and one by his third. I descended from a very large, tall and stout race of beings, much larger than the generality of people in other parts of the globe, being commonly considerable above six feet in height, and every way well proportioned.

.   .   .   .

Before I dismiss [my] country, I must first inform my reader what I remember concerning this place. A large river runs through this country in a westerly course. The land for a great way on each side is flat and level, hedged in by a considerable rise in the country at a great distance from it. It scarce ever rains there, yet the land is fertile; great dews fall in the night which refresh the soil. About the latter end of June or first of July, the river begins to rise, and gradually increases until it has inundated the country for a great distance, to the height of seven or eight feet. This brings on a slime which enriches the land surprisingly. When the river has subsided, the natives begin to sow and plant, and the vegetation is exceeding rapid. Near this rich river my guardian's land lay. He possessed, I cannot exactly tell how much, yet this I am certain of respecting it, that he owned an immense tract. He possessed likewise a great many cattle and goats. During my stay with him I was kindly used, and with as much tenderness, for what I saw, as his only son, although I was an entire stranger to him, remote from friends and relatives. The principal occupations of the inhabitants there were the cultivation of the soil and the care of their flocks. They were a people pretty similar in every respect to that of mine, except in their persons, which were not so tall and stout. They appeared to be very kind and friendly. I will now return to my departure from that place.

My father sent a man and horse after me. After settling with my guardian for keeping me, he took me away and went for home. It was then about one year since my mother brought me here. Nothing remarkable occurred to us on our journey until we arrived safe home. I found then that the difference between my parents had been made up previous to their sending for me. On my return, I was received both by my father and mother with great joy and affection, and was once more restored to my paternal dwelling in peace and happiness. I was then about six years old.

Not more than six weeks had passed after my return, before a message was brought by an inhabitant of the place where I lived the preceding year to my father, that that place had been invaded by a numerous army, from a nation not far distant, furnished with musical instruments, and all kinds of arms then in use; that they were instigated by some white nation who equipped and sent them to subdue and possess the country; that his nation had made no preparation for war, having been for a long time in profound peace; that they could not defend themselves against such a formidable train of invaders, and must, therefore, necessarily evacuate their lands to the fierce enemy, and fly to the protection of some chief; and that if he would permit them they would come under his rule and protection when they had to retreat from their own possessions. He was a kind and merciful prince, and therefore consented to these proposals.

He had scarcely returned to his nation with the message before the whole of his people were obliged to retreat from their country and come to my father's dominions. He gave them every privilege and all the protection his government could afford. But they had not been there longer than four days before news came to them that the invaders had laid waste their country, and were coming speedily to destroy them in my father's territories. This affrighted them, and therefore they immediately pushed off to the southward, into the unknown countries there, and were never more heard of.

Two days after their retreat, the report turned out to be but too true. A detachment from the enemy came to my father and informed him that the whole army was encamped not far from his dominions, and would invade the territory and deprive his people of their liberties and rights, if he did not comply with the following terms. These were, to pay them a large sum of money, three hundred fat cattle, and a great number of goats, sheep, asses, etc.

My father told the messenger he would comply rather than that his subjects should be deprived of their rights and privileges, which he was not then in circumstances to defend from so sudden an invasion. Upon turning out those articles, the enemy pledged their faith and honor that they would not attack him. On these he relied, and therefore thought it unnecessary to be on his guard against the enemy. But their pledges of faith and honor proved no better than those of other unprincipled hostile nations, for a few days after, a certain relation of the king came and informed him that the enemy who sent terms of accommodation to him, and received tribute to their satisfaction, yet meditated an attack upon his subjects by surprise, and that probably they would commence their attack in less than one day, and concluded with advising him, as he was not prepared for war, to order a speedy retreat of his family and subjects. He complied with this advice.

The same night which was fixed upon to retreat, my father and his family set off about the break of day. The king and his two younger wives went in one company, and my mother and her children in another. We left our dwellings in succession, and my father's company went on first. We directed our course for a large shrub plain, some distance off, where we intended to conceal ourselves from the approaching enemy, until we could refresh ourselves a little. But we presently found that our retreat was not secure. For having struck up a little fire for the purpose of cooking victuals, the enemy, who happened to be encamped a little distance off, had sent out a scouting party who discovered us by the smoke of the fire, just as we were extinguishing it and about to eat. As soon as we had finished eating, my father discovered the party and immediately began to discharge arrows at them. This was what I first saw, and it alarmed both me and the women, who, being unable to make any resistance, immediately betook ourselves to the tall, thick reeds not far off, and left the old king to fight alone. For some time I beheld him from the reeds defending himself with great courage and firmness, till at last he was obliged to surrender himself into their hands.

They then came to us in the reeds, and the very first salute I had from them was a violent blow on the head with the fore part of a gun, and at the same time a grasp round the neck. I then had a rope put about my neck, as had all the women in the thicket with me, and were immediately led to my father, who was likewise pinioned and haltered for leading. In this condition we were all led to the camp. The women and myself, being submissive, had tolerable treatment from the enemy, while my father was closely interrogated respecting his money, which they knew he must have. But as he gave them no account of it, he was instantly cut and pounded on his body with great inhumanity, that he might be induced by the torture he suffered to make the discovery. All this availed not in the least to make him give up his money, but he despised all the tortures which they inflicted, until the continued exercise and increase of torment obliged him to sink and expire. He thus died without informing his enemies where his money lay. I saw him while he was thus tortured to death. The shocking scene is to this day fresh in my memory, and I have often been overcome while thinking on it. He was a man of remarkable stature. I should judge as much as six feet and six or seven inches high, two feet across the shoulders, and every way well proportioned. He was a man of remarkable strength and resolution, affable, kind and gentle, ruling with equity and moderation.

The army of the enemy was large, I should suppose consisting of about six thousand men. Their leader was called Baukurre. After destroying the old prince, they decamped and immediately marched towards the sea, lying to the west, taking with them myself and the women prisoners. In the march, a scouting party was detached from the main army. To the leader of this party I was made waiter, having to carry his gun, etc. As we were a-scouting, we came across a herd of fat cattle consisting of about thirty in number. These we set upon and immediately wrested from their keepers, and afterwards converted them into food for the army. The enemy had remarkable success in destroying the country wherever they went. For as far as they had penetrated they laid the habitations waste and captured the people. The distance they had now brought me was about four hundred miles. All the march I had very hard tasks imposed on me, which I must perform on pain of punishment. I was obliged to carry on my head a large flat stone used for grinding our corn, weighing, as I should suppose, as much as twenty-five pounds; besides victuals, mat and cooking utensils. Though I was pretty large and stout of my age, yet these burdens were very grievous to me, being only six years and a half old.

We were then come to a place called Malagasco. When we entered the place, we could not see the least appearance of either houses or inhabitants, but on stricter search found that instead of houses above ground they had dens in the sides of hillocks, contiguous to ponds and streams of water. In these we perceived they had all hid themselves, as I suppose they usually did on such occasions. In order to compel them to surrender, the enemy contrived to smoke them out with faggots. These they put to the entrance of the caves and set them on fire. While they were engaged in this business, to their great surprise some of them were desperately wounded with arrows which fell from above on them. This mystery they soon found out. They perceived that the enemy discharged these arrows through holes on the top of the dens directly into the air. Their weight brought them back, point downwards, on their enemies' heads, whilst they were smoking the inhabitants out. The points of their arrows were poisoned, but their enemy had an antidote for it which they instantly applied to the wounded part. The smoke at last obliged the people to give themselves up. They came out of their caves, first spatting the palms of their hands together, and immediately after extended their arms, crossed at their wrists, ready to be bound and pinioned. I should judge that the dens above mentioned were extended about eight feet horizontally into the earth, six feet in height, and as many wide. They were arched overhead and lined with earth, which was of the clay kind and made the surface of their walls firm and smooth.

The invaders then pinioned the prisoners of all ages and sexes indiscriminately, took their flocks and all their effects, and moved on their way towards the sea. On the march, the prisoners were treated with clemency, on account of their being submissive and humble. Having come to the next tribe, the enemy laid siege and immediately took men, women, children, flocks, and all their valuable effects. They then went on to the next district, which was contiguous to the sea, called in Africa, Anamaboo. The enemies' provisions were then almost spent, as well as their strength. The inhabitants, knowing what conduct they had pursued, and what were their present intentions, improved the favorable opportunity, attacked them, and took enemy, prisoners, flocks and all their effects. I was then taken a second time. All of us were then put into the castle and kept for market. On a certain time, I and other prisoners were put on board a canoe, under our master, and rowed away to a vessel belonging to Rhode Island, commanded by Captain Collingwood, and the mate, Thomas Mumford. While we were going to the vessel, our master told us to appear to the best possible advantage for sale. I was bought on board by one Robert-son Mumford, steward of said vessel, for four gallons of rum and a piece of calico, and called VENTURE, on account of his having purchased me with his own private venture. Thus I came by my name. All the slaves that were bought for that vessel's cargo were two hundred and sixty.

2

The British Colonies of North America

After considering why people from the Old World came to America, we should also consider how well they fared once here. In what ways were their lives better or worse? Obviously, their experiences depended on many personal variables, and British North America contained enormous cultural and institutional diversity. Settlers also came with varying skills and resources and often encountered circumstances that were unfamiliar and therefore challenging to them. In addition, colonial leaders and promoters were motivated and informed by a wide variety of aims and ideas.

It is always difficult to generalize from individual cases. Were these typical? Were they exceptional? There was, of course, no Gallup poll in seventeenth-century America, and so we cannot know whether the early settlers were glad or sorry that they had come to the New World. But is there any way we can estimate how most European settlers felt about their decision to cross the Atlantic? What facts can we use to make such an evaluation?

First we shall look at the economic circumstances encountered by four early settlers. What positive and negative experiences do they report? Next, we shall turn to the political institutions of the colonies, to see how these compared to those of the mother country and to explore their reasons for innovation. Then we will look at the important question of religion, to explore the critical issue of tolerance, or lack thereof, and its role in shaping America. Finally, we will also explore the social structure of British North America, to evaluate how traditional matters of class and caste were resolved in the new environment.

2.1: Paradise or Hell: Economic Survival and Opportunity (1609, 1623, 1666, 1725)

Jamestown, Virginia, the first permanent English colony in North America, was founded in May 1607, when three ships arrived from England and set ashore 105 European males on a spit of land near a malarial swamp. The settlement did not thrive, and, especially during the "Starving Time," as the winter of 1609 was known, the settlers suffered terribly from hunger and disease. The selection below (which was actually written in 1624) vividly describes these early afflictions.

Does the document offer clues to why the early Virginia settlers experienced such hardships? Consider the fact that this was one of the first English attempts to establish a permanent colony in America. Also note the reliance on the Native Americans for help. What does this dependence suggest about the competence of this group of Europeans? Did this dependence persist? Or was it a temporary phase in the settlement process?

The Generall Historie of Virginia: The Fourth Booke[1]

JOHN SMITH

To make plaine the True Proceedings of the Historie for 1609.

We must follow the examinations of Doctor Simons, and two learned Orations published by the Companie; with the relation of the Right Honourable the Lord De la Ware.

What happened in the first government after the alteration, in the time of Captaine George Piercie their Governor.

The day before Captaine Smith returned[2] for England with the ships, Captaine Davis arrived in a small Pinace, with some sixteene proper men more: To these were added a company from James towne, under the command of Captaine John Sickelmore alias Ratliffe, to inhabit Point Comfort. Captaine Martin and Captaine West, having lost their boats and neere halfe their men among the Salvages, were returned to James towne; for the Salvages no sooner understood Smith was gone, but they all revolted, and did spoile and murther all they incountered.

Now wee were all constrained to live onely on what Smith had onely for his owne Companie,[3] or the rest had consumed their proportions. And now they had twentie Presidents with all their appurtenances: Master Piercie, our new President, was so sicke hee could neither goe nor stand. But ere all was consumed, Captaine West and Captaine Sickelmore, each with a small ship and thirtie or fortie men well appointed, sought abroad to trade. Sickelmore upon the confidence of Powhatan,[4] with about thirtie others as carelesse as himselfe, were all slaine; onely Jeffrey Shortridge escaped; and Pokahontas the Kings daughter saved a boy called Henry Spilman, that lived many

John Smith, "The Generall Historie of Virginia," Lyon Gardner Tyler, ed., *Narratives of Early Virginia, 1606–1625* (New York: Charles Scribner's Sons, 1930), pp. 294–96.

[1]Footnotes renumbered.
[2]About October 4, 1609.
[3]That is the portion of the settlers retained at Jamestown.
[4]Chief of the Powhatan Confederacy—ED.

yeeres after, by her meanes, amongst the Patawomekes. Powhatan still, as he found meanes, cut off their Boats, denied them trade: so that Captaine West set saile for England. Now we all found the losse of Captaine Smith, yea his greatest maligners could now curse his losse: as for corne provision and contribution from the Salvages, we had nothing but mortall wounds, with clubs and arrowes; as for our Hogs, Hens, Goats, Sheepe, Horse, or what lived, our commanders, officers and Salvages daily consumed them, some small proportions sometimes we tasted, till all was devoured; then swords, armes, pieces, or any thing, wee traded with the Salvages, whose cruell fingers were so oft imbrewed in our blouds, that what by their crueltie, our Governours indiscretion, and the losse of our ships, of five hundred within six moneths after Captaine Smiths departure, there remained not past sixtie men, women and children, most miserable and poore creatures; and those were preserved for the most part, by roots, herbes, acornes, walnuts, berries, now and then a little fish: they that had startch in these extremities, made no small use of it; yea, even the very skinnes of our horses. Nay, so great was our famine, that a Salvage we slew and buried, the poorer sort tooke him up againe and eat him; and so did divers one another boyled and stewed with roots and herbs: And one amongst the rest did kill his wife, powdered[5] her, and had eaten part of her before it was knowne; for which hee was executed, its hee well deserved: now whether shee was better roasted, boyled or carbonado'd, I know not; but of such a dish as powdered wife I never heard of. This was that time, which still to this day[6] we called the starving time; it were too vile to say, and scarce to be beleeved, what we endured: but the occasion was our owne, for want of providence industrie and government, and not the barrennesse and defect of the Countrie, as is generally supposed; for till then in three yeeres, for the numbers were landed us, we had never from England provision sufficient for six moneths, though it seemed by the bils of loading sufficient was sent us, such a glutton is the Sea, and such good fellowes the Mariners; we as little tasted of the great proportion sent us, as they of our want and miseries, yet notwithstanding they ever overswayed and ruled the businesse, though we endured all that is said, and chiefly lived on what this good Countrie naturally afforded. Yet had wee beene even in Paradice it selfe with these Governours, it would not have beene much better withe us; yet there was amongst us, who had they had the government as Captaine Smith appointed, but that they could not maintaine it, would surely have kept us from those extremities of miseries. This in ten daies more, would have supplanted us all with death.

But God that would not this Countrie should be unplanted, sent Sir Thomas Gates, and Sir George Sommers with one hundred and fiftie people most happily preserved by the Bermudas to preserve us: strange it is to say how miraculously they were preserved in a leaking ship, as at large you may reade in the insuing Historie of those Ilands.

The Plaint of an English Bondsman (1623)

The settlement at Jamestown managed to survive, and the Virginia colony as a whole eventually even prospered, especially after the introduction of tobacco culture in 1612. But that did not mean that every

---

[5]Salted.
[6]1624.

settler throve even then. The following selection is a pitiful cry from Richard Ffrethorne, a young man who was brought to Virginia to work as an indentured servant for the planters, probably for the typical period of four years.

As an indentured servant, Ffrethorne had volunteered to come to America. What seems to have gone wrong with his plans? Was his fate the result of bad luck or personal fecklessness? Or did the still primitive, infant society make demands that Europeans found difficult? Do you think his fate was typical of indentured servants in colonial America?

(We do not know if Richard Ffrethorne's plea for rescue was heard by his parents in England, to whom he addressed this letter.)

A Virginia Settler Regrets Coming

RICHARD FFRETHORNE

I have nothing to Comfort me, nor ther is nothing to be gotten here but sicknes, and death, except that one had money to lay out in some thinges for profit; But I have nothing at all, no not a shirt to my backe, but two Ragges nor no Clothes, but one poore suite, nor but one paire of shooes, but one paire of stockins, but one Capp, but two bands, my Cloke is stollen by one of my owne fellowes, and to his dying hower would not tell mee what he did with it but some of my fellows saw him have butter and beife out of a ship, which my Cloke I doubt [not] paid for, so that I have not a penny, nor a penny Worth to helpe me to either spice, or sugar, or strong Waters, without the which one cannot lyve here, for as strong beare in England doth fatten and strengthen them so water here doth wash and weaken theis here, onelie keepe life and soule togeather. but I am not halfe a quarter so strong as I was in England, and all is for want of victualls, for I doe protest unto you, that I have eaten more in a day at home then I have allowed me here for a Weeke. You have given more then my dayes allowance to a beggar at the doore; and if Mr Jackson had not releived me, I should bee in a poore Case, but he like a ffather and shee like a loveing mother doth still helpe me, for when wee goe up to James Towne that is 10 myles of us, there lie all the ships that Come to the land, and there they must deliver their goods, and when wee went up to Towne as it may bee on Moonedaye, at noone, and come there by night, then load the next day by noone, and goe home in the afternoone, and unload, and then away againe in the night, and bee up about midnight, then if it rayned, or blowed never so hard wee must lye in the boate on the water, and have nothing but alitle bread, for when wee go into the boate wee have a loafe allowed to two men, and it is all if we staid there 2 dayes, which is hard, and must lye all that while in the boate, but that Goodman Jackson pityed me & made me a Cabbin to lye in always when I come up, and he would give me some poore Jacks home with me which Comforted mee more then pease, or water gruell. Oh they bee

Susan Myra Kingsbury, ed., *The Records of the Virginia Company of London* (1906) (Washington, DC: U.S. Government Printing Office, 1938), vol. 5, pp. 59, 62.

verie godlie folkes, and love me verie well, and will doe anie thing for me, and he much marvailed that you would send me a servaunt to the Companie, he saith I had beene better knockd on the head, and Indeede so I fynd it now to my greate greife and miserie, and saith, that if you love me you will redeeme me suddenlie, for wch I doe Intreate and begg. . . .

O that you did see may daylie and hourelie sighes, grones, and teares, and thumpes that I afford mine owne brest, and rue and Curse the time of my birth with holy Job. I thought no head had beene able to hold so much water as hath and doth dailie flow from mine eyes, But this is Certaine I never felt the want of ffather and mother till now, but now deare ffrends full well I knowe and rue it although it were too late before I knew it.

A Former Indentured Servant Praises the System (1666)

Clearly not every indentured servant in America found his experience intolerable. George Alsop, who came to Maryland in the 1660s, was one bondsman who considered his years in the colony a rewarding experience, as he states in the following selection. Does Alsop's description seem believable? We today would surely find the restrictions imposed on bond servants galling. But this was an era when many poor men and women were forced to defer to their "betters" and when economic freedom was hedged with harsh restrictions. Note as well that the work from which this excerpt is drawn was addressed to Lord Baltimore, the "Absolute Lord and Proprietary of the Provinces of Mary-Land and Avelon in America." Does this tell us anything about the motives behind Alsop's observations?

A Settler in Maryland Endorses His Experience[1]

GEORGE ALSOP

They whose abilities cannot extend to purchase their own transportation [from England] over into Mary-Land, (and surely he that cannot command so small a sum for so great a matter, his life must needs be mighty low and dejected) I say they may for the debarment of a four years sordid liberty, go over into this Province and there live plentiously well. And what's a four years Servitude to advantage a man all the remainder of his dayes, making his predecessors happy in his sufficient abilities, which he attained to partly by the restrainment of so small a time?

Now those that commit themselves unto the care of the Merchant to carry them over, they need not trouble themselves with any inquisitive search touching their Voyage; for there is such an honest care and provision made for them all the time

Clayton Colman Hall, ed., *Narratives of Early Maryland, 1633–1684* (New York: Charles Scribner's Sons, 1910), pp. 356–59.
[1]Footnotes renumbered.

they remain aboard the Ship, and are sailing over, that they want for nothing that is necessary and convenient.

The Merchant commonly before they go aboard the Ship, or set themselves in any forwardness for their Voyage, has Conditions of Agreements drawn between him and those that by a voluntary consent become his Servants, to serve him, his Heirs or Assigns, according as they in their primitive acquaintance have made their bargain, some two, some three, some four years; and whatever the Master or Servant tyes himself up to here in England by Condition, the Laws of the Province will force a performance of when they come there: Yet here is this Priviledge in it when they arrive, If they dwell not with the Merchant they made their first agreement withall, they may choose whom they will serve their prefixed time with; and after their curiosity has pitcht on one whom they think fit for their turn, and that they may live well withall, the Merchant makes an Assignment of the Indenture over to him whom they of their free will have chosen to be their Master, in the same nature as we here in England (and no otherwise) turn over Covenant Servants or Apprentices from one Master to another. Then let those whose chaps are always breathing forth those filthy dregs of abusive exclamations, which are Lymbeckt from their sottish and preposterous brains, against this Country of Mary-Land, saying, That those which are transported over thither, are sold in open Market for Slaves, and draw in Carts like Horses; which is so damnable an untruth, that if they should search to the very Center of Hell, and enquire for a Lye of the most antient and damned stamp, I confidently believe they could not find one to parallel this: For know, That the Servants here in Mary-Land of all Colonies, distant or remote Plantations, have the least cause to complain, either for strictness of Servitude, want of Provisions, or need of Apparel: Five dayes and a half in the Summer weeks is the alotted time that they work in; and for two months, when the Sun predominates in the highest pitch of his heat, they claim an antient and customary Priviledge, to repose themselves three hours in the day within the house, and this is undeniably granted to them that work in the Fields.

In the Winter time, which lasteth three months (*viz.*) December, January, and February, they do little or no work or imployment, save cutting of wood to make good fires to sit by, unless their Ingenuity will prompt them to hunt the Deer, or Bear, or recreate themselves in Fowling, to slaughter the Swans, Geese, and Turkeys (which this Country affords in a most plentiful manner:) For every Servant has a Gun, Powder and Shot allowed him, to sport him withall on all Holidayes and leasurable times, if he be capable of using it, or be willing to learn.

Now those Servants which come over into this Province, being Artificers, they never (during their Servitude) work in the Fields, or do any other imployment save that which their Handicraft and Mechanick endeavours are capable of putting them upon, and are esteem'd as well by their Masters, as those that imploy them, above measure. He that's a Tradesman here in Mary-Land (though a Servant), lives as well as most common Handicrafts do in London, though they may want something of that Liberty which Freemen have, to go and come at their pleasure; yet if it were rightly understood and considered, what most of the Liberties of the several poor Tradesmen are taken up about, and what a care and trouble attends that thing they call Liberty, which according to the common translation is but Idleness, and (if weighed in the Ballance of a just Reason) will be found to be much heavier and cloggy then the four years restrainment of a Mary-Land Servitude. He that lives in the nature of a Servant in this Province, must serve but four years by the Custom of the Country; and when the expiration of his time speaks him a Freeman, there's a Law in the Province, that enjoyns his Master whom he hath served to give him Fifty Acres of Land, Corn to serve him a whole year, three Sutes of Apparel, with things necessary to them, and Tools to work withall; so that they are no sooner free, but they are ready to set up for themselves, and when once entred, they live passingly well.

The Women that go over into this Province as Servants, have the best luck here as in any place of the world besides; for they are no sooner on shoar, but they are courted into a Copulative Matrimony, which some of them (for aught I know) had they not come to such a Market with their Virginity, might have kept it by them untill it had been mouldy, unless they had let it out by a yearly rent to some of the Inhabitants of Lewknors-lane,[2] or made a Deed of Gift of it to Mother Coney, having only a poor stipend out of it, untill the Gallows or Hospital called them away. Men have not altogether so good luck as Women in this kind, or natural preferment, without they be good Rhetoricians, and well vers'd in the Art of perswasion, then (probably) they may ryvet themselves in the time of their Servitude into the private and reserved favour of their Mistress, if Age speak their Master deficient.

In short, touching the Servants of this Province, they live well in the time of their Service, and by their restrainment in that time, they are made capable of living much better when they come to be free; which in several other parts of the world I have observed, That after some servants have brought their indented and limited time to a just and legal period by Servitude, they have been much more incapable of supporting themselves from sinking into the Gulf of a slavish, poor, fettered, and intangled life, then all the fastness of their prefixed time did involve them in before.

A Well-Blessed Land (1725)

For some Europeans, clearly the move to colonial America was a success. The document below, a letter by an Irish Quaker immigrant to Pennsylvania friends and relatives back home, reflects a happy experience. Why was Robert Parke so pleased with Pennsylvania? Note the date. How long had the colony been settled by the time the letter was written? Might the time factor help explain the positive response? Parke was a free man rather than an indentured servant. Might his status, as compared to Richard Ffrethorne's, have affected how he fared?

[2]A disreputable neighborhood in London.

Pennsylvania Is a Good Country

ROBERT PARKE

Chester Township the—of the 10th Mo. 1725.

Dear Sister Mary Valentine:

This goes with a Salutation of Love to thee, Brother Thomas and the children & in a word to all friends, Relations & well Wishers in Generall as if named, hoping it may find you all in good health, as I with all our family in Generall are in at this present writing & has been since our arival, for we have not had a day's Sickness in the Family Since we came into the Country, blessed be God for it. My father in Particular has not had his health better these ten years than Since he Came here, his ancient age considered. Our Irish Acquaintance in general are well Except Thoe: Lightfoot who Departed this Life at Darby in a Good old age About 4 weeks Since. Thee writes in thy Letter that there was a talk went back to Ireland that we were not Satisfyed in coming here, which was Utterly false: now let this Suffice to Convince you. In the first place he that carried back this Story was an Idle fellow, & one of our Ship-Mates, but not thinking this country Suitable to his Idleness, went back. . . . He is Sort of a Lawyer, or Rather a Lyar as I may term him, therefore I wod not have you give credit to Such false reports for the future, for there is not one of the family but what likes the country very well & wod If we were in Ireland again come here Directly it being the best country for working folk & tradesmen of any in the world. But for Drunkards and Idlers, they cannot live well any where. It is likewise an Extradin. healthy country. . . . Land is of all Prices Even from ten Pounds, to one hundred Pounds a hundred, according to the goodness or else the situation thereof, & Grows dearer every year by Reason of Vast Quantities of People that come here yearly from Several Parts of the world, therefore thee & thy family or any that I wish well I wod desire to make what Speed you can to come here the Sooner the better. We have traveled over a Pretty deal of this country to seek the Land, & [though] we met with many fine Tracts of Land here & there in the country, yet my father being curious & somewhat hard to Please Did not buy any Land until the Second day of 10th mo: Last and then he bought a Tract of Land consisting of & five hundred Acres for which he gave 350 pounds. It is Excellent good land but none cleared, Except about 20 Acres, with a small log house and Orchard Planted, we are going to clear some of it Directly, for our next Sumer's fallow. We might have bought Land much Cheaper but not so much to our Satisfaction. We stayed in Chester 3 months & then we Rented a Place 1 mile from Chester, with a good brick house & 200 Acres of Land for [—] pound a year, where we continue till next May. We have sowed about 200 Acres of wheat & 7 acres of rye this season. We sowed but a bushel on an acre, 3 pecks is Enough on new ground. I am grown an Experienced Plowman & my brother Abell is Learning. Jonathan & thy Son John

Charles A. Hanna, *The Scotch-Irish in North Britain, North Ireland, and North America* (New York: G. P. Putnam's Sons, 1902), pp. 64–67.

drives for us. He is grown a Lusty fellow Since thou Saw him. We have the finest plows here that Can be. We plowed up our Sumer's fallows in May & June, with a Yoak of Oxen & 2 horses & they goe with as much Ease as Double the number in Ireland. We sow our wheat with 2 horses. A boy of 12 or 14 years old Can hold Plow here, a man Comonly holds & Drives himself. They plow an Acre, nay some Plows 2 Acres a day. They sow Wheat & Rye in August or September. We have had a crop of oats, barley & very good flax & hemp, Indian Corn & buckwheat all of our own Sowing & Planting this last summer. We also planted a bushel of white Potatoes Which Cost us 5 Shills. & we had 10 or 12 bushels Increase. This country yields Extraordinary Increase of all sorts of Grain Likewise—for nicholas hooper had of 3 Acres of Land & at most 3 bushels of Seed above 80 bushels Increase so that it is as Plentiful a Country as any Can be if people will be Industrious. . . . All Sorts of Provisions are Extraordinary Plenty in Philadelphia market, where Country people bring in their comodities. Their markets are on 4th day and 7th day. This country abounds in fruit, Scarce an house but has an Apple, Peach & cherry or-chard. As for chestnuts, Wallnuts, & hasel nuts, Strawberrys, Billberrys & Mulber-rys they grow wild in the woods and fields in Vast Quantities. They also make great Preparations against harvest; both Roast & boyled, Cakes & Tarts & Rum, stand at the Lands End, so that they may Eat and Drink at Pleasure. A Reaper has 2 Shills. & 3 pence a day, a mower has 2 Shills. & 6 pence & a pint of Rum beside meat & drink of the best; for no workman works without their Victuals in the bargain throughout the Country. A Laboring man has 18 or 20 pence a day in Winter. The Winters are not so cold as we Expected nor the Sumers so Extreme hot as formerly, for both Sumer and Winter are moderater than they ever were known. In Sumer time they wear nothing but a Shirt Linnen drawers Trousers, which are breeches and stockings all in one made of Linnen; they are fine Cool wear in Sumer. As to what thee writt about the Governours Opening Letters it is Utterly false & nothing but a Lye & any one Except bound Servants may go out of the Country when they will & Servants when they Serve their time may Come away If they please but it is rare any are such fools to leave the Country Except men's business require it. They pay 9 Pounds for their Passage (of this money) to go to Ireland. There is 2 fairs, yearly & 2 markets weekly in Philadelphia also 2 fairs yearly in Chester & Likewise in new castle, but they Sell no Cattle nor horses, no living Creatures, but altogether Merchant's Goods, as hatts, Linnen & woolen Cloth, handkerchiefs, knives, Scizars, tapes & treds buckels, Ribonds & all Sorts of necessarys fit for our wooden Country & here all young men and women that wants wives or husbands may be Supplyed. Lett this Suffice for our fairs. As to meetings they are so plenty one may ride to their choice. I desire thee to bring or Send me a bottle of good Oyle fit for guns, thee may buy it in Dublin. . . . Dear Sister I wod not have thee Doupt the truth of what I write, for I know it to be true Tho I have not been long here. I wod have you Cloath yourselves well with Woolen & Linnen, Shoes & Stockings & hats for Such things are dear hear, & yet a man will Sooner Earn a suit of Cloths here than in Ireland, by Reason workman's Labour is so Dear. . . . I wod have you bring for your own Use 2 or 3 good falling Axes, a pair of beetle rings & 3 Iron wedges, for they are of good Service here. Your Plow Irons will not answer here, therefore you had better bring 1 or 2 hundred Iron. You may bring your Plow Chains as they are also a good—Iron. . . . Dear Sister I desire thee may tell my old friend Samuel Thornton that he could give so much credit to my words & find no Iffs nor ands in my Letter, that in Plain terms he could not do better than to Come here, for both his & his wife's trade are Very good here. The best way for him to do is to pay what money he Can Conveniently Spare at that side & Engage himself to Pay the rest at this Side & when he Comes here if he Can get no friend to lay down the money for him, when it Comes to the worst, he may hire out 2 or 3 children. & I wod have him Cloath his family as well as his Small Ability will allow. Thee may tell him what things are proper to bring with him both for his Sea Store & for his Use in this Country. I wod have him Procure 3 or 4 Lusty Servants & Agree to pay their passage at this Side he might sell 2 & pay the others' passage with the money. I fear my good will to him will be of Little Effect by reason he is So hard of beleif, but thou mayest Assure him from me that if I had not a particular Respect for him & his family I Should not have writ so much for his Encouragement.

2.2:   The Political Economy: Old Regime or Innovation? (1624, 1629, 1663)

What political and legal innovations resulted from the creation of colonies? The original charters and laws of the colonies are clearly products of the seventeenth century, but novel circumstances led to inevitable deviation from British practice over time. In short, the founders of colonies usually intended to replicate British political institutions, but a new environment and the sizable geographic separation of the colonies from the mother country led to divergence. The first document in this section, The Ordinance for Virginia (1624) reflects this dilemma. Which principles of British political theory can easily be discerned in its early sections? What innovations can be implied in the "second council" labeled "The General Assembly"? What circumstances necessitated this invention? Most importantly, what legal prescriptions are made relating lawmaking in the colony to the mother country? What long-range implications would these be likely to have?

The second document, while Dutch in origin, exemplifies legal precedent established in most British colonies—that of endowing certain individuals with exceptional property rights and/or other principles that may be described as aristocratic. How do the legal status and property standings of the "patroons" re-create conditions of Europe's ancient regime? Do these conditions seem more medieval than modern to you? If so, how? In addition to advantages of property, what other privileges did this colonial elite enjoy? Can you identify examples in other colonies where similar privileges were legalized by charters?

Finally, although each colony had its own unique charter that led to political particularism and variety, the Navigation Acts did attempt to impose a certain degree of unity or cohesion on the system. The third selection is from the Navigation Act of 1663. What political assumptions about the relationship of colonies to the mother country lay behind this act? Remember, these acts were designed to "regulate" trade and commerce. What economic assumptions do they reveal? Does the system seem readily transferable from theory into practice? Which specific provisions of the act do you find most interesting? Why?

After reading all three sections, how would you describe the legal framework of the colonies? If they were an attempt to reassert royal authority and feudal traditions, what loopholes could possibly undermine these intentions? Why might it have been difficult for the Crown to maintain its traditional prerogatives in the New World?

Ordinance for Virginia
(July 24, 1621)

An ordinance and Constitution of the Treasurer, Council, and Company in England, for a Council of State and General Assembly. Dated July 24, 1621.

To all People, to whom these Presents shall come, be seen, or heard The Treasurer, Council, and Company of Adventurers and Planters for the City of *London* for the first colony of *Virginia,* send Greeting. Know ye that we, the said Treasurer, Council, and Company, taking into our careful Consideration the present State, of the said Colony of *Virginia,* and intending, by the Divine Assistance, to settle such a Form of Government there as may be to the greatest Benefit and Comfort of the People, and whereby all Injustice, Grievances, and Oppression may be prevented and kept off as much as possible from the said Colony, have thought fit to make our Entrance, by ordering and establishing such Supreme Councils, as may not only be assisting to the Governor for the time being, in the Administration of Justice, and the executing of other Duties for this office belonging, but also, by their vigilant care and Prudence, may provide, as well for a Remedy of all Inconveniences, growing from time to time, as also for advancing of Increase, Strength, Stability, and Prosperity of the said Colony:

II. We therefore, the said Treasurer, Council, and Company, by Authority directed to us from his Majesty under the Great Seal, upon mature Deliberation, do hereby order and declare, that, from hence forward, there shall be Two SUPREME COUNCILS in *Virginia,* for the better Government of the said Colony aforesaid.

III. The one of which Councils, to be called THE COUNCIL OF STATE (and whose Office shall chiefly be assisting, with their Care, Advise, and Circumspection, to the said Governor) shall be chosen, nominated, placed and displaced, from time to time,

F. N. Thorpe, ed., *Federal and State Constitutions,* Vol. VII, p. 3810 ff.

by Us, the said Treasurer, Council, and Company, and our Successors: Which Council of State shall consist, for the present, only of these Persons, as are here inserted, *viz.* Sir *Francis Wyat,* Governor of *Virginia,* Captain *Francis West,* Sir *George Yeardley,* Knight, Sir *William Neuce,* Knight Marshal of *Virginia,* Mr. *George Sandys,* Treasurer, Mr. *George Thorpe,* Deputy of the College, Captain *Thomas Neuce,* Deputy for the Company, Mr. *Pawlet,* Mr. *Leech,* Captain *Nathaniel Powel,* Mr. *Harwood,* Mr. *Samuel Macock,* Mr. *Christopher Davison,* Secretary, *Doctor Pots* Physician to the Company, Mr. *Roger Smith,* Mr. *John Berkley,* Mr. *John Rolfe,* Mr. *Ralph Hamer,* Mr. *John Pountis,* Mr. *Michael Lapworth.* Which said Counsellors and Council we earnestly pray and desire, and in his Majesty's Name strictly charge and command, that (all Factions, Partialities, and sinister Respect laid aside) they bend their Care and Endeavors to assist the said Governor; first and principally in the Advancement of the Honour and Service of God, and the Enlargement of his Kingdom amongst the Heathen People; and next, in erecting of the said Colony in due obedience to his Majesty, and all lawful Authority from his Majesty's Directions; and lastly, in maintaining the said People in Justice and *Christian* Conversation amongst themselves, and in Strength and Ability to withstand their Enemies. And this Council, to be always, or for the most Part, residing about or near the Governor.

IV. The other Council, more generally to be called by the Governor, once yearly, and no oftener, but for very extraordinary and important occasions, shall consist, for the present, of the said Council of State, and of two Burgesses out of every Town, Hundred, or other particular Plantation, to be respectively chosen by the Inhabitants; Which Council shall be called THE GENERAL ASSEMBLY, wherein (as also in the said Council of State) all Matter shall be decided, determined, and ordered, by the greater Part of the Voices then present; reserving to the Governor always a Negative Voice. And this General Assembly shall have free Power to treat, consult, and conclude, as well of all emergent Occasions concerning the Publick Weal of the said Colony and every Part thereof, as also to make, ordain, and enact such general Laws and Orders, for the Behoof of the said Colony, and the good Government thereof, as shall, from time to time, appear necessary or requisite;

V. Whereas in all other Things, we require the said General Assembly, as also the said Council of State, to imitate and follow the Policy of the Form of Government—Laws, Customs, and Manner of Trial, and other Administration of Justice, used in the Realm of *England,* as near as may be, even as ourselves, by his Majesty's Letters Patent, are required.

VI. Provided, that no Law or Ordinance, made in the said General Assembly, shall be or continue in Force or Validity, unless the same shall be solemnly ratified and confirmed, in a General Quarter Court of the said Company here in England and so ratified, be returned to them under our Seal; It being our Intent to afford the like Measure also unto the said Colony, that after the Government of the said Colony shall once have been well framed, and settled accordingly, which is to be done by Us, as by Authority derived from his Majesty, and the same shall have been so by Us declared, no Orders of Court afterwards shall bind the said Colony, unless they be ratified in like Manner in the General Assemblies. IN WITNESS whereof we have here unto set our Common Seal, the 24th of *July* 1621, and in the Year of the Reign of our Sovereign Lord, JAMES, King of *England,* &c., the —— and of Scotland the ——

Charter of Freedoms and Exemptions to Patroons
(June 7, 1629)

III. All such shall be acknowledged Patroons of New Netherland who shall, within the space of four years next after they have given notice to any of the Chambers of the Company here, or to the Commander or Council there, undertake to plant a Colonie there of fifty souls, upwards of fifteen years old; one-fourth part within one year, and within three years after the sending of the first, making together four years, the remainder, to the full number of fifty persons . . . ; but it is to be observed that the Company reserve the Island of the Manhattes to themselves.

IV. They shall, from the time they make known the situation of the places where they propose to settle Colonies, have the preference to all others of the absolute property of such lands as they have there chosen; but in case the situation should not afterwards please them, or they should have been mistaken as to the quality of the land, they may, after remonstrating concerning the same to the Commander and Council there, be at liberty to choose another place.

V. The Patroons, by virtue of their power, shall and may be permitted, at such places as they shall settle their Colonies, to extend their limits four leagues along the shore, that is, on one side of a navigable river, or two leagues on each side of a river, and so far into the country as the situation of the occupiers will permit; provided and conditioned that the Company keep to themselves the lands lying and remaining between the limits of Colonies, to dispose thereof, when and at such time as they shall think proper, in such manner that no person shall be allowed to come within seven or eight leagues of them without their consent, unless the situation of the land thereabout be such that the Commander and Council, for good reasons, should order otherwise. . . .

VI. They shall forever possess and enjoy all the lands lying within the aforesaid limits, together with the fruits, rights, minerals, rivers and fountains thereof; as also the chief command and lower jurisdictions, fishing, fowling and grinding, to the exclusion of all others, to be holden from the Company as a perpetual inheritance, without it ever devolving again to the Company, and in case it should devolve, to be redeemed and repossessed with twenty guilders per Colonie, to be paid to this Company, at the Chamber here or to their Commander there, within a year and six weeks after the same occurs, each at the Chamber where he originally sailed from; and further, no person or persons whatsoever shall be privileged to fish and hunt but the Patroons and such as they shall permit. And in case any one should in time prosper so much as to found one or more cities, he shall have power and authority to estab-

E. B. O'Callaghan, ed., *Documents Relative to the Colonial History of the State of New York,* Vol. II, p. 553 ff.

lish officers and magistrates there, and to make use of the title of his Colonie, according to his pleasure and to the quality of the persons. . . .

X. The Patroons and colonists shall be privileged to send their people and effects thither, in ships belonging to the Company, provided they take the oath, and pay to the Company for bringing over the people, as mentioned in the first article. . . .

XII. Inasmuch as it is intended to people the Island of the Manhattes first, all fruits and wares that are produced on the lands situate on the North river, and lying thereabout, shall, for the present, be brought there before being sent elsewhere, . . .

XIII. All the Patroons of Colonies in New Netherland, and of Colonies on the Island of Manhattes, shall be at liberty to sail and traffic all along the coast, from Florida to Terra Neuf, provided that they do again return with all such goods as they shall get in trade to the Island of Manhattes, and pay five per cent duty to the Company, in order, if possible, that, after the necessary inventory of the goods shipped be taken, the same may be sent hither. . . .

XV. It shall be also free for the aforesaid Patroons to traffic and trade all along the coast of New Netherland and places circumjacent, with such goods as are consumed there, and receive in return for them all sorts of merchandise that may be had there, except beavers, otters, minks, and all sorts of peltry, which trade the Company reserve to themselves. But the same shall be permitted at such places where the Company have no factories, conditioned that such traders shall be obliged to bring all the peltry they can procure to the Island of Manhattes, in case it may be, at any rate, practicable, and there deliver to the Director, to be by him shipped hither with the ships and goods; or, if they should come here without going there, then to give notice thereof to the Company, that a proper account thereof may be taken, in order that they may pay to the Company one guilder for each merchantable beaver and otter skin; the property, risk and all other charges remaining on account of the Patroons or owners.

XVI. All coarse wares that the Colonists of the Patroons there shall consume, such as pitch, tar, weed-ashes, wood, grain, fish, salt, hearthstone and such like things shall be conveyed in the Company's ships, at the rate of eighteen guilders per last. . . .

XVIII. The Company promises the colonists of the Patroons that they shall be free from customs, taxes, excise, imposts or any other contributions for the space of ten years; and after the expiration of the said ten years, at the highest, such customs as the goods pay here for the present. . . .

XX. From all judgments given by the Courts of the Patroons for upwards of fifty guilders, there may be an appeal to the Company's Commander and Council in New Netherland.

XXI. In regard to such private persons as on their own account, . . . shall be inclined to go thither and settle, they shall, with the approbation of the Director and Council there, be at liberty to take up and take possession of as much land as they shall be able properly to improve, . . .

XXIII. Whosoever, whether colonists of Patroons for their Patroons, or free persons for themselves, or others for their masters, shall discover any shores, bays or other fit places for erecting fisheries, or the making of salt ponds, they may take possession thereof, and begin to work on them as their own absolute property, to the exclusion of all others. And it is consented to that the Patroons of colonists may send ships along the coast of New Netherland, on the cod fishery, . . .

XXVI. Whoever shall settle any Colonie out of the limits of the Manhattes Island, shall be obliged to satisfy the Indians for the land they shall settle upon, and they may extend or enlarge the limits of their Colonies if they settle a proportionate number of colonists thereon.

XXVII. The Patroons and colonists shall in particular, and in the speediest manner, endeavor to find out ways and means whereby they may support a Minister and Schoolmaster, that thus the service of God and zeal for religion may not grow cool and be neglected among them, and they shall, for the first, procure a Comforter of the sick there. . . .

XXIX. The Colonists shall not be permitted to make any woolen, linen or cotton cloth, nor weave any other stuffs there, on pain of being banished, and as perjurers, to be arbitrarily punished.

XXX. The Company will use their endeavors to supply the colonists with as many Blacks as they conveniently can, on the conditions hereafter to be made, in such manner, however, that they shall not be bound to do it for a longer time than they shall think proper.

XXXI. The Company promise to finish the fort on the Island of the Manhattes, and to put it in a posture of defence without delay.

The Navigation Act of 1663

V. And in regard his Majesty's plantations beyond the seas are inhabited and peopled by his subjects of this his kingdom of England; for the maintaining a greater correspondence and kindness between them, and keeping them in a firmer dependence upon it, and rendering them yet more beneficial and advantageous unto it in the further employment and increase of English shipping and seamen, vent of English woollen and other manufactures and commodities, rendering the navigation to and from the same more safe and cheap, and making this kingdom a staple, not only of the commodities of those plantations, but also of the commodities of other countries and places, for the supplying of them; and it being the usage of other nations to keep their plantations trade to themselves.

VI. Be it enacted, and it is hereby enacted, that from and after the five and twentieth day of March one thousand six hundred sixty-four, no commodity of the growth, production, or manufacture of Europe shall be imported into any land, island, plantation, colony, territory, or place to his Majesty belonging, or which shall hereafter belong unto or be in the possession of his Majesty, his heirs and successors, in Asia, Africa, or America (Tangier only excepted) but what shall be *bona fide,* and without fraud, laden and shipped in England, Wales, or the town of Berwick upon Tweed, and in English built shipping . . . ; and whereof the master and three fourths of the mariners at least are English, and which shall be carried directly thence to the said lands, islands, plantations, colonies, territories, or places, and from no other place or places whatsoever; any law, statute, or usage to the contrary notwithstanding;

Statutes at Large, adapted from Pickering (ed.), pp. 243–4.

(2) under the penalty of the loss of all such commodities of the growth, production, or manufacture of Europe, as shall be imported into any of them from any other place whatsoever, by land or water; and if by water, of the ship or vessel also in which they were imported, with all her guns, tackle, furniture, ammunition, and apparel; one third part to his Majesty, his heirs and successors; one third part to the governor of such land, island, plantation, colony, territory, or place, into which such goods were imported, if the said ship, vessel, or goods be there seized or informed against and sued for; or otherwise that third part also to his Majesty, his heirs and successors; and the other third part to him or them who shall seize, inform, or sue for the same in any of his Majesty's courts in such of the said lands, islands, colonies, plantations, territories, or places where the offence was committed, or in any court of record in England, by bill, information, plaint, or other action, wherein no essoin, protection, or wager of law shall be allowed.

VII. Provided always, and be it hereby enacted by the authority aforesaid, that it shall and may be lawful to ship and lade in such ships, and so navigated, as in the foregoing clause is set down and expressed, in any part of Europe, salt for the fisheries of New England and Newfoundland, and to ship and lade in the Madeira's wines of the growth thereof, and to ship and lade in the Western islands of Azores wines of the growth of the said islands, and to ship and take in servants or horses in Scotland or Ireland, and to ship or lade in Scotland all sorts of victual of the growth or production of Scotland, and to ship or lade in Ireland all sorts of victual of the growth or production of Ireland, and the same to transport into any of the said lands, islands, plantations, colonies, territories, or places; anything in the foregoing clause to the contrary in any wise notwithstanding.

VIII. And for the better prevention of frauds, be it enacted and it is hereby enacted, that from and after the five and twentieth day of March one thousand six hundred sixty and four, every person or persons importing by land any goods or commodities whatsoever into any the said lands, islands, plantations, colonies, territories, or places, shall deliver to the governor of such land, island, plantation, colony, territory, or place, or to such person or officer as shall be by him thereunto authorized and appointed, within four and twenty hours after such importation, his and their names and surnames, and a true inventory and particular of all such goods or commodities; (2) and no ship or vessel coming to any such land, island, plantation, colony, territory, or place, shall lade or unlade any goods or commodities whatsoever, until the master or commander of such ship or vessel shall first have made known to the governor of such land, island, plantation, colony, territory, or place, or such other person or officer as shall be by him thereunto authorized and appointed, the arrival of the said ship or vessel, with her name, and the name and surname of her master or commander, and have shown to him that she is an English built ship, or made good by producing such certificate, as abovesaid, that she is a ship or vessel *bona fide* belonging to England, Wales, or the town of Berwick, and navigated with an English master, and three fourth parts of the mariners at least Englishmen, and have delivered to such governor or other person or officer a true and perfect inventory or invoice of her lading, together with the place or places in which the said goods were laden or taken into the said ship or vessel. . . .

2.3: Religious Toleration (1636, 1677, 1661, 1644, 1782)

America's role as refuge for victims of religious persecution is a historical commonplace. Puritans, Quakers, Baptists, German Pietists, Catholics, Jews, and others fled from Europe to the New World during the colonial period to escape religious persecution and find freedom to worship as they wished. But was their quest successful? Was America a safe haven for those persecuted for religion's sake? Did the religious refugees find the freedom they sought?

Clearly religious outsiders from Europe who established their own colonies found genuine sanctuary. Orthodox Puritans were safe in Massachusetts; Quakers were not penalized in Pennsylvania. But what about the others? Did the American colonies as a whole provide room for religious diversity? Or did they prove to be just as intolerant as Europe toward those who did not conform to the local majority? Was colonial America generally, then, a religiously tolerant community?

The original Puritan leaders of Massahusetts Bay had little use for the toleration of religious views deemed heretical. In the first selection, one of the earliest Puritan leaders, John Cotton, explains how the religious community should be defined and why its laws must be enforced. The second selection provides an example of a law passed to translate this vision into reality. But not all agreed. In the third example, Roger Williams presents arguments quite contrary to Cotton's. Williams supported religious toleration quite vehemently. The final selection, by Crévecoeur, presents a rather more casual observation as to how over time conflicts may have ocasionally been resolved. In what areas of public debate do these arguments echo today? Are the principles similar?

God Did Not Ordain Democracy Fit for Church or Commonwealth (1636)

JOHN COTTON

It is very suitable to Gods all-sufficient wisdom, and to the fullness and perfection of Holy Scriptures, not only to prescribe perfect rules for the right ordering of a private mans soul to everlasting blessedness with himself, but also for the right ordering of a mans family, yea, of the commonwealth too, so far as both of them are

"God Did Not Ordain Democracy Fit for Church or Commonwealth," John Cotton, 1636. Reprinted from Samuel L. Caldwell, ed., *Publications of the Narragansett Club* (Providence, RI, 1867). Series 1, Volume III.

subordinate to spiritual ends, and yet avoid both the churches usurpation upon civil jurisdictions, *in ordine and spiritualia,* and the commonwealths invasion upon ecclesiastical administrations, *in ordine* to civil peace, and conformity to the civil state. Gods institutions (such as the government of church and of commonwealth be) may be close and compact, and co-ordinate one to another, and yet not confounded. God hath so framed the state of church government and ordinances, that they may be compatible to any commonwealth, though never so much disordered in his frame. But yet when a commonwealth hath liberty to mold his own frame (*scriptura plenitudinem adoro*) I conceive the Scripture hath given full direction for the right ordering of the same, and that, in such sort as may best maintain the *euexia* of the church. Mr. Hooker doth often quote a saying out of Mr. Cartwright (though I have not read it in him) that no man fashioneth his house to his hangings, but his hangings to his house. It is better that the commonwealth be fashioned to the setting forth of Gods house, which is his church: than to accommodate the church frame to the civil state. Democracy, I do not conceive that ever God did ordain as a fit government either for church or commonwealth. If the people be governors, who shall be governed? As for monarchy, and aristocracy, they are both of them clearly approved, and directed in Scripture, yet so as referreth the sovereignty to himself, and setteth up Theocracy in both, as the best form of government in the commonwealth, as well as in the church.

The law, which your Lordship instanceth in [that none shall be chosen to magistracy among us, but a church member] was made and enacted before I came into the country; but I have hitherto wanted sufficient light to plead against it. The rule that directeth the choice of supreme governors, is of like equity and weight in all magistrates, that one of their brethren (not a stranger) should be set over them. Deut. 17. 15. and Jethro's counsel to Moses was approved of God, that the judges, and officers to be set over the people, should be men fearing God. Exod. 18. 21. and Solomon maketh it the joy of a commonwealth, when the righteous are in authority, and their mourning when the wicked rule, Prov. 29. 21. Job 34. 30. Your Lordship's fear, that this will bring in papal excommunication, is just, and pious: but let your Lordship be pleased again to consider whether the consequence be necessary. *Turpius ejictur quam non admittitur:* nonmembership may be a just cause of nonadmission to the place of magistracy, but yet, ejection out of his membership will not be a just cause of ejecting him out of his magistry. A godly woman, being to make choice of an husband, may justly refuse a man that is either cast out of church fellowship, or is not yet received into it, but yet, when she is once given to him, she may not reject him then, for such defect. Mr. Humfrey was chosen for an assistant (as I hear) before the colony came over hither: and, though he be not as yet joined into church fellowship (by reason of the unsettledness of the congregation where he liveth) yet the commonwealth do still continue his magistry to him, as knowing he waiteth for opportunity of enjoying church-fellowship shortly.

When your Lordship doubteth, that this course will draw all things under the determination of the church, *in ordine ad spiritualia* (seeing the church is to determine who shall be members, and none but a member may have to do in the government of a commonwealth) be pleased (I pray you) to conceive, that magistrates are neither chosen to office in the church, nor do govern by directions from the church, but by civil laws, and those enacted in general courts, and executed in courts of justice, by the governors and assistants. In all which, the church (as the church) hath nothing to do: only, it prepareth fit instruments both to rule, and to choose rulers, which is no ambition in the church, nor dishonor to the commonwealth, the apostle, on the contrary, thought it a great dishonor and reproach to the church of Christ, if it were not able to yield able judges to hear and determine all causes amongst their brethren. *i, Cor.* 6. i. to 5. which place alone seemeth to me fully to decide this question: for it plainly holdeth forth this argument: It is a shame to the church to want able judges of civil matters (as v. 5) and an audacious act in any church member voluntarily to go for judgment, other where than before the saints (as v. 1.) then it will be no arrogance nor folly in church members, nor prejudice to the commonwealth, if voluntarily they never choose any civil judges but from amongst the saints, such as church members are called to be. But the former is clear: and how then can the latter be avoided. If this therefore be (as your Lordship rightly conceiveth one of the main objections if not the only one) which hindereth this commonwealth from the entertainment of the propositions of those worthy gentlemen, we entreat them, in the name of the Lord Jesus, to consider, in meekness of wisdom, it is not any conceit, or will of ours, but the holy counsel and will of the Lord Jesus (whom they seek to serve as well as we) that overruleth us in this case: and we trust will overrule them also, that the Lord only may be exalted amongst all his servants. What pity and grief were it, that the observance of the will of Christ should hinder good things from us!

But your Lordship doubteth, that if such a rule were necessary, then the church estate and the best ordered commonwealth in the world were not compatible. But let not your Lordship so conceive. For, the church submitteth itself to all the laws and ordinances of men, in what commonwealth soever they come to dwell. But it is one thing, to submit unto what they have no calling to reform: another thing, voluntarily to ordain a form of government, which to the best discerning of many of us (for I speak not of myself) is expressly contrary to rule. Nor need your Lordship fear (which yet I speak with submission to your Lordships better judgment) that this course will lay such a foundation, as nothing but a mere democracy can be built upon it. Bodine confesseth, that though it be *status popularis,* where a people choose their own governors; yet the government is not a democracy, if it be administered, not by the people, but by the governors, whether one (for then it is a monarchy, though elective) or by many, for then (as you know) it is aristocracy. In which respect it is, that church government is justly denied (even by Mr. Robinson) to be democratical, though the people choose their own officers and rulers.

Nor need we fear, that this course will, in time, cast the commonwealth into distractions, and popular confusions. For (under correction) these three things do not undermine, but do mutually and strongly maintain one another (even those three which we principally aim at) authority in magistrates, liberty in people, purity in the church. Purity, preserved in the church, will preserve well-ordered liberty in the people, and both of them establish well-balanced authority in the magistrates. God is the author of all these three, and neither is himself the God of confusion, nor are the ways the ways of confusion, but of peace.

What our brethren (magistrates or ministers, or leading freeholders) will answer to the rest of the propositions, I shall better understand before the gentlemans return from Connecticut, who brought them over. Mean while, two of the principal of them, the general court hath already condescended unto. (1) In establishing a standing council, who, during their lives, should assist the governor in managing the chiefest affairs of this little state. They have chosen, for the present, only two (Mr. Winthrop and Mr. Dudley) not willing to choose more, till they see what further better choice the Lord will send over to them, that so they may keep an open door, for such desirable gentlemen as your Lordship mentioneth. (2) They have granted the governor and assistants a negative voice, and reserved to the freemen the like liberty also. Touching other things, I hope to give your Lordship further account, when the gentleman returneth.

He being now returned, I have delivered to him an answer to the rest of your demands, according to the minds of such leading men amongst us, as I thought meet to consult withal, concealing your name from any, except two or three, who alike do concur in a joint desire of yielding to any such propositions as your Lordship demandeth, so far as with allowance from the word they may, beyond which I know your Lordship would not require any thing.

Now the Lord Jesus Christ (the prince of peace) keep and bless your Lordship, and dispose of all your times and talents to his best advantage: and let the covenant of his grace and peace rest upon your honourable family and posterity, throughout all generations.

Thus, humbly craving pardon for my boldness and length, I take leave and rest,

Your Honours to serve in Christ Jesus,
J. C.

Massachusetts Proscribes Quakers (May 24, 1677)

As an addition to the last law relating to Quakers meeting, the constables of every town are hereby required to make diligent search in their respective towns, especially on the Lord's day, in all suspected places and houses, and where they know or may be informed that any Quakers are met to celebrate their irregular and prohibited worship, and are hereby empowered to break open any door where peaceable entrance is denied them, and such persons as shall be found at such meetings shall be apprehended and proceeded with and punished as the law provides in that case. And every constable neglecting his duty herein, and being legally convicted thereof, shall forfeit the sum of forty shillings to the use of the county. And for all such persons as shall be prosecuted or complained of for absenting themselves from the

N. B. Shurtleff, ed., *Records of the Governor and Company of the Massachusetts Bay in New England, 1628–1686,* Vol. IV, Pt. I, p. 82.

public allowed worship of God on the Lord's day, and will not so much as affirm they were there or necessarily absent by the providence of God, it shall be adjudged a conviction and the breach of the law and punished accordingly.

Royal Order to Send Accused Quakers to England (September 9, 1661)

Charles R. Trusty and well-beloved, we greet you well.

Having been informed that several of our subjects among you, called Quakers, have been and are imprisoned by you, whereof some have been executed and others, as has been represented to us, are in danger to undergo the like, we have thought fit to signify our pleasure in that behalf for the future, and do hereby require, that if there be any of those people called Quakers among you not already condemned to suffer death, or other corporal punishment, or that are imprisoned and obnoxious to the like condemnation, you forebear to proceed any farther therein; but that you forthwith send the said persons, whether condemned or imprisoned, over into this our kingdom of England, together with their respective crimes or offenses laid to their charge, to the end such course may be taken with them here as shall be agreeable to our laws and their demerits. And for so doing, these our letters shall be your warrant and sufficient discharge.

Given at our court at Whitehall, the 9th day of September 1661 in the 13th year of our reign.

By His Majesty's command,
William Morris.

To our trusty and well-beloved John Endicott, Esquire, and to all and every other the governor or governors of our plantation of New England; and of all the colonies thereunto belonging, that now are or hereafter shall be. And to all and every the ministers and officers there of our said plantation and colonies whatsoever in the continent of New England.

Roger Williams Responds to John Cotton (1644)

ROGER WILLIAMS

First, That the blood of so many hundred thousand souls of Protestants and Papists, spilt in the Wars of present and former Ages, for their respective Consciences, is not required nor accepted by Jesus Christ the Prince of Peace.

Secondly, Pregnant Scriptures and Arguments are throughout the Work proposed against the Doctrine of persecution for cause of Conscience.

Collections, Massachusetts Historical Society, 4th Ser., Vol. IX, pp. 159–160.

"Roger Williams Responds to John Cotton, The Bloudy Tenant of Persecution, for Cause of Conscience, discussed in a conference between Truth and Peace, 1644." Reprinted from Samuel L. Caldwell, ed., *Publications of The Narragansett Club* (Providence, RI, 1867), Series 1, Volume III.

Thirdly, Satisfactory Answers are given to Scriptures, and objections produced by Mr. Calvin, [Mr.] Beza, Mr. Cotton, and the Ministers of the New English Churches and others former and later, tending to prove the Doctrine of persecution for cause of Conscience.

Fourthly, The Doctrine of persecution for cause of Conscience, is proved guilty of all the blood of the Souls crying for vengeance under the Altar.

Fifthly, All Civil States with their Officers of justice in their respective constitutions and administrations are proved essentially Civil, and therefore not Judges, Governors or Defenders of the Spiritual or Christian state and Worship.

Sixthly, It is the will and command of God, that (since the coming of his Son the Lord Jesus) a permission of the most Paganish, Jewish, Turkish, or Anti-Christian consciences and worships, be granted to all men in all Nations and Countries: and they are only to be fought against with that Sword which is only (in Soul matters) able to conquer, to wit, the Sword of Gods Spirit, the Word of God.

Seventhly, The state of the Land of Israel, the Kings and people thereof in Peace & War, is proved figurative and ceremonial, and no pattern nor precedent for any Kingdom or civil state in the world to follow.

Eighthly, God requireth not an uniformity of Religion to be enacted and enforced in any civil state; which enforced uniformity (sooner or later) is the greatest occasion of civil War, ravishing of conscience, persecution of Christ Jesus in his servants, and of the hypocrisy and destruction of millions of souls.

Ninthly, In holding an enforced uniformity of Religion in a civil state, we must necessarily disclaim our desires and hopes of the Jews conversion to Christ.

Tenthly, An enforced uniformity of Religion throughout a Nation or civil state, confounds the Civil and Religious, denies the principles of Christianity and civility, and that Jesus Christ is come in the Flesh.

Eleventhly, The permission of other consciences and worships than a state professeth, only can (according to God) procure a firm and lasting peace (good assurance being taken according to the wisdom of the civil state for uniformity of civil obedience from all sorts).

Twelfthly, lastly, true civility and Christianity may both flourish in a state or Kingdom, notwithstanding the permission of diverse and contrary consciences, either of Jew or Gentile.

American Diversity: American Tolerance (1782)

HECTOR ST. JOHN DE CRÈVECOEUR

As I have endeavoured to shew you how Europeans become Americans; it may not be disagreeable to shew you likewise how the various Christian sects introduced, wear out, and how religious indifference becomes prevalent. When any considerable number of a particular sect happen to dwell contiguous to each other, they immediately erect a temple, and there worship the Divinity agreeably to their own

Hector St. John de Crèvecoeur, *Letters from an American Farmer* (London: 1782), pp. 54–70.

peculiar ideas. Nobody disturbs them. If any new sect springs up in Europe, it may happen that many of its professors will come and settle in America. As they bring their zeal with them, they are at liberty to make proselytes if they can, and to build a meeting and to follow the dictates of their consciences; for neither the government nor any other power interferes. If they are peaceable subjects, and are industrious, what is it to their neighbours how and in what manner they think fit to address their prayers to the Supreme Being? But if the sectaries are not settled close together, if they are mixed with other denominations, their zeal will cool for want of fuel, and will be extinguished in a little time. Then the Americans become as to religion, what they are as to country, allied to all. In them the name of Englishman, Frenchman, and European is lost, and in like manner, the strict modes of Christianity as practised in Europe are lost also. This effect will extend itself still farther hereafter, and though this may appear to you as a strange idea, yet it is a very true one. I shall be able perhaps hereafter to explain myself better, in the meanwhile, let the following example serve as my first justification.

Let us suppose you and I to be travelling; we observe that in this house, to the right, lives a Catholic, who prays to God as he has been taught, and believes in transubstantion [sic]; he works and raises wheat, he has a large family of children, all hale and robust; his belief, his prayers offend nobody. About one mile farther on the same road, his next neighbour may be a good honest plodding German Lutheran, who addresses himself to the same God, the God of all, agreeably [sic] to the modes he has been educated in, and believes in consubstantiation [sic]; by so doing he scandalizes nobody; he also works in his fields, embellishes the earth, clears swamps, &c. What has the world to do with his Lutheran principles? He persecutes nobody, and nobody persecutes him, he visits his neighbours, and his neighbours visit him. Next to him lives a seceder, the most enthusiastic of all sectaries; his zeal is hot and fiery, but separated as he is from others of the same complexion, he has no congregation of his own to resort to, where he might cabal and mingle religious pride with worldly obstinacy. He likewise raises good crops, his house is handsomely painted, his orchard is one of the fairest in the neighbourhood. How does it concern the welfare of the country, or of the province at large, what this man's religious sentiments are, or really whether he has any at all? He is a good farmer, he is a sober, peaceable, good citizen: William Penn himself would not wish for more. This is the visible character, the invisible one is only guessed at, and is nobody's business. Next again lives a Low Dutchman, who implicitly believes the rules laid down by the synod of Dort.[1] He conceives no other idea of a clergyman than that of an hired man; if he does his work well he will pay him the stipulated sum; if not he will dismiss him, and do without his sermons, and let his church be shut up for years. But notwithstanding this coarse idea, you will find his house and farm to be the neatest in all the country; and you will judge by his waggon and fat horses, that he thinks more of the affairs of this world than of those of the next. He is sober and laborious, therefore he is all he ought to be as to the affairs of this life; as for those

---

[1]A convocation of orthodox Dutch Calvinists in 1618–1619 that condemned the views of Jacob Arminius and envisioned strict Calvinist views—ED.

of the next, he must trust to the great Creator. Each of these people instruct their children as well as they can, but these instructions are feeble compared to those which are given to the youth of the poorest class in Europe. Their children will therefore grow up less zealous and more indifferent in matters of religion than their parents. The foolish vanity, or rather the fury of making Proselytes, is unknown here; they have no time, the seasons call for all their attention, and thus in a few years, this mixed neighbourhood will exhibit a strange religious medley, that will be neither pure Catholicism nor pure Calvinism. A very perceptible indifference even in the first generation, will become apparent; and it may happen that the daughter of the Catholic will marry the son of the seceder, and settle by themselves at a distance from their parents. What religious education will they give their children? A very imperfect one. If there happens to be in the neighbourhood any place of worship, we will suppose a Quaker's meeting; rather than not shew their fine clothes, they will go to it, and some of them may perhaps attach themselves to that society. Others will remain in a perfect state of indifference; the children of these zealous parents will not be able to tell what their religious principles are, and their grandchildren still less. The neighbourhood of a place of worship generally leads them to it, and the action of going thither, is the strongest evidence they can give of their attachment to any sect. The Quakers are the only people who retain a fondness for their own mode of worship; for be they ever so far separated from each other, they hold a sort of communion with the society, and seldom depart from its rules, at least in this country. Thus all sects are mixed as well as all nations; thus religious indifference is imperceptibly disseminated from one end of the continent to the other; which is at present one of the strongest characteristics of the Americans. Where this will reach no one can tell, perhaps it may leave a vacuum fit to receive other systems. Persecution, religious pride, the love of contradiction, are the food of what the world commonly calls religion. These motives have ceased here: zeal in Europe is confined; here it evaporates in the great distance it has to travel; there it is a grain of powder inclosed, here it burns away in the open air, and consumes without effect.

2.4: Class Tensions and Slavery in Colonial America (1629, 1664, 1739)

In Section 2.2 we presented legal distinctions made in charters on behalf of the colonial elites. Such distinctions were not always accepted without resistance, however. In the first selection, a Dutch settler presents a critical view of planter society, analyzing its inherent problems and tensions and relating them to existing class and caste relationships. Class distinctions as observed by this traveler were not merely customs or social mores. The second reading is drawn from Virginia laws, which attempted to define the status of servants. How do these compare with regulations and customs pertaining to slaves? Poor people responded to such assertions in a variety of ways; what forms of resistance can be inferred from the concerns of the lawmakers? Do the laws seem just? Are they enforceable? A particularly extreme form of resistance to authority occurred in 1676 when a group of Backwoodsmen, referred to as the "common people," challenged colonial authorities in an uprising known as Bacon's Rebellion. What additional class tensions are reflected in Nathaniel Bacon's "Declaration of the People"? What regional tensions emerged within colonies? Why were relations between East and West often strained within the individual colonies? How could Indian affairs become an important variable in colonial power and politics? Finally, no institution had greater impact on colonial culture than slavery, particularly in regions where it was widespread. The final two selections in this section reveal the brutality of slavery, even though both the Maryland Statute and the description of Stano's Rebellion were written by white men.

A Traveler Disapproves of the Chesapeake Planters (1679)[1]

JASPAR DANCKAERTS

Jaspar Danckaerts was a native of Zeeland in Holland who came to America in 1679 as an agent of the Labadists, a small Protestant sect established by French mystic Jean de Labadie. Danckaerts and his companion, Peter Sluyter, were seeking a site for a Labadist colony, where this pious group could worship without official interference. The two agents traveled through the former Dutch colony of New Netherland, visited New England, and then scouted the Chesapeake region. The following document is an excerpt from Danckaerts's journal describing life on the Chesapeake in Maryland toward the end of the seventeenth century.

Danckaerts is critical of the Maryland planters' habits and is not impressed by the way they conducted their affairs. It is of course possible that objective observers would agree with his estimates of seventeenth-century Maryland society, but it is also possible that his views were governed by prejudice. Why might a man of his background have found the customs of the Chesapeake planters less than admirable? Can his judgment be accepted without question?

All of Maryland that we have seen, is high land, with few or no meadows, but possessing such a rich and fertile soil, as persons living there assured me that they had

Jaspar Danckaerts, ed., *Journal of Jaspar Danckaerts,* 1679–1680, B. B. James and J. F. Jameson (New York: Charles Scribner's Sons, 1913), pp. 133–37.
[1]Footnotes renumbered.

raised tobacco off the same piece of land for thirty consecutive years. The inhabitants, who are generally English, are mostly engaged in this production. It is their chief staple, and the money with which they must purchase every thing they require, which is brought to them from other English possessions in Europe, Africa and America. There is, nevertheless, sometimes a great want of these necessaries, owing to the tobacco market being low, or the shipments being prevented by some change of affairs in some quarter, particularly in Europe, or indeed to both causes, as was the case at this time, whereby there sometimes arises a great scarcity of such articles as are most necessary, as we saw when there. So large a quantity of tobacco is raised in Maryland and Virginia, that it is one of the greatest sources of revenue to the crown by reason of the taxes which it yields. Servants and negroes are chiefly employed in the culture of tobacco, who are brought from other places to be sold to the highest bidders, the servants for a term of years only, but the negroes forever, and may be sold by their masters to other planters as many times as their masters choose, that is, the servants until their term is fulfilled, and the negroes for life. These men, one with another, each make, after they are able to work, from 2,500 pounds to 3,000 pounds and even 3,500 pounds of tobacco a year, and some of the masters and their wives who pass their lives here in wretchedness, do the same. The servants and negroes after they have worn themselves down the whole day, and come home to rest, have yet to grind and pound the grain, which is generally maize, for their masters and all their families as well as themselves, and all the negroes, to eat. Tobacco is the only production in which the planters employ themselves, as if there were nothing else in the world to plant but that, and while the land is capable of yielding all the productions that can be raised anywhere, so far as the climate of the place allows. As to articles of food, the only bread they have is that made of Turkish wheat or maize, and that is miserable. They plant this grain for that purpose everywhere. It yields well, not a hundred, but five or six hundred for one; but it takes up much space, as it is planted far apart like vines in France. This grain, when it is to be used for men or for similar purposes, has to be first soaked, before it is ground or pounded, because the grains being large and very hard, cannot be broken under the small stones of their light hand-mills; and then it is left so coarse it must be sifted. They take the finest for bread, and the other for different kinds of groats, which, when it is cooked, is called *sapaen* or *homina.* The meal intended for bread is kneaded moist without leaven or yeast, salt or grease, and generally comes out of the oven so that it will hardly hold together, and so blue and moist that it is as heavy as dough; yet the best of it when cut and roasted, tastes almost like warm white bread, at least it then seemed to us so. This corn is also the only provender for all their animals, be it horses, oxen, cows, hogs, or fowls, which generally run in the woods to get their food, but are fed a little of this, mornings and evenings during the winter when there is little to be had in the woods; though they are not fed too much, for the wretchedness, if not cruelty, of such living, affects both man and beast. This is said not without reason, for a master having a sick servant, and there are many so, and observing from his declining condition, he would finally die, and that there was no probability of his enjoying any more service from him, made him, sick and languishing as he was, dig his own grave, in which he was to be laid a few days afterwards, in order not to busy any of the others with it, they having their hands full in attending to the tobacco.[2]

A few vegetables are planted, but they are of the coarsest kinds and are cultivated in the coarsest manner, without knowledge or care, and they are, therefore, not properly raised, and do not amount to much as regards the production, and still less as to their use. Some have begun to plant orchards, which all bear very well, but are not properly cultivated. The fruit is for the greater part pressed, and makes good cider, of which the largest portion becomes soured and spoiled through their ignorance or negligence, either from not putting it into good casks, or from not taking proper care of the liquor afterwards. Sheep they have none, although they have what is requisite for them if they chose. It is a matter of conjecture whether you will find any milk or butter even in summer; we have not found any there at this season of the year. They bestow all their time and care in producing tobacco; each cask or hogshead, as they call it, of which pays two English shillings on exportation, and on its arrival in England, two pence a pound, besides the fees for weighing and other expenses here, and freight and other charges beyond sea. When, therefore, tobacco only brings four or five pence, there is little or nothing left for the owner.

The lives of the planters in Maryland and Virginia are very godless and profane. They listen neither to God nor his commandments, and have neither church nor cloister. Sometimes there is some one who is called a minister, who does not as elsewhere, serve in one place, for in all Virginia and Maryland there is not a city or a village[3]—but travels for profit, and for that purpose visits the plantations through the country, and there addresses the people; but I know of no public assemblages being held in these places; you hear often that these ministers are worse than anybody else, yea, are an abomination.

When the ships arrive with goods, and especially with liquors, such as wine and brandy, they attract everybody, that is, masters, to them, who then indulge so abominably together, that they keep nothing for the rest of the year, yea, do not go away as long as there is any left, or bring anything home with them which might be useful to them in their subsequent necessities. It must therefore go hard with the household, and it is a wonder if there be a single drop left for the future. They squander so much in this way, that they keep no tobacco to buy a shoe or a stocking for their children, which sometimes causes great misery. While they take so little care for provisions, and are otherwise reckless, the Lord sometimes punishes them with insects, flies, and worms, or with intemperate seasons, causing great famine, as happened a few years ago in the time of the last Dutch war with the English,[4] when the Lord sent so many weevils that all their grain was eaten up as well as almost all the other productions of the field, by reason of which such a great famine was caused

---

[2]Despite these criticisms as to slavery, it appears, if we can accept the hostile testimony of Dittelbach, *Verval en Val der Labadisten* (Amsterdam, 1692), that [Peter] Sluyter, when in control of the Labadist plantation at Bohemia Manor, employed slave labor without hesitation and with some harshness.
[3]No cities, of course, but some villages.
[4]The war of 1672–1674. But the attack on the Hoere-kill (Whorekill, now Lewes, Delaware) was not an act of war against the Dutch, but an attack by Marylanders on inhabitants who were under the jurisdiction of the Duke of York, in a territory disputed between him and Lord Baltimore.

that many persons died of starvation, and a mother killed her own child and ate it, and then went to her neighbors, calling upon them to come and see what she had done, and showing them the remains of her child, whereupon she was arrested and condemned to be hung. When she sat or stood on the scaffold, she cried out to the people, in the presence of the governor, that she was now going to God, where she would render an account, and would declare before him that what she had done she did in the mere delirium of hunger, for which the governor alone should bear the guilt; inasmuch as this famine was caused by the weevils, a visitation from God, because he, the governor, undertook in the preceding summer an expedition against the Dutch residing on the South River, who maintained themselves in such a good posture of defense, that he could accomplish but little; when he went to the Hoere-kill on the west side of that river, not far from the sea, where also he was not able to do much; but as the people subsisted there only by cultivating wheat, and had at this time a fine and abundant harvest in the fields—and from such harvests the people of Maryland generally, and under such circumstances as these particularly, were fed—he set fire to it, and all their other fruits, whether of the trees or the field; whereby he committed two great sins at the same time, namely, against God and his goodness, and against his neighbors, the Dutch, who lost it, and the English who needed it; and had caused more misery to the English in his own country, than to the Dutch in the enemy's country. This wretched woman protesting these words substantially against the governor, before Heaven and in the hearing of every one, was then swung up.

In addition to what the tobacco itself pays on exportation, which produces a very large sum, every hundred acres of land, whether cultivated or not, has to pay one hundred pounds of tobacco a year, and every person between sixteen and sixty years of age must pay three shillings a year. All animals are free of taxation, and so are all productions except tobacco.

It remains to be mentioned that those persons who profess the Roman Catholic religion have great, indeed, all freedom in Maryland, because the governor makes profession of that faith, and consequently there are priests and other ecclesiastics who travel and disperse themselves everywhere, and neglect nothing which serves for their profit and purpose. The priests of Canada take care of this region, and hold correspondence with those here, as is supposed, as well as with those who reside among the Indians. It is said there is not an Indian fort between Canada and Maryland, where there is not a Jesuit who teaches and advises the Indians, who begin to listen to them too much; so much so, that some people in Virginia and Maryland as well as in New Netherland, have been apprehensive lest there might be an outbreak, hearing what has happened in Europe,[5] as well as among their neighbors at Boston; but they hope the result of the troubles there will determine many things elsewhere. The Lord grant a happy issue there and here, as well as in other parts of the world, for the help of His own elect, and the glory of His name.

---

[5]The reference is to the Popish Plot in England; in respect to Boston, it is probably to King Philip's War, 1675–1676, and the hostilities along the Maine coast in 1677, though there is no reason to attribute these to French or Jesuit instigation. Yet possibly the great fire of August 8–9, 1679, is meant.

Laws Regulating Servants (March, 1642/43)

Whereas many great abuses and much detriment have been found to arise both against the law of God and likewise to the service of many masters of families in the colony occasioned through secret marriages of servants, their masters and mistresses being not any way made privy thereto, as also by committing of fornication. For preventing the like abuses hereafter, be it enacted and confirmed by this Grand Assembly that what man servant soever has since January, one thousand six hundred and forty, or hereafter shall secretly marry with any maid or woman servant without the consent of her master or mistress, if she be a widow, he or they so offending shall, in the first place, serve out his or their time or times with his or their masters or mistresses and after shall serve his or their master or mistress one complete year more for such offense committed; and the maid or woman servant, so marrying without consent as aforesaid, shall, for such her offense, double the time of service with her master and mistress. And a freeman so offending shall give satisfaction to the master or mistress by doubling the value of the service and pay a fine of five hundred pounds of tobacco to the parish where such offense shall be committed. And it is also further enacted and confirmed, by the authority of this Grand Assembly, that if any man servant shall commit the act of fornication with any maid or woman servant, he shall, for his offense, besides the punishment by the law appointed in like cases, give satisfaction for the loss of her service by one whole year's service when he shall be free from his master according to his indentures. And if it so fall out that a freeman offended, as formerly, he shall be compelled to make satisfaction to the master or mistress of the said woman servant by his service for one complete year or otherwise give, forthwith, such valuable consideration as the commissioners in their discretion shall think fit.

Act XXI

Whereas complaints are at every quarter court exhibited against divers persons who entertain and enter into covenants with runaway servants and freemen who have formerly hired themselves to others to the great prejudice, if not the utter undoing, of divers poor men, thereby also encouraging servants to run from their masters and obscure themselves in some remote plantations. Upon consideration had for the future preventing of the like injurious and unjust dealings, be it enacted and confirmed that what person or persons soever shall entertain any person as hireling or sharer or upon any other conditions, for one whole year without certificate from the commander or any one commissioner of the place that he or she is free from any engagement of service, the person so hiring without such certificate, as aforesaid, shall, for every night that he or she entertains any servant, either as hireling or otherwise, forfeit to the master or mistress of the said servant twenty pounds of tobacco and for every freeman which he or she shall forfeit to the party who had first hired him twenty pounds of tobacco for every night detained. And for every freeman which he or she entertains, though he has not formerly hired himself to another,

W. W. Hening, ed., *Statutes at Large of Virginia*, Vol. 1, pp. 252–255.

without certificate as aforesaid, and in all these cases the party hired shall receive such censure and punishment as shall be thought fit by the Governor and Council; always provided that if any such runaway servants or hired freemen shall produce a certificate wherein it appears that they are freed from their former master's service or from any such engagement respectively, if, afterwards, it shall be proved that the said certificates are counterfeit, then the retainer not to suffer according to the penalty of this act, but such punishment shall be inflicted upon the forger and procurer thereof as the Governor and Council shall think fit.

Act XXII

Whereas there are divers loitering runaways in the colony who very often absent themselves from their master's service and sometimes in two or three months cannot be found, whereby their said masters are at great charge in finding them and many times even to the loss of their year's labor before they be had. Be it, therefore, enacted and confirmed that all runaways that shall absent themselves from their said master's service shall be liable to make satisfaction by service at the end of their times by indenture, viz., double the time of service so neglected, and, in some cases more, if the commissioners for the place appointed shall find it requisite and convenient. And if such runaways shall be found to transgress the second time or oftener, if it shall be duly proved against them, that then they shall be branded in the cheek with the letter R. and pass under the statute of incorrigible rogues; provided, notwithstanding, that where any servants shall have just cause of complaint against their masters or mistresses by harsh or unchristianlike usage or other ways, for want of diet or convenient necessaries, that then it shall be lawful for any such servant or servants to repair to the next commissioner to make his or their complaint. And if the said commissioner shall find, by good and sufficient proofs, that the said servant's cause of complaint is just, the said commissioner is hereby required to give order for the warning of any such master or mistress before the commissioners in their several county courts where the matter in difference shall be decided, as they in their discretions shall think fit, and that care be had that no such servant or servants be misused by their masters or mistresses where they shall find the cause of complaint to be just. Be it further also enacted that if any servant, running away as aforesaid, shall carry either piece, powder, and shot and leave either all or any of them with the Indians, and being thereof lawfully convicted, shall suffer death as in case of felony.

Law Binding Out Children (October 1646)

Whereas sundry laws and statues, by act of Parliament established, have, with great wisdom, ordained, for the better educating of youth in honest and profitable trades and manufactures, as also to avoid sloath and idleness wherewith such young children are easily corrupted, as also for relief of such parents whose poverty extends not to give them breeding, that the justices of the peace should, at their discretion, bind out children to tradesmen or husbandmen to be brought up in some good and

W. W. Hening, ed., *Statutes at Large of Virginia*, Vol. 1, pp. 336–337.

lawful calling. And whereas God Almighty, among many his other blessings, has vouchsafed increase of children to this colony, who now are multiplied to a considerable number, who, if instructed in good and lawful trades, may much improve the honor and reputation of the country and no less their own good and their parents comfort. But forasmuch as for the most part the parents, either through fond indulgence or perverse obstinacy, are most averse and unwilling to part with their children. Be it, therefore, enacted by authority of this Grand Assembly, according to the aforesaid laudable custom in the kingdom of England, that the commissioners of the several counties respectively do, at their discretion, make choice of two children in each county of the age of eight or seven years at the least, either male or female, which are to be sent up to James City, between this and June next, to be employed in the public flax houses under such master and mistress as shall be there appointed in carding, knitting, and spinning, etc. And that the said children be furnished from the said county with six barrels of corn, two coverlets, or one rug and one blanket, one bed, one wooden bowl or tray, two pewter spoons, a sow shote of six months old, two laying hens, with convenient apparel, both linen and woolen, with hose and shoes. And for the better provision of housing for the said children, it is enacted that there be two houses built by the first of April next of forty feet long apiece with good and substantial timber. The houses to be twenty feet broad apiece, eight feet high in the pitch and a stack of brick chimneys standing in the midst of each house, and that they be lofted with sawn boards and made with convenient partitions. And it is further thought fit that the commissioners have caution not to take up any children but from such parents who, by reason of their poverty, are disabled to maintain and educate them. Be it likewise agreed that the Governor has agreed with the Assembly for the sum of 10,000 pounds of tobacco to be paid him the next crop to build and finish the said houses in manner and form before expressed.

The Declaration of the People

For having upon specious pretences of public works, raised unjust taxes upon the commonalty for the advancement of private favourites and other sinister ends, but no visible effects in any measure adequate.

For not having during the long time of his government in any measure advanced this hopeful colony, either by fortification, towns or trade.

For having abused and rendered contemptible the majesty of justice, of advancing to places of judicature scandalous and ignorant favourites.

For having wronged his Majesty's prerogative and interest by assuming the monopoly of the beaver trade.

By having in that unjust gain bartered and sold his Majesty's country and the lives of his loyal subjects to the barbarous heathen.

For having protected, favoured and emboldened the Indians against his Majesty's most loyal subjects, never contriving, requiring, or appointing any due or proper means of satisfaction for their many invasions, murders, and robberies committed upon us.

Reprinted from *The Virginia Magazine of History and Biography,* Volume I (1894), pp. 55–61.

For having, when the army of the English was just upon the track of the Indians, which now in all places burn, spoil, and murder, and when we might with ease have destroyed them who then were in open hostility, for having expressly counter-manded and sent back our army by passing his word for the peaceable demeanor of the said Indians, who immediately prosecuted their evil intentions, committing horrid murders and robberies in all places, being protected by the said engagement and word passed of him, the said Sir William Berkeley, having ruined and made desolate a great part of his Majesty's country, have now drawn themselves into such obscure and remote places and are by their successes so emboldened and confirmed, and by their confederacy so strengthened that the cries of blood are in all places, and the terror and consternation of the people so great, that they are now become not only a difficult, but a very formidable enemy who might with ease have been destroyed, etc. When upon the loud outcries of blood, the Assembly had with all care raised and framed an army for the prevention of future mischiefs and safeguard of his Majesty's colony.

For having with only the privacy of some few favourites, without acquainting the people, only by the alternation of a figure, forged a commission by we know not what hand, not only without but against the consent of the people, for raising and effecting of civil wars and distractions, which being happily and without bloodshed prevented.

For having the second time attempted the same thereby calling down our forces from the defence of the frontiers, and most weak exposed places, for the prevention of civil mischief and ruin amongst ourselves, whilst the barbarous enemy in all places did invade, murder, and spoil us, his Majesty's most faithful subjects.

Of these, the aforesaid articles, we accuse Sir William Berkeley, as guilty of each and every one of the same, and as one who has traitorously attempted, violated and injured his Majesty's interest here, by the loss of a great part of his colony, and many of his faithful and loyal subjects by him betrayed, and in a barbarous and shameful manner exposed to the incursions and murders of the heathen.

And we further declare these, the ensuing persons in this list, to have been his wicked, and pernicious counsellors, aiders and assisters against the commonality in these our cruel commotions:

Sir Henry Chicherly, Knt.	Jos. Bridger
Col. Charles Wormley	Wm. Clabourne
Phil. Dalowell	Thos. Hawkins, Jr.
Robert Beverly	William Sherwood
Robert Lee	Jos. Page, Clerk
Thos. Ballard	Jo. Cliffe, Clerk
William Cole	Hubberd Farrell
Richard Whitacre	John West
Nicholas Spencer	Thos. Reade
Mathew Kemp	

And we do further demand, that the said Sir William Berkeley, with all the persons in this list, be forthwith delivered up, or surrender themselves, within four days after the notice hereof, or otherwise we declare as followeth: that in whatsoever house, place, or ship any of the said persons shall reside, be hid, or protected, we do declare that the owners, masters, or inhabitants of the said places, to be confederates and traitors to the people, and the estates of them, as also of all the aforesaid persons, to be confiscated. This we, the commons of Virginia, do declare desiring a prime union amongst ourselves, that we may jointly, and with one accord defend ourselves against the common enemy. And let not the faults of the guilty be the reproach of the innocent, or the faults or crimes of the oppressors divide and separate us, who have suffered by their oppressions.

These are therefore in his Majesty's name, to command you forthwith to seize the persons above mentioned as traitors to the king and country, and them to bring to Middle Plantation, and there to secure them, till further order, and in case of opposition, if you want any other assistance, you are forthwith to demand it in the name of the people of all the counties of Virginia.

signed
NATH BACON, Gen'l.
By the Consent of the People.

Maryland Statute on Negroes and Other Slaves (1664)

Surviving statements by colonial slaves about the particulars of their lives are extremely rare. Few could write, and their oppressors had little interest in preserving their opinions or recording their protests. But colonial statutes pertaining to slavery, as well as numerous accounts by whites, attest dramatically to its harshness. Also, at times, the slaves themselves did express their feelings about their circumstances in a way that could not be hidden or ignored—through organized revolt.

Bee itt Enacted by the Right Honourable the Lord Proprietary, by the advice and Consent of the upper and lower house of this present Generall Assembly, That all Negroes or other slaves already within the Province And all Negroes and other slaves to bee hereafter imported into the Province shall serve Durante Vita. And all Children born of any Negro or other slave shall be Slaves as their fathers were for the terme of their lives. And forasmuch as divers freeborne English women forgettfull of their free Condition and to the disgrace of our Nation doe intermarry with Negro Slaves, by which alsoe divers suites may arise touching the Issue of such woemen and a great damage doth befall the Masters of such Negros—for prevention whereof and for deterring such freeborne women from such shamefull Matches, Bee itt further Enacted by the Authority advice and Consent aforesaid, That whatsoever free borne woman shall inter marry with any slave from and after the Last day of this present Assembly shall Serve the master of such slave dureing

William H. Browne, ed., *Archives of Maryland* (Baltimore: Maryland Historical Society, 1883), pp. 533–534.

the life of her husband, And that all the Issue of such freeborne woemen soe marryed shall be Slaves as their fathers were. And Bee itt further Enacted that all the Issues of English or other freeborne woemen that have already marryed Negroes shall
serve the Masters of their Parents till they be Thirty years of age and noe longer.

George Oglethorpe on the Stono Rebellion (1739)

GEORGE OGLETHORPE

*There were a number of slave revolts during the colonial era. The
most serious was the Stono Rebellion in South Carolina in 1739, when
thirty whites and forty-four blacks lost their lives. Earlier, in 1712, an
armed uprising of slaves in New York City had been put down by the
militia, and twenty-one of the rebels were hanged.*

*What can you conclude about the way slaves were probably treated
based upon this and the previous reading? What image is conveyed of
white authority? In light of harsh punishments and intense social control, do you think armed revolt could have been a common recourse of
colonial slaves?*

Sometime since there was a Proclamation published at Augustine, in which the
King of Spain (then at Peace with Great Britain) promised Protection and Freedom
to all Negroes Slaves that would resort thither. Certain Negroes belonging to Captain Davis escaped to Augustine, and were received there. They were demanded by
General Oglethorpe who sent Lieutenant Demere to Augustine, and the Governour
assured the General of his sincere Friendship, but at the same time showed his Orders from the Court of Spain, by which he was to receive all Run away Negroes. Of
this other Negroes having notice, as it is believed, from the Spanish Emissaries,
four or five who were Cattel-Hunters, and knew the Woods, some of whom belonged to Captain Macpherson, ran away with His Horses, wounded his Son and
killed another Man. These marched f [*sic*] for Georgia, and were pursued, but the
Rangers being then newly reduced [*sic*] the Countrey people could not overtake
them, though they were discovered by the Saltzburghers, as they passed by
Ebenezer [a religious community near Savannah, founded by German dissenters].
They reached Augustine, one only being killed and another wounded by the Indians
in their flight. They were received there with great honours, one of them had a
Commission given to him, and a Coat faced with Velvet. Amongst the Negroe
Slaves there are a people brought from the Kingdom of Angola in Africa, many of
these speak Portugueze [which Language is as near Spanish as Scotch is to
English,] by reason that the Portugueze have considerable Settlement, and the
Jesuits have a Mission and School in that Kingdom and many Thousands of the Ne-
groes there profess the Roman Catholic Religion. Several Spaniards upon diverse

Allen D. Candler, ed., *The Colonial Records of the State of Georgia.* 26 vols. (Atlanta: Chas. D. Byrd.
1913), 22:232–236.

Pretences have for some time past been strolling about Carolina, two of them, who will give no account of themselves have been taken up and committed to Jayl in Georgia. The good reception of the Negroes at Augustine was spread about, Several attempted to escape to the Spaniards, & were taken, one of them was hanged at Charles Town. In the latter end of July last Don Pedro, Colonel of the Spanish Horse, went in a Launch to Charles Town under pretence of a message to General Oglethorpe and the Lieutenant Governour.

On the 9th day of September last being Sunday which is the day the Planters allow them to work for themselves, Some Angola Negroes assembled, to the number of Twenty: and one who was called Jemmy was their Captain, they suprized a Warehouse belonging to Mr. Hutchenson at a place called Stonehow [*sic*—]: they there killed Mr. Robert Bathurst, and Mr. Gibbs, plundered the House and took a pretty many small Arms and Powder, which were there for Sale. Next they plundered and burnt Mr. Godfrey's house, and killed him, his Daughter and Son. They then turned back and marched Southward along Pons Pons, which is the Road through Georgia to Augustine, they passed Mr. Wallace's Tavern towards day break, and said they would not hurt him, for he was a good Man and kind to his Slaves, but they broke open and plundered Mr. Lemy's House, and killed him, his wife and Child. They marched on towards Mr. Rose's resolving to kill him; but he was saved by a Negroe, who having hid him went out and pacified the others. Several Negroes joyned them, they calling out Liberty, marched on with Colours displayed, and two Drums beating, pursuing all the white people they met with, and killing Man Woman and Child when they could come up to them. Collonel Bull Lieutenant Governour of South Carolina, who was then riding along the Road, discovered them, was pursued and with much difficulty escaped & raised the Countrey. They burnt Colonel Hext's house and killed his Overseer and his Wife. They then burnt Mr. Sprye's house, then Mr. Sacheverell's, and then Mr. Nash's house, all lying upon the Ponts Pons Road, and killed all the white People they found in them. Mr. Bullock got off, but they burnt his House, by this time many of them were drunk with the Rum they had taken in the Houses. They increased every minute by new Negroes coming to them, so that they were above Sixty, some say a hundred, on which they halted in a field, and set to dancing, Singing and beating Drums, to draw more Negroes to them, thinking they were now victorious over the whole Province, having marched ten miles & burnt all before them without Opposition, but the Militia being raised, the Planters with great briskness pursued them and when they came up, dismounting; charged them on foot. The Negroes were soon routed, though they behaved boldly several being killed on the Spot, many ran back to their Plantations thinking they had not been missed, but they were there taken and [*sic*] Shot, Such as were taken in the field also, were after being examined, shot on the Spot, And this is to be said to the honour of the Carolina Planters, that notwithstanding the Provocation they had received from so many Murders, they did not torture one Negroe, but only put them to an easy death. All that proved to be forced & were not concerned in the Murders & Burnings were pardoned, And this sudden Courage in the field & the Humanity afterwards hath had so good an Effect that there hath been no farther Attempt, and the very Spirit of Revolt seems over.

About 30 escaped from the fight, of which ten marched about 30 miles Southward, and being overtaken by the Planters on horseback, fought stoutly for some time and were all killed on the Spot. The rest are yet untaken. In the whole action about 40 Negroes and 20 whites were killed. The Lieutenant Governour sent an account of this to General Oglethorpe, who met the advices on his return from the Indian Nation. He immediately ordered a Troop of Rangers to be ranged, to patrole through Georgia, placed some Men in the Garrison at Palichocolas, which was before abandoned, and near which the Negroes formerly passed, being the only place where Horses can come to swim over the River Savannah for near 100 miles, ordered out the Indians in pursuit, and a Detachment of the Garrison at Port Royal to assist the Planters on any Occasion, and published a Proclamation ordering all the Constables &c. of Georgia to pursue and seize all Negroes, with a Reward for any that should be taken. It is hoped these measures will prevent any Negroes from getting down to the Spaniards.—

❖ *3* ❖

Native Americans

Long before Europeans and Africans came to America, people from northeastern Asia had crossed to the Western Hemisphere by a land bridge that connected Siberia to Alaska. By the time of Columbus they numbered perhaps as many as 50 million people spread across the two American continents and the adjacent islands. Believing at first that the Americas were an eastern extension of Asia, Europeans called these people *Indians.* Many of their descendants, however, prefer the name *Native Americans.*

Europeans were ambivalent about the indigenous people of the New World. On the one hand the "natives" seemed uncivilized beings whose customs were alien and often "brutish." Even worse, they were heathens, ignorant of Christian revelation, and so, unless converted, consigned to eternal damnation.

But there was another side of the European response as well. Europeans could not help admiring many Native American qualities, although this admiration often rested on ascribed attributes they did not always have. Above all, many Europeans admired their supposed directness and simplicity, their closeness to nature. They were not really brutish creatures, these observers said, but "noble savages" (to use British poet John Dryden's expression) whose individual and collective characteristics put those of Europeans to shame.

The documents in this section present a range of European views of the Native American population during the years of early contact. Unfortunately we do not have any corresponding statements from Native Americans of this era about the Europeans. Keep in mind, however, the frequency of the bloody Indian wars of colonial America. They do more than hint at what the indigenous people felt toward the transatlantic invaders.

3.1:   A Professor Disparages the Native Americans of Virginia (1724)

In 1716 Hugh Jones, with a master's degree from Oxford University, came to Williamsburg, the capital of Virginia, to teach mathematics at the College of William and Mary. In 1721 he returned to England for three years and while there wrote The Present State of Virginia, *from which this selection is taken.*

Jones's observations were based on his actual contact with the Virginia Indians, but they are clearly imbued with the prejudices of a European. Can you detect "Euro-centered" opinions here? What are they? Is his description predominantly negative? Although Jones was a teacher, he was also an Anglican minister. Do any of his views reflect the fact that he was a Christian clergyman?

Characteristics of the Indians[1]

HUGH JONES

As to the government and life of the Indians they live in a kind of patriachal [sic] manner, variously diversifyed, not unlike the tribes and families mentioned in the Old Testament. Every small town is a petty kingdom governed by an absolute monarch, assisted and advised by his great men, selected out of the gravest, oldest, bravest, and richest; if I may allow their dear-skins, peak and roenoak (black and white shells with holes, which they wear on strings about their arms and necks) to be wealth.

Sometimes there are general emperors, who have several petty kingdoms in some measure under their protection and power.

They dwell in towns some twenty, some a hundred miles, and some farther from one another, each town having a particular jargon and peculiar customs; though for the most part they agree in certain signs, expressions, and manners.

They are frequently at war with all their neighbours, or most of them, and treat their captive prisoners very barbarously; either by scalping them (which I have seen) by ripping off the crown of the head, which they wear on a thong by their side as a signal trophee and token of victory and bravery, or sometimes they tie their prisoners, and lead them bound to their town, where with the most joyful solemnity they kill them, often by thrusting in several parts of their bodies scewers of light-wood which burn like torches. The poor victim all the while (which is sometimes

[1]Footnotes deleted.

two or three days) not shewing the least symptom of grief, nor sign of pain, but bearing it with a scornful sullenness.

In their rejoicings and wardances they with the most antick gestures, in the most frightful dress, with a hideous noise, enumerate the enemies, that they have murdered, and such like exploits.

They attack always by surprize, and will never stand their ground when discovered; but fly to ambush, whither the enemy may pursue with peril of his life.

They are made for running very swiftly, and are nicely dextrous at fishing, hunting, and fowling; whereby they support themselves and families with venison, fish, wild turkies, etc.

The women do all the hard labour, such as cutting down the trees, planting corn, etc. carrying burthens, and all their other work; the men only hunting, fishing and fowling, eating, drinking, dancing and sleeping.

The boys still use bows and arrows for exercise, with which they are very dextrous; but the men always use fire-arms, which with ammunition they buy of us with their dear-skins, going rarely out unarmed.

They are so wonderfully quick-sighted, that they will swiftly pursue by eye the track of any thing among the trees, in the leaves and grass, as an hound does by the scent, where we can't perceive the least mark or footstep.

They cohabit in some hundreds of families, and fix upon the richest ground to build their wooden houses, which they place in a circular form, meanly defended with pales, and covered with bark; the middle area (or forum) being for common uses and publick occasions. The women in order to plant their Indian corn and tobacco (to clear the ground of trees) cut the bark round; so that they die and don't shade the ground, and decay in time.

Wherever we meet with an old Indian field, or place where they have lived, we are sure of the best ground. They all remove their habitation for fear of their enemies, or for the sake of game and provision.

They have small sweating houses like ovens; out of which when they are almost smothered with heat, they run into a river, which they always contrive to build their towns near.

This practice in all distempers often kills vast numbers in sicknesses which are new to them.

They have no notion of providing for futurity; for they eat night and day whilst their provision lasts, falling to as soon as they awake, and falling asleep again as soon as they are well crammed.

Their fish, flesh, and fowl, they either barbacue on an high gridiron, or broil on sharp sticks before a fire, which they always keep in the middle of their cabbin; and they lie upon boards and skins raised like benches round about their room.

Their drink is water unless they can get rum; with which they make themselves the greatest beasts, never ceasing as long as they have liquor to drink, and can keep awake.

I have known, when cows have been given them, that they let them go dry for laziness in neglecting to milk them, and die in the winter for want of fodder.

They commonly wear a dear-skin, putting their arms through the holes of the shoulder, with a flap tyed before and behind to cover their nakedness; though they buy often matchcoats or blankets now, to defend them from the wet and cold, and think themselves very fine in such coats as our common soldiers wear, or of any taudry colours: besides this, some pin pieces of red or blue cloth about their legs, and make moccassons or leather purses for their feet, with which they can travel in the woods, without danger of thorns or stumps. For all the country is but one continued forest, with patches of some hundred acres here and there cleared; either being formerly seated by Indians, or the trees being burnt in fire-hunting, or cut down for plantations.

Their children almost as soon as born, are tyed flat on their backs to a board; and so may be flung on the ground or put to lean against any thing, or be slung over their neck in travelling, or hung upon a bough, as occasion requires.

This occasions them to be exactly strait; so that it is a miracle to see a crooked or deformed Indian.

Their hair is very black, coarse and long; and they are all over daubed frequently with bear's oil.

Each nation has some distinguishing mark, especially in the cut or tie of their hair, in which they are very whimsical and comical.

They often wear shells hanging upon their breasts with feathers or a deer's tail in their bored ears or hair, with a wolf or fox-skin for a snapsack; with other odd accoutrements.

In their opinion, they are finest when dressed most ridiculously or terribly. Thus some have their skins all over curiously wrought with blewish lines and figures, as if done with gun-powder and needles, and all of them delight in being painted; so that when they are very fine, you may see some of them with their hair cut off on one side, and a long lock on the other. The crown being crested and bedaubed with red lead and oil; their forehead being painted white, and it may be their nose black, and a circle of blue round one eye, with the cheek red, and all the other side of the face yellow, or in some such fantastical manner. These colours they buy of us, being persuaded to despise their own, which are common and finer.

They are treacherous, suspicious and jealous, difficult to be persuaded or imposed upon, and very sharp, hard in dealing, and ingenious in their way, and in things that they naturally know, or have been taught; though at the first they are very obstinate, and unwilling to apprehend or learn novelties, and seem stupid and silly to strangers.

An instance of their resolute stupidity and obstinacy in receiving a new custom, I have seen in the prodigious trouble of bringing them to sell their skins, and buy gunpowder by weight; for they could not apprehend the power and justice of the stilliard; but with the scales at lenth they apprehended it tolerably well; though at first they insisted upon as much gunpowder as the skin weighed, which was much more than their demand in measure. They have geographical notions, as to the situation of their own country, and will find the way to very remote places in a surprizing manner; steering by the course of the rivers, etc. or by the trees, whose north side is easily known by the moss.

Thus I know, that Wickmannatauchee (a great king among the southern Indians) when I saw just before, and since, when he made his escape from his enemy Indians at Christanna, where his queen and abundance of his people were slain, and he tyed in order to be carried away prisoner; yet broke loose, and ran directly home several hundred miles stark-naked, without arms or provision, in the month of March, when the trees afforded no fruit; neither did he go near any other nation, till he got to his own; therefore I suppose roots were his provision, and water his liquor, unless by some cunning method (with which they abound) he caught fish, fowl, or venison; and as for fire I know they can kindle that by rubbing of certain sticks together.

They count their time by days, or by the return of the moon, and cohonks, a sort of wild geese. They walk one after another in a line, are very serious in debates, speak but one at a time; and in negotiations all agree to what either proposes or approves of, and are not easily imposed upon; and when affronted, they highly resent injuries, and being treacherous are no more to be trusted than tame lions, who can't wholly lose their savage hearts.

They have tolerable good notions of natural justice, equity, honour, and honesty, to the rules whereof the great men strictly adhere; but their common people will lye, cheat, and steal.

They seldom commit violence upon the English, but when provoked, or put on by others. . . .

The Indians have a blind worship and sacrifice, priests, and physicians, and expiation, with howling lamentations and purgation at their burials: all which I have seen at the funeral of their slain at Christanna, whom they buried thus; having made holes like sawpits, and lined them with bark and sticks, they wrapped the bodies in the best cloth they could buy with the skins of the deceased, and laid them in the graves, with all the cloths, skins and nicknacks of the dead: then they covered the body hollow with sticks, and flung in the earth with mournful noise; so the bodies lay as in coffins.

The priest or physician in curing the wounded, made an hideous noise, singing certain charms, with particular actions and forms of incantation, to which he ascribed the cure, though I believe this is done only to blind the common Indians; for I observed he did not begin his operation, till he had been in the woods. Then he shut us all out for an hour, and when we were readmitted, I perceived he had been using certain roots and herbs that I knew not.

Upon enquiry, we have from them these their notions of the state of the dead.

They believe that they go to Mohomny that lives beyond the sun, if they have not been wicked, nor like dogs nor wolves, that is, not unchast, then they believe that Mohomny sends them to a plentiful country abounding with fish, flesh, and fowls, the best of their kind, and easy to be caught; but if they have been naughty, then he sends them to a poor barren country, where be many wolves and bears, with a few nimble deer, swift fish and fowls, difficult to be taken; and when killed, being scarce any thing but skin and bones.

They allow polygamy if the man can maintain his family, as I have been informed.

They punish adultery in a woman by cutting off her hair, which they fix upon a long pole without the town; which is such a disgrace that the party is obliged to fly and becomes a victim to some enemy, a slave to some rover, or perishes in the woods.

3.2: A Pennsylvanian Calls the Native Americans "Devils" (1782)

From the seventeenth century onward, whites have implicitly denied Indians' rights to exclusive possession of the North American continent. At times they have made the case for the priority of the interests of the whites explicit, as in the selection below.[1] The statement is from a letter by Hugh Henry Brackenridge, a Pennsylvanian who wrote one of the first successful American novels.

Although himself a cultivated man, Brackenridge lived in Pittsburgh, then a crude frontier town. Do you think the fact that he was from the "west" of his day influenced Brackenridge's opinions? Does he make a convincing case for the right of Europeans to dispossess the Indians? Few of us would condone a "might makes right" moral code. But then we must ask whether Indian rights should have prevailed over those of the transatlantic intruders? Consider the implications for you and your family of a "yes" answer.

The Indians Have No Exclusive Claim to America

HUGH HENRY BRACKENRIDGE

With the narrative enclosed, I subjoin some observations with regard to the animals, vulgarly called Indians. It is not my intention to write any labored essay; for at so great a distance from the city, and so long unaccustomed to write, I have scarcely resolution to put pen to paper. Having an opportunity to know something of the character of this race of men, from the deeds they perpetrate daily round me, I think proper to say something on the subject. Indeed, several years ago, and before I left your city, I had thought different from some others with respect to the right of soil, and the propriety of forming treaties and making peace with them.

In the United States Magazine in the year 1777, I published a dissertation denying them to have a right in the soil. I perceive a writer in your very elegant and useful paper, has taken up the same subject, under the signature of "Caractacus," and unanswerably shown, that their claim to the extensive countries of America, is wild and inadmissible. I will take the liberty in this place, to pursue this subject a little.

On what is their claim founded?—Occupancy. A wild Indian with his skin painted red, and a feather through his nose, has set his foot on the broad continent of North and South America; a second wild Indian with his ears cut in ringlets, or his nose slit like a swine or a malefactor, also sets his foot on the same extensive tract

---

Hugh Henry Brackenridge to the editor of the *Freeman's Journal,* in Wilcomb Washburn, ed. *Indian and White Man* (New York: New York University Press, 1964), pp. 111–27.

[1]Unfortunately, it is impossible to find a statement of this position that dates before the end of the eighteenth century, though it is clear that, judging by actions, the view goes back much further.

of soil. Let the first Indian make a talk to his brother, and bid him take his foot off the continent, for he being first upon it, had occupied the whole, to kill buffaloes, and tall elks with long horns. This claim in the reasoning of some men would be just, and the second savage ought to depart in his canoe, and seek a continent where no prior occupant claimed the soil. Is this claim of occupancy of a very early date? When Noah's three sons, Shem, Ham, and Japhet, went out to the three quarters of the old world, Ham to Africa, Shem to Asia, Japhet to Europe, did each claim a quarter of the world for his residence? Suppose Ham to have spent his time fishing or gathering oysters in the Red Sea, never once stretching his leg in a long walk to see his vast dominions, from the mouth of the Nile, across the mountains of Ethiopia and the river Niger to the Cape of Good Hope, where the Hottentots, a cleanly people, now stay; or supposing him, like a Scots pedlar, to have traveled over many thousand leagues of that country; would this give him a right to the soil? In the opinion of some men it would establish an exclusive right. Let a man in more modern times take a journey or voyage like Patrick Kennedy and others to the heads of the Mississippi or Missouri rivers, would he gain a right ever after to exclude all persons from drinking the waters of these streams? Might not a second Adam make a talk to them and say, is the whole of this water necessary to allay your thirst, and may I also drink of it?

The whole of this earth was given to man, and all descendants of Adam have a right to share it equally. There is no right of primogeniture in the laws of nature and of nations. There is reason that a tall man, such as the chaplain in the American army we call the High Priest, should have a large spot of ground to stretch himself upon; or that a man with a big belly, like a goodly alderman of London, should have a larger garden to produce beans and cabbage for his appetite, but that an agile, nimble runner, like an Indian called the Big Cat, at Fort Pitt, should have more than his neighbors, because he has traveled a great space, I can see no reason.

I have conversed with some persons and found their mistakes on this subject, to arise from a view of claims by individuals in a state of society, from holding a greater proportion of the soil than others; but this is according to the laws to which they have consented; an individual holding one acre, cannot encroach on him who has a thousand, because he is bound by the law which secures property in this un-equal manner. This is the municipal law of the state under which he lives. The member of a distant society is not excluded by the laws from a right to the soil. He claims under the general law of nature, which gives a right, equally to all, to so much of the soil as is necessary for subsistence. Should a German from the closely peopled country of the Rhine, come into Pennsylvania, more thinly peopled, he would be justifiable in demanding a settlement, though his personal force would not be sufficient to effect it. It may be said that the cultivation of melioration of the earth, gives a property in it. No—if an individual has engrossed more than is neces-sary to produce grain for him to live upon, his useless gardens, fields and pleasure walks, may be seized upon by the person who, not finding convenient ground else-where, choose to till them for his support.

It is a usual way of destroying an opinion by pursuing it to its consequence. In the present case we may say, that if the visiting one acre of ground could give a right to it, the visiting of a million would give a right on the same principle; and thus a few surly ill natured men, might in the earlier ages have excluded half the human race from a settlement, or should any have fixed themselves on a territory, visited before they had set a foot on it, they must be considered as invaders of the rights of others.

It is said that an individual, building a house or fabricating a machine has an exclusive right to it, and why not those who improve the earth? I would say, should man build houses on a greater part of the soil, than falls to his share, I would, in a state of nature, take away a proportion of the soil and the houses from him, but a machine or any work of art, does not lessen the means of subsistence to the human race, which an extensive occupation of the soil does.

Claims founded on the first discovery of soil are futile. When gold, jewels, manufacturers, or any work of men's hands is lost, the finder is entitled to some reward, that is, he has some claims on the thing found, for a share of it.

When by industry or the exercise of genius, something unusual is invented in medicine or in other matters, the author doubtless has a claim to an exclusive profit by it, but who will say the soil is lost, or that any one can found a claim by discovering it. The earth with its woods and rivers still exist, and the only advantage I would allow to any individual for having cast his eye first on any particular part of it, is the privilege of making the first choice of situation. I would think the man a fool and unjust, who would exclude me from drinking the waters of the Mississippi river, because he had first seen it. He would be equally so who would exclude me from settling in the country west of the Ohio, because in chasing a buffalo he had been first over it.

The idea of an exclusive right to the soil in the natives had its origin in the policy of the first discoverers, the kings of Europe. Should they deny the right of the natives from their first treading on the continent, they would take away the right of discovery in themselves, by sailing on the coast. As the vestige of the moccasin in one case gave a right, so the cruise in the other was the foundation of a claim.

Those who under these kings, derived grants were led to countenance the idea, for otherwise why should kings grant or they hold extensive tracts of country. Men become enslaved to an opinion that has been long entertained. Hence it is that many wise and good men will talk of the right of savages to immense tracts of soil.

What use do these ring, streaked, spotted and speckled cattle make of the soil? Do they till it? Revelation said to man, "Thou shalt till the ground." This alone is human life. It is favorable to population, to science, to the information of a human mind in the worship of God. Warburton[2] has well said, that before you can make an Indian a christian you must teach him agriculture and reduce him to a civilized life. To live by tilling is *more humano,* by hunting is *more bestiarum.* I would as soon admit a right in the buffalo to grant lands, as in Killbuck, the Big Cat, the Big Dog, or any of the ragged wretches that are called chiefs and sachems. What would you think of going to a big lick or place where the beasts collect to lick saline nitrous earth and water, and addressing yourself to a great buffalo to grant you land? It is true he could not make the mark of the stone or the mountain reindeer, but he could set his cloven foot to the instrument like the great Ottomon, the father of the Turks,

---

[2]Probably William Warburton, the Anglican Bishop of Gloucester, England—ED.

when he put his signature to an instrument, he put his large hand and spreading fingers in the ink and set his mark to the parchment. To see how far the folly of some would go, I had once a thought of supplicating some of the great elks or buffaloes that run through the woods, to make me a grant of a hundred thousand acres of land and prove he had brushed the weeds with his tail, and run fifty miles.

I wonder if Congress or the different States would recognize the claim? I am so far from thinking the Indians have a right to the soil, that not having made a better use of it for many hundred years, I conceive they have forfeited all pretence to claim, and ought to be driven from it.

With regard to forming treaties or making peace with this race, there are many ideas:

They have the shapes of men and may be of the human species, but certainly in their present state they approach nearer the character of Devils; take an Indian, is there any faith in him? Can you bind him by favors? Can you trust his word or confide in his promise? When he makes war upon you, when he takes you prisoner and has you in his power will he spare you? In this he departs from the law of nature, by which, according to baron Montesquieu[3] and every other man who thinks on the subject, it is unjustifiable to take away the life of him who submits; the conqueror in doing otherwise becomes a murderer, who ought to be put to death. On this principle are not the whole Indian nations murderers?

Many of them may have not had an opportunity of putting prisoners to death, but the sentiment which they entertain leads them invariably to this when they have it in their power or judge it expedient; these principles constitute them murderers, and they ought to be prevented from carrying them into execution, as we would prevent a common homicide, who should be mad enough to conceive himself justifiable in killing men.

The tortures which they exercise on the bodies of their prisoners, justify extermination. Gelo of Syria made war on the Carthaginians because they oftentimes burnt human victims, and made peace with them on conditions they would cease from this unnatural and cruel practice. If we could have any faith in the promises they make we could suffer them to live, provided they would only make war amongst themselves, and abandon their hiding or lurking on the pathways of our citizens, emigrating unarmed and defenceless inhabitants; and murdering men, women and children in a defenceless situation; and on their ceasing in the meantime to raise arms no more among the American Citizens.

3.3: William Penn Urges Kindness Toward Native Americans (1683)

Until well into the eighteenth century, relations between whites and Native Americans were more peaceable in Pennsylvania than anywhere else. The following selection by William Penn, founder of the Pennsylvania colony, suggests why this was so.

---

[3]Charles de Secondat Montesquieu, a prominent French philosopher of the early eighteenth century—ED.

Was it significant, in considering good Indian-white relations, that Pennsylvania was established under Quaker auspices? What was the Quaker view of power and authority? What was the Quaker view of racial differences? In the end, did it make a difference for the Indians of Pennsylvania that the colony's early rulers were Quakers? Or were they submerged there too?

William Penn Admires the Indians

WILLIAM PENN

XI. The *Natives* I shall consider in their Persons, Language, Manners, Religion and Government, with my sence of their Original. For their Persons, they are generally tall, streight, well-built, and of singular Proportion; they tread strong and clever, and mostly walk with a lofty Chin: Of Complexion, Black, but by design, as the Gypsies in England: They grease themselves with Bears-fat clarified, and using no defence against Sun or Weather, their skins must needs be swarthy; Their Eye is little and black, not unlike a straight-look't Jew: The thick Lip and flat Nose, so frequent with the East-Indians and Blacks, are not common to them; for I have seen as comely European-like faces among them of both, as on your side the Sea; and truly an Italian Complexion hath not much more of the White, and the Noses of several of them have as much of the Roman.

XII. Their Language is lofty, yet narrow, but like the Hebrew; in Signification full, like Short-hand in writing; one word serveth in the place of three, and the rest are supplied by the Understanding of the Hearer: Imperfect in their Tenses, wanting in their Moods, Participles, Adverbs, Conjunctions, Interjections: I have made it my business to understand it, that I might not want an Interpreter on any occasion: And I must say, that I know not a Language spoken in Europe, that hath words of more sweetness or greatness, in Accent and Emphasis, than theirs. . . .

XIII. Of their Customs and Manners there is much to be said; I will begin with Children. So soon as they are born, they wash them in Water, and while very young, in cold Weather to chuse, they Plunge them in the Rivers to harden and embolden them. Having wrapt them in a Clout, they lay them on a straight thin Board, a little more than the length and breadth of the Child, and swadle it fast upon the Board to make it straight; wherefore all Indians have flat Heads; and thus they carry them at their Backs. The Children will go very young, at nine Moneths commonly; they wear only a small Clout round their Waste, till they are big; if Boys, they go a Fishing till ripe for the Woods, which is about Fifteen; then they Hunt, and after having given some Proofs of their Manhood, by a good return of Skins, they may Marry, else it is a shame to think of a Wife. The Girls stay with their Mothers, and

Albert Cook Myers, ed., *Narratives of Early Pennsylvania, West Jersey, and Delaware* (New York: Charles Scribner's Sons, 1912), pp. 230–36.

help to hoe the Ground, plant Corn and carry Burthens; and they do well to use them to that Young, they must do when they are Old; for the Wives are the true Servants of their Husbands; otherwise the Men are very affectionate to them.

XIV. When the Young Women are fit for Marriage, they wear something upon their Heads for an Advertisement, but so as their Faces are hardly to be seen, but when they please: The Age they Marry at, if Women, is about thirteen and fourteen; if Men, seventeen and eighteen; they are rarely elder.

XV. Their Houses are Mats, or Barks of Trees set on Poles, in the fashion of an English Barn, but out of the power of the Winds, for they are hardly higher than a Man; they lie on Reeds or Grass. In Travel they lodge in the Woods about a great Fire, with the Mantle of Duffils they wear by day, wrapt about them, and a few Boughs stuck round them.

XVI. Their Diet is Maze, or Indian Corn, divers ways prepared: sometimes Roasted in the Ashes, sometimes beaten and Boyled with Water, which they call *Homine;* they also make Cakes, not unpleasant to eat: They have likewise several sorts of Beans and Pease that are good Nourishment; and the Woods and Rivers are their Larder.

XVII. If an European comes to see them, or calls for Lodging at their House or *Wigwam* they give him the best place and first cut. If they come to visit us, they salute us with an *Itah* which is as much as to say, Good be to you, and set them down, which is mostly on the Ground close to their Heels, their Legs upright; may be they speak not a word more, but observe all Passages: If you give them any thing to eat or drink, well, for they will not ask; and be it little or much, if it be with Kindness, they are well pleased, else they go away sullen, but say nothing.

XVIII. They are great Concealers of their own Resentments, brought to it, I believe, by the Revenge that hath been practised among them; in either of these, they are not exceeded by the Italians. A Tragical Instance fell out since I came into the Country; A King's Daughter thinking her self slighted by her Husband, in suffering another Woman to lie down between them, rose up, went out, pluck't a Root out of the Ground, and ate it, upon which she immediately dyed; and for which, last Week he made an Offering to her Kindred for Attonement and liberty of Marriage; as two others did to the Kindred of their Wives, that dyed a natural Death: For till Widdowers have done so, they must not marry again. Some of the young Women are said to take undue liberty before Marriage for a Portion; but when marryed, chaste; when with Child, they know their Husbands no more, till delivered; and during their Moneth, they touch no Meat, they eat, but with a Stick, least they should defile it; nor do their Husbands frequent them, till that time be expired.

XIX. But in Liberality they excell, nothing is too good for their friend; give them a fine Gun, Coat, or other thing, it may pass twenty hands, before it sticks; light of Heart, strong Affections, but soon spent; the most merry Creatures that live, Feast and Dance perpetually; they never have much, nor want much: Wealth circulateth like the Blood, all parts partake; and though none shall want what another hath, yet exact Observers of Property. Some Kings have sold, others presented me with several parcels of Land; the Pay or Presents I made them, were not hoarded by the particular Owners, but the neighbouring Kings and their Clans being present when the Goods were brought out, the Parties chiefly concerned consulted, what and to whom they should give them? To every King then, by the hands of a Person for that work appointed, is a proportion sent, so sorted and folded, and with that Gravity, that is admirable. Then that King sub-divideth it in like manner among his Dependents, they hardly leaving themselves an Equal share with one of their Subjects: and be it on such occasions, at Festivals, or at their common Meals, the Kings distribute, and to themselves last. They care for little, because they want but little; and the Reason is, a little contents them: In this they are sufficiently revenged on us; if they are ignorant of our Pleasures, they are also free from our Pains. They are not disquieted with Bills of Lading and Exchange, nor perplexed with Chancery-Suits and Exchequer-Reckonings. We sweat and toil to live; their pleasure feeds them, I mean, their Hunting, Fishing and Fowling, and this Table is spread every where; they eat twice a day, Morning and Evening; their Seats and Table are the Ground. Since the European came into these parts, they are grown great lovers of strong Liquors, Rum especially, and for it exchange the richest of their Skins and Furs: If they are heated with Liquors, they are restless till they have enough to sleep; that is their cry. Some more, and I will go to sleep; but when Drunk, one of the most wretchedst Spectacles in the world.

XX. In sickness impatient to be cured, and for it give any thing, especially for their Children, to whom they are extreamly natural; they drink at those times a *Teran* or Decoction of some Roots in spring Water; and if they eat any flesh, it must be of the Female of any Creature; If they dye, they bury them with their Apparel, be they Men or Women, and the nearest of Kin fling in something precious with them, as a token of their Love: Their Mourning is blacking of their faces, which they continue for a year; They are choice of the Graves of their Dead; for least they should be lost by time, and fall to common use, they pick off the Grass that grows upon them, and heap up the fallen Earth with great care and exactness.

XXI. These poor People are under a dark Night in things relating to Religion, to be sure, the Tradition of it; yet they believe a God and Immortality, without the help of Metaphysicks; for they say, There is a great King that made them, who dwells in a glorious Country to the Southward of them, and that the Souls of the good shall go thither, where they shall live again. Their Worship consists of two parts, Sacrifice and *Cantico.* Their Sacrifice is their first Fruits; the first and fattest Buck they kill, goeth to the fire, where he is all burnt with a Mournful Ditty of him that performeth the Ceremony, but with such marvellous Fervency and Labour of Body, that he will even sweat to a foam. The other part is their *Cantico,* performed by round-Dances, sometimes Words, sometimes Songs, then Shouts, two being in the middle that begin, and by Singing and Drumming on a Board direct the Chorus: Their Postures in the Dance are very Antick and differing, but all keep measure. This is done with equal Earnestness and Labour, but great appearance of Joy. In the Fall, when the Corn cometh in, they begin to feast one another; there have been two great Festivals already, to which all come that will: I was at one my self; their Entertainment was a green Seat by a Spring, under some shady Trees, and twenty Bucks, with hot Cakes of new Corn, both Wheat and Beans, which they make up in a square form, in the leaves of the Stem, and bake them in the Ashes: And after that they fell to Dance, But they that go, must carry a small Present in their Money, it may be six Pence, which is made of the Bone of a Fish; the black is with them as Gold, the white, Silver; they call it all *Wampum.*

XXII.   Their Government is by Kings, which they call *Sachema,* and those by Succession, but always of the Mothers side; for Instance, the Children of him that is now King, will not succeed, but his Brother by the Mother, or the Children of his Sister, whose Sons (and after them the Children of her Daughters) will reign; for no Woman inherits; the Reason they render for this way of Descent, is, that their Issue may not be spurious.

XXIII. Every King hath his Council, and that consists of all the Old and Wise men of his Nation, which perhaps is two hundred People: nothing of Moment is undertaken, be it War, Peace, Selling of Land or Traffick, without advising with them; and which is more, with the Young Men too. 'Tis admirable to consider, how Powerful the Kings are, and yet how they move by the Breath of their People. I have had occasion to be in Council with them upon Treaties for Land, and to adjust the terms of Trade; their Order is thus: The King sits in the middle of an half Moon, and hath his Council, the Old and Wise on each hand; behind them, or at a little distance, sit the younger Fry, in the same figure. Having consulted and resolved their business, the King ordered one of them to speak to me; he stood up, came to me, and in the Name of his King saluted me, then took me by the hand, and told me, That he was ordered by his King to speak to me, and that now it was not he, but the King that spoke, because what he should say, was the King's mind. He first pray'd me, To excuse them that they had not complyed with me the last time; he feared, there might be some fault in the Interpreter, being neither Indian nor English; besides, it was the Indian Custom to deliberate, and take up much time in Council, before they resolve; and that if the Young People and Owners of the Land had been as ready as he, I had not met with so much delay. Having thus introduced his matter, he fell to the Bounds of the Land they had agreed to dispose of, and the Price, (which now is little and dear, that which would have bought twenty Miles, not buying now two.) During the time that this Person spoke, not a man of them was observed to whisper or smile; the Old, Grave, the Young, Reverend in their Deportment; they do speak little, but fervently, and with Elegancy: I have never seen more natural Sagacity, considering them without the help, (I was agoing to say, the spoil) of Tradition; and he will deserve the Name of Wise, that Outwits them in any Treaty about a thing they understand. When the Purchase was agreed, great Promises past between us of Kindness and good Neighbourhood, and that the Indians and English must live in Love, as long as the Sun gave light. Which done, another made a Speech to the Indians, in the Name of all the *Sachamakers* or Kings, first to tell them what was done; next, to charge and command them, To Love the Christians, and particularly live in Peace with me, and the People under my Government: That many Governours had been in the River, but that no Governour had come himself to live and stay here before; and having now such a one that had treated them well, they should never do him or his any wrong. At every sentence of which they shouted, and said, Amen, in their way.

XXIV. The Justice they have is Pecuniary: In case of any Wrong or evil Fact, be it Murther it self, they Attone by Feasts and Presents of their *Wampon,* which is proportioned to the quality of the Offence or Person injured, or of the Sex they are of: for in case they kill a Woman, they pay double, and the Reason they render, is, That she breedeth Children, which Men cannot do. 'Tis rare that they fall out, if Sober; and if Drunk, they forgive it, saying, It was the Drink, and not the Man, that abused them.

XXV. We have agreed, that in all Differences between us, Six of each side shall end the matter: Don't abuse them, but let them have Justice, and you win them: The worst is, that they are the worse for the Christians, who have propagated their Vices, and yielded them Tradition for ill, and not for good things. But as low an Ebb as they are at, and as glorious as their Condition looks, the Christians have not out-liv'd their sight with all their Pretensions to an higher Manifestation: What good then might not a good People graft, where there is so distinct a Knowledge left between Good and Evil? I beseech God to incline the Hearts of all that come into these parts, to out-live the Knowledge of the Natives, by a fixt Obedience to their greater Knowledge of the Will of God, for it were miserable indeed for us to fall under the just censure of the poor Indian Conscience, while we make profession of things so far transcending.

3.4: A Moravian Missionary Praises Native American Values (1777)

The Reverend John Heckewelder was a clergyman of the Moravian denomination, a pious Protestant sect that traced its roots to fifteenth-century Central Europe. Moravians came to America in the 1740s and settled in Pennsylvania. From Bethlehem, their hub, they soon dispatched missionaries to the Indians.

Heckewelder spent many years among the frontier tribes during the last half of the eighteenth century and wrote an account of his experiences. The following selection describes Indian hospitality and Indian attitudes toward private property. Do these views help explain why Native Americans and people of European ancestry often clashed? Is there a resemblance between Indian attitudes toward nature during the eighteenth century and views of modern environmentalists? Why might there be such a similarity? Would it be fair to describe the effort to convert the Indians to the Christian faith as an implicit act of disrespect?

Indians and Nature

JOHN HECKEWELDER

Not satisfied with paying this first of duties to the Lord of all, in the best manner they are able, the Indians also endeavour to fulfil the views which they suppose he had in creating the world. They think that he made the earth and all that it contains for the common good of mankind; when he stocked the country that he gave them with plenty of game, it was not for the benefit of a few, but of all. Every thing was given in common to the sons of men. Whatever liveth on the land, whatsoever groweth out of the earth, and all that is in the rivers and waters flowing through the same, was given jointly to all, and every one is entitled to his share. From this principle, hospitality flows as from its source. With them it is not a virtue but a strict duty. Hence they are never in search of excuses to avoid giving, but freely supply their neighbour's wants from the stock prepared for their own use. They give and are hospitable to all, without exception, and will always share with each other and often with the stranger, even to their last morsel. They rather would lie down themselves on an empty stomach, than have it laid to their charge that they had neglected their duty, by not satisfying the wants of the stranger, the sick or the needy. The stranger has a claim to their hospitality, partly on account of his being at a distance from his family and friends, and partly because he has honoured them by his visit, and ought to leave them with a good impression upon his mind; the sick and the poor because they have a right to be helped out of the common stock: for if the meat they have been served with, was taken from the woods, it was common to all before the hunter took it; if corn or vegetables, it had grown out of the common ground, yet not by the power of man, but by that of the Great Spirit. Besides, on the principle, that all are descended from one parent, they look upon themselves as but one great family, who therefore ought at all times and on all occasions, to be serviceable and kind to each other, and by that means make themselves acceptable to the head of the universal family, the great and good Mannitto. Let me be permitted to illustrate this by an example.

John Heckewelder, *Account of the History, Manners and Customs of the Indian Nations, Who Once Inhabited Pennsylvania and the Neighboring States* (Philadelphia: The American Philosophical Society, 1819), pp. 85–87.

Some travelling Indians having in the year 1777, put their horses over night to pasture in my little meadow, at Gnadenhutten on the Muskingum, I called on them in the morning to learn why they had done so. I endeavoured to make them sensible of the injury they had done me, especially as I intended to mow the meadow in a day or two. Having finished my complaint, one of them replied: "My friend, it seems you lay claim to the grass my horses have eaten, because you had enclosed it with a fence: now tell me, who caused the grass to grow? Can *you* make the grass grow? I think not, and no body can except the great Mannitto. He it is who causes it to grow both for my horses and for yours! See, friend! the grass which grows out of the earth is common to all; the game in the woods is common to all. Say, did you never eat venison and bear's meat?—"Yes, very often."—Well, and did you ever hear me or any other Indian complain about that? No; then be not disturbed at my horses having eaten only once, of what you call *your* grass, though the grass my horses did eat, in like manner as the meat you did eat, was given to the Indians by the Great Spirit. Besides, if you will but consider, you will find that my horses did not eat *all* your grass. For friendship's sake, however, I shall never put my horses in your meadow again."

The Indians are not only just, they are also in many respects a generous people, and cannot see the sick and the aged suffer for want of clothing. To such they will give a blanket, a shirt, a pair of leggings, mocksens, &c. Otherwise, when they make presents, it is done with a view to receive an equivalent in return, and the receiver is given to understand what that ought to be. In making presents to strangers, they are content with some trifle in token of remembrance; but when they give any thing to a trader, they at least expect double the value in return, saying that he can afford to do it, since he had cheated them so often.

They treat each other with civility, and shew much affection on meeting after an absence. When they meet in the forenoon, they will compliment one another with saying, "a good morning to you!" and in the afternoon "a good evening." In the act of shaking hands with each other, they strictly attend to the distinguishing names of relations, which they utter at the time; as for instance, "a good morning, father, grandfather, uncle, aunt, cousin," and so down to a small grandchild. They are also in the habit of saluting old people no ways related to them, by the names of grandfather and grandmother, not in a tone of condescending superiority or disguised contempt, but as a genuine mark of the respect which they feel for age. The common way of saluting where no relationship exists, is that of "friend;" when, however, the young people meet, they make use of words suitable to their years or stage in life; they will say "a good morning, comrade, favourite, beloved, &c." Even the children salute each other affectionately. "I am glad to see you," is the common way in which the Indians express themselves to one another after a short absence; but on meeting after a long absence, on the return of a messenger or a warrior from a critical or dangerous expedition, they have more to say; the former is saluted in the most cordial manner with some such expression: "I thank the Great Spirit, that he has preserved our lives to this time of our happily meeting again. I am, indeed, very glad to see you." To which the other will reply: "you speak the truth; it is through the favour of the great and good Spirit that we are permitted to meet. I am equally glad to see you." To the latter will be said: "I am glad that the Great Spirit has preserved your life and granted you a safe return to your family."

3.5:   Treaties and Alliances (1684, 1742)

Contact between European settlers and Native Americans took place on both global and decentralized levels. Native Americans became tragically engulfed in European imperial contests, and ultimately, individual colonies negotiated treaties or alliances with individual native tribes—often playing them off against their neighbors or rivals.

The attached documents reveal the complexity of settler–native relations. What can we determine about these relations from these documents? Were natural resources such as land and game abundant, or was human society in stiff competition over their control? What levels of trust and integrity existed in settler–native relations, and what long-term trends might you expect to develop based upon the reading of these documents?

Iroquois Chiefs Address the Governors of New York and Virginia (1684)

[Spokesman for the Onondagas and Cayugas:]

Brother Corlear,

Your Sachem is a great Sachem, and we are but a small People; but when the English came first to Manhatan [New York], to Aragiske [Virginia] and to Yakokranagary [Maryland], they were then but a small People, and we were great. Then, because we found you a good People, we treated you kindly, and gave you Land; we hope therefore, now that you are great, and we small, you will protect us from the French. If you do not, we shall lose all our Hunting and Bevers: The French will get all the Bevers. The Reason they are now angry with us is, because we carry our Bever to our Brethren.

We have put our Lands and ourselves under the Protection of the great Duke of York, the Brother of your great Sachem, who is likewise a great Sachem.

We have annexed the Susquehana River, which we won with the sword, to this Government; and we desire it may be a Branch of the great Tree that grows in this Place, the Top of which reaches the Sun, and its Branches shelter us from the French, and all other Nations. Our Fire burns in your Houses, and your Fire burns with us; we desire it may be so always. But we will not that any of the great Penn's People settle upon the Susquehana River, for we have no other Land to leave to our Children.

Our young Men are Soldiers, and when they are provoked, they are like Wolves in the Woods, as you, Sachem of Virginia, very well know.

Cadwallader Colden, *The History of the Five Nations of Canada* (London, 1755), vol. 1, pp. 46–51.

We have put ourselves under the great Sachem Charles, that lives on the other Side the great Lake. We give you these two white dressed Deer-skins, to send to the great Sachem, that he may write on them, and put a great red Seal to them, to confirm what we now do; and put the Susquehana River above the Falls, and all the rest of our Land under the great Duke of York, and give that Land to none else. Our Brethren, his People, have been like Fathers to our Wives and Children, and have given us Bread when we were in Need of it; we will not therefore join ourselves, or our Land, to any other Government but this. We desire Corlear, our Governor, may send this our Proposition to the great Sachem Charles, who dwells on the other Side the great Lake, with this Belt of Wampum, and this other smaller Belt to the Duke of York his Brother: And we give you, Corlear, this Bever, that you may send over this Proposition.

You great Man of Virginia, we let you know, that great Penn did speak to us here in Corlear's House by his Agents, and desired to buy the Susquehana River of us, but we would not hearken to him, for we had fastened it to this Government.

We desire you therefore to bear witness of what we now do, and that we now confirm what we have done before. Let your Friend, that lives on the other Side the great Lake, know this, that we being a free People, though united to the English, may give our Lands, and be joined to the Sachem we like best. We give this Bever to remember what we say.

[Spokesman for the Senecas:]

We have heard and understood what Mischief hath been done in Virginia; we have it as perfect as if it were upon our Fingers Ends. O Corlear! we thank you for having been our Intercessor, so that the Axe has not fallen upon us.

And you Assarigoa, great Sachem of Virginia, we thank you for burying all Evil in the Pit. We are informed, that the Mohawks, Oneydoes, Onnondagas, and Cayugas, have buried the Axe already; now we that live remotest off, are come to do the same, and to include in this Chain the Cahnawaas, your Friends. We desire therefore, that an Axe, on our Part, may be buried with one of Assarigoa's. O Corlear! Corlear! we thank you for laying hold on one End of the Axe; and we thank you, great Governor of Virginia, not only for throwing aside the Axe, but more especially for your putting all Evil from your Heart. Now we have a new Chain, a strong and a straight Chain, that cannot be broken. The Tree of Peace is planted so firmly, that it cannot be moved, let us on both Sides hold the Chain fast.

We understand what you said of the great Sachem, that lives on the other Side the great Water.

You tell us, that the Cahnawaas will come hither, to strengthen the Chain. Let them not make any Excuse, that they are old and feeble, or that their Feet are sore. If the old Sachems cannot, let the young Men come. We shall not fail to come hither, tho' we live farthest off, and then the new Chain will be stronger and brighter.

We understand, that because of the Mischief that has been done to the People and Castles of Virginia and Maryland, we must not come near the Heads of your Rivers, now near your Plantations; but keep at the Foot of the Mountains; for tho' we lay down our Arms, as Friends, we shall not be trusted for the future, but looked on as Robbers. We agree however to this Proposition, and shall wholly stay away from Virginia: And this we do in Gratitude to Corlear, who has been at so great Pains to persuade you, great Governor of Virginia, to forget what is past. You are wise in giving Ear to Corlear's good Advice, for we shall now go a Path which was never trod before.

We have now done speaking to Corlear, and the Governor of Virginia; let the Chain be for ever kept clean and bright by him, and we shall do the same.

The other Nations from the Mohawks Country to the Cayugas, have delivered up the Susquehana River, and all that Country, to Corlear's Government. We confirm what they have done by giving this Belt.

An Iroquois Chief Discusses the Treaty of Rights (1742)

Canassateego:

Brethren, the Governor and Council, and all present,

According to our Promise we now propose to return you an Answer to the several Things mentioned to us Yesterday, and shall beg Leave to speak to publick Affairs first, tho' they were what you spoke to last. On this Head you Yesterday put us in Mind, first, of William Penn's early and constant Care to cultivate Friendship with all the Indians; of the Treaty we held with one of his Sons, about ten Years ago; and of the Necessity there is at this Time of keeping the Roads between us clear and free from all Obstructions. We are all very sensible of the kind Regard that good Man William Penn had for all the Indians, and cannot but be pleased to find that his Children have the same. We well remember the Treaty you mention, held with his Son on his Arrival here, by which we confirmed our League of Friendship, that is to last as long as the Sun and Moon endure. In Consequence of this, we, on our Part, shall preserve the Road free from all Incumbrances; in Confirmation whereof we lay down this String of Wampum. . . .

Brethren, we received from the Proprietor Yesterday, some Goods in Consideration of our Release of the Lands on the West-side of the Susquehannah. It is true, we have the full Quantity according to Agreement; but if the Proprietor had been here himself, we think, in Regard of our Numbers and Poverty, he would have made an Addition to them. If the Goods were only to be divided amongst the Indians present, a single Person would have but a small Portion; but if you consider what Numbers are left behind, equally entitled with us to a Share, there will be extremely little. We therefore desire, if you have the Keys of the Proprietor's Chest, you will open it, and take out a little more for us.

We know our Lands are now become more valuable. The white People think we do not know their Value; but we are sensible that the Land is everlasting, and the few Goods we receive for it are soon worn out and gone. For the future, we will sell

Julian P. Boyd., ed., *Indian Treaties Printed by Benjamin Franklin, 1736–1762.* (Philadelphia: The Historical Society of Pennsylvania, 1938.).

no Lands but when the Proprietor is in the Country; and we will know beforehand, the Quantity of the Goods we are to receive. Besides, we are not well used with respect to the Lands still unsold by us. Your People daily settle on these Lands, and spoil our Hunting. We must insist on your removing them, as you know they have no Right to settle to the Northward of Kittochtinny-Hills. In particular, we renew our Complaints against some People who are settled at the Juniata, a Branch of the Susquehannah, and all the Banks of that River, as far as Mahaniay; and we desire they may be forthwith made to go off the Land, for they do great Damage to our Cousins the Delawares.

We have further to observe, with respect to the Lands lying on the Westside of the Susquehannah, that though the Proprietor has paid us for what his People possess, yet some Parts of that Country have been taken up by Persons, whose Place of Residence is to the South of this Province, from whom we have never received any Consideration. This Affair was recommended to you by our Chiefs at our last Treaty; and you then, at our earnest Desire, promised to write a Letter to that Person who has the Authority over those People, and to procure us his Answer. As we have never heard from you on this Head, we want to know what you have done in it. If you have not done any Thing, we now *renew* our Request, and desire you will inform the Person whose People are seated on our Lands, that that Country belongs to us, in Right of Conquest—we having bought it with our Blood, and taken it from our Enemies in fair War; and we expect, as Owners of that Land, to receive such a Consideration for it as the Land is worth. We desire you will press him to send a positive Answer. Let him say Yes or No. If he says Yes, we will treat with him; if No, we are able to do ourselves Justice; and we will do it, by going to take Payment ourselves.

It is customary with us to make a Present of Skins, whenever we renew our Treaties. We are ashamed to offer our brethren so few, but your Horses and Cows have eat the Grass our Deer used to feed on. This has made them scarce, and will, we hope, plead in Excuse for our not bringing a larger Quantity. If we could have spared more, we would have given more, but we are really poor; and desire you'll not consider the Quantity, but few as they are, accept them in Testimony of our Regard.

Lieutenant Governor Thomas:

Brethren,

We thank you for the many Declarations of Respect you have given us, in this solemn Renewal of our Treaties. We receive, and shall keep your String and Belts of Wampum, as Pledges of your Sincerity, and desire those we gave you may be carefully preserved, as Testimonies of ours.

In answer to what you say about the Proprietaries: they are all absent, and have taken the Keys of their Chest with them; so that we cannot, on their Behalf, enlarge the Quantity of Goods. Were they here, they might perhaps be more generous; but we cannot be liberal for them. The Government will, however, take your Request into Consideration; and in Regard to your Poverty, may perhaps make you a Present. . . .

The Number of Guns, as well as every Thing else, answers exactly with the Particulars specified in your Deed of Conveyance, which is more than was agreed to be given you. It was your own Sentiments, that the Lands on the West-side of the Susquehannah, were not so valuable as those on the East; and an Abatement was to be made, proportionable to the Difference in Value. But the Proprietor overlooked this, and ordered the full Quantity to be delivered, which you will look on as a Favour.

It is very true, that Lands are of late becoming more valuable; but what raises their Value? Is it not entirely owing to the Industry and Labour used by the white People, in their Cultivation and Improvement? Had not they come amongst you, these Lands would have been of no Use to you, any further than to maintain you. And is there not, now you have sold so much, enough left for all the Purposes of Living? What you say of the Goods, that they are soon worn out, is applicable to every Thing; but you know very well, that they cost a great deal of Money; and the Value of Land is no more, than it is worth in Money.

3.6:   The Paxton Boys and Native American Extermination (1764)

In 1763 Pennsylvania, for many years the model of good Native American–white relations, witnessed one of the most deplorable incidents of white brutality against Native Americans during the colonial era. The perpetrators were the so-called Paxton Boys, a group of hot-headed frontier farmers, mostly of Scotch-Irish stock, who deeply resented the refusal of the Quaker-dominated legislature in Philadelphia to protect them against Indian attack. Claiming that the Conestoga Indians, converts to Christianity, were selling guns to the hostile frontier tribes, in 1763 they descended on the unarmed Conestogas, and, despite the colonial authorities' attempt to provide protection, massacred most of them without regard to age or sex.

Benjamin Franklin, by now a prominent man of affairs in Philadelphia, penned the eloquent denunciation of the Paxton Boys' brutal assault that follows. No figure in our history so closely approximates the American ideal of common decency as Franklin. Some would say his outrage does credit to our national tradition of fairness. Does it? Does the incident say anything about the differences between frontier attitudes toward Indians and those of the older, settled regions?

The perpetrators were never punished, in spite of governor John Penn's offer of a reward for their capture. Does this failure reveal anything about white attitudes?

A Narrative of the Late Massacres, in Lancaster County, of a Number of Indians, Friends of This Province, by Persons Unknown. With Some Observations on the Same. Printed in the Year MDCCLXIV.

BENJAMIN FRANKLIN

These *Indians* were the Remains of a Tribe of the *Six Nations,* settled at *Conestogoe,* and thence called *Conestogoe Indians.* On the first Arrival of the *English* in *Pennsylvania,* Messengers from this Tribe came to welcome them, with Presents of Venison, Corn, and Skins; and the whole Tribe entered into a Treaty of Friendship with the first Proprietor, William Penn, which was to last "as long as the Sun should shine, or the Waters run in the Rivers."

This Treaty has been since frequently renewed, and the *Chain brightened,* as they express it, from time to time. It has never been violated, on their Part or ours, till now. As their Lands by Degrees were mostly purchased, and the Settlements of the White People began to surround them, the Proprietor assigned them lands on the Manor of *Conestogoe,* which they might not part with; there they have lived many years in Friendship with their White Neighbours, who loved them for their peaceable inoffensive Behaviour.

It has always been observed, that *Indians,* settled in the Neighbourhood of White People, do not increase, but diminish continually. This Tribe accordingly went on diminishing, till there remained in their Town on the Manor, but 20 persons, viz. 7 Men, 5 Women, and 8 Children, Boys and Girls.

Of these, *Shehaes* was a very old Man, having assisted at the second Treaty held with them, by Mr. Penn, in 1701, and ever since continued a faithful and affectionate Friend to the *English;* He is said to have been an exceeding good Man, considering his Education, being naturally of a most kind, benevolent Temper.

Peggy was *Shehaes's* Daughter; she worked for her aged Father, continuing to live with him, though married, and attended him with filial Duty and Tenderness.

John was another good old Man; his Son *Harry* helped to support him.

George and *Will Soc* were two Brothers, both young Men.

John Smith, a valuable young Man of the *Cayuga* Nation, who became acquainted with *Peggy, Shehaes's* Daughter, some few Years since, married her, and settled in that Family. They had one Child, about three Years old.

Betty, a harmless old Woman; and her son *Peter,* a likely young Lad.

Sally, whose *Indian* name was *Wyanjoy,* a Woman much esteemed by all that knew her, for her prudent and good Behaviour in some very trying situations of Life. She was a truly good and an amiable Woman, had no Children of her own, but, a distant Relation dying, she had taken a Child of that Relation's, to bring up as her own, and performed towards it all the Duties of an affectionate Parent.

Benjamin Franklin, *The Writings of Benjamin Franklin,* A. H. Smyth, ed. (New York: The Macmillan Company, 1905–7), vol. 4, pp. 289–93.

The Reader will observe, that many of their Names are *English*. It is common with the *Indians* that have an affection for the *English,* to give themselves, and their Children, the Names of such *English* Persons as they particularly esteem.

This little Society continued the Custom they had begun, when more numerous, of addressing every new Governor, and every Descendant of the first Proprietor, welcoming him to the Province, assuring him of their Fidelity, and praying a Continuance of that Favour and Protection they had hitherto experienced. They had accordingly sent up an Address of this Kind to our present Governor, on his Arrival; but the same was scarce delivered, when the unfortunate Catastrophe happened, which we are about to relate.

On *Wednesday,* the 14th of *December,* 1763, Fifty-seven Men, from some of our Frontier Townships, who had projected the Destruction of this little Commonwealth, came, all well mounted, and armed with Firelocks, Hangers and Hatchets, having travelled through the Country in the Night, to *Conestogoe* Manor. There they surrounded the small Village of *Indian* Huts, and just at Break of Day broke into them all at once. Only three Men, two Women, and a young Boy, were found at home, the rest being out among the neighbouring White People, some to sell the Baskets, Brooms and Bowls they manufactured, and others on other Occasions. These poor defenceless Creatures were immediately fired upon, stabbed, and hatcheted to Death! The good *Shehaes,* among the rest, cut to Pieces in his Bed. All of them were scalped and otherwise horribly mangled. Then their Huts were set on Fire, and most of them burnt down. Then the Troop, pleased with their own Conduct and Bravery, but enraged that any of the poor *Indians* had escaped the Massacre, rode off, and in small Parties, by different Roads, went home.

The universal Concern of the neighbouring White People on hearing of this Event, and the Lamentations of the younger *Indians,* when they returned and saw the Desolation, and the butchered half-burnt Bodies of their murdered Parents and other Relations, cannot well be expressed.

The Magistrates of *Lancaster* sent out to collect the remaining *Indians,* brought them into the Town for their better Security against any farther Attempt; and it is said condoled with them on the Misfortune that had happened, took them by the Hand, comforted and *promised them Protection.* They were all put into the Workhouse, a strong Building, as the Place of greatest Safety.

When the shocking News arrived in Town, a Proclamation was issued by the Governor, in the following Terms, viz.

"Whereas I have received Information, that on *Wednesday,* the Fourteenth Day of this Month, a Number of People, armed, and mounted on Horseback, unlawfully assembled together, and went to the *Indian* Town in the *Conestogoe* Manor, in *Lancaster County,* and without the least Reason or Provocation, in cool Blood, barbarously killed six of the *Indians* settled there, and burnt and destroyed all their Houses and Effects: And whereas so cruel and inhuman an Act, committed in the Heart of this Province on the said *Indians,* who have lived peaceably and inoffensively among us, during all our late Troubles, and for many Years before, and were justly considered as under the Protection of this Government and its Laws, calls loudly for the vigorous Exertion of the civil Authority, to detect the

Offenders, and bring them to condign Punishment; I have therefore, by and with the Advice and Consent of the Council, thought fit to issue this Proclamation, and do hereby strictly charge and enjoin all Judges, Justices, Sheriffs, Constables, Officers Civil and Military, and all other His Majesty's liege Subjects within this Province, to make diligent Search and Enquiry after the Authors and Perpetrators of the said Crime, their Abettors and Accomplices, and to use all possible Means to apprehend and secure them in some of the publick Gaols of this Province, that they may be brought to their Trials, and be proceeded against according to Law.

"And whereas a Number of other *Indians,* who lately lived on or near the Frontiers of this province, being willing and desirous to preserve and continue the ancient Friendship, which heretofore subsisted between them and the good People of this Province, have, at their own earnest Request, been removed from their Habitations, and brought into the County of *Philadelphia* and seated for the present, for their better Security, on the *Province Island,* and in other places in the Neighbourhood of the City of *Philadelphia,* where Provision is made for them at the public Expence; I do therefore hereby strictly forbid all Persons whatsoever, to molest or injure any of the said *Indians,* as they will answer the contrary at their Peril.

"Given under my Hand, and the Great Seal of the said Province, at Philadelphia, *the Twenty-second Day of* December, *Anno Domini One Thousand Seven Hundred and Sixty-three, and in the Fourth Year of His Majesty's Reign.*

"JOHN PENN.

"By his Honour's Command,
"JOSEPH SHIPPEN, *Jun., Secretary.*
"God save the King."

Notwithstanding this Proclamation, those cruel Men again assembled themselves, and hearing that the remaining fourteen *Indians* were in the Workhouse at *Lancaster,* they suddenly appeared in that Town, on the 27th of *December.* Fifty of them, armed as before, dismounting, went directly to the Workhouse, and by Violence broke open the Door, and entered with the utmost Fury in their Countenances. When the poor Wretches saw they had *no Protection* nigh, nor could possibly escape, and being without the least Weapon for Defence, they divided into their little Families, the Children clinging to the Parents; they fell on their Knees, protested their Innocence, declared their Love to the *English,* and that, in their whole Lives, they had never done them Injury; and in this Posture they all received the Hatchet! Men, Women and little Children were every one inhumanly murdered!—in cold Blood!

The barbarous Men who committed the atrocious Fact, in defiance of Government, of all Laws human and divine, and to the eternal Disgrace of their Country and Colour, then mounted their Horses, huzza'd in Triumph, as if they had gained a Victory, and rode off—*unmolested!*

The Bodies of the Murdered were then brought out and exposed in the Street, till a Hole could be made in the Earth to receive and cover them.

But the Wickedness cannot be covered, the Guilt will lie on the whole Land, till Justice is done on the Murderers. THE BLOOD OF THE INNOCENT WILL CRY TO HEAVEN FOR VENGEANCE.

It is said that, *Shehaes* being before told, that it was to be feared some *English* might come from the Frontier into the Country, and murder him and his People; he replied, "It is impossible: there are *Indians,* indeed, in the Woods, who would kill me and mine, if they could get at us, for my Friendship to the *English;* but the *English* will wrap me in their Matchcoat, and secure me from all Danger." How unfortunately was he mistaken!

❖ *4* ❖

Patriot Versus Loyalist

The patriot (Whig) cause that propelled the American colonies toward independence was not universally admired or embraced. Many colonists preferred the loyalist (Tory) view that considered British policy benign and dismissed the angry and unruly attacks against Britain after 1763 as undeserved. When the tensions of the imperial crisis finally sparked armed revolt in 1775, about a quarter of the American people chose the loyalist road.

The documents below record the discordant voices, British and American, patriot and loyalist, of the political debate that swirled through the empire in the years following England's peace with France in 1763. In evaluating them try to detect, beneath the debaters' formal logic, the different assumptions of each. Both sides often emphasize rights. But what about interests? What conflicting interests were at stake in the conflict over the future of America within the empire?

4.1: The Stamp Act Congress Denounces Taxation Without Representation (1765)

Conflict over American political autonomy was probably inevitable as the English-speaking colonies matured and grew in population and wealth. Yet a significant incident was required to trigger a British-American imperial crisis. That incident came in March 1765 with the passage by Parliament of the Stamp Act, placing taxes, in the form of a stamp, on legal and commercial documents, college diplomas, playing cards, dice, newspapers, advertisements, almanacs, and calendars.

The measure was intended to force the Americans to share the cost of defending the empire and to relieve the British taxpayer of a crushing burden. It produced an explosion of wrath in America. Reaction ranged

*from dignified petitions and remonstrances to riots and physical vio-
lence against defenders of British policies and the tax collectors appointed to administer the law. The most effective weapons against the
tax were consumer boycotts of British goods and nonimportation agreements by the port merchants against British suppliers.*

*In October 1765, at the urging of the Massachusetts General Court,
representatives of nine colonies met in New York as the Stamp Act
Congress and adopted the resolutions below addressed to the king and
the British government. What are the Americans' chief arguments
against the Stamp Act? Do the stated reasons for their objections include all the real reasons? Is the tone of the document respectful? Do
the Americans seem to revere the empire and their status as Britons?
Do you detect any signs of a desire for independence?*

*(The allusion at the end of the document to "any other acts of par-
liament" refers primarily to the Sugar Act of 1764, which placed new
taxes on various imports into the colonies and established a corps of
imperial officials to enforce the measure.)*

Declarations of the Stamp Act Congress

STAMP ACT CONGRESS

The members of this congress, sincerely devoted, with the warmest sentiments of
affection and duty to his Majesty's person and government; inviolably attached to
the present happy establishment of the Protestant succession, and with minds deeply
impressed by a sense of the present and impending misfortunes of the British
colonies on this continent; . . . make the following declarations, of our humble opinion, respecting the most essential rights and liberties of the colonists, and of the
grievances under which they labour, by reason of several late acts of Parliament.

I. That his Majesty's subjects in these colonies, owe the same allegiance to
the Crown of Great Britain, that is owing from his subjects born within the realm,
and all due subordination to that august body, the Parliament of Great Britain.

II. That his Majesty's liege subjects in these colonies are entitled to all the inherent rights and liberties of his natural born subjects within the kingdom of Great
Britain.

III. That it is inseparably essential to the freedom of a people, and the un-
doubted right of Englishmen, that no taxes should be imposed on them, but with
their own consent, given personally, or by their representatives.

IV. That the people of these colonies are not, and from their local circumstances, cannot be represented in the House of Commons in Great Britain.

John Alman, ed., "The Declarations of the Stamp Act Congress," *Collection of Interesting, Authentic Papers Relative to the Disputes between Britain and America* (London, n.p., 1777), vol. 5, no. 1, pp. 11–13.

V. That the only representatives of the people of these colonies, are persons chosen therein, by themselves; and that no taxes ever have been, or can be constitutionally imposed on them, but by their respective legislature.

VI. That all supplies to the Crown, being free gifts of the people, it is unreasonable and inconsistent with the principles and spirit of the British constitution, for the people of Great Britain to grant to his Majesty the property of the colonists.

VII. That trial by jury is the inherent and invaluable right of every British subject in these colonies.

VIII. That the late Act of Parliament, entitled, An Act for granting and applying certain Stamp Duties, ... by imposing taxes on the inhabitants of these colonies, and the said Act, and several other Acts, by extending the jurisdiction of the courts of admiralty beyond its ancient limits, have a manifest tendency to subvert the rights and liberties of the colonists.

IX. That the duties imposed by several late Acts of Parliament, from the peculiar circumstances of these colonies, will be extremely burdensome and grievous, and from the scarcity of specie, the payment of them absolutely impracticable.

X. That as the profits of the trade of these colonies ultimately centre in Great Britain, to pay for the manufactures which they are obliged to take from thence, they eventually contribute very largely to all supplies granted there to the Crown.

XI. That the restrictions imposed by several late Acts of Parliament, on the trade of these colonies, will render them unable to purchase the manufactures of Great Britain.

XII. That the increase, prosperity and happiness of these colonies, depend on the full and free enjoyment of their rights and liberties, and an intercourse with great Britain, mutually affectionate and advantageous.

XIII. That it is the right of the British subjects in these colonies, to petition the king or either house of Parliament.

Lastly, that it is the indispensable duty of these colonies to the best of sovereigns, to the mother country, and to themselves, to endeavor by a loyal and dutiful address to his Majesty, and humble applications to both houses of Parliament, to procure the repeal of the Act for granting and applying certain stamp duties, of all clauses of any other Acts of Parliament, whereby the jurisdiction of the admiralty is extended as aforesaid, and of the other late Acts for the restriction of American commerce.

4.2 A Constitutional Crisis: Virtual and Actual Representation (1765)

Pamphleteers, activists, and lawyers soon came to debate the distinctions between actual and virtual representation. This context over legal meanings and philosophical assumptions became an integral part of the constitutional crisis. Benjamin Franklin had represented several colonies as an agent to Parliament as of the writing of this let-

ter in 1765. What does Franklin say of actual and virtual representa-tion? What rights of British subjects does Franklin see endangered by the current political initiatives of Great Britain? What is the relation-ship between the rights of common consent and petition on the one hand and what we would describe as property rights on the other?

Invectives Against the Americans

BENJAMIN FRANKLIN

To the PRINTER.

I would fain know what good purpose can be answered, by the frequent invectives published in your and other papers against the Americans. Do these small writers hope to provoke the nation by their oratory, to embrue its hands in the blood of its, perhaps mistaken children? And if this should be done, do they imagine it could be of any advantage to this country? Do they expect to convince the Americans, and reduce them to submission, by their flimsey arguments of *virtual representation,* and of *Englishmen by fiction of law only,* mixed with insolence, contempt and abuse? Can it be supposed that such treatment will make them rest satisfied with the unlimited claim set up, of a power to tax them *ad libitum,* without their consent; while they are to work only for us, and our profit; restrained in their foreign trade by our laws, however profitable it might be to them; forbidden to manufacture their own produce, and obliged to purchase the work of our artificers at our own prices? Is this the state we wish to keep them in? And can it be thought such writings (which are unfortunately reprinted in all *their* papers) will induce them to bear it with greater patience, and during a longer period of time?

The gentle terms of *republican race, mixed rabble of Scotch, Irish and foreign vagabonds, descendants of convicts, ungrateful rebels,* &c. are some of the sweet flowers of English rhetorick, with which our colonists have of late been regaled. Surely, if we are so much their superiors, we should shew the superiority of our breeding by our better manners! Our slaves they may be thought: But every master of slaves ought to know, that though all the slave possesses is the property of the master, his *goodwill* is his own, he bestows it where he pleases; and it is of *some im-portance* to the master's *profit,* if he can obtain that *good-will* at the cheap rate of a few kind words, with fair and gentle usage.

These people, however, are not, never were, nor ever will be our slaves. The first settlers of New England particularly, were English gentlemen of fortune, who, being Puritans, left this country with their families and followers, in times of perse-cution, for the sake of enjoying, though in a wilderness, the blessings of civil and religious liberty; of which they retain to this day, as high a sense as any Briton whatsoever; and possess as much virtue, humanity, civility, and, let me add, *loyalty to their Prince,* as is to be found among the like number of people in any part of the world; and the other colonies merit and maintain the same character. They should then be treated with *decency* and with *candour.*

Benjamin Franklin, *The Gazetteer and New Daily Advertiser,* December 28, 1765.

Your correspondent Vindex Patriæ, who is indeed more of a reasoner than a railer, has nevertheless thought fit to assert, that "their refusing submission to the stamp act, proceeds *only* from their *ambition* of becoming *independent;* and that it is plain the colonies have no other aim but a *total enfranchisement* from obedience to our Parliament." These are strong charges; but the proofs of such ambitious and rebellious views no where appear in his paper. He has, however, condescended to give us his proofs of another point, viz. "That the colonies have no tenderness for their mother country;" (and of course I suppose, the mother country is to have none for them.) "The sugar, teas, and other commodities, says he, which they daily buy from St. Eustatia and Monte Christi, in particular, are too *convincing proofs,* that they have *no tenderness* for their mother country." May one ask this profound writer; are sugar and teas the produce of the mother country? does not she herself buy her teas from strangers? were the north americans to buy all the sugars they consume, even of our own Islands, would not that raise the price of such sugars upon us here in England? is not then their buying them of Foreigners, if it proves any thing, a Proof rather of their tenderness for their mother country? but the grocerly argument of tea and sugar, is not inferior to the lawyerly argument with which he demonstrates, that, "by a *fiction* between us and the colonists, Connecticut is in England, and therefore represented in the British parliament." I am afraid the common Americans will be as much at a loss as I am, to understand what he means by his *estoppers,* and his *averments,* and therefore not in the least convinced by his demonstration. They will only find out upon the whole, that he is not their friend; and perhaps conclude from that and his learning in the law, that he is one of their *virtual representatives* by *fiction* in P—t:

I hope, however, to see prudent measures taken by our rulers, such as may heal and not widen our breaches. The Americans, I am sure, for I know them, have not the least desire of independence; they submit, in general, to all the laws we make for them; they desire only a continuance of what they think a *right,* the privilege of manifesting their loyalty by granting their own money, when the occasions of their prince shall call for it. This right they say they have always enjoyed and exercised, and never misused; and they think it wrong that any body of men whatever, should claim a power of giving what is not their own, and make to themselves a merit with the sovereign and their own constituents, by granting away the property of others who have no representatives in that body, and therefore make no part of the *common consent in parliament,* by which alone, according to *magna charta* and the *petition of right,* taxes can be legally laid upon the subject. These are their notions. They may be errors; 'tis a part of our common constitution perhaps not hitherto sufficiently considered. 'Tis fit for the discussion of wise and learned men, who will, I doubt not, settle it wisely and benevolently. Cowardice and cruelty are indeed almost inseparable companions, and none are more ready to propose sending out fleets and armies, and to expose friends and foes to one common carnage, than such pusilanimous men as would tremble at a sword drawn in their presence tho' with the most peaceable Intention. But Britons, as a people, are equally brave and generous; prodigal of their blood and treasure where there are just calls for its expence; and by no means niggards of those rights, liberties and privileges, that make the subjects of Britain the envy and admiration of the universe.   N. N.

4.3:   The Boston Town Meeting Presents the Patriot Case (1772)

Between 1765, when the Stamp Act Congress met, and 1772, when the Boston Town Meeting adopted the resolutions below, seven eventful, contentious years had intervened. Nevertheless, by 1772 many of the points of friction between Britain and America had been smoothed over, mostly by British concessions—including repeal of the Stamp Act—and the patriot cause had receded. This calm dismayed a group of Boston firebrands, headed by the militant Samuel Adams, who believed that a fundamental alteration of British-American political relationships was necessary. When the Massachusetts royal governor Thomas Hutchinson announced that the crown would be paying his salary, a change that freed him from financial dependence on the Massachusetts legislature, Adams saw his chance to reignite anti-British feelings and actions. The document below, written by Joseph Warren, a physician who would die fighting the redcoats at Bunker Hill, catches the mood of the patriot zealots.

What new complaints against British policy have been added to the charges of the Stamp Act Congress? What do the references to hats, slitting mills, and wool signify? What do the Boston patriots mean when they refer to an "American Episcopate"? Do the new complaints seem exaggerated?

A List of Infringements and Violations of Rights[1]

JOSEPH WARREN

We cannot help thinking, that an enumeration of some of the most open infringements of our rights, will by every candid person be judged sufficient to justify whatever measures have been already taken, or may be thought proper to be taken, in order to obtain a redress of the grievances under which we labour. . . .

1. The British Parliament have assumed the power of legislation for the colonists in all cases whatsoever, without obtaining the consent of the inhabitants, which is ever essentially necessary to the right establishment of such a legislative.
2. They have exerted that assumed power, in raising a revenue in the colonies without their consent; thereby depriving them of that right which every man has to keep his own earnings in his own hands until he shall in person, or by his Representative, think fit to part with the whole or any portion of it. . . .

Boston Town Records, 1770–1777 (Eighteenth Report of the Boston Record Commissioners, n.p. 1887), pp. 90–92.

[1]Footnotes deleted.

3. A number of new officers, unknown in the charter of this Province, have been appointed to superintend this revenue, whereas by our charter the Great and General Court or Assembly of this Province has the sole right of appointing all civil officers, excepting only such officers, the election and constitution of whom is in said charter expressly excepted; among whom these officers are not included.

4. These officers are by their commission invested with powers altogether unconstitutional, and entirely destructive to that security which we have a right to enjoy; and to the last degree dangerous, not only to our property, but to our lives. For the Commissioners of His Majesty's Customs in America, or any three of them, are by their commission impowered, 'by writing under their hands and seales to constitute and appoint inferior officers in all and singular the ports within the limits of their commissions'. Each of these petty officers so made is intrusted with power more absolute and arbitrary than ought to be lodged in the hands of any man or body of men whatsoever. . . .

   Thus our houses and even our bed chambers are exposed to be ransacked, our boxes, chests, and trunks broke open, ravaged and plundered by wretches, whom no prudent man would venture to employ even as menial servants; whenever they are pleased to say they *suspect* there are in the house wares, etc., for which the dutys have not been paid. Flagrant instances of the wanton exercise of this power, have frequently happened in this and other seaport towns. By this we are cut off from that domestick security which renders the lives of the most unhappy in some measure agreable. . . .

5. Fleets and armies have been introduced to support these unconstitutional officers in collecting and managing this unconstitutional revenue; and troops have been quarter'd in this metropolis for that purpose. Introducing and quartering standing armies in a free country in times of peace without the consent of the people either by themselves or by their representatives, is and always has been deemed a violation of their rights as freemen; and of the charter or compact made between the King of Great Britain, and the people of this province, whereby all the rights of British subjects are confirmed to us.

6. The Revenue arising from this tax unconstitutionally laid, and committed to the management of persons arbitrarily appointed and supported by an armed force quartered in a free city, has been in part applyed to the most destructive purposes. It is absolutely necessary in a mixt government like that of this Province, that a due proportion or balance of power should be established among the several branches of legislative. Our ancestors received from King William and Queen Mary a charter by which it was understood by both parties in the contract, that such a proportion or balance was fixed; and therefore everything which renders any one branch of the legislative more independent of the other two than it was originally designed, is an alteration of the constitution as settled by the charter; and as it has been untill the establishment of this revenue, the constant practise of the General Assembly to provide for the support of government, so it is an essential part of our constitution, as it is a necessary means of preserving an equilibrium, without which we cannot continue a free state.

   In particular it has always been held that the dependence of the Governor of this Province upon the General Assembly for his support, was necessary for the preservation of this equilibrium; nevertheless His Majesty has been pleased to apply fifteen hundred pounds sterling annually out of the American revenue, for the support of the Governor of this Province independent of the Assembly, whereby the ancient connection between him and this people is weakened, the confidence in the Governor lessened and the equilibrium destroyed, and the constitution essentially altered.

   And we look upon it highly probable from the best intelligence we have been able to obtain, that not only our Governor and Lieuvetenant Governor, but the Judges of the Superior Court of Judicature, as also the King's Attorney and Solicitor

General are to receive their support from this grievous tribute. This will if accomplished compleat our slavery. . . .

7. We find ourselves greatly oppressed by instructions sent to our Governor from the Court of Great Britain, whereby the first branch of our legislature is made merely a ministerial engine. And the Province has already felt such effects from these instructions, as we think justly intitle us to say that they threaten an entire destruction of our liberties, and must soon, if not checked, render every branch of our government a useless burthen upon the people. We shall point out some of the alarming effects of these instructions which have already taken place.

   In consequence of instructions, the Governor has called and adjourned our General Assemblies to a place highly inconvenient to the members, and grately disadvantageous to the interest of the Province, even against his own declared intention.

   In consequence of instructions, the Assembly has been prorogued from time to time, when the important concerns of the Province required their meeting.

   In obedience to instructions, the General Assembly was anno 1768 dissolved by Governor Bernard, because they would not consent to rescind the resolution of a former house, and thereby sacrifise the rights of their constituents.

   By an instruction, the honourable His Majesty's Council are forbid to meet and transact matters of publick concern as a Council of advice to the Governor, unless called by the Governor; and if they should from a zealous regard to the interest of the province so meet at any time, the Governor is ordered to negative them at the next election of Councellors. . . .

   His Excellency has also pleaded instructions for giving up the provincial fortress, Castle William, into the hands of troops, over whom he had declared he had no controul, and that at a time when they were menaceing the Slaughter of the inhabitants of the Town, and our streets were stained with the blood which they had barbariously shed. . . .

8. The extending the power of the Courts of Vice Admirality to so enormous a degree as deprives the people in the colonies in a great measure of their inestimable right to tryals by juries: which has ever been justly considered as the grand bulwark and security of English property. . . .

9. The restraining us from erecting slitting mills for manufacturing our iron, the natural produce of this country, is an infringement of that right with which God and nature have invested us, to make use of our skill and industry in procuring the necessaries and conveniences of life. And we look upon the restraint laid upon the manufacture and transportation of hatts to be altogether unreasonable and grievous. Although by the charter all havens, rivers, ports, waters, etc., are expressly granted the inhabitants of the Province and their successors, to their only proper use and behoof forever, yet the British Parliament passed an Act, whereby they restrain us from carrying our wool, the produce of our own farms, even over a ferry; whereby the inhabitants have often been put to the expence of carrying a bag of wool near an hundred miles by land, when passing over a river or water of one quarter of a mile, of which the Province are the absolute proprietors, would have prevented all that trouble.

10. The Act passed in the last session of the British Parliament, intitled, An Act for the better preserving his Majestys Dock Yards, Magizines, Ships, Ammunition and Stores, is, as we apprehend a violent infringement of our rights. By this Act any one of us may be taken from his family, and carried to any part of Great Britain, there to be tried whenever it shall be pretended that he has been concerned in burning or otherwise destroying any boat or vessel, or any materials for building, etc., any naval or victualling store, etc., belonging to His Majesty. . . .

11. As our Ancestors came over to this Country that they might not only enjoy their civil but their religious rights, and particularly desired to be free from the prelates,

who in those times cruilly persecuted all who differed in sentiment from the established Church; we cannot see without concern the various attempts which have been made and are now making, to establish an American Episcopate. Our Episcopal brethren of the colonies do enjoy, and rightfully ought ever to enjoy, the free exercise of their religeon, we cannot help fearing that they who are so warmly contending for such an establishment, have views altogether inconsistent with the universal and peaceful enjoyment of our Christian privileges. And doing or attempting to do anything which has even the remotest tendency to endanger this enjoyment, is justly looked upon a great grievance, and also an infringement of our rights, which is not barely to exercise, but peaceably and securely to enjoy, that liberty wherewith Christ has made us free.

And we are further of Opinion that no power on Earth can justly give either temporal or spiritual jurisdiction within this Province, except the great and General Court. We think therefore that every design for establishing the jurisdiction of a bishop in this Province, is a design both against our civil and religeous rights. And we are well informed, that the more candid and judicious of our brethren of the Church of England in this and the other colonies, both clergy and laity, conceive of the establishing an American Episcopate both unnecessary and unreasonable.

12. Another grievance under which we labour is the frequent alteration of the bounds of the colonies by decisions before the King and Council, explanatory of former grants and charters. This not only subjects men to live under a constitution to which they have not consented, which in itself is a great grievance; but moreover under color that the right of soil is affected by such declarations, some governors, or ministers, or both in conjunction, have pretended to grant in consequence of a mandamus many thousands of acres of lands appropriated near a century past; and rendered valuable by the labors of the present cultivators and their ancestors. There are very notable instances of setlers, who having first purchased the soil of the natives, have at considerable expence obtained confermation of title from this Province; and on being transferred to the jurisdiction of the Province of New Hampshire have been put to the trouble and cost of a new grant or confermation from thence; and after all this there has been a third declaration of royal will, that they should henceforth be considered as pertaining to the Province of New York. The troubles, expences, and dangers which hundreds have been put to on such occasions, cannot here be recited; but so much may be said, that they have been most cruelly harrassed, and even threatned with a military force, to dragoon them into a compliance with the most unreasonable demands.

4.4:   An American Radical Reevaluates the English Constitution (1776)

Few publications in history have had the dramatic impact of Thomas Paine's Common Sense, *which played a key role in swaying public opinion in favor of independence in 1776. This 47-page pamphlet, written by one of the Revolution's most radical spokesmen, both challenged the theoretical foundations of the English Constitution and presented patriots with numerous practical advantages for breaking with the Crown. Like the Declaration of Independence that followed it,* Common Sense *saw the monarchy, not Parliament, as the root of the*

*unfolding constitutional crisis. As both skillful propagandist and prac-
tical philosopher, Paine's writing reveals the transformation of Whig
philosophy into bold new directions.*

*In reading this selection, ask yourself why this small tract was so in-
fluential. Would you describe it as a theoretical discourse, a practical
one, or both? Are these arguments indeed presented by a voice of
"common sense" or by an academic philosopher? Does Paine arouse
your sentiments against King George III personally or against "the
system" in general? Most of all, how would our government measure
up to these questions if asked today?*

Common Sense

THOMAS PAINE

OF MONARCHY AND HEREDITARY SUCCESSION

MANKIND being originally equals in the order of creation, the equality could only be
destroyed by some subsequent circumstance; the distinctions of rich, and poor, may
in a great measure be accounted for, and that without having recourse to the harsh
ill sounding names of oppression and avarice. Oppression is often the *consequence,*
but seldom or never the *means* of riches; and though avarice will preserve a man
from being necessitiously poor, it generally makes him too timorous to be wealthy.

But there is another and greater distinction for which no truly natural or religious
reason can be assigned, and that is, the distinction of men into KINGS and SUBJECTS.
Male and female are the distinctions of nature, good and bad the distinctions of
heaven; but how a race of men came into the world so exalted above the rest, and
distinguished like some new species, is worth enquiring into, and whether they are
the means of happiness or of misery to mankind.

In the early ages of the world, according to the scripture chronology, there were
no kings; the consequence of which was there were no wars; it is the pride of kings
which throw mankind into confusion. Holland without a king hath enjoyed more
peace for this last century than any of the monarchical governments in Europe. Antiquity favors the same remark; for the quiet and rural lives of the first patriarchs
hath a happy something in them, which vanishes away when we come to the history
of Jewish royalty.

Government by kings was first introduced into the world by the Heathens, from
whom the children of Israel copied the custom. It was the most prosperous invention the Devil ever set on foot for the promotion of idolatry. The Heathens paid divine honors to their deceased kings, and the christian world hath improved on the

Thomas Paine, *Common Sense: Addressed to the Inhabitants of America.* (Philadelphia: W. & T. Brad-
ford, 1776).

plan by doing the same to their living ones. How impious is the title of sacred majesty applied to a worm, who in the midst of his splendor is crumbling into dust!

As the exalting one man so greatly above the rest cannot be justified on the equal rights of nature, so neither can it be defended on the authority of scripture; for the will of the Almighty, as declared by Gideon and the prophet Samuel, expressly disapproves of government by kings. All antimonarchical parts of scripture have been very smoothly glossed over in monarchical governments, but they undoubtedly merit the attention of countries which have their governments yet to form. *"Render unto Cæsar the things which are Cæsar's"* is the scripture doctrine of courts, yet it is no support of monarchical government, for the Jews at that time were without a king, and in a state of vassalage to the Romans.

Near three thousand years passed away from the Mosaic account of the creation, till the Jews under a national delusion requested a king. Till then their form of government (except in extraordinary cases, where the Almighty interposed) was a kind of republic administred by a judge and the elders of the tribes. Kings they had none, and it was held sinful to acknowledge any being under that title but the Lord of Hosts. And when a man seriously reflects on the idolatrous homage which is paid to the persons of Kings, he need not wonder, that the Almighty ever jealous of his honor, should disapprove of a form of government which so impiously invades the prerogative of heaven.

Monarchy is ranked in scripture as one of the sins of the Jews, for which a curse in reserve is denounced against them. The history of that transaction is worth attending to.

The children of Israel being oppressed by the Midianites, Gideon marched against them with a small army, and victory, thro' the divine interposition, decided in his favour. The Jews elate with success, and attributing it to the generalship of Gideon, proposed making him a king, saying, *Rule thou over us, thou and thy son and thy son's son.* Here was temptation in its fullest extent; not a kingdom only, but an hereditary one, but Gideon in the piety of his soul replied, *I will not rule over you, neither shall my son rule over you.* The Lord shall rule over you. Words need not be more explicit; Gideon doth not *decline* the honor, but denieth their right to give it; neither doth he compliment them with invented declarations of his thanks, but in the positive stile of a prophet charges them with disaffection to their proper Sovereign, the King of heaven.

About one hundred and thirty years after this, they fell again into the same error. The hankering which the Jews had for the idolatrous customs of the Heathens, is something exceedingly unaccountable; but so it was, that laying hold of the misconduct of Samuel's two sons, who were entrusted with some secular concerns, they came in an abrupt and clamorous manner to Samuel, saying, *Behold thou art old, and thy sons walk not in thy ways, now make us a king to judge us like all the other nations.* And here we cannot but observe that their motives were bad, viz. that they might be *like* unto other nations, i.e. the Heathens, whereas their true glory laid in being as much *unlike* them as possible. *But the thing displeased Samuel when they said, Give us a king to judge us; and Samuel prayed unto the Lord, and the Lord said unto Samuel, Hearken unto the voice of the people in all that they say unto thee, for they have not rejected thee, but they have rejected me,* THAT I SHOULD NOT REIGN OVER THEM. *According to all the works which they have done since the day that I brought them up out of Egypt, even unto this day; wherewith they have forsaken me and served other Gods; so do they also unto thee. Now therefore hearken unto their voice, howbeit, protest solemnly unto them and shew them the manner of the king that shall reign over them, i.e.* not of any particular king, but the general manner of the kings of the earth, whom Israel was so eagerly copying after. And notwithstanding the great distance of time and difference of manners, the character is still in fashion. *And Samuel told all the words of the Lord unto the people, that asked of him a king. And he said, This shall be the manner of the king that shall reign over you; he will take your sons and appoint them for himself, for his chariots, and to be his horsemen, and some shall run before his chariots* (this description agrees with the present mode of impressing men) *and he will appoint him captains over thousands and captains over fifties, and will set them to ear his ground and to reap his harvest, and to make his instruments of war, and instruments of his chariots; and he will take your daughters to be confectionaries, and to be cooks and to be bakers* (this describes the expence and luxury as well as the oppression of kings) *and he will take your fields and your olive yards, even the best of them, and give them to his servants; and he will take the tenth of your feed, and of your vineyards, and give them to his officers and to his servants* (by which we see that bribery, corruption and favoritism are the standing vices of kings) *and he will take the tenth of your men servants, and your maid servants, and your goodliest young men and your asses, and put them to his work; and he will take the tenth of your sheep, and ye shall be his servants, and ye shall cry out in that day because of your king which ye shall have chosen,* AND THE LORD WILL NOT HEAR YOU IN THAT DAY. This accounts for the continuation of monarchy; neither do the characters of the few good kings which have lived since, either sanctify the title, or blot out the sinfulness of the origin; the high encomium given of David takes no notice of him *officially as a king,* but only as a *man* after God's own heart. *Nevertheless the People refused to obey the voice of Samuel, and they said, Nay, but we will have a king over us, that we may be like all the nations, and that our king may judge us, and go out before us, and fight our battles.* Samuel continued to reason with them, but to no purpose; he set before them their ingratitude, but all would not avail; and seeing them fully bent on their folly, he cried out, *I will call unto the Lord, and he shall send thunder and rain* (which then was a punishment, being in the time of wheat harvest) *that ye may perceive and see that your wickedness is great which ye have done in the sight of the Lord,* IN ASKING YOU A KING. *So Samuel called unto the Lord, and the Lord sent thunder and rain that day, and all the people greatly feared the Lord and Samuel. And all the people said unto Samuel, Pray for thy servants unto the Lord thy God that we die not, for* WE HAVE ADDED UNTO OUR SINS THIS EVIL, TO ASK A KING. These portions of scripture are direct and positive. They admit of no equivocal construction. That the Almighty hath here entered his protest against monarchical government is true, or the scripture is false. And a man hath good reason to believe that there is as much of king-craft, as priest-craft, in withholding the scripture from the public in Popish countries. For monarchy in every instance is the Popery of government.

To the evil of monarchy we have added that of hereditary succession; and as the first is a degradation and lessening of ourselves, so the second, claimed as a matter of right, is an insult and an imposition on posterity. For all men being originally equals, no *one* by *birth* could have a right to set up his own family in perpetual preference to all others for ever, and though himself might deserve *some* decent degree of honors of his cotemporaries, yet his descendants might be far too unworthy to inherit them. One of the strongest *natural* proofs of the folly of hereditary right in kings, is, that nature disapproves it, otherwise she would not so frequently turn it into ridicule by giving mankind an *ass for a lion.*

Secondly, as no man at first could possess any other public honors than were bestowed upon him, so the givers of those honors could have no power to give away the right of posterity, and though they might say "We choose you for *our* head," they could not, without manifest injustice to their children, say "that your children and your childrens children shall reign over *overs* for ever." Because such an unwise, unjust, unnatural compact might (perhaps) in the next succession put them under the government of a rogue or a fool. Most wise men, in their private sentiments, have ever treated hereditary right with contempt; yet it is one of those evils, which when once established is not easily removed; many submit from fear, others from superstition, and the more powerful part shares with the king the plunder of the rest.

This is supposing the present race of kings in the world to have had an honorable origin; whereas it is more than probable, that could we take off the dark covering of antiquity, and trace them to their first rise, that we should find the first of them nothing better than the principal ruffian of some restless gang, whose savage manners or pre-eminence in subtility obtained him the title of chief among plunderers; and who by increasing in power, and extending his depredations, overawed the quiet and defenceless to purchase their safety by frequent contributions. Yet his electors could have no idea of giving hereditary right to his descendants, because such a perpetual exclusion of themselves was incompatible with the free and unrestrained principles they professed to live by. Wherefore, hereditary succession in the early ages of monarchy could not take place as a matter of claim, but as something casual or complimental; but as few or no records were extant in those days, and traditionary history stuffed with fables, it was very easy, after the lapse of a few generations, to trump up some superstitious tale, conveniently timed, Mahomet like, to cram hereditary right down the throats of the vulgar. Perhaps the disorders which threatened, or seemed to threaten, on the decease of a leader and the choice of a new one (for elections among ruffians could not be very orderly) induced many at first to favor hereditary pretensions; by which means it happened, as it hath happened since, that what at first was submitted to as a convenience, was afterwards claimed as a right.

England, since the conquest, hath known some few good monarchs, but groaned beneath a much larger number of bad ones; yet no man in his senses can say that their claim under William the Conqueror is a very honorable one. A French bastard landing with an armed banditti, and establishing himself king of England against the consent of the natives, is in plain terms a very paltry rascally original.—It certainly hath no divinity in it. However, it is needless to spend much time in exposing the folly of hereditary right, if there are any so weak as to believe it, let them promiscuously worship the ass and lion, and welcome. I shall neither copy their humility, nor disturb their devotion.

Yet I should be glad to ask how they suppose kings came at first? The question admits but of three answers, viz. either by lot, by election, or by usurpation. If the first king was taken by lot, it establishes a precedent for the next, which excludes hereditary succession. Saul was by lot, yet the succession was not hereditary, neither does it appear from that transaction there was any intention it ever should. If the first king of any country was by election, that likewise establishes a precedent for the next; for to say, that the *right* of all future generations is taken away, by the act of the first electors, in their choice not only of a king, but of a family of kings for ever, hath no parallel in or out of scripture but the doctrine of original sin, which supposes the free will of all men lost in Adam; and from such comparison, and it will admit of no other, hereditary succession can derive no glory. For as in Adam all sinned, and as in the first electors all men obeyed; as in the one all mankind were subjected to Satan, and in the other to Sovereignty; as our innocence was lost in the first, and our authority in the last; and as both disable us from reassuming some former state and privilege, it unanswerably follows that original sin and hereditary succession are parellels. Dishonorable rank! Inglorious connexion! Yet the most subtile sophist cannot produce a juster simile.

As to usurpation, no man will be so hardy as to defend it; and that William the Conqueror was an usurper is a fact not to be contradicted. The plain truth is, that the antiquity of English monarchy will not bear looking into.

But it is not so much the absurdity as the evil of hereditary succession which concerns mankind. Did it ensure a race of good and wise men it would have the seal of divine authority, but as it opens a door to the *foolish,* the *wicked,* and the *improper,* it hath in it the nature of oppression. Men who look upon themselves born to reign, and others to obey, soon grow insolent; selected from the rest of mankind their minds are early poisoned by importance; and the world they act in differs so materially from the world at large, that they have but little opportunity of knowing its true interests, and when they succeed to the government are frequently the most ignorant and unfit of any throughout the dominions.

Another evil which attends hereditary succession is, that the throne is subject to be possessed by a minor at any age; all which time the regency, acting under the cover of a king, have every opportunity and inducement to betray their trust. The same national misfortune happens, when a king worn out with age and infirmity, enters the last stage of human weakness. In both these cases the public becomes a prey to every miscreant, who can tamper successfully with the follies either of age or infancy.

The most plausible plea, which hath ever been offered in favour of hereditary succession, is, that it preserves a nation from civil wars; and were this true, it would be weighty; whereas, it is the most barefaced falsity ever imposed upon mankind. The whole history of England disowns the fact. Thirty kings and two minors have reigned in that distracted kingdom since the conquest, in which time there have been (including the Revolution) no less than eight civil wars and nineteen rebellions. Wherefore instead of making for peace, it makes against it, and destroys the very foundation it seems to stand on.

The contest for monarchy and succession, between the houses of York and Lancaster, laid England in a scene of blood for many years. Twelve pitched battles, besides skirmishes and sieges, were fought between Henry and Edward. Twice was Henry prisoner to Edward, who in his turn was prisoner to Henry. And so uncertain is the fate of war and the temper of a nation, when nothing but personal matters are the ground of a quarrel, that Henry was taken in triumph from a prison to a palace, and Edward obliged to fly from a place to a foreign land; yet, as sudden transitions of temper are seldom lasting, Henry in his turn was driven from the throne, and Edward recalled to succeed him. The parliament always following the strongest side.

This contest began in the reign of Henry the Sixth, and was not entirely extinguished till Henry the Seventh, in whom the families were united. Including a period of 67 years, viz. from 1422 to 1489.

In short, monarchy and succession have laid (not this or that kingdom only) but the world in blood and ashes. 'Tis a form of government which the word of God bears testimony against, and blood will attend it.

If we inquire into the business of a king, we shall find that in some countries they have none; and after sauntering away their lives without pleasure to themselves or advantage to the nation, withdraw from the scene, and leave their successors to tread the same idle round. In absolute monarchies the whole weight of business, civil and military, lies on the king; the children of Israel in their request for a king, urged this plea "that he may judge us, and go out before us and fight our battles." But in countries where he is neither a judge nor a general, as in England, a man would be puzzled to know what *is* his business.

The nearer any government approaches to a republic the less business there is for a king. It is somewhat difficult to find a proper name for the government of England. Sir William Meredith calls it a republic; but in its present state it is unworthy of the name, because the corrupt influence of the crown, by having all the places in its disposal, hath so effectually swallowed up the power, and eaten out the virtue of the house of commons (the republican part in the constitution) that the government of England is nearly as monarchical as that of France or Spain. Men fall out with names without understanding them. For it is the republican and not the monarchical part of the constitution of England which Englishmen glory in, viz. the liberty of choosing an house of commons from out of their own body—and it is easy to see that when republican virtue fails, slavery ensues. Why is the constitution of England sickly, but because monarchy hath poisoned the republic, the crown hath engrossed the commons?

In England a king hath little more to do than to make war and give away places; which in plain terms, is to impoverish the nation and set it together by the ears. A pretty business indeed for a man to be allowed eight hundred thousand sterling a year for, and worshipped into the bargain! Of more worth is one honest man to society and in the sight of God, than all the crowned ruffians that ever lived.

4.5:   The Declaration
of Independence (1776)

*Another four years brought the Declaration of Independence, the final
political break with Britain. This followed the outbreak of actual hostilities and the loss of lives, both British and American, in several
colonies. Written primarily by Thomas Jefferson, delegate to the Continental Congress from Virginia, the document summarized the accumulated reasons for the drastic American action.*

*A part of the Declaration is an indictment of specific British "abuses
and usurpations." It refers both to longstanding grievances and to immediate ones, especially the punitive measures adopted by Britain following the Boston Tea Party in late 1773. Objective scholars today
would discount much of this section of the Declaration as exaggerated
rhetoric. More important, however, is the second paragraph. In this
section Jefferson presents, in a few dozen words, a theory of government that formed the philosophical foundation for the Revolution.
What is this theory? Was it widely held in its day? From what sources
did it derive? Has it influenced political thinking since that era?*

⌣

The Declaration of Independence

THOMAS JEFFERSON

In Congress, July 4, 1776,

The Unanimous Declaration of the Thirteen United States of America.

When in the Course of human events, it becomes necessary for one people to dissolve the political bands which have connected them with another, and to assume
among the Powers of the earth, the separate and equal station to which the Laws of
Nature and of Nature's God entitle them, a decent respect to the opinions of
mankind requires that they should declare the causes which impel them to the separation.

We hold these truths to be self-evident, that all men are created equal, that they
are endowed by their Creator with certain unalienable Rights, that among these are
Life, Liberty and the pursuit of Happiness. That to secure these rights, Governments are instituted among Men, deriving their just powers from the consent of the
governed, That whenever any Form of Government becomes destructive of these
ends, it is the Right of the People to alter or to abolish it, and to institute new Government, laying its foundation on such principles and organizing its powers in such
form, as to them shall seem most likely to effect their Safety and Happiness. Prudence, indeed, will dictate that Governments long established should not be

changed for light and transient causes; and accordingly all experience hath shown, that mankind are more disposed to suffer, while evils are sufferable, than to right themselves by abolishing the forms to which they are accustomed. But when a long train of abuses and usurpations, pursuing invariably the same Object evinces a design to reduce them under absolute Despotism, it is their right, it is their duty, to throw off such Government, and to provide new Guards for their future security.— Such has been the patient sufferance of these Colonies; and such is now the necessity which constrains them to alter their former Systems of Government. The history of the present King of Great Britain is a history of repeated injuries and usurpations, all having in direct object the establishment of an absolute Tyranny over these States. To prove this, let Facts be submitted to a candid world.

He has refused his Assent to Laws, the most wholesome and necessary for the public good.

He has forbidden his Governors to pass Laws of immediate and pressing importance, unless suspended in their operation till his Assent should be obtained; and when so suspended, he has utterly neglected to attend to them.

He has refused to pass other Laws for the accommodation of large districts of people, unless those people would relinquish the right of Representation in the Legislature, a right inestimable to them and formidable to tyrants only.

He has called together legislative bodies at places unusual, uncomfortable, and distant from the depository of their Public Records, for the sole purpose of fatiguing them into compliance with his measures.

He has dissolved Representative Houses repeatedly, for opposing with manly firmness his invasions on the rights of the people.

He has refused for a long time, after such dissolutions, to cause others to be elected; whereby the Legislative Powers, incapable of Annihilation, have returned to the People at large for their exercise; the State remaining in the mean time exposed to all the dangers of invasion from without, and convulsions within.

He has endeavoured to prevent the population of these States; for that purpose obstructing the Laws of Naturalization of Foreigners; refusing to pass others to encourage their migration hither, and raising the conditions of new Appropriations of Lands.

He has obstructed the Administration of Justice, by refusing his Assent to Laws for establishing Judiciary Powers.

He has made Judges dependent on his Will alone, for the tenure of their offices, and the amount and payment of their salaries.

He has erected a multitude of New Offices, and sent hither swarms of Officers to harass our People, and eat out their substance.

He has kept among us, in times of peace, Standing Armies without the Consent of our legislature.

He has affected to render the Military independent of and superior to the Civil Power.

He has combined with others to subject us to a jurisdiction foreign to our constitution, and unacknowledged by our laws; giving his Assent to their acts of pretended legislation:

For quartering large bodies of armed troops among us:

For protecting them, by a mock Trial, from Punishment for any Murders which they should commit on the Inhabitants of these States:

For cutting off our Trade with all parts of the world:

For imposing taxes on us without our Consent:

For depriving us in many cases, of the benefits of Trial by Jury:

For transporting us beyond Seas to be tried for pretended offences:

For abolishing the free System of English Laws in a neighbouring Province, establishing therein an Arbitrary government, and enlarging its Boundaries so as to render it at once an example and fit instrument for introducing the same absolute rule into these Colonies:

For taking away our Charters, abolishing our most valuable Laws, and altering fundamentally the Forms of our Governments:

For suspending our own Legislature, and declaring themselves invested with Power to legislate for us in all cases whatsoever.

He has abdicated Government here, by declaring us out of his Protection and waging War against us.

He has plundered our seas, ravaged our Coasts, burnt our towns, and destroyed the lives of our people.

He is at this time transporting large armies of foreign mercenaries to compleat the works of death, desolation and tyranny, already begun with circumstances of Cruelty & perfidy scarcely paralleled in the most barbarous ages, and totally unworthy the Head of a civilized nation.

He has constrained our fellow Citizens taken Captive on the high Seas to bear Arms against their Country, to become the executioners of their friends and Brethren, or to fall themselves by their Hands.

He has excited domestic insurrections amongst us, and has endeavoured to bring on the inhabitants of our frontiers, the merciless Indian Savages, whose known rule of warfare, is an undistinguished destruction of all ages, sexes and conditions.

In every stage of these Oppressions We have Petitioned for Redress in the most humble terms: Our repeated Petitions have been answered only by repeated injury. A Prince, whose character is thus marked by every act which may define a Tyrant, is unfit to be the ruler of a free People.

Nor have We been wanting in attention to our British brethren. We have warned them from time to time of attempts by their legislature to extend an unwarrantable jurisdiction over us. We have reminded them of the circumstances of our emigration and settlement here. We have appealed to their native justice and magnanimity, and we have conjured them by the ties of our common kindred to disavow these usurpations, which, would inevitably interrupt our connections and correspondence. They too have been deaf to the voice of justice and of consanguinity. We must, therefore, acquiesce in the necessity, which denounces our Separation, and hold them, as we hold the rest of mankind, Enemies in War, in Peace Friends.

We, therefore, the Representatives of the united States of America, in General Congress, Assembled, appealing to the Supreme Judge of the world for the rectitude of our intentions, do, in the Name, and by Authority of the good People of these Colonies, solemnly publish and declare, That these United Colonies are, and of Right ought to be Free and Independent States; that they are Absolved from all Allegiance to the British Crown, and that all political connection between them and the State of Great Britain, is and ought to be totally dissolved; and that as Free and Independent States, they have full Power to levy War, conclude Peace, contract Alliances, establish Commerce, and to do all other Acts and Things which Independent States may of right do. And for the support of this Declaration, with a firm reliance on the Protection of Divine Providence, we mutually pledge to each other our Lives, our Fortunes and our sacred Honor.

JOHN HANCOCK.

New Hampshire
JOSIAH BARTLETT,
WM. WHIPPLE,
MATTHEW THORNTON.

Massachusetts-Bay
SAML. ADAMS,
JOHN ADAMS,
ROBT. TREAT PAINE,
ELBRIDGE GERRY.

Rhode Island
STEP. HOPKINS,
WILLIAM ELLERY.

Connecticut
ROGER SHERMAN,
SAM'EL HUNTINGTON,
WM. WILLIAMS,
OLIVER WOLCOTT.

Georgia
BUTTON GWINNETT,
LYMAN HALL,
GEO. WALTON.

Maryland
SAMUEL CHASE,
WM. PACA,
THOS. STONE,
CHARLES CARROLL
OF Carrollton.

Virginia
GEORGE WYTHE,
RICHARD HENRY LEE,
TH. JEFFERSON,
BENJA. HARRISON,
THS. NELSON, JR.,
FRANCIS LIGHTFOOT LEE,
CARTER BRAXTON.

New York
WM. FLOYD,
PHIL. LIVINGSTON,
FRANS. LEWIS,
LEWIS MORRIS.

Pennsylvania
ROBT. MORRIS,
BENJAMIN RUSH,
BENJA. FRANKLIN,
JOHN MORTON,
GEO. CLYMER,
JAS. SMITH,
GEO. TAYLOR,
JAMES WILSON,
GEO. ROSS.

Delaware
CAESAR RODNEY,
GEO. READ,
THO. M'KEAN.

North Carolina
WM. HOOPER,
JOSEPH HEWES,
JOHN PENN.

South Carolina
EDWARD RUTLEDGE,
THOS. HEYWARD, JUNR.,
THOMAS LYNCH, JUNR.,
ARTHUR MIDDLETON.

New Jersey
RICHD. STOCKTON,
JNO. WITHERSPOON,
FRAS. HOPKINSON,
JOHN HART,
ABRA. CLARK.

4.6:   The Radicalism of the American Revolution (1776)

Many American historians—notably Bernard Bailyn, Pauline Meier, and Gordon Wood—have emphasized the importance of ideology during the Revolutionary Period. Set in motion by the Constitutional Crisis, ideas that were often rooted in the British Whig tradition of dissent acquired radical new possibilities in an American context. New state constitutions, each written to replace the old colonial charters, clearly reflected the remarkable pervasiveness and radicalism of revolutionary thought during the 1770s and 1780s.

Do the rights Virginia proclaimed in June 1776 seem familiar? Where else was reference made to these rights? What makes this document "radical"? Which specific rights contained in the Bill constitute significant deviations from the conventional English constitutional thinking of the day?

The Virginia Bill of Rights, June 12, 1776

A declaration of rights made by the representatives of the good people of Virginia, assembled in full and free convention; which rights do pertain to them and their posterity, as the basis and foundation of government.

1. That all men are by nature equally free and independent, had have certain inherent rights, of which, when they enter into a state of society, they cannot by any compact deprive or divest their posterity; namely, the enjoyment of life and liberty, with the means of acquiring and possessing property, and pursuing and obtaining happiness and safety.

2. That all power is vested in, and consequently derived from, the people; that magistrates are their trustees and servants, and at all times amenable to them.

3. That government is, or ought to be instituted for the common benefit, protection, and security of the people, nation, or community; of all the various modes and forms of government, that is best which is capable of producing the greatest degree of happiness and safety, and is most effectually secured against the danger of maladministration; and that when any government shall be found inadequate or contrary to these purposes, a majority of the community hath an indubitable, unalienable and indefeasible right to reform, alter or abolish it, in such manner as shall be judged most conducive to the public weal.

4. That no man, or set of men, are entitled to exclusive or separate emoluments or privileges from the community, but in consideration of publick services; which,

Poore, ed., *The Federal and State Constitutions,* (Washington, DC: United States Government Printing Offices, 1878), Part II, pp. 1908–1909.

not being descendible, neither ought the offices of magistrate, legislator or judge to be hereditary.

5. That the legislative and executive powers of the state should be separate and distinct from the judiciary; and that the members of the two first may be restrained from oppression, by feeling and participating the burthens of the people, they should, at fixed periods, be reduced to a private station, return into that body from which they were originally taken, and the vacancies be supplied by frequent, certain, and regular elections, in which all, or any part of the former members to be again eligible or ineligible, as the laws shall direct.

6. That elections of members to serve as representatives of the people in assembly, ought to be free; and that all men having sufficient evidence of permanent common interest with, and attachment to the community, have the right of suffrage, and cannot be taxed or deprived of their property for publick uses, without their own consent, or that of their representatives so elected, nor bound by any law to which they have not, in like manner, assented for the public good.

7. That all power of suspending laws, or the execution of laws, by any authority without consent of the representatives of the people, is injurious to their rights, and ought not to be exercised.

8. That in all capital or criminal prosecutions a man hath a right to demand the cause and nature of his accusation, to be confronted with the accusers and witnesses, to call for evidence in his favour, and to a speedy trial by an impartial jury of his vicinage, without whose unanimous consent he cannot be found guilty; nor can he be compelled to give evidence against himself; that no man be deprived of his liberty, except by the law of the land or the judgment of his peers.

9. That excessive bail ought not to be required, nor excessive fines imposed, nor cruel and unusual punishments inflicted.

10. That general warrants, whereby an officer or messenger may be commanded to search suspected places without evidence of a fact committed, or to seize any person or persons not named, or whose offence is not particularly described and supported by evidence, are grievous and oppressive, and ought not to be granted.

11. That in controversies respecting property, and in suits between man and man, the ancient trial by jury is preferable to any other, and ought to be held sacred.

12. That the freedom of the press is one of the great bulwarks of liberty, and can never be restrained but by despotick governments.

13. That a well-regulated militia, composed of the body of the people trained to arms, is the proper, natural and safe defence of a free state; that standing armies in time of peace should be avoided as dangerous to liberty; and that in all cases the military should be under strict subordination to, and governed by, the civil power.

14. That the people have a right to uniform government; and, therefore, that no government separate from, or independent of the government of Virginia, ought to be erected or established within the limits thereof.

15. That no free government, or the blessings of liberty, can be preserved to any people, but by a firm adherence to justice, moderation, temperance, frugality and virtue, and by frequent recurrence to fundamental principles.

16. That religion, or the duty which we owe to our Creator, and the manner of discharging it, can be directed only by reason and conviction, not by force or violence; and therefore all men are equally entitled to the free exercise of religion, according to the dictates of conscience; and that it is the mutual duty of all to practise Christian forbearance, love, and charity towards each other.

4.7:   Parliament's Official View (1766)

As Parliament repealed the Stamp Act, early in 1766, it also proclaimed its authority over the colonies by passing The Declaratory Act. Whereas the repeal of the Stamp Act resolved the immediate political crisis at hand, the Declaratory Act assured that the constitutional issues raised would remain unresolved.

What does the Declaratory Act attempt to say? Are its assumptions reasonable? Why would the colonists remain baffled by it?

The Declaratory Act, March 18, 1766

An act for the better securing the dependency of his Majesty's dominions in America *upon the crown and parliament of* Great Britain.

WHEREAS *several of the houses of representatives in his Majesty's colonies and plantations in* America, *have of late, against law, claimed to themselves, or to the general assemblies of the same, the sole and exclusive right of imposing duties and taxes upon his Majesty's subjects in the said colonies and plantations; and have, in pursuance of such claim, passed certain votes, resolutions, and orders, derogatory to the legislative authority of parliament, and inconsistent with the dependency of the said colonies and plantations upon the crown of* Great Britain: . . . be it declared . . . , That the said colonies and plantations in *America* have been, are, and of right ought to be, subordinate unto, and dependent upon the imperial crown and parliament of *Great Britain;* and that the King's majesty, by and with the advice and consent of the lords spiritual and temporal, and commons of *Great Britain,* in parliament assembled, had, hath, and of right ought to have, full power and authority to make laws and statutes of sufficient force and validity to bind the colonies and people of *America,* subjects of the crown of *Great Britain,* in all cases whatsoever.

II. And be it further declared . . . , That all resolutions, votes, orders, and proceedings, in any of the said colonies or plantations, whereby the power and authority of the parliament of *Great Britain,* to make laws and statutes as aforesaid, is denied, or drawn into question, are, and are hereby declared to be, utterly null and void to all intents and purposes whatsoever.

D. Pickering, *Statutes at Large,* vol. XXVII, pp. 19–20.

4.8: A British Official Argues for Taxing Americans (1766)

The stamp tax and the other imperial measures to raise revenues in America appeared very different when viewed from the eastern side of the Atlantic. In 1766 Thomas Whately, a British treasury official, wrote Considerations on the Trade and Finances of This Kingdom, *excerpted below, to explain why both justice and necessity required the new imperial taxes and trade regulations after the end of the French and Indian War in 1763.*

Are Whately's arguments convincing? Did the Americans really benefit by the British military victory over France? Should the colonists have contributed more to the cost of the French and Indian War? Might there have been a better way for them to have contributed to common imperial needs than the methods the British government tried to impose?

British Policies Are Just

THOMAS WHATELY

[O]f all the Measures which were pursued for the Benefit of Trade, those were by far the most important which respected the Colonies, who have of late been the Darling Object of the Mother Country's Care: We are not yet recovered from a War undertaken solely for their Protection: Every Object for which it was begun, is accomplished; and still greater are obtained than at first were even thought of; but whatever may be the Value of the Acquisitions in *America,* the immediate Benefit of them is to the Colonies; and this Country [Britain] feels it only in their Prosperity; for though the Accessions of Trade and of Territory which were obtained by the Peace, are so many Additions to the Empire and the Commerce of *Great Britain* at large, yet they principally affect that Part of her Dominions, and that Branch of her Trade, to which they immediately relate [the American colonies]. To improve these Advantages, and to forward still further the peculiar Interests of the Colonies, was the chief Aim of the Administration in the Period now before me. . . .

Were there no other Ground to require a Revenue from the Colonies, than as a Return for these Obligations, it would alone be a sufficient Foundation: Add to these the Advantages obtained for them by the Peace; add the Debt incurred by [Britain in] a War undertaken in their Defense only; the Distress thereby brought upon the [British] Finances, upon the Credit both publick and private, upon the Trade, and upon the people of this Country; and it must be acknowledged that no Time was ever so seasonable for claiming their Assistance. The Distribution is too

Thomas Whately, *Considerations on the Trade and Finances of This Kingdom* (London: G. Wilkie, 1766), pp. 66–72.

unequal, of Benefits only to the Colonies, and all the Burthens upon the Mother Country; and yet no more was desired than that they should contribute to the Preservation of the Advantages they have received, and take upon themselves a small Share of the [military] Establishment necessary for their own Protection: Upon these Principles several new Taxes were laid upon the Colonies: Many were indeed . . . rather Regulations of Trade than Funds of Revenue: But some were intended to answer both Purposes. . . .

But it was never intended to impose on them any Share of the National Debt: They were never called upon to defray any Part of our domestic civil Expenses: the Legislature [Parliament] only required of them to contribute to the Support of those Establishments, which are equally interesting to all the Subjects of *Great Britain.* The Charge of the Navy, Army, and Ordinance, of *Africa* and of *America,* is about £3,000,000 *per ann.* These, surely, are general; they are as important to the Colonies as to the Mother Country; as necessary to their Protection, as conducive to their Welfare, as to our own: If all share the Benefit, they should also share the Burthen; the whole ought not to be borne by a Part. . . .

. . . We have their All, they say; all that they can gain, all that they can raise is sent hither to purchase *British* Manufactures, and we must therefore be content to see their Demand diminish, by so much as any Revenue we require may amount to: But does their All really even center in *Great Britain?* Their illicit Trade was computed during the last Peace to be about a Third of their actual Imports; and the Money diverted from that to the Establishment is surely no national Loss. . . .

The Argument is nearly the same, it is only weaker, when instead of the Consumption of the Colonies, the Consequence of that Consumption, their Debt to this Country, is pleaded, and the new Duties are represented as depriving them of the Means of discharging it: the Complaint would be just if a Revenue had been exacted from them without furnishing of the means for raising it: But the Peace, and the measures taken since for improving the Advantages of it, have done much more: for it would be rating the Cessions made by *France* very low indeed, if the Security which is the Consequence of them; if the vast Accession of Territory; if the Intercourse [commerce] opened with the *Indians,* their greater Demand for Cloathing, Arms, Spirits, and other Commodities, and the Monopoly of their Return in Beaver, Furs, and all sorts of Peltry; if the Improvements of the Cod, Seal, and Sea-Cow Fishery, [and other major commercial gains to America derived from the victory over France and the treaty of 1763] . . . . By all these Means we have increased the Abilities of the Colonies to purchase our Manufactures, . . . and to discharge their Debts in *Great Britain.* All Objections therefore to the Taxing them, as affecting their Trade, are resolvable at last into a Complaint, that we have not done more for them. . . .

The only remaining Argument worth Notice is, that restraints being laid upon the Trade of the Colonies, they ought therefore be exempted from contributing to the Revenue: A very general Argument indeed, equally applicable to all Times, and to all Taxes: but which would not be a just Inference even from a Supposition that they had no other Trade than to their Mother Country; and is preposterous when applied to a People whose Lands through all their various Soils and Climates are

luxuriantly rich in almost all the Productions of the Earth, who besides their inex-
haustible Fisheries, and besides their Intercourse with *Great Britain,* carry on a
most exhaustive Traffick with the *West-Indies,* with *Africa,* and with all Parts of
Europe to the southward of Cape *Finisterre;* and whose Seas are from all these
Causes throng'd with Ships, and their Rivers floating with Commerce. This flourishing State of their Commerce contradicts all the Complaints which have been
made of the Restraints laid upon it. For such Restraints have subsisted from a very
early Period, and under them that Trade has been established and enlarged, which is
now pretended they oppress. . . .

If from what has been said it appears, that no Principle of Finance or of Commerce forbids the Taxing of the Colonies for the Purposes of Revenue only; it must
on the other Hand be admitted that the Circumstances of this Country [Britain] call
for every Aid which any of its Subjects can give: And there is a peculiar Propriety
in requiring it from the *Americans,* who have contributed so little and for whom so
much has been done. . . .

4.9: A British View of "No Taxation without Representation" (1765)

*Whately's argument for imperial taxes emphasized the need to share
economic burdens. Other defenders of British policy took issue with
the American claim that taxation without representation violated the
age-old rights of English subjects. In the selection that follows Soame
Jenyns, a member of Parliament, criticizes the American argument by
an appeal to both history and precedent. In truth, Jenyns's facts are
correct: Few people in England, including most adult men, had the
vote, and yet all had to submit to taxes. But was the American case different from that of the disfranchised English taxpayers? How would
you have answered Jenyns?*

"No Taxation with Representation" Is an Invalid Argument

SOAME JENYNS

The great capital argument, which I find on this subject, and which, like an elephant
at the head of a Nabob's army, being once overthrown, must put the whole into confusion, is this: that no Englishman is, or can be taxed, but by his own consent: by
which must be meant one of these three propositions; either that no Englishman can
be taxed without his own consent as an individual; or that no Englishman can be
taxed without the consent of the persons he chuses to represent him; or that no
Englishman can be taxed without the consent of the majority of all those, who are

Soame Jenyns, *The Works of Soame Jenyns,* ed. Charles N. Cole (London, n.p. 1790), vol. 2, pp. 191–94.

elected by himself and others of his fellow-subjects to represent them. Now let us impartially consider, whether any one of these propositions are in fact true: if not, then this wonderful structure which has been erected upon them, falls at once to the ground, and like another Babel, perishes by a confusion of words, which the builders themselves are unable to understand.

First then, that no Englishman is or can be taxed but by his own consent as an individual: this is so far from being true, that it is the very reverse of truth, for no man that I know of is taxed by his own consent; and an Englishman, I believe, is as little likely to be so taxed, as any man in the world.

Secondly, that no Englishman is, or can be taxed, but by the consent of those persons, whom he has chose to represent him; for the truth of this I shall appeal only to the candid representatives of those unfortunate counties which produce cyder, and shall willingly acquiesce under their determination.

Lastly, that no Englishman is, or can be taxed, without the consent of the majority of those, who are elected by himself, and others of his fellow-subjects, to represent them. This is certainly as false as the other two; for every Englishman is taxed, and not one in twenty represented: copyholders, leaseholders, and all men possessed of personal property only, chuse no representatives: Manchester, Birmingham, and many more of our richest and most flourishing trading towns send no members to parliament, consequently cannot consent by their representatives, because they chuse none to represent them; yet are they not Englishmen? or are they not taxed?

I am well aware, that I shall hear Locke, Sidney, Seldon, and many other great names quoted, to prove that every Englishman, whether he has a right to vote for a representative or not, is still represented in the British parliament; in which opinion they all agree: on what principle of common sense this opinion is founded I comprehend not, but on the authority of such respectable names I shall acknowledge its truth; but then I will ask one question, and on that I will rest the whole merits of the cause: Why does not this imaginary representation extend to America as well as over the whole island of Great Britain? If it can travel three hundred miles, why not three thousand? if it can jump over rivers and mountains, why cannot it sail over the ocean? If the towns of Manchester and Birmingham sending no representatives to parliament, are notwithstanding there represented, why are not the cities of Albany and Boston equally represented in that assembly? Are they not alike British subjects? are they not Englishmen? or are they only Englishmen when they solicit for protection, but not Englishmen when taxes are required to enable this country to protect them? . . .

One method indeed has been hinted at, and but one, that might render the exercise of this power in a British parliament just and legal, which is the introduction of representatives from the several colonies into that body; but as this has never seriously been proposed, I shall not here consider the impracticability of this method, nor the effects of it, if it could be practiced; but only say, that I have lately seen so many specimens of the great powers of speech, of which these American gentlemen are possessed, that I should be much afraid, that the sudden importation of so much eloquence at once, would greatly endanger the safety of the government of this country; or in terms more fashionable, though less understood, this our most excellent constitution. If we can avail ourselves of these taxes on no other condition, I shall never look upon it as a measure of frugality; being perfectly satisfied, that in the end, it may be much cheaper for us to pay their army, than their orators.

4.10: American Loyalists Defend Britain (1774, 1775)

American Tories, who after 1776 preferred the name loyalists, were a large fraction of the entire population. Many belonged to certain specific categories: recent arrivals from Britain, colonial officeholders, Anglican ministers, and those who had retained close ties with the mother country, either emotional or economic.

Two of the most articulate Tories were the Anglican ministers Samuel Seabury and Jonathan Boucher, the first from New York, the second from Maryland. In the selections below they express their dismay at the defiant mood of their fellow Americans toward Parliament and the king. What are the underlying political and social assumptions shared by the two clergymen? Can you see a connection between their allegiance to the Anglican church, which in the new United States, would take the name "Episcopal," and their views of the proper relations of subject and ruler?

Anglican Ministers Defend Britain's Position

SAMUEL SEABURY AND JONATHAN BOUCHER

Samuel Seabury

In every government there must be a supreme, absolute authority lodged somewhere. In arbitrary governments this power is in the monarch; in aristocratical governments, in the nobles; in democratical in the people; or the deputies of their electing. . . .

Upon supposition that every English colony enjoyed a legislative power independent of the parliament; and that the parliament has no just authority to make laws to bind them, this absurdity will follow—that there is no power in the British empire, which has authority to make laws for the whole empire; i. e. we have an empire, without government; or which amounts to the same thing, we have a government which has no supreme power. All our colonies are independent of each other:

Samuel Seabury, *A View of the Controversy Between Great Britain and Her Colonies* (New York, n.p. 1774), p. 6.

Suppose them independent of the British parliament,—what power do you leave to govern the whole? None at all. You split and divide the empire into a number of petty, insignificant states. This is the direct, the necessary tendency of refusing submission to acts of parliament. Every man who can see one inch beyond his nose, must see this consequence. And every man who endeavors to accelerate the independency of the colonies on the British parliament, endeavors to accelerate the ruin of the British empire.

To talk of being liege subjects to King George, while we disavow the authority of parliament is another piece of whiggish nonsense. I love my King as well as any whig in America or England either, and am as ready to yield him all lawful submission: But while I submit to the King, I submit to the authority of the laws of the state, whose guardian the King is. The difference between a good and a bad subject, is only this, that the one obeys, the other transgresses the law. The difference between a loyal subject and a rebel, is, that the one yields obedience to, and faithfully supports the supreme authority of the state, and the other endeavours to overthrow it. If we obey the laws of the King, we obey the laws of the parliament. If we disown the authority of the parliament, we disown the authority of the King. There is no medium without ascribing powers to the King which the constitution know nothing of:—without making him superior to the laws, and setting him above all restraint. These are some of the ridiculous absurdities of American whiggism. . . .

I will here, Sir, venture to deliver my sentiments upon the line that ought to be drawn between the supremacy of Great-Britain, and the dependency of the colonies. And I shall do it with the more boldness, because, I know it to be agreeable to the opinions of many of the warmest advocates for America, both in England and in the colonies, in the time of the stamp-act.—I imagine that if all internal taxation be vested in our own legislatures, and the right of regulating trade by duties, bounties, etc. be left in the power of the Parliament; and also the right of enacting all general laws for the good of all the colonies, that we shall have all the security for our rights, liberties and property, which human policy can give us: The dependence of the colonies on the mother country will be fixed on a firm foundation; the sovereign authority of Parliament, over all the dominions of the empire will be established, and the mother-country and all her colonies will be knit together, in one GRAND, FIRM, AND COMPACT BODY.

Jonathan Boucher

It can, I think, admit of no dispute, that an accommodation between the Colonies and the Mother Country, on almost any terms, is infinitely more to be desired by both countries than even the most signal successes in war. In the latter way, to succeed is to become a separate people; not as Abram and Lot became a separate people, whilst yet they continued to be friends; but having no longer any community either of interest or affection, as perfect aliens to each other, and, in short, as totally distinct and separate nations. There seems no possibility of any middle course. . . .

Jonathan Boucher, *A View of the Causes and Consequences of the American Revolution* (London, n.p. 1797), p. 16.

Were the question to be determined by present expediency, it is possible the arguments in favour of a separation might be found to be the strongest. But, as such a separation would be a new thing in the world, . . . and as also there are in this vast continent many thousands of respectable men, who, considering allegiance [to the British crown] as a duty, find it impossible to bring themselves to retain or relinquish it just as a mere convenience may seem to suggest, we hope at least to be permitted to pause before we determine.

There is an objection of no ordinary magnitude at the very threshold of this novel proposal. It has never been proved, nor, in my humble opinion, can it ever be proved, that the Parent State can do what is asked; that is to say, can, without a breach of the Constitution, voluntarily withdraw or forbear it's [*sic*] government over America. Allegiance and protection are not merely reciprocal duties, entirely dependent the one on the other. Each duty continues to be equally obligatory, and in force, whether the other be performed or not. . . .

The only rational idea of civil liberty, or (which is the same thing) of a legitimate and good government . . . is, when the great body of the people are trained and led habitually to submit to and acquiesce in some fixed and steady principles of conduct. It is essential, moreover, to Liberty, that such principles shall be of power sufficient to controul the arbitrary and capricious wills of mankind; which, whenever they are not so controuled, are found to be dangerous and destructive to the best interests of society. The primary aim, therefore, of all well-framed Constitutions is, to place man, as it were, out of the reach of his own power, and also out of the power of others as weak as himself, by placing him under the power of law. To counteract that aim (and to do so is the object of all self-constituted assemblies) is to carry back social man to his supposed original independence, and to throw him once more into what has been called a state of Nature. In our own case, it is violently pulling down an old, well-poised Constitution, arbitrarily to introduce, in its stead, what, if it be no anarchy, must at best be a democracy. Now, it ought never to be out of the recollection of mankind, that democracies, even when established without either tumult or tyranny, and by the very general though perhaps not unanimous consent of the community, not contended with an equality of rights, in theory at least, naturally aim at an equality of possessions. . . .

This popular notion, that government was originally formed by the consent or by a compact of the people, rests on, and is supported by, another similar notion, not less popular, nor better founded. This other notion is, that the whole human race is born equal; and that no man is naturally inferior or, in any respect, subjected to another; and that he can be made subject to another only by his own consent. . . . Man differs from man in every thing that can be supposed to lead to supremacy and subjection, *as one star differs from another star in glory.* . . . A musical instrument composed of chords, keys, or pipes, all perfectly equal in size and power, might as well be expected to produce harmony, as a society composed of members all perfectly equal to be productive of harmony and peace. If (according to the idea of the advocates of this chimerical scheme of equality) no man could rightfully *be compelled to come in* and be a member even of a government to be formed by a regular compact, but by his own individual consent; it clearly follows, from the same principles, that neither could he rightfully be made or compelled to submit to the ordinances of any government already formed, to which he has not individually or actually consented. On the principle of equality, neither his parents, nor even the vote of a majority of the society . . . can have any such authority over any man. . . . The same principle of equality that exempts him from being governed without his own consent, clearly entitles him to recall and resume that consent whenever he sees fit; and he alone has a right to judge when and for what reasons it may be resumed.

All government, whether lodged in one or in many, is, in its nature, absolute and irresistible. . . . Without some paramount and irresistible power, there can be no government. In our Constitution, this supremacy is vested in the King and the Parliament; and, subordinate to them, in our Provincial Legislatures. If you were now released from this constitutional power, you must differ from all others "of the human race," if you did not soon find yourselves under a necessity of submitting to a power no less absolute, though vested in other persons, and a government differently constituted.

4.11: The American Revolution as a Social Movement (1776, 1777)

How did the American Revolution affect the lives of ordinary people? Was it a movement primarily concerned with society's upper ranks, or was its reach more profound? In recent years, scholars have paid great attention to how the Revolution affected the ordinary, poor people whose voices we seldom encounter when studying the eloquent writings and speeches of the Founding Fathers. Moreover, how did the Revolution affect those outside the direct exercise of political power, namely women, slaves, and Native Americans?

Do the enclosed selections reveal a pattern of debate consistent with the concerns of society's leaders? Did the Revolution raise expectations? To what degree were these fulfilled?

Abigail Adams on Women's Rights (1776)

Abigail to John

. . . I long to hear that you have declared an independancy—and by the way in the new Code of Laws which I suppose it will be necessary for you to make I desire you would Remember the Ladies, and be more generous and favourable to them than your ancestors. Do not put such unlimited power into the hands of the Husbands. Remember all Men would be tyrants if they could. If perticuliar care and attention is

Charles Francis Adams, *Familiar Letters of John Adams and his Wife Abigail Adams* (Boston: Houghton Mifflin & Co., 1876), March 31, 1776.

not paid to the Laidies we are determined to foment a Rebelion, and will not hold ourselves bound by any Laws in which we have no voice, or Representation.

That your Sex are Naturally Tyrannical is a Truth so thoroughly established as to admit of no dispute, but such of you as wish to be happy willingly give up the harsh title of Master for the more tender and endearing one of Friend. Why then, not put it out of the power of the vicious and the Lawless to use us with cruelty and indignity with impunity. Men of Sense in all Ages abhor those customs which treat us only as the vassals of your Sex. Regard us then as Beings placed by providence under your protection and in immitation of the Supreem Being make use of that power only for our happiness.

John to Abigail

. . . As to your extraordinary Code of Laws, I cannot but laugh. We have been told that our Struggle has loosened the bands of Government every where. That Children and Apprentices were disobedient—that schools and Colleges were grown turbulent— that Indians slighted their Guardians and Negroes grew insolent to their Masters. But your Letter was the first Intimation that another Tribe more numerous and powerfull than all the rest were grown discontented—This is rather too coarse a Compliment but you are so saucy, I wont blot it out.

Depend upon it, We know better than to repeal our Masculine systems. Altho they are in full Force, you know they are little more than Theory. We dare not exert our Power in its full Latitude. We are obliged to go fair, and softly, and in Practice you know We are the subjects. We have only the Name of Masters, and rather than give up this, which would compleatly subject Us to we shall find no difference; neither can any just cause be assigned why we should punish in the one case and pardon in the other. Let them call me rebel, and welcome, I feel no concern from it; but I should suffer the misery of devils, were I to make a whore of my soul by swearing allegiance to one whose character is that of a sottish, stupid, stubborn, worthless, brutish man. I conceive likewise a horrid idea in receiving mercy from a being, who at the last day shall be shrieking to the rocks and mountains to cover him, and fleeing with terror from the orphan, the widow, and the slain of America.

There are cases which cannot be overdone by language, and this is one. There are persons too who see not the full extent of the evil which threatens them, they solace themselves with hopes that the enemy, if they succeed, will be merciful. It is the madness of folly, to expect mercy from those who have refused to do justice; and even mercy, where conquest is the object, is only a trick of war; the cunning of the fox is as murderous as the violence of the wolf; and we ought to guard equally against both. . . .

I thank God that I fear not. I see no real cause for fear. I know our situation well, and can see the way out of it. . . . By perseverance and fortitude we have the prospect of a glorious issue; by cowardice and submission, the sad choice of a variety of evils—a ravaged country—a depopulated city—habitations without safety, and slavery without hope—our homes turned into barracks and bawdy-houses for Hessians, and a future race to provide for, whose fathers we shall doubt of. Look on this picture and weep over it! and if there yet remains one thoughtless wretch who believes it not, let him suffer it unlamented. . . .

Prince Hall, a Former Slave (1777)

To the Honorable Council & House of Representatives
for the State of Massachusetts-Bay in General Court
assembled January 13th 1777.

The Petition of a great number of Negroes who are detained in a state of Slavery in the Bowels of a free & Christian Country Humbly Shewing

That your Petitioners apprehend that they have, in common with all other Men, a natural & unalienable right to that freedom, which the great Parent of the Universe hath bestowed equally on all Mankind, & which they have never forfeited by any compact or agreement whatever—But they were unjustly dragged, by the cruel hand of Power, from their dearest friends, & some of them even torn from the embraces of their tender Parents. From a populous, pleasant and plentiful Country—& in Violation of the Laws of Nature & of Nation & in defiance of all the tender feelings of humanity, brought hither to be sold like Beasts of Burden, & like them condemned to slavery for Life—Among a People professing the mild Religion of Jesus—A People not insensible of the sweets of rational freedom—Nor without spirit to resent the unjust endeavours of others to reduce them to a State of Bondage & Subjection—Your Honors need not to be informed that a Life of Slavery, like that of your petitioners, deprived of every social privilege, of every thing requisite to render Life even tolerable, is far worse than Non-Existence—In imitation of the laudable example of the good People of these States, your Petitioners have long & patiently waited the event of Petition after Petition by them presented to the legislative Body of this State, & can not but with grief reflect that their success has been but too similar—They can not but express their astonishment, that it has never been considered, that every principle from which America has acted in the course of her unhappy difficulties with Great-Britain, pleads stronger than a thousand arguments in favor of your Petitioners. They therefore humbly beseech your Honors, to give this Petition its due weight & consideration, & cause an Act of the Legislature to be passed, whereby they may be restored to the enjoyment of that freedom which is the natural right of all Men—& their Children (who were born in this Land of Liberty) may not be held as Slaves after they arrive at the age of twenty one years—So may the Inhabitants of this State (no longer chargeable with the inconsistency of acting, themselves, the part which they condemn & oppose in others) be prospered in their present glorious struggles for Liberty; & have those blessings secured to them by Heaven, of which benevolent minds can not wish to deprive their fellow Men.

And your Petitioners, as in Duty Bound shall ever pray.

Lancaster Hill
Peter Bess
Brister Slenten   Negroes Petition to the Honble
Prince Hall   Gen Assembly—Mass.

Massachusetts Historical Collections. Fifth Series, No. 3 (Boston, 1788).

Jack Purpont *his mark*

Nero Suneto *his mark*

Newport Symner *his mark*

Job Lock

March 18
Judge Sargeant
M. Balton
M. Appleton
Coll. Brooks
M. Stony
W. Lowell
Matter Atlege
W. Davis

❖ 5 ❖

The Constitution

We who live under the federal Constitution seldom question its wisdom and effectiveness. But its creation and adoption in 1787–1788 provoked major battles among Americans. To some it seemed imprudent and unnecessary; the loose confederation of near sovereign states established by the Articles of Confederation during the Revolution was good enough. A stronger central government, such people worried, might tyrannize the states and the people themselves.

Supporters of the new frame of government, on the other hand—the "federalists"[1]—believed it essential to remedy American weakness at home and abroad. The new United States, they insisted, was in danger of becoming a collection of squabbling, petty states, a laughingstock among nations, unable to protect its sovereignty or further its people's interests and prosperity.

The delegates to the Constitutional Convention that met in Philadelphia during the summer of 1787 required that the system they created be submitted to the states. The state governments in turn, they assumed, would submit it to special state ratifying conventions. When nine of these had ratified, the Constitution would become operative. It was during the ratification process from late September 1787 to mid-summer 1788 that the public debate over adoption raged most vociferously.

Pro- or antiratification opinion was not distributed at random. Nor was it solely a matter of individual temperament, although personal attitudes toward freedom versus authority obviously played a part in determining people's positions. Citizens saw advantages or disadvantages for themselves or their group in the new Constitution, however they defined these benefits or drawbacks. Compared to the existing Confederation, a

---

[1]"Federalist" at this point meant a supporter of the Constitution. By the mid-1790s it had come to mean a supporter of a new political party that was opposed to the Jeffersonian Republicans.

new, stronger central government promised to be more solvent, to be more effective internationally, to exert greater power over the economy, and to be more forceful in preventing threats to social order. Inevitably, expanded influence for the central government seemed likely to confer gains on some, losses on others.

There was also the matter of national pride. Thousands who had fought and sacrificed for independence had a stake in a government that could effectively express collective American aspirations, a role that the government of the Articles of Confederation seemed unable to play.

On the other hand, many Americans had no sense of national solidarity. Their chief loyalty was to their local communities, especially to their states. These, not some abstract entity controlled by a remote authority in some national capital, were their "countries." They also feared the effects of a strong central government on freedom. As originally composed, the Constitution had no guarantees of citizens' rights against the new federal government. Critics thought it might well become an instrument of tyranny.

See if you can detect the primary motivation of the writers in the selections that follow. What lay behind their arguments for or against the Constitution?

5.1: Drafting the Constitution (1787)

George Washington, elected president of the convention that met in Philadelphia during the summer of 1787, wrote this letter as a preamble explaining why the delegates had come together. In addition to drafting the Constitution, the delegates also proposed a method for ratification. How democratic was this process? Did the means employed by the founding fathers justify the ends? What problems did the fledgling nation face under the Articles of Confederation that they hoped would be solved by the new Constitution? In your opinion, was the Constitution, as its defenders have often claimed, the fulfillment of the sentiments and purposes of the American Revolution, or was it what Anti-Federalists and later detractors termed a "counter-Revolution"?

The document itself has received the devoted attention of millions over the past two centuries. What philosophical principles inspire it? How does it define sovereignty, and what is its view of human nature? In what ways is it a product of the enlightenment? What roles do the following concepts play in how the new government will work: separation of powers, checks and balances, minority rights, and virtue?

Many have described the Constitution as a "living document," meaning that it can change over time. Based on your understanding of how the U.S. government works today, are you surprised by any constitutional features, either included or excluded? Finally, how has our view of the Bill of Rights evolved over time? Do we interpret the first ten amendments the same way the framers did?

Letter from the Constitutional Convention to the President of Congress

GEORGE WASHINGTON

In Convention, September 17, 1787.

SIR, WE have now the honor to submit to the consideration of the United States in Congress assembled, that Constitution which has appeared to us the most adviseable.

The friends of our country have long seen and desired, that the power of making war, peace and treaties, that of levying money and regulating commerce, and the correspondent executive and judicial authorities should be fully and effectually vested in the general government of the Union: but the impropriety of delegating such extensive trust to one body of men is evident—Hence results the necessity of a different organization.

It is obviously impracticable in the foederal government of these States; to secure all rights of independent sovereignty to each, and yet provide for the interest and safety of all—Individuals entering into society, must give up a share of liberty to preserve the rest. The magnitude of the sacrifice must depend as well on situation and circumstance, as on the object to be obtained. It is at all times difficult to draw with precision the line between those rights which must be surrendered, and those which may be reserved; and on the present occasion this difficulty was encreased by a difference among the several States as to their situation, extent, habits, and particular interests.

In all our deliberations on this subject we kept steadily in our view, that which appears to us the greatest interest of every true American, the consolidation of our Union, in which is involved our prosperity, felicity, safety, perhaps our national existence, This important consideration, seriously and deeply impressed on our minds, led each State in the Convention to be less rigid on points of inferior magnitude, than might have been otherwise expected; and thus the Constitution, which we now present, is the result of a spirit of amity, and of that mutual deference and concession which the peculiarity of our political situation rendered indispensible.

That it will meet the full and entire approbation of every State is not perhaps to be expected; but each will doubtless consider, that had her interests been alone consulted, the consequences might have been particularly disagreeable or injurious to others; that it is liable to as few exceptions as could reasonably have been expected, we hope and believe; that it may promote the lasting welfare of that country so dear to us all, and secure her freedom and happiness, is our most ardent wish.

Adapted from Bernard Bailyn (ed.), *The Debate on the Constitution, Part One.* New York: The Library of America, pp. 965–966.

With great respect, WE have the honor to be SIR, Your Excellency's most Obedient and humble servants.

> George Washington, President.
> By unanimous Order of the
> Convention

Resolutions of the Convention Concerning the Ratification and Implementation of the Constitution

In Convention Monday September 17th. 1787.

Present The States of New Hampshire, Massachusetts, Connecticut, Mr. Hamilton from New York, New Jersey, Pennsylvania, Delaware, Maryland, Virginia, North Carolina, South Carolina and Georgia.

RESOLVED, That the preceeding Constitution be laid before the United States in Congress assembled, and that it is the Opinion of this Convention, that it should afterwards be submitted to a Convention of Delegates, chosen in each State by the People thereof, under the Recommendation of its Legislature, for their Assent and Ratification; and that each Convention assenting to, and ratifying the Same, should give Notice thereof to the United States in Congress assembled.

Resolved, That it is the Opinion of this Convention, that as soon as the Conventions of nine States shall have ratified this Constitution, the United States in Congress assembled should fix a Day on which Electors should be appointed by the States which shall have ratified the same, and a Day on which the Electors should assemble to vote for the President, and the Time and Place for commencing Proceedings under this Constitution. That after such Publication the Electors should be appointed, and the Senators and Representatives elected: That the Electors should meet on the Day fixed for the Election of the President, and should transmit their Votes certified, signed, sealed and directed, as the Constitution requires, to the Secretary of the United States in Congress assembled, that the Senators and Representatives should convene at the Time and Place assigned; that the Senators should appoint a President of the Senate, for the sole Purpose of receiving, opening and counting the Votes for President; and, that after he shall be chosen, the Congress, together with the President, should, without Delay, proceed to execute this Constitution.

> By the Unanimous Order of the Convention
> W. Jackson Secretary.   George Washington, President.

The Constitution

We the People of the United States, in Order to form a more perfect Union, establish Justice, insure domestic Tranquility, provide for the common defence, promote the general Welfare, and secure the Blessings of Liberty to ourselves and our Posterity, do ordain and establish this Constitution for the United States of America.

Adapted from Bernard Bailyn (ed.), *The Debate on the Constitution, Part One.* New York: The Library of America, pp. 967ff.

Article. I.

Section. 1. All legislative Powers herein granted shall be vested in a Congress of the United States, which shall consist of a Senate and House of Representatives.

Section. 2. The House of Representatives shall be composed of Members chosen every second Year by the People of the several States, and the Electors in each State shall have the Qualifications requisite for Electors of the most numerous Branch of the State Legislature.

No Person shall be a Representative who shall not have attained to the Age of twenty five Years, and been seven Years a Citizen of the United States, and who shall not, when elected, be an Inhabitant of that State in which he shall be chosen.

Representatives and direct Taxes shall be apportioned among the several States which may be included within this Union, according to their respective Numbers, which shall be determined by adding to the whole Number of free Persons, including those bound to Service for a Term of Years, and excluding Indians not taxed, three fifths of all other Persons. The actual Enumeration shall be made within three Years after the first Meeting of the Congress of the United States, and within every subsequent Term of ten Years, in such Manner as they shall by Law direct. The Number of Representatives shall not exceed one for every thirty Thousand, but each State shall have at Least one Representative; and until such enumeration shall be made, the State of New Hampshire shall be entitled to chuse three, Massachusetts eight, Rhode-Island and Providence Plantations one, Connecticut five, New-York six, New Jersey four, Pennsylvania eight, Delaware one, Maryland six, Virginia ten, North Carolina five, South Carolina five, and Georgia three.

When vacancies happen in the Representation from any State, the Executive Authority thereof shall issue Writs of Election to fill such Vacancies.

The House of Representatives shall chuse their Speaker and other Officers; and shall have the sole Power of Impeachment.

Section. 3. The Senate of the United States shall be composed of two Senators from each State, chosen by the Legislature thereof, for six Years; and each Senator shall have one Vote.

Immediately after they shall be assembled in Consequence of the first Election, they shall be divided as equally as may be into three Classes. The Seats of the Senators of the first Class shall be vacated at the Expiration of the second Year, of the second Class at the Expiration of the fourth Year, and of the third Class at the Expiration of the sixth Year, so that one third may be chosen every second Year; and if Vacancies happen by Resignation, or otherwise, during the Recess of the Legislature of any State, the Executive thereof may make temporary Appointments until the next Meeting of the Legislature, which shall then fill such Vacancies.

No Person shall be a Senator who shall not have attained to the Age of thirty Years, and been nine Years a Citizen of the United States, and who shall not, when elected, be an Inhabitant of that State for which he shall be chosen.

The vice President of the United States shall be President of the Senate, but shall have no Vote, unless they be equally divided.

The Senate shall chuse their other Officers, and also a President pro tempore, in the Absence of the Vice President, or when he shall exercise the Office of President of the United States.

The Senate shall have the sole Power to try all Impeachments. When sitting for that Purpose, they shall be on Oath or Affirmation. When the President of the United States is tried, the Chief Justice shall preside: And no Person shall be convicted without the Concurrence of two thirds of the Members present.

Judgment in Cases of Impeachment shall not extend further than to removal from Office, and disqualification to hold and enjoy any Office of honor, Trust or Profit under the United States: but the Party convicted shall nevertheless be liable and subject to Indictment, Trial, Judgment and Punishment, according to Law.

Section. 4. The Times, Places and Manner of holding Elections for Senators and Representatives, shall be prescribed in each State by the Legislature thereof; but the Congress may at any time by Law make or alter such Regulations, except as to the Places of chusing Senators.

The Congress shall assemble at least once in every Year, and such Meeting shall be on the first Monday in December, unless they shall by Law appoint a different Day.

Section. 5. Each House shall be the Judge of the Elections, Returns and Qualifications of its own Members, and a Majority of each shall constitute a Quorum to do Business; but a smaller Number may adjourn from day to day, and may be authorized to compel the Attendance of absent Members, in such Manner, and under such Penalties as each House may provide.

Each House may determine the Rules of its Proceedings, punish its members for disorderly Behaviour, and, with the Concurrence of two thirds, expel a Member.

Each House shall keep a Journal of its Proceedings, and from time to time publish the same, excepting such Parts as may in their Judgment require Secrecy; and the Yeas and Nays of the Members of either House on any question shall, at the Desire of one fifth of those Present, be entered on the Journal.

Neither House, during the Session of Congress, shall, without the Consent of the other, adjourn for more than three days, nor to any other Place than that in which the two Houses shall be sitting.

Section. 6. The Senators and Representatives shall receive a Compensation for their Services, to be ascertained by Law, and paid out of the Treasury of the United States. They shall in all Cases, except Treason, Felony and Breach of the Peace, be privileged from Arrest during their Attendance at the Session of their respective Houses, and in going to and returning from the same; and for any Speech or Debate in either House, they shall not be questioned in any other Place.

No Senator or Representative shall, during the Time for which he was elected, be appointed to any civil Office under the Authority of the United States which shall have been created, or the Emoluments whereof shall have been encreased during such time; and no Person holding any Office under the United States, shall be a Member of either House during his Continuance in Office.

Section. 7. All Bills for raising Revenue shall originate in the House of Representatives; but the Senate may propose or concur with Amendments as on other Bills.

Every Bill which shall have passed the House of Representatives and the Senate shall, before it become a Law, be presented to the President of the United States; If he approve he shall sign it, but if not he shall return it, with his Objections to that House in which it shall have originated, who shall enter the Objections at large on their Journal, and proceed to reconsider it. If after such Reconsideration two thirds of that House shall agree to pass the Bill, it shall be sent, together with the Objections, to the other House, by which it shall likewise be reconsidered, and if approved by two thirds of that House, it shall become a Law. But in all such Cases the Votes of both Houses shall be determined by yeas and Nays, and the Names of the Persons voting for and against the Bill shall be entered on the Journal of each House respectively. If any Bill shall not be returned by the President within ten Days (Sundays excepted) after it shall have been presented to him, the Same shall be a Law, in like Manner as if he had signed it, unless the Congress by their Adjournment prevent its Return, in which Case it shall not be a Law.

Every Order, Resolution, or Vote to which the Concurrence of the Senate and House of Representatives may be necessary (except on a question of Adjournment) shall be presented to the President of the United States; and before the Same shall take Effect, shall be approved by him, or being disapproved by him, shall be repassed by two thirds of the Senate and House of Representatives, according to the rules and Limitations prescribed in the Case of a Bill.

Section. 8. The Congress shall have Power To lay and collect Taxes, Duties, Imposts and Excises, to pay the Debts and provide for the common Defence and general Welfare of the United States; but all Duties, Imposts and Excises shall be uniform throughout the United States;

To borrow Money on the credit of the United States;

To regulate Commerce with foreign Nations, and among the several States, and with the Indian Tribes;

To establish an uniform Rule of Naturalization, and uniform Laws on the subject of Bankruptcies throughout the United States;

To coin Money, regulate the Value thereof, and of foreign Coin, and fix the Standard of Weights and Measures;

To provide for the Punishment of counterfeiting the Securities and current Coin of the United States;

To establish Post Offices and post Roads;

To promote the Progress of Science and useful Arts, by securing for limited Times to authors and Inventors the exclusive Right to their respective Writings and Discoveries;

To constitute Tribunals inferior to the supreme Court;

To define and punish Piracies and Felonies committed on the high Seas, and Offences against the Law of Nations;

To declare War, grant Letters of Marque and Reprisal, and make Rules concerning Captures on Land and Water;

To raise and support Armies, but no Appropriation of Money to that Use shall be for a longer Term than two Years;

To provide and maintain a Navy;

To make Rules for the Government and Regulation of the land and naval Forces;

To provide for calling forth the Militia to execute the Laws of the Union, suppress Insurrections and repel Invasions;

To provide for organizing, arming, and disciplining, the Militia, and for governing such Part of them as may be employed in the Service of the United States, reserving to the States respectively, the Appointment of the Officers, and the Authority of training the Militia according to the discipline prescribed by Congress;

To exercise exclusive Legislation in all Cases whatsoever, over such District (not exceeding ten Miles square) as may, by Cession of particular States, and the Acceptance of Congress, become the Seat of the Government of the United States, and to exercise like Authority over all Places purchased by the Consent of the Legislature of the State in which the same shall be, for the Erection of Forts, Magazines, Arsenals, dock-Yards, and other needful buildings;—And

To make all Laws which shall be necessary and proper for carrying into Execution the foregoing Powers, and all other Powers vested by this Constitution in the Government of the United States, or in any Department or Officer thereof.

Section. 9. The Migration or Importation of such Persons as any of the States now existing shall think proper to admit, shall not be prohibited by the Congress prior to the Year one thousand eight hundred and eight, but a Tax or duty may be imposed on such Importation, not exceeding ten dollars for each Person.

The Privilege of the Writ of Habeas Corpus shall not be suspended, unless when in Cases of Rebellion or Invasion the public Safety may require it.

No Bill of Attainder or ex post facto Law shall be passed.

No Capitation, or other direct, Tax shall be laid, unless in Proportion to the Census or Enumeration herein before directed to be taken.

No Tax or Duty shall be laid on Articles exported from any State.

No Preference shall be given by any Regulation of Commerce or Revenue to the Ports of one State over those of another: nor shall Vessels bound to, or from, one State, be obliged to enter, clear, or pay Duties in another.

No Money shall be drawn from the Treasury, but in Consequence of Appropriations made by Law; and a regular Statement and Account of the Receipts and Expenditures of all public Money shall be published from time to time.

No Title of Nobility shall be granted by the United States: And no Person holding any Office of Profit or Trust under them, shall, without the Consent of the Congress, accept of any present, Emolument, Office, or Title, of any kind whatever, from any King, Prince, or foreign State.

Section. 10. No State shall enter into any Treaty, Alliance, or Confederation; grant Letters of Marque and Reprisal; coin Money; emit Bills of Credit; make any Thing but gold and silver Coin a Tender in Payment of Debts; pass any Bill of Attainder, ex post facto Law, or Law impairing the Obligation of Contracts, or grant any Title of Nobility.

No State shall, without the Consent of the Congress, lay any Imposts or Duties on Imports or Exports, except what may be absolutely necessary for executing it's inspection Laws: and the net Produce of all Duties and Imposts, laid by any State on Imports or Exports, shall be for the Use of the Treasury of the United States; and all such Laws shall be subject to the Revision and Controul of the Congress.

No State shall, without the Consent of Congress, lay any Duty of Tonnage, keep Troops, or Ships of War in time of Peace, enter into any Agreement or Compact with another State, or with a foreign Power, or engage in War, unless actually invaded, or in such imminent Danger as will not admit of delay.

Article. II.

Section. 1. The executive Power shall be vested in a President of the United States of America. He shall hold his Office during the Term of four Years, and, together with the Vice President, chosen for the same Term, be elected, as follows

Each State shall appoint, in such Manner as the Legislature thereof may direct, a Number of Electors, equal to the whole Number of Senators and Representatives to which the State may be entitled in the Congress: but no Senator or Representative, or Person holding an Office of Trust or Profit under the United States, shall be appointed an Elector.

The Electors shall meet in their respective States and vote by Ballot for two Persons, of whom one at least shall not be in Inhabitant of the same State with themselves. And they shall make a List of all the Persons voted for, and of the Number of Votes for each; which List they shall sign and certify, and transmit sealed to the Seat of the Government of the United States, directed to the President of the Senate. The President of the Senate shall, in the Presence of the Senate and House of Representatives, open all the Certificates, and the Votes shall then be counted. The Person having the greatest Number of Votes shall be the President, if such Number be a Majority of the whole Number of Electors appointed; and if there be more than one who have such Majority, and have an equal Number of Votes, then the House of Representatives shall immediately chuse by Ballot one of them for President; and if no Person have a Majority, then from the five highest on the List the said House shall in like Manner chuse the President. But in chusing the President, the Votes shall be taken by States, the Representation from each State having one Vote; A quorum for this Purpose shall consist of a Member or Members from two thirds of the States, and a Majority of all the States shall be necessary to a Choice. In every Case, after the Choice of the President, the Person having the greatest Number of Votes of the Electors shall be the Vice President. But if there should remain two or more who have equal Votes, the Senate shall chuse from them by Ballot the Vice President.

The Congress may determine the Time of chusing the Electors, and the Day on which they shall give their Votes; which Day shall be the same throughout the United States.

No Persons except a natural born Citizen, or a Citizen of the United States, at the time of the Adoption of this Constitution, shall be eligible to the Office of President; neither shall any Person be eligible to that office who shall not have attained to the Age of thirty five Years, and been fourteen Years a Resident within the United States.

In Case of the Removal of the President from Office, or of his Death, Resignation, or Inability to discharge the Powers and Duties of the said Office, the Same shall devolve on the Vice President, and the Congress may by Law provide for the Case of Removal, Death, Resignation or Inability, both of the President and Vice President, declaring what Officer shall then act as President, and such Officer shall act accordingly, until the Disability be removed, or a President shall be elected.

The President shall, at stated Times, receive for his Services, a Compensation, which shall neither be encreased nor diminished during the Period for which he shall have been elected, and he shall not receive within that Period any other Emolument from the United States, or any of them.

Before he enter on the Execution of his Office, he shall take the following Oath or Affirmation:—"I do solemnly swear (or affirm) that I will faithfully execute the Office of President of the United States, and will to the best of my Ability, preserve, protect and defend the Constitution of the United States."

Section. 2. The President shall be Commander in Chief of the Army and Navy of the United States, and of the Militia of the several States, when called into the actual Service of the United States; he may require the Opinion, in writing, of the principal Officer in each of the executive Departments, upon any Subject relating to the Duties of their respective Offices, and he shall have Power to grant Reprieves and Pardons for Offences against the United States, except in Cases of Impeachment.

He shall have Power, by and with the Advice and Consent of the Senate, to make Treaties, provided two thirds of the Senators present concur; and he shall nominate, and by and with the Advice and Consent of the Senate, shall appoint Ambassadors, other public Ministers and Consuls, Judges of the supreme Court, and all other Officers of the United States, whose Appointments are not herein otherwise provided for, and which shall be established by Law: but the Congress may by Law vest the Appointment of such inferior Officers, as they think proper, in the President alone, in the Courts of Law, or in the Heads of Departments.

The President shall have Power to fill up all Vacancies that may happen during the Recess of the Senate, by granting Commissions which shall expire at the End of their next Session.

Section. 3. He shall from time to time give to the Congress Information of the State of the Union, and recommend to their Consideration such Measures as he shall judge necessary and expedient; he may, on extraordinary Occasions, convene both Houses, or either of them, and in Case of Disagreement between them, with Respect to the Time of Adjournment, he may adjourn them to such Time as he shall think proper; he shall receive ambassadors and other public Ministers; he shall take

Care that the Laws be faithfully executed, and shall Commission all the Officers of the United States.

Section. 4. The President, Vice President and all civil Officers of the United States, shall be removed from Office on Impeachment for, and Conviction of Treason, Bribery, or other high Crimes and Misdemeanors.

Article. III.

Section. 1. The judicial Power of the United States, shall be vested in one supreme Court, and in such inferior Courts as the Congress may from time to time ordain and establish. The Judges, both of the supreme and inferior Courts, shall hold their Offices during good Behaviour, and shall, at stated Times, receive for their Services, a Compensation, which shall not be diminished during their Continuance in Office.

Section. 2. The judicial Power shall extend to all Cases, in Law and Equity, arising under this Constitution, the Laws of the United States, and Treaties made, or which shall be made, under their Authority;—to all Cases affecting Ambassadors, other public Ministers and Consuls;—to all Cases of admiralty and maritime Jurisdiction;—to Controversies to which the United States shall be a Party;—to Controversies between two or more States—between a State and Citizens of another State;—between Citizens of different States,—between Citizens of the same State claiming Lands under Grants of different States, and between a State, or the Citizens thereof, and of foreign States, Citizens or Subjects.

In all Cases affecting Ambassadors, other public Ministers and Consuls, and those in which a State shall be Party, the supreme Court shall have original Jurisdiction. In all the other Cases before mentioned, the supreme Court shall have appellate Jurisdiction, both as to Law and Fact, with such Exceptions, and under such Regulations as the Congress shall make.

The Trial of all Crimes, except in Cases of Impeachment, shall be by Jury; and such Trial shall be held in the State where the said Crimes shall have been committed; but when not committed within any State, the Trial shall be at such Place or Places as the Congress may by Law have directed.

Section. 3. Treason against the United States, shall consist only in levying War against them, or in adhering to their enemies, giving them Aid and Comfort. No Person shall be convicted of Treason unless on the Testimony of two Witnesses to the same overt Act, or on Confession in open Court.

The Congress shall have Power to declare the Punishment of Treason, but no Attainder of Treason shall work Corruption of Blood, or Forfeiture except during the Life of the Person attained.

Article. IV.

Section. 1. Full Faith and Credit shall be given in each State to the public Acts, Records, and judicial Proceedings of every other State. And the Congress may by general Laws prescribe the Manner in which such Acts, Records and Proceedings shall be proved, and the Effect thereof.

Section. 2. The Citizens of each State shall be entitled to all privileges and Immunities of Citizens in the several States.

A Person charged in any State with Treason, Felony, or other Crime, who shall flee from Justice, and be found in another State, shall on Demand of the executive Authority of the State from which he fled, be delivered up, to be removed to the State having Jurisdiction of the Crime.

No Person held to Service or Labour in one State, under the Laws thereof, escaping into another, shall, in Consequence of any Law or Regulation therein, be discharged from such Service or Labour, but shall be delivered up on Claim of the Party to whom such Service or Labour may be due.

Section. 3. New States may be admitted by the Congress into this Union; but no new State shall be formed or erected within the Jurisdiction of any other State; nor any State be formed by the Junction of two or more States, or Parts of States, without the Consent of the Legislatures of the States concerned as well as of the Congress.

The Congress shall have Power to dispose of and make all needful rules and Regulations respecting the Territory or other Property belonging to the United States; and nothing in this Constitution shall be so construed as to Prejudice any Claims of the United States, or of any particular State.

Section. 4. The United States shall guarantee to every State in this Union a Republican Form of Government, and shall protect each of them against Invasion; and on Application of the Legislature, or of the Executive (when the Legislature cannot be convened) against domestic Violence.

Article. V.

The Congress, whenever two thirds of both Houses shall deem it necessary, shall propose Amendments to this Constitution, or, on the Application of the Legislatures of two thirds of the several States, shall call a Convention for proposing Amendments, which, in either Case, shall be valid to all Intents and Purposes, as Part of this Constitution, when ratified by the Legislatures of three fourths of the several States, or by Conventions in three fourths thereof, as the one or the other Mode of Ratification may be proposed by the Congress; Provided that no Amendment which may be made prior to the Year One thousand eight hundred and eight shall in any Manner affect the first and fourth Clauses in the Ninth Section of the first Article; and that no State, without its Consent, shall be deprived of it's equal Suffrage in the Senate.

Article. VI.

All Debts contracted and Engagements entered into, before the Adoption of this Constitution, shall be as valid against the United States under this Constitution, as under the Confederation.

This Constitution, and the Laws of the United States which shall be made in Pursuance thereof; and all Treaties made, or which shall be made, under the Authority of the United States, shall be the supreme Law of the Land; and the Judges in every State shall be bound thereby, any Thing in the Constitution or Laws of any State to the Contrary notwithstanding.

The Senators and Representatives before mentioned, and the Members of the several State Legislatures, and all executive and judicial Officers; both of the United States and of the several States, shall be bound by Oath or Affirmation, to support this Constitution; but no religious test shall ever be required as a Qualification to any Office or public Trust under the United States.

Article. VII.

The Ratification of the Conventions of nine States, shall be sufficient for the Establishment of this Constitution between the States so ratifying the Same.

DONE in convention by the Unanimous consent of the States present the seventeenth Day of September in the Year of our Lord one thousand seven hundred and Eighty seven and of the Independance of the United States of America the Twelfth In Witness whereof We have hereunto subscribed our Names,

Attest William Jackson Secretary

Go: Washington—Presidt.
and deputy from Virginia

Delaware
- Geo: Read
- Gunning Bedford junr
- John Dickinson
- Richard Bassett
- Jaco: Broom

Maryland
- James McHenry
- Dan of St Thos. Jenifer
- Danl Carroll

Virginia
- John Blair—
- James Madison Jr.

North Carolina
- Wm. Blount
- Richd. Dobbs Spaight.
- Hu Williamson

South Carolina
- J. Rutledge
- Charles Cotesworth Pinckney
- Charles Pinckney
- Pierce Butler

Georgia
- William Few
- Abr Baldwin

New Hampshire
- John Langdon
- Nicholas Gilman

Massachusetts
- Nathaniel Gorham
- Rufus King

Connecticut
- Wm: Saml. Johnson
- Roger Sherman

New York . . . Alexander Hamilton

New Jersey
- Wil: Livingston
- David Brearley
- Wm. Paterson.
- Jona: Dayton

Pennsylvania
- B. Franklin
- Thomas Mifflin
- Robt Morris
- Geo. Clymer
- Thos. FitzSimons
- Jared Ingersoll
- James Wilson
- Gouv. Morris

ARTICLES in Addition to, and Amendment of, the Constitution of the United States of America, proposed by Congress, and ratified by the Legislatures of the several States, pursuant to the fifth Article of the original Constitution.

Article I.

Congress shall make no law respecting an establishment of religion, or prohibiting the free exercise thereof; or abridging the freedom of speech or of the press; or the right of the people peaceably to assemble, and to petition the Government for a redress of grievances.

Article II.

A well regulated Militia, being necessary to the security of a free State, the right of the people to keep and bear Arms, shall not be infringed.

Article III.

No Soldier shall, in time of peace be quartered in any house, without the consent of the Owner, nor in time of war, but in a manner to be prescribed by law.

Article IV.

The right of the people to be secure in their persons, houses, papers, and effects, against unreasonable searches and seizures, shall not be violated and no Warrants shall issue, but upon probable cause, supported by Oath or affirmation, and particularly describing the place to be searched, and the persons or things to be seized.

Article V.

No person shall be held to answer for a capital, or otherwise infamous crime, unless on a presentment or indictment of a Grand Jury, except in cases arising in the land or naval forces, or in the Militia, when in actual service in time of War or public danger; nor shall any person be subject for the same offence to be twice put in jeopardy of life or limb; nor shall be compelled in any criminal case to be a witness against himself, nor be deprived of life, liberty, or property, without due process of law; nor shall private property be taken for public use, without just compensation.

Article VI.

In all criminal prosecutions, the accused shall enjoy the right to a speedy and public trial, by an impartial jury of the State and district wherein the crime shall have been committed, which district shall have been previously ascertained by law, and to be informed of the nature and cause of the accusation; to be confronted with the witnesses against him; to have compulsory process for obtaining witnesses in his favor, and to have the Assistance of Counsel for his defence.

Article VII.

In Suits at common law, where the value in controversy shall exceed twenty dollars, the right of trial by jury shall be preserved, and no fact tried by a jury, shall be otherwise reexamined in any Court of the United States, than according to the rules of the common law.

Article VIII.

Excessive bail shall not be required, nor excessive fines imposed, nor cruel and unusual punishments inflicted.

Article IX.

The enumeration in the Constitution, of certain rights, shall not be construed to deny or disparage others retained by the people.

Article X.

The powers not delegated to the United States by the Constitution, nor prohibited by it to the States, are reserved to the States respectively, or to the people.

Articles I.–X. proposed to the states by Congress, September 25, 1789
Ratification completed, December 15, 1791
Ratification declared, March 1, 1792

5.2: Patrick Henry Denounces the Constitution (1788)

By the time the Virginia convention came to debate the adoption of the Constitution on June 2, 1788, most of the nine states needed to put the document into effect had already ratified it. Still, the formation of a national government without Virginia was unthinkable: It was the largest state, and its leaders had been at the forefront of the patriot cause.

One of the most formidable opponents of the Constitution in Virginia was the patriot firebrand Patrick Henry. In a speech to the state ratification convention, Henry drew a dramatic contrast between power and liberty: Government could either exercise power effectively or protect individual freedom; it could not do both. Was he right? Does a strong government inevitably endanger liberty? Is the preservation of liberty the most important goal of government? Did the consolidated government Henry feared actually trample on rights? on states' rights? on individual rights? What revisions of the original document may have reduced fears of federal power over individuals?

Interestingly, in the 1790s, possibly out of admiration for the Federalist president George Washington, Henry became a member of the political party that favored expanding the new Constitution to maximize the power and authority of the government it had created.

Virginia Should Reject the Constitution

PATRICK HENRY

Mr. Chairman, the public mind, as well as my own, is extremely uneasy at the proposed change of government. Give me leave to form one of the number of those who wish to be thoroughly acquainted with the reasons of this perilous and uneasy situation, and why we are brought hither to decide on this great national question. I consider myself as the servant of the people of this commonwealth, as a sentinel over their rights, liberty, and happiness. I represent their feelings when I say that they are exceedingly uneasy at being brought from that state of full security, which they enjoyed, to the present delusive appearance of things. A year ago, the minds of our citizens were at perfect repose. Before the meeting of the late federal Convention at Philadelphia, a general peace and a universal tranquillity prevailed in this country; but, since that period, they are exceedingly uneasy and disquieted. When I wished for an appointment to this Convention, my mind was extremely agitated for the situation of public affairs. I conceived the republic to be in extreme danger. If our situation be thus uneasy, whence has arisen this fearful jeopardy? It arises from this fatal system; it arises from a proposal to change our government—a proposal that goes to the utter annihilation of the most solemn engagements of the states. . . .

. . . Make the best of this new government—say it is composed by any thing but inspiration—you ought to be extremely cautious, watchful, jealous of your liberty; for, instead of securing your rights, you may lose them forever. If a wrong step be now made, the republic may be lost forever. If this new government will not come up to the expectation of the people, and they shall be disappointed, their liberty will be lost, and tyranny must and will arise. I repeat it again, and I beg gentlemen to consider, that a wrong step, made now, will plunge us into misery, and our republic will be lost. It will be necessary for this Convention to have a faithful historical detail of the facts that preceded the session of the federal Convention, and the reasons that actuated its members in proposing an entire alteration of government, and to demonstrate the dangers that awaited us. If they were of such awful magnitude as to warrant a proposal so extremely perilous as this, I must assert, that this Convention has an absolute right to a thorough discovery of every circumstance relative to this great event. And here I would make this inquiry of those worthy characters who composed a part of the late federal Convention. I am sure they were fully impressed with the necessity of forming a great consolidated government, instead of a confederation. That this is a consolidated government is demonstrably clear; and the danger of such a government is, to my mind, very striking. I have the highest veneration for those gentlemen; but, sir, give me leave to demand, What right had they to say, *We, the people?* My political curiosity, exclusive of my anxious solicitude for the public welfare, leads me to ask: Who authorized them to speak the language of, *We, the people,* instead of, *We, the states?* States are the

Jonathan Elliot, ed., *The Debates in the Several State Conventions on the Adoption of the Federal Constitution* (Washington, DC: J. Elliot, 1840), vol. 3, pp. 21–22, 44–46, 58–60, 65–66.

characteristics and the soul of confederation. If the states be not the agents of this compact, it must be one great, consolidated, national government, of the people of all the states. . . .

. . . Here is a resolution as radical as that which separated us from Great Britain. It is radical in this transition; our rights and privileges are endangered, and the sovereignty of the states will be relinquished: and cannot we plainly see that this is actually the case? The rights of conscience, trial by jury, liberty of the press, all your immunities and franchises, all pretensions to human rights and privileges, are rendered insecure, if not lost, by this change, so loudly talked of by some, and inconsiderately by others. Is this tame relinquishment of rights worthy of freemen? Is it worthy of that manly fortitude that ought to characterize republicans? It is said eight states have adopted this plan. I declare that if twelve states and a half had adopted it, I would, with manly firmness, and in spite of an erring world, reject it. You are not to inquire how your trade may be increased, nor how you are to become a great and powerful people, but how your liberties can be secured; for liberty ought to be the direct end of your government. . . .

. . . We are come hither to preserve the poor commonwealth of Virginia, if it can be possibly done: something must be done to preserve your liberty and mine. The Confederation, this same despised government, merits, in my opinion, the highest encomium: it carried us through a long and dangerous war; it rendered us victorious in that bloody conflict with a powerful nation; it has secured us a territory greater than any European monarch possesses: and shall a government which has been thus strong and vigorous, be accused of imbecility, and abandoned for want of energy? Consider what you are about to do before you part with the government. Take longer time in reckoning things; revolutions like this have happened in almost every country in Europe; similar examples are to be found in ancient Greece and ancient Rome—instances of the people losing their liberty by their own carelessness and the ambition of a few. We are cautioned by the honorable gentleman, who presides, against faction and turbulence. I acknowledge that licentiousness is dangerous, and that it ought to be provided against: I acknowledge, also, the new form of government may effectually prevent it: yet there is another thing it will as effectually do— it will oppress and ruin the people. . . .

. . . An opinion has gone forth, we find, that we are contemptible people: the time has been when we were thought otherwise. Under the same despised government, we commanded the respect of all Europe: wherefore are we now reckoned otherwise? The American spirit has fled from hence: it has gone to regions where it has never been expected; it has gone to the people of France, in search of a splendid government—a strong, energetic government. Shall we imitate the example of those nations who have gone from a simple to a splendid government? Are those nations more worthy of our imitation? What can make an adequate satisfaction to them for the loss they have suffered in attaining such a government—for the loss of their liberty? If we admit this consolidated government, it will be because we like a great, splendid one. Some way or other we must be a great and mighty empire; we must have an army, and a navy, and a number of things. When the American spirit was in its youth, the language of America was different: liberty, sir, was then the primary object. We are descended from a people whose government was founded on liberty: our glorious forefathers of Great Britain made liberty the foundation of every thing. That country is become a great, mighty, and splendid nation; not because their government is strong and energetic, but, sir, because liberty is its direct end and foundation. We drew the spirit of liberty from our British ancestors: by that spirit we have triumphed over every difficulty. But now, sir, the American spirit, assisted by the ropes and chains of consolidation, is about to convert this country into a powerful and mighty empire. If you make the citizens of this country agree to become the subjects of one great consolidated empire of America, your government will not have sufficient energy to keep them together. Such a government is incompatible with the genius of republicanism. There will be no checks, no real balances, in this government. What can avail your specious, imaginary balances, your rope-dancing, chain-rattling, ridiculous ideal checks and contrivances? But, sir, we are not feared by foreigners; we do not make nations tremble. Would this constitute happiness, or secure liberty? I trust, sir, our political hemisphere will ever direct their operations to the security of those objects.

Consider our situation, sir: go to the poor man, and ask him what he does. He will inform you that he enjoys the fruits of his labor, under his own fig-tree, with his wife and children around him, in peace and security. Go to every other member of society,—you will find the same tranquil ease and content; you will find no alarms or disturbances. Why, then, tell us of danger, to terrify us into an adoption of this new form of government? And yet who knows the dangers that this new system may produce? They are out of the sight of the common people: they cannot foresee latent consequences. I dread the operation of it on the middling and lower classes of people: it is for them I fear the adoption of this system. I fear I tire the patience of the committee; but I beg to be indulged with a few more observations. When I thus profess myself an advocate for the liberty of the people, I shall be told I am a designing man, that I am to be a great man, that I am to be a demagogue; and many similar illiberal insinuations will be thrown out: but, sir, conscious rectitude outweighs those things with me. I see great jeopardy in this new government. I see none from our present one. . . .

This Constitution is said to have beautiful features; but when I come to examine these features, sir, they appear to me horribly frightful. Among other deformities, it has an awful squinting; it squints towards monarchy; and does not this raise indignation in the breast of every true American?

Your President may easily become king. Your Senate is so imperfectly constructed that your dearest rights may be sacrificed by what may be a small minority; and a very small minority may continue forever unchangeably this government, although horridly defective. Where are your checks in this government? Your strongholds will be in the hands of your enemies. It is on a supposition that your American governors shall be honest, that all the good qualities of this government are founded, but its defective and imperfect construction puts it in their power to perpetrate the worse of mischiefs, should they be bad men; and, sir, would not all the world, from the eastern to the western hemisphere, blame our distracted folly in resting our rights upon the contingency of our rulers being good or bad? Show me that age and country where the rights and liberties of the people were placed on the sole chance of their rulers being good men, without a consequent loss of liberty! I say that the loss of that dearest privilege has ever followed, with absolute certainty, every such mad attempt.

If your American chief be a man of ambition and abilities, how easy is it for him to render himself absolute! The army is in his hands, and if he be a man of address, it will be attached to him, and it will be the subject of long meditation with him to seize the first auspicious moment to accomplish his design; and sir, will the American spirit solely relieve you when this happens? I would rather infinitely—and I am sure most of this Convention are of the same opinion—have a king, lords, and commons, than a government so replete with such insupportable evils. If we make a king, we may prescribe the rules by which he shall rule his people, and interpose such checks as shall prevent him from infringing them; but the President, in the field, at the head of his army, can prescribe the terms on which he shall reign master, so far that it will puzzle any American ever to get his neck from under the galling yoke. I cannot with patience think of this idea. If ever he violates the laws, one of two things will happen: he will come at the head of his army, to carry every thing before him; or he will give bail, or do what Mr. Chief Justice will order him. If he be guilty, will not the recollection of his crimes teach him to make one bold push for the American throne? Will not the immense difference between being master of every thing, and being ignominiously tried and punished, powerfully excite him to make this bold push? But, sir, where is the existing force to punish him? Can he not, at the head of his army, beat down every opposition? Away with your President! we shall have a king: the army will salute him monarch: your militia will leave you, and assist in making him king, and fight against you: and what have you to oppose this force? What will then become of you and your rights? Will not absolute despotism ensue? . . .

I beg pardon of this house for having taken up more time than came to my share, and I thank them for the patience and polite attention with which I have been heard. If I shall be in the minority, I shall have those painful sensations which arise from a conviction of *being overpowered in a good cause.* Yet I will be a peaceable citizen. My head, my hand, and my heart, shall be at liberty to retrieve the loss of liberty, and remove the defects of that system in a constitutional way. I wish not to go to violence, but will wait with hopes that the spirit which predominated in the revolution is not yet gone, nor the cause of those who are attached to the revolution yet lost. I shall therefore patiently wait in expectation of seeing that government changed, so as to be compatible with the safety, liberty, and happiness, of the people.

5.3:   The Constitution as a Usurpation (1787)

Richard Henry Lee was another Virginian who opposed the Constitution. He and Patrick Henry had been closely allied in the struggle against Great Britain and continued to be allies in the fight to derail the Constitution. In the following essay, the first of his anti-Constitution series collected as Letters of the Federal Farmer, *Lee attacks both the motives and the methods of his opponents.*

What does he mean by "aristocratical men"? Who, for example, might be included in that group? Did the craftsmen, small shopkeepers, and "mechanics" of the cities vote for pro-Constitution delegates to the states' adoption conventions?

The Constitution Will Encourage Aristocracy

RICHARD HENRY LEE

The present moment discovers a new face in our affairs. Our object has been all along to reform our federal system, and to strengthen our governments—to establish peace, order, and justice in the community—but a new object now presents. The plan of government now proposed is evidently calculated totally to change, in time, our condition as a people. Instead of being thirteen republics, under a federal head, it is clearly designed to make us one consolidated government. Of this, I think, I shall fully convince you in my following letters on this subject. This consolidation of the states has been the object of several men in this country for some time past. Whether such a change can ever be effected, in any manner; whether it can be effected without convulsions and civil wars; whether such a change will not totally destroy the liberties of this country—time only can determine.

To have a just idea of the government before us, and to show that a consolidated one is the object in view, it is necessary not only to examine the plan, but also its history, and the politics of its particular friends.

The Confederation was formed when great confidence was placed in the voluntary exertions of individuals, and of the respective states; and the framers of it, to guard against usurpation, so limited and checked the powers that, in many respects they are inadequate to the exigencies of the union. We find, therefore, members of Congress urging alterations in the federal system almost as soon as it was adopted. It was early proposed to vest Congress with powers to levy an impost, to regulate trade, &c., but such was that known to be the caution of the states in parting with power, the vestment even of these was proposed to be under several checks and limitations. During the war

Richard Henry Lee, *Letters of the Federal Farmer to a Republican, October 8, 1787* (New York: Thomas Greenleaf, 1787), pp. 6–8.

the general confusion and the introduction of paper money infused in the minds of people vague ideas respecting government and credit. We expected too much from the return of peace, and of course we have been disappointed. Our governments have been new and unsettled; and several legislatures, by making tender, suspension, and paper money laws, have given just cause of uneasiness to creditors. By these and other causes, several orders of men in the community have been prepared, by degrees, for a change of government; and this very abuse of power in the legislatures, which in some cases has been charged upon the democratic part of the community, has furnished aristocratical men with those very weapons, and those very means, with which in great measure they are rapidly effecting their favorite object. And should an oppressive government be the consequence of the proposed change, [posterity] may reproach not only a few overbearing, unprincipled men, but those parties in the states which have misused their powers.

The conduct of several legislatures, touching paper money and tender laws, has prepared many honest men for changes in government which otherwise they would not have thought of—when by the evils, on the one hand, and by the secret instigations of artful men, on the other, the minds of men were become sufficiently uneasy, a bold step was taken which is usually followed by a revolution or a civil war. A general convention for mere commercial purposes was moved for—the authors of this measure saw that the people's attention was turned solely to the amendment of the federal system; and that, had the idea of a total change been started, probably no state would have appointed members to the convention. The idea of destroying ultimately the state government and forming one consolidated system could not have been admitted. A convention, therefore, merely for vesting in Congress power to regulate trade was proposed. This was pleasing to the commercial towns, and the landed people had little or no concern about it. September, 1786, a few men from the middle states met at Annapolis and hastily proposed a convention to be held in May, 1787, for the purpose, generally, of amending the Confederation. This was done before the delegates of Massachusetts and of the other states arrived. Still not a word was said about destroying the old constitution and making a new one. The states still unsuspecting and not aware that they were passing the Rubicon, appointed members to the new convention, for the sole and express purpose of revising and amending the Confederation—and, probably not one man in ten thousand in the United States till within these ten or twelve days, had an idea that the old ship was to be destroyed, and he put to the alternative of embarking in the new ship presented, or of being left in danger of sinking. The States, I believe, universally supposed the convention would report alterations in the Confederation which would pass an examination in Congress, and after being agreed to there, would be confirmed by all the legislatures, or be rejected.

Virginia made a very respectable appointment and placed at the head of it the first man in America. In this appointment there was a mixture of political characters; but Pennsylvania appointed principally those men who are esteemed aristocratical. Here the favorite moment for changing the government was evidently discerned by a few men, who seized it with address. Ten other states appointed, and tho' they chose men principally connected with commerce and the judicial department, yet they appointed many good republican characters—had they all attended we should now see, I am persuaded, a better system presented. The nonattendance of eight or nine men who were appointed members of the convention, I shall ever consider as a very unfortunate event to the United States. Had they attended, I am pretty clear that the result of the convention would not have had that strong tendency to aristocracy now discernible in every part of the plan. There would not have been so great an accumulation of powers, especially as to the internal police of this country, in a few hands as the constitution reported proposes to vest in them—the young visionary men and the consolidating aristocracy would have been more restrained than they have been. Eleven states met in the convention and after four months close attention presented the new constitution, to be adopted or rejected by the people. The uneasy and fickle part of the community may be prepared to receive any form of government; but I presume the enlightened and substantial part will give any constitution presented for their adoption a candid and thorough examination; and silence those designing or empty men who weakly and rashly attempt to precipitate the adoption of a system of so much importance. We shall view the convention with proper respect—and, at the same time that we reflect there were men of abilities and integrity in it, we must recollect how disproportionately the democratic and aristocratic parts of the community were represented. Perhaps the judicious friends and opposers of the new constitution will agree that it is best to let it rely solely on its own merits, or be condemned for its own defects.

5.4: "The Father of the Constitution" Defends His Offspring (1787, 1788)

If any one person was the guiding hand behind the Philadelphia deliberations that shaped the Constitution, it was James Madison of Virginia. In June 1788, Madison was called on to defend his handiwork in the Virginia adoption convention against the attack of Patrick Henry and others.

In the section of Madison's defense excerpted below, he responds to Henry's attacks on the taxing powers conferred on the proposed new government. He reviews the severe handicaps the Articles of Confederation imposed on the ability of the general government to pay its bills. He also describes the financial and economic plight of the nation under the Confederation, as perceived by a nationalist.

In what ways, according to Madison, did the weak revenue-raising power of the Confederation government hurt the American nation? Do you see any connection between the antifederalists' fears of the taxing power of the new general government and the opposition to Britain after 1763? Was the conferring of greater taxing power on the new federal government in some ways a retreat from the "Spirit of '76"?

If a stronger central government were to be created by this new constitution, what would become of minorities or particular interests? Would they lose their autonomy in the new majority? And what of the nature of factions, the specific driving forces that seemed to place selfish interests before the public good? Could these be better controlled by the new government? In Federalist Paper Number 10, *Madison argued that the new Constitution could indeed better address these issues.*

The Constitution Should Be Ratified

JAMES MADISON

Mr. Chairman, in considering this great subject, I trust we shall find that part which gives the general government the power of laying and collecting taxes indispensable, and essential to the existence of any efficient or well-organized system of government: if we consult reason, and be ruled by its dictates, we shall find its justification there: if we review the experience we have had, or contemplate the history of nations, here we find ample reasons to prove its expediency. There is little reason to depend for necessary supplies on a body which is fully possessed of the power of withholding them. If a government depends on other governments for its revenues—if it must depend on the voluntary contributions of its members—its existence must be precarious. A government which relies on thirteen independent sovereignties for the means of its existence, is a solecism in theory and a mere nullity in practice. Is it consistent with reason that such a government can promote the happiness of any people? It is subversive of every principle of sound policy, to trust the safety of a community with a government totally destitute of the means of protecting itself or its members. Can Congress, after the repeated unequivocal proofs it has experienced of the utter inutility and inefficacy of requisitions, reasonably expect that they would be hereafter effectual or productive? Will not the same local interests, and other causes, militate against a compliance? Whoever hopes the contrary must ever be disappointed. The effect, sir, cannot be changed without a removal of the cause. Let each county in this commonwealth be supposed free and independent; let your revenues depend on requisitions of proportionate quotas from them; let application be made to them repeatedly:—is it to be presumed that they would comply, or that an adequate collection could be made from partial compliances? It is now difficult to collect taxes from them: how much would that difficulty be enhanced, were you to depend solely on their generosity! I appeal to the reason of every gentleman here, whether he is not persuaded that the present Confederation is

Jonathan Elliot, ed., *The Debates in the Several State Conventions on the Adoption of the Federal Constitution* (Washington, DC: J. Elliot, 1840), vol. 3, pp. 128–29, 135–36, 147–49.

as feeble as the government of Virginia would be in that case: to the same reason I appeal, whether it be compatible with prudence to continue a government of such manifest and palpable debility. . . .

I agree with the honorable gentleman (Mr. Henry) that national splendor and glory are not our objects; but does he distinguish between what will render us secure and happy at home, and what will render us respectable abroad? If we be free and happy at home, we shall be respectable abroad.

The Confederation is so notoriously feeble, that foreign nations are unwilling to form any treaties with us; they are apprized that our general government cannot perform any of its engagements, but that they may be violated at pleasure by any of the states. Our violation of treaties already entered into proves this truth unequivocally. No nation will, therefore, make any stipulations with Congress, conceding any advantages of importance to us: they will be the more averse to entering into engagements with us, as the imbecility of our government enables them to derive many advantages from our trade, without granting us any return. But were this country united by proper bands, in addition to other great advantages, we could form very beneficial treaties with foreign states. But this can never happen without a change in our system. Were we not laughed at by the minister of that nation, from which we may be able yet to extort some of the most salutary measures for this country? Were we not told that it was necessary to temporize till our government acquired consistency? Will any nation relinquish national advantages to us? You will be greatly disappointed, if you expect any such good effects from this contemptible system. Let us recollect our conduct to that country from which we have received the most friendly aid [France]. How have we dealt with that benevolent ally? Have we complied with our most sacred obligations to that nation? Have we paid the interest punctually from year to year? Is not the interest accumulating, while not a shilling is discharged of the principal? The magnanimity and forbearance of that ally are so great that she has not called upon us for her claims, even in her own distress and necessity. This, sir, is an additional motive to increase our exertions. At this moment of time a very considerable amount is due from us to that country and others.

[Here Mr. Madison mentioned the amount of the debts due to different foreign nations.]

We have been obliged to borrow money even to pay the interests of our debts. This is a ruinous and most disgraceful expedient. Is this a situation on which America can rely for security and happiness? How are we to extricate ourselves? The honorable member told us we might rely on the punctuality and friendship of the states, and that they will discharge their quotas for the future. The contributions of the states have been found inadequate from the beginning, and are diminishing instead of increasing. From the month of June, 1787, till June, 1788, they have only paid 276,641 dollars into the federal treasury for the purposes of supporting the national government, and discharging the interest of the national debts—a sum so very insufficient, that it must greatly alarm the friends of their country. Suggestions and strong assertions dissipate before these facts. I shall no longer fatigue the committee at this time, but will resume the subject as early as I can.

Regulating the Violence of Faction
Federalist Paper #10

JAMES MADISON

To the People of the State of New York:

Among the numerous advantages promised by a well-constructed Union, none deserves to be more accurately developed than its tendency to break and control the violence of faction. The friend of popular governments never finds himself so much alarmed for their character and fate, as when he contemplates their propensity to this dangerous vice. He will not fail, therefore, to set a due value on any plan which, without violating the principles to which he is attached, provides a proper cure for it. The instability, injustice, and confusion introduced into the public councils, have, in truth, been the mortal diseases under which popular governments have everywhere perished; as they continue to be the favorite and fruitful topics from which the adversaries to liberty derive their most specious declamations. The valuable improvements made by the American constitutions on the popular models, both ancient and modern, cannot certainly be too much admired; but it would be an unwarrantable partiality, to contend that they have as effectually obviated the danger on this side, as was wished and expected. Complaints are everywhere heard from our most considerate and virtuous citizens, equally the friends of public and private faith, and of public and personal liberty, that our governments are too unstable, that the public good is disregarded in the conflicts of rival parties, and that measures are too often decided, not according to the rules of justice and the rights of the minor party, but by the superior force of an interested and overbearing majority. However anxiously we may wish that these complaints had no foundation, the evidence of known facts will not permit us to deny that they are in some degree true. It will be found, indeed, on a candid review of our situation, that some of the distresses under which we labor have been erroneously charged on the operation of our governments; but it will be found, at the same time, that other causes will not alone account for many of our heaviest misfortunes; and, particularly, for that prevailing and increasing distrust of public engagements, and alarm for private rights, which are echoed from one end of the continent to the other. These must be chiefly, if not wholly, effects of the unsteadiness and injustice with which a factious spirit has tainted our public administrations.

By a faction, I understand a number of citizens, whether amounting to a majority or minority of the whole, who are united and actuated by some common impulse of passion, or of interest, adverse to the rights of other citizens, or to the permanent and aggregate interests of the community.

There are two methods of curing the mischiefs of faction: the one, by removing its causes; the other, by controlling its effects.

There are again two methods of removing the causes of faction: the one, by destroying the liberty which is essential to its existence; the other, by giving to every citizen the same opinions, the same passions, and the same interests.

Reprinted from Alexander Hamilton and James Madison, eds., *The Federalist on the New Constitution* (New York: George F. Hopkins, 1802), pp. 55–58.

It could never be more truly said than of the first remedy, that it was worse than the disease. Liberty is to faction what air is to fire, an aliment without which it instantly expires. But it could not be less folly to abolish liberty, which is essential to political life, because it nourishes faction, than it would be to wish the annihilation of air, which is essential to animal life, because it imparts to fire its destructive agency.

The second expedient is as impracticable as the first would be unwise. As long as the reason of man continues fallible, and he is at liberty to exercise it, different opinions will be formed. As long as the connection subsists between his reason and his self-love, his opinions and his passions will have a reciprocal influence on each other; and the former will be objects to which the latter will attach themselves. The diversity in the faculties of men, from which the rights of property originate, is not less an insuperable obstacle to a uniformity of interests. The protection of these faculties is the first object of government. From the protection of different and unequal faculties of acquiring property, the possession of different degrees and kinds of property immediately results; and from the influence of these on the sentiments and views of the respective proprietors, ensues a division of the society into different interests and parties.

The latent causes of faction are thus sown in the nature of man; and we see them everywhere brought into different degrees of activity, according to the different circumstances of civil society. A zeal for different opinions concerning religion, concerning government, and many other points, as well of speculation as of practice; an attachment to different leaders ambitiously contending for pre-eminence and power; or to persons of other descriptions whose fortunes have been interesting to the human passions, have, in turn, divided mankind into parties, inflamed them with mutual animosity, and rendered them much more disposed to vex and oppress each other than to co-operate for their common good. So strong is this propensity of mankind to fall into mutual animosities, that where no substantial occasion presents itself, the most frivolous and fanciful distinctions have been sufficient to kindle their unfriendly passions and excite their most violent conflicts. But the most common and durable source of factions has been the various and unequal distribution of property. Those who hold and those who are without property have ever formed distinct interests in society. Those who are creditors, and those who are debtors, fall under a like discrimination. A landed interest, a manufacturing interest, a mercantile interest, a moneyed interest, with many lesser interests, grow up of necessity in civilized nations, and divide them into different classes, actuated by different sentiments and views. The regulation of these various and interfering interests forms the principal task of modern legislation, and involves the spirit of party and faction in the necessary and ordinary operations of the government.

5.5: Alexander Hamilton on Pro- and Anti-Constitution Forces (1787)

Alexander Hamilton was a New York delegate to the Constitutional Convention. An intense nationalist, he had condemned the document that emerged from the deliberations at Philadelphia as too weak, too tilted toward local rights. Despite such misgivings, however, he much preferred it to the Articles of Confederation, and fought hard for its adoption by his state. Together with James Madison and John Jay, Hamilton authored a set of brilliant newspaper articles designed to convince New Yorkers of the wisdom of adopting the new frame of government. These became the famous Federalist Papers, *one of the best commentaries on the Constitution to this day. Hamilton also participated in the actual New York convention debates.*

The following brief selection is a frank, private memo that Hamilton composed soon after the Philadelphia convention had adjourned that summarizes what he anticipated would be the alignment of pro- and anti-Constitution sentiment in the country. Are Hamilton's remarks biased? What is he referring to when he speaks of "the depredations which the democratic spirit is apt to make on property"? Who are the "Creditors of the United States" he mentions, and why are they supposedly interested in a stronger national government?

Conjectures About the New Constitution

ALEXANDER HAMILTON

The new constitution has in favour of its success these circumstances—a very great weight of influence of the persons who framed it, particularly in the universal popularity of General Washington—the good will of the commercial interest throughout the states which will give all its efforts to the establishment of a government capable of regulating protecting and extending the commerce of the Union—the good will of most men of property in the several states who wish a government of the union able to protect them against domestic violence and the depredations which the democratic spirit is apt to make on property; and who are besides anxious for the respectability of the nation—the hopes of the Creditors of the United States that a general government possessing the means of doing it will pay the debt of the Union—a strong belief in the people at large of the insufficiency of the present confederation to preserve the existence of the Union and of the necessity of the union to their safety and prosperity; of course a strong desire of a change and a predisposition to receive well the propositions of the Convention.

Against its success is to be put the dissent of two or three important men in the Convention; who will think their characters pledged to defeat the plan—the influence of many *inconsiderable* men in possession of considerable offices under the state governments who will fear a diminution of their consequence, power and emolument by the establishment of the general government and who can hope for nothing there—the influence of some *considerable* men in office possessed of talents and popularity who partly from the same motives and partly from a desire of *playing a part* in a convul-

Alexander Hamilton, "Conjectures about the New Constitution," *The Papers of Alexander Hamilton,* Harold Syrett, ed. (New York: Columbia University Press, 1962), vol. 4, pp. 275–77. © Columbia University Press, New York.

sion for their own aggrandisement will oppose the quiet adoption of the new government—(some considerable men out of office, from motives of (am)bition may be disposed to act the same part)—add (to) these causes the disinclination of the people to taxes, and of course to a strong government—the opposition of all men much in debt who will not wish to see a government established one object of which is to restrain the means of cheating Creditors—the democratical jealousy of the people which may be alarmed at the appearance of institutions that may seem calculated to place the power of the community in few hands and to raise a few individuals to stations of great preeminence—and the influence of some foreign powers who from different motives will not wish to see an energetic government established throughout the states.

In this view of the subject it is difficult to form any judgment whether the plan will be adopted or rejected. It must be essentially [a] matter of conjecture. The present appearances and all other circumstances considered the probability seems to be on the side of its adoption.

But the causes operating against its adoption are powerful and there will be nothing astonishing in the Contrary.

If it do not finally obtain, it is probable the discussion of the question will beget such struggles animosities and heats in the community that this circumstance conspiring with the *real necessity* of an essential change in our present situation will produce civil war. Should this happen, whatever parties prevail it is probable governments very different from the present in their principles will be established. A dismemberment of the Union and monarchies in different portions of it may be expected. It may however happen that no civil war will take place; but several republican confederacies be established between different combinations of the particular states.

A reunion with Great Britain, from universal disgust at a state of commotion, is not impossible, though not much to be feared. The most plausible shape of such a business would be the establishment of a son of the present monarch in the supreme government of this country with a family compact.

If the government be adopted, it is probable general Washington will be the President of the United States. This will insure a wise choice of men to administer the government and a good administration. A good administration will conciliate the confidence and affection of the people and perhaps enable the government to acquire more consistency than the proposed constitution seems to promise for so great a Country. It may then triumph altogether over the state governments and reduce them to an intire subordination, dividing the larger states into smaller districts. The *organs* of the general government may also acquire additional strength.

If this should not be the case, in the course of a few years, it is probable that the contests about the boundaries of power between the particular governments and the general government and the *momentum* of the larger states in such contests will produce a dissolution of the Union. This after all seems to be the most likely result.

But it is almost arrogance in so complicated a subject, depending so intirely on the incalculable fluctuations of the human passions, to attempt even a conjecture about the event.

It will be Eight or Nine months before any certain judgment can be formed respecting the adoption of the Plan.

❖ 6 ❖

Federalist Versus Republican

The founders of the United States planned well for a new national government, but they left out one vital piece: political parties. In every modern democracy voters with similar social, economic, political, ideological, and cultural views have combined into parties to win elections and enact programs that reflect their ideals and interests.

Yet the early leaders of the American republic deplored parties as divisive and likely to be corrupt and self-serving. They made no provision for them in their new frame of government. But parties soon appeared. They coalesced around a cluster of issues, domestic and foreign, that would divide the young nation.

At home the most urgent concerns of the new government led by President George Washington were the financial problems that had beset its predecessor: the lack of revenue, the unpaid government debts, the disarray in the nation's currency, and America's financial reputation abroad. The man Washington placed in charge of the nation's finances was Alexander Hamilton, the New York lawyer who had helped get the Constitution adopted in his home state, even though it was too weak for his tastes. As secretary of the Treasury, Hamilton would push a program of federal taxes, debt refunding, a protective tariff, and a national bank designed to transform the economic base of American society.

The new republic was also forced to reorder its relations with other nations. The United States faced problems with Spain over the navigation of the Mississippi and with Britain over Indian relations, unpaid debts, exclusion of Americans from traditional trade routes, and continued military occupation of American territory in the West.

Even more tangled were America's associations with France, which after 1789 experienced the shattering political, social, and ideological upheaval known as the French Revolution. Franco-American relations would become particularly nettlesome when France, under its revolutionary leaders, went to war with Austria, Prussia, and England in 1792–1793 and sought to involve the United States on its side. In charge of the Washington administration's foreign policy was Secretary of State Thomas Jefferson, the chief author of the Declaration of Independence. Jefferson would take a pro-French, anti-British position, although he would refuse to sacrifice American interests for the sake of the French republic.

Fierce partisan differences over finance and foreign policy would become the bases for the first American political parties. Behind these policy differences would be philosophical differences over human nature and ideological disagreements over the best form of government. Hamilton and Jefferson would become the leaders of the two political organizations, the Federalists and Republicans,[1] respectively.

In the selections that follow, you should look beyond the disagreements over specific policies and programs to underlying conflicts of interest or ideology. What major economic changes in America did the successful enactment of Hamilton's program imply? What alternative did the Jeffersonian Republicans represent? Who stood to gain from Hamilton's financial and economic program? Who stood to lose? Why did some Americans favor France over Britain and vice versa?

---

[1]These Republicans should not be confused with the supporters of the Republican Party organized in the 1850s to oppose the spread of slavery. It is this later party that is the ancestor of the Republicans of today.

6.1: Alexander Hamilton's Economic Reports (1790–1791)

In 1790–1791 Secretary of Treasury Alexander Hamilton, at Congress's bidding, prepared a series of reports recommending legislation to deal with pressing national economic issues. There were three major reports, two of which (excerpted here), the First *and Second Reports on* Public Credit,[1] *formed the bases for immediate path-breaking legislation: the Funding Act of 1790 and the act establishing the Bank of the United States. A third, the* Report on Manufactures, *did not produce a quick legislative response, but it expressed even more clearly than the other two documents the Hamiltonian attitude toward America's future economic and social course. In it Hamilton casts himself in the role of the first modern economic planner. This report became an arsenal of arguments for those determined to encourage the growth*

---

[1]"The Second Report on Public Credit" is also often called "The Report on a National Bank."

of domestic manufactures in the United States. Eventually, its protectionist philosophy was also incorporated into specific legislation, although long after Hamilton was dead.

The First Report on Public Credit *dealt with the unpaid debts of the Revolution. These were of three kinds: debts owed by the United States to foreign countries, debts owed by the United States to its own citizens, and debts owed by the thirteen states to American creditors. Some states had taxed their own citizens to pay their debts; others had not. All the debts of the national government, those owed both at home and abroad, had fallen into arrears, and many of the debt certificates had been sold by the original possessors to speculators for whatever they would bring.*

Hamilton, in the first report, starts by making a case for the prompt and full payment of all the new nation's public debts. He then seeks to deal with the controversies over how to pay the domestic debt, both state and national. In his arguments are embedded certain attitudes toward creditors and debtors, toward the role of government in the economy, toward the business community, and toward America's future. What are these? The Secretary of the Treasury strongly favored the federal "assumption" of the unpaid debts of the states. Why does he argue for this position? What would taxpayers in states that had already paid their debts probably feel about such an assumption plan?

The first report already hinted at Hamilton's view of the larger economic role of a "funded" debt, that is, a consolidated federal debt, backed by provisions to pay interest and principle, into which the old debts could be converted. In his second report he more explicitly links this new funded debt with certain larger economic goals through a federally chartered central bank that would accept the new securities as paid-in capital. The bank would then issue paper money backed by these securities. What hopes does Hamilton have for this paper money? What are his larger economic goals? How would the new national bank further them? In what ways would the national bank help the government itself as contrasted to the economy in general?

Given Hamilton's bias toward commerce and industry, how do you explain his tribute in his Report on Manufactures *to agriculture? Was he being realistic in his hope that sectional differences over manufactures need not be disruptive? Is his vision of a transformed American economic future an attractive one? Could America have avoided the outcome he anticipated? Which of the eleven methods to encourage manufactures he suggests did Americans ultimately use most widely?*

The First Report on Public Credit, January 9, 1790

ALEXANDER HAMILTON

In the opinion of the Secretary [Hamilton] . . . [we must consider certain] plain and undeniable truths.

That exigencies are to be expected to occur, in the affairs of nations, in which there will be a necessity for borrowing.

That loans in times of public danger, especially from foreign war, are found [to be] an indispensable resource even to the wealthiest of them.

And that in a country which, like this, is possessed of little active wealth, or in other words, little monied capital, the necessity for that resource, must, in such emergencies, be proportionately urgent. . . .

And as . . . the necessity for borrowing in particular emergencies cannot be doubtful, so, . . . it is equally evident that to be able to borrow upon good terms, it is essential that the credit of a nation should be well established.

For, when the credit of a country is in any degree questionable, it will never fail to give an extravagant premium . . . upon all the loans it has occasion to make. . . .

If the maintenance of public credit, then, be truly so important, the next inquiry which suggests itself is: By what means is it to be effected? The ready answer to which question is, by good faith; by a punctual performance of contracts. . . .

To justify and preserve their confidence; to promote the increasing respectability of the American name; to answer the calls of justice; to restore landed property to its due value; to furnish new resources, both to agriculture and commerce; to cement more closely the union of the states; to add to their security against foreign attack; to establish public order on the basis of an upright and liberal policy;—these are the great and invaluable ends to be secured by a proper and adequate provision . . . for the support of the public credit. . . .

The advantage to the public creditors, from the increased value of that part of their property which constitutes the public debt, needs no explanation.

But there is a consequence of this, less obvious, though not less true, in which every citizen is interested. It is a well-known fact, that, in countries in which the national debt is properly funded, and an object of established confidence, it answers most of the purposes of money. Transfers of stock or public debt are there equivalent to payments in specie [i.e., gold and silver]. The same thing would, in all probability, happen here under the like circumstances.

The benefits of this are various and obvious:

First.—Trade is extended by it. . . .
Secondly.—Agriculture and manufactures are also promoted by it. . . .
Thirdly.—The interest of money will be lowered by it. . . .

And from a combination of these effects, additional aids will be furnished to labor, to industry, and to arts of every kind. . . .

Henry Cabot Lodge, ed., *The Works of Alexander Hamilton* (New York: G. P. Putnam's Sons, 1904), vol. 2, pp. 227–296.

Having now taken a concise view of the inducements to a proper provision of the public debt, the next inquiry which presents itself is: What ought to be the nature of such a provision . . . ?

It is agreed on all hands, that that part of the debt which . . . is denominated the foreign debt, ought to be provided for, according to the precise terms of the contracts relating to it. The discussions, which can arise, therefore, will have reference essentially to the domestic part of it. . . .

[The question has arisen] whether a discrimination ought not to be made between original holders of the public securities, and present possessors by purchase. Those who advocate a discrimination are for making a full provision for the securities of the former, at their nominal [i.e., face] value; but contend, that the latter ought to receive no more than the cost to them and the interest. . . .

In favor of this scheme, it is alleged, that it would be unreasonable to pay twenty shillings in the pound [i.e., full face value] to one who had not given more for it than three or four. And it is added, that it would be hard to aggravate the misfortune of the first owner, who, probably through necessity, parted with his property at so great a loss, by obliging him to contribute to the profit of the person, who has speculated on his distresses.

The Secretary . . . is induced to reject the doctrine [this argument] contains, as equally unjust and impolitic, as highly injurious, even to the original holders of public securities; as ruinous to public credit.

It is inconsistent with justice, because in the first place, it is a breach of contract; in violation of the rights of a fair purchaser.

The nature of the contract in its origin, is, that the public will pay the sum expressed in the security, to the first holder, or his *assignee.* The *intent* in making the security assignable, is, that the proprietor may be able to make use of his property, by selling it for as much as it *may be worth in the market,* and that the buyer be *safe* in the purchase.

Every buyer therefor stands exactly in the place of the seller, has the same right with him in the identical sum expressed in the security. . . .

That he is to be considered as a fair purchaser, results from this: Whatever necessity the seller may have been under, was occasioned by the government in not making proper provision for its debts. The buyer had no agency in it and therefore ought not to suffer. He is not even chargeable with having taken an undue advantage. He paid what the commodity was worth on the market and took the risks of reimbursement upon himself. . . .

That the case of those, who parted with their securities from necessity, is a hard one, cannot be denied. But . . . they knew, that by the terms of the contract . . . , the public were bound to pay those to whom they should convey their title, the sums stipulated to be paid to them; and that as citizens of the United States, they were to bear their proportion of the contribution to that purpose. This, by the act of assignment, they tacitly agreed to do. . . .

The impolicy of discrimination [between original holder and later speculative purchaser] results from two considerations; one, that it proceeds upon a principle destructive of the *quality* of the public debt . . . which is essential to the capacity for answering the purpose of money—that is the *security of transfer;* the other, as because it includes a breach of faith, it renders property in the funds [i.e., in the public securities] less valuable; consequently induces lenders to demand a higher premium [i.e., interest] for what they lend and produces every other inconvenience of a bad state of public credit. . . .

But there is still a point in view in which it will appear perhaps even more exceptionable than in either of the former. It would be repugnant to an express provision of the Constitution of the United States. This provision is that "all debts contracted and engagements entered into before the adoption of this Constitution shall be as valid against the United States under this Constitution, as under the confederation," which amounts to a constitutional ratification of the contract respecting the debt, in the state in which they existed under the confederation. And resorting to that standard, there can be no doubt, that the rights of assignees and original holders, must be considered equal. . . .

The Secretary . . . proceeds to examine whether a difference ought to be permitted [between United States creditors and] . . . those of the states. . . .

The Secretary . . . entertains a full conviction, that assumption of the debts of the particular states by the union, will be a measure of sound policy and substantial justice.

It would . . . contribute . . . to an orderly, stable and satisfactory arrangement of the national finances. . . .

If all the public creditors receive their dues from one source, distributed with an equal hand, their interest will be the same. And having the same interests, they will unite in support of the fiscal arrangements of the government. . . .

If on the contrary there are distinct provisions [for paying the federal and the state debts], there will be distinct interests, drawing different ways. That union and concert of views, among the [public] creditors, which in every government is of great importance to their security, and to that of the public credit, will not only not exist, but will likely give place to mutual jealousy and opposition. And from this cause, the operation of the system which may be adopted, both by the particular states, and by the union in relation to their respective debts, will be in danger of being counteracted. . . .

Persuaded, as the Secretary is, that the proper funding of the present debt, will render it a national blessing: Yet he is so far from acceding to the position . . . that "public debts are public benefits"—a position inviting to prodigality, and liable to dangerous abuse—that he ardently wishes to see it incorporated as a fundamental maxim . . . that the creation of debt should always be accompanied by the means of extinguishment. This he regards as the true secret for rendering public credit immortal.

The Second Report on Public Credit, December 13, 1790

ALEXANDER HAMILTON

The . . . Secretary further . . . reports that . . . a National Bank is an institution of primary importance to the proper administration of the finances, and would be of the greatest utility in the operations connected with the support of the public credit. . . .

Henry Cabot Lodge, ed., *The Works of Alexander Hamilton* (New York: G. P. Putnam's Sons, 1904), vol. 2, pp. 337–351.

The following are among the principal advantages of a bank.

First. The augmentation of the active or productive capital of a country. Gold and silver, when they are employed merely as the instruments of exchange . . . have not been improperly denoted dead stock [i.e., unproductive]: but when deposited in banks, to become the basis of a paper circulation, . . . they then acquire life, or, in other words, an active and productive quality. . . . It is evident, for instance, that the money, which a merchant keeps in his chest, waiting for a favorable opportunity to employ it, produces nothing 'till that opportunity arrives. But if . . . he either deposits it in a bank or invests it in the stock of a bank, it yields a profit, during the interval. . . . His money thus deposited or invested is a fund, upon which himself and others can borrow to a much larger amount. It is a well established fact, that banks in good credit can circulate a far greater sum than the actual quantum of their capital in gold and silver. The extent of the possible excess seems indeterminate; though it has been conjecturally stated at the proportions of three to one. . . .

Secondly. Greater facility to the government in obtaining pecuniary aids, especially in sudden emergencies. . . . The capitals of a great number of individuals are [through banks], collected to a point, and placed under one direction. . . . [T]his mass is always ready, and can at once be put in motion, in aid of the government. . . .

Thirdly. The facilitating of the payment of taxes. This advantage is produced in two ways. Those who are in a situation to have access to the bank can have the assistance of loans to answer with punctuality the public calls upon them. . . . The other way . . . is the increasing of the quantity of circulating medium and the quickening of circulation. . . . And it is evident, that, whatever enhances the quantity of circulating money adds to the ease with which every industrious member of the community may acquire that portion of it of which he stands in need; and enables him to better pay his taxes, as well as supply his other wants. Even where the circulation of the bank paper [i.e., paper money issued by the banks] is not general, it must still have the same effect, though in a less degree, for whatever furnishes additional supplies to the channels of circulation, in one quarter, naturally contributes to keep the streams fuller elsewhere. . . . Banks tend to facilitate the payment of taxes, and to exemplify their utility to business of every kind, in which money is an agent. . . .

The combination of a portion of the public debt in the formation of capital, is the principal thing, of which an explanation is requisite. The chief object of this is, to enable the creation of a capital sufficiently large to be the basis of an extensive circulation, and an adequate security for it. . . . [T]he original plan of the Bank of North America[1] contemplated a capital of ten millions of dollars. . . . But to collect such a sum in this country in gold and silver, into one depository, may, without hesitation, be pronounced impracticable. Hence the necessity of an auxiliary which the public debt at once presents.

This part of the fund will be always ready to come in aid of the specie. It will more and more command a ready sale; and can therefore expeditiously be turned into coin if an exigency of the bank should at any time require it. This quality of

---

[1]The Bank of North America, the first private commercial bank in the United States, was chartered by the Confederation Congress in 1781 to help with the financing of the Revolution. It accomplished less than its organizers hoped—ED.

prompt convertibility into coin, renders it an equivalent for that necessary agent of bank circulation; and distinguishes it from a fund in land.[2]

The Report on Manufactures, December 5, 1791

ALEXANDER HAMILTON

The expediency of encouraging manufactures in the United States . . . appears at this time to be pretty generally admitted. . . . [T]he restrictive regulations which in foreign markets abridge the vent [i.e., export] of the increasing surplus of our Agricultural produce, serve to beget an earnest desire, that a more extensive demand for that surplus may be created at home. . . .

There . . . are . . . respectable patrons of opinions unfriendly to the encouragement of manufactures. The following are . . . the arguments by which these opinions are defended. [Hamilton summarizes the views of those opposed to encouraging manufactures, which are as follows: (1) especially in a country like the United States, with "immense tracts of fertile territory," no other occupation is as productive as agriculture; (2) for government to encourage manufactures is "to transfer the natural current of industry from a more to a less beneficial channel"; (3) America's abundant land relative to its small population makes it difficult to recruit workers for manufactures, since people will prefer the independence of farming to the "less independent condition of an artisan"; and (4) is somehow, despite these facts, government can by "heavy duties, prohibitions, bounties, or by other forced expedients" give a "premature spring" to manufactures, it "will only sacrifice the interests of the community to those of particular classes." He then resumes his own arguments.]

It ought readily to be conceded that the cultivation of the earth, as the primary and most certain source of national supply; as the immediate and chief source of sustenance to man; as the principal source of those materials which constitute the nutriment of other kinds of labor; as including a state most favourable to the freedom and independence of the human mind—one, perhaps, most conducive to the multiplication of the human species; has intrinsically a strong claim to preeminence over every other kind of industry.

But, that it has a title to any thing like an exclusive predilection, in any country, ought to be admitted with great caution. That it is even more productive than every other branch of Industry requires more evidence, than has yet been given in support of the position. . . .

It is now proper to . . . enumerate the principal circumstances from which it may be inferred that manufacturing establishments not only occasion a positive augmentation of the produce and revenue of the society, but that they contribute essentially

Henry Cabot Lodge, ed., *The Works of Alexander Hamilton* (New York: G. P. Putnam's Sons, 1904), vol. 4, pp. 70–198.

[2]The reference here is to the controversial land banks established in several colonies before 1776 to provide a circulating medium. These were generally not successful—ED.

to rendering them greater than they could possibly be, without such establishments. These circumstances are:

1. The division of labor.
2. An extension of the use of machinery.
3. Additional employment to classes of the community not ordinarily engaged in the business.
4. The promotion of emigration from foreign countries.
5. The furnishing greater scope for the diversity of talents and dispositions, which discriminate men from each other.
6. The affording a more ample and variable field for enterprise.
7. The creating, in some instances, a new, and securing, in all, a more certain and steady demand for the surplus produce of the soil. . . .

Not only the wealth; but the independence and security of a country, appear to be materially connected with the prosperity of manufactures. Every nation, with a view to those great objects, ought to endeavor to possess within itself all the essentials of national supply. These comprise the means of subsistence, habitation, clothing, and defence. . . .

It is not uncommon to meet with an opinion, that, though the promoting of manufactures may be the interest of a part of the Union, it is contrary to that of another part. The Northern and Southern regions are sometimes represented as having adverse interests in this respect. Those are called manufacturing, these agricultural States: and a species of opposition is imagined to subsist between the manufacturing and agricultural interests. . . .

Ideas of a contrariety of interests between the Northern and Southern regions of the Union are, in the main, as unfounded as they are mischievous. The diversity of circumstances on which such a contrariety is usually predicated, authorizes a directly contrary conclusion. Mutual wants constitute one of the strongest links of political connexion. . . .

If the Northern and Middle States should be the principal scenes of such [manufacturing] establishments, they would immediately benefit the more Southern, by creating a demand for productions. . . . These productions . . . are timber, flax, hemp, cotton, wool, raw silk, indigo, iron, lead, fur, hides, skins and coals. . . .

The extensive cultivation of cotton, can, perhaps, hardly be expected but from the previous establishment of domestic manufactories [i.e., workshops] of the article. . . .

A full view having now been taken of the inducements to the promotion of manufactures in the United States, . . . it is proper . . . to consider the means by which it may be effected. . . .

1. *Protecting duties—or duties on those foreign articles which are the rivals of the domestic ones intended to be encouraged. . . .*
2. *Prohibitions of rival articles, or duties equivalent to prohibitions. . . .*
3. *Prohibitions of the exportation of the materials of manufactures. . . .*
4. *Pecuniary Bounties. . . .*
5. *Premiums. . . .*

6. *The exemption of the materials of manufactures from duty.* . . .
7. *Drawbacks of the duties which are imposed on the materials of manufactures.* . . .
8. *The encouragement of new inventions and discoveries at home, and of the introduction into the United States of such as may have been made in other countries; particularly, those which relate to machinery.* . . .
9. *Judicious regulations for the inspection of manufactured commodities.* . . .
10. *The facilitating of pecuniary remittances from place to place.* . . .
11. *The facilitating of the transportation of commodities.* . . .

In countries where there is great private wealth, much may be effected by the voluntary contributions of patriotic individuals; but in a community situated like that of the United States, the public purse must apply the deficiency of private resource. In what can it be so useful, as in prompting and improving the efforts of industry?

6.2: Thomas Jefferson and the American Arcadia (1784)

Thomas Jefferson himself never expressed his views of America's social and economic future as comprehensively as did Hamilton, his chief rival. But the following selection from his only full-length book, Notes on the State of Virginia, *written in 1784, captures his attitudes as expressed shortly after the peace with Britain confirming America's independence.*

Considering his origins and background, why might Jefferson, more than Hamilton, be a defender of agriculture over manufactures? Why does Jefferson oppose manufactures? Why does he seem fearful of cities? As president, did any of his major policies reinforce the vision of America's future he expressed here? Is Jefferson's view of human nature implicit in the document?

Query XIX: Manufactures[1]

THOMAS JEFFERSON

The Present State of Manufactures, Commerce, Interior and Exterior Trade?

We never had an interior trade of any importance. Our exterior commerce has suffered very much from the beginning of the present contest. During this time we have manufactured within our families the most necessary articles of cloathing. Those of cotton will bear some comparison with the same kinds of manufacture in Europe; but those of wool, flax and hemp are very coarse, unsightly, and unpleasant: and such is our attachment to agriculture, and such our preference for foreign

Thomas Jefferson, *Notes on the State of Virginia,* in *The Writings of Thomas Jefferson,* Paul Leicester Ford, ed. (New York: G. P. Putnam's Sons, 1894), vol. 3, pp. 268–69.
[1]Footnotes deleted.

manufacturers, that be it wise or unwise, our people will certainly return as soon as they can, to the raising raw materials, and exchanging them for finer manufactures than they are able to execute themselves.

The political œconomists of Europe have established it as a principle that every state should endeavour to manufacture for itself: and this principle, like many others, we transfer to America, without calculating the difference of circumstance which should often produce a difference of result. In Europe the lands are either cultivated, or locked up against the cultivator. Manufacture must therefore be resorted to of necessity not of choice, to support the surplus of their people. But we have an immensity of land courting the industry of the husbandman. Is is best then that all our citizens should be employed in its improvement, or that one half should be called off from that to exercise manufactures and handicraft arts for the other? Those who labour in the earth are the chosen people of God, if ever he had a chosen people, whose breasts he has made his peculiar deposit for substantial and genuine virtue. It is the focus in which he keeps alive that sacred fire, which otherwise might escape from the face of the earth. Corruption of morals in the mass of cultivators is a phænomenon of which no age nor nation has furnished an example. It is the mark set on those, who not looking up to heaven, to their own soil and industry, as does the husbandman, for their subsistance [*sic*], depend for it on the casualties and caprice of customers. Dependance begets subservience and venality, suffocates the germ of virtue, and prepares fit tools for the designs of ambition. This, the natural progress and consequence of the arts, has sometimes perhaps been retarded by accidental circumstances: but, generally speaking, the proportion which the aggregate of the other classes of citizens bears in any state to that of its husbandmen, is the proportion of its unsound to its healthy parts, and is a good-enough barometer whereby to measure its degree of corruption. While we have land to labour then, let us never wish to see our citizens occupied at a work-bench, or twirling a distaff. Carpenters, masons, smiths, are wanting in husbandry: but, for the general operations of manufacture, let our workshops remain in Europe. It is better to carry provisions and materials to workmen there, than bring them to the provisions and materials, and with them their manners and principles. The loss by the transportation of commodities across the Atlantic will be made up in happiness and permanence of government. The mobs of great cities add just so much to the support of pure government, as sores do to the strength of the human body. It is the manners and spirit of a people which preserve a republic in vigour. A degeneracy in these is a canker which soon eats to the heart of its laws and constitution.

6.3: Thomas Jefferson Attacks the Hamiltonian System (1790)

During the years 1785–1789 Jefferson served as American minister to France. Appointed while abroad by Washington as the first Secretary of State, he returned home in 1789 to find himself in the middle of the debate over the Hamiltonian program. The following document is an excerpt from "The Anas," a journal Jefferson kept at the time and later revised, in which he fiercely attacks the Hamiltonian system and the party, the Federalists, that coalesced around it.

One part of the indictment was that the Hamiltonians were "monarchists." In what sense could the funding system be considered monarchist? Another charge was that the Hamiltonians were corrupt men motivated largely by their lust for personal gain. How does this conflict with the arguments of Hamilton for his financial programs? Were Jefferson's claims of corruption valid, or were they primarily the charges of a political partisan unhappy at the successes of an opponent?

The Vile Hamiltonian System

THOMAS JEFFERSON

I returned from that mission [to France] in the 1st. year of the new government, having landed in Virginia in Dec. [17]89 & proceeded to N. York [the nation's first capital] in March [17]90 to enter on the office of Secretary of State. Here certainly I found a state of things which, of all I had ever contemplated, I the least expected. I had left France in the first year of its revolution, in the fervor of natural rights, and zeal for reformation. My conscientious devotion to these rights could not be heightened, but it had been aroused and excited by daily exercise. The president [George Washington] received me cordially, and my Colleagues & the circle of principal citizens, apparently, with welcome. The courtesies of dinner parties given me as a stranger newly arrived among them placed me at once in their familiar society. But I cannot describe the wonder and mortification with which the table conversations filled me. Politics were the chief topic, and a preference for kingly, over republican, government, was evidently the favorite sentiment. An apostate I could not be; nor yet a hypocrite: and I found myself, for the most part, the only advocate on the republican side of the question, unless, among the guests, there chanced to be some member of that party from the legislative Houses [i.e., Congress]. Hamilton's financial system had then passed. It had two objects: 1st as a puzzle, to exclude popular understanding & inquiry. 2dly, as a machine for the corruption of the legislature; for he avowed the opinion that man could be governed by one of two motives only, force or interest: force he observed, in this country, was out of the question; and the interests therefore of the members must be laid hold of, to keep the legislature in unison with the Executive [i.e., the president]. And with grief and shame it must be acknowledged that his machine was not without effect. That even in this, the birth of our government,

Thomas Jefferson, *The Writings of Thomas Jefferson,* Paul Leicester Ford, ed. (New York: G. P. Putnam's Sons, 1895), vol. 1, pp. 159–66.

some members were found sordid enough to bend their duty to their interests, and to look after personal, rather than public good.

It is well-known that, during the [Revolutionary] war, the greatest difficulty we encountered was the want of money or means, to pay our soldiers who fought, or our farmers, manufacturers & merchants who furnished the necessary supplies of food & clothing for them. After the expedient of paper money had exhausted itself, certificates of debt were given to the individual creditors, with the assurance of payment, so soon as the U.S. be able. But the distresses of these people often obliged them to part with these for the half, the fifth, and even a tenth of their value; and speculators had made a trade of cozening them from the holders, by the most fraudulent practices and persuasions that they would never be paid. In the bill for funding & paying these, Hamilton made no difference between the original holders & the fraudulent purchasers of this paper. Great & just repugnance arose in putting these two classes of creditors on the same footing, and great exertions were used to pay to the former the full value, and to the latter the price only which he had paid, with interest.

But this would have prevented the game which was to be played, & for which the minds of greedy members were already tutored and prepared. When the trial of strength . . . had indicated the form in which the bill would finally pass, this being known within doors sooner than without, and especially than to those who were in distant parts of the Union, the base scramble began. Couriers & relay horses by land and swift sailing pilot boats by sea, were flying in all directions. Active partners & agents were associated & employed in every state, town, and country neighborhood, and this paper was bought up at 5 [shillings] and even low 2 [shillings] in the pound [i.e., from one-fourth to one-tenth of face value] before the holder knew that Congress had already provided for its redemption at par. Immense sums were thus filched from the poor & ignorant, and fortunes accumulated by those who had themselves been poor enough before.

[Jefferson attacks the assumption of state debts by the federal government as another example of the perfidy of the Hamiltonian funding program. He excuses his own role in inducing the southern states to accept assumption by claiming that he was new to the issue, having been abroad when it was first discussed and having yielded out of ignorance to Hamilton's plea that unless the assumption passed the union would be dissolved. His explanation downplays the deal he helped arrange between the Hamiltonians and the southern states to locate the future national capital on the Potomac River in exchange for accepting assumption.]

. . . [A]nd so the assumption was passed, and 20 millions of stock divided among favored states and thrown in as pabulum [i.e., food] to the stock-jobbing herd. This added to the number of votaries [i.e., supporters] to the treasury and made its Chief [Hamilton] the master of every vote in the legislature that might give the government the direction suited to his political views. I know well . . . that nothing like a majority in Congress had yielded to this corruption. Far from it. But a division, not very unequal, had already taken place in the honest part of that body, between the parties styled republican and federal. The latter being monarchists in principle, adhered to Hamilton of course, as their leader in that principle, and this mercenary phalanx added to them ensured always a majority in both houses: so that the whole action of the legislature was now under the direction of the treasury. Still the machine was not compleat. The effect of the funding system, & of the assumption, would be temporary. It would be lost with the loss of the individual members whom it had enriched, and some engine of influence more permanent must be contrived, while those myrmidons [i.e., henchmen] were yet in place to carry it thro' all opposition. This engine was the Bank of the U.S. . . . . While the government remained at Philadelphia, a selection of members of both houses were constantly kept as Directors, who, on every question interesting to that institution, or to the views of the federal head, voted at the will of the head; and, together with the stockholding members, could always make the federal [Federalist] vote that of the majority. By this combination, legislative expositions [i.e., interpretations] were given to the constitution, and all the administrative laws were shaped on the model of England & so passed. . . .

Here then was the real ground of the [Republican] opposition which was made to the course of the [Federalist] administration. Its object was to preserve the legislature pure and independent of the executive, to restrain the administration to republican forms and principles, and not permit the constitution to be construed into a monarchy, and to be warped in practice into all the principles and pollutions of their favorite English model. Nor was this an opposition to Gen'l Washington. He was true to the republican charge confided to him; & has solemnly and repeatedly protested to me, in our private conversations, that he would lose the last drop of blood in support of it, and he did this the oftener, and with the more earnestness because he knew my suspicions of Hamilton's designs against it; & wished to quiet them. For he was not aware of the drift, or of the effect of Hamilton's schemes. Unversed in financial projects & calculations, & budgets, his approbation of them was bottomed on his confidence in the man. But Hamilton was not only a monarchist, but for a monarchy bottomed on corruption. . . . Hamilton was indeed a singular character. Of acute understanding, disinterested, honest, and honorable in all private transactions, amiable in society, and duly valuing virtue in private life, yet so bewitched & perverted by the British example, as to be under thoro' conviction that corruption was essential to the government of a nation.

6.4: The Jeffersonians Embrace the French (1793)

In 1789 forces long repressed rose up to challenge the "Old Regime," the ancient order of privilege that reigned in France. In 1790 the French insurgents established a constitutional monarchy and abolished most of the prerogatives and trappings of aristocracy. In 1792 the revolutionaries deposed the French king and replaced the age-old

*monarchy with a republic based on many of the same concepts of nat-
ural rights that had inspired the Americans in 1776. The following
year they tried Louis XVI for treason and beheaded him. Marie An-
toinette, his frivolous queen, soon followed him to the guillotine.*

*France's conservative neighbors were appalled by the revolution
and its excesses. In 1792, even before Louis's execution, revolutionary
France found itself at war with Austria and Prussia and in the following year with Great Britain. For the next twenty years the French and
their allies were embroiled in almost constant warfare in Europe and
wherever French influence reached, against a coalition of forces bit-
terly opposed to their policies and principles.*

*From the outset the wars of the French Revolution had an important
ideological dimension. The leaders of France, at least until 1795, were
militant secular democrats who loathed organized religion as well as
social and political inequality. Yet at the same time they had little respect for civil liberties. The revolutionary leaders used terror to cow
their opponents. Thousands of aristocrats and clergy fled France for
exile in more hospitable lands, including America. Many who remained suffered the same fate as the king and queen. Before long the
war between France and its enemies came to be seen as a struggle between two fundamentally different political philosophies, one that celebrated stability, hierarchy, and traditional religion, another that
cherished change, equality, and secularism.*

*At first most Americans cheered the French Revolution. But as it be-
came more radical, the French republic became a divisive force in American political life. This effect was magnified by the 1778 Franco-American
treaty of alliance that the French claimed obliged the Americans to support them in their new war with Britain and their other enemies.*

*Thomas Jefferson himself had been in Paris as minister to France at
the outbreak of the revolution and had applauded the sweeping political changes he witnessed. After he returned to America, he continued
to give them his support.*

*The following letter from Secretary of State Jefferson to William
Short, U.S. minister to the Netherlands, expresses his cordial feelings
toward the French republic. Jefferson and his subordinate obviously
disagreed over the Jacobins, the most militant faction among the
French revolutionary leaders and the group most committed to using
violent deeds against the revolution's enemies.*

*How does Jefferson condone the bloodshed unleashed by the Ja-
cobins? Does he himself seem an extremist? Do his views support the
principle that a good end justifies any means to achieve it?*

In Praise of the French Jacobins

THOMAS JEFFERSON

To William Short

Philadelphia Jan 3. 1793.

Dear Sir,—My last private letter to you was of Oct. 16. since which I have received your No. 103, 107, 108, 109, 110, 112, 113, & 114 and yesterday your private one of Sep 15, came to hand. The tone of your letters had for some time given me pain, on account of the extreme warmth with which they censured the proceedings of the Jacobins of France. I considered that sect as the same with the Republican patriots, & the Feuillants[1] as the Monarchical patriots, well known in the early part of the revolution, & but little distant in their views, both having in object the establishment of a free constitution, & differing only on the question whether their chief Executive should be hereditary or not. The Jacobins (as since called) yielded to the Feuillants & tried the experiment of retaining their hereditary Executive. The experiment failed completely, and would have brought on the reestablishment of despotism had it been pursued. The Jacobins saw this, and that the expunging that officer was of absolute necessity. And the Nation was with them in opinion, for however they might have been formerly for the constitution framed by the first assembly, they were come over from their hope in it, and were now generally Jacobins. In the struggle which was necessary, many guilty persons fell without the forms of trial, and with them some innocent. These I deplore as much as any body, & shall deplore some of them to the day of my death. But I deplore them as I should have done had they fallen in battle. It was necessary to use the arm of the people, a machine not quite so blind as balls and bombs, but blind to a certain degree. A few of their cordial friends met at their hands the fate of enemies. But time and truth will rescue & embalm their memories, while their posterity will be enjoying that very liberty for which they would never have hesitated to offer up their lives. The liberty of the whole earth was depending on the issue of the contest, and was ever such a prize won with so little innocent blood? My own affections have been deeply wounded by some of the martyrs to this cause, but rather than it should have failed, I would have seen half the earth desolated. Were there but an Adam & Eve left in every country, & left free, it would be better than as it now is. I have expressed to you my sentiments, because they are really those of 99. in an hundred of our citizens. The universal feasts, and rejoicings which have lately been had on account of the successes of the French shewed the genuine effusions of their hearts. You have been wounded by the sufferings of your friends, and have by this circumstance been hurried into a temper of mind which would be extremely disrelished if known to your countrymen. The *reserve of the President of the United States* had never permitted

Thomas Jefferson, *The Writings of Thomas Jefferson,* Paul Leicester Ford, ed. (New York: G. P. Putnam's Sons, 1895), vol. 1, pp. 153–56.

[1]A moderate group, later suppressed by the Jacobins—ED.

me to discover the light in which he viewed it, and as I was more anxious that you should satisfy him than me, I had still avoided explanations with you on the subject. But your 113, induced him to break silence and to notice the extreme acrimony of your expressions. He added that he had been informed the sentiments you expressed *in your conversations* were equally offensive to our allies, & that you should consider yourself as the representative of your country and that what you say might be imputed to your constituents. He desired me therefore to write to you on this subject. He added that he considered *France as the sheet anchor of this country and its friendship as a first object.* There are in the U.S. some characters of opposite principles; some of them are high in office, others possessing great wealth, and all of them hostile to France and fondly looking to England as the staff of their hope. These I named to you on a former occasion. Their prospects have certainly not brightened. Excepting them, this country is entirely republican, friends to the constitution, anxious to preserve it and to have it administered according to it's [*sic*] own republican principles. The little party above mentioned have espoused it only as a stepping stone to monarchy, and have endeavored to approximate it to that in it's [*sic*] administration in order to render it's [*sic*] final transition more easy. The successes of republicanism in France have given the coup de grace to their prospects, and I hope to their projects.—I have developed to you faithfully the sentiments of your country, that you may govern yourself accordingly. I know your republicanism to be pure, and that it is no decay of that which has embittered you against it's [*sic*] votaries in France, but too great a sensibility at the partial evil which it's [*sic*] object has been accomplished there. I have written to you in the stile to which I have been always accustomed with you, and which perhaps it is time I should lay aside. But while old men are sensible enough of their own advance in years, they do not sufficiently recollect it in those whom they have seen young. In writing too the last private letter which will probably be written under present circumstances, in contemplating that your correspondence will shortly be turned over to I know not whom, but certainly to some one not in the habit of considering your interests with the same fostering anxieties I do, I have presented things without reserve, satisfied you will ascribe what I have said to it's true motive, use it for your own best interest, and in that fulfil completely what I had in view.

6.5: The Federalists Denounce the French Revolution (1793)

One opponent of the French cause was Thomas Jefferson's successor as American minister to France, Gouverneur Morris. From a distinguished New York family, Morris had been a delegate to the Constitutional Convention, where he had supported a strong central government. Like Jefferson, he was in Paris when the revolution first erupted. But unlike the red-haired Virginian, he supported the besieged monarchy. He later became a Federalist senator from New York.

In the following letter to George Washington, Morris discloses his loathing for the tactics of the revolutionary leaders. How do you explain his sympathy for the queen? Was Morris correct in his prediction that France would end up being governed by "a single despot"?

Deploring the Excesses of the French Revolution

GOUVERNEUR MORRIS

To George Washington

Paris, October 18th, 1793

My Dear Sir,

You will see by the official correspondence, that your orders are complied with, and that your intentions are fulfilled. Permit me on this occasion to remark, that had the people of America been well informed of the state of things on this side of the Atlantic, no one would have dared to adopt the conduct which M. Genêt[1] has pursued. In reading the few gazettes which have reached me, I am surprised to see so little sound intelligence.

The present government is evidently a despotism both in principle and practice. The Convention[2] now consists of only a part of those, who were chosen to frame a constitution. These, after putting under arrest their fellows, claim all power, and have delegated the greater part of it to a *Committee of Safety.* You will observe, that one of the ordinary measures of government is to send out Commissioners with unlimited authority. They are invested with power to remove officers elected by the people, and put others in their places. This power, as well as that of imprisoning on suspicion, is liberally exercised. The revolutionary tribunal established here to judge on general principles, gives unbounded scope to will. It is an emphatic phrase in fashion among the patriots [i.e., the revolution's supporters] that *terror is the order of the day.* Some years have elapsed since Montesquieu[3] wrote that the principle of arbitrary government is *fear.*

The Queen was executed the day before yesterday. Insulted during her trial and reviled during her last moments, she behaved with dignity throughout. This execution will, I think, give to future hostilities a deeper dye, and unite more intimately the allied powers [at war with France]. It will silence the opposition of those, who

---

Jared Sparks, *The Life of Gouverneur Morris with Selections from His Correspondence* (Boston: Gray and Bowen, 1832), vol. 2, pp. 369–70.

[1]Edmond Charles Genêt was sent in 1792 as French minister to the United States, charged with inducing the Americans to aid the French republic against its enemies. He became the center of debate in America between the friends and the enemies of revolutionary France, and was eventually recalled at the request of the American government. To spare him punishment in France, however, he was allowed to stay in the United States—ED.

[2]The body created in 1791 to draw up a new constitution for France that would embody the changed political order. It represented a range of political views from royalists to Jacobins—ED.

[3]Charles de Secondat Montesquieu, a French political philosopher, is considered the source of the theory of checks and balances—ED.

would not listen to the dismemberment of this country, and, therefore it may be concluded that the blow by which she died was directed from a distance.

But whatever may be the lot of France in remote futurity, and putting aside the military events, it seems evident that she must be governed by a single despot. Whether she will pass through that point through the medium of a triumvirate, [a partnership of three leaders], or other small body of men, seems as yet undetermined. I think it most probable that she will. A great and awful crisis seems to be near at hand. A blow is, I am told, meditated which will shroud in grief and horror a guilty land. Already the prisons are surcharged with persons who consider themselves victims. Nature recoils, and I yet hope that these ideas are circulated only to inspire fear. I am, &c.

Gouverneur Morris

6.6:   Freedom of Expression: The Press (1798, 1804)

Could the fledgling government endure criticism? Would it collapse in the face of dissent, particularly when a major controversy, such as embroilment in foreign wars, threatened? The Early Republic displayed two tendencies. Federalists tended to fear the effects of freedom of the press; an excessive manifestation of this can be found in the Alien and Sedition Acts, which were passed by the Adams Administration. Not all Americans shared these fears, however, and Thomas Jefferson's letter to John Tyler reflects the alternative view that ultimately triumphed as the national aspiration.

The Alien and Sedition Acts (1798)

1. The Naturalization Act (June 18, 1798)

An Act supplementary to and to amend the act, intituled "An act to establish an uniform rule of naturalization;" and to repeal the act heretofore passed on that subject.

SECTION 1. *Be it enacted . . .* , That no alien shall be admitted to become a citizen of the United States, or of any state, unless . . . he shall have declared his intention to become a citizen of the United States, five years, at least, before his admission, and shall, at the time of his application to be admitted, declare and prove, to the satisfaction of the court having jurisdiction in the case, that he has resided within the United States fourteen years, . . .

U. S. Statutes at Large, Vol. I, p. 566 ff.

2. The Alien Act (June 25, 1798)

An Act concerning Aliens.

SEC. 1. *Be it enacted . . . ,* That it shall be lawful for the President of the United States at any time during the continuance of this act, to *order* all such *aliens* as he shall judge dangerous to the peace and safety of the United States, or shall have reasonable grounds to suspect are concerned in any treasonable or secret machinations against the government thereof, to depart out of the territory of the United States, within such time as shall be expressed in such order, which order shall be served on such alien by delivering him a copy thereof, or leaving the same at his usual abode, and returned to the office of the Secretary of State, by the marshal or other person to whom the same shall be directed. And in case any alien, so ordered to depart, shall be found at large within the United States after the time limited in such order for his departure, and not having obtained a *license* from the President to reside therein, or having obtained such *license* shall not have conformed thereto, every such alien shall, on conviction thereof, be imprisoned for a term not exceeding three years, and shall never after be admitted to become a citizen of the United States. *Provided always, and be it further enacted,* that if any alien so ordered to depart shall prove to the satisfaction of the President, by evidence to be taken before such person or persons as the President shall direct, who are for that purpose hereby authorized to administer oaths, that no injury or danger to the United States will arise from suffering such alien to reside therein, the President may grant a *license* to such alien to remain within the United States for such time as he shall judge proper, and at such place as he may designate. And the President may also require of such alien to enter into a bond to the United States, in such penal sum as he may direct, with one or more sufficient sureties to the satisfaction of the person authorized by the President to take the same, conditioned for the good behavior of such alien during his residence in the United States, and not violating his license, which license the President may revoke, whenever he shall think proper.

Sec. 2. *And be it further enacted,* That it shall be lawful for the President of the United States, whenever he may deem it necessary for the public safety, to order to be removed out of the territory thereof, any alien who may or shall be in prison in pursuance of this act; and to cause to be arrested and sent out of the United States such of those aliens as shall have been ordered to depart therefrom and shall not have obtained a license as aforesaid, in all cases where, in the opinion of the President, the public safety requires a speedy removal. And if any alien so removed or sent out of the United States by the President shall voluntarily return thereto, unless by permission of the President of the United States, such alien on conviction thereof, shall be imprisoned so long as, in the opinion of the President, the public safety may require. . . .

Sec. 6. *And be it further enacted,* That this act shall continue and be in force for and during the term of two years from the passing thereof.

U. S. Statutes at Large, Vol. I, p. 570 ff.

3. The Alien Enemies Act (July 6, 1798)

An Act respecting Alien Enemies.

Section 1. *Be it enacted . . . ,* That whenever there shall be a declared war between the United States and any foreign nation or government, or any invasion or predatory incursion shall be perpetrated, attempted, or threatened against the territory of the United States, by any foreign nation or government, . . . all natives, citizens, denizens, or subjects of the hostile nation or government, being males of the age of fourteen years and upwards, who shall be within the United States, and not actually naturalized, shall be liable to be apprehended, restrained, secured and removed, as alien enemies. And the President of the United States shall be, and he is hereby authorized, . . . to direct the conduct to be observed, on the part of the United States, towards the aliens who shall become liable, as aforesaid; the manner and degree of the restraint to which they shall be subject, and in what cases, and upon what security their residence shall be permitted, and to provide for the removal of those, who, not being permitted to reside within the United States, shall refuse or neglect to depart therefrom; and to establish any other regulations which shall be found necessary in the premises and for the public safety: . . .

4. The Sedition Act (July 14, 1798)

An Act in addition to the act, entitled "An act for the punishment of certain crimes against the United States."

Sec. 1. *Be it enacted . . . ,* That if any persons shall unlawfully combine or conspire together, with intent to oppose any measure or measures of the government of the United States, which are or shall be directed by proper authority, or to impede the operation of any law of the United States, or to intimidate or prevent any person holding a place or office in or under the government of the United States, from undertaking, performing or executing his trust or duty; and if any person or persons, with intent as aforesaid, shall counsel, advise or attempt to procure any insurrection, riot, unlawful assembly, or combination, whether such conspiracy, threatening, counsel, advice, or attempt shall have the proposed effect or not, he or they shall be deemed guilty of a high misdemeanor, and on conviction, before any court of the United States having jurisdiction thereof, shall be punished by a fine not exceeding five thousand dollars, and by imprisonment during a term not less than six months nor exceeding five years; and further, at the discretion of the court may be holden to find sureties for his good behaviour in such sum, and for such time, as the said court may direct.

Sec. 2. That if any person shall write, print, utter, or publish, or shall cause or procure to be written, printed, uttered or published, or shall knowingly and willingly assist or aid in writing, printing, uttering or publishing any false, scandalous and malicious writing or writings against the government of the United States, or either house of the Congress of the United States, or the President of the United States,

U. S. Statutes at Large, Vol. I, p. 577 ff.
U. S. Statutes at Large, Vol. I, p. 596–7

with intent to defame the said government, or either house of the said Congress, or the said President, or to bring them, or either of them, into contempt or disrepute; or to excite against them, or either or any of them, the hatred of the good people of the United States, or to stir up sedition within the United States, or to excite any unlawful combinations therein, for opposing or resisting any law of the United States, or any act of the President of the United States, done in pursuance of any such law, or of the powers in him vested by the constitution of the United States, or to resist, oppose, or defeat any such law or act, or to aid, encourage or abet any hostile designs of any foreign nation against the United States, their people or government, then such person, being thereof convicted before any court of the United States having jurisdiction thereof, shall be punished by a fine not exceeding two thousand dollars, and by imprisonment not exceeding two years.

Sec. 3. That if any person shall be prosecuted under this act, for the writing or publishing any libel aforesaid, it shall be lawful for the defendant, upon the trial of the cause, to give in evidence in his defence, the truth of the matter contained in the publication charged as a libel. And the jury who shall try the cause, shall have a right to determine the law and the fact, under the direction of the court, as in other cases.

Thomas Jefferson on Freedom of the Press from Letter

To Judge John Tyler

Washington, June 28, 1804

DEAR SIR,—Your favor of the 10th instant has been duly received. Amidst the direct falsehoods, the misrepresentations of truth, the calumnies and the insults resorted to by a faction to mislead the public mind, and to overwhelm those entrusted with its interests, our support is to be found in the approving voice of our conscience and country, in the testimony of our fellow citizens, that their confidence is not shaken by these artifices. When to the plaudits of the honest multitude, the sober approbation of the sage in his closet is added, it becomes a gratification of an higher order. It is the sanction of wisdom superadded to the voice of affection. The terms, therefore, in which you are so good as to express your satisfaction with the course of the present administration cannot but give me great pleasure. I may err in my measures, but never shall deflect from the intention to fortify the public liberty by every possible means, and to put it out of the power of the few to riot on the labors of the many. No experiment can be more interesting than that we are now trying, and which we trust will end in establishing the fact, that man may be governed by reason and truth. Our first object should therefore be, to leave open to him all the avenues to truth. The most effectual hitherto found, is the freedom of the press. It is therefore,

Merrill D. Peterson, ed., *The Writings of Thomas Jefferson* (New York: The Library of America, 1984), pp. 1146–8.

the first shut up by those who fear the investigation of their actions. The firmness with which the people have withstood the late abuses of the press, the discernment they have manifested between truth and falsehood, show that they may safely be trusted to hear everything true and false, and to form a correct judgment between them. As little is it necessary to impose on their senses, or dazzle their minds by pomp, splendor, or forms. Instead of this artificial, how much surer is that real respect, which results from the use of their reason, and the habit of bringing everything to the test of common sense.

I hold it, therefore, certain, that to open the doors of truth, and to fortify the habit of testing everything by reason, are the most effectual manacles we can rivet on the hands of our successors to prevent their manacling the people with their own consent. The panic into which they were artfully thrown in 1798, the frenzy which was excited in them by their enemies against their apparent readiness to abandon all the principles established for their own protection, seemed for awhile to countenance the opinions of those who say they cannot be trusted with their own government. But I never doubted their rallying; and they did rally much sooner than I expected. On the whole, that experiment on their credulity has confirmed my confidence in their ultimate good sense and virtue.

I lament to learn that a like misfortune has enabled you to estimate the afflictions of a father on the loss of a beloved child. However terrible the possibility of such another accident, it is still a blessing for you of inestimable value that you would not even then descend childless to the grave. Three sons, and hopeful ones too, are a rich treasure. I rejoice when I hear of young men of virtue and talents, worthy to receive, and likely to preserve the splendid inheritance of self-government, which we have acquired and shaped for them.

The complement of midshipmen for the Tripoline squadron, is full; and I hope the frigates have left the Capes by this time. I have, however, this day, signed warrants of midshipmen for the two young gentlemen you recommended. These will be forwarded by the Secretary of the Navy. He tells me that their first services will be to be performed on board the gun boats.

Accept my friendly salutations, and assurances of great esteem and respect.

6.7: Washington and the Success of the Great Experiment (1789, 1796)

In the final analysis, George Washington played a crucial role in the success of the "Great Experiment." His effective leadership, continuous awareness of the importance of precedent, and, most of all, personal commitment to the ideals and values of the Revolution rescued the young republic from much of the turbulence, instability, and internecine violence nations emerging from revolutions usually experience. The first selection is from Washington's First Inaugural Address and reflects both the idealism and exceptionalism that he and many others felt about the American experience. The second selection, his Farewell Address, is clearly tempered by the sobering experience of having tried to translate these ideals into reality during his two terms as president.

What themes connect both speeches? What were the ideals and beliefs that Washington felt all Americans should cherish? What fears and doubts clearly troubled Washington when he left office? Are any of the themes running through either speech relevant to us today?

From Washington's First Inaugural Address April 30, 1789

Fellow-Citizens of the Senate and of the House of Representatives:

Among the vicissitudes incident to life no event could have filled me with greater anxieties than that of which the notification was transmitted by your order, and received on the 14th day of the present month. On the one hand, I was summoned by my country, whose voice I can never hear but with veneration and love, from a retreat which I had chosen with the fondest predilection, and, in my flattering hopes, with an immutable decision, as the asylum of my declining years—a retreat which was rendered every day more necessary as well as more dear to me by the addition of habit to inclination, and of frequent interruptions in my health to the gradual waste committed on it by time. On the other hand, the magnitude and difficulty of the trust to which the voice of my country called me, being sufficient to awaken in the wisest and most experienced of her citizens a distrustful scrutiny into his qualifications, could not but overwhelm with despondence one who (inheriting inferior endowments from nature and unpracticed in the duties of civil administration) ought to be peculiarly conscious of his own deficiencies. In this conflict of emotions all I dare aver is that it has been my faithful study to collect my duty from a just appreciation of every circumstance by which it might be affected. All I dare hope is that if, in executing this task, I have been too much swayed by a grateful remembrance of former instances, or by an affectionate sensibility to this transcendent proof of the confidence of my fellow-citizens, and have thence too little consulted my incapacity as well as disinclination for the weighty and untried cares before me, my error will be palliated by the motives which mislead me, and its consequences be judged by my country with some share of the partiality in which they originated.

. . . [I]n obedience to the public summons, . . . it would be peculiarly improper to omit in this first official act my fervent supplications to that Almighty Being who rules over the universe, . . . No people can be bound to acknowledge and adore the Invisible Hand which conducts the affairs of men more than those of the United States. Every step by which they have advanced to the character of an independent nation seems to have been distinguished by some token of providen-tial agency; . . .

. . . [I] behold the surest pledges that as on one side no local prejudices or attachments, no separate views nor party animosities, will misdirect the comprehensive

George Washington, Inaugural Address, April 30, 1789, New York City. *Messages and Papers,* James D. Richardson, ed. (Washington, DC: United States Government Printing Office, 1896), vol. I, p. 51.

and equal eye which ought to watch over this great assemblage of communities and interests, so, on another, that the foundation of our national policy will be laid in the pure and immutable principles of private morality, and the preëminence of free government be exemplified by all the attributes which can win the affections of its citizens and command the respect of the world. I dwell on this prospect with every satisfaction which an ardent love for my country can inspire, since there is no truth more thoroughly established than that there exists in the economy and course of nature an indissoluble union between virtue and happiness; between duty and advantage; between the genuine maxims of an honest and magnanimous policy and the solid rewards of public prosperity and felicity; since we ought to be no less persuaded that the propitious smiles of Heaven can never be expected on a nation that disregards the eternal rules of order and right which Heaven itself has ordained; and since the preservation of the sacred fire of liberty and the destiny of the republican model of government are justly considered, perhaps, as *deeply,* as *finally,* staked on the experiment intrusted to the hands of the American people.

From Washington's Farewell Address
September 17, 1796

UNITED STATES, *September 17, 1796.*
Friends and Fellow-Citizens:

. . . [E]very day the increasing weight of years admonishes me more and more that the shade of retirement is as necessary to me as it will be welcome. Satisfied that if any circumstances have given peculiar value to my services they were temporary, I have the consolation to believe that, while choice and prudence invite me to quit the political scene, patriotism does not forbid it. . . .

Here, perhaps, I ought to stop. But a solicitude for your welfare which can not end with my life, and the apprehension of danger natural to that solicitude, urge me on an occasion like the present to offer to your solemn contemplation and to recommend to your frequent review some sentiments which are the result of much reflection, of no inconsiderable observation, and which appear to me all important to the permanency of your felicity as a people. . . .

Interwoven as is the love of liberty with every ligament of your hearts, no recommendation of mine is necessary to fortify or confirm the attachment.

The unity of government which constitutes you one people is also now dear to you. It is justly so, for it is a main pillar in the edifice of your real independence, the support of your tranquillity at home, your peace abroad, of your safety, of your prosperity, of that very liberty which you so highly prize. But as it is easy to foresee that from different causes and from different quarters much pains will be taken, many artifices employed, to weaken in your minds the conviction of this truth, as this is the point in your political fortress against which the batteries of internal and

George Washington, "Farewell Address," September 17, 1796. *Messages and Papers,* Vol. I, James D. Richardson, ed. (Washington, DC: United States Government Printing Office, 1896), p. 213ff.

external enemies will be most constantly and actively (though often covertly and insidiously) directed, it is of infinite moment that you should properly estimate the immense value of your national union to your collective and individual happiness; that you should cherish a cordial, habitual, and immovable attachment to it; accustoming yourselves to think and speak of it as of the palladium of your political safety and prosperity; watching for its preservation with jealous anxiety; discountenancing whatever may suggest even a suspicion that it can in any event be abandoned, and indignantly frowning upon the first dawning of every attempt to alienate any portion of our country from the rest or to enfeeble the sacred ties which now link together the various parts. . . .

The independence and liberty you possess are the work of joint councils and joint efforts, of common dangers, sufferings, and successes.

But these considerations, however powerfully they address themselves to your sensibility, are greatly outweighed by those which apply more immediately to your interest. Here every portion of our country finds the most commanding motives for carefully guarding and preserving the union of the whole.

The *North,* in an unrestrained intercourse with the *South,* protected by the equal laws of a common government, finds in the productions of the latter great additional resources of maritime and commercial enterprise and precious materials of manufacturing industry. The *South,* in the same intercourse, benefiting by the same agency of the *North,* sees its agriculture grow and its commerce expand. Turning partly into its own channels the seamen of the *North,* it finds its particular navigation invigorated; and while it contributes in different ways to nourish and increase the general mass of the national navigation, it looks forward to the protection of a maritime strength to which itself is unequally adapted. The *East,* in a like intercourse with the *West,* already finds, and in the progressive improvement of interior communications by land and water will more and more find, a valuable vent for the commodities which it brings from abroad or manufactures at home. The *West* derives from the *East* supplies requisite to its growth and comfort, and what is perhaps of still greater consequence, it must of necessity owe the *secure* enjoyment of indispensable *outlets* for its own productions to the weight, influence, and the future maritime strength of the Atlantic side of the Union, directed by an indissoluble community of interest as *one nation.* Any other tenure by which the *West* can hold this essential advantage, whether derived from its own separate strength or from an apostate and unnatural connection with any foreign power, must be intrinsically precarious.

While, then, every part of our country thus feels an immediate and particular interest in union, all the parts combined can not fail to find in the united mass of means and efforts greater strength, greater resource, proportionably greater security from external danger, a less frequent interruption of their peace by foreign nations, and what is of inestimable value, they must derive from union an exemption from those broils and wars between themselves which so frequently afflict neighboring countries not tied together by the same governments, which their own rivalships alone would be sufficient to produce, but which opposite foreign alliances, attachments, and intrigues would stimulate and imbitter. Hence, likewise, they will avoid the necessity of those overgrown military establishments which, under any form of government, are inauspicious to liberty, and which are to be regarded as particularly hostile to republican liberty. In this sense it is that your union ought to be considered as a main prop of your liberty, and that the love of the one ought to endear to you the preservation of the other. . . .

[T]here will always be reason to distrust the patriotism of those who in any quarter may endeavor to weaken its bands.

In contemplating the causes which may disturb our union it occurs as matter of serious concern that any ground should have been furnished for characterizing parties by *geographical* discriminations—*Northern* and *Southern, Atlantic* and *Western*—whence designing men may endeavor to excite a belief that there is a real difference of local interests and views. One of the expedients of party to acquire influence within particular districts is to misrepresent the opinions and aims of other districts. You can not shield yourselves too much against the jealousies and heartburnings which spring from these misrepresentations; they tend to render alien to each other those who ought to be bound together by fraternal affection. . . .

I have already intimated to you the danger of parties in the State, with particular reference to the founding of them on geographical discriminations. Let me now take a more comprehensive view, and warn you in the most solemn manner against the baneful effects of the spirit of partly generally.

This spirit, unfortunately, is inseparable from our nature, having its root in the strongest passions of the human mind. It exists under different shapes in all governments, more or less stifled, controlled, or repressed; but in those of the popular form it is seen in its greatest rankness and is truly their worst enemy. . . .

It serves always to distract the public councils and enfeeble the public administration. It agitates the community with illfounded jealousies and false alarms; kindles the animosity of one part against another: forments occasionally riot and insurrection. It opens the door to foreign influence and corruption, which find a facilitated access to the government itself through the channels of party passion. Thus the policy and the will of one country are subjected to the policy and will of another.

There is an opinion that parties in free countries are useful checks upon the administration of the government, and serve to keep alive the spirit of liberty. This within certain limits is probably true; and in governments of a monarchical cast patriotism may look with indulgence, if not with favor, upon the spirit of party. But in those of the popular character, in governments purely elective, it is a spirit not to be encouraged. From their natural tendency it is certain there will always be enough of that spirit for every salutary purpose; and there being constant danger of excess, the effort ought to be by force of public opinion to mitigate and assuage it. A fire not to be quenched, it demands a uniform vigilance to present its bursting into a flame, lest, instead of warming, it should consume.

It is important, likewise, that the habits of thinking in a free country should inspire caution in those intrusted with its administration to confine themselves within their respective constitutional spheres, avoiding in the exercise of the powers of one department to encroach upon another. The spirit of encroachment tends to consolidate the powers of all the departments in one, and thus to create, whatever the form of government, a real despotism. . . . If in the opinion of the people the distribution or modification of the constitutional powers be in any particular wrong, let it be corrected by an amendment in the way which the Constitution designates. But let there be no change by usurpation; for though this in one instance may be the instrument of good, it is the customary weapon by which free governments are destroyed. The precedent must always greatly overbalance in permanent evil any partial or transient benefit which the use can at any time yield.

Of all the dispositions and habits which lead to political prosperity, religion and morality are indispensable supports. In vain would that man claim the tribute of patriotism who should labor to subvert these great pillars of human happiness—these firmest props of the duties of men and citizens. The mere politician, equally with the pious man, ought to respect and to cherish them. A volume could not trace all their connections with private and public felicity. Let it simply be asked, Where is the security for property, for reputation, for life, if the sense of religious obligation *desert* the oaths which are the instruments of investigation in courts of justice? And let us with caution indulge the supposition that morality can be maintained without religion. Whatever may be conceded to the influence of refined education on minds of peculiar structure, reason and experience both forbid us to expect that national morality can prevail in exclusion of religious principle.

It is substantially true that virtue or morality is a necessary spring of popular government. The rule indeed extends with more or less force to every species of free government. Who that is a sincere friend to it can look with indifference upon attempts to shake the foundation of the fabric? Promote, then, as an object of primary importance, institutions for the general diffusion of knowledge. In proportion as the structure of a government gives force to public opinion, it is essential that public opinion should be enlightened.

As a very important source of strength and security, cherish public credit. One method of preserving it is to use it as sparingly as possible, avoiding occasions of expense by cultivating peace, but remembering also that timely disbursements to prepare for danger frequently prevent much greater disbursements to repel it; avoiding likewise the accumulation of debt, not only by shunning occasions of expense, but by vigorous exertions in time of peace to discharge the debts which unavoidable wars have occasioned, not ungenerously throwing upon posterity the burthen which we ourselves ought to bear. . . .

Observe good faith and justice toward all nations. Cultivate peace and harmony with all. Religion and morality enjoin this conduct. And can it be that good policy does not equally enjoin it? It will be worthy of a free, enlightened, and at no distant period a great nation to give to mankind the magnanimous and too novel example of a people always guided by an exalted justice and benevolence. Who can doubt that in the course of time and things the fruits of such a plan would richly repay any temporary advantages which might be lost by a steady adherence to it? Can it be that Providence has not connected the permanent felicity of a nation with its virtue?

The experiment, at least, is recommended by every sentiment which ennobles human nature. Alas! is it rendered impossible by its vices?

In the execution of such a plan nothing is more essential than that permanent, inveterate antipathies against particular nations and passionate attachments for others should be excluded, and that in place of them just and amicable feelings toward all should be cultivated. The nation which indulges toward another an habitual hatred or an habitual fondness is in some degree a slave. It is a slave to its animosity or to its affection, either of which is sufficient to lead it astray from its duty and its interest. Antipathy in one nation against another disposes each more readily to offer insult and injury, to lay hold of slight causes of umbrage, and to be haughty and intractable when accidental or trifling occasions of dispute occur. . . .

The great rule of conduct for us in regard to foreign nations is, in extending our commercial relations to have with them as little *political* connection as possible. So far as we have already formed engagements let them be fulfilled with perfect good faith. Here let us stop.

Europe has a set of primary interests which to us have none or a very remote relation. Hence she must be engaged in frequent controversies, the causes of which are essentially foreign to our concerns. Hence, therefore, it must be unwise in us to implicate ourselves by artificial ties in the ordinary vicissitudes of her politics or the ordinary combinations and collisions of her friendships or enmities.

Our detached and distant situation invites and enables us to pursue a different course. If we remain one people, under an efficient government, the period is not far off when we may defy material injury from external annoyance; when we may take such an attitude as will cause the neutrality we may at any time resolve upon to be scrupulously respected; when belligerent nations, under the impossibility of making acquisitions upon us, will not lightly hazard the giving us provocation; when we may choose peace or war, as our interest, guided by justice, shall counsel.

Why forego the advantages of so peculiar a situation? Why quit our own to stand upon foreign ground? Why, by interweaving our destiny with that of any part of Europe, entangle our peace and prosperity in the toils of European ambition, rivalship, interest, humor, or caprice?

It is our true policy to steer clear of permanent alliances with any portion of the foreign world, so far, I mean, as we are now at liberty to do it; for let me not be understood as capable of patronizing infidelity to existing engagements. I hold the maxim no less applicable to public than to private affairs that honesty is always the best policy. I repeat, therefore, let those engagements be observed in their genuine sense. But in my opinion it is unnecessary and would be unwise to extend them.

Taking care always to keep ourselves by suitable establishments on a respectable defensive posture, we may safely trust to temporary alliances for extraordinary emergencies. . . .

Though in reviewing the incidents of my Administration I am unconscious of intentional error, I am nevertheless too sensible of my defects not to think it probable that I may have committed many errors. Whatever they may be, I fervently beseech the Almighty to avert or mitigate the evils to which they may tend. I shall also carry with me the hope that my country will never cease to view them with indulgence, and that, after forty-five years of my life dedicated to its service with an upright zeal, the faults of incompetent abilities will be consigned to oblivion, as myself must soon be to the mansions of rest.

Relying on its kindness in this as in other things, and actuated by that fervent love toward it which is so natural to a man who views in it the native soil of himself and his progenitors for several generations, I anticipate with pleasing expectation that retreat in which I promise myself to realize without alloy the sweet enjoyment of partaking in the midst of my fellow-citizens the benign influence of good laws under a free government—the ever-favorite object of my heart, and the happy reward, as I trust, of our mutual cares, labors, and dangers.

G°. WASHINGTON.

❖ 7 ❖

Pioneers and Native Americans

From the very outset the United States was a huge country. It became still larger through the Louisiana Purchase (1803), the purchase of Florida (1819), the Mexican Cession (1848), the acquisition of Oregon (1848), and the Gadsden Purchase (1853). By 1860, the nation had grown to almost 3 million square miles.

Beyond the coastal band of dense settlement in the early republic, most of this vast expanse was initially without many inhabitants of Old World extraction. To contemporary whites it seemed an empty,[1] bounteous resource that offered escape from troubles in the older East and new opportunities for attaining wealth. In the "West," Americans could earn a second chance.

One of the epochal developments of the early nation was the opening of the trans-Appalachian West to white settlement after the War of 1812. During the years between 1815 and the start of the Civil War, millions of acres of western lands were wrested from Indian control and carved into farms and plantations. Bustling cities rose where Indian villages or virgin forest had existed. By 1849 seventeen new states had been added to the original thirteen, almost all in the great interior valley drained by the Mississippi and its tributaries.

What was the fate of the thousands of people who pulled up stakes and headed west during these years? And what about the Indian inhabitants of the region? How did the pre-Civil War westward movement of whites[2] affect them?

Eastern Americans have always been ambivalent about the West. To some it has seemed the place that best expressed the American spirit. To

---

[1]It was, of course, not empty, but inhabited by many Native American tribes. Few whites, however, took their claims seriously—as you will see—ED.
[2]And many blacks as well, mostly as slaves brought by their owners—ED.

others it has been the abode of savagery, the region where imported civilization quickly decayed. The documents below deal with this dialogue.

7.1: Opening the Great American Desert: The Lewis and Clark Expedition (1803)

Little was known about the geography of central North America as the nineteenth century began. The Louisiana Purchase (1803) transformed the prospects of the new United States of America and gave concrete meaning to both Jefferson's and Hamilton's continental aspirations.

The Lewis and Clark expedition was designed as a scientific and diplomatic mission and proved to be one of Jefferson's most important personal concerns. In the following letter, Jefferson instructs Lewis as to the goals and methods of the expedition. The passage reveals an encounter with an unknown world, rich with prophetic issues about to unfold. How much did Americans know about their continent's geographic and scientific dimension in 1803? What profound ecological issues would emerge in the years to come? Most of all, the "great American wilderness" was not uninhabited; millions of native Americans lived there. What were Jefferson's directives and personal feelings about American relations with the Indians? Were Jefferson's views humanistic? What challenges did the future hold?

Expedition to the Pacific

Instructions to Captain Lewis

THOMAS JEFFERSON

June 20, 1803

To Merryweather Lewis, Esq., Captain of the 1st Regiment of Infantry of the United States of America.

Your situation as Secretary of the President of the United States has made you acquainted with the objects of my confidential message of Jan. 18, 1803, to the legislature. You have seen the act they passed, which, tho' expressed in general terms, was meant to sanction those objects, and you are appointed to carry them into execution.

Instruments for ascertaining by celestial observations the geography of the country thro' which you will pass, have been already provided. Light articles for barter, & presents among the Indians, arms for your attendants, say for from 10 to 12 men,

Merrill D. Peterson, ed., *The Writings of Thomas Jefferson,* (New York: The Library of America, 1984), pp. 1126–32.

boats, tents, & other travelling apparatus, with ammunition, medicine, surgical in-struments & provision you will have prepared with such aids as the Secretary at War can yield in his department; & from him also you will receive authority to en-gage among our troops, by voluntary agreement, the number of attendants above mentioned, over whom you, as their commanding officer are invested with all the powers the laws give in such a case.

As your movements while within the limits of the U.S. will be better directed by occasional communications, adapted to circumstances as they arise, they will not be noticed here. What follows will respect your proceedings after your departure from the U.S.

Your mission has been communicated to the Ministers here from France, Spain, & Great Britain, and through them to their governments; and such assurances given them as to it's objects as we trust will satisfy them. The country of Louisiana having been ceded by Spain to France, the passport you have from the Minister of France, the representative of the present sovereign of the country, will be a protection with all it's subjects: And that from the Minister of England will entitle you to the friendly aid of any traders of that allegiance with whom you may happen to meet.

The object of your mission is to explore the Missouri river, & such principal stream of it, as, by it's course & communication with the water of the Pacific Ocean may offer the most direct & practicable water communication across this continent, for the purposes of commerce.

Beginning at the mouth of the Missouri, you will take observations of latitude and longitude at all remarkable points on the river, & especially at the mouths of rivers, at rapids, at islands & other places & objects distinguished by such natural marks & characters of a durable kind, as that they may with certainty be recognized hereafter. The courses of the river between these points of observation may be sup-plied by the compass, the log-line & by time, corrected by the observations them-selves. The variations of the compass too, in different places should be noticed.

The interesting points of the portage between the heads of the Missouri & the water offering the best communication with the Pacific Ocean should be fixed by observation & the course of that water to the ocean, in the same manner as that of the Missouri.

Your observations are to be taken with great pains & accuracy, to be entered dis-tinctly, & intelligibly for others as well as yourself, to comprehend all the elements necessary, with the aid of the usual tables to fix the latitude & longitude of the places at which they were taken, & are to be rendered to the war office, for the pur-pose of having the calculations made concurrently by proper persons within the U.S. Several copies of these as well as of your other notes, should be made at leisure times & put into the care of the most trustworthy of your attendants, to guard by multiplying them against the accidental losses to which they will be exposed. A further guard would be that one of these copies be written on the paper of the birch, as less liable to injury from damp than common paper.

The commerce which may be carried on with the people inhabiting the line you will pursue, renders a knolege of these people important. You will therefore endeavor to make yourself acquainted, as far as a diligent pursuit of your journey shall admit.

with the names of the nations & their numbers;

the extent & limits of their possessions;

their relations with other tribes or nations;

their language, traditions, monuments;

their ordinary occupations in agriculture, fishing, hunting, war, arts, & the implements for these;

their food, clothing, & domestic accommodations;

the diseases prevalent among them, & the remedies they use;

moral and physical circumstance which distinguish them from the tribes they know;

peculiarities in their laws, customs & dispositions;

and articles of commerce they may need or furnish & to what extent.

And considering the interest which every nation has in extending & strengthening the authority of reason & justice among the people around them, it will be useful to acquire what knolege you can of the state of morality, religion & information among them, as it may better enable those who endeavor to civilize & instruct them, to adapt their measures to the existing notions & practises of those on whom they are to operate.

Other objects worthy of notice will be

the soil & face of the country, its growth & vegetable productions; especially those not of the U.S.

the animals of the country generally, & especially those not known in the U.S. The remains & accounts of any which may be deemed rare or extinct;

the mineral productions of every kind; but more particularly metals, limestone, pit coal & saltpetre; salines & mineral waters, noting the temperature of the last & such circumstances as may indicate their character; volcanic appearances;

climate as characterized by the thermometer, by the proportion of rainy, cloudy & clear days, by lightening, hail, snow, ice, by the access & recess of frost, by the winds, prevailing at different seasons, the dates at which particular plants put forth or lose their flowers, or leaf, times of appearance of particular birds, reptiles or insects.

Altho' your route will be along the channel of the Missouri, yet you will endeavor to inform yourself by inquiry, of the character and extent of the country watered by its branches, and especially on it's southern side. The north river or Rio Bravo which runs into the gulph of Mexico, and the north river, or Rio colorado, which runs into the gulph of California, are understood to be the principal streams heading opposite to the waters of the Missouri, & running Southwardly. Whether the dividing grounds between the Missouri & them are mountains or flatlands, what are their distance from the Missouri, the character of the intermediate country, & the people inhabiting it, are worthy of particular enquiry. The northern waters of the Missouri are less to be enquired after, because they have been ascertained to a considerable degree, and are still in a course of ascertainment by English traders & travellers. But if you can learn anything certain of the most northern source of the Mississippi, & of it's position relative to the lake of the woods, it will be interesting to us. Some account too of the path of the Canadian traders from the Mississippi, at the mouth of the Ouisconsin river, to where it strikes the Missouri and of the soil and rivers in it's course, is desirable.

In all your intercourse with the natives treat them in the most friendly & conciliatory manner which their own conduct will admit; allay all jealousies as to the object of your journey, satisfy them of it's innocence, make them acquainted with the position, extent, character, peaceable & commercial dispositions of the U.S., of our wish to be neighborly, friendly & useful to them, & of our dispositions to a commercial intercourse with them; confer with them on the points most convenient as mutual emporiums, & the articles of most desirable interchange for them & us. If a few of their influential chiefs, within practicable distance, wish to visit us, arrange such a visit with them, and furnish them with authority to call on our officers, on their entering the U.S. to have them conveyed to this place at the public expense. If any of them should wish to have some of their young people brought up with us, & taught such arts as may be useful to them, we will receive, instruct & take care of them. Such a mission, whether of influential chiefs, or of young people, would give some security to your own party. Carry with you some matter of the kine-pox, inform those of them with whom you may be of it's efficacy as a preservative from the small-pox; and instruct & encourage them in the use of it. This may be especially done wherever you may winter.

As it is impossible for us to foresee in what manner you will be received by those people, whether with hospitality or hostility, so is it impossible to prescribe the exact degree of perseverance with which you are to pursue your journey. We value too much the lives of citizens to offer them to probably destruction. Your numbers will be sufficient to secure you against the unauthorized opposition of individuals, or of small parties: but if a superior force, authorized or not authorized, by a nation, should be arrayed against your further passage, & inflexibly determined to arrest it, you must decline it's further pursuit, & return. In the loss of yourselves, we should lose also the information you will have acquired. By returning safely with that, you may enable us to renew the essay with better calculated means. To your own discretion therefore must be left the degree of danger you may risk, & the point at which you should decline, only saying we wish you to err on the side of your safety, & to bring back your party safe, even if it be with less information.

As far up the Missouri as the white settlements extend, an intercourse will probably be found to exist between them and the Spanish posts at St. Louis, opposite Cahokia, or Ste. Genevieve opposite Kaskaskia. From still farther up the river, the traders may furnish a conveyance for letters. Beyond that you may perhaps be able to engage Indians to bring letters for the government to Cahokia or Kaskaskia on promising that they shall there receive such special compensation as you shall have stipulated with them. Avail yourself of these means to communicate to us at seasonable intervals a copy of your journal, notes & observations of every kind, putting into cipher whatever might do injury if betrayed.

Should you reach the Pacific Ocean inform yourself of the circumstances which may decide whether the furs of those parts may not be collected as advantageously at the head of the Missouri (convenient as is supposed to the waters of the Colorado & Oregon or Columbia) as at Nootka Sound or any other point of that coast; & that trade be consequently conducted through the Missouri & U.S. more beneficially than by the circumnavigation now practised.

On your arrival on that coast endeavor to learn if there be any port within your reach frequented by the sea-vessels of any nation, and to send two of your trusted people back by sea, in such way as shall appear practicable, with a copy of your notes. And should you be of opinion that the return of your party by the way they went will be eminently dangerous, then ship the whole, & return by sea by way of Cape Horn or the Cape of Good Hope, as you shall be able. As you will be without money, clothes or provisions, you must endeavor to use the credit of the U.S. to obtain them; for which purpose open letters of credit shall be furnished you authorizing you to draw on the Executive of the U.S. or any of its officers in any part of the world, in which drafts can be disposed of, and to apply with our recommendations to the consuls, agents, merchants or citizens of any nation with which we have intercourse, assuring them in our name that any aids they may furnish you, shall be honorably repaid and on demand. Our consuls Thomas Howes at Batavia in Java, William Buchanan of the Isles of France and Bourbon & John Elmslie at the Cape of Good Hope will be able to supply your necessities by drafts on us.

Should you find it safe to return by the way you go, after sending two of your party round by sea, or with your whole party, if no conveyance by sea can be found, do so; making such observations on your return as may serve to supply, correct or confirm those made on your outward journey.

In re-entering the U.S. and reaching a place of safety, discharge any of your attendants who may desire & deserve it: procuring for them immediate paiment of all arrears of pay & cloathing which may have incurred since their departure & assure them that they shall be recommended to the liberality of the Legislature for the grant of a souldier's portion of land each, as proposed in my message to Congress: & repair yourself with your papers to the seat of government.

To provide, on the accident of your death, against anarchy, dispersion & the consequent danger to your party, and total failure of the enterprise, you are hereby authorized by any instrument signed & written in your own hand to name the person among them who shall succeed to the command on your decease, & by like instruments to change the nomination from time to time, as further experience of the characters accompanying you shall point out superior fitness: and all the power & authorities given to yourself are, in the event of your death transferred to & vested in the successor so named, with further power to him, & his successors in like manner to name each his successor, who, on the death of his predecessor shall be invested with all the powers & authorities given to yourself.

Given under my hand at the city of Washington, this 20th day of June, 1803.

7.2:   The Pioneer Experience (1818)

Once past the initial pioneer phase, how did the emigrants to the West fare? One of our best sources on the early nineteenth-century frontier is the account of Morris Birkbeck, an Englishman who traveled through the West just after 1815. Birkbeck was not just a visitor. He came to America with his large family as a permanent immigrant and settled on land in Illinois. In the selection below he describes both the bright and the dark side of the pioneer farmer's experiences. Which do you think was the more typical? In the absence of opinion polls, how could you determine whether people probably gained or lost by their move west?

The Life of the Western Farmer

MORRIS BIRKBECK

June 8. We were detained at Washington [in western Pennsylvania] by the indisposition of one of our party, and to-day proceeded only twenty-two miles to Ninian Beall's tavern. We now consider ourselves, though east of the Ohio, to have made an inroad on the western territory: a delightful region;—healthy, fertile, romantic.

Our host has a small and simple establishment, which his civility renders truly comfortable. His little history may serve as an example of the natural growth of property in this young country.

He is about thirty; has a wife and three fine and healthy children: his father is a farmer; that is to say, a proprietor, living five miles distant. From him he received five hundred dollars, and "began the world," in true style of American enterprize, by taking a cargo of flour to New Orleans, about two thousand miles, gaining a little more than this expences, and a stock of knowledge. Two years ago he had increased his property to nine hundred dollars; purchased this place; a house, stable, &c. and two hundred and fifty acres of land (sixty-five of which are cleared and laid down to grass,) for three thousand five hundred dollars, of which he has already paid three thousand, and will pay the remaining five hundred next year. He is now building a good stable, and going to improve his house. His property is at present worth seven thousand dollars; having gained, or rather grown, five thousand five hundred dollars in two years, with prospects of future accumulation to his utmost wishes. Thus it is that people here grow wealthy without extraordinary exertion, and without anxiety.

.   .   .   .

August 1. Dagley's, twenty miles north of Shawnee Town [in Indiana]. After viewing several beautiful prairies, so beautiful with their surrounding woods as to seem

Morris Birkbeck, *Notes on a Journey in America from the Coast of Virginia to the Territory of Illinois* (London: James Ridgeway, 1818), pp. 50–51, 120–21.

like the creation of fancy, gardens of delight in a dreary wilderness; and after losing our horses and spending two days recovering them, we took a hunter as our guide, and proceeded across the Little Wabash, to explore the country between that river and the Skillet-fork.

Since we left the Fox [Indian] settlement . . . cultivation has been very scanty, many miles intervening between the little "clearings." This may therefore be truly called a new country.

These lonely settlers are poorly off;—their bread corn must be ground thirty miles off, requiring three days to carry to the mill, and bring back, the small horse-load of three bushels. Articles of family manufacture are very scanty, and what they purchase is of the meanest quality and excessively dear: yet they are friendly and willing to share their simple fare with you. . . . To struggle with privations has now become the habit of their lives, most of them having made several successive plunges into the wilderness; and they begin already to talk of selling their "improvements," and getting farther "back," on finding that emigrants of another description are thickening about them.

7.3:   Indian Removal (1825–1835)

If the pre-Civil War westward movement was a mixed experience for white settlers from the East and Europe, it was a complete disaster for the Native Americans who lived beyond the Appalachians. These peoples, divided into numerous tribes, or nations, occupied land and resources coveted by the white settlers. Between 1815 and 1860 they were largely evicted from their ancestral lands and pushed further west into unfamiliar regions by a concerted government policy of Indian "removal."

At first the removal policy was ad hoc and piecemeal, designed to accommodate whites pressing against a given Indian-occupied tract. After 1825 it became a systematic effort to herd all the eastern Indians beyond the Mississippi so that their vacated land might be carved into farms and towns for white settlers.

In the four items that follow we see the process from the point of view of white settlers, the federal government, and the Native Americans themselves.

Most white settlers considered the Indians a savage, bloodthirsty race. In the first item below, Timothy Flint endorses this view and describes the way settlers dealt with Indian attack. His is the classic picture of brave pioneers and "wild" Indians that for many years colored our history. Are his stories of Indian attacks false? How would you explain those attacks? What would have to be added to Flint's account to make it a rounded picture of Indian-white relations?

The second item, an 1832 petition to Congress by Florida settlers, suggests the material reason for Indian removal. What special factors might have influenced the petitioners' attitudes? What other sorts of material considerations would have influenced white expulsionists?

The federal government's removal plans are described in the third item, an 1825 statement by Secretary of War John C. Calhoun, later the preeminent champion of southern rights. Was Calhoun's program completely indifferent to the claims of justice or the needs of the so-called five civilized nations? Is he weeping crocodile tears for the Indians? Does the Secretary of War reveal cultural biases? If so, what were they?

The Indians themselves protested the removal policy. Especially eloquent and forceful were those of the so-called five civilized tribes, composed of the Choctaw, Chickasaw, Cherokee, Creeks, and Seminole, Indian nations that occupied choice lands in the Southeast. The Cherokees particularly had borrowed the best of white culture (and some of the worst as well) and combined it with their own. Possessing large herds of cattle, gristmills, sawmills, schools, a written language, and, alas, even slaves, they were able to put up a formidable legal struggle against the officials of Georgia and the federal government. The 1830 petition below was one step in their case against removal farther west.

Do the Indians make their case convincingly? President Andrew Jackson believed that the Indians occupied far too much land considering their numbers. Is this argument for the need for the Indians to surrender land to the whites valid?

The Indians Are Savages

TIMOTHY FLINT

In the immense extent of frontier, which I have visited, I have heard many an affecting tale of the horrible barbarities and murders of the Indians, precisely of a character with those, which used to be recorded in the early periods of New England history. I saw two children, the only members of a family—consisting of a father, mother, and a number of children—that were spared by the Indians. It was on the river Femme-Osage. A party of Sacs and Foxes, that had been burning and murdering in the vicinity, came upon the house, as the father was coming in from abroad.

Timothy Flint, *Recollections of the Last Ten Years Passed in Occasional Residences and Journeyings in the Valley of the Mississippi* (Boston: Cummings, Hilliard and Company, 1826), pp. 160–62.

They shot him, and he fled, wounded, a little distance, and fell. They then toma-hawked the wife, and mangled her body. She had been boiling the sap of the sugar-maple. The Indians threw two of the children into the boiling kettles. The younger of the two orphans that I saw, was but three years old. His sister two years older, drew him under the bed before they were seen by the Indians. It had, in the fashion of the country, a cotton counterpane that descended to the floor. The howling of these demons, the firing, the barking of the dogs, the shrieking of the children that became their victims, never drew from these poor things, that were trembling under the bed, a cry, or the smallest noise. The Indians thrust their knives through the bed, that nothing concealed there, might escape them, and went off, through fear of pur-suit, leaving these desolate beings unharmed.

You will see the countenances of the frontier people, as they relate numberless tragic occurrences of this sort, gradually kindling. There seems, between them and the savages, a deep-rooted enmity, like that between the seed of the woman and the serpent. They would be more than human, if retaliation were not sometimes the consequence. They tell you, with a certain expression of countenance, that in former days when they met an Indian in the woods, they were very apt to see him suffer under the falling-sickness. This dreadful state of things has now passed away, and I have seldom heard of late of a murder committed by the whites upon the Indians. Twenty years ago, the Indians and whites both considered, when casual rencounters took place in the woods, that it was a fair shot upon both sides. A volume would not contain the cases of these unrecorded murders.

The narrations of a frontier circle, as they draw round their evening fire, often turn upon the exploits of the old race of men, the heroes of the past days, who wore hunting shirts, and settled the country. Instances of undaunted heroism, of desperate daring, and seemingly of more than mortal endurance, are recorded of these people. In a boundless forest full of panthers and bears, and more dreadful Indians, with not a white within a hundred miles, a solitary adventurer penetrates the deepest wilder-ness, and begins to make the strokes of his axe resound among the trees. The Indi-ans find him out, ambush, and imprison him. A more acute and desperate warrior than themselves, they wish to adopt him, and add his strength to their tribe. He feigns contentment, uses the savage's insinuations, outruns him in the use of his own ways of management, but watches his opportunity, and when their suspicion is lulled, and they fall asleep, he springs upon them, kills his keepers, and bounds away into unknown forests, pursued by them and their dogs. He leaves them all at fault, subsists many days upon berries and roots, and finally arrives at his little clearing, and resumes his axe. In a little palisade, three or four resolute men stand a siege of hundreds of assailants, kill many of them, and mount calmly on the roof of their shelter, to pour water upon the fire, which burning arrows have kindled there, and achieve the work amidst a shower of balls. A thousand instances of that stern and unshrinking courage which had shaken hands with death, of that endurance which defied all the inventions of Indian torture, are recorded of these wonderful men. The dread of being roasted alive by the Indians, called into action all their hid-den energies and resources.

The Indian Removal Act of 1830

An Act to Provide for an Exchange of Lands with the Indians Residing in any of the States or Territories, and for their Removal West of the River Mississippi.

Be it enacted by the Senate and House of Representatives of the United States of America, in Congress assembled, That it shall and may be lawful for the President of the United States to cause so much of any territory belonging to the United States, west of the river Mississippi, not included in any state or organized territory, and to which the Indian title has been extinguished, as he may judge necessary, to be divided into a suitable number of districts, for the reception of such tribes or nations of Indians as may choose to exchange the lands where they now reside, and remove there; and to cause each of said districts to be so described by natural or artificial marks, as to be easily distinguished from every other.

Section II

And be it further enacted, That it shall and may be lawful for the President to exchange any or all of such districts, so to be laid off and described, with any tribe or nation of Indians now residing within the limits of any of the states or territories, and with which the United States have existing treaties, for the whole or any part or portion of the territory claimed and occupied by such tribe or nation, within the bounds of any one or more of the states or territories, where the land claimed and occupied by the Indians, is owned by the United States, or the United States are bound to the state within which it lies to extinguish the Indian claim thereto.

Section III

And be it further enacted, That in the making of any such exchange or exchanges, it shall and may be lawful for the President solemnly to assure the tribe or nation with which the exchange is made, that the United States will forever secure and guaranty to them, and their heirs or successors, the country so exchanged with them; and if they prefer it, that the United States will cause a patent or grant to be made and executed to them for the same: Provided always, That such lands shall revert to the United States, if the Indians become extinct, or abandon the same.

Section IV

And be it further enacted, That if, upon any of the lands now occupied by the Indians, and to be exchanged for, there should be such improvements as add value to the land claimed by any individual or individuals of such tribes or nations, it shall and may be lawful for the President to cause such value to be ascertained by appraisement or otherwise, and to cause such ascertained value to be paid to the person or persons rightfully claiming such improvements. And upon the payment of

Adapted from Anthony F.C. Wallace, *The Long Bitter Trail* (New York: Hill and Wang, 1993), pp. 125-8, Appendix B.

such valuation, the improvements so valued and paid for, shall pass to the United States, and possession shall not afterwards be permitted to any of the same tribe.

Section V

And be it further enacted, That upon the making of any such exchange as is contemplated by this act, it shall and may be lawful for the President to cause such aid and assistance to be furnished to the emigrants as may be necessary and proper to enable them to remove to, and settle in, the country for which they may have exchanged; and also, to give them such aid and assistance as may be necessary for their support and subsistence for the first year after their removal.

Section VI

And be it further enacted, That it shall and may be lawful for the President to cause such tribe or nation to be protected, at their new residence, against all interruption or disturbance from any other tribe or nation of Indians, or from any other person or persons whatever.

Section VII

And be it further enacted, That it shall and may be lawful for the President to have the same superintendence and care over any tribe or nation in the country to which they may remove, as contemplated by this act, that he is now authorized to have over them at their present places of residence: Provided, That nothing in this act contained shall be construed as authorizing or directing the violation of any existing treaty between the United States and any of the Indian tribes.

Section VIII

And be it further enacted, That for the purpose of giving effect to the provisions of this act, the sum of five hundred thousand dollars is hereby appropriated, to be paid out of any money in the treasury, not otherwise appropriated.

Approved, May 28, 1830.

Memorial to Congress by Inhabitants of the Territory

[Referred March 26, 1832]

To the Hon. the Senate & House of Representatives of the United States In Congress Assembled

The Memorial of the undersigned humbly shewith; that your memorialists Inhabitants Florida, are and have been for a long time greatly annoyed by the Semenole or Florida Indians; who are constantly wandering from their own Country and trespassing upon the property of the Whites: Their depredations upon our stock; are so frequent and ex-

Clarence E. Carter, ed., *The Territorial Papers of the United States* (Washington, DC: Government Printing Office, 1959), vol. 24, pp. 678–79.

tensive, that we cannot for a moment, feel any thing like Security, in relation to this description of our property & unless some measures are adopted by the Government to give us protection, we see no alternative left, but to abandon the settlements we have made at much expence & toil & retire to situation affording greater safety & less troublesome neighbours. We apprehend that unless the Indians are entirely removed from our Territory to some distant position, the evil in view, can not be effectfully remedied. The wildness & unsettled character of the frontier, (being in extent more than three hundred miles) between the whites and Indians, afford much ample facility for them to indulge their national disposition to wander, that it will be next to impossible to confine them within their own Territorial limits:—But were it possible to restrain & keep them at home, there is still to be found a most weighty objection to their continuing to occupy, (as they now do) a tract of Country, within the geographical boundaries, of our Territory: in the fact, that absconding Slaves, find ready security among the Indians & such aid as is amply sufficient, to enable them successfully to alude the best efforts of their masters to recover them. It is believed that their are at this time, fifty or more runaway negroes in the Indian nation, who have taken refuge their since the treaty of 1823; to whom the Indians give protection, (in the way of secrecy at least) notwithstanding they are in that treaty obligated by a solemn pledge to apprehend & surrender all Slaves who may seek shelter in their Country. So long as a state of things thus dangerous to the interests of the inhabitants of Florida continues she cannot hope for prosperity or improvement: It cannot be expected that people of property will settle in a Country where there is so little security in relation to their property. We humbly pray therefore that your honourable body will take the matter into consideration and award to us such relief as is in your opinion necessary & proper.

Justification for "Removal"

JOHN C. CALHOUN

Of the four southern tribes, two of them (the Cherokees and Choctaws) have already allotted to them a tract of country west of the Mississippi. That which has been allotted to the latter is believed to be sufficiently ample for the whole nation, should they emigrate; and if an arrangement, which is believed not to be impracticable, could be made between them and the Chickasaws, who are their neighbors, and of similar habits and dispositions, it would be sufficient for the accommodation of both. A sufficient country should be reserved to the west of the Cherokees on the Arkansas, as a means of exchange with those who remain on the east. To the Creeks might be allotted a country between the Arkansas and the Canadian river, which limits the northern boundary of the Choctaw possessions in that quarter. There is now pending with the Creeks a negotiation, under the appropriation of the last session, with a prospect that the portion of that nation which resides within the limits of Georgia may be induced, with the consent of the nation, to cede the country which they now occupy for a portion of the one which it is proposed to allot for the Creek nation on the west of the Mississippi. Should the treaty prove successful, its stipulations will provide for the means of carrying it into effect, which will render any additional provision, at present, unnecessary. It will be proper to open new communications with the Cherokees, Choctaws, and Chickasaws, for the purpose of explaining to them the views of the Government, and inducing them to remove beyond the Mississippi, on the principles and conditions which may be proposed to the other tribes. It is known that there are many individuals of each of the tribes who are desirous of settling west of the Mississippi, and, should it be thought advisable, there can be no doubt that (if, by an adequate appropriation, the means were afforded the Government of bearing their expense) they would emigrate. Should it be thought that the encouragement of such emigration is desirable, the sum of $40,000, at least, would be required to be appropriated for this object, to be applied under the discretion of the President of the United States. The several sums which have been recommended to be appropriated, if the proposed arrangement should be adopted, amount to $95,000. The appropriation may be made either general or specific, as may be considered most advisable.

I cannot, however, conclude without remarking, that no arrangement ought to be made which does not regard the interest of the Indians as well as our own; and that, to protect the interest of the former, decisive measures ought to be adopted to prevent the hostility which must almost necessarily take place, if left to themselves, among tribes hastily brought together, of discordant character, and many of which are actuated by feelings far from being friendly towards each other. But the preservation of peace between them will not alone be sufficient to render their condition as eligible in their new situation as it is in their present. Almost all of the tribes proposed to be affected by the arrangement are more or less advanced in the arts of civilized life, and there is scarcely one of them which has not the establishments of schools in the nation, affording, at once, the means of moral, religious, and intellectual improvement. These schools have been established, for the most part, by religious societies, with the countenance and aid of the Government; and, on every principle of humanity, the continuance of similar advantages of education ought to be extended to them in their new residence. There is another point which appears to be indispensable to be guarded, in order to render the condition of this race less afflicting. One of the greatest evils to which they are subject is that incessant pressure of our population, which forces them from seat to seat, without allowing time for that moral and intellectual improvement, for which they appear to be naturally eminently susceptible. To guard against this evil, so fatal to the race, there ought to be the strongest and the most solemn assurance that the country given them should be theirs, as a permanent home for themselves and their posterity, without being disturbed by the encroachments of our citizens. To such assurance, if there should be added a system, by which the Government, without destroying their independence, would gradually unite the several tribes under a simple but enlightened system of government and laws formed on the principles of our own, and to which, as their own people would partake in it, they would, under the influence of the contemplated improvement, at no distant day, become prepared, the arrangements which have been proposed would prove to the Indians and their posterity a permanent blessing. It is believed that, if they could be assured that peace and friendship would be maintained among the several tribes; that the advantages of education, which they now enjoy, would be extended to them; that they should have a permanent and solemn guaranty for their possessions, and receive the countenance and aid of the Government for the gradual extension of its privileges to them, there would be among all the tribes a disposition to accord with the views of the Government. There are now, in most of the tribes, well educated, sober, and reflecting individuals, who are afflicted at the present condition of the Indians, and despondent at their future prospects. Under the operation of existing causes, they behold the certain degradation, misery, and even the final annihilation of their race, and, no doubt, would gladly embrace any arrangement which would promise to elevate them in the scale of civilization, and arrest the destruction which now awaits them. It is conceived that one of the most cheap, certain, and desirable modes of effecting the object in view, would be for Congress to establish fixed principles, such as have been suggested, as the basis of the proposed arrangement; and to authorize the President to convene, at some suitable point, all of the well-informed, intelligent, and influential individuals of the tribes to be affected by it, in order to explain to them the views of the Government, and to pledge the faith of the nation to the arrangements that might be adopted. Should such principles be established by Congress, and the President be vested with suitable authority to convene the individuals as proposed, and suitable provision be made to meet the expense, great confidence is felt that a basis of a system might be laid, which, in a few years, would entirely effect the object in view, to the mutual benefit of the Government and the Indians; and which, in its operations, would effectually arrest the calamitous course of events to which they must be subject, without a radical change in the present system. Should it be thought advisable to call such a convention, as one of the means of effecting the object in view, an additional appropriation of $30,000 will be required; making, in the whole, $125,000 to be appropriated.

All of which is respectfully submitted.

J. C. Calhoun

The Indians Protest Against Removal

CHEROKEE PETITIONERS

We are aware that some persons suppose it will be for our advantage to remove beyond the Mississippi. We think otherwise. Our people universally think otherwise. Thinking that it would be fatal to their interests, they have almost to a man sent their memorial to Congress, deprecating the necessity of a removal. This question was distinctly before their minds when they signed their memorial. Not an adult person can be found, who has not an opinion on the subject; and if the people were

Ebenezer C. Tracy, *Memoir of the Life of Jeremiah Evarts* (Boston: Crocker and Brewster, 1845), pp. 149–58.

to understand distinctly, that they could be protected against the laws of the neighboring States, there is probably not an adult person in the nation, who would think it best to remove; though possibly a few might emigrate individually. There are doubtless many who would flee to an unknown country, however beset with dangers, privations and sufferings, rather than be sentenced to spend six years in a Georgia prison for advising one of their neighbors not to betray his country. And there are others who could not think of living as outlaws in their native land, exposed to numberless vexations, and excluded from being parties or witnesses in a court of justice. It is incredible that Georgia should ever have enacted the oppressive laws to which reference is here made, unless she had supposed that something extremely terrific in its characters was necessary, in order to make the Cherokees willing to remove. We are not willing to remove; and if we could be brought to this extremity, it would be, not by argument; not because our judgment was satisfied; not because our condition will be improved—but only because we cannot endure to be deprived of our national and individual rights, and subjected to a process of intolerable oppression.

We wish to remain on the land of our fathers. We have a perfect and original right to claim this, without interruption or molestation. The treaties with us, and laws of the United States made in pursuance of treaties, guaranty our residence, and our privileges, and secure us against intruders. Our only request is, that these treaties may be fulfilled, and these laws executed.

But if we are compelled to leave our country, we see nothing but ruin before us. The country west of the Arkansas territory is unknown to us. From what we can learn of it, we have no prepossessions in its favor. All the inviting parts of it, as we believe, are preoccupied by various Indian nations, to which it has been assigned. They would regard us as intruders, and look upon us with an evil eye. The far greater part of that region is, beyond all controversy, badly supplied with wood and water; and no Indian tribe can live as agriculturists without these articles. All our neighbors, in case of our removal, though crowded into our near vicinity, would speak a language totally different from ours, and practice different customs. The original possessors of that region are now wandering savages, lurking for prey in the neighborhood. They have always been at war, and would be easily tempted to turn their arms against peaceful emigrants. Were the country to which we are urged much better than it is represented to be, and were it free from the objections which we have made to it, still it is not the land of our birth, nor of our affections. It contains neither the scenes of our childhood, nor the graves of our fathers.

❖ 8 ❖

Capital Versus Labor

Western growth did not devitalize New England and the middle Atlantic states as many people from these sections feared it would. Instead, in the decades before the Civil War, the Northeast experienced a burst of economic growth and change that soon made it the most dynamic and prosperous part of the country, the pioneer of an industrial regime that would eventually penetrate every corner of the nation.

The most significant economic advance of these years was the replacement of the small handicraft shop by the system of factories employing masses of wage workers tending power-driven machines under one roof. The first American factories in the modern sense were spinning mills in southern New England that produced cotton thread and yarn. The machines were run by water power and were based on British models brought to America by immigrants who carried the plans in their heads. These mills usually employed whole families, including children, much as did the contemporary farm.

In 1815 the Boston Manufacturing Company, headed by Francis Cabot Lowell, began to operate at Waltham, Massachusetts, using the power generated by the Charles River. Employing mostly young, unmarried women, the Waltham mills produced finished cloth and sold it at good prices to a receptive market. So profitable was the enterprise that the promoters soon established factories at other power sites. The most elaborate development was the multimill factory complex and residential town located on the Merrimack River and named after Francis Lowell. The Lowell community soon became the emblem of the new industrial revolution, and visitors in droves came to the neat, bustling little city to observe and to marvel at its enterprise and its social harmony.

The New England textile industry was only one sector of a broad front of economic change. The half-century following 1810 ushered in a transportation revolution based on turnpikes, canals, steamboats, and railroads that broke down isolation and knit the nation into a single economic entity. It witnessed the beginnings of mechanization in grain-growing on the prairies and the arrival of the telegraph, presaging a communications revolution. Before long the nation was transformed from a collection of self-sufficient communities to a market economy where goods moved freely and cheaply hundreds of miles between consumers and producers. Presiding over the process was a new class of entrepreneurs who, through their wealth and vigor, expanded the influence of capitalist institutions and values in a nation already committed to the pursuit of riches and material abundance.

The new economic surge clearly increased overall wealth. It also magnified inequality and created social strains. The documents below focus on the great economic changes taking place in the North as the nation advanced through the half-century preceding the Civil War. The observers include both defenders of the new business system and those who opposed it. Their views open anew the issue of business values versus human values that is still alive today.

8.1: The Lowell System (1842, 1845, 1846)

The directors of the Boston Manufacturing Company tapped an underused pool of labor for their new mills: unmarried rural Yankee women. These young women came to Lowell, Chicopee, Lawrence, Holyoke, and the other textile mill towns to work for a few years while accumulating savings to help their families or to provide themselves with a marriage dowry. To reassure parents and entice "operatives," the mill owners housed the young women in clean, chaperoned boarding houses and provided them with schools, lecture halls, libraries, churches, and even, in the case of Lowell, a subsidy to publish a newspaper (The Lowell Offering).

The selections below highlight two opposing views of the labor system in the Lowell-type mills. The first, by Charles Dickens, is highly favorable. Dickens was already a famous writer when he visited America in 1842, and wherever he went he was treated as a celebrity. Americans sought to show him their best, but the English novelist was not to be deceived. When he returned home, he wrote a highly critical account of America and a scathing novel set in the contemporary United States.

What audience is Dickens writing for in this piece from his American Notes? *His tone suggests that his readers may be skeptical of what he reports about the "Lowell girls." Why might he think that? What frame of reference regarding textile mills would his audience already have? Was Dickens apt to be an objective observer of the Lowell mill workers? Do his views of America make his conclusions more or less believable? Do you know whether in his writings generally Dickens was sympathetic to the poor and exploited? How might his views of his own country's working class affect your evaluation of his conclusions?*

The second, more negative view comes from a group of brief pieces written by "mill girls" themselves. They date from 1845–1846, a few years after Dickens's visit to America. The first four items are by young women who worked in the mills in Exeter, New Hampshire; the last two are from Lowell operatives.

What are the complaints of the young women? Are they entirely economic? What other criticisms of their treatment do they make? To what does the mention of the Lowell girls' rebellion refer? How do you square Dickens's views with those in these documents? Note the difference in dates between Dickens's account and the attacks of the young women. Could the passage of time have accounted for the change?

A Positive View of the Lowell Girls

CHARLES DICKENS

These girls, as I have said, were all well dressed: and that phrase necessarily includes extreme cleanliness. They had serviceable bonnets, good warm cloaks, and shawls; and were not above clogs and patterns. Moreover, there were places in the mill in which they could deposit these things without injury; and there were conveniences for washing. They were healthy in appearance, many of them remarkably so, and had the manners and deportment of young women: not of degraded brutes of burden. If I had seen in one of those mills (but I did not, though I looked for something of this kind with a sharp eye), the most lisping, mincing, affected, and ridiculous young creature that my imagination could suggest. I should have thought of the careless, moping, slatternly, degraded, dull reverse (I *have* seen that), and should have been still well pleased to look upon her.

The rooms in which they worked, were as well ordered as themselves. In the windows of some, there were green plants, which were trained to shade the glass; in all, there was as much fresh air, cleanliness, and comfort, as the nature of the occupation would possibly admit of. Out of so large a number of females, many of whom were only then just verging upon womanhood, it may be reasonably supposed that some were delicate and fragile in appearance: no doubt there were. But I solemnly declare, that from all the crowd I saw in the different factories that day, I cannot recall or separate one young face that gave me a painful impression; nor one young

Charles Dickens, *American Notes and Pic-Nic Papers* (Philadelphia: T. B. Paterson and Brothers, 1842), pp. 40–41.

girl whom, assuming it to be matter of necessity that she should gain her daily bread by the labour of her hands, I would have removed from those works if I had had the power.

.   .   .   .

I am now going to state three facts, which will startle a large class of readers on this side of the Atlantic, very much.

Firstly, there is a joint-stock piano in a great many of the boarding-houses. Secondly, nearly all these young ladies subscribe to circulating libraries. Thirdly, they have got up among themselves a periodical called THE LOWELL OFFERING, "A repository of original articles, written exclusively by females actively employed in the mills,"—which is duly printed, published, and sold; and whereof I brought away from Lowell four hundred good solid pages, which I have read from beginning to end.

The large class of readers, startled by these facts, will exclaim, with one voice, "How very preposterous!" On my deferentially inquiring why, they will answer, "These things are above their station." In reply to that objection, I would beg to ask what their station is.

It is their station to work. And they *do* work. They labour in these mills, upon an average, twelve hours a day, which is unquestionably work, and pretty tight work too. Perhaps it is above their station to indulge in such amusements, on any terms. Are we quite sure that we in England have not formed our ideas of the "station" of working people, from accustoming ourselves to the contemplation of that class as they are, and not as they might be? I think that if we examine our own feelings, we shall find that the pianos, and the circulating libraries, and even THE LOWELL OFFERING, startle us by their novelty, and not by their bearing upon any abstract question of right or wrong.

The "Factory Girls" Tell Their Own Story[1]

The Operatives' Life

The numerous class of females who are operatives in mills, are required to devote *fifteen twenty-fourths* of every working day to the laborious task incumbent upon them, being thirteen hours of incessant toil, and two hours devoted to meals &c. Is not this fact a painful one? Is it not degrading to the age in which we live? It indicates that barbarism still exists among us, and it would be well for some people to take moral and humane lessons from savage life even. It is not a matter of marvel, that the Lowell girls should rebel against such treatment and petition the legislature of Massachusetts to establish a ten hour system: neither is it surprising that the federal *wise-acres,* who constituted that body, considered it inexpedient to legislate upon the subject—*they* do not legislate for the protection of the *poor,* but for the

Philip Foner, ed., *The Factory Girls* (Urbana: The University of Illinois Press, 1977), pp. 79–85. © 1977 by The University of Illinois Press.
[1]Footnotes deleted.

protection of the *rich;* the *gold* that lies within their grasp benumbs their sensibilities; and prevents the administration of that *justice* which humanity demands. We
begin to doubt the utility or justice of any legislation for the protection of capital;
indeed, if *barbarism* is to be the result of *protection,* we trust that the enlightened
and philanthropic inhabitants of this country will cheerfully dispense with such *aid,*
and, (as experience teaches it,) consider that legislation for the benefit of the *few,* is
inimical to the best interests of the *whole.*

Think of girls being obliged to labor *thirteen* hours each working day, for a net
compensation of *two cents per hour,* which is above the average net wages, being
$1.56 per week. Two cents per hour for severe labor! Is not such a lesson enough to
make an American curse the hour, when in an evil mood our lawmakers first
granted a charter to enable the *few* to wield the wealth and power of *hundreds?* Is it
not necessary to the maintenance of our rights, that some change be speedily effected in those laws by which our corporations are governed? We trust the friends
of *equal rights,* will petition our legislature to make such a revision of these laws, as
will cause the more general distribution of those benefits which were designed for
all. If such a course is taken, let the tyrants tremble.

A Factory Girl's Album

Exeter, N.H., June 20, 1846

Independence

Dialogue of a Lowell girl with the overseer of a factory:—"Well, Mr. Buck, I am
informed that you wish to cut down my wages?" "Yes, such is my determination."
"Do you suppose that I would go into that room to work again, at lower price than I
received before?" "Why, it's no more than fair and reasonable, considering the hard
times." "Well, all I have to say is, that before I'll do it, I'll see you in Tophet, pump-
ing thunder at three cents a clap!" It is needless to say that she was invited to resume her duties.

A Factory Girl's Album

Exeter, N.H., September 19, 1846

Beauties of Factory Life

Hundreds of operatives who work in our mills, are scarcely paid sufficient to board
themselves, and are obliged to dress poorly, or, run in debt for their clothing. The
consequence is, they become discouraged—lose confidence in themselves, and
then, regardless of consequences, abandon their virtue to obtain favors. A goodly
proportion of those in large cities, who inhabit "dens of shame," are first initiated
into this awful vice in manufacturing places. Soon after, most of them commence
the downward road to destruction—they become known, and are compelled to leave
their work in the mills and emigrate to large cities. We repeat what we have often
done—girls leave not your homes in the country. It will be better for you to stay at
home on your fathers farms than to run the risk of being ruined in a manufacturing
village—Man. Pal.

How painfully true is the above. Many young, amiable and virtuous girls are yearly initiated into a life of vice and shame, through the baneful influences of the present corrupt factory system in New England. And when we hear of the depraved condition of those whom we had formerly known as the fairest of their sex, but who have since gone astray through dire necessity, or been duped by the arts of the wily men who frequent manufacturing villages, we are led to exclaim in the language of [William] Cowper,

> *My ear is pained,*
> *My soul is sick with every day's report*
> *Of wrong and outrage with which earth is filled.*
> *There is no flesh for man; the natural bond*
> *of brotherhood is severed as the flax,*
> *That falls asunder at the touch of fire.*

Factory Girl's Album

Exeter, N.H., October 31, 1846

Letter from a Local Factory Girl

I write to let the public know the cruel story of a sister operative of mine in Lowell. She is a young woman who had been employed in one of the factories of that city and left it, for the purpose of removing to another of the mills in which she thought she could labor with much better satisfaction to herself. But on application for work at that mill, she was denied employment, because the overseer (*driver* in the Southern term) of the mill she had left, had denounced her to the overseers (or drivers) of every mill in the place, as a girl not worthy to be employed. She applied to each mill in the city for employment, but was repulsed at all in succession for the same reason that employment was refused her at the first one. She sued the driver in a civil suit for slander, but was defeated in her suit for damages because the mill owners had established amongst themselves a rule, which custom had made law, making the ill-report of the overseer of one mill imperative cause of rejection by all the mills of the place;—for which ill-report as reason is asked of the overseer, and it stands by itself unexplained, final and imperative.

The issue of this case proves the existence of a rule and combination among the Lowell corporation that prevents any person upon leaving a corporation from obtaining work in any other corporation, if, *in the opinion of the overseer* of the corporation where the person formerly worked, he or she is not a suitable person to be employed. And it is of no consequence what induces that opinion—bad temper, immoral conduct, or nothing, on the part of the girl, or private pique, the gratification of an envious favorite, revenge for disappointed lechery, or any other cause, no matter how trivial or how wicked, on the part of the overseer—it may and does result in hunting and driving a girl out of the city if the overseer chooses to exercise his power over her density and her reputation.

Now I defy the most vehement ranters against Southern slavery to produce a section of the "black code" of any State, which makes more of a slave in the Southern plantation driver the female negro who has a master and an owner to protect her, than under the rule above established by the mill owners of Lowell, and as "priviledged communications" *made supreme over the common law of the State,* are the thousands of unprotected white females of Lowell slaves to the overseers of a dozen or two of cotton mills, who hold not only the bread, but the characters of those girls, in the palms of their hands, and can do with them as any passion may dictate or any caprice suggest, with perfect impunity of the law, and safety from all consequences to themselves.

When chartered and specially protected monopolies obtain such power and exercise such outrageous tyranny over the *women* of the U. States, making their laws of *custom* and *"privilege"* paramount to the common law of the land, placing thousands of virtuous and noble females under worse than Turkish subjection to the male tyrants of the cotton mills, who associated millions pension United States Senators and buy up legislators "like cattle in the market," it is indeed high time for the men of the United States, if there are any left this side of the Rio Grande, to seriously inquire whether these things are tending, and whether there is no remedy for such a slavish condition of *American white women?*

A Factory Girl in the Nashua Corporation

Nashua (N.H.) Gazette, October 1, 1846

Are the Operatives Well Off?

Mr. Editor:

We are told by gentlemen both in this country and abroad that the Lowell factory operatives are exceedingly well off. Good wages, sure pay, not very hard work, comfortable food and lodgings, and such unparalleled opportunities for intellectual cultivation, (why, they even publish a Magazine there!!) what more can one desire? Really gentlemen! would you not reckon your wives and sisters fortunate if they could by any possibility be elevated into the situation of operatives? When in the tender transports of first love, you paint for the fairest and fondest of mortal maidens a whole life of uninterrupted joy, do you hope for her as the supremest felicity, the lot of a factory girl? The operatives are well enough off!—Indeed! Do you receive them in your parlors, are they admitted to visit your families, do you raise your hats to them in the street, in a word, are they your *equals?*

Oliva

Lowell, Sept. 16, 1845

The Voice of the Sufferers

It is a subject of comment and general complaint, among the operatives, that while they tend three or four looms, where they used to tend but two, making nearly twice the number of yards of cloth, the pay is not increased to them, while the increase, to the owners is very great. Is this just? Twenty-five cents per week for each week, additional pay, would not increase the cost of the cloth, one mill a yard; no, not the half of a mill.

Now while I am penning this paragraph, a young lady enters my room with "Oh dear! Jane, I am sick and what shall I do? I have worked for three years, and never gave out, before. I stuck to my work, until I fainted at my loom. The Doctor says I must quit work and run about and amuse myself; but I have nowhere to go, and do not know what to do with myself." I have given the language, as it struck my ear; the conversation going on behind me. It is but the feelings of a thousand homeless, suffering females, this moment chanting "the Voice of Industry in this wilderness of sin."

One of the Vast Army of Sufferers

Voice of Industry, March 13, 1846

The "Beauties of Factory Life"

Mr. Editor:

Those who write so effusively about the "Beauties of Factory Life," tell us that we are indeed happy creatures, and how truly grateful and humbly submissive we should be. Can it be that any of us are so stupified as not to realize the exalted station and truly delightful influences which we enjoy? If so, let them take a glance at pages 195 and 196 of Rev. H. Miles' book, and they will surely awake to gratitude and be content. Pianos, teachers of music, evening schools, lectures, libraries and all these sorts of advantages are, says he, enjoyed by the operatives. (Query—when do they find time for all or any of these? When exhausted nature demands repose?) Very pretty picture that to write about; but we who work in the factory know the sober reality to be quite another thing altogether.

After all, it is easier to write a book than it is to *do* right. It is easier to smooth over and plaster up a deep festering rotten system, which is sapping the life-blood of our nation, widening and deepening the yawning gulf which will ere long swallow up the laboring classes in dependent servitude and serfdom, like that of Europe, than it is to probe to the very bottom of this death-spreading monster.

Juliana

Voice of Industry, June 12, 1846

8.2: An Economist Defends Capitalism (1835)

From Alexander Hamilton's day until our own, many Americans have believed economic growth to be the only valid formula for national affluence. Economic progress, it is argued, benefits not only the capitalists but also their employees. To hinder it in any way is to assure poverty for all.

The following selection is from a book by Philadelphian Henry C. Carey, a respected writer on economic subjects of the pre-Civil War era. Carey later became a supporter of the protective tariff, but at this point he still believed in unqualified free trade and laissez-faire.

What is the gist of Carey's argument? Is it convincing? Has it been widely applied in the United States? During what periods in particular has the formula enjoyed wide support?

Worker Benefit from High Profits

HENRY C. CAREY

Wages and profits have been represented by many political economists as natural antagonists, the Ormuzd and Ahriman[1] of political economy, one of which could rise only at the expense of the other. Such has been the belief of the great mass of the people who receive wages, which belief has given rise to trades' unions, so numerous in England, and obtaining in the United States; as well as to the cry of *the poor against the rich*. A large portion of those who pay, as well as those who receive wages, believe that the rate is altogether arbitrary, and that changes may be made at will. To this belief we are indebted for the numerous "strikes," or "turns out" we have seen, the only effect of which has been loss to both employers and workmen. Had the journeymen tailors of London understood the laws by which the distribution of the proceeds between the workman and the capitalist is regulated, they would have saved themselves and their employers the enormous loss that has arisen out of their recent combination, and would have retained their situations instead of seeing themselves pushed from their stools by the influx of Germans, who seized gladly upon the places vacated by their English fellow workmen. Believing, as they do, that their wages are depressed for the benefit of their employers, they believe also that those employers are bound to give them a portion of their profits in the advance of wages, when, in fact, the employers are also sufferers by the same causes which produce the depression, and are unable to advance them, however willing they may be. If the real causes of the depression were understood, instead of combining against their employers, they would unite with them to free their country from those restrictions and interferences which produce the effect of which they complain, and would thus secure permanent advantage, instead of a temporary advance of wages, which is all that can be hoped for from combination, even if successful, which is rarely the case. Fortunately, in the United States there have been fewer interferences, and there is therefore less to alter, than in any other country; and if the workmen and labourers could be made to understand the subject, they would see that the division between themselves and the capitalist, or the rate of wages, is regulated by a law immutable as are those which govern the motion of the Heavenly bodies; that attempts at legislative interference can produce only disadvantageous effects; and, that the only mode of increasing wages is by rendering labour more productive, which can only be accomplished by allowing every man to

Henry C. Carey, *Essay on the Rate of Wages with an Examination of the Causes of the Differences in the Condition of the Labouring Population throughout the World* (Philadelphia: Carey, Lea, and Blanchard, 1835), pp. 15–18.

[1]That is, the A to Z of political economy—ED.

employ his capital and talent in the way which he deems most advantageous to himself. They would see that all attempts on the part of the capitalist, to reduce wages below the natural rate, as well as all on their part to raise it above that rate, must fail, as any such reduction must be attended with an unusual rate of profit to the employer, which must, in its turn, beget competition among the possessors of capital, and raise the rate of wages; while such elevation in any employment must reduce the rate of profit so far as to drive capital therefrom, and reduce wages again to the proper standard.

They should see in the fact that the great majority of the master workmen have risen by their own exertions to the situations they at present occupy, abundant evidence that nothing is wanting to them but industry and economy. They should desire nothing but freedom of action for themselves, and that security both of person and property which prompts the capitalist to investment; and so far should they be from entertaining feelings of jealousy towards those who, by industry and economy, succeed in making themselves independent, that they should see with pleasure the increase of capital, certain that such increase must produce new demands for their labour, accompanied by increased comfort and enjoyment for them. With such a system the population of this country might increase still more rapidly than it has done; the influx of people from abroad might be triple or quadruple what it has been, and each successive year find the comforts of the labouring population in a regular course of increase, as the same causes which drive the labourers of Europe here, to seek that employment and support denied them at home, impel the capitalist to seek here a market for his capital, at the higher rate of interest which our system enables us to pay him with profit to ourselves.

8.3: The Workingmen's Party Indicts Capitalism (1840)

It is an open question among scholars whether a majority of wage earners accepted the entrepreneurial spirit of the pre–Civil War age. We do know that many voted for the Whigs, clearly the party that best exemplified that spirit. But it is also clear that there was a strong insurgent voice among the men and women who toiled in the shops and factories of the era.

Below is an eloquent dissent from the position that Henry C. Carey represents. It is from an 1841 address of the Workingmen's Party of Charlestown, Massachusetts to "their brethren" throughout the state and nation.

The "Workies" (as they were called) claim special consideration from the community at large. On what bases? It is often said that American working people did not feel class resentment very strongly. Does this document support that view? The authors of this statement suggest that the condition of the laboring classes in America was deteriorating at this time. Was it? Were times good in 1840? How representative of labor attitudes is this document do you suppose? How would you estimate how prevalent such views were among wage workers?

Workers Are Exploited and Oppressed

THE WORKINGMEN'S PARTY OF CHARLESTOWN, MASSACHUSETTS

BRETHREN:—The time seems to have arrived, when we, the real workingmen of the country, should pause, and survey our condition; ascertain our actual state, what are our rights, and the means of securing their full enjoyment.

We are in this country, as in all others, the great majority of the population. We are the real producers. By our toil and sweat, our skill and industry, is produced all the wealth of the community. We have felled the primeval forests of this western world, converted them into fruitful fields, and planted the rose in the wilderness. We have erected these cities and villages which smile where lately was the Indian's wigwam, or the lair of the wild beast. We have called into existence American manufacturers, and been the instruments by which Commerce has amassed her treasures; our labor has digged the canals, and constructed the railways, which are intersecting the country in all directions, and opening its resources. We have built and manned the ships which navigate every ocean, and furnished the houses of the rich with all their comforts and luxuries. Our labor has done it all. And yet what is our condition? We toil on from morning to night, from one year's end to another, increasing our exertions with each year, and with each day, and still we are the poor and dependent. Here, as everywhere else, they, who pocket the proceeds of our labor, look upon us as the lower class, and term us the mob. We are but laborers, operatives, *vulgar* workingmen. We are poor. Our wages barely suffice to supply us the necessaries of life. We rarely have either leisure or opportunity to cultivate our minds, or to acquire that general knowledge of men and things, which no human being should grow up without. We are doomed by our position to grow up ignorant, and often in total neglect of all our nobler endowments. Our rights and interests attract no general attention. Legislators have no leisure to attend to our wants. And politicians have no further concern with us, than to wheedle us out of our votes by fair speeches and vague promises. The great concern is to take care of the rich and prosperous, the educated and powerful—of those who fill the high places of society, ride in carriages, sit on cushioned seats, and feast their dainty palates on luxuries culled from every clime. The wants of these are urgent. *Their* rights, privileges, and interests will brook no delay. But we, we, who bear all the burdens of society, pay all the revenues of Government, and the incomes of the rich, why we may go our way till a more convenient season.

"Address of the Workingmen's Party of Charlestown, Massachusetts to Their Brethren throughout the Commonwealth and the Union, 1840," *Boston Quarterly Review*, vol. 4 (January 1841), pp. 119–23.

Now, Brethren, against this state of things, we enter a loud, an indignant protest. Our pockets may be empty, our faces may be sunburnt, and our hands may be hard; but we are men, with the souls of men, and the rights of men. There is a spirit within us, that assures us we were not born to be slaves; that we were not made merely to toil and sweat, to endure hunger, and cold, and nakedness, and death, that the few might grow fat on our labors and sufferings, and then turn round and kick us. We feel that we were made for something better, and that we have a right to aspire to something higher. An apostle has said, "If any man will not work, neither shall he eat." And this we believe should apply to one man as well as to another. Why, if we must bear all the burthens of society, shall we not in common justice enjoy all its blessings?

Brethren, we have reflected on our condition, and we have come to the conclusion, that it is not the true condition of men. We are made of the same blood with those who work us as they do their horses and oxen, and who value us only for the profit they can derive from our labors. As pure blood courses in our veins as in theirs; as generous, as noble emotions swell our bosoms, and we have by nature capacities, to say the least, every way equal to theirs. Why then are they regarded as the better sort? Why then do they fatten on our labors? Why then are they rich and we poor? Why shall not our condition be as good as theirs? Why shall they call themselves our masters, and work us for their profit? . . .

How stands the case with us? We labor more hours and with more intensity than we did formerly. We are aided by the discoveries of science and the introduction of machinery which gives to our labor a thousand fold additional power of production; and yet our condition relatively to the capitalist does by no means become better. There is scarcely a country in Europe where, in proportion to the labor they perform, the laboring classes are worse off than they are here. If we worked no more hours in a day, no more days in a week, and with no more intensity, than do the Italian peasants, we should find ourselves in a condition scarcely superior to theirs. We receive only about the same proportion of the proceeds of our labor.

Moreover everything is tending to reduce the workingmen of this country to the condition they are sunk to in the old world. And what is that condition? In England, Scotland, and Wales, fourteen millions of the population, it is said, are obliged to subsist on an annual income of about ninety dollars a year and under. Five millions of these subsist on an annual income of less than twenty-five dollars each. In some counties in England, prior to the new poor laws, the paupers amounted to 63 per cent on the whole population, and in Liverpool every third individual was in indigence. Of Ireland, we need say nothing more than that one third of the whole population experience a deficiency of even third rate potatoes for thirty weeks out of fifty-two. In France, out of a population of about thirty-two millions, nearly thirty-one millions receive an annual income of under seventy-five dollars each; seven millions five hundred thousand, under twenty-five dollars; seven millions five hundred thousand, about eighteen dollars each. The expense of living is higher in England than in this country, and probably about one fourth less in France. But what must be the condition of the laboring classes even in France, where it is better than in England, and perhaps as good as in any country in Europe with the exception of Belgium?

Now, what saves us from a similar condition? We are saved from a similar condition mainly by the paucity of our numbers, and the superior freedom of our industry, which creates a greater competition among capitalists, and therefore a greater demand for laborers. But this competition is less among manufacturers than it was. The principal manufacturers having adopted in regard to labor nearly uniform prices, rarely bid upon one another. The multiplication of large corporations is rapidly changing the whole character of our laboring population, by bringing them under the control of corporate bodies. These corporations check individual enterprise, lessen competition between individual capitalists, bind the capitalists together in close affinity of interest, and enable them to exert a sovereign control over the prices of labor. Let these corporations continue to increase for a few years longer, and they will be able to reduce our wages to the minimum of human subsistence. There will grow up around them a population bearing but little resemblance to that which won our political independence. It will be enfeebled in mind and body, and without either the mental or physical energy to shift its employment, or to make a firm stand for the amelioration of its condition.

Hitherto the great mass of our laboring population has been bred in the agricultural districts, and consequently could easily shift from the city or the factory village to the farm. But this will not continue to be the case for another generation. Nor is this all. Lands are monopolized; the whole earth is foreclosed. However well disposed the laborer might be to cultivate the soil, he has not the means of becoming its owner. He has no spot on which to erect him a cabin, or on which he may raise a few potatoes to feed his wife and little ones; for the broad hands of the few cover it all over.

Nor can we stop here. It would seem that the more we produced the better should be our condition. But this is not the fact except for short seasons. We suffer from over-production. To-day the supply is small, and the demand is brisk, we find employment and receive tolerable wages. But a hundred capitalists have rushed simultaneously into the work of producing; all hands are employed; forthwith the demand is supplied; the market is glutted; sales are diminished; and the diminished sales return upon us in the shape of a reduction of wages. To make up for this reduction of wages, we must labor more hours, or with greater intensity, and increase the amount of our production; and this increased amount of production, returns upon us again in the shape of a still farther reduction of our wages; and thus on, till they are reduced to the lowest point compatible with our existence.

Brethren, put these things together, and tell us, if the natural tendency in this country is not to reduce us, and that at no distant day, to the miserable condition of the laboring classes in the old world? We stand on the declivity; we have already begun to descend! What is to save us?

Brethren, this is a question of fearful import to us and our children. It is a question we must put to ourselves in sober earnest. It is a question we must put *now,* for a little more delay and it will be TOO LATE. Is it not already too late? God forbid! We will not believe it too late; but we feel that not a moment is to be lost. Now or never, must our salvation be secured. How shall it be done?

Brethren, our salvation must, through the blessing of God, come from ourselves. It is useless to expect it from those whom our labors enrich. It is for their interest to augment our numbers and our poverty. It is their interest to purchase our labor at the lowest rate possible; it is ours to sell it at the highest rate possible. Their interest and ours, then, stand in direct opposition to each other. The greater our numbers, the more necessitous our condition, the greater is the facility with which they can obtain laborers, and the lower the price they are obliged to pay for labor. The fewer our numbers, the more independent our condition, the higher is the price we can demand and obtain for our labor. This refutes the pretensions of the aristocracy, that their interests and ours are one and the same. As men, as human beings, no doubt their interest and ours are the same; but their interests as capitalists, and ours as laborers, are directly opposite, and mutually destructive. In fact there is less identity of interest between the capitalists and us, than there is between the master and the slave. The slave is the master's property, and it is for the master's interest to take care of his property; it is for his interest to give his slave a sufficiency of food, and to be careful not to overwork him; for the sickness or death of his slave would be a loss of property. The same principle, which leads a man to take good care of his horses, sheep, and oxen, would lead him to take good care of his slaves. But the capitalist has no other interest in us, than to get as much labor out of us as possible. We are hired men, and hired men, like hired horses, have no souls. If a man owns the horse he drives, he will take care not to injure him; but if the horse be a hired one, what he will do, is told in a common saying. "Hired horses have no souls; drive on." "Hired men have no souls; drive on." If we sicken and die, the loss is ours, not the employer's. *There are enough more ready to take our places.*

Brethren, we conjure you, therefore, not to believe a word of what is said about your interest and that of your employers being the same. Your interests and theirs are in the nature of things, hostile and irreconcilable. Then do not look to them for relief. Be not so mad as to suppose that they will voluntarily work out your salvation for you. You must expect them to be governed mainly by their own interests, and must never rely on their doing, as a body, what it is not for their interest to do. If then you have ever expected the capitalist, the accumulator, contractor, and employer, to conspire to elevate your condition, expect it no longer. As well might the poor and depressed have expected the Gospel, which is good news to the poor, from the scribes and pharisees, the chief priests and elders, who crucified Jesus for proclaiming it.

❖ *9* ❖

Jacksonian Democracy

The inauguration of Andrew Jackson as president in 1829 marked the appearance of a new political force in America. Following the War of 1812 the Federalists had virtually disappeared as a party, leaving the Jeffersonian Republicans without organized opposition for a decade or more. However much they gave lip service to the "people's" sovereignty, the Jeffersonian leaders were well-educated gentlemen who governed in the name of the people without being men of the people. In this era, elections were often weakly contested, and voter turnouts were usually low. The public trusted its patrician leaders and saw little reason to become embroiled in political campaigns that promised little change.

Jackson's advent transformed the nation's political culture. Andy Jackson, the victor of the Battle of New Orleans, the famous Indian fighter, was a hero to the masses. Unlike his predecessors, he was a self-made man from a humble background. He was also the first president from the new West and carried to Washington its rough vigor, egalitarianism, and suspicion of eastern business enterprise.

Jackson polarized American politics by his deeds and personality. Hotheaded and contentious, vengeful toward his enemies and fiercely loyal to his friends, he was a high-handed and overbearing man. His political opponents called him "King Andrew" and likened themselves to the Whig opponents of King George III during the Revolution. But his enemies were not moved solely by personal dislike. They also deplored his attacks on the Second Bank of the United States and his opposition to federal aid to "internal improvements." Most of all, they decried what they considered his pandering to the ignorant and unruly masses. In the eyes of the Whig opposition, the Democrats, as the Jackson party came to be called, represented the nation's "leveling" forces, hostile to wealth, order, and good breeding. The Jacksonians, they said, stood for the triumph of numbers over merit.

200

Jackson's friends naturally saw "Old Hickory" in a different light. He was a man of the people, an opponent of the rich and powerful. The Democrats reversed the Whig estimate of the emerging new parties. The Whigs were the "silk-stocking" party of the social elite, who used government favors to advance their narrow and privileged economic interests.

Modern scholars are often skeptical of these party characterizations. Some see the Jacksonian leaders as recruits from the same class of rich lawyers, landowners, and merchants as their Whig counterparts. Others detect an important entrepreneurial component in the Jackson party. In this view the Jacksonians represent a class of newer business promoters who opposed the efforts of better established groups to retain their advantages and privileges. If anything, they better represented the spirit of free market capitalism than their adversaries.

Whatever the sources of Jackson's support, by the time "Old Hickory" left office in 1837 a "second-party system" of Whigs and Democrats had taken shape that would last until the mid-1850s. Both new parties were coalitions, and their ideology and sociocultural composition overlapped. Yet contemporaries would feel that it made a difference whether the Whigs or Democrats won, and they would show this at the polls. The two new political organizations would each win the passionate loyalty of large blocks of citizens. Election turnouts would soar; political campaigns would become exciting contests marked by pageantry and florid oratory.

9.1: Andrew Jackson Vetoes the Bank Bill (1832)

No political act did so much to define the party conflicts of the Jackson era as King Andrew's veto of the bill to recharter the Second Bank of the United States. Established in 1816 in the flush of nationalist fervor that followed the War of 1812, the bank, under its third president, Nicholas Biddle, had become stern regulator of the nation's monetary system and a force for stability and economic growth. In 1831 Biddle and his supporters sought to get Congress to renew the bank's charter, due to expire in 1836. Congress obliged in July 1832, but Jackson vetoed the bill, setting off a major national debate.

The bank issue deeply divided the nation. On one side were the "agrarians," who detested all banks in general as sources of chicanery and corruption, and the Bank of the United States in particular as a "monster," controlled by the rich and possessing powers to manipulate the politicians and negate the popular will. Allied with these agrarians were various business groups, especially in the South and West, that resented Biddle's restrictive financial policies for curtailing their profits. On the other side of the bank issue were those like Henry Clay and Daniel Webster, who favored Hamiltonian policies of federal aid and guidance to economic growth and considered the bank a bulwark of sound money and orderly expansion. Eastern bankers and merchants usually favored the national bank as well.

The following document is a condensed version of Jackson's 1832 veto message. It was actually ghosted by Amos Kendall, a member of Jackson's "kitchen cabinet," his group of informal advisers, and by Roger Taney, the Democratic attorney general, but it accurately expressed the president's views.

Some of Jackson's attack on the bank centers on fears of foreign control of the American economy. Were these charges valid? Other arguments concern the dubious constitutionality of a federal charter for a bank and the extent to which the bill violated states' rights. But the central theme, emphasized in this excerpt, is that the bank is a source of privilege for some at the expense of "the humble members of society." Was this charge demagoguery, or was it a valid view of the bank's role in contemporary America? Do large private corporations pose a hazard to a democratic society, or are they indispensable for prosperity?

Why I Vetoed the BUS Recharter

ANDREW JACKSON

The present corporate body, denominated the president, directors, and company of the Bank of the United States, will have existed at the time this act is intended to take effect twenty years. It enjoys an exclusive privilege of banking under the authority of the General Government, a monopoly of its favor and support, and, as a necessary consequence, almost a monopoly of the foreign and domestic exchange. The powers, privileges, and favors bestowed upon it in the original charter, by increasing the value of the stock far above its par value, operated as a gratuity of many millions to the stockholders. . . .

The act before me proposes another gratuity to the holders of the same stock, and in many cases to the same men, of at least seven millions more. . . . It is not our own citizens only who are to receive the bounty of our Government. More than eight millions of the stock of this bank are held by foreigners. By this act the American Republic proposes virtually to make them a present of some millions of dollars. For these gratuities to foreigners and to some of our own opulent citizens the act secures no equivalent whatever. They are the certain gains of the present stockholders under the operation of this act, after making full allowance for the payment of the bonus.

Every monopoly and all exclusive privileges are granted at the expense of the public, which ought to receive a fair equivalent. The many millions which this act

James D. Richardson, *A Compilation of the Messages and Papers of the Presidents* (New York: Bureau of National Literature, 1897), vol. 3, pp. 1139–54.

proposes to bestow on the stockholders of the existing bank must come directly or indirectly out of the earnings of the American people. . . .

It is not conceivable how the present stockholders can have any claim to the special favor of the Government. The present corporation has enjoyed its monopoly during the period stipulated in the original contract. If we must have such a corporation, why should not the Government sell out the whole stock and thus secure to the people the full market value of the privileges granted? Why should not Congress create and sell twenty-eight millions of stock, incorporating the purchasers with all the powers and privileges secured in this act and putting the premium upon the sales into the Treasury?

But this act does not permit competition in the purchase of this monopoly. It seems to be predicated on the erroneous idea that the present stockholders have a prescriptive right not only to the favor but to the bounty of Government. It appears that more than a fourth part of the stock is held by foreigners and the residue is held by a few hundred of our own citizens, chiefly of the richest class. For their benefit does this act exclude the whole American people from competition in the purchase of this monopoly and dispose of it for many millions less than it is worth. This seems the less excusable because some of our citizens not now stockholders petitioned that the door of competition might be opened, and offered to take a charter on terms much more favorable to the Government and country.

But this proposition, although made by men whose aggregate wealth is believed to be equal to all the private stock in the existing bank, has been set aside, and the bounty of our Government is proposed to be again bestowed on the few who have been fortunate enough to secure the stock and at this moment wield the power of the existing institution. I can not perceive the justice or policy of this course. If our Government must sell monopolies, it would seem to be its duty to take nothing less than their full value, and if gratuities must be made once in fifteen or twenty years let them not be bestowed on the subjects of a foreign government nor upon a designated and favored class of men in our own country. It is but justice and good policy, as far as the nature of the case will admit, to confine our favors to our own fellow-citizens, and let each in his turn enjoy an opportunity to profit by our bounty. In the bearings of the act before me upon these points I find ample reasons why it should not become a law. . . .

Is there no danger to our liberty and independence in a bank that in its nature has so little to bind it to our country? The president of the bank has told us that most of the State banks exist by its forbearance. Should its influence become concentered, as it may under the operation of such an act as this, in the hands of a self-elected directory whose interests are identified with those of the foreign stockholders, will there not be cause to tremble for the purity of our elections in peace and for the independence of our country in war? Their power would be great whenever they might choose to exert it; but if this monopoly were regularly renewed every fifteen or twenty years on terms proposed by themselves, they might seldom in peace put forth their strength to influence elections or control the affairs of the nation. But if any private citizen or public functionary should interpose to curtail its powers or prevent a renewal of its privileges, it can not be doubted that he would be made to feel its influence.

Should the stock of the bank principally pass into the hands of the subjects of a foreign country, and we should unfortunately become involved in a war with that country, what would be our condition? Of the course which would be pursued by a bank almost wholly owned by the subjects of a foreign power, and managed by those whose interests, if not affections, would run in the same direction there can be no doubt. All its operations within would be in aid of the hostile fleets and armies without. Controlling our currency, receiving our public moneys, and holding thousands of our citizens in dependence, it would be more formidable and dangerous than the naval and military power of the enemy.

If we must have a bank with private stockholders, every consideration of sound policy and every impulse of American feeling admonishes that it should be *purely American.* Its stockholders should be composed exclusively of our own citizens, who at least ought to be friendly to our Government and willing to support it in times of difficulty and danger. . . .

The bank is professedly established as an agent of the executive branch of the Government, and its constitutionality is maintained on that ground. Neither upon the propriety of present action nor upon the provisions of this act was the Executive consulted. It has had no opportunity to say that it neither needs nor wants a agent clothed with such powers and favored by such exemptions. There is nothing in its legitimate functions which makes it necessary or proper. Whatever interest or influence, whether public or private, has given birth to this act, it can not be found either in the wishes or necessities of the executive department, by which present action is deemed premature, and the powers conferred upon its agent not only unnecessary, but dangerous to the Government and country.

It is to be regretted that the rich and powerful too often bend the acts of government to their selfish purposes. Distinctions in society will always exist under every just government. Equality of talents, of education, or of wealth can not be produced by human institutions. In the full enjoyment of the gifts of Heaven and the fruits of superior industry, economy, and virtue, every man is equally entitled to protection by law; but when the laws undertake to add to these natural and just advantages artificial distinctions, to grant titles, gratuities, and exclusive privileges, to make the rich richer and the potent more powerful, the humble members of society—the farmers, mechanics, and laborers—who have neither the time nor the means of securing like favors to themselves, have a right to complain of the injustice of their Government. There are no necessary evils in government. Its evils exist only in its abuses. If it would confine itself to equal protection, and, as Heaven does its rains, shower its favors alike on the high and the low, the rich and the poor, it would be an unqualified blessing. In the act before me there seems to be a wide and unnecessary departure from these just principles.

Nor is our Government to be maintained or our Union preserved by invasions of the rights and powers of the several States. In thus attempting to make our General Government strong we make it weak. Its true strength consists in leaving individuals and States as much as possible to themselves—in making itself felt, not in its power, but in its beneficence; not in its control, but in its protection; not in binding the States more closely to the center, but leaving each to move unobstructed in its proper orbit.

Experience should teach us wisdom. Most of the difficulties our Government now encounters and most of the dangers which impend over our Union have sprung from an abandonment of the legitimate objects of Government by our national legislation, and the adoption of such principles as are embodied in this act. Many of our rich men have not been content with equal protection and equal benefits, but have besought us to make them richer by act of Congress. By attempting to gratify their desires we have in the results of our legislation arrayed section against section, interest against interest, and man against man, in a fearful commotion which threatens to shake the foundations of our Union. It is time to pause in our career to review our principles, and if possible revive that devoted patriotism and spirit of compromise which distinguished the sages of the Revolution and the fathers of our Union. If we can not at once, in justice to interests vested under improvident legislation, make our Government what it ought to be, we can at least take a stand against all new grants of monopolies and exclusive privileges, against any prostitution of our Government to the advancement of the few at the expense of the many, and in favor of compromise and gradual reform in our code of laws and system of political economy.

9.2: Daniel Webster Replies to the Veto (1832)

Within hours of Andrew Jackson's veto of the bill to renew the charter of the Second Bank, Daniel Webster, Whig senator from Massachusetts, rose to defend the bank. Webster had a personal interest in its fate: He was an attorney for the bank, one of its frequent borrowers, and a close friend of Nicholas Biddle, the bank's president. As we read the selection below, we must take these facts into consideration, yet we should judge Webster's arguments on their merits. Does he deal effectively with Jackson's criticisms? What, in Webster's view, were the bank's advantages to the country at large?

Daniel Webster Defends the BUS

DANIEL WEBSTER

Mr. President I will not conceal my opinion that the affairs of the country are approaching an important and dangerous crisis. At the very moment of almost unparalleled general prosperity, there appears an unaccountable disposition to destroy the most useful and most approved institutions of the government. Indeed, it seems to be in the midst of all this national happiness that some are found openly to question the advantages of the Constitution itself; and many more ready to embarrass the exercise of its just power, weaken its authority, and undermine its foundations. How

Daniel Webster, *Works of Daniel Webster,* ed. (Boston: Charles C. Little and James Brown, 1851), vol. 3, pp. 423–47.

far these notions may be carried it is impossible yet to say. We have before us the practical result of one of them. The bank has fallen, or is to fall. . . .

Before proceeding to the constitutional question, there are some other topics, treated in the [veto] message, which ought to be noticed. It commences by an inflamed statement of what it calls the "favor" bestowed upon the original bank by the government, or, indeed, as it is phrased, the "monopoly of its favor and support"; and through the whole message all possible changes are rung on the "gratuity," the "exclusive privileges," and "monopoly," of the bank charter. Now, Sir, the truth is, that the powers conferred on the bank are such, and no others, as are usually conferred on similar institutions. They constitute no monopoly, although some of them are of necessity, and with propriety, exclusive privileges. "The original act," says the message, "operated as a gratuity of many millions to the stockholders." What fair foundation is there for this remark? The stockholders received their charter, not gratuitously, but for a valuable consideration in money, prescribed by Congress, and actually paid. At some times the stock has been above *par,* at other times below *par,* according to prudence in management, or according to commercial occurrences. But if, by a judicious administration of its affairs, it had kept its stock always above *par,* what pretence would there be, nevertheless, for saying that such augmentation of its value was a "gratuity" from government? The message proceeds to declare, that the present act proposes another donation, another gratuity, to the same men, of at least seven millions more. It seems to me that this is an extraordinary statement, and an extraordinary style of argument, for such a subject and on such an occasion. In the first place, the facts are all assumed; they are taken for true without evidence. There are no proofs that any benefit to that amount will accrue to the stockholders, nor any experience to justify the expectation of it. It rests on random estimates, or mere conjecture. But suppose the continuance of the charter should prove beneficial to the stockholders; do they not pay for it? They give twice as much for a charter of fifteen years, as was given before for one of twenty. And if the proposed *bonus,* or premium, be not, in the President's judgment, large enough, would he, nevertheless, on such a mere matter of opinion as that, negative the whole bill? May not Congress be trusted to decide even on such a subject as the amount of the money premium to be received by government for a charter of this kind?

But, Sir, there is a larger and a much more just view of this subject. The bill was not passed for the purpose of benefiting the present stockholders. Their benefit, if any, is incidental and collateral. Nor was it passed on any idea that they had a right to a renewed charter, although the message argues against such right, as if it had been somewhere set up and asserted. No such right has been asserted by any body. Congress passed the bill, not as a bounty or a favor to the present stockholders, nor to comply with any demand of right on their part; but to promote great public interests, for great public objects. Every bank must have some stockholders, unless it be such a bank as the President has recommended, and in regard to which he seems not likely to find much concurence of other men's opinions; and if the stockholders, whoever they may be, conduct the affairs of the bank prudently, the expectation is always, of course, that they will make it profitable to themselves, as well as useful to the public. If a bank charter is not to be granted, because, to some extent, it may be profitable to the stockholders, no charter can be granted. The objection lies against all banks.

Sir, the object aimed at by such institutions is to connect the public safety and convenience with private interests. It has been found by experience, that banks are safest under private management, and that government banks are among the most dangerous of all inventions. Now, Sir, the whole drift of the message is to reverse the settled judgment of all the civilized world, and to set up government banks, independent of private interest or private control. For this purpose the message labors, even beyond the measure of all its other labors, to create jealousies and prejudices, on the ground of the alleged benefit which individuals will derive from the renewal of this charter. Much less effort is made to show that government, or the public, will be injured by the bill, than that individuals will profit by it. Following up the impulses of the same spirit, the message goes on gravely to allege, that the act, as passed by Congress, proposes to make a *present* of some millions of dollars to foreigners, because a portion of the stock is held by foreigners. Sir, how would this sort of argument apply to other cases? The President has shown himself not only willing, but anxious, to pay off the three per cent stock of the United States at *par,* notwithstanding that it is notorious that foreigners are owners of the greater part of it. Why should he not call that a donation to foreigners of many millions? . . .

From the commencement of the government, it has been thought desirable to invite, rather than to repel, the introduction of foreign capital. Our stocks have all been open to foreign subscriptions; and the State banks, in like manner, are free to foreign ownership. Whatever State has created a debt has been willing that foreigners should become purchasers, and desirous of it. How long is it, Sir, since Congress itself passed a law vesting new powers in the President of the United States over the cities in this District, for the very purpose of increasing their credit abroad, the better to enable them to borrow money to pay their subscriptions to the Chesapeake and Ohio Canal? It is easy to say that there is danger to liberty, danger to independence, in a bank open to foreign stockholders, because it is easy to say any thing. But neither reason nor experience proves any such danger. The foreign stockholder cannot be a director. He has no voice even in the choice of directors. His money is placed entirely in the management of the directors appointed by the President and Senate and by the American stockholders. So far as there is dependence or influence either way, it is to the disadvantage of the foreign stockholder. He has parted with the control over his own property, instead of exercising control over the property or over the actions of others. . . .

In order to justify its alarm for the security of our independence, the message supposes a case. It supposes that the bank should pass principally into the hands of the subjects of a foreign country, and that we should be involved in war with that country, and then it exclaims, "What would be our condition?" Why, Sir, it is plain that all the advantages would be on our side. The bank would still be our institution, subject to our own laws, and all its directors elected by ourselves; and our means would be enhanced, not by the confiscation and plunder, but by the proper use, of the foreign capital in our hands. And, Sir, it is singular enough, that this very state of war, from which this argument against a bank is drawn, is the very thing which, more than all others, convinced the country and the government of the necessity of a national bank. So much was the want of such an institution felt in the late war, that the subject engaged the attention of Congress, constantly, from the declaration of that war down to the time when the existing bank was actually established; so that in this respect, as well as in others, the argument of the message is directly opposed to the whole experience of the government, and to the general and long-settled convictions of the country. . . .

Mr. President, we have arrived at a new epoch. We are entering on experiments, with the government and the Constitution of the country, hitherto untried, and of fearful and appalling aspect. This message calls us to the contemplation of a future which little resembles the past. Its principles are at war with all that public opinion has sustained, and all which the experience of the government has sanctioned. It denies first principles; it contradicts truths, heretofore received as indisputable. It denies to the judiciary the interpretation of law, and claims to divide with Congress the power of originating statutes. It extends the grasp of executive pretension over every power of the government. But this is not all. It presents the chief magistrate of the Union in the attitude of arguing away the powers of that government over which he has been chosen to preside; and adopting for this purpose modes of reasoning which, even under the influence of all proper feeling towards high official station, it is difficult to regard as respectable. It appeals to every prejudice which may betray men into a mistaken view of their own interests, and to every passion which may lead them to disobey the impulses of their understanding. It urges all the specious topics of State rights and national encroachment against that which a great majority of the States have affirmed to be rightful, and in which all of them have acquiesced. It sows, in an unsparing manner, the seeds of jealousy and ill-will against that government of which its author is the official head. It raises a cry, that liberty is in danger, at the very moment when it puts forth claims to powers heretofore unknown and unheard of. It effects alarm of the public freedom, when nothing endangers that freedom so much as its own unparalleled pretenses. This, even, is not all. It manifestly seeks to inflame the poor against the rich; it wantonly attacks whole classes of the people, for the purpose of turning against them the prejudices and the resentments of other classes. It is a state paper which finds no topic too exciting for its use, no passion too inflammable for it address and its solicitation.

Such is this message. It remains now for the people of the United States to choose between the principles here avowed and their government. These cannot subsist together. The one or the other must be rejected. If the sentiments of the message shall receive general approbation, the Constitution will have perished even earlier than the moment which its enemies originally allowed for the termination of its existence. It will not have survived to its fiftieth year.

9.3:   Jacksonian Enterprise (1837)

Not all Jacksonians accepted the antibusiness bias displayed in the 1832 veto message. Clearly many of Old Hickory's staunchest supporters hated the bank, not as a symbol of business as such, but as a monopoly that stifled other enterprises, both other banks and other business ventures generally.

One Jacksonian of this temper was Roger Taney, Jackson's close friend and a member of his cabinet. It was Secretary of Treasury Taney who, on Jackson's orders, removed the government deposits in the Second Bank in 1833 and placed them in the "pet banks" (state banks favored by the Jacksonians), thereby administering the final blow to the bank. In 1836 Jackson appointed Taney as chief justice of the Supreme Court, where he served until his death in 1864.

As chief justice, Taney used the Supreme Court to overturn legal monopolies and assert freedom of enterprise. One blow for the doctrine of laissez faire was his decision in Charles River Bridge v. Warren Bridge in 1837. The case decided a suit brought by the stockholders of a toll bridge, the Charles River Bridge in Boston, to stop construction of an adjacent and competing bridge, the Warren Bridge. The plaintiffs insisted that their charter from the state conferred on them an exclusive privilege and that the charter for the new bridge violated that privilege. In the decision excerpted here Taney decided against the Charles River Bridge company.

On what grounds did Taney base his decision? In what way did his decision reflect the spirit of enterprise of the age? What might have been the course of economic development in the United States if the Supreme Court had upheld the exclusive charter of the Charles River Bridge?

The Chief Justice Defends Economic Progress

ROGER TANEY

Borrowing, as we have done, our system of jurisprudence from the English law . . . it would present a singular spectacle, if, while the courts in England are restraining, within the strictest limits, the spirit of monopoly, and exclusive privileges in nature of monopolies, and confining corporations to the privileges plainly given to them in their charter, the courts of this country should be found enlarging these privileges by implication; and construing a statute more unfavorably to the public, and to the rights of the community, than would be done in a like case in an English court of justice.

But we are not now left to determine for the first time the rules by which public grants are to be construed in this country. The subject has already been considered in this court, and the rules of construction above stated fully established. In the case of the *United States* v. *Arredondo,* 8 Pet. 738, the leading cases upon this subject are

Cases Argued and Decided in the Supreme Court of the United States (Rochester, NY: The Lawyers' Co-Operative Publishing Company, 1926), Book 9, pp. 551–53.

collected together by the learned judge who delivered the opinion of the court, and the principle recognized that, in grants by the public nothing passes by implication. . . .

But the case most analogous to this, and in which the question came more directly before the court, is the case of *Providence Bank* v. *Billings,* 4 Pet. 514, which was decided in 1830. In that case it appeared that the legislature of Rhode Island had chartered the bank, in the usual form of such acts of incorporation. The charter contained no stipulation on the part of the State that it would not impose a tax on the bank, nor any reservation of the right to do so. It was silent on this point. Afterwards a law was passed imposing a tax on all banks in the State, and the right to impose this tax was resisted by the Providence Bank upon the ground that if the State could impose a tax, it might tax so heavily as to render the franchise of no value, and destroy the institution; that the charter was a contract, and that a power which may in effect destroy the charter is inconsistent with it, and is impliedly renounced in granting it. But the court said that the taxing power is of vital importance and essential to the existence of government, and that the relinquishment of such a power is never to be assumed. . . . The case now before the court is, in principle, precisely the same. It is a character from a state; the act of incorporation is silent in relation to the contested power. The argument in favor of the proprietors of the Charles River bridge, is the same, almost in words, with that used by the Providence Bank; that is, that the power claimed by the state, if it exists, may be so used as to destroy the value of the franchise they have granted to the corporation. The argument must receive the same answer; and the fact that the power has been already exercised, so as to destroy the value of the franchise, cannot in any degree affect the principle. The existence of the power does not, and cannot, depend upon the circumstance of its having been exercised or not.

It may, perhaps, be said, that in the case of the Providence Bank, this court were speaking of the taxing power; which is of vital importance to the very existence of every government. But the object and end of all government is to promote the happiness and prosperity of the community by which it is established; and it can never be assumed, that the government intended to diminish its power of accomplishing the end for which it was created. And in a country like ours, free, active and enterprising, continually advancing in numbers and wealth, new channels of communication are daily found necessary, both for travel and trade, and are essential to the comfort, convenience and prosperity of the people. A state ought never to be presumed to surrender this power, because, like the taxing power, the whole community have an interest in preserving it undiminished. And when a corporation alleges, that a state has surrendered, for seventy years, its power of improvement and public accommodation, in a great and important line of travel, along which a vast number of its citizens must daily pass, the community have a right to insist, in the language of this court, above quoted, "that its abandonment ought not to be presumed, in a case, in which the deliberate purpose of the state to abandon it does not appear." The continued existence of a government would be of no great value, if, by implications and presumptions, it was disarmed of the powers necessary to accomplish the ends of its creation, and the functions it was designed to perform, transferred to the hands of privileged corporations. The rule of construction announced by the court, was not confined to the taxing power, nor is it so limited, in the opinion delivered. On the contrary, it was distinctly placed on the ground, that the interests of the community were concerned in preserving, undiminished, the power then in question; and whenever any power of the state is said to be surrendered or diminished, whether it be the taxing power, or any other affecting the public interest, the same principle applies, and the rule of construction must be the same. No one will question, that the interests of the great body of the people of the state, would, in this instance, be affected by the surrender of this great line of travel to a single corporation, with the right to exact toll, and exclude competition, for seventy years. While the rights of private property are sacredly guarded, we must not forget, that the community also have rights, and that the happiness and well-being of every citizen depends on their faithful preservation.

Adopting the rule of construction above stated as the settled one, we proceed to apply it to the charter of 1785 to the proprietors of the Charles River bridge. This act of incorporation is in the usual form, and the privileges such as are commonly given to corporations of that kind. It confers on them the ordinary faculties of a corporation, for the purpose of building the bridge; and establishes certain rates of toll, which the company are authorized to take. This is the whole grant. There is no exclusive privilege given to them over the waters of Charles river, above or below their bridge; no right to erect another bridge themselves, nor to prevent other persons from erecting one, no engagement from the State, that another shall not be erected; and no undertaking not to sanction competition, nor to make improvements that may diminish the amount of its income. Upon all these subjects the charter is silent; and nothing is said in it about a line of travel, so much insisted on in the argument, in which they are to have exclusive privileges. No words are used from which an intention to grant any of these rights can be inferred. If the plaintiff is entitled to them, it must be implied, simply from the nature of the grant, and cannot be inferred from the words by which the grant is made. . . .

The inquiry then is, does the charter contain such a contract on the part of the State? Is there any such stipulation to be found in that instrument? It must be admitted on all hands, that there is none—no words that even relate to another bridge, or to the diminution of their tolls, or to the line of travel. If a contract on that subject can be gathered from the charter, it must be by implication, and cannot be found in the words used. Can such an agreement be implied? The rule of construction before stated is an answer to the question. In characters of this description, no rights are taken from the public, or given to the corporation, beyond those which the words of the charter, by their natural and proper construction, purport to convey. There are no words which import such a contract as the plaintiffs in error contend for, and none can be implied; and the same answer must be given to them that was given by this court to the Providence Bank. The whole community are interested in this inquiry, and they have a right to require that the power of promoting their comfort and convenience, and of advancing the public prosperity, by providing safe, convenient, and cheap ways for the transportation of produce and the purposes of travel, shall not be construed to have been surrendered or diminished by the State, unless it shall appear by plain words that it was intended to be done. . . .

Indeed, the practice and usage of almost every State in the Union old enough to have commenced the work of internal improvement, is opposed to the doctrine contended for on the part of the plaintiffs in error. Turnpike roads have been made in succession, on the same line of travel; the later ones interfering materially with the profits of the first. These corporations have, in some instances, been utterly ruined by the introduction of newer and better modes of transportation and travelling. In some cases, railroads have rendered the turnpike roads on the same line of travel so entirely useless, that the franchise of the turnpike corporation is not worth preserving. Yet in none of these cases have the corporations supposed that their privileges were invaded, or any contract violated on the part of the State. . . .

And what would be the fruits of this doctrine of implied contracts on the part of the States, and of property in a line of travel by a corporation, if it should now be sanctioned by this court? To what results would it lead us? If it is to be found in the charter to this bridge, the same process of reasoning must discover it, in the various acts which have been passed, within the last forty years, for turnpike companies. . . . If this court should establish the principles now contended for, what is to become of the numerous railroads established on the same line of travel with turnpike companies, and which have rendered the franchises of the turnpike corporations of no value? Let it once be understood that such charters carry with them these implied contracts, and give this unknown and undefined property in a line of travelling, and you will soon find the old turnpike corporations awakening from their sleep and calling upon this court to put down the improvements which have taken their place. The millions of property which have been invested in railroads and canals upon lines of travel which had been before occupied by turnpike corporations will be put in jeopardy. We shall be thrown back to the improvements of the last century, and obliged to stand still until the claims of the old turnpike corporations shall be satisfied, and they shall consent to permit these States to avail themselves of the lights of modern science, and to partake of the benefit of those improvements which are now adding to the wealth and prosperity, and the convenience and comfort, of every other part of the civilized world. . . .

Judgment affirmed.

STORY, J., delivered a dissenting opinion in which THOMPSON, J., concurred.

9.4: Democratic Egalitarianism (1836)

Just as there was an entrepreneurial wing of the Democratic Party, there was also a radical wing. In New York it took form as the "Loco Focos,"[1] a group that went beyond the regular Democrats in demanding equality. For a time the Loco Focos remained loyal Democrats, although fighting

[1]The term comes from the name for a new form of self-lighting matches. These were used by the radical Democrats to light candles at a Tammany Hall meeting in 1835, when the New York regulars turned out the gas lights to force their equal rights opponents to adjourn a gathering called to reject the regulars' candidates and party platform.

the Tammany Hall conservatives who represented the conservative "regulars," for supremacy within the New York Democratic Party. In 1836 they held a separate state convention at Utica, established the Equal Rights Party, and nominated a separate ticket for state offices.

The following letter was written by Isaac S. Smith of Buffalo on the occasion of his nomination for governor by the Utica convention. What political principles does Smith support? What are his economic principles? From what ideas or sources does he derive these principles? Why does he emphasize paper money so strongly? Why does he also emphasize education? In what sense might Smith be considered a radical? Do the view of the Loco Focos have any resonance today? (Note the resemblance between Smith's views and those of the Charlestown "Workies" in Chapter 8.)

The Positions of the Loco Focos

ISAAC S. SMITH

Buffalo, September 29th, 1836

Gentlemen:—

Your letter of the 26th instant, in behalf of the convention of Mechanics, Farmers, and Workingmen, accompanied by a Declaration of rights adopted by them at Utica, and presented for my consideration, is before me.

Fully approving the resolution which requires of candidates for elective offices, avowals of their political principles, I cheerfully state the following as mine.

The first great political truth to be impressed on the minds of our youth is, that they are born free, and that no acts of legislation should deprive them of perfect equality in rights. This principle will constantly stimulate those of humble birth to compete with the favorites of fortune, and teach them that without personal merit, no one can have just claims to honorable distinction.

Although the first declaration, that "all men are created free and equal," is subscribed to by a vast majority, yet our legislatures have not framed their acts in conformity to it: I allude to their acts of incorporation, generally granted to active and intriguing partisans, who make a trade of electioneering, and find their zeal and fidelity rewarded by valuable monopolies and lucrative offices.

Our legislatures can have no more right to take from the people and confer upon individuals, special and exclusive privileges, than they have to confer titles of nobility.

Indirect taxes on articles of necessity, or which by habit have become so, as well as all demands for personal services without equivalents, which operate oppressively on the poor, and are not felt by the rich, are unjust, and should not exist.

Francis Byrdsall, *The History of the Loco Foco or Equal Rights Party* (New York: Clement & Packard, 1842), pp. 75–76.

All wealth is an accumulation of surplus labor, from which alone the expenses and burthens of government should be borne. No person possessing mental or physical ability, can have a *moral* right to consume that which he does not in some manner contribute to produce.

None of our institutions have so strong a tendency to create and perpetuate the odious distinctions betwixt the rich and the poor, as the paper money banks. Those incorporations, and others are not more meritorious, and yet equally monopolizing, have been the greatest cause of truckling and corruption in legislatures.

The worst feature in the proceedings of the past legislatures, has been the wasteful appropriation of large sums, ostensibly for public improvements, but in reality for party purposes; and the granting of charters for banks, with which to strengthen the hands of party leaders. The great majority of the people have but little interest individually in these plunderings of the many for the benefit of the few.

The genius of our institutions requires that the majority shall govern, therefore no legislature can in all cases bind their successors.

The doctrine of vested rights, as heretofore promulgated, is dangerous, and cannot be sustained.

I conceive the term, *paper money,* an absurdity; therefore, I would sanction nothing but silver and gold as a circulating medium. Bankers' notes of large denominations, and bills of exchange, which must exist, cannot come within my definition of circulating medium. My creed is to leave commercial men to manage their own affairs.

As the difference in education is one great cause of the distinctions in society, and as our own and the experience of other countries show that a well educated community is the least liable to anarchy; that nothing approaching equality can exist between ignorance and intelligence, I deem it essential to the perpetuation of the best of our institutions, and to promote the happiness of generations to come, that our common schools be established upon a basis that will insure to every child the advantages of equal education. At this time, it is not possible in most parts of our country to obtain any more than the rudiments of the plainest education, unless the children be sent from home, and provided for at a great expense in the towns; this expense being beyond the means of most men, their children neglected, and being comparatively in ignorance, must eventually become the proper subjects for demagogues.

Those who produce all the wealth should not submit to have their families kept in ignorance and degradation, and the common schools held in disrepute, while the public bounty is showered upon those for the education of the aristocratical few. Too much cannot be done for common schools.

As a citizen, having their interests warmly at heart, I approve the Declaration of Rights made by the Mechanics, Farmers and Workingmen, transmitted by you to me; and as they have thought the use of my name would benefit the cause, I do not feel at liberty to decline the nomination with which they have honored me.

I am very respectfully yours,

Isaac S. Smith.

To Messrs. E. G. Barney, John Commerford, Daniel Gorham, F. Byrdsall, W. F. Piatt.

9.5: A "Knickerbocker" Gentleman Flays the "Rabble" (1836, 1837)

Philip Hone was a rich merchant of New York during the Jackson era. He was a self-made man, but his wealth gained him entrée into the social circle of the city's Knickerbocker elite, the descendants of the old New York families, many of Dutch extraction. Hone was a devout Whig. He despised Jackson and closely associated with the Whig leaders Henry Clay, Daniel Webster, and William Henry Seward. His social views were those of the "silk-stocking" element in the Whig party: aristocratic and antiegalitarian.

Hone kept a diary from the late 1820s until his death in the 1850s. It is a remarkable view of a rich, conservative New Yorker—his ideas, his politics, his amusements, his business activities, his relations with his family and friends. In his journal Hone chronicled the growing assertiveness of the "common" folk as expressed in their attitudes toward their elected representatives and their employers. In the following diary entries for 1836 and 1837, he describes a New York judge's response to a strike of tailors to raise their wages and Mayor William Beach Lawrence's New Year's reception in 1837. Is Hone's attitude toward the tailors' strike more than snobbery? What stronger term might be more accurate? What is his tone concerning the mayor's reception? What do you suppose those whom Hone disparages would say about the reception?

A Whig Gentleman's View of the Working Class

PHILIP HONE

Monday, June 6 [1836].—

Journeymen Tailors. In corroboration of the remarks which I have occasionally made of late, on the spirit of faction and contempt of the laws which pervades the community at this time, is the conduct of the journeymen tailors instigated by a set of vile foreigners (principally English), who, unable to endure the restraint of wholesome laws, well administered in their own country, take refuge here, establish trade unions, and villify Yankee judges and juries. Twenty odd of these "knights of the thimble" were convicted at the oyer and terminer [i.e., a criminal court] of a conspiracy to raise their wages and to prevent any of the craft from working at prices less than those for which they "struck." Judge Edwards gave notice that he

Philip Hone, *The Diary of Philip Hone, 1828–1857,* Allan Nevins, ed. (New York: Dodd, Mead and Company, 1927), vol. 1, pp. 211–12, 235–36.

would proceed to sentence them this day, but in consequence of the continuance of Robinson's trial the court postponed the sentence until Friday.

This, however, being the day on which it was expected, crowds of people have been collected in the park, ready for any mischief to which they may have been instigated, and a most diabolical and inflammatory handbill was circulated yesterday, headed by a coffin. The board of Aldermen held an informal meeting this evening, at which a resolution was adopted authorizing the mayor to offer a reward for the discovery of the author, printer, publisher, or distributor of this incendiary publication. The following was the handbill:—

"The *Rich* Against the *Poor!*

"Judge Edwards, the tool of the aristocracy, against the people! Mechanics and Workingmen! A deadly blow has been struck at your *Liberty!* The prize for which your fathers fought has been robbed from you! The freemen of the North are now on a level with the slaves of the South! With no other privilege than laboring, that drones may fatten on your life-blood! Twenty of your brethren have been found guilty for presuming to resist a reduction of their wages! And Judge Edwards has charged an American jury, and agreeably to that charge, they have established the precedent that workingmen have no right to regulate the price of labor, or, in other words, the rich are the only judges of the wants of the poor man. On Monday, June 6, 1836, at ten o'clock, these freemen are to receive their sentence, to gratify the hellish appetites of the aristocrats!

"On Monday, the liberty of the workingmen will be interred! Judge Edwards is to chant the requiem! Go! Go! Every freeman and workingman and hear the hollow and the melancholy sound of the earth on the coffin of equality! Let the courtroom, the City Hall, yea! the whole park be filled with *mourners.* But remember, offer no violence to Judge Edwards. Bend meekly, and receive the chain wherewith you are to be bound! Keep the peace! Above all things, keep the peace!"

Tuesday, Jan. 3 [1837].—

Mr. [William Beach] Lawrence, the Mayor, kept open house yesterday, according to custom from time immemorable, but the manners as well as the times have sadly changed. Formerly gentlemen visited the mayor, saluted him by an honest shake of the hand, paid him the compliment of the day, and took their leave; one out of twenty perhaps taking a single glass of wine or cherry bounce and a morsel of pound cake or New Year's cookies. But that respectable functionary is now considered the mayor of a party, and the rabble considering him "hail fellow well met," use his house as a Five Points[1] tavern. Mr. Lawrence has been much annoyed on former occasions, but the scene yesterday defies description. At ten o'clock the doors were beset by a crowd of importunate *sovereigns,* some of whom had already laid the foundations of *regal* glory and expected to become *royally* drunk at the hospitable house of His Honor. The rush was tremendous; the tables were taken by storm, the bottles emptied in a moment. Confusion, noise, and quarreling ensued,

---

[1] A crime-ridden area of New York city—ED.

until the mayor with the assistance of his police cleared the house and locked the doors, which were not reopened until every eatable and drinkable were removed, and a little decency and order restored.

I called soon after this change had taken place. The mayor related the circumstances to me with strong indignation, and I hope the evil will be remedied hereafter. All this comes of Mr. Lawrence being the mayor of a party and not of the city. Every scamp who has bawled out "Huzza for Lawrence" and "Down With the Whigs" considered himself authorized to use him and his house and furniture at his pleasure; to wear his hat in his presence, to smoke and spit upon his carpet, to devour his beef and turkey, and wipe his greasy fingers upon the curtains, to get drunk with his liquor, and discharge the reckoning with riotous shouts of "Huzza for our mayor." *We* put him in and *we* are entitled to the use of him. Mr. Lawrence (party man as he is) is too much of a gentleman to submit to this, and sometimes wishes his constituents and his office all to the devil, if I am not greatly mistaken, and if he rejects (as he has now done) their kind tokens of brotherly affection, they will be for sending him there ere long, and will look out for somebody of their own class less troubled than him with aristocratical notions of decency, order, and sobriety.

❖ *10* ❖

The Ferment of Reform

The generation preceding the Civil War was one of extraordinarily rapid change. These were years when thousands of immigrants, primarily from Ireland and Germany, descended on American shores. In 1854 alone 460,000 aliens arrived in the United States at a time when the nation's total population was only 26.5 million. It was an era of economic transformation, especially in the North. In the 1790s the first spinning mills for cotton yarn were established in New England. Twenty years later the first integrated textile factories began pouring out acres of cotton cloth. Canals and steamboats meanwhile made the movement of freight and people in the nation's interior relatively swift and efficient. The railroads arrived in the late 1830s, and by 1860 the country was covered by a network of track on which freight and passenger cars moved as fast as fifty miles an hour. An information revolution was also underway. In May 1844 Samuel F. B. Morse transmitted the proceedings of the Democratic Party's national convention from Baltimore to Washington over the lines of the brand new electric telegraph. Two years later Richard Hoe invented the rotary printing press, thus making possible vast runs of daily newspapers selling at a penny a copy.

The slave-holding South was largely impervious to these improvements, but they converted the North into a social caldron where new ideas and movements bubbled constantly to the surface of daily life. Many of these movements emphasized improving the world through legislation. Others sought personal regeneration through augmented personal resolve. Still others urged withdrawal from the corrupting world into miniature experimental societies of the virtuous. Thousands of people were swept up in the wave of zeal to remake the world. "We are all a little wild here with numberless projects of social reform," Ralph Waldo Emerson, the Concord philosopher, wrote the English essayist Thomas Carlyle in 1840. "Not a reading man but has a draft of a new community in his waistcoat pocket."

Not every American welcomed the enthusiasm for social change. Many deplored the "isms" breaking out all over, especially those like abolitionism and feminism, which threatened to subvert institutions deeply intrenched in the social system. The documents below deal with various aspects of the pre–Civil War reform surge. Inevitably they leave out large areas of the many-sided reform wave of the era, but they do concern several of the most important. The selections also include several critiques of the reformers and their causes.

10.1: Abolitionism (1831)

Few of the pre–Civil War reform movements had such a powerful impact on the nation as abolitionism. Attacks on slavery go back as far as the early eighteenth century. The assault grew more intense during the era of the American Revolution and expanded into a movement that effectively terminated the "peculiar institution" north of the Mason-Dixon line by the 1820s. Although it survived in the South, uneasiness with slavery led to a wave of personal emancipations by slave owners and a liberalization of southern slave codes. During this period antislavery advocates supported the gradual emancipation of the country's remaining slaves and sought to press their program by appealing to the consciences of southerners and slaveholders.

This moderate movement changed abruptly on January 1, 1831, with the appearance of a new antislavery publication, The Liberator, *published in Boston. Its editor was William Lloyd Garrison, a Massachusetts-born printer and editor, whose antislavery convictions derived from those of Benjamin Lundy, a Quaker abolitionist. Garrison rejected Lundy's mild tone and gentle tactics, however. He demanded "immediate" abolition, by which he meant that the process of freeing the slaves must begin at once, not being phased in as had been done earlier in the northern states. He harshly condemned both slavery and slaveholders, and rejected a view then common among antislavery advocates that freed blacks should be sent back to Africa ("colonized"). In 1833 Garrison founded the American Antislavery Society, which soon had scores of local affiliates all over the North that helped spread the antislavery message widely. By the end of the decade the antislavery societies had several thousand members, including a contingent of free blacks, men and women, who were among the most committed and effective members. By this time the antislavery movement had fissured into feuding groups, several of which deplored Garrison and his followers.*

The document that follows is the opening editorial of The Liberator,
*in effect Garrison's prospectus. Do you think his tone helped or hurt
the antislavery cause? What would you expect the reaction to the Gar-
risonian challenge to be in the North? In the South? Among other antislavery advocates? In fighting a malevolent institution like slavery, is
it better to be militant or compassionate?*

Manifesto of a New Antislavery Movement[1]

WILLIAM LLOYD GARRISON

To the Public.

In the month of August, I issued proposals for publishing "THE LIBERATOR" in
Washington City; but the enterprise, though hailed in different sections of the country, was palsied by public indifference. Since that time, the removal of the *Genius of
Universal Emancipation*[2] to the Seat of Government has rendered less imperious the
establishment of a similar periodical in that quarter.

During my recent tour for the purpose of exciting the minds of the people by a series of discourses on the subject of slavery, every place that I visited gave fresh evidence of the fact, that a greater revolution in public sentiment was to be effected in
the free States—*and particularly in New-England*—than at the South. I found contempt more bitter, opposition more active, detraction more relentless, prejudice
more stubborn, and apathy more frozen, than among slave-owners themselves. Of
course, there were individual exceptions to the contrary. This state of things afflicted, but did not dishearten me. I determined, at every hazard, to lift up the standard of emancipation in the eyes of the nation, *within sight of Bunker Hill and in the
birthplace of liberty.* That standard is now unfurled; and long may it float, unhurt by
the spoliations of time or the missiles of a desperate foe—yea, till every chain be
broken, and every bondman set free! Let Southern oppressors tremble—let their secret abettors tremble—let their Northern apologists tremble—let all the enemies of
the persecuted blacks tremble.

I deem the publication of my original Prospectus unnecessary, as it has obtained
a wide circulation. The principles therein inculcated will be steadily pursued in this
paper, excepting that I shall not array myself as the political partisan of any man. In
defending the great cause of human rights, I wish to derive the assistance of all reli-
gions and of all parties.

Assenting to the "self-evident truth" maintained in the American Declaration of
Independence, "that all men are created equal, and endowed by their Creator with
certain inalienable rights—among which are life, liberty, and the pursuit of happi-

William Lloyd Garrison, 1805–1879: The Story of His Life Told by His Children (New York: The Century Company, 1885), vol. 1, pp. 224–26.
[1]Original footnotes deleted.
[2]The antislavery publication of Garrison's mentor, Benjamin Lundy—ED.

ness," I shall strenuously contend for the immediate enfranchisement of our slave population. In Park-Street Church [in Boston], on the Fourth of July, 1829, in an address on slavery, I unreflectingly assented to the popular but pernicious doctrine of *gradual* abolition. I seize this opportunity to make a full and unequivocal recantation, and thus publicly to ask pardon of my God, of my country, and of my brethren the poor slaves, for having uttered a sentiment so full of timidity, injustice, and absurdity. A similar recantation, from my pen, was published in the *Genius of Universal Emancipation* at Baltimore, in September, 1829. My conscience is now satisfied.

I am aware that many object to the severity of my language; but is there not cause for severity? I *will be* as harsh as truth, and as uncompromising as justice. On this subject, I do not wish to think, or speak, or write, with moderation. No! No! Tell a man whose house is on fire to give a moderate alarm; tell him to moderately rescue his wife from the hands of the ravisher; tell the mother to gradually extricate her babe from the fire into which it has fallen;—but urge me not to use moderation in a cause like the present. I am in earnest—I will not equivocate—I will not excuse—I will not retreat a single inch—AND I WILL BE HEARD. The apathy of the people is enough to make every statue leap from its pedestal, and to hasten the resurrection of the dead.

It is pretended, that I am retarding the cause of emancipation by the coarseness of my invective and the precipitancy of my measures. *The charge is not true.* On this question my influence,—humble as it is,—is felt at this moment to a considerable extent, and shall be felt in coming years—not perniciously, but beneficially—not as a curse, but as a blessing; and posterity will bear testimony that I was right. I desire to thank God, that he enables me to disregard "the fear of man which bringeth a snare," and to speak his truth in its simplicity and power. And here I close with this fresh dedication:

> "*Oppression! I have seen thee, face to face,*
> *And met thy cruel eye and cloudy brow;*
> *But thy soul-withering glance I fear not now—*
> *For dread to prouder feelings doth give place*
> *Of deep abhorrence! Scorning the disgrace*
> *Of slavish knees that at thy footstool bow,*
> *I also kneel—but with far other vow*
> *Do hail thee and thy herd of hirelings base:—*
> *I swear, while life-blood warms my throbbing veins,*
> *Still to oppose and thwart, with heart and hand,*
> *Thy brutalising sway—till Afric's chains*
> *Are burst, and Freedom rules the rescued land,—*
> *Trampling Oppression and his iron rod:*
> *Such is the vow I take—SO HELP ME GOD!*"

WILLIAM LLOYD GARRISON.

BOSTON, January 1, 1831.

10.2: Women's Rights (1848)

American women were prominent in many of the pre–Civil War reform organizations and movements. During the earliest years of the nineteenth century, they had been active in Christian missionary and tract publishing societies dedicated to uplifting the "heathen" at home or on the remote shores of Oregon, Africa, or Asia. When the reform wave broadened during the 1830s, women established parallel all-female reform societies and auxiliaries to help with fund-raising and housekeeping services for the male-run organizations.

However devoted to social change, many of the male reformers refused to accept women as full equals. When dedicated female antislavery advocates like Angelina Grimké[1] sought to address mixed male-female audiences, they were renounced by all but the followers of William Lloyd Garrison, the most radical of the abolitionist leaders. At the 1840 World Anti-Slavery Convention in London, American women abolitionists were denied seats and were relegated to the gallery. It was at this London convention that Elizabeth Cady Stanton and Lucretia Mott met and began the association that would alter the fundamental relations between men and women.

In 1848 Stanton, backed by Mott, issued a call for a meeting to consider women's rights at Seneca Falls, New York. The Seneca Falls convention assembled in a year when much of the Euro-American world was in great social and political ferment. Moreover, the small community near Rochester was in the heart of the "Burned Over" district of western New York where waves of evangelical revivals had shaken people out of accustomed beliefs and modes of behavior. It was the right time and right setting for a call to revolutionary change.

The convention's Declaration of Sentiments was modeled after the Declaration of Independence, but it is a statement of feminist grievances and an eloquent indictment of "woman's" oppressors.

In what ways were American women oppressed in 1848? . . . Almost a century and a half has elapsed since the Seneca Falls convention. Has the feminist description of a male-dominated American society changed drastically? Since women have long since acquired the vote, how do you explain the sense of oppression some women still feel?

---

[1]Angelina and Sarah Grimké were two South Carolina sisters who despised the slavery of their home state and fled to Philadelphia in the 1820s. There they became Quakers and activists in the antislavery movement. Angelina later married the eloquent abolitionist Theodore Dwight Weld, one of Garrison's more moderate colleagues.

The Seneca Falls Declaration of Sentiments and Resolutions
July 19, 1848

1. Declaration of Sentiments

When, in the course of human events, it becomes necessary for one portion of the family of man to assume among the people of the earth a position different from that which they have hitherto occupied, but one to which the laws of nature and of nature's God entitle them, a decent respect to the opinions of mankind requires that they should declare the causes that impel them to such a course.

We hold these truths to be self-evident: that all men and women are created equal; that they are endowed by their Creator with certain inalienable rights; that among these are life, liberty, and the pursuit of happiness; that to secure these rights governments are instituted, deriving their just powers from the consent of the governed. Whenever any form of government becomes destructive of these ends, it is the right of those who suffer from it to refuse allegiance to it, and to insist upon the institution of a new government, laying its foundation on such principles, and organizing its powers in such form, as to them shall seem most likely to effect their safety and happiness. Prudence, indeed, will dictate that governments long established should not be changed for light and transient causes; and accordingly all experience hath shown that mankind are more disposed to suffer while evils are sufferable, than to right themselves by abolishing the forms to which they are accustomed. But when a long train of abuses and usurpations, pursuing invariably the same object, evinces a design to reduce them under absolute despotism, it is their duty to throw off such government, and to provide new guards for their future security. Such has been the patient sufferance of the women under this government, and such is now the necessity which constrains them to demand the equal station to which they are entitled.

The history of mankind is a history of repeated injuries and usurpations on the part of man toward woman, having in direct object the establishment of an absolute tyranny over her. To prove this, let facts be submitted to a candid world.

He has never permitted her to exercise her inalienable right to the elective franchise.

He has compelled her to submit to laws, in the formation of which she had no voice.

He has withheld from her rights which are given to the most ignorant and degraded men—both natives and foreigners.

Having deprived her of this first right of a citizen, the elective franchise, thereby leaving her without representation in the halls of legislation, he has oppressed her on all sides.

He has made her, if married, in the eye of the law, civilly dead.

He has taken from her all right in property, even to the wages she earns.

Elizabeth Cady Stanton, et al., *The Declaration of Sentiments and Resolutions of the Seneca Falls Convention, July 19, 1848.* (New York: Robert J. Johnston Printer, 1870), pp. 20–21.

He has made her, morally, an irresponsible being, as she can commit many crimes with impunity, provided they be done in the presence of her husband. In the covenant of marriage, she is compelled to promise obedience to her husband, he becoming, to all intents and purposes, her master—the law giving him power to deprive her of her liberty, and to administer chastisement.

He has so framed the laws of divorce, as to what shall be the proper causes, and in case of separation, to whom the guardianship of the children shall be given, as to be wholly regardless of the happiness of women—the law, in all cases, going upon a false supposition of the supremacy of man, and giving all power into his hands.

After depriving her of all rights as a married woman, if single, and the owner of property, he has taxed her to support a government which recognizes her only when her property can be made profitable to it.

He has monopolized nearly all the profitable employments, and from those she is permitted to follow, she receives but a scanty remuneration. He closes against her all the avenues to wealth and distinction which he considers most honorable to himself. As a teacher of theology, medicine, or law, she is not known.

He has denied her the facilities for obtaining a thorough education, all colleges being closed against her.

He allows her in Church, as well as State, but a subordinate position, claiming Apostolic authority for her exclusion from the ministry, and, with some exceptions, from any public participation in the affairs of the Church.

He has created a false public sentiment by giving to the world a different code of morals for men and women, by which moral delinquencies which exclude women from society, are not only tolerated, but deemed of little account in man.

He has usurped the prerogative of Jehovah himself, claiming it as his right to assign for her a sphere of action, when that belongs to her conscience and to her God.

He has endeavored, in every way that he could, to destroy her confidence in her own powers, to lessen her self-respect and to make her willing to lead a dependent and abject life.

Now, in view of this entire disfranchisement of one-half the people of this country, their social and religious degradation—in view of the unjust laws above mentioned, and because women do feel themselves aggrieved, oppressed, and fraudulently deprived of their most sacred rights, we insist that they have immediate admission to all the rights and privileges which belong to them as citizens of the United States.

In entering upon the great work before us, we anticipate no small amount of misconception, misrepresentation, and ridicule; but we shall use every instrumentality within our power to effect our object. We shall employ agents, circulate tracts, petition the State and National legislatures, and endeavor to enlist the pulpit and the press in our behalf. We hope this Convention will be followed by a series of Conventions embracing every part of the country.

2. Resolutions

WHEREAS, The great precept of nature is conceded to be, that "man shall pursue his own true and substantial happiness." Blackstone in his Commentaries remarks, that this law of Nature being coeval with mankind, and dictated by God himself, is of course superior in obligation to any other. It is binding over all the globe, in all countries and at all times; no human laws are of any validity if contrary to this, and such of them as are valid, derive all their force, and all their validity, and all their authority, mediately and immediately, from this original; therefore,

Resolved, That all laws which prevent woman from occupying such a station in society as her conscience shall dictate, or which place her in a position inferior to that of man, are contrary to the great precept of nature, and therefore of no force or authority.

Resolved, That woman is man's equal—was intended to be so by the Creator, and the highest good of the race demands that she should be recognized as such.

Resolved, That the women of this country ought to be enlightened in regard to the laws under which they live, that they may no longer publish their degradation by declaring themselves satisfied with their present position, nor their ignorance, by asserting that they have all the rights they want.

Resolved, That inasmuch as man, while claiming for himself intellectual superiority, does accord to woman moral superiority, it is pre-eminently his duty to encourage her to speak and teach, as she has an opportunity, in all religious assemblies.

Resolved, That the same amount of virtue, delicacy, and refinement of behavior that is required of woman in the social state, should also be required of man, and the same transgressions should be visited with equal severity on both man and woman.

Resolved, That the objection of indelicacy and impropriety, which is so often brought against woman when she addresses a public audience, comes with a very ill-grace from those who encourage, by their attendance, her appearance on the stage, in the concert, or in feats of the circus.

Resolved, That woman has too long rested satisfied in the circumscribed limits which corrupt customs and a perverted application of the Scriptures have marked out for her, and that it is time she should move in the enlarged sphere which her great Creator has assigned her.

Resolved, That it is the duty of the women of this country to secure to themselves their sacred right to the elective franchise.

Resolved, That the equality of human rights results necessarily from the fact of the identity of the race in capabilities and responsibilities.

Resolved, That the speedy success of our cause depends upon the zealous and untiring efforts of both men and women, for the overthrow of the monopoly of the pulpit, and for the securing to women an equal participation with men in the various trades, professions, and commerce.

Resolved, therefore, That, being invested by the creator with the same capabilities, and the same consciousness of responsibility for their exercise, it is demonstrably the right and duty of woman, equally with man, to promote every righteous cause by every righteous means; and especially in regard to the great subjects of morals and religion, it is self-evidently her right to participate with her brother in teaching them, both in private and in public, by writing and by speaking, by any instrumentalities proper to be used, and in any assemblies proper to be held; and this being a self-evident truth growing out of the divinely implanted principles of human nature, any custom or authority adverse to it, whether modern or wearing the hoary sanction of antiquity, is to be regarded as a self-evident falsehood, and at war with mankind.

10.3: Dorothea L. Dix and the Plight of the Mentally Ill (1843)

Among the most vigorous and determined reformers of the pre–Civil War era was Dorothea L. Dix, a Maine-born schoolteacher who abandoned her profession in 1835 when her health failed. In 1841 Dix discovered her true vocation when, in the course of teaching a Sunday school class in the House of Correction in East Cambridge, Massachusetts, she discovered that the authorities had packed a group of mentally ill people into filthy, unheated cells where they had been neglected and mistreated.

Dix spent the next two years investigating the condition of the mentally ill poor in Massachusetts, and her revulsion and horror grew. In 1843 she addressed a memorial to the state legislature, which is excerpted below, describing her findings and requesting an appropriation to provide more humane and medically useful treatment facilities for these unfortunate people. The state responded by expanding the existing Worcester Insane Asylum.

Dix soon extended her horizons beyond her own state and became the standard-bearer of a new movement to provide clean, well equipped, well administered "asylums" where the mentally ill could find havens and receive treatment. During the next decade she helped induce eleven state legislatures to appropriate funds to build asylums and even convinced Congress to approve a federal land grant to support care of the mentally ill. This measure was vetoed by President Franklin Pierce, however. Dix was also interested in the emerging nursing profession, and during the Civil War she served the Union as Superintendent of Women Nurses.

Why does Dix appear so humble in her petition? The horrendous conditions she describes may seem ample explanation for her activities, but were they new conditions? How had Americans provided for the mentally impaired in earlier periods? Had the conditions Dix recounts existed for many years? Why might a person like Dix have been particularly empathetic toward those she describes? Did the state-supported asylum system she helped create achieve the results she desired? What has happened to that system in recent years?

Memorial to the Legislature of Massachusetts

DOROTHEA L. DIX

GENTLEMEN,

I respectfully ask to present this Memorial, believing that the *cause,* which actuates to and sanctions so unusual a movement, presents no equivocal claim to public consideration and sympathy. Surrendering to calm and deep convictions of duty my habitual views of what is womanly and becoming, I proceed briefly to explain what has conducted me before you unsolicited and unsustained, trusting, while I do so, that the memorialist will be speedily forgotten in the memorial.

About two years since leisure afforded opportunity, and duty prompted me to visit several prisons and alms-houses in the vicinity of this metropolis. I found, near Boston, in the Jails and Asylums for the poor, a numerous class brought into unsuitable connexion with criminals and the general mass of Paupers. I refer to Idiots and Insane persons, dwelling in circumstances not only adverse to their own physical and moral improvement, but productive of extreme disadvantages to all other persons brought into association with them. I applied myself diligently to trace the causes of these evils, and sought to supply remedies. As one obstacle was surmounted, fresh difficulties appeared. Every new investigation has given depth to the conviction that it is only by decided, prompt, and vigorous legislation the evils to which I refer, and which I shall proceed more fully to illustrate, can be remedied. I shall be obliged to speak with great plainness, and to reveal many things revolting to the taste, and from which my woman's nature shrinks with peculiar sensitiveness. But truth is the highest consideration. *I tell what I have seen*—painful and shocking as the details often are—that from them you may feel more deeply the imperative obligation which lies upon you to prevent the possibility of a repetition or continuance of such outrages upon humanity. If I inflict pain upon you, and move you to horror, it is to acquaint you with sufferings which you have the power to alleviate, and make you hasten to the relief of the victims of legalized barbarity.

I come to present the strong claims of suffering humanity. I come to place before the Legislature of Massachusetts the condition of the miserable, the desolate, the outcast: I come as the advocate of helpless, forgotten, insane and idiotic men and women; of beings, sunk to a condition from which the most unconcerned would start with real horror; of beings wretched in our Prisons, and more wretched in our Alms-Houses. And I cannot suppose it needful to employ earnest persuasion, or stubborn argument, in order to arrest and fix attention upon a subject, only the more strongly pressing in its claims, because it is revolting and disgusting in its details.

I must confine myself to few examples, but am ready to furnish other and more complete details, if required. If my pictures are displeasing, coarse, and severe, my subjects, it must be recollected, offer no tranquil, refined, or composing features.

Dorothea L. Dix, Memorial to the Legislature of Massachusetts, 1843. In *On Behalf Of the Insane Poor: Selected Reports* (New York: Arno Press, 1971), pp. 3–9.

The condition of human beings, reduced to the extremest states of degradation and misery, cannot be exhibited in softened language, or adorn a polished page.

I proceed, Gentlemen, briefly to call your attention to the *present* state of Insane Persons confined within this Commonwealth, in *cages, closets, cellars, stalls, pens! Chained, naked, beaten with rods,* and *lashed* into obedience!

As I state cold, severe *facts,* I feel obliged to refer to persons, and definitely to indicate localities. But it is upon my subject, not upon localities or individuals, I desire to fix attention; and I would speak as kindly as possible of all Wardens, Keepers, and other responsible officers, believing that *most* of these have erred not through hardness of heart and wilful cruelty, so much as want of skill and knowledge, and want of consideration. Familiarity with suffering, it is said, blunts the sensibilities, and where neglect once finds a footing other injuries are multiplied. This is not all, for it may justly and strongly be added that, from the deficiency of adequate means to meet the wants of these cases, it has been an absolute impossibility to do justice in this matter. Prisons are not constructed in view of being converted into County Hospitals, and Alms-Houses are not founded as receptacles for the Insane. And yet, in the face of justice and common sense, Wardens are by law compelled to receive, and the Masters of Alms-Houses not to refuse, Insane and Idiotic subjects in all stages of mental disease and privation.

It is the Commonwealth, not its integral parts, that is accountable for most of the abuses which have lately, and do still exist. I repeat it, it is defective legislation which perpetuates and multiplies these abuses.

In illustration of my subject, I offer the following extracts from my Notebook and Journal:—

Springfield

In the jail, one lunatic woman, furiously mad, a state pauper, improperly situated, both in regard to the prisoners, the keepers, and herself. It is a case of extreme self-forgetfulness and oblivion to all the decencies of life; to describe which, would be to repeat only the grossest scenes. She is much worse since leaving Worcester. In the almshouse of the same town is a woman apparently only needing judicious care, and some well-chosen employment, to make it unnecessary to confine her in solitude, in a dreary unfurnished room. Her appeals for employment and companionship are most touching, but the mistress replied, 'she had no time to attend to her.'
. . .

Plympton

One insane, three idiots; condition wretched.

Besides the above, I have seen many who, part of the year, are chained or caged. The use of cages all but universal; hardly a town but can refer to some not distant period of using them: chains are less common: negligences frequent: wilful abuse less frequent than sufferings proceeding from ignorance, or want of consideration. I encountered during the last three months many poor creatures wandering reckless and unprotected through the country. Innumerable accounts have been sent me of persons who had roved away unwatched and unsearched after;

and I have heard that responsible persons, controlling the almshouses, have not thought themselves culpable in sending away from their shelter, to cast upon the chances of remote relief, insane men and women. These, left on the highways, un-friended and incompetent to control or direct their own movements, sometimes have found refuge in the hospital, and others have not been traced. But I cannot particularize; in traversing the state I have found hundreds of insane persons in every variety of circumstance and condition; many whose situation could not and need not be improved; a less number, but that very large, whose lives are the sad-dest pictures of human suffering and degradation. I give a few illustrations; but de-scription fades before reality.

Danvers

November; visited the almshouse; a large building, much out of repair; understand a new one is in contemplation. Here are from fifty-six to sixty inmates; one idiotic; three insane; one of the latter in close confinement at all times.

Long before reaching the house, wild shouts, snatches of rude songs, impreca-tions, and obscene language, fell upon the ear, proceeding from the occupant of a low building, rather remote from the principal building to which my course was di-rected. Found the mistress, and was conducted to the place, which was called '*the home*' of the *forlorn* maniac, a young woman, exhibiting a condition of neglect and misery blotting out the faintest idea of comfort, and outraging every sentiment of decency. She had been, I learnt, "a respectable person; industrious and worthy; dis-appointments and trials shook her mind, and finally laid prostrate reason and self-control; she became a maniac for life! She had been at Worcester Hospital for a considerable time, and had been returned as incurable." The mistress told me she understood that, while there, she was "comfortable and decent." Alas! what a change was here exhibited! She had passed from one degree of violence and degra-dation to another, in swift progress; there she stood, clinging to, or beating upon, the bars of her caged apartment, the contracted size of which afforded space only for in-creasing accumulations of filth, a *foul* spectacle; there she stood with naked arms and dishevelled hair; the unwashed frame invested with fragments of unclean gar-ments, the air so extremely offensive, though ventilation was afforded on all sides save one, that it was not possible to remain beyond a few moments without retreat-ing for recovery to the outward air. Irritation of body, produced by utter filth and exposure, incited her to the horrid process of tearing off her skin by inches; her face, neck, and person, were thus disfigured to hideousness; she held up a fragment just rent off; to my exclamation of horror, the mistress replied, "oh, we can't help it; half the skin is off sometimes; we can do nothing with her; and it makes no differ-ence what she eats, for she consumes her own filth as readily as the food which is brought her."

It is now January; a fortnight since, two visitors reported that most wretched outcast as "wallowing in dirty straw, in a place yet more dirty, and without cloth-ing, without fire. Worse cared for than the brutes, and wholly lost to consciousness of decency!" Is the whole story told? What was seen, is; what is reported is not. These gross exposures are not for the pained sight of one alone; all, all, coarse, brutal men, wondering, neglected children, old and young, each and all, witness this lowest, foulest state of miserable humanity. And who protects her, that worse than Paria outcast, from other wrongs and blacker outrages? I do not *know* that such *have been.* I do know that they are to be dreaded, and that they are not guarded against.

Some may say these things cannot be remedied; these furious maniacs are not to be raised from these base conditions. I *know* they are; could give *many* examples; let *one* suffice. A young woman, a pauper, in a distant town, *Sandisfield,* was for years a raging maniac. A cage, chains, and *the whip,* were the agents for controlling her, united with harsh tones and profane language. Annually, with others (the town's poor) she was put up at auction, and bid off at the lowest price which was declared for her. One year, not long past, an old man came forward in the number of applicants for the poor wretch; he was taunted and ridiculed; "what would he and his old wife do with such a mere beast?" "My wife says yes," replied he, "and I shall take her." She was given to his charge; he conveyed her home; she was washed, neatly dressed, and placed in a decent bed-room, furnished for comfort and opening into the kitchen. How altered her condition! As yet *the chains* were not off. The first week she was somewhat restless, at times violent, but the quiet kind ways of the old people wrought a change; she received her food decently; forsook acts of violence, and no longer uttered blasphemous or indecent language; after a week, the chain was lengthened, and she was received as a companion into the kitchen. Soon she engaged in trivial employments. "After a fortnight," said the old man, "I knocked off the chains and made her a free woman." She is at times excited, but not violently; they are careful of her diet; they keep her very clean; she calls them "father" and "mother." Go there now and you will find her "clothed," and though not perfectly in her "right mind," so far restored as to be a safe and comfortable inmate.

Newburyport

Visited the almshouse in June last; eighty inmates; seven insane, one idiotic. Commodious and neat house; several of the partially insane apparently very comfortable; two very improperly situated, namely, an insane man, not considered incurable, in an out-building, whose room opened up on what was called 'the dead room, affording in lieu of companionship with the living, a contemplation of corpses! The other subject was a woman in a *cellar.* I desired to see her; much reluctance was shown. I pressed the request; the Master of the House stated that she was *in the cellar;* that she was *dangerous to be approached;* that 'she had lately attacked his wife;' and *was often naked.* I persisted; 'if you will not go with me, give me the keys and I will go alone.' Thus importuned, the outer doors were opened. I descended the stairs from within; a strange, unnatural noise seemed to proceed from beneath our feet; at the moment I did not much regard it. My conductor proceeded to remove a padlock, while my eye explored the wide space in quest of the poor woman. All for a moment was still. But judge my horror and amazement, when a door to a closet *beneath* the *staircase* was opened, revealing in the imperfect light a female apparently wasted to a skeleton, partially wrapped in blankets, furnished for the narrow bed on which she was sitting; her countenance furrowed, not by age, but suffering, was the image of distress; in that contracted space, unlighted, unventilated, she poured forth the wailings of despair: mournfully she extended her arms and appealed to me, "why am I consigned to hell? dark—dark—I used to pray, I used to read the Bible—I have done no crime in my heart; I had friends, why have all forsaken me!—my God! my God! why hast *thou* forsaken me!" Those groans, those wailings come up daily, mingling, with how many others, a perpetual and sad memorial. When the good Lord shall require an account of our stewardship, what shall all and each answer!

Perhaps it will be inquired how long, how many days or hours was she imprisoned in these confined limits? *For years!* In another part of the cellar were other small closets, only better, because higher through the entire length, into one of which she by turns was transferred, so as to afford opportunity for fresh whitewashing, &c.

10.4:   Sarah Josepha Hale on Women and Peace Societies (1840)

Although educated, middle-class women were disproportionately represented in virtually all the reform societies, they were undoubtedly a minority of their group. Most women, as most people generally, were probably indifferent to all public causes. And others actively opposed the female reformers as unappealing social disrupters and betrayers of their sex.

One conservative female voice of this era was Sarah Josepha Hale, literary editor of the popular and successful magazine for women, the Lady's Book. *Hale fought for better education for women and deplored restrictions on married women, but she also opposed the women's suffrage activists and the militant female reformers, who to her seemed "unwomanly." In the selection below she advises her readers against joining peace societies and against adopting the ways of the more extreme "non-resisters," who were opposed to all war regardless of cause. ("Peace societies" were part of a movement begun during the late 1820s to abolish war. It eventually attracted the attention of William Lloyd Garrison as well as Elizabeth Cady Stanton and the Grimké sisters, who joined its extreme pacifist, "non-resister" wing opposed to all war, defensive as well as offensive.)*

Why is Hale's editorial focused on George Washington? What does she believe the proper stand on peace for women to take? Why does she believe that peace may have its problems too? How might Hale's position at the magazine have influenced her views of reform?

Ought Ladies to Form Peace Societies?

SARAH JOSEPHA HALE

We had the honour of a letter, some time since, from a distinguished advocate of the peace cause, on the above subject. The writer blamed the ladies of America, particularly the literary ladies, severely, for the encouragement they give to the warlike spirit among men. Mrs. Hemans[1] poetry was denounced in round terms, mothers were accused of kindling the martial enthusiasm of their sons by allowing them drums as playthings, and the opportunity of seeing military parades, and worse than these, it was affirmed, was the character and example of our Washington, to which these young aspirants for fame were always referred, as to a pattern of perfection.

Now it appears to us that the name of Washington is a surer check to the fierce and fiend-like passions enkindled by war, and to the lust of conquest, than all the prudential arguments which were ever urged by the advocates of peace. His example has thrown shame on the selfish ambition of warriors who, for their own glory, poured out the blood of their soldiers, and freed their country from foreign oppressors only to fix a more galling yoke of servitude to themselves. Public opinion has a *new and moral model for a hero*. It is a model that will accelerate the reign of peace. It has made justice, self-denial, and humanity necessary to the soldier. The example of Washington withered the laurels of Bonaparte; it prevented Bolivar from placing a crown on his head. The war, therefore, in which Washington triumphed, should be kept in remembrance by every one who wishes the advancement of the world in knowledge, peace and happiness. From the history of that period, all may learn their duties as men, citizens, Christians. But the picture must be exhibited, if we wish to have it examined. Mothers must tell their sons of the virtues of Washington, of the trials he endured, the wars in which he was engaged, if they wish them to profit by the example of prudence, justice, fortitude, moderation and *piety* which he has left as a most precious legacy to his countrymen.

And if the history of our Revolution must be withheld from our sons, lest they should acquire an admiration for war, we must also prohibit the Bible from being read, for we are there assured that God has taught "hands to war," and given "strength for the battle." And we as fully believe that God blessed the labours of our patriots, and directed the movements of our armies, as he did those of Israel of old, and that we are bound to remember his goodness and give him grateful thanks for inspiring the colonists with courage to resist their oppressors, thus exhibiting an example to the world of the holy patriotism of a people called to be free, and the pattern of a perfect hero.

We fully agree with our respected correspondent that this subject of "peculiar worth" is one which ought deeply to interest our own sex. Though the sins of war are chiefly perpetrated by men, the sufferings fall most heavily on the women. Devoutly do we wish the reign of universal peace; but we do not think that the cause

Sarah Josepha Hale, "Ought Ladies to Form Peace Societies?" *Lady's Book,* vol. 21 (July–December 1840), pp. 88–89.
[1]Felicia Hemans, a minor pre–Civil War poet—ED.

will be materially advanced by the formation of "Ladies Peace Societies;" nor, indeed, by urging on men to become professors of the "non-resistance principle." In all humility, we would suggest that *peace* has its dangers and temptations as well as war. It is far more likely that the virtues and liberties of our country will be destroyed by the luxuries of the former than the wasting of the latter. The tree which grew stronger for the tempest will in the hot sunshine droop and wither; the cankerworm may destroy what the lion could not have overturned.

Our peace societies must exert their influence in suppressing the peculiar vices which prosperity engenders, those which spring from idleness, security, and abundance, before they will deserve to be esteemed as of much benefit to public morals. What advantage is it to stay the thunderbolt, if the impure vapours are permitted to accumulate? The lightning might destroy a few lives, the pestilence will sweep away multitudes. All history attests the fact, that luxury, such as grows rank among the people of a Republic, only in times of peace, is more baneful than the ambition of renown. Greece, Rome, Venice, all perished by the corruptions of wealth, not the crimes of war. Carthage only, of all the ancient Republics, was destroyed in battle; that would not have occurred had not the soldiers of Hannibal been enervated by the luxuries of peace at Capus.

It appears to us, therefore, that our American ladies will act the wiser part to teach their children to be temperate in all things, to do, in all cases as they would wish to be done by, to practise self-denial and the noble spirit of forgiveness towards their enemies, and of ready kindness to every one, than to spend their time in discussions on the propriety of a "Congress of nations in settling the peace of the world," or even devising how they shall prevent their little sons from looking on a military review. We deem it better that woman should study the things which make for peace at home, rather than devote her thoughts to the dissemination of peace principles abroad. Is she careful to promote peace in her own family and neighbourhood, is she gentle, kind, and charitable in her opinion of others? She may be sure that she is fulfilling the duties assigned by her divine *Teacher,* and that these humble duties, when performed in a right spirit, will be blessed to the promotion of his kingdom of peace on earth.

10.5: A Utopian Community (1841)

Utopian experiments thrived in the North during the antebellum period. Communal endeavors often embraced programs of political or social improvement and were replete with religious overtones or purposes. At their heart was usually a longing for the perfectibility of humanity on earth.

The Brook Farm Association, established in Roxbury, Massachusetts, attracted several of the day's most prominent American writers, including Nathaniel Hawthorne. The community espoused the principles of transcendentalism, which provided the basis for the writings of

Emerson, Thoreau, and Whitman. Hawthorne later provided a fictional account of his experience at Brook Farm in his novel The Blithedale Romance *(1852).*

What does the Brook Farm Constitution tell us of this community? How do its principles seem similar to and different from communal experiments today?

The Constitution of the Brook Farm Association

In order more effectually to promote the great purposes of human culture; to establish the external relations of life on a basis of wisdom and purity; to apply the principles of justice and love to our social organization in accordance with the laws of Divine Providence; to substitute a system of brotherly coöperation for one of selfish competition; to secure to our children and those who may be entrusted to our care, the benefits of the highest physical, intellectual and moral education, which in the progress of knowledge the resources at our command will permit; to institute an attractive, efficient, and productive system of industry; to prevent the exercise of worldly anxiety, by the competent supply of our necessary wants; to diminish the desire of excessive accumulation, by making the acquisition of individual property subservient to upright and disinterested uses; to guarantee to each other forever the means of physical support, and of spiritual progress; and thus to impart a greater freedom, simplicity, truthfulness, refinement, and moral dignity, to our mode of life;—we the undersigned do unite in a voluntary Association, and adopt and ordain the following articles of agreement, to wit:

Article I

Sec. 1. The name of this Association shall be "THE BROOK-FARM ASSOCIATION FOR INDUSTRY AND EDUCATION." All persons who shall hold one or more shares in its stock, or whose labor and skill shall be considered an equivalent for capital, may be admitted by the vote of two-thirds of the Association, as members thereof.

Sec. 2. No member of the Association shall ever be subjected to any religious test; nor shall any authority be assumed over individual freedom of opinion by the Association, nor by any one member over another; nor shall any one be held accountable to the Association, except for such overt acts, omissions of duty, as violate the principles of justice, purity, and love, on which it is founded; and in such cases the relation of any member may be suspended, or discontinued, at the pleasure of the Association.

"The Constitution of the Brook Farm Association." In O. B. Frothingham, *Transcendentalism in New England* (New York: G. P. Putnam's Sons, 1876), p. 159ff.

Article II

Sec. 1. The members of this Association shall own and manage such real and personal estate in joint stock proprietorship, divided into shares of one hundred dollars, each, as may from time to time be agreed on. . . .

Sec. 4. The shareholders on their part, for themselves, their heirs and assigns, do renounce all claim on any profits accruing to the Association for the use of their capital invested in the stock of the Association, except five per cent, interest on the amount of stock held by them, payable in the manner described in the preceding section.

Article III

Sec. 1. The Association shall provide such employment for all its members as shall be adapted to their capacities, habits, and tastes; and each member shall select and perform such operations of labor, whether corporal or mental, as shall be deemed best suited to his own endowments, and the benefit of the Association.

Sec. 2. The Association guarantees to all its members, their children, and family dependents, house-rent, fuel, food, and clothing, and the other necessaries of life, without charge, not exceeding a certain fixed amount to be decided annually by the Association; no charge shall ever be made for support during inability to labor from sickness or old age, or for medical or nursing attendance, except in case of shareholders, who shall be charged therefor . . . but no charge shall be made to any members for education or the use of library and public rooms. . . .

Article V

Sec. 1. The government of the Association shall be vested in a board of Directors, divided into four departments as follows; 1st., General Direction; 2d, Direction of Education; 3d., Direction of Industry; 4th, Direction of Finance; consisting of three persons each. . . .

Sec. 5. The departments of Education and Finance shall be under the control each of its own Direction, which shall select, and in concurrence with the General Direction, shall appoint such teachers, officers, and agents, as shall be necessary to the complete and systematic organization of the department. No Directors or other officers shall be deemed to possess any rank superior to the other members of the Association, nor shall they receive any extra remuneration for their official services.

Sec. 6. The department of Industry shall be arranged in groups and series, as far as practicable, and shall consist of three primary series: to wit, Agricultural, Mechanical, and Domestic Industry. The chief of each series shall be elected every two months by the members thereof. . . .

10.6:   Unitarianism and Christian Benevolence (1836)

Religious fervor pervaded nineteenth century reform. Unitarianism con-
stituted an approach to Christianity that emphasized God's goodness to
humanity and the opportunity of individuals to live freely and perfect the
society around them. Unitarianism was based in optimism, universalism,
and confidence in humanistic progress.

The Blessings of Christianity

WILLIAM ELLERY CHANNING

Among the many and inestimable blessings of Christianity, I regard as not the least the new sentiment with which it teaches man to look upon his fellow beings; the new interest which it awakens in us toward everything human; the new importance which it gives to the soul; the new relation which it establishes between man and man. In this respect it began a mighty revolution, which has been silently spreading itself through society, and which, I believe, is not to stop until new ties shall have taken the place of those which have hitherto, in the main, connected the human race. Christianity has as yet but begun its work of reformation.Under its influences a new order of society is advancing, surely though slowly; and this beneficent change it is to accomplish in no small measure by revealing to men their own na-ture, and teaching them to "honor all" who partake it.

As yet Christianity has done little, compared with what it is to do, in establishing the true bond of union between man and man. The old bonds of society still con-tinue in a great degree. They are instinct, interest, force. The true tie, which is mu-tual respect, calling forth mutual, growing, never-failing acts of love, is as yet little known. A new revelation, if I may so speak, remains to be made; or rather, the truths of the old revelation in regard to the greatness of human nature are to be brought out from obscurity and neglect. The soul is to be regarded with a religious reverence hitherto unfelt; and the solemn claims of every being to whom this divine principle is imparted are to be established on the ruins of those pernicious princi-ples, both in church and state, which have so long divided mankind into the classes of the abject many and the self-exalting few.

There is nothing of which men know so little as themselves. They understand in-comparably more of the surrounding creation, of matter and of its laws, than of that spiritual principle to which matter was made to be the minister, and without which the outward universe would be worthless. . . . Men have as yet no just respect for themselves, and of consequence no just respect for others. The true bond of society is thus wanting; and accordingly there is a great deficiency of Christian benevo-lence. There is, indeed, much instinctive, native benevolence, and this is not to be despised; but the benevolence of Jesus Christ, which consists in a calm purpose to

The Works of William Elery Channing (Boston, 1886), pp. 109–13, 120–21.

suffer and, if need be, to die, for our fellow creatures, the benevolence of Christ on the cross, which is the true pattern to the Christian, this is little known; and what is the cause? It is this. We see nothing in human beings to entitle them to such sacrifices; we do not think them worth suffering for. Why should we be martyrs for beings who awaken in us little more of moral interest than the brutes?

I hold that nothing is to make man a true lover of man but the discovery of something interesting and great in human nature. We must see and feel that a human being is something important, and of immeasurable importance. We must see and feel the broad distance between the spiritual life within us and the vegetable or animal life which acts around us. I cannot love the flower, however beautiful, with a disinterested affection which will make me sacrifice to it my own prosperity. . . .

To show the grounds on which the obligation to honor all men rests, I might take a minute survey of that human nature which is common to all, and set forth its claims to reverence. But, leaving this wide range, I observe that there is one principle of the soul which makes all men essentially equal, which places all on a level as to means of happiness, which may place in the first rank of human beings those who are the most depressed in worldly condition, and which therefore gives the most depressed a title to interest and respect. I refer to the sense of duty, to the power of discerning and doing right, to the moral and religious principle, to the inward monitor which speaks in the name of God, to the capacity of virtue or excellence. This is the great gift of God. We can conceive no greater. In seraph and archangel, we can conceive no higher energy than the power of virtue, or the power of forming themselves after the will and moral perfections of God. This power breaks down all barriers between the seraph and the lowest human being; it makes them brethren. Whoever has derived from God this perception and capacity of rectitude has a bond of union with the spiritual world stronger than all the ties of nature. He possesses a principle which, if he is faithful to it, must carry him forward forever, and insures to him the improvement and happiness of the highest order of beings. . . .

Having shown, in the preceding remarks, that there is a foundation in the human soul for the honor enjoined in our text toward all men, I proceed to observe that, if we look next into Christianity, we shall find this duty enforced by new and still more solemn considerations. This whole religion is a testimony to the worth of man in the sight of God, to the importance of human nature, to the infinite purposes for which we were framed. God is there set forth as sending to the succor of his human family his Beloved Son, the bright image and representative of his own perfections; and sending him, not simply to roll away a burden of pain and punishment (for this, however mangified in systems of theology, is not his highest work), but to create men after that divine image which he himself bears, to purify the soul from every stain, to communicate to it new power over evil, and to open before it immortality as its aim and destination—immortality, by which we are to understand, not merely a perpetual, but an ever-improving and celestial being. Such are the views of Christianity. And these blessings it proffers, not to a few, not to the educated, not to the eminent, but to all human beings, to the poorest and the most fallen; and we know that, through the power of its promises, it has in not a few instances raised the most fallen to true greatness, and given them in their present virtue and peace an earnest of the Heaven which it unfolds. Such is Christianity. Men, viewed in the light of this religion, are beings cared for by God, to whom he has given his Son, on whom he pours forth his Spirit, and whom he has created for the highest good in the universe, for participation in his own perfections and happiness. My friends, such is Christianity. Our skepticism as to our own nature cannot quench the bright light which that religion sheds on the soul and on the prospects of mankind; and just as far as we receive its truth, we shall honor all men. . . .

. . . I would only say, "Honor all men." Honor man, from the beginning to the end of his earthly course. Honor the child. Welcome into being the infant with a feeling of its mysterious grandeur, with the feeling that an immortal existence has begun, that a spirit has been kindled which is never to be quenched. Honor the child. On this principle all good education rests. Never shall we learn to train up the child till we take it in our arms, as Jesus did, and feel distinctly that "of such is the kingdom of heaven." In that short sentence is taught the spirit of the true system of education; and for want of understanding it, little effectual aid, I fear, is yet given to the heavenly principle in the infant soul.—Again. Honor the poor. This sentiment of respect is essential to improving the connection between the more and less prosperous conditions of society. This alone makes beneficence truly godlike. Without it, almsgiving degrades the receiver. We must learn how slight and shadowy are the distinctions between us and the poor; and that the last in outward condition may be first in the best attributes of humanity. . . .

. . . The great revelation which man now needs is a revelation of man to himself. The faith which is most wanted is a faith in what we and our fellow beings may become—a faith in the divine germ or principle in every soul. In regard to most of what are called the mysteries of religion, we may innocently be ignorant. But the mystery within ourselves, the mystery of our spiritual, accountable, immortal nature, it behooves us to explore. Happy are they who have begun to penetrate it, and in whom it has awakened feelings of awe toward themselves, and of deep interest and honor toward their fellow creatures.

10.7: A Southerner Denounces Northern Reform and Social Experimentation (1857)

Many northerners were critical of the reformers and their efforts. To some they seemed ridiculous and naïve zealots, while to others they seemed dangerous fanatics who were certain to do more harm than good.

Few Americans, however, were as skeptical of the impulse to improve and purify society as were southern intellectuals. One of the most ardent antagonists of the reform movements was George Fitzhugh, a Virginia lawyer and occasional newspaper editor, who had rejected entirely the Jeffersonian liberalism that had imbued his home state a half-century before. Fitzhugh believed that all creative societies in the past had relied on slaves and that no society could achieve a high level of civilization without men and women to do its degrading, but essential, dirty work. The North's vaunted freedom, he argued, simply papered over a system of wage slavery that reduced white people to the same status as southern black slaves. That freedom also unleashed licentiousness, infidelity, and greed.

As the selection that follows shows, Fitzhugh despised the northern reformers and blamed them for undermining the foundations of society and destroying traditional Christian values. Fitzhugh links the various "isms" to abolitionism. Is he correct? Did the other reform movements and social experiments derive from abolitionism? Or were they merely parallel impulses? Does Fitzhugh's warning against the dangers of freedom have any validity? Or was he merely defending a benighted and besieged system of human oppression? Have voices similar to his in recent years emphasized the dangers of institutional reform and social experimentation?

In What Slavery Ends

GEORGE FITZHUGH

Mr. [Thomas] Carlyle[1] very properly contends that abolition and the other social movements of the day propose little or no government as the moral panacea that is to heal and save a suffering world. [Pierre Joseph] Proudhon[2] expressly advocates anarchy; and Stephen Pearl Andrews, the ablest of American socialistic and abolition philosophers, elaborately attacks all existing social relations, and all legal and government restraints, and proposes No-Government as their substitute. He is the author of the Free Love experiment in New York, and a co-laborer and eulogist of similar experiments in villages or settlements in Ohio, Long Island and other places in the North and Northwest. He is a follower of Josiah Warren[3] who was associated with [Robert] Owen[4] of Lanark at New Harmony. We do not know that there is any essential difference between his system and that which has been for many years past practically carried out in Oneida County, New York, by the Perfectionists, who construe the Bible into authority for the unrestrained indulgence of every sensual appetite. The doctrines of [Charles] Fourier,[5] of Owen and Fanny Wright,[6] and the

---

[1] A conservative nineteenth-century British essayist—ED.

[2] A radical nineteenth-century French social theorist—ED.

[3] An early nineteenth-century American labor reformer—ED.

[4] A British industrialist and philanthropist who came to America in 1824 and founded a utopian socialist community, New Harmony, in Indiana—ED.

[5] A nineteenth-century French social thinker who inspired numerous socialist communities in America—ED.

[6] Frances Wright was an English reformer and "free thinker" who collaborated with Robert Owen in the New Harmony experiment—ED.

other early Socialists, all lead to No-Government and Free Love. 'Tis probable they foresaw and intended this result, but did not suggest or propose it to a world then too wicked and unenlightened to appreciate its beatific purity and loveliness. The materials as well as the proceedings of the infidel, woman's rights, negro rights, free-everything and anti-every school, headed and conducted in Boston by [William Lloyd] Garrison, [Theodore] Parker,[7] [Wendell] Phillips,[8] and their associated women and negroes, show that they too are busy with "assiduous wedges" in loosening the whole frame of society, and preparing for the glorious advent of Free Love and No-Government. All the Infidel and Abolition papers in the North betray a similar tendency. The Abolitionists of New York, headed by Gerrit Smith and Wm. Goodell, are engaged in precisely the same projects, but being Christians, would dignify Free Love and No-Government with the appellation of a Millennium. Probably half the Abolitionists at the North expect a great social revolution soon to occur by the advent of the Millennium. If they would patiently await that event, instead of attempting to get it up themselves, their delusions, however ridiculous, might at least be innocuous. But these progressive Christian Socialists differ not at all from the Infidel Socialists of Boston. They are equally intent and busy in pulling down the priesthood, and abolishing or dividing all property—seeing that whether the denouement be Free Love or a Millennium, the destruction of all existing human relations and human institutions is prerequisite to their full fruition.

Many thousand as have been of late years the social experiments attempting to practice community of property, of wives, children, &c., and numerous as the books inculcating and approving such practices, yet the existence and growth of Mormonism[9] is of itself stronger evidence than all other of the tendency of modern free society towards No-Government and Free Love. In the name of polygamy, it has practically removed all restraints to the intercourse of sexes, and broken up the Family. It promises, too, a qualified community of property and a fraternal association of labor. It beats up monthly thousands of recruits from free society in Europe and America, but makes not one convert in the slaveholding South. Slavery is satisfied and conservative. Abolition, finding that all existing legal, religious, social and governmental institutions restrict liberty and occasion a quasi-slavery, is resolved not to stop short of the subversion of all those institutions, and the inauguration of Free Love and No-Government. The only cure for all this is for free society sternly to recognize slavery as right in principle, and necessary in practice, with more or less of modification, to the very existence of government, of property, of religion, and of social existence.

We shall not attempt to reconcile the doctrines of the Socialists, which propose to remove all legal restraints, with their denunciations of Political Economy. Let Alone [i.e., laissez faire] is the essence of Political Economy and the whole creed of

[7]A Unitarian minister of Boston active in the abolitionist movement—ED.
[8]A Massachusetts abolitionist and disciple of Garrison—ED.
[9]Followers of the prophet Joseph Smith who, in the 1820s, discovered a "lost" Book of Mormon, which inspired him to establish a new religion. The Mormons, for a time, believed in "plural marriage" or polygamy—ED.

most of the Socialists. The Political Economists, Let Alone, for a fair fight, for universal rivalry, antagonism, competition, and cannibalism. They say the eating up the weaker members of society, the killing them out by capital and competition, will improve the breed of men and benefit society. They foresee the consequences of their doctrine, and are consistent. [Thomas] Hobbes[10] saw men devouring one another, under their system, two hundred years ago, and we all see them similarly engaged now. The Socialists promise that when society is wholly disintegrated and dissolved, by inculcating good principles and "singing fraternity over it," all men will cooperate, love, and help one another.

They place men in positions of equality, rivalry, and antagonism, which must result in extreme selfishness of conduct, and yet propose this system as a cure for selfishness. To us their reasonings seem absurd.

Yet the doctrines so prevalent with Abolitionists and Socialists, of Free Love and Free Lands, Free Churches, Free Women and Free Negroes—of No-Marriage, No-Religion, No-Private Property, No-Law and No-Government, are legitimate deductions, if not obvious corollaries from the leading and distinctive axiom of political economy—Laissez Faire, or Let Alone.

All the leading Socialists and Abolitionists of the North, we think, agree with Fanny Wright, that the gradual changes which have taken place in social organization from domestic slavery to prædial serfdom and thence to the present system of free and competitive society, have been mere transitive states, each placing the laborer in a worse condition than that of absolute slavery, yet valuable as preparing the way for a new and more perfect social state. They value the present state of society the more highly because it is intolerable, and must the sooner usher in a Millennium or Utopia.

---

[10]Hobbes was a seventeenth-century English philosopher who believed people to be driven by personal interest and kept from mutual destruction only by strong government—ED.

❖ *11* ❖

Defining the American Character

"What then is the American, this new man?" our first reading asks. A simple answer has always been, and remains, hard to find. From the earliest stages, it was clear that British North America would be settled by a great variety of peoples; diverse groups from Europe and Africa mixed with yet a third heterogenous group, Native Americans. As the British colonies became an independent nation that quickly grew in size and complexity, nineteenth-century immigration patterns and westward expansion further intensified this rich diversity. The American Revolution had added an interesting and unique twist to such differences of culture, language, race, ethnicity, and religion—new institutions seemed to legitimate a new egalitarianism, which appeared to most observers a significant departure from familiar European models. Finally, the physical environment of America spanned vast territories that encompassed great differences in climate, natural resources, and economic possibilities.

Some European travelers visiting America in the nineteenth century liked what they saw; others hated it and couldn't wait to return home. Nonetheless, all seemed to agree on one basic point: The United States of America was radically different from Europe. Americans, in turn, if unable to define precisely who they were, understood and took emerging national pride in what they were not: Europeans. Throughout the United States, even in the plantation regions of the South, a new democratic spirit seemed present everywhere. This spirit expressed itself in the popular embrace of participatory political institutions, and the boundaries of class and status dwindled markedly. If some of America's aristocrats were ambivalent or reluctant to embrace this emerging egalitarian mood, others celebrated it. Universal white male suffrage, widespread opportunity to own land or amass other property, and labor shortages contributed to the acceptance and eventual triumph of the "common man."

What made Americans so different? Was it the heterogeneity of its people or the novelty of its institutions? What historic forces were most influential? What role did environment and natural resources play in helping to forge the new nation's unique identity? Was economic opportunity a myth or a reality, and did political democracy really play a functional role?

11.1: American Diversity (1782, 1855)

Hector St. John de Crèvecoeur's Letters from an American Farmer *(1782) provides one of the nation's earliest and richest celebrations of diversity. In the famous letter "What is an American?" the author asserts that the American is a new man, not to be found elsewhere and given to unique circumstances. What does St. John de Crèvecoeur view as the ancestry of the American? What forces influenced his current development? What role has nature and environment played in the American experience? Would you say that the author is optimistic or pessimistic about this new experience? Most of all, what cultural and social characteristics are unique to America? Why are they so praiseworthy?*

Walt Whitman has been hailed by many as our national poet. His Leaves of Grass *(1855, 1891) broke new literary ground with the use of free verse and celebrated the ideals of democratic culture. Whitman thrilled to the variety of the American experience and devoted his career to asserting the ideal of the common man with vivid and enthusiastic imagery. How does Whitman describe the nation in this selection of his poetry? What are the underlying reasons for his optimism and confidence?*

What Is an American?

HECTOR ST. JOHN DE CRÈVECOEUR

What, then, is the American, this new man? He is neither an European nor the descendant of an European; hence that strange mixture of blood, which you will find in no other country. I could point out to you a family whose grandfather was an Englishman, whose wife was Dutch, whose son married a French woman, and whose present four sons have now four views of different nations. *He* is an American, who, leaving behind him all his ancient prejudices and manners, receives new ones from the new mode of life he has embraced, the new government he obeys,

Hector St. John de Crèvecoeur, *Letters from an American Farmer* (New York: Fox, Duffield and Company 1904), pp. 54–61.

and the new rank he holds. He becomes an American by being received in the broad lap of our great Alma Mater. Here individuals of all nations are melted into a new race of men, whose labours and posterity will one day cause great changes in the world. Americans are the western pilgrims who are carrying along with them that great mass of arts, sciences, vigour, and industry which began long since in the East; they will finish the great circle. The Americans were once scattered all over Europe; here they are incorporated into one of the finest systems of population which has ever appeared, and which will hereafter become distinct by the power of the different climates they inhabit. The American ought therefore to love this country much better than that wherein either he or his forefathers were born. Here the rewards of his industry follow with equal steps the progress of his labour; his labour is founded on the basis of nature, self-interest; can it want a stronger allurement? Wives and children, who before in vain demanded of him a morsel of bread, now, fat and frolicsome, gladly help their father to clear those fields whence exuberant crops are to arise to feed and to clothe them all, without any part being claimed, either by a despotic prince, a rich abbot, or a mighty lord. Here religion demands but little of him: a small voluntary salary to the minister and gratitude to God; can he refuse these? The American is a new man, who acts upon new principles; he must therefore entertain new ideas and form new opinions. From involuntary idleness, servile dependence, penury, and useless labour, he has passed to toils of a very different nature, rewarded by ample subsistence. This is an American.

British America is divided into many provinces, forming a large association scattered along a coast of 1,500 miles extent and about 200 wide. This society I would fain examine, at least such as it appears in the middle provinces; if it does not afford that variety of tinges and gradations which may be observed in Europe, we have colours peculiar to ourselves. For instance, it is natural to conceive that those who live near the sea must be very different from those who live in the woods; the intermediate space will afford a separate and distinct class.

Men are like plants; the goodness and flavour of the fruit proceeds from the peculiar soil and exposition in which they grow. We are nothing but what we derive from the air we breathe, the climate we inhabit, the government we obey, the system of religion we profess, and the nature of our employment. Here you will find but few crimes; these have acquired as yet no root among us. I wish I were able to trace all my ideas; if my ignorance prevents me from describing them properly, I hope I shall be able to delineate a few of the outlines; which is all I propose.

Those who live near the sea feed more on fish than on flesh and often encounter that boisterous element. This renders them more bold and enterprising; this leads them to neglect the confined occupations of the land. They see and converse with a variety of people; their intercourse with mankind becomes extensive. The sea inspires them with a love of traffic, a desire of transporting produce from one place to another, and leads them to a variety of resources which supply the place of labour. Those who inhabit the middle settlements, by far the most numerous, must be very different; the simple cultivation of the earth purifies them, but the indulgences of the government, the soft remonstrances of religion, the rank of independent free-holders, must necessarily inspire them with sentiments, very little known in Europe among a people of the same class. What do I say? Europe has no such class of men; the early knowledge they acquire, the early bargains they make, give them a great degree of sagacity. As freemen, they will be litigious; pride and obstinacy are often the cause of lawsuits; the nature of our laws and governments may be another. As citizens, it is easy to imagine that they will carefully read the newspapers, enter into every political disquisition, freely blame or censure governors and others. As farmers, they will be careful and anxious to get as much as they can, because what they get is their own. As northern men, they will love the cheerful cup. As Christians, religion curbs them not in their opinions; the general indulgence leaves every one to think for themselves in spiritual matters; the law inspects our actions; our thoughts are left to God. Industry, good living, selfishness, litigiousness, country politics, the pride of freemen, religious indifference, are their characteristics. If you recede still farther from the sea, you will come into more modern settlements; they exhibit the same strong lineaments, in a ruder appearance. Religion seems to have still less influence, and their manners are less improved.

Now we arrive near the great woods, near the last inhabited districts; there men seem to be placed still farther beyond the reach of government, which in some measure leaves them to themselves. How can it pervade every corner, as they were driven there by misfortunes, necessity of beginnings, desire of acquiring large tracks of land, idleness, frequent want of economy, ancient debts; the reunion of such people does not afford a very pleasing spectacle. When discord, want of unity and friendship, when either drunkenness or idleness prevail in such remote districts, contention, inactivity, and wretchedness must ensue. There are not the same remedies to these evils as in a long-established community. The few magistrates they have are in general little better than the rest; they are often in a perfect state of war; that of man against man, sometimes decided by blows, sometimes by means of the law; that of man against every wild inhabitant of these venerable woods, of which they are come to dispossess them. There men appear to be no better than carnivorous animals of a superior rank, living on the flesh of wild animals when they can catch them, and when they are not able, they subsist on grain. He who would wish to see America in its proper light and have a true idea of its feeble beginnings and barbarous rudiments must visit our extended line of frontiers, where the last settlers dwell and where he may see the first labours of settlement, the mode of clearing the earth, in all their different appearances, where men are wholly left dependent on their native tempers and on the spur of uncertain industry, which often fails when not sanctified by the efficacy of a few moral rules. There, remote from the power of example and check of shame, many families exhibit the most hideous parts of our society. They are a kind of forlorn hope, preceding by ten or twelve years the most respectable army of veterans which come after them. In that space, prosperity will polish some, vice and the law will drive off the rest, who, uniting again with others like themselves, will recede still farther, making room for more industrious people, who will finish their improvements, convert the log-house into a convenient habitation, and rejoicing that the first heavy labours are finished, will change in a few years that hitherto barbarous country into a fine, fertile, well-regulated district. Such is our progress; such is the march of the Europeans toward the interior parts of this continent. In all societies there are off-casts; this impure part serves as our precursors or pioneers; my father himself was one of that class, but he came upon honest principles and was therefore one of the few who held fast; by good conduct and temperance, he transmitted to me his fair inheritance, when not above one in fourteen of his contemporaries had the same good fortune.

Forty years ago, this smiling country was thus inhabited; it is now purged, a general decency of manners prevails throughout, and such has been the fate of our best countries.

Exclusive of those general characteristics, each province has its own, founded on the government, climate, mode of husbandry, customs, and peculiarity of circumstances. Europeans submit insensibly to these great powers and become, in the course of a few generations, not only Americans in general, but either Pennsylvanians, Virginians, or provincials under some other name. Whoever traverses the continent must easily observe those strong differences, which will grow more evident in time. The inhabitants of Canada, Massachusetts, the middle provinces, the southern ones, will be as different as their climates; their only points of unity will be those of religion and language.

Leaves of Grass (1855 edition)

WALT WHITMAN

I am of old and young, of the foolish as much as the wise.
Regardless of others, ever regardful of others,
Maternal as well as paternal, a child as well as a man,
Stuffed with the stuff that is coarse, and stuffed with
    the stuff that is fine,
One of the great nation, the nation of many nations—the
    smallest the same and the largest the same,
A southerner soon as a northerner, a planter nonchalant and hospitable,
A Yankee bound my own way . . . . ready for trade . . . .
    my joints the limberest joints on earth and the sternest
    joints on earth,
A Kentuckian walking the vale of the Elkhorn in my
    deerskin leggings,
A boatman over the lakes or bays or along coasts . . . . a
    Hoosier, a Badger, a Buckeye,
A Louisianian or Georgian, a poke-easy from sandhills and
    pines,

Walt Whitman, *Leaves of Grass* (Brooklyn: [s.n.] 1855), pp. 42–43.

*At home on Canadian snowshoes or up in the bush, or with
    fishermen off Newfoundland,*
*At home in the fleet of iceboats, sailing with the rest and
    tacking,*
*At home on the hills of Vermont or in the woods of Maine
    or the Texan ranch,*
*Comrade of Californians . . . . comrade of free
    northwesterners, loving their big proportions,*
*Comrade of raftsmen and coalmen—comrade of all who
    shake hands and welcome to drink and meat;*
A learner with the simplest, a teacher of the thoughtfulest,
A novice beginning experient of myriads of seasons,
Of every hue and trade and rank, of every caste and religion,
*Not merely of the New World but of Africa Europe or Asia
    . . . . a wandering savage,*
*A farmer, mechanic, or artist . . . . a gentleman, sailor,
    lover or quaker,*
A prisoner, fancy-man, rowdy, lawyer, physician or priest:

I resist anything better than my own diversity,
And breathe the air and leave plenty after me,
And am not stuck up, and am in my place.

11.2:   A European Traveler Observes America's English Cultural Heritage (1835)

*Alexis de Tocqueville visited America in 1831 on a mission to study
prisons and other institutions. His massive study,* Democracy in
America, *published in 1835 and 1840, has long been considered one
of the most quotable sources on the nature and distinctness of the
American experience. Constantly asking questions about American institutions and always seeking to define the elusive American "character," Tocqueville believed that its English cultural heritage had been
the most important factor in influencing the identity of the American
character.*

*Tocqueville found potent opportunities in America's historical cir-
cumstances. What were they? What negative factors influenced European development but were less oppressive in the New World? What
distinctions did Tocqueville draw between the settlement of New England and Virginia? Which did he prefer? Finally, how would you best
summarize Tocqueville's emphasis on the importance of the role of religion in this passage?*

Democracy in America

ALEXIS DE TOCQUEVILLE

After the birth of a human being his early years are obscurely spent in the toils or pleasures of childhood. As he grows up the world receives him, when his manhood begins, and he enters into contact with his fellows. He is then studied for the first time, and it is imagined that the germ of the vices and the virtues of his maturer years is then formed.

This, if I am not mistaken, is a great error. We must begin higher up; we must watch the infant in his mother's arms; we must see the first images which the external world casts upon the dark mirror of his mind; the first occurrences which he witnesses; we must hear the first words which awaken the sleeping powers of thought, and stand by his earliest efforts, if we would understand the prejudices, the habits, and the passions which will rule his life. The entire man is, so to speak, to be seen in the cradle of the child.

The growth of nations presents something analogous to this; they all bear some marks of their origin; and the circumstances which accompanied their birth and contributed to their rise, affect the whole term of their being.

If we were able to go back to the elements of states, and to examine the oldest monuments of their history, I doubt not that we should discover the primary cause of the prejudices, the habits, the ruling passions, and in short of all that constitutes what is called the national character: we should then find the explanation of certain customs which now seem at variance with prevailing manners, of such laws as conflict with established principles, and of such incoherent opinions as are here and there to be met with in society, like those fragments of broken chains which we sometimes see hanging from the vault of an edifice, and supporting nothing. This might explain the destinies of certain nations which seem borne along by an unknown force to ends of which they themselves are ignorant. But hitherto facts have been wanting to researches of this kind: the spirit of inquiry has only come upon communities in their latter days; and when they at length turned their attention to contemplate their origin, time had already obscured it, or ignorance and pride adorned it with truth-concealing fables.

America is the only country in which it has been possible to witness the natural and tranquil growth of society, and where the influence exercised on the future condition of states by their origin is clearly distinguishable.

At the period when the peoples of Europe landed in the New World their national characteristics were already completely formed; each of them had a physiognomy of its own; and as they had already attained that stage of civilization at which men are led to study themselves, they have transmitted to us a faithful picture of their opinions, their manners, and their laws. The men of the sixteenth century are almost as well known to us as our contemporaries. America consequently exhibits in the broad light of day the phaenomena which the ignorance or rudeness of earlier ages conceals from our researches. Near enough to the time when the states of America

Alexis de Tocqueville, *Democracy in America* (New York: Allard and Saunders, 1838), pp. 1–18.

were founded to be accurately acquainted with their elements, and sufficiently removed from that period to judge of some of their results, the men of our own day seem destined to see further than their predecessors into the series of human events. Providence has given us a torch which our forefathers did not possess, and has allowed us to discern fundamental causes in the history of the world which the obscurity of the past concealed from them.

If we carefully examine the social and political state of America after having studied its history, we shall remain perfectly convinced that not an opinion, not a custom, not a law, I may even say not an event, is upon record which the origin of that people will not explain. The readers of this book will find the germ of all that is to follow in the present chapter, and the key to almost the whole work.

The emigrants who came at different periods to occupy the territory now covered by the American Union, differed from each other in many respects; their aim was not the same, and they governed themselves on different principles.

These men had, however, certain features in common, and they were all placed in an analogous situation. The tie of language is perhaps the strongest and the most durable that can unite mankind. All the emigrants spoke the same tongue; they were all offsets from the same people. Born in a country which had been agitated for centuries by the struggles of faction, and in which all parties had been obliged in their turn to place themselves under the protection of the laws, their political education had been perfected in this rude school, and they were more conversant with the notions of right, and the principles of true freedom, than the greater part of their European contemporaries. At the period of the first emigrations, the parish system, that fruitful germ of free institutions, was deeply rooted in the habits of the English; and with it the doctrine of the sovereignty of the people had been introduced even into the bosom of the monarchy of the House of Tudor.

The religious quarrels which have agitated the Christian world were then rife. England had plunged into the new order of things with headlong vehemence. The character of its inhabitants, which had always been sedate and reflecting, became argumentative and austere. General information had been increased by intellectual debate, and the mind had received a deeper cultivation. Whilst religion was the topic of discussion, the morals of the people were reformed. All these national features are more or less discoverable in the physiognomy of those adventurers who came to seek a new home on the opposite shores of the Atlantic.

Another remark, to which we shall hereafter have occasion to recur, is applicable not only to the English, but to the French, the Spaniards, and all the Europeans who successively established themselves in the New World. All these European colonies contained the elements, if not the development, of a complete democracy. Two causes led to this result. It may safely be advanced, that on leaving the mother-country the emigrants had in general no notion of superiority over one another. The happy and the powerful do not go into exile, and there are no surer guarantees of equality among men than poverty and misfortune. It happened, however, on several occasions that persons of rank were driven to America by political and religious quarrels. Laws were made to establish a gradation of ranks; but it was soon found that the soil of America was entirely opposed to a territorial aristocracy.

To bring that refractory land into cultivation, the constant and interested exertions of the owner himself were necessary; and when the ground was prepared, its produce was found to be insufficient to enrich a master and a farmer at the same time. The land was then naturally broken up into small portions, which the proprietor cultivated for himself. Land is the basis of an aristocracy, which clings to the soil that supports it; for it is not by privileges alone, nor by birth, but by landed property handed down from generation to generation, that an aristocracy is constituted. A nation may present immense fortunes and extreme wretchedness; but unless those fortunes are territorial, there is no aristocracy, but simply the class of the rich and that of the poor.

All the British colonies had then a great degree of similarity at the epoch of their settlement. All of them, from their first beginning, seemed destined to witness the growth, not of the aristocratic liberty of their mother-country, but of that freedom of the middle and lower orders of which the history of the world has as yet furnished no complete example.

In this general uniformity several striking differences were however discernible, which it is necessary to point out. Two branches may be distinguished in the Anglo-American family which have hitherto grown up without entirely commingling; the one in the South, the other in the North.

Virginia received the first English colony; the emigrants took possession of it in 1607. The idea that mines of gold and silver are the sources of national wealth was at that time singularly prevalent in Europe; a fatal delusion, which has done more to impoverish the nations which adopted it, and has cost more lives in America, than the united influence of war and bad laws. The men sent to Virginia were seekers of gold, adventurers without resources and without character, whose turbulent and restless spirits endangered the infant colony, and rendered its progress uncertain. The artisans and agriculturists arrived afterwards; and although they were a more moral and orderly race of men, they were in nowise above the level of the inferior classes in England. No lofty conceptions, no intellectual system directed the foundation of these new settlements. The colony was scarcely established when slavery was introduced, and this was the main circumstance which has exercised so prodigious an influence on the character, the laws, and all the future prospects of the South.

Slavery, as we shall afterwards show, dishonors labor; it introduces idleness into society, and, with idleness, ignorance and pride, luxury and distress. It enervates the powers of the mind, and benumbs the activity of man. The influence of slavery, united to the English character, explains the manners and the social condition of the Southern States.

In the North, the same English foundation was modified by the most opposite shades of character; and here I may be allowed to enter into some details. The two or three main ideas which constitute the basis of the social theory of the United States were first combined in the Northern British colonies, more generally denominated the states of New England. The principles of New England spread at first to the neighboring states; they then passed successively to the more distant ones; and at length they imbued the whole Confederation. They now extend their influence beyond its limits over the whole American world. The civilization of New England has been like a beacon lit upon a hill, which after it has diffused its warmth around, tinges the distant horizon with its glow.

The foundation of New England was a novel spectacle, and all the circumstances attending it were singular and original. The large majority of colonies have been first inhabited either by men without education and without resources, driven by their poverty and their misconduct from the land which gave them birth, or by speculators and adventurers greedy of gain. Some settlements cannot even boast so honorable an origin; St. Domingo was founded by buccaneers; and, at the present day, the criminal courts of England supply the population of Australia.

The settlers who established themselves on the shores of New England all belonged to the more independent classes of their native country. Their union on the soil of America at once presented the singular phaenomenon of a society containing neither lords nor common people, neither rich nor poor. These men possessed, in proportion to their number, a greater mass of intelligence than is to be found in any European nation of our own time. All, without a single exception, had received a good education, and many of them were known in Europe for their talents and their acquirements. The other colonies had been founded by adventurers without family; the emigrants of New England brought with them the best elements of order and morality, they landed in the desert accompanied by their wives and children. But what most especially distinguished them was the aim of their undertaking. They had not been obliged by necessity to leave their country, the social position they abandoned was one to be regretted, and their means of subsistence were certain. Nor did they cross the Atlantic to improve their situation or to increase their wealth; the call which summoned them from the comforts of their homes was purely intellectual; and in facing the inevitable sufferings of exile, their object was the triumph of an idea.

The emigrants, or, as they deservedly styled themselves, the Pilgrims, belonged to that English sect, the austerity of whose principles had acquired for them the name of Puritans. Puritanism was not merely a religious doctrine, but it corresponded in many points with the most absolute democratic and republican theories. It was this tendency which had aroused its most dangerous adversaries. Persecuted by the Government of the mother-country, and disgusted by the habits of a society opposed to the rigor of their own principles, the Puritans went forth to seek some rude and unfrequented part of the world, where they could live according to their own opinions, and worship God in freedom. . . .

The remarks I have made will suffice to display the character of Anglo-American civilization in its true light. It is the result (and this should be constantly present to the mind) of two distinct elements, which in other places have been in frequent hostility, but which in America have been admirably incorporated and combined with one another. I allude to the spirit of Religion and the spirit of Liberty.

The settlers of New England were at the same time ardent sectarians and daring innovators. Narrow as the limits of some of their religious opinions were, they were entirely free from political prejudices.

Hence arose two tendencies, distinct but not opposite, which are constantly discernible in the manners as well as in the laws of the country.

It might be imagined that men who sacrificed their friends, their family, and their native land to a religious conviction, were absorbed in the pursuit of the intellectual advantages which they purchased at so dear a rate. The energy, however, with which they strove for the acquirements of wealth, moral enjoyment, and the comforts as well as liberties of the world, is scarcely inferior to that with which they devoted themselves to heaven.

Political principles, and all human laws and institutions were moulded and altered at their pleasure; the barriers of the society in which they were born were broken down before them; the old principles which had governed the world for ages were no more; a path without a term, and a field without an horizon were opened to the exploring and ardent curiosity of man: but at the limits of the political world he checks his researches, he discreetly lays aside the use of his most formidable faculties, he no longer consents to doubt or to innovate, but carefully abstaining from raising the curtain of the sanctuary, he yields with submissive respect to truths which he will not discuss.

Thus in the moral world, everything is classed, adapted, decided and foreseen; in the political world everything is agitated, uncertain, and disputed: in the one is a passive, though a voluntary, obedience: in the other an independence, scornful of experience and jealous of authority.

These two tendencies, apparently so discrepant, are far from conflicting; they advance together, and mutually support each other.

Religion perceives that civil liberty affords a noble exercise to the faculties of man, and that the political world is a field prepared by the Creator for the efforts of the intelligence. Contented with the freedom and the power which it enjoys in its own sphere, and with the place which it occupies, the empire of religion is never more surely established than when it reigns in the hearts of men unsupported by aught beside its native strength.

Religion is no less the companion of liberty in all its battles and its triumphs; the cradle of its infancy, and the divine source of its claims. The safe-guard of morality is religion, and morality is the best security of law as well as the surest pledge of freedom.

11.3: Voices of Cultural Nationalism (1834, 1837)

In the early days of the new republic, talented young Americans interested in the arts or letters frequently studied and spent much of their professional careers in Europe, where "high culture" flourished. By the 1830s, strong voices demanded that America assert its own independence culturally, as it had previously done politically. The 1840s witnessed a continued growth in the demand for "cultural nationalism," and the 1850s saw its achievement in the creation of an

American literature come of age in the writings of Melville, Whitman, Emerson, and many others. Painting and architecture reached similar new heights, and distinctly American styles emerged in all cultural forms.

George Bancroft became the young nation's first widely read professional historian, and his massive History of the United States from the Discovery of the American Continent *appeared in installments over a staggering period of fifty years. When finally finished, it contained 1.7 million words. A vocal proselytizer of cultural nationalism, Bancroft viewed American institutions created by the Revolution as unique and blessed by Providence. The enclosed selection from the Introduction to his* History *captures his assumptions and pride. What made America so exceptional? Why was Bancroft so pleased with the American experiment? He says little of Europe in this passage. Why? What does he mean when he says that America had developed under a "favoring Providence"?*

In the second passage, Ralph Waldo Emerson refers to American uniqueness in the famous "American Scholar" address he gave at Harvard University in 1837. Imploring Americans to be more culturally and intellectually independent, his words also reflect a sense of exceptionalism and separateness, in which American institutions are to play a key role. What are the reasons for Emerson's confidence, and in what ways are his thoughts similar to Bancroft's? Foremost, how does Emerson envision the American scholar—as an academician, or in a significantly broader role?

The History of the United States from the Discovery of the American Continent

GEORGE BANCROFT

The United States of America constitute an essential portion of a great political system, embracing all the civilized nations of the earth. At a period when the force of moral opinion is rapidly increasing, they have the precedence in the practice and the defence of the equal rights of man. The sovereignty of the people is here a conceded axiom, and the laws, established upon that basis, are cherished with faithful patriotism. While the nations of Europe aspire after change, our constitution engages the fond admiration of the people, by which it has been established. Prosperity follows the execution of even justice; invention is quickened by the freedom of competition; and labor rewarded with sure and unexampled returns. Domestic peace is main-

George Bancroft, *The History of the United States from the Discovery of the Continent,* Centenary Edition (Boston: Little, Brown and Company, 1876), vol. I, pp. 1–3.

tained without the aid of a military establishment; public sentiment permits the existence of but few standing troops, and those only along the seaboard and on the frontiers. A gallant navy protects our commerce, which spreads its banners on every sea, and extends its enterprise to every clime. Our diplomatic relations connect us on terms of equality and honest friendship with the chief powers of the world; while we avoid entangling participation in their intrigues, their passions, and their wars. Our national resources are developed by an earnest culture of the arts of peace. Every man may enjoy the fruits of his industry; every mind is free to publish its convictions. Our government, by its organization, is necessarily identified with the interests of the people, and relies exclusively on their attachment for its durability and support. Even the enemies of the state, if there are any among us, have liberty to express their opinions undisturbed; and are safely tolerated, where reason is left free to combat their errors. Nor is the constitution a dead letter, unalterably fixed: it has the capacity for improvement; adopting whatever changes time and the public will may require, and safe from decay, so long as that will retains its energy. New states are forming in the wilderness; canals, intersecting our plains and crossing our highlands, open numerous channels to internal commerce; manufactures prosper along our watercourses; the use of steam on our rivers and railroads annihilates distance by the acceleration of speed. Our wealth and population, already giving us a place in the first rank of nations, are so rapidly cumulative, that the former is increased fourfold, and the latter is doubled, in every period of twenty-two or twenty-three years. There is no national debt; the community is opulent; the government economical; and the public treasury full. Religion, neither persecuted nor paid by the state, is sustained by the regard for public morals and the convictions of an enlightened faith. Intelligence is diffused with unparalleled universality; a free press teems with the choicest productions of all nations and ages. There are more daily journals in the United States than in the world beside. A public document of general interest is, within a month, reproduced in at least a million of copies, and is brought within the reach of every freeman in the country. An immense concourse of emigrants of the most various lineage is perpetually crowding to our shores; and the principles of liberty, uniting all interests by the operation of equal laws, blend the discordant elements into harmonious union. Other governments are convulsed by the innovations and reforms of neighboring states; our constitution, fixed in the affections of the people, from whose choice it has sprung, neutralizes the influence of foreign principles, and fearlessly opens an asylum to the virtuous, the unfortunate, and the oppressed of every nation.

And yet it is but little more than two centuries since the oldest of our states received its first permanent colony. Before that time the whole territory was an unproductive waste. Throughout its wide extent the arts had not erected a monument. Its only inhabitants were a few scattered tribes of feeble barbarians, destitute of commerce and of political connection. The axe and the ploughshare were unknown. The soil, which had been gathering fertility from the repose of centuries, was lavishing its strength in magnificent but useless vegetation. In the view of civilization the immense domain was a solitude.

It is the object of the present work to explain how the change in the condition of our land has been brought about; and, as the fortunes of a nation are not under the control of blind destiny, to follow the steps by which a favoring Providence, calling our institutions into being, has conducted the country to its present happiness and glory.

The American Scholar

RALPH WALDO EMERSON

Another sign of our times, also marked by an analogous political movement, is, the new importance given to the single person. Every thing that tends to insulate the individual,—to surround him with barriers of natural respect, so that each man shall feel the world is his, and man shall treat with man as a sovereign state with a sovereign state;—tends to true union as well as greatness. "I learned," said the melancholy Pestalozzi, "that no man in God's wide earth is either willing or able to help any other man." Help must come from the bosom alone. The scholar is that man who must take up into himself all the ability of the time, all the contributions of the past, all the hopes of the future. He must be an university of knowledges. If there be one lesson more than another, which should pierce his ear, it is, The world is nothing, the man is all; in yourself is the law of all nature, and you know not yet how a globule of sap ascends; in yourself slumbers the whole of Reason; it is for you to know all, it is for you to dare all. Mr. President and Gentlemen, this confidence in the unsearched might of man belongs, by all motives, by all prophecy, by all preparation, to the American Scholar. We have listened too long to the courtly muses of Europe. The spirit of the American freeman is already suspected to be timid, imitative, tame. Public and private avarice make the air we breathe thick and fat. The scholar is decent, indolent, complaisant. See already the tragic consequence. The mind of this country, taught to aim at low objects, eats upon itself. There is no work for any but the decorous and the complaisant. Young men of the fairest promise, who begin life upon our shores, inflated by the mountain winds, shined upon by all the stars of God, find the earth below not in unison with these,—but are hindered from action by the disgust which the principles on which business is managed in spire, and turn drudges, or die of disgust,—some of them suicides. What is the remedy? They did not yet see, and thousands of young men as hopeful now crowding to the barriers for the career, do not yet see, that, if the single man plant himself indomitably on his instincts, and there abide, the huge world will come round to him. Patience,—patience;—with the shades of all the good and great for company; and for solace, the perspective of your own infinite life; and for work, the study and the communication of principles, the making those instincts prevalent, the conversion of the world. Is it not the chief disgrace in the world, not to be an unit;—not to be

Ralph Waldo Emerson, The American Scholar. An Oration before the Phi Beta Kappa Society at Cambridge (MA), August 31, 1837. Reprinted from Ralph Waldo Emerson, *Nature. Addresses and Lectures* (Boston: Houghton Mifflin Company, 1903), pp. 113–115.

reckoned one character;—not to yield that peculiar fruit which each man was created to bear, but to be reckoned in the gross, in the hundred, or the thousand, of the party, the section, to which we belong; and our opinion predicted geographically, as the north, or the south? Not so, brothers and friends,—please God, ours shall not be so. We will walk on our own feet; we will work with our own hands; we will speak our own minds. The study of letters shall be no longer a name for pity, for doubt, and for sensual indulgence. The dread of man and the love of man shall be a wall of defense and a wreath of joy around all. A nation of men will for the first time exist, because each believes himself inspired by the Divine Soul which also inspires all men.

11.4:   The Significance of the Frontier in American History (1893)

In addition to a revolutionary past that created new institutions, and an unprecedented intermingling of humanity that formed its people, the United States faced yet another unique circumstance that strongly influenced its identity—environment. As a natural phenomenon, the American landscape is vast and diverse. It is also filled with extremes and in its pristine form capable of enormous hostility toward human life. Add to this rugged environmentalism the political organization of what was called "Indian Territory" and the insatiable appetite of countless American citizens to migrate west in hopes of developing land and finding greater economic opportunity and one has the phenomenon of the frontier, a major theme in nineteenth-century American life.

In this address to the American Historical Association in 1893, Frederick Jackson Turner summarized the key beliefs behind his life's work as a historian—that the frontier was the most significant factor in establishing the American character and that westward expansion provided a mechanism by which democratic institutions and values were perpetuated and constantly born anew. How did the frontier make America different from Europe? How did Turner view the frontier's environment? What assumptions does Turner make about civilization and the "primitive"? How, in the long run, did environmental conditions come to transform institutions, and how did human adaptation to the environment shape values and culture? How does Turner's view of the American character compare and contrast to the previous readings in this chapter?

Report to the American Historical Association

FREDERICK JACKSON TURNER

In a recent bulletin of the Superintendent of the Census for 1890 appear these significant words: "Up to and including 1880 the country had a frontier of settlement, but at present the unsettled area has been so broken into by isolated bodies of settlement that there can hardly be said to be a frontier line. In the discussion of its extent, its westward movement, etc., it can not, therefore, any longer have a place in the census reports." This brief official statement marks the closing of a great historic movement. Up to our own day American history has been in a large degree the history of the colonization of the Great West. The existence of an area of free land, its continuous recession, and the advance of American settlement westward, explain American development.

Behind institutions, behind constitutional forms and modifications, lie the vital forces that call these organs into life and shape them to meet changing conditions. The peculiarity of American institutions is the fact that they have been compelled to adapt themselves to the changes of an expanding people—to the changes involved in crossing a continent, in winning a wilderness, and in developing at each area of this progress out of the primitive economic and political conditions of the frontier into the complexity of city life. Said Calhoun in 1817, "We are great, and rapidly—I was about to say fearfully—growing!" So saying, he touched the distinguishing feature of American life. All peoples show development; the germ theory of politics has been sufficiently emphasized. In the case of most nations, however, the development has occurred in a limited area; and if the nation has expanded, it has met other growing peoples whom it has conquered. But in the case of the United States we have a different phenomenon. Limiting our attention to the Atlantic coast, we have the familiar phenomenon of the evolution of institutions in a limited area, such as the rise of representative government; the differentiation of simple colonial governments into complex organs; the progress from primitive industrial society, without division of labor, up to manufacturing civilization. But we have in addition to this a recurrence of the process of evolution in each western area reached in the process of expansion. Thus American development has exhibited not merely advance along a single line, but a return to primitive conditions on a continually advancing frontier line, and a new development for that area. American social development has been continually beginning over again on the frontier. This perennial rebirth, this fluidity of American life, this expansion westward with its new opportunities, its continuous touch with the simplicity of primitive society, furnish the forces dominating American character. The true point of view in the history of this nation is not the Atlantic coast, it is the Great West. Even the slavery struggle, which is made so exclusive an object of attention by writers like Professor von Holst, occupies its important place in American history because of its relation to westward expansion.

Frederick Jackson Turner, *Report of the American Historical Association for 1893* (Washington, 1894), pp. 199–227. Address delivered at the meeting of the American Historical Association in Chicago, July 12, 1893.

In this advance, the frontier is the outer edge of the wave—the meeting point between savagery and civilization. Much has been written about the frontier from the point of view of border warfare and the chase, but as a field for the serious study of the economist and the historian it has been neglected.

The American frontier is sharply distinguished from the European frontier—a fortified boundary line running through dense populations. The most significant thing about the American frontier is, that it lies at the hither edge of free land. In the census reports it is treated as the margin of that settlement which has a density of two or more to the square mile. The term is an elastic one, and for our purposes does not need sharp definition. We shall consider the whole frontier belt, including the Indian country and the outer margin of the "settled area" of the census reports. This paper will make no attempt to treat the subject exhaustively; its aim is simply to call attention to the frontier as a fertile field for investigation, and to suggest some of the problems which arise in connection with it.

In the settlement of America we have to observe how European life entered the continent, and how America modified and developed that life and reacted on Europe. Our early history is the study of European germs developing in an American environment. Too exclusive attention has been paid by institutional students to the Germanic origins, too little to the American factors. The frontier is the line of most rapid and effective Americanization. The wilderness masters the colonist. It finds him a European in dress, industries, tools, modes of travel, and thought. It takes him from the railroad car and puts him in the birch canoe. It strips off the garments of civilization and arrays him in the hunting shirt and the moccasin. It puts him in the log cabin of the Cherokee and Iroquois and runs an Indian palisade around him. Before long he has gone to planting Indian corn and plowing with a sharp stick; he shouts the war cry and takes the scalp in orthodox Indian fashion. In short, at the frontier the environment is at first too strong for the man. He must accept the conditions which it furnishes, or perish, and so he fits himself into the Indian clearings and follows the Indian trails. Little by little he transforms the wilderness, but the outcome is not the old Europe, not simply the development of Germanic germs, any more than the first phenomenon was a case of reversion to the Germanic mark. The fact is that here is a new product that is American. At first, the frontier was the Atlantic coast. It was the frontier of Europe in a very real sense. Moving westward, the frontier became more and more American. As successive terminal moraines result from successive glaciations, so each frontier leaves it traces behind it, and when it becomes a settled area the region still partakes of the frontier characteristics. Thus the advance of the frontier has meant a steady movement away from the influence of Europe, a steady growth of independence on American lines. And to study this advance, the men who grew up under these conditions, and the political, economic, and social results of it, is to study the really American part of our history.

In the course of the seventeenth century the frontier was advanced up the Atlantic river courses, just beyond the "fall line," and the tidewater region became the settled area. In the first half of the eighteenth century another advance occurred. Traders followed the Delaware and Shawnese Indians to the Ohio as early as the end of the first quarter of the century. Gov. Spotswood, of Virginia, made an expedition in 1714 across the Blue Ridge. The end of the first quarter of the century saw the advance of the Scotch-Irish and the Palatine Germans up the Shenandoah Valley into the western part of Virginia, and along the Piedmont region of the Carolinas. The Germans in New York pushed the frontier of settlement up the Mohawk to German Flats. In Pennsylvania the town of Bedford indicates the line of settlement. Settlements soon began on the New River, or the Great Kanawha, and on the sources of the Yadkin and French Broad. The King attempted to arrest the advance by his proclamation of 1763, forbidding settlements beyond the sources of the rivers flowing into the Atlantic; but in vain. In the period of the Revolution the frontier crossed the Alleghenies into Kentucky and Tennessee, and the upper waters of the Ohio were settled. When the first census was taken in 1790, the continuous settled area was bounded by a line which ran near the coast of Maine, and included New England except a portion of Vermont and New Hampshire. New York along the Hudson and up the Mohawk about Schenectady, eastern and southern Pennsylvania, Virginia well across the Shenandoah Valley, and the Carolinas and eastern Georgia. Beyond this region of continuous settlement were the small settled areas of Kentucky and Tennessee, and the Ohio, with the mountains intervening between them and the Atlantic area, thus giving a new and important character to the frontier. The isolation of the region increased its peculiarly American tendencies, and the need of transportation facilities to connect it with the East called out important schemes of internal improvement, which will be noted farther on. The "West," as a self-conscious section, began to evolve.

From decade to decade distinct advances of the frontier occurred. By the census of 1820 the settled area included Ohio, southern Indiana and Illinois, southeastern Missouri, and about one-half of Louisiana. This settled area had surrounded Indian areas, and the management of these tribes became an object of political concern. The frontier region of the time lay along the Great Lakes, where Astor's American Fur Company operated in the Indian trade, and beyond the Mississippi, where Indian traders extended their activity even to the Rocky Mountains; Florida also furnished frontier conditions. The Mississippi River region was the scene of typical frontier settlements.

The rising steam navigation on western waters, the opening of the Erie Canal, and the westward extension of cotton culture added five frontier states to the Union in this period. Grund, writing in 1836, declares: "It appears then that the universal disposition of Americans to emigrate to the western wilderness, in order to enlarge their dominion over inanimate nature, is the actual result of an expansive power which is inherent in them, and which by continually agitating all classes of society is constantly throwing a large portion of the whole population on the extreme confines of the State, in order to gain space for its development. Hardly is a new State or Territory formed before the same principle manifests itself again and gives rise to a further emigration; and so is it destined to go on until a physical barrier must finally obstruct its progress."

In the middle of this century the line indicated by the present eastern boundary of Indian Territory, Nebraska, and Kansas marked the frontier of the Indian country. Minnesota and Wisconsin still exhibited frontier conditions, but the distinctive frontier of the period is found in California, where the gold discoveries had sent a sudden tide of adventurous miners, and in Oregon, and the settlements in Utah. As the frontier had leaped over the Alleghenies, so now it skipped the Great Plains and the

Rocky Mountains; and in the same way that the advance of the frontiersmen beyond the Alleghenies had caused the rise of important questions of transportation and internal improvement, so now the settlers beyond the Rocky Mountains needed means of communication with the East, and in the furnishing of these arose the settlement of the Great Plains and the development of still another kind of frontier life. Railroads, fostered by land grants, sent an increasing tide of immigrants into the Far West. The United States Army fought a series of Indian wars in Minnesota, Dakota, and the Indian Territory.

By 1880 the settled area had been pushed into northern Michigan, Wisconsin, and Minnesota, along Dakota rivers, and in the Black Hills region, and was ascending the rivers of Kansas and Nebraska. The development of mines in Colorado had drawn isolated frontier settlements into that region, and Montana and Idaho were receiving settlers. The frontier was found in these mining camps and the ranches of the Great Plains. The superintendent of the census for 1890 reports, as previously stated, that the settlements of the West lie so scattered over the region that there can no longer be said to be a frontier line.

In these successive frontiers we find natural boundary lines which have served to mark and to affect the characteristics of the frontiers, namely: the "fall line;" the Allegheny Mountains; the Mississippi; the Missouri where its direction approximates north and south: the line of the arid lands, approximately the ninety-ninth meridian; and the Rocky Mountains. The fall line marked the frontier of the seventeenth century; the Alleghenies that of the eighteenth; the Mississippi that of the first quarter of the nineteenth; the Missouri that of the middle of this century (omitting the California movement); and the belt of the Rocky Mountains and the arid tract, the present frontier. Each was won by a series of Indian wars.

At the Atlantic frontier one can study the germs of processes repeated at each successive frontier. We have the complex European life sharply precipitated by the wilderness into the simplicity of primitive conditions. The first frontier had to meet its Indian question, its question of the disposition of the public domain, of the means of intercourse with older settlements, of the extension of political organization, of religious and educational activity. And the settlement of these and similar questions for one frontier served as a guide for the next. The American student needs not to go to the "prim little townships of Sleswick" for illustrations of the law of continuity and development. For example, he may study the origin of our land policies in the colonial land policy; he may see how the system grew by adapting the statutes to the custom of the successive frontiers. He may see how the mining experience in the lead regions of Wisconsin, Illinois, and Iowa was applied to the mining laws of the Sierras, and how our Indian policy has been a series of experimentations on successive frontiers. Each tier of new states has found in the older ones material for its constitutions. Each frontier has made similar contributions to American character, as will be discussed farther on.

But with all these similarities there are essential differences, due to the place element and the time element. It is evident that the farming frontier of the Mississippi Valley presents different conditions from the mining frontier of the Rocky Mountains. The frontier reached by the Pacific Railroad, surveyed into rectangles, guarded by the United States Army, and recruited by the daily immigrant ship, moves forward at a swifter pace and in a different way than the frontier reached by the birch canoe or the pack horse. The geologist traces patiently the shores of ancient seas, maps their areas, and compares the older and the newer. It would be a work worth the historian's labors to mark these various frontiers and in detail compare one with another. Not only would there result a more adequate conception of American development and characteristics, but invaluable additions would be made to the history of society.

Loria, the Italian economist, has urged the study of colonial life as an aid in understanding the stages of European development, affirming that colonial settlement is for economic science what the mountain is for geology, bringing to light primitive stratifications. "America," he says, "has the key to the historical enigma which Europe has sought for centuries in vain, and the land which has no history reveals luminously the course of universal history." There is much truth in this. The United States lies like a huge page in the history of society. Line by line as we read this continental page from West to East we find the record of social evolution. It begins with the Indian and the hunter; it goes on to tell of the disintegration of savagery by the entrance of the trader, the pathfinder of civilization; we read the annals of the pastoral stage in ranch life; the exploitation of the soil by the raising of unrotated crops of corn and wheat in sparsley settled farming communities; the intensive culture of the denser farm settlement; and finally the manufacturing organization with city and factory system. This page is familiar to the student of census statistics, but how little of it has been used by our historians. Particularly in eastern States this page is a palimpsest. What is now a manufacturing State was in an earlier decade an area of intensive farming. Earlier yet it had been a wheat area, and still earlier the "range" had attracted the cattleherder. Thus Wisconsin, now developing manufacture, is a State with varied agricultural interests. But earlier it was given over to almost exclusive grain-raising, like North Dakota at the present time.

Each of these areas has had an influence in our economic and political history; the evolution of each into a higher stage has worked political transformations. But what constitutional historian has made any adequate attempt to interpret political facts by the light of these social areas and changes? . . .

We may next inquire what were the influences on the East and on the Old World. A rapid enumeration of some of the more noteworthy effects is all that I have time for.

First, we note that the frontier promoted the formation of a composite nationality for the American people. The coast was preponderantly English, but the later tides of continental immigration flowed across to the free lands. This was the case from the early colonial days. The Scotch-Irish and the Palatine Germans, or "Pennsylvania Dutch," furnished the dominant element in the stock of the colonial frontier. With these peoples were also the freed indented servants, or redemptioners, who at the expiration of their time of service passed to the frontier. Governor Spotswood of Virginia writes in 1717, "The inhabitants of our frontiers are composed generally of such as have been transported hither as servants, and, being out of their time, settle themselves where land is to be taken up and that will produce the necessarys of life with little labour." Very generally these redemptioners were of non-English stock. In the crucible of the frontier the immigrants were Americanized, liberated, and fused into a mixed race, English in neither nationality nor characteristics. The process has gone on from the early days to our own. Burke and other writers in the middle of the eighteenth century believed that Pennsylvania was "threatened with the danger of being wholly foreign in language, manners, and perhaps even inclinations." The German and Scotch-Irish elements in the frontier of the South were only less great. In the middle of the present century the German element in Wisconsin was already so considerable that leading publicists looked to the creation of a German state out of the commonwealth by concentrating their colonization. Such examples teach us to beware of misinterpreting the fact that there is a common English speech in America into a belief that the stock is also English. . . .

From the conditions of frontier life came intellectual traits of profound importance. The works of travelers along each frontier from colonial days onward describe certain common traits, and these traits have, while softening down, still persisted as survivals in the place of their origin, even when a higher social organization succeeded. The result is that to the frontier the American intellect owes its striking characteristics. That coarseness and strength combined with acuteness and inquisitiveness; that practical, inventive turn of mind, quick to find expedients; that masterful grasp of material things, lacking in the artistic but powerful to effect great ends; that restless, nervous energy; that dominant individualism, working for good and for evil, and withal that buoyancy and exuberance which comes from freedom—these are traits of the frontier, or traits called out elsewhere because of the existence of the frontier. Since the days when the fleet of Columbus sailed into the waters of the New World, America has been another name for opportunity, and the people of the United States have taken their tone from the incessant expansion which has not only been open but has even been forced upon them. He would be a rash prophet who should assert that the expansive character of American life has now entirely ceased. Movement has been its dominant fact, and, unless this training has no effect upon a people, the American energy will continually demand a wider field for its exercise. But never again will such gifts of free land offer themselves. For a moment, at the frontier, the bonds of custom are broken and unrestraint is triumphant. There is not *tabula rasa*. The stubborn American environment is there with its imperious summons to accept its conditions; the inherited ways of doing things are also there; and yet, in spite of environment, and in spite of custom, each frontier did indeed furnish a new field of opportunity, a gate of escape from the bondage of the past; and freshness, and confidence, and scorn of older society, impatience of its restraints and its ideas, and indifference to its lessons, have accompanied the frontier. What the Mediterranean Sea was to the Greeks, breaking the bond of custom, offering new experiences, calling out new institutions and activities, that, and more, the ever retreating frontier has been to the United States directly, and to the nations of Europe more remotely. And now, four centuries from the discovery of America, at the end of a hundred years of life under the Constitution, the frontier has gone, and with its going has closed the first period of American history.

❖ *12* ❖

The Mexican War

The generation preceding the Civil War was a time of explosive physical growth for the United States. During the 1840s and 1850s, the country added 1.2 million square miles to its geographical limits. The largest block of new territory by far was wrenched from our southern neighbor, Mexico—through annexation of Texas in 1845 and by the Mexican Cession following victory in war in 1848.

Our relations with Mexico during these years were at best morally dubious. Long after wresting its independence from Spain in the 1820s, Mexico remained a poor, weak, and chaotic nation. The government in Mexico City was in constant flux as conflicting elites fought for control. The rapid shifts disturbed relations with the United States. Mexico's internal turmoil led to the loss of American lives and the destruction of American property.

The most serious Mexican American difficulties, however, concerned the borderlands. The Mexican government's hold on its sparsely populated, distant northern borders—the region adjoining the United States—was at best feeble. Mexico's weakness seemed America's opportunity. Encouraged by development-minded officials in Mexico City (*federalistas*), Americans began to drift into the borderlands soon after Mexican independence. In 1835 one group of Texas settlers, initially welcomed by Mexican authorities, rose in revolt against the central government when new, unfriendly officials (*centralistas*) came to power. After defeating the Mexican army, the secessionists established the Texas Republic. In 1845 the United States, to Mexico's dismay, annexed Texas as a state of the Union.

The remaining borderlands—California and New Mexico—remained tempting prizes to Americans. In 1846, for reasons explored below, the United States went to war with Mexico. For the Americans, victory followed victory, and in 1848 the defeated Mexicans ceded the two vast border provinces to the United States for the sum of $15 million.

Contemporaries differed over the causes of the Mexican War. Not surprisingly there were fundamental disagreements between citizens of the two republics. But Americans also disagreed among themselves. The following documents express a variety of attitudes concerning the origins of the Mexican War and the justice of the American cause.

12.1:   Manifest Destiny (1845)

Clearly many Americans in the period 1830 to 1860 believed that some irresistible moral, economic, demographic, or geographic imperative sanctioned the extension of their country's borders to include much of the North American continent. This view was given a name in 1845 by John L. O'Sullivan, a New York Democratic newspaper editor. It was America's "manifest destiny," O'Sullivan proclaimed, to extend its territory from coast to coast and from the arctic to the tropics.

O'Sullivan published the following editorial in the summer of 1845, soon after Congress had voted to annex Texas to the United States. Although the decision had been made, criticism continued, and O'Sullivan sought to defend the decision. But his remarks go beyond the matter of Texas annexation to embrace the issue of United States expansion generally. O'Sullivan is sensitive to several charges against the expansionists. What are these charges? Does he answer them convincingly in the case of Texas? What is his explanation for American expansionism? How does a transcontinental railroad fit into O'Sullivan's view of American destiny? It has often been said that arguments such as O'Sullivan's are merely crude rationalizations for greed and other self-serving drives. Do they in fact merely disguise more selfish motives? Or were they sincere beliefs that by themselves served to spur action?

Manifest Destiny

JOHN L. O'SULLIVAN

It is time now for opposition to the Annexation of Texas to cease, all further agitation of the waters of bitterness and strife, at least in connexion with this question,—even though it may perhaps be required of us as a necessary condition of the freedom of our institutions, that we must live on for ever in a state of unpausing struggle and excitement upon some subject of party division or other. But, in regard

John L. O'Sullivan, "Annexation," *The United States Magazine and Domestic Review,* vol. 17 (July and August, 1845), pp. 5–10.

to Texas, enough has now been given to Party. It is time for the common duty of Patriotism to the Country to succeed;—or if this claim will not be recognized, it is at least time for common sense to acquiesce with decent grace in the inevitable and the irrevocable.

Texas is now ours. Already, before these words are written, her Convention has undoubtedly ratified the acceptance, by her Congress, of our proffered invitation into the Union; and made the requisite changes in her already republican form of constitution to adopt it to its future federal relations. Her star and her stripe may already be said to have taken their place in the glorious blazon of our common nationality; and the sweep of our eagle's wing already includes within its circuit the wide extent of her fair and fertile land. She is no longer to us a mere geographical space—a certain combination of coast, plain, mountain, valley, forest and stream. She is no longer to us a mere country on the map. She comes within the dear and sacred designation of Our Country; no longer a *"pays,"* she is a part of *"la patrie,"* and that which is at once a sentiment and a virtue,[1] Patriotism, already begins to thrill for her too within the national heart. . . .

Why, were other reasoning wanting, in favor of now elevating this question of the reception of Texas into the Union, out of the lower region of our past party dissensions, up to its proper level of a high and broad nationality, it surely is to be found, found abundantly, in the manner in which other nations have undertaken to intrude themselves into it, between us and the proper parties to the case, in a spirit of hostile interference against us, for the avowed object of thwarting our policy and hampering our power, limiting our greatness and checking the fulfillment of our manifest destiny to overspread the continent allotted by Providence for the free development of our yearly multiplying millions. . . .

It is wholly untrue, and unjust to ourselves, the pretence that the Annexation has been a measure of spoliation, unrightful and unrighteous—of military conquest under forms of peace and law—of territorial aggrandizement at the expense of justice, and justice due by a double sanctity to the weak. This view of the question is wholly unfounded, and has been before so amply refuted in these pages, as well as in a thousand other modes, that we shall not again dwell upon it. The independence of Texas was complete and absolute. It was an independence, not only in fact but of right. No obligation of duty towards Mexico tended in the least degree to restrain our right to effect the desired recovery of the fair province once our own—whatever motives of policy might have prompted a more deferential consideration of her feelings and her pride, as involved in the question. If Texas became peopled with an American population, it was by no contrivance of our government, but on the express invitation of that of Mexico herself; accompanied with such guaranties of State independence, and the maintenance of a federal system analogous to our own, as constituted a compact fully justifying the strongest measures of redress on the part of those afterwards deceived in this guaranty, and sought to be enslaved under

---

[1]O'Sullivan is here distinguishing essentially between a slice of geography and a nation—ED.

the yoke imposed by its violation. She was released, rightfully and absolutely released, from all Mexican allegiance, or duty of cohesion to the Mexican political
body, by the acts and fault of Mexico herself, and Mexico alone. There never was a
clearer case. It was not revolution; it was resistance to revolution; and resistance
under such circumstances as left independence the necessary resulting state, caused
by the abandonment of those with whom her former federal association had existed.
What then can be more preposterous than all this clamor by Mexico and the Mexican interest, against Annexation, as a violation of any rights of hers, any duties of
ours? . . .

California will, probably, next fall away from the loose adhesion which, in such
a country as Mexico, holds a remote province in a slight equivocal kind of dependence on the metropolis. Imbecile and distracted, Mexico never can exert any
real governmental authority over such a country. The impotence of the one and the
distance of the other, must make the relation one of virtual independence; unless,
by stunting the province of all natural growth, and forbidding that immigration
which can alone develop its capabilities and fulfil the purposes of its creation,
tyranny may retain a military dominion which is no government in the legitimate
sense of the term. In the case of California this is now impossible. The Anglo-
Saxon foot is already on its borders. Already the advance guard of the irresistible
army of Anglo-Saxon emigration has begun to pour down upon it, armed with the
plough and the rifle, and marking its trail with schools and colleges, courts and
representative halls, mills and meeting-houses. A population will soon be in actual
occupation of California, over which it will be idle for Mexico to dream of dominion. They will necessarily become independent. All this without agency of our
government, without responsibility of our people—in the natural flow of events,
the spontaneous working of principles, and the adaptation of the tendencies and
wants of the human race to the elemental circumstances in the midst of which they
find themselves placed. And they will have a right to independence—to self-
government—to the possession of the homes conquered from the wilderness by
their own labors and dangers, sufferings and sacrifices—a better and a truer right
than the artificial title of sovereignty in Mexico a thousand miles distant, inheriting from Spain a title good only against those who have none better. Their right
to independence will be the natural right of self-government belonging to any
community strong enough to maintain it—distinct in position, origin and character, and free from any mutual obligations of membership of a common political
body, binding it to others by the duty of loyalty and compact of public faith. This
will be their title to independence; and by this title, there can be no doubt that the
population now fast streaming down upon California will both assert and maintain
that independence. Whether they will then attach themselves to our Union or not,
is not to be predicted with any certainty. Unless the projected rail-road across the
continent to the Pacific be carried into effect, perhaps they may not; though even
in that case, the day is not distant when the Empires of the Atlantic and Pacific
would again flow together into one, as soon as their inland border should approach
each other. But that great work, colossal as appears the plan on its first suggestion,
cannot remain long unbuilt. Its necessity for this very purpose of binding and

holding together in its iron clasp our fast settling Pacific region with that of the Mississippi valley—the natural facility of the route—the ease with which any amount of labor for the construction can be drawn in from the overcrowded populations of Europe, to be paid in the lands made valuable by the progress of the work itself—and its immense utility to the commerce of the world with the whole eastern coast of Asia, alone almost sufficient for the support of such a road—these considerations give assurance that the day cannot be distant which shall witness the conveyance of the representatives from Oregon and California to Washington within less time than a few years ago was devoted to a similar journey by those from Ohio; while the magnetic telegraph will enable the editors of the "San Francisco Union," the "Astoria Evening Post," or the "Nootka Morning News" to set up in type the first half of the President's Inaugural, before the echoes of the latter half shall have died away beneath the lofty porch of the Capitol, as spoken from his lips.

Away, then, with all idle French talk of *balances of power* on the American Continent. There is no growth in Spanish America! Whatever progress of population there may be in the British Canadas, is only for their own early severance of their present colonial relation to the little island three thousand miles across the Atlantic; soon to be followed by Annexation, and destined to swell the still accumulating momentum of our progress. And whatsoever may hold the balance, though they should cast into the opposite scale all the bayonets and cannon, not only of France and England, but of Europe entire, how would it kick the beam against the simple solid weight of the two hundred and fifty or three hundred millions—and American millions—destined to gather beneath the flutter of the stripes and stars, in the fast hastening year of the Lord 1845?

12.2: James K. Polk Calls for War Against Mexico (1846)

President James K. Polk, a Tennessee Democrat, was one of the most ardent expansionists of this period. Determined to fulfill America's territorial destiny in the Southwest, he preferred buying land to fighting for it. In late 1845 Polk sent John Slidell to Mexico to settle outstanding U.S. claims against Mexico for loss of American lives and property and to negotiate the purchase of California. But when the Mexicans refused to receive Slidell, Polk felt free to consider other ways of satisfying his territorial ambitions.

At the time of the Texas annexation, the United States claimed that the new state's valid southwestern boundary was the Rio Grande del Norte rather than the Nueces River, as the Mexicans insisted. Most historians now conclude that the American view was incorrect, but to back up the American assertion, in 1846 Polk ordered U.S. troops to occupy the disputed region between the rivers. The Mexicans, already angry over the Texas annexation and convinced that they stood a good chance to humble the Americans in a military encounter, determined to attack. On April 25, 1846, the Mexican commander at Matamoros crossed the Rio Grande and assaulted an American army patrol, inflicting sixteen casualties.

Polk was ready to go to war before he heard of the attack. But as he prepared his war message to Congress, news of the clash arrived in Washington and provided far better ammunition than any he previously had, and he used it. The document below is an excerpt from Polk's request for a declaration of war by Congress.

Is the statement of grievances against Mexico sincere, or does it seem contrived or hypocritical? Was Polk being honest when he declared that he desired "to establish peace with Mexico on liberal and honourable terms"? Or was this merely a cloak for American ambition?

Polk's War Message

JAMES K. POLK

The strong desire to establish peace with Mexico on liberal and honourable terms, and the readiness of this Government to regulate and adjust our boundary and other causes of difference with that power on such fair and equitable principles as would lead to permanent relations of the most friendly nature, induced me in September last [1845] to seek the reopening of diplomatic relations between the two countries. Every measure adopted on our part had for its object the furtherance of these desired results. In communicating to Congress a succinct statement of the injuries we had suffered from Mexico, and which have been accumulating during a period of more than twenty years, every expression that could tend to inflame the people of Mexico or defeat or delay a pacific result was carefully avoided. An envoy of the United States [John Slidell] repaired to Mexico with full powers to adjust every existing difference. But though present on Mexican soil by agreement between the two Governments, invested with full powers, and bearing evidence of the most friendly dispositions, his mission has been unavailing. The Mexican Government not only refused to see him or listen to his propositions, but after a long-continued series of menaces have at last invaded our territory and shed the blood of our fellow-citizens on our own soil. . . .

Thus the Government of Mexico, though solemnly pledged by official acts in October last to receive and accredit an American envoy, violated their plighted faith and refused the offer of a peaceful adjustment of our difficulties. . . .

James D. Richardson, ed., *A Compilation of the Messages and Papers of the Presidents* (New York: Bureau of National Literature, 1896), vol. 5, pp. 2287–93.

I informed you that upon the earnest appeal of the Congress and the convention of Texas I had ordered an efficient military force to take a position between "the Nueces and the [Rio Grande] Del Norte." This had become necessary to meet a threatened invasion of Texas by the Mexican forces, for which extensive military preparations had been made. The invasion was threatened solely because Texas had determined, in accordance with a solemn resolution of the Congress of the United States, to annex herself to our Union, and under these circumstances it was plainly our duty to extend our protection over her citizens and soil. . . .

Meanwhile Texas, by the final action of our Congress, had become an integral part of our Union. The Congress of Texas, by its act of December 19, 1836, had declared the Rio del Norte to be the boundary of that Republic. . . . It became, therefore, of urgent necessity to provide for the defense of that portion of our country. Accordingly, on the 13th of January last instructions were issued to the general in command of these troops to occupy the left bank of the Del Norte. This river, which is the southwestern boundary of the State of Texas, is an exposed frontier. From this quarter invasion was threatened; upon it and in its immediate vicinity, in the judgment of high military experience, are the proper stations for the protecting forces of the Government. . . .

The movement of the troops to the Del Norte was made by the commanding general under positive instructions to abstain from all aggressive acts toward Mexico or Mexican citizens and to regard the relations between that Republic and the United States as peaceful unless she should declare war or commit acts of hostility indicative of a state of war. He was specially directed to protect private property and respect personal rights.

The Army moved from Corpus Christi on the 11th of March, and on the 28th of that month arrived on the left bank of the Del Norte opposite to Matamoras, where it encamped on a commanding position, which has since been strengthened by the erection of fieldworks. A depot has also been established at Point Isabel, near the Brazos Santiago, 30 miles in rear of the encampment. The selection of his position was necessarily confided to the judgment of the general in command.

The Mexican forces at Matamoras assumed a belligerent attitude, and on the 12th of April General Ampudia, then in command, notified General [Zachary] Taylor to break up his camp within twenty-four hours and to retire beyond the Nueces River, and in the event of his failure to comply with these demands announced that arms, and arms alone, must decide the question. But no open act of hostility was committed until the 24th of April. On that day General Arista, who had succeeded to the command of the Mexican forces, communicated to General Taylor that "he considered hostilities commenced and should prosecute them." A party of dragoons of 63 men and officers were on the same day dispatched from the American camp up the Rio del Norte, on its left bank, to ascertain whether the Mexican troops had crossed or were preparing to cross the river, "became engaged with a large body of these troops, and after a short affair, in which some 16 were killed and wounded, appear to have been surrounded and compelled to surrender."

The grievous wrongs perpetrated by Mexico upon our citizens throughout a long period of years remain unredressed, and solemn treaties pledging her public faith for this redress have been disregarded. A government either unable or unwilling to enforce the execution of such treaties fails to perform one of its plainest duties. . . .

We have been exerting our best efforts to propitiate her good will. Upon the pretext that Texas, a nation as independent as herself, thought proper to unite its destinies with our own, she has affected to believe that we have severed her rightful territory, and in official proclamations and manifestoes has repeatedly threatened to make war upon us for the purpose of reconquering Texas. In the meantime we have tried every effort at reconciliation. The cup of forbearance had been exhausted even before the recent information from the frontier of the Del Norte. But now, after reiterated menaces, Mexico has passed the boundary of the United States, has invaded our territory and shed American blood upon the American soil. She has proclaimed that hostilities have commenced, and that the two nations are now at war.

As war exists, and, notwithstanding all our efforts to avoid it, exists by the act of Mexico herself, we are called upon by every consideration of duty and patriotism to vindicate with decision the honor, the rights, and the interests of our country.

12.3:   The Mexican View (1850)

Needless to say, Mexicans did not share the American view of the 1846–1848 war—as the selection below, by a group of patriotic Mexican scholars and journalists, shows. What factors do the Mexican commentators focus on in making their case against U.S. actions toward their country? Is their case convincing? Does it leave out some of the relevant background to the Mexican American dispute? Do you detect any begrudging admiration of the United States in their remarks?

The Mexican View of the War

RAMON ALCARAZ

To explain then in a few words the true origin of the war, it is sufficient to say that the insatiable ambition of the United States, favored by our weakness, caused it. But this assertion, however veracious and well founded, requires the confirmation which we will present, along with some former transactions, to the whole world. This evidence will leave no doubt of the correctness of our impressions.

In throwing off the yoke of the mother country, the United States of the North appeared at once as a powerful nation. This was the result of their excellent elementary principles of government established while in colonial subjection. The Republic announced at its birth, that it was called upon to represent an important part in the world of Columbus. Its rapid advancement, its progressive increase, its

Ramon Alcaraz et al., *The Other Side, or Notes for the History of the War Between Mexico and the United States,* trans. by Albert C. Ramsey (New York, n.p., 1850), pp. 2–3, 30–32.

wonderful territory, the uninterrupted augmentation of its inhabitants, and the formidable power it had gradually acquired, were many proofs of its becoming a colossus, not only for the feeble nations of Spanish America, but even for the old populations of the ancient continent.

The United States did not hope for the assistance of time in their schemes of aggrandizement. From the days of their independence they adopted the project of extending their dominions, and since then, that line of policy has not deviated in the slightest degree. This conduct, nevertheless, was not perceptible to the most enlightened: but reflecting men, who examined events, were not slow in recognising it. Conde de Aranda,[1] from whose perception the ends which the United States had resolved upon were not concealed, made use of some celebrated words. These we shall now produce as a prophecy verified by events. "This nation has been born a pigmy: in the time to come, it will be a giant, and even a colossus, very formidable in these vast regions. Its first step will be an appropriation of the Floridas to be master of the Gulf of Mexico."

The ambition of the North Americans has not been in conformity with this. They desired from the beginning to extend their dominion in such manner as to become the absolute owners of almost all this continent. In two ways they could accomplish their ruling passion: in one by bringing under their laws and authority all America to the Isthmus of Panama; in another, in opening an overland passage to the Pacific Ocean, and making good harbors to facilitate its navigation. By this plan, establishing in some way an easy communication of a few days between both oceans, no nation could compete with them. England herself might show her strength before yielding the field to her fortunate rival, and the mistress of the commercial world might for a while be delayed in touching the point of greatness to which she aspires.

In the short space of some three quarters of a century events have verified the existence of these schemes and their rapid development. The North American Republic has already absorbed territories pertaining to Great Britain, France, Spain, and Mexico. It has employed every means to accomplish this—purchase as well as usurpation, skill as well as force, and nothing has restrained it when treating of territorial acquisition. Louisiana, the Floridas, Oregon, and Texas, have successively fallen into its power. . . .

While the United States seemed to be animated by a sincere desire not to break the peace, their acts of hostility manifested very evidently what were their true intentions. Their ships infested our coasts; their troops continued advancing upon our territory, situated at places which under no aspect could be disputed. Thus violence and insult were united: thus at the very time they usurped part of our territory, they offered to us the hand of treachery, to have soon the audacity to say that our obstinacy and arrogance were the real causes of the war.

To explain the occupation of the Mexican territory by the troops of General [Zachary] Taylor, the strange idea occurred to the United States that the limits of

---

[1]Pedro de Aranda, a Mexican patriot of the early nineteenth century who participated in the revolt against Spain that brought Mexico its independence—ED.

Texas extended to the Rio Grande del Norte. This opinion was predicted upon two distinct principles: one, that the Congress of Texas had so declared it in December, in 1836; and another, that the river mentioned had been the natural line of Louisiana. To state these reasons is equivalent at once to deciding the matter; for no one could defend such palpable absurdities. The first, which this government prizing its intelligence and civilization, supported with refined malice, would have been ridiculous in the mouth of a child. Whom could it convince that the declaration of the Texas Congress bore a legal title for the acquisition of the lands which it appropriated to itself with so little hesitation? If such a principle were recognised, we ought to be very grateful to these gentlemen senators who had the kindness to be satisfied with so little. Why not declare the limits of the rebel state extended to San Luis, to the capital, to our frontier with Guatemala?

The question is so clear in itself that it would only obscure by delaying to examine it further. We pass then to the other less nonsensical than the former. In the first place to pretend that the limits of Louisiana came to the Rio Grande, it was essential to confound this province with Texas, which never can be tolerated. In the beginning of this article we have already shown the ancient and peaceable possession of Spain over the lands of the latter. Again, this same province, and afterwards State of Texas, never had extended its territory to the Rio Grande, being only to the Nueces, in which always had been established the boundary. Lastly, a large part of the territory situated on the other side of the Grande, belonged, without dispute or doubt, to other states of the Republic—to New Mexico, Tamaulipas, Coahuila, and Chihuahua.

Then, after so many and such plain proceedings, is there one impartial man who would not consider the forcible occupation of our territory by the North American arms a shameful usurpation? Then further, this power desired to carry to the extreme the sneer and the jest. When the question had resolved itself into one of force which is the *ultima ratio* of nations as well as of kings, when it had spread desolation and despair in our populations, when many of our citizens had perished in the contest, the bloody hand of our treacherous neighbors was turned to present the olive of peace. The Secretary of State, Mr. Buchanan, on the 27th of July, 1846, proposed anew, the admission of an Envoy to open negotiations which might lead to the concluding of an honorable peace. The national government answered that it could not decide, and left it to Congress to express its opinion of the subject. Soon to follow up closely the same system of policy, they ordered a commissioner with the army, which invaded us from the east, to cause it to be understood that peace would be made when our opposition ceased. Whom did they hope to deceive with such false appearances? Does not the series of acts which we have mentioned speak louder than this hypocritical language? By that test then, as a question of justice, no one who examines it in good faith can deny our indisputable rights. Among the citizens themselves, of the nation which has made war on us, there have been many who defended the cause of the Mexican Republic. These impartial defenders have not been obscure men, but men of the highest distinction. Mexico has counted on the assistance, ineffectual, unfortunately, but generous and illustrious, of a [Henry]

Clay, [John Quincy] Adams, a [Daniel] Webster, a [n Albert] Gallatin; that is to say, on the noblest men, the most appreciated for their virtues, for their talents, and for their services. Their conduct deserves our thanks, and the authors of this work have a true pleasure in paying, in this place, the sincere homage of their gratitude.

Such are the events that abandoned us to a calamitous war; and, in the relation of which, we have endeavored not to distort even a line of the private data consulted, to prove, on every occasion, all and each of our assertions.

From the acts referred to, it has been demonstrated to the very senses, that the real and effective cause of this war that afflicted us was the spirit of aggrandizement of the United States of the North, availing itself of its power to conquer us. Impartial history will some day illustrate for ever the conduct observed by this Republic against all laws, divine and human, in an age that is called one of light, and which is, notwithstanding, the same as the former—one of *force and violence.*

12.4: Dissent at Home (1846, 1847)

Opposition to the war against Mexico in the United States itself came from two chief sources: Whigs and northern antislavery adherents.

The first selection below is by the Massachusetts poet James Russell Lowell. His antiwar poem, written in rural Yankee dialect, expresses the views of Hosea Biglow, a fictional character Lowell uses as his spokesman. In fact, farmer Biglow spoke for many in New England and other parts of the Northeast. What is the theory of the Mexican War advanced by Biglow? Was it correct? What factors might explain the sectional split implied here? What do the last two lines suggest about why some northerners objected to new slave territory? (You must make allowances for Lowell's use of the term "nigger." Unfortunately, the expression was widely employed in American speech in this period.)

The second selection comes from a speech by Ohio Whig leader Thomas Corwin to the United States Senate in 1847, on the occasion of a bill to appropriate additional money to finance the war. Politics clearly influenced Corwin's attitude; other Whig politicians, including Congressman Abraham Lincoln of Illinois, were equally skeptical of the war, which they saw as a Democratic venture. But do partisan politics alone explain Corwin's harsh tone? Opponents called the Ohio senator unpatriotic, but is there something authentically American about his response? Does Corwin dispose effectively of the argument that Americans needed more room for living space?

The Mexican War Is on Behalf of Slavery

JAMES RUSSELL LOWELL

'T would n't suit them Southun fellers,
    They're a dreffle[1] graspin' set,
We must ollers[2] blow the bellers[3]
    Wen they want their irons het[4];
May be it's all right ez preachin',
    But my narves it kind o' grates,
Wen I see the overreachin'
    O' them nigger-driven' States. . . .

Ez fer war, I call it murder,—
    There you hev it plain an' flat;
I don't want to go no furder
    Than my Testyment fer that;
God hez sed so plump an' fairly,
    It's ez long ez it is broad,
    An' you've gut to git up airly
Ef you want to take in God. . . .

Wut's the use o' meetin'-goin'
    Every Sabbath, wet or dry,
Ef it's right to go amowin'
    Feller-men like oats an' rye?
I dunno but wut it's pooty
    Trainin' round in botail coats,—
But it's curus Christian dooty
    This 'ere cuttin' folks' throats.

They may talk o' Freedom's airy[5]
    Tell they're pupple in the face,—
It's a grand gret cemetary
    For the barthrights of our race;
They jest want this Californy
    So's to lug new slave-states in
To abuse ye, an' to scorn ye,
    An' to plunder ye like sin.

Aint it cute[6] to see a Yankee
    Take sech everlastin' pains,
All to get the Devil's thankee
    Helpin' on 'em weld their chains!
Wy, it's jest ez clear ez figgers,
    Clear ez one an' one make two,
Chaps thet make black slaves o' niggers
    Want to make wite slaves o' you.

James Russell Lowell, *The Biglow Papers* (Boston: Houghton Mifflin Company, 1891), pp. 64–70.

[1]Dreadfull—ED.
[2]Always—ED.
[3]Bellows—ED.
[4]Heated—ED.
[5]Freedom's nest, which is the United States, the home of freedom—ED.
[6]Here the word means clever, in a facetious way—ED.

The War with Mexico Is Morally Wrong

THOMAS CORWIN

Mr. President, I . . . beg the indulgence of the Senate to some reflections on the particular bill now under consideration. I voted for a bill somewhat like the present at the last session—our army was then in the neighborhood of our line. I then hoped that the President did sincerely desire a peace. Our army had not then penetrated far into Mexico, and I did hope, that with the two millions then proposed, we might get peace, and avoid the slaughter, the shame, the crime, of an aggressive, unprovoked war. But now you have overrun half of Mexico—you have exasperated and irritated her people—you claim indemnity for all expenses incurred in doing this mischief, and boldly ask her to give up New Mexico and California; and, as a bribe to her patriotism, seizing on her property, you offer three millions to pay the soldiers she has called out to repel your invasion, on condition that she will give up to you at least one-third of her whole territory. . . .

But, sir, let us see what, as the chairman of the Committee on Foreign Relations explains it, we are to get by the combined processes of conquest and treaty.

What is the territory, Mr. President, which you propose to wrest from Mexico? It is consecrated to the heart of the Mexican by many a well-fought battle with his old Castilian master. His Bunker Hills, and Saratogas, and Yorktowns, are there! The Mexican can say, "There I bled for liberty! and shall I surrender that consecrated home of my affections to the Anglo-Saxon invaders? What do they want with it? They have Texas already. They have possessed themselves of the territory between the Nueces and the Rio Grande. What else do they want? To what shall I point my children as memorials of that independence which I bequeath to them when those battlefields shall have passed from my possession?"

Sir, had one come and demanded Bunker Hill of the people of Massachusetts, had England's Lion ever showed himself there, is there a man over thirteen and under ninety who would not have been ready to meet him? Is there a river on this continent that would not have run red with blood? Is there a field but would have been piled high with the unburied bones of slaughtered Americans before these consecrated battlefields of liberty should have been wrested from us? But this same American goes into a sister republic and says to poor, weak Mexico, "Give up your territory, you are unworthy to possess it; I have got one-half already, and all I ask of you is to give up the other!" England might as well, in the circumstances I have described, have come and demanded of us, "Give up the Atlantic slope—give up this trifling territory from the Alleghany [sic] Mountains to the sea; it is only from Maine to St. Mary's—only about one-third of your republic, and the least interesting portion of it." What would be the response? They would say, we must give this up to John Bull. Why? "He wants room." The Senator from Michigan says he must have this. Why, my worthy Christian brother, on what principle of justice? "I want room!"

Congressional Globe, 29th Cong., 2d sess., 1847, Appendix, pp. 216–17.

Sir, look at this pretence of want of room. With twenty millions of people, you have about one thousand millions of acres of land, inviting settlement by every conceivable argument, bringing them down to a quarter of a dollar an acre, and allowing every man to squat where he pleases. But the Senator from Michigan says we will be two hundred millions in a few years, and we want room. If I were a Mexican I would tell you, "Have you not room in your own country to bury your dead men? If you come into mine, we will greet you with bloody hands, and welcome you to hospitable graves."

Why, says the chairman of this Committee on Foreign Relations, it is the most reasonable thing in the world! We ought to have the Bay of San Francisco. Why? Because it is the best harbor on the Pacific! It has been my fortune, Mr. President, to have practiced a good deal in criminal courts in the course of my life, but I never yet heard a thief, arraigned for stealing a horse, plead that it was the best horse that he could find in the country! We want California. What for? Why, says the Senator from Michigan, we will have it; and the Senator from South Carolina, with a very mistaken view, I think, of policy, says you can't keep our people from going there. I don't desire to prevent them. Let them go and seek their happiness in whatever country or clime it pleases them.

All I ask of them is, not to require this Government to protect them with that banner consecrated to war waged for principles—eternal, enduring truth. Sir, it is not meet that our old flag should throw its protecting folds over expeditions for lucre or for land. But you still say you want room for your people. This has been the plea of every robber chief from Nimrod to the present hour.

❖ *13* ❖

Slavery and the "Old South"

The "Old South"—the slave states before 1860—was diverse in economy, geography, class, race, religion, and culture. Yet the institution of slavery gave it both a cohesion and a uniqueness that set it apart from the rest of the United States.

No segment of the American past has been the focus of so much misunderstanding and myth as the Old South. To the average American today the name summons up images of vast cotton plantations with their slaves and masters. This picture may seem benign or malignant, depending on the race or ideology of the viewer, but it is, in any case, a simplistic view of a complex reality.

There were, of course, masters and slaves in the Old South, and the relations of the two formed a fundamental fact of the region's social and economic life. It is important to know how each viewed the other and how each perceived the circumstances under which they lived. But there were other significant members of Old South society besides slaveholders and slaves. We know that most southern whites were not slaveowners. Did they support the "peculiar institution," the South's distinctive system of chattel slavery? And what opinions did nonsoutherners have about Dixie? The Old South was defined to some degree by those on the outside who observed and criticized its institutions. What did the people of the free North have to say about the institutions and values of the region?

The selections below provide a sampling of contemporary opinion regarding the Old South. Judging from these documents, how should we perceive the society that developed in the slave states before the Civil War?

13.1:   Slavery from the Victim's Viewpoint (1848)

Among our best sources for evidence on how slavery affected slaves are the descriptions of slave refugees. Hundreds of slaves escaped the South each year, especially from the border states of Virginia, Maryland, Kentucky, and Missouri. A small proportion of these fugitives were literate men and women who wrote about their lives under the "peculiar institution." These poignant firsthand accounts found a sympathetic audience and were popular with the growing number of antislavery advocates in the North.

One of the best of these slave autobiographies is the Narrative of William Brown, A Fugitive Slave, *published in 1848, some thirteen years after Brown escaped from slavery. Like most slaves, Brown received no formal education, but he became a talented writer who published a number of books including a novel, the first by an African American.*

The following excerpt is the first two chapters of Brown's Narrative. *It contains descriptions of physical cruelty. But it also reveals the psychological costs of slavery. What are these, as depicted by Brown? Brown describes several brutal slaveowners. Does he suggest that some slave masters were better than these cruel men?*

The second reading presents a woman's perspective on slavery, exposing one of the most painful and bitter aspects of its tyranny: the sexual exploitation of enslaved women by white slave owners.

My Life as a Slave

WILLIAM BROWN

I was born in Lexington, Ky. The man who stole me as soon as I was born, recorded the births of all the infants which he claimed to be born [on] his property, in a book which he kept for that purpose. My mother's name was Elizabeth. She had seven children, viz.: Solomon, Leander, Benjamin, Joseph, Millford, Elizabeth, and myself. No two of us were children of the same father. My father's name, as I learned from my mother, was George Higgins. He was a white man, a relative of my master, and connected with some of the first families in Kentucky.

My master owned about forty slaves, twenty-five of whom were field hands. He removed from Kentucky to Missouri when I was quite young, and settled thirty or forty miles above St. Charles, on the Missouri, where, in addition to his practice as

William Brown, *Narrative of William Brown, A Fugitive Slave* (Boston: Published at the Anti-Slavery Office, 1848), pp. 1–7.

a physician, he carried on milling, merchandizing and farming. He had a large farm, the principal productions of which were tobacco and hemp. The slave cabins were situated on the back part of the farm, with the house of the overseer, whose name was Grove Cook, in their midst. He had the entire charge of the farm, and having no family, was allowed a woman to keep house for him, whose business it was to deal out the provisions for the hands.

A woman was also kept at the quarters to do the cooking for the field hands, who were summoned to their unrequited toil every morning at four o'clock, by the ringing of a bell, hung on post near the house of the overseer. They were allowed half an hour to eat their breakfast, and get to the field. At half past four a horn was blown by the overseer, which was his signal to commence work; and every one that was not on the spot at the time, had to receive ten lashes from the negro-whip, with which the overseer always went armed. The handle was about three feet long, with the butt-end filled with lead, and the lash, six or seven feet in length, made of cow-hide, with platted wire on the end of it. This whip was put in requisition very frequently and freely, and a small offence on the part of a slave furnished an occasion for its use. During the time that Mr. Cook was overseer, I was a house servant—a situation preferable to that of a field hand, as I was better fed, better clothed, and not obliged to rise at the ringing of the bell, but about half an hour after. I have often laid and heard the crack of the whip, and the screams of the slave. My mother was a field hand, and one morning was ten or fifteen minutes behind the others in getting into the field. As soon as she reached the spot where they were at work, the overseer commenced whipping her. She cried, "Oh! pray—Oh! pray—Oh! pray"— these are generally the words of slaves, when imploring mercy at the hands of their oppressors. I heard her voice, and knew it, and jumped out of my bunk, and went to the door. Though the field was some distance from the house, I could hear every crack of the whip, and every groan and cry of my poor mother. I remained at the door, not daring to venture any further. The cold chills ran over me, and I wept aloud. After giving her ten lashes, the sound of the whip ceased, and I returned to my bed, and found no consolation but in my tears. Experience has taught me that nothing can be more heart-rending than for one to see a dear and beloved mother or sister tortured, and to hear their cries, and not be able to render them assistance. But such is the position which an American slave occupies.

My master, being a politician, soon found those who were ready to put him into office, for the favors he could render them; and a few years after his arrival in Missouri he was elected to a seat in the legislature. In his absence from home everything was left in charge of Mr. Cook, the overseer, and he soon became more tyrannical and cruel. Among the slaves on the plantation was one by the name of Randall. He was a man about six feet high, and well-proportioned, and known as a man of great strength and power. He was considered the most valuable and able-bodied slave on the plantation; but no matter how good or useful a slave may be, he seldom escapes the lash. But it was not so with Randall. He had been on the plantation since my earliest recollection, and I had never known of his being flogged. No thanks were due to the master or overseer for this. I have often heard him declare that no white man should ever whip him—that he would die first.

Cook, from the time that he came upon the plantation, had frequently declared that he could and would flog any nigger that was put into the field to work under him. My master had repeatedly told him not to attempt to whip Randall, but he was determined to try it. As soon as he was left sole dictator, he thought the time had come to put his threats into execution. He soon began to find fault with Randall, and threatened to whip him if he did not do better. One day he gave him a very hard task—more than he could possibly do; and at night, the task not being performed, he told Randall that he should remember him the next morning. On the following morning, after the hands had taken breakfast, Cook called out to Randall, and told him that he intended to whip him, and ordered him to cross his hands and be tied. Randall asked why he wished to whip him. He answered, because he had not finished his task the day before. Randall said that the task was too great, or he should have done it. Cook said it made no difference—he should whip him. Randall stood silent for a moment, and then said, "Mr. Cook, I have always tried to please you since you have been on the plantation, and I find you are determined not to be satisfied with my work, let me do as well as I may. No man has laid hands on me, to whip me, for the last ten years, and I have long since come to the conclusion not to be whipped by any man living." Cook, finding by Randall's determined look and gestures, that he would resist, called three of the hands from their work, and commanded them to seize Randall, and tie him. The hands stood still;—they knew Randall—and they also knew him to be a powerful man, and were afraid to grapple with him. As soon as Cook had ordered the men to seize him, Randall turned to them, and said—"Boys, you all know me; you know that I can handle any three of you, and the man that lays hands on me shall die. This white man can't whip me himself, and therefore he has called you to help him." The overseer was unable to prevail upon them to seize and secure Randall, and finally ordered them all to go to their work together.

Nothing was said to Randall by the overseer for more than a week. One morning, however, while the hands were at work in the field, he came into it, accompanied by three friends of his, Thompson, Woodbridge and Jones. They came up to where Randall was at work, and Cook ordered him to leave his work, and go with them to the barn. He refused to go; whereupon he was attacked by the overseer and his companions, when he turned upon them, and laid them, one after another, prostrate on the ground. Woodbridge drew out his pistol, and fired at him, and brought him to the ground by a pistol ball. The others rushed upon him with their clubs, and beat him over the head and face, until they succeeded in tying him. He was then taken to the barn, and tied to a beam. Cook gave him over one hundred lashes with a heavy cowhide, had him washed with salt and water, and left him tied during the day. The next day he was untied, and taken to a blacksmith's shop, and had a ball and chain attached to his leg. He was compelled to labor in the field, and perform the same amount of work that the other hands did. When his master returned home, he was much pleased to find that Randall had been subdued in his absence.

Soon afterwards, my master removed to the city of St. Louis, and purchased a farm four miles from there, which he placed under the charge of an overseer by the name of Friend Haskell. He was a regular Yankee from New England. The Yankees are noted for making the most cruel overseers.

My mother was hired out in the city, and I was also hired out there to Major Freeland, who kept a public house. He was formerly from Virginia, and was a horse-racer, cock-fighter, gambler, and withal an inveterate drunkard. There were ten or twelve servants in the house, and when he was present, it was cut and slash—knock down and drag out. In his fits of anger, he would take up a chair, and throw it at a servant; and in his more rational moments, when he wished to chastise one, he would tie them up in the smoke-house, and whip them; after which, he would cause a fire to be made of tobacco stems, and smoke them. This he called *"Virginia play."*

I complained to my master of the treatment which I received from Major Freeland; but it made no difference. He cared nothing about it, so long as he received the money for my labor. After living with Major Freeland five or six months, I ran away, and went into the woods back of the city; and when night came on, I made my way to my master's farm, but was afraid to be seen, knowing that if Mr. Haskell, the overseer, should discover me, I should be again carried back to Major Freeland; so I kept in the woods. One day, while in the woods, I heard the barking and howling of dogs, and in a short time they came so near that I knew them to be the bloodhounds of Major Benjamin O'Fallon. He kept five or six, to hunt runaway slaves with.

As soon as I was convinced that it was them, I knew there was no chance of escape. I took refuge in the top of a tree, and the hounds were soon at its base, and there remained until the hunters came up in a half or three quarters of an hour afterwards. There were two men with the dogs, who, as soon as they came up, ordered me to descend. I came down, was tied, and taken to St. Louis jail. Major Freeland soon made his appearance, and took me out, and ordered me to follow him, which I did. After we returned home, I was tied up in the smoke-house, and was very severely whipped. After the major had flogged me to his satisfaction, he sent out his son Robert, a young man eighteen or twenty years of age, to see that I was well smoked. He made a fire of tobacco stems, which soon set me to coughing and sneezing. This, Robert told me, was the way his father used to do to his slaves in Virginia. After giving me what they conceived to be a decent smoking, I was untied and again set to work.

Robert Freeland was a "chip of the old block." Though quite young, it was not unfrequently that he came home in a state of intoxication. He is now, I believe, a popular commander of a steamboat on the Mississippi river. Major Freeland soon after failed in business, and I was put on board the steamboat Missouri, which plied between St. Louis and Galena. The commander of the boat was William B. Culver. I remained on her during the sailing season, which was the most pleasant time for me that I had ever experienced. At the close of navigation I was hired to Mr. John Colburn, keeper of the Missouri Hotel. He was from one of the free states; but a move inveterate hater of the negro I do not believe ever walked God's green earth. This hotel was at that time one of the largest in the city, and there were employed in it twenty or thirty servants, mostly slaves.

Mr. Colburn was very abusive, not only to the servants, but to his wife also, who was an excellent woman, and one from whom I never knew a servant to receive a harsh word; but never did I know a kind one to a servant from her husband. Among the slaves employed in the hotel was one by the name of Aaron, who belonged to Mr. John F. Darby, a lawyer. Aaron was the knife-cleaner. One day, one of the knives was put on the table, not as clean as it might have been. Mr. Colburn, for this offence, tied Aaron up in the wood-house, and gave him over fifty lashes on the bare back with a cow-hide, after which, he made me wash him down with rum. This seemed to put him into more agony than the whipping. After being untied he went home to his master, and complained of the treatment which he had received. Mr. Darby would give no heed to anything he had to say, but sent him directly back. Colburn, learning that he had been to his master with complaints, tied him up again, and gave him a more severe whipping than before. The poor fellow's back was literally cut to pieces; so much so, that he was not able to work for ten or twelve days.

There was, also, among the servants, a girl whose master resided in the country. Her name was Patsey. Mr. Colburn tied her up one evening, and whipped her until several of the boarders came out and begged him to desist. The reason for whipping her was this. She was engaged to be married to a man belonging to Major William Christy, who resided four or five miles north of the city. Mr. Colburn had forbid her to see John Christy. The reason of this was said to be the regard which he himself had for Patsey. She went to meeting that evening, and John returned home with her. Mr. Colburn had intended to flog John, if he came within the inclosure; but John knew too well the temper of his rival, and kept at a safe distance:—so he took vengeance on the poor girl. If all the slave-drivers had been called together, I do not think a more cruel man than John Colburn—and he too a northern man—could have been found among them.

While living at the Missouri hotel, a circumstance occurred which caused me great unhappiness. My master sold my mother, and all her children, except myself. They were sold to different persons in the city of St. Louis.

The Trials of Girlhood

HARRIET JACOBS

During the first years of my service in Dr. Flint's family, I was accustomed to share some indulgences with the children of my mistress. Though this seemed to me no more than right, I was grateful for it, and tried to merit the kindness by the faithful discharge of my duties. But I now entered on my fifteenth year—a sad epoch in the life of a slave girl. My master began to whisper foul words in my ear. Young as I was, I could not remain ignorant of their import. I tried to treat them with indifference or contempt. The master's age, my extreme youth, and the fear that his

Harriet Jacobs, *Incidents in the Life of a Slave Girl. Written By Herself.* L. Maria Child, ed., (Boston, 1861).

conduct would be reported to my grandmother, made him bear this treatment for many months. He was a crafty man, and resorted to many means to accomplish his purposes. Sometimes he had stormy, terrific ways, that made his victims tremble; sometimes he assumed a gentleness that he thought must surely subdue. Of the two, I preferred his stormy moods, although they left me trembling. He tried his utmost to corrupt the pure principles my grandmother had instilled. He peopled my young mind with unclean images, such as only a vile monster could think of. I turned from him with disgust and hatred. But he was my master. I was compelled to live under the same roof with him—where I saw a man forty years my senior daily violating the most sacred commandments of nature. He told me I was his property; that I must be subject to his will in all things. My soul revolted against the mean tyranny. But where could I turn for protection? No matter whether the slave girl be as black as ebony or as fair as her mistress. In either case, there is no shadow of law to protect her from insult, from violence, or even from death; all these are inflicted by fiends who bear the shape of men. The mistress, who ought to protect the helpless victim, has no other feelings towards her but those of jealousy and rage. The degradation, the wrongs, the vices, that grow out of slavery, are more than I can describe. They are greater than you would willingly believe. Surely, if you credited one half the truths that are told you concerning the helpless millions suffering in this cruel bondage, you at the north would not hlep to tighten the yoke. You surely would refuse to do for the master, on your own soil, the mean and curel work which trained bloodhounds and the lowest class of whites do for him at the south.

Every where the years bring to all enough of sin and sorrow; but in slavery the very dawn of life is darkened by these shadows. Even the little child, who is accustomed to wait on her mistress and her children, will learn, before she is twelve years old, why it is that her mistress hates such and such a one among the slaves. Perhaps the child's own mother is among those hated ones. She listens to violent outbreaks of jealous passion, and cannot help understanding what is the cause. She will become prematurely knowing in evil things. Soon she will learn to tremble when she hears her master's footfall. She will be compelled to realize that she is no longer a child. If God has bestowed beauty upon her, it will prove her greatest curse. That which commands admiration in the white woman only hastens the degradation of the female slave. I know that some are too much brutalized by slavery to feel the humiliation of their position; but many slaves feel it most acutely, and shrink from the memory of it. I cannot tell how much I suffered in the presence of these wrongs, nor how I am still pained by the retrospect. My master met me at every turn, reminding me that I belonged to him, and swearing by heaven and earth that he would compel me to submit to him. If I went out for a breath of fresh air, after a day of unwearied toil, his footsteps dogged me. If I knelt by my mother's grave, his dark shadow fell on me even there. The light heart which nature had given me became heavy with sad forebodings. The other slaves in my master's house noticed the change. Many of them pitied me; but none dared to ask the cause. They had no need to inquire. They knew too well the guilty practices under that roof; and they were aware that to speak of them was an offense that never went unpunished.

I longed for some one to confide in. I would have given the world to have laid my head on my grandmother's faithful bosom, and told her all my troubles. But Dr. Flint swore he would kill me, if I was not as silent as the grave. Then, although my grandmother was all in all to me, I feared her as well as loved her. I had been accustomed to look up to her with a respect bordering upon awe. I was very young, and felt shamefaced about telling her such impure things, especially as I knew her to be very strict on such subjects. Moreover, she was a woman of a high spirit. She was usually very quiet in her demeanor; but if her indignation was once roused, it was not very easily quelled. I had been told that she once chased a white gentleman with a loaded pistol, because he insulted one of her daughters. I dreaded the consequences of a violent outbreak; and both pride and fear kept me silent. But though I did not confide in my grandmother, and even evaded her vigilant watchfulness and inquiry, her presence in the neighborhood was some protection to me. Though she had been a slave, Dr. Flint was afraid of her. He dreaded her scorching rebukes. Moreover, she was known and patronized by many people; and he did not wish to have his villany made public. It was lucky for me that I did not live on a distant plantation, but in a town not so large that the inhabitants were ignorant of each other's affairs. Bad as are the laws and customs in a slaveholding community, the doctor, as a professional man, deemed it prudent to keep up some outward show of decency.

O, what days and nights of fear and sorrow that man caused me! Reader, it is not to awaken sympathy for myself that I am telling you truthfully what I suffered in slavery. I do it to kindle a flame of compassion in your hearts for my sisters who are still in bondage, suffering as I once suffered.

I once saw two beautiful children playing together. One was a fair white child; the other was her slave, and also her sister. When I saw them embracing each other, and heard their joyous laughter, I turned sadly away from the lovely sight. I foresaw the inevitable blight that would fall on the little slave's heart. I knew how soon her laughter would be changed to sighs. The fair child grew up to be a still fairer woman. From childhood to womanhood her pathway was blooming with flowers, and overarched by a sunny sky. Scarcely one day of her life had been clouded when the sun rose on her happy bridal morning.

How had those years dealt with her slave sister, the little playmate of her childhood? She, also, was very beautiful; but the flowers and sunshine of love were not for her. She drank the cup of sin, and shame, and misery, whereof her persecuted race are compelled to drink.

In view of these things, why are ye silent, ye free men and women of the north? Why do your tongues falter in maintenance of the right? Would that I had more ability! But my heart is so full, and my pen is so weak! There are noble men and women who plead for us, striving to help those who cannot help themselves. God bless them! God give them strength and courage to go on! God bless those, every where, who are laboring to advance the cause of humanity!

13.2: A Southern Apologist Views Slavery (1859)

*For a generation following the Revolution, many southern whites har-
bored serious moral reservations about slavery. By the 1830s these
reservations began to erode, however, and by the 1850s slavery had
gone from being regarded as a necessary evil to a positive good by
most white southerners. By the Civil War the South had forged a complex proslavery defense that obliterated almost all former doubts.*

*One of the most effective defenders of slavery was Edward A. Pollard,
a Virginia journalist. In the following selection from a volume of letters
to a fictional northern friend, Pollard depicts slaves and slavery as most
Southern whites preferred to see them. How would you characterize the
slave types that Pollard sketches? Were his descriptions invalid on their
face? Compare Pollard's Aunt Debby with William Brown's Randall in
the previous selection. How did they differ in their response to the white
master class? Is Aunt Debby a believable character?*

Happy "Darkies"

EDWARD A. POLLARD

But it is not my purpose to trouble you with a dissertation on "the vexed question,"
or the social system of the South, or any of the political aspects of Slavery. I merely
design to employ a few leisure hours in a series of unpretending sketches of the
condition, habits, and peculiarities of the negro-slave. The field, you know, has furnished a number of books; and I am sure, my dear C., that you are too sensible of
the large share of public attention *niggers* occupy in this country to slight them. Besides, I am thoroughly convinced that the negro portraits of the fiction writers are,
most of them, mere caricatures, taking them all, from [Harriet Beecher Stowe's]
"Uncle Tom's Cabin," down to the latest reply thereto—"a book" from a Virginia
authoress, in which the language put in the mouth of her leading character is a mixture of Irish idioms with the dialect of the Bowery. Who ever heard a Southern
negro say, as the Virginia lady's sable hero does, "The tip-top of the morning to
you, young ladies!" or "What's to pay now?" Nor will we find any of Mrs. Stowe's
Uncle Toms in the South, at least so far as the religious portraiture goes. The negro,
in his religion, is not a solemn old gentleman, reading his Bible in corners and praying in his closet: his piety is one of fits and starts, and lives on prayer-meetings,
with its rounds of *'zortations,* shoutings, and stolen sweets of baked pig.

You already know my opinion of the peculiarities of the negro's condition in the
South, in the provision made for his comfort, and in the attachment between him

Edward A. Pollard, *Black Diamonds Gathered in the Darkey Homes of the South* (New York: Pudney
and Russell, 1859), pp. 20–25.

and his master. The fact is, that, in wandering from my native soil to other parts of the world, I have seen slavery in many forms and aspects. We have all heard enough of the colliers and factory operatives of England, and the thirty thousand costermongers [peddlars] starving in the streets of London; as also of the serfs and crown-peasants of Russia, who are considered not even as chattels, but as part of the land, and who have their wives selected for them by their masters. I have seen the hideous slavery of Asia. I have seen the coolies of China "housed on the wild sea with wilder usages," or creeping with dejected faces into the suicide houses of Canton. I have seen the Siamese slave creeping in the presence of his master on all-fours—a human quadruped. It was indeed refreshing, after such sights, to get back to the Southern institution, which strikes one after so many years of absence, with a novelty that makes him appreciate more than ever the evidences of comfort and happiness on the plantations of the South.

The first unadulterated negro I had seen for a number of years (having been absent for the most of that time on a foreign soil), was on the railroad cars in Virginia. He looked like *home*. I could have embraced the old uncle, but was afraid the passengers, from such a demonstration, might mistake me for an abolitionist. I looked at him with my face aglow, and my eyelids touched with tears. How he reminded me of my home—of days gone by—that poetry of youth, "when I was a boy," and wandered with my sable playmates over the warm, wide hills of my sweet home, and along the branches, fishing in the shallow waters with a crooked pin! But no romancing with the past! So we continue our journey onward to "the State of railways and revolvers."

Arrived in Georgia, I find plenty of the real genuine *woolly-heads,* such as don't part their hair in the middle, like Mass'r [Charles] Fremont. My first acquaintance is with Aunt Debby. I insist upon giving her a shake of the hand, which she prepares for by deprecatingly wiping her hand on her apron. Aunt Debby is an aged colored female of the very highest respectability, and, with her white apron, and her head mysteriously enveloped in the brightest of bandannas, she looks (to use one of her own rather obscure similes) "like a new pin." She is very fond of usurping the authority of her mistress below stairs, and has the habit of designating every one of her own color, not admitted to equality, as *"de nigger."* Aunt Debby is rather spoiled, if having things her own way means it. If at times her mistress is roused to dispute her authority, Aunt Debby is sure to resume the reins when quiet ensues. "Debby," cries her mistress, "what's all this noise in the kitchen—what are you whipping Lucy for?" "La, missis, I'se jest makin' her 'have herself. She too busy *walling* her eyes at me, and spilt the water on the steps." Among the children, Aunt Debby is a great character. She is, however, very partial; and her favorite is little Nina, whom she calls (from what remote analogy we are at a loss to conjecture) "her *jelly-pot*." I flatter myself that I am in her good graces. Her attention to me has been shown by a present of ground-peas, and accessions of fat lightwood to my fire in the morning.

The religious element is very strong in Aunt Debby's character, and her *repertoire* of pious minstrelsy is quite extensive. Her favorite hymn is in the following words, which are repeated over and over again:

"Oh run, brother, run! Judgement day is comin'!
Oh run, brother, run! Why don't you come along?
The road so rugged, and the hill so high—
And my Lord call me home,
To walk the golden streets of my New Jerusalem."

Aunt Debby's religion is of that sort—always begging the Lord to take her up to glory, and professing the greatest anxiety to go *right now!* This religious enthusiasm, however, is not to be taken at its word.

You have doubtless heard the anecdote of Caesar, which is too good not to have been told more than once; though even if you have heard the story before, it will bear repetition for its moral. Now, Caesar one day had caught it, not from Brutus, but from Betty—an allegorical coquette in the shape of a red cowhide. On retiring to the silence of his cabin at night, Caesar commenced to soliloquize, rubbing the part of his body where the castigation had been chiefly administered, and bewailing his fate with tragic desperation, in the third person. "Caesar," said he, "most done gone—don't want to live no longer! Jist come, good Lord, swing low de chariot, and take dis chile away! Caesar ready to go—he *wants* to go!" An irreverent darkey outside, hearing these protestations, tapped at the door. "Who dar?" replied Caesar, in a low voice of suppressed alarm. "De angel of de Lord come for Caesar, 'cordin to request." The dread summons had indeed come, thought Caesar; but blowing out the light with a sudden whiff, he replied, in an unconcerned tone, *"De nigger don't live here."*

There is one other trait wanting to complete Aunt Debby's character. Though at an advanced age, she is very coquettish; and keeps a regular assault on a big lout of the name of Sam, whom she affects to despise as "jist 'de meanest nigger de Lord ever put breath in." I overheard some words between them last holiday. "I'se a white man to-day," says Sam, "and I'se not gwine to take any of your imperence, old ooman;" at the same time, taking the familiar liberty of poking his finger into her side like a brad-awl. "Get 'long, Sa-ten!" replied Aunt Debby, with a shove, but a smile at the same time, to his infernal majesty. And then they both fell to laughing for the space of half a minute, although I must confess, that I could not understand what they were laughing at.

Aunt Debby may serve you, my dear C., as a picture of the happy, contented, Southern slave. Some of your Northern politicians would represent the slaves of the South as sullen, gloomy, isolated from life—in fact, pictures of a living death. Believe me, nothing could be further from the truth. Like Aunt Debby, they have their little prides and passions, their amusements, their pleasantries, which constitute the same sum of happiness as in the lives of their masters.

13.3: The Southern Plantation Idyll (1832)

Most white southerners not only defended slavery as such; they also defended the white society it carried on its back. The following selection is from a novel by John Pendleton Kennedy, a native of Baltimore related through his mother to several aristocratic families of Virginia. Kennedy was not a typical defender of the southern plantation idyll, but his book, Swallow Barn, *a novel in the form of letters, helped construct the myth of the gracious, happy plantation where everyone, masters and slaves alike, lived a genial and civilized, if deferential, existence.*

Kennedy's hero, Frank Meriwether, is an idealized type. What are his chief characteristics? Do you think there were actually people like Meriwether in the antebellum South? Were there plantations like Swallow Barn? Or were they—the Meriwethers and the Swallow Barns—all creations of southern propaganda?

(It is worth noting that after the Civil War Kennedy became a Republican!)

The Southern Plantation Idyll

JOHN PENDLETON KENNEDY

Swallow Barn is an aristocratical old edifice which sits, like a brooding hen, on the southern bank of the James River. It looks down upon a shady pocket or nook, formed by an indentation of the shore, from a gentle acclivity thinly sprinkled with oaks whose magnificent branches afford habitation to sundry friendly colonies of squirrels and woodpeckers.

This time-honored mansion was the residence of the family of Hazards. But in the present generation, the spells of love and mortgage have translated the possession to Frank Meriwether, who having married Lucretia, the eldest daughter of my late Uncle Walter Hazard, and lifted some gentleman-like incumbrances which had been sleeping for years upon the domain, was thus inducted into the proprietary rights. The adjacency of his own estate gave a territorial feature to this alliance, of which the fruits were no less discernible in the multiplication of negroes, cattle, and poultry, than in a flourishing clan of Meriwethers.

The main building is more than a century old. It is built with thick brick walls, but one story in height, and surmounted by a double-faced or hipped roof, which gives the idea of a ship bottom upwards. Later buildings have been added to this, as the wants or ambition of the family have expanded. These are all constructed of wood, and seem to have been built in defiance of all laws of congruity, just as convenience required. But they form altogether an agreeable picture of habitation, suggesting the idea of comfort in the ample space they fill, and in their conspicuous adaptation to domestic uses.

John Pendleton Kennedy, *Swallow Barn, Or, A Sojourn in the Old Dominion* (Philadelphia: J. B. Lippincott, 1861), pp. 22–35.

The hall door is an ancient piece of walnut, which has grown too heavy for its hinges, and by its daily travel has furrowed the floor in a quadrant, over which it has an uneasy journey. It is shaded by a narrow porch, with a carved pediment upheld by massive columns of wood, somewhat split by the sun. An ample court-yard, inclosed by a semi-circular paling, extends in front of the whole pile, and is traversed by a gravel road leading from a rather ostentatious iron gate, which is swung between two pillars of brick surmounted by globes of cut stone. Between the gate and the house a large willow spreads its arched and pendent drapery over the grass. A bridle rack stands within the inclosure, and near it a ragged horse-nibbled plum-tree—the current belief being that a plum-tree thrives on ill usage—casts its skeleton shadow on the dust. . . .

Appendant to this homestead is an extensive tract of land which stretches some three or four miles along the river, presenting alternately abrupt promontories mantled with pine and dwarf oak, and small inlets terminating in swamps. Some sparse portions of forest vary the landscape, which, for the most part, exhibits a succession of fields clothed with Indian corn, some small patches of cotton or tobacco plants, with the usual varieties of stubble and fallow grounds. These are inclosed by worm fences of shrunken chestnut, where lizards and ground-squirrels are perpetually running races along the rails.

A few hundred steps from the mansion, a brook glides at a snail's pace towards the river, holding its course through a wilderness of laurel and alder, and creeping around islets covered with green mosses. Across the stream is thrown a rough bridge, which it would delight a painter to see; and not far below it an aged sycamore twists its roots into a grotesque framework to the pure mirror of a spring, which wells up its cool waters from a bed of gravel and runs gurgling to the brook. There it aids in furnishing a cruising ground to a squadron of ducks who, in defiance of all nautical propriety, are incessantly turning up their sterns to the skies. On the grass which skirts the margin of the spring, I observe the family linen is usually spread out by some three or four negro women, who chant shrill music over their wash-tubs, and seem to live in ceaseless warfare with sundry little besmirched and bow-legged blacks, who are never tired of making somersets, and mischievously pushing each other on the clothes laid down to dry. . . .

The master of this lordly domain is Frank Meriwether. He is now in the meridian of life—somewhere about forty-five. Good cheer and an easy temper tell well upon him. The first has given him a comfortable, portly figure, and the latter a contemplative turn of mind, which inclines him to be lazy and philosophical.

He has some right to pride himself on his personal appearance, for he has a handsome face, with a dark blue eye and a fine intellectual brow. His head is growing scant of hair on the crown, which induces him to be somewhat particular in the management of his locks in that locality, and these are assuming a decided silvery hue.

It is pleasant to see him when he is going to ride to the Court House on business occasions. He is then apt to make his appearance in a coat of blue broadcloth, astonishingly glossy, and with an unusual amount of plaited ruffle strutting through the folds of a Marseilles waistcoat. A worshipful finish is given to this costume by a large straw hat, lined with green silk. There is a magisterial fulness in his garments which betokens condition in the world, and a heavy bunch of seals, suspended by a chain of gold, jingles as he moves, pronouncing him a man of superfluities.

It is considered rather extraordinary that he has never set up for Congress: but the truth is, he is an unambitious man, and has a great dislike to currying favor—as he calls it. And, besides, he is thoroughly convinced that there will always be men enough in Virginia willing to serve the people, and therefore does not see why he should trouble his head about it. Some years ago, however, there was really an impression that he meant to come out. By some sudden whim, he took it into his head to visit Washington during the session of Congress, and returned, after a fortnight, very seriously distempered with politics. He told curious anecdotes of certain secret intrigues which had been discovered in the affairs of the capital, gave a clear insight into the views of some deep-laid combinations, and became, all at once, painfully florid in his discourse, and dogmatical to a degree that made his wife stare. Fortunately, this orgasm soon subsided, and Frank relapsed into an indolent gentleman of the opposition; but it had the effect to give a much more decided cast to his studies, for he forthwith discarded the "Richmond Whig" from his newspaper subscription, and took to "The Enquirer,"[1] like a man who was not to be disturbed by doubts. And as it was morally impossible to believe all that was written on both sides, to prevent his mind from being abused, he from this time forward took a stand against the re-election of Mr. [John Quincy] Adams to the Presidency, and resolved to give an implicit faith to all alleged facts which set against his administration. The consequence of this straight-forward and confiding deportment was an unexpected complimentary notice of him by the Executive of the State. He was put into the commission of the peace, and having thus become a public man against his will, his opinions were observed to undergo some essential changes. He now thinks that a good citizen ought neither to solicit nor decline office; that the magistracy of Virginia is the sturdiest pillar which supports the fabric of the Constitution; and that the people, "though in their opinions they may be mistaken, in their sentiments they are never wrong;"—with some such other dogmas as, a few years ago, he did not hold in very good repute. In this temper, he has of late embarked on the millpond of county affairs, and nothwithstanding his amiable character and his doctrinary republicanism, I am told he keeps the peace as if he commanded a garrison, and administers justice like a Cadi. . . .

A landed proprietor, with a good house and a host of servants, is naturally a hospitable man. A guest is one of his daily wants. A friendly face is a necessary of life, without which the heart is apt to starve, or a luxury without which it grows parsimonious. Men who are isolated from society by distance, feel these wants by an instinct, and are grateful for the opportunity to relieve them. In Meriwether, the sentiment goes beyond this. It has, besides, something dialectic in it. His house is open to every body, as freely almost as an inn. But to see him when he has had the good

---

[1]The *Whig* was a partisan of the nationalist and moderate Whig party; The *Enquirer* was the more pro-South Democratic paper—ED.

fortune to pick up an intelligent, educated gentleman,—and particularly one who listens well!—a respectable, assentatious stranger!—All the better if he has been in the Legislature, or better still, if in Congress. Such a person caught within the purlieus of Swallow Barn, may set down one week's entertainment as certain—inevitable, and as many more as he likes—-the more the merrier. He will know something of the quality of Meriwether's rhetoric before he is gone.

Then again, it is very pleasant to see Frank's kind and considerate bearing towards his servants and dependents. His slaves appreciate this, and hold him in most affectionate reverence, and, therefore, are not only contented, but happy under his dominion. . . .

He thinks lightly of the mercantile interest, and, in fact, undervalues the manners of the large cities generally. He believes that those who live in them are hollow-hearted and insincere, and wanting in that substantial intelligence and virtue, which he affirms to be characteristic of the country. He is an ardent admirer of the genius of Virginia, and is frequent in his commendation of a toast in which the state is compared to the mother of the Gracchi[2]:—indeed, it is a familiar thing with him to speak of the aristocracy of talent as only inferior to that of the landed interest,—the idea of a free-holder inferring to his mind a certain constitutional pre-eminence in all the virtues of citizenship, as a matter of course.

13.4: A Nonslaveholding Southerner Attacks the "Peculiar Institution" (1857)

Not all white southerners supported slavery. A minority deplored the institution, and a very few even publicly denounced it. Among the most vocal white southern opponents of the "peculiar institution" was Hinton Rowan Helper, a North Carolinian from the mountainous western part of the state, where there were few slaves and almost no plantations. Helper spoke in the name of the southern white small farmer, who, in his view, suffered severely from the domination of the planter "oligarchy." He was, however, no friend to blacks and indeed advocated their expulsion from the United States!

In 1857 Helper blasted the slaveowners in a volume that no one in the South would publish. The Impending Crisis of the South *finally came out under antislavery auspices and was adopted as a Republican campaign document in the 1860 presidential election. As if that were not bad enough in the eyes of white Southerners, the volume seemed to condone a bloody uprising of slaves against their masters. Overnight Helper became a pariah in his home section.*

What are the charges Helper levels against slavery? Do they overlap those expressed by William Brown above? Does Helper add other

---

[2]Agrarian reformers of the late Roman Republic—ED.

items to the indictment of slavery besides cruelty? Was his view that slavery hurt the South's nonslaveholding whites correct? Do you know if slavery made the pre–Civil War South overall poorer than the North?

Slavery Hurts Non-Slaveholding Whites

HINTON ROWAN HELPER

As a striking illustration of the selfish and debasing influences which slavery exercises over the hearts and minds of slaveholders themselves, we will here state the fact that, when we, the non-slaveholders, remonstrate against the continuance of such a manifest wrong and inhumanity—a system of usurpation and outrage so obviously detrimental to *our* interests—they fly into a terrible passion, exclaiming, among all sorts of horrible threats, which are not unfrequently executed, "It's none of your business!"—meaning to say thereby that their slaves do not annoy us, that slavery affects no one except the masters and their chattels personal and that *we* should give ourselves no concern about it, whatever! To every man of common sense and honesty of purpose the preposterousness of this assumption is so evident, that any studied attempt to refute it would be a positive insult. Would it be none of our business, if they were to bring the small-pox into the neighborhood, and, with premeditated design, let "foul contagion spread"? Or, if they were to throw a pound of strychnine into a public spring, would that be none of our business? Were they to turn a pack of mad dogs loose on the community, would we be performing the part of good citizens by closing ourselves within doors for the space of nine days, saying nothing to anybody? Small-pox is a nuisance; strychnine is a nuisance; mad dogs are a nuisance; slavery is a nuisance; slaveholders are a nuisance, and so are slave-breeders; it is our business, nay, it is our imperative duty, to abate nuisances; we propose, therefore, with the exception of strychnine, which is the least of all these nuisances, to exterminate this catalogue from beginning to end.

We mean precisely what our words express, when we say we believe thieves are, as a general rule, less amenable to the moral law than slaveholders; and here is the basis of our opinion: Ordinarily, thieves wait until we acquire a considerable amount of property, and then they steal a dispensable part of it; but they deprive no one of physical liberty, nor do they fetter the mind; slaveholders, on the contrary, by clinging to the most barbarous relic of the most barabrous age, bring disgrace on themselves, their neighbors, and their country, depreciate the value of their own and others' lands, degrade labor, discourage energy and progress, prevent non-slaveholders from accumulating wealth, curtail their natural rights and privileges, doom their children to ignorance, and all its attendant evils, rob the negroes of their freedom, throw a damper on every species of manual and intellectual enterprise, that is not projected under their own roofs and for their own advantage, and, by other means equally at variance with the principles of justice, though but an in-

Hinton Rowan Helper, *The Impending Crisis of the South: How to Meet It* (New York: Burdick Brothers, 1857), pp. 139–41, 380–82.

significant fractional part of the population, they constitute themselves the sole arbiters and legislators for the entire South. Not merely so; the thief rarely steals from more than one man out of an hundred; the slaveholder defrauds ninety and nine, and the hundredth does not escape him. Again, thieves steal trifles from rich men; slaveholders oppress poor men, and enact laws for the perpetuation of their poverty. Thieves practice deceit on the wise; slaveholders take advantage of the ignorant.

We contend, moreover, that slaveholders are more criminal than common murderers. We know all slaveholders would not wilfully imbue their hands in the blood of their fellow-men; but it is a fact, nevertheless, that all slaveholders are under the shield of a perpetual license to murder. This license they have issued to themselves. According to their own infamous statutes, if the slave raises his hand to ward off an unmerited blow, they are permitted to take his life with impunity. We are personally acquainted with three ruffians who have become actual murderers under circumstances of this nature. One of them killed two negroes on one occasion; the other two have murdered but one each. Neither of them has ever been subjected to even the preliminaries of a trial; not one of them has ever been arrested; their own private explanations of the homicides exculpated them from all manner of blame in the premises. They had done nothing wrong in the eyes of the community. The negroes made an effort to shield themselves from the tortures of a merciless flagellation, and were shot dead on the spot. Their murderers still live, and are treated as honorable members of society! No matter how many slaves or free negroes may witness the perpetration of these atrocious homicides, not one of them is ever allowed to lift up his voice in behalf of his murdered brother. In the South, negroes, whether bond or free, are never, under any circumstances, permitted to utter a syllable under oath, except for or against persons of their own color; their testimony against white persons is of no more consequence than the idle zephyr of the summer. . . .

Black slave labor, though far less valuable, is almost invariably better paid than free white labor. The reason is this: The fiat of the oligarchy has made it *fashionable* to "have negroes around," and there are, we are grieved to say, many non-slaveholding whites, (lickspittles), who, in order to retain on their premises a hired slave whom they falsely imagine secures to them not only the appearance of wealth, but also a position of high social standing in the community, keep themselves in a perpetual strait.

Last Spring, we made it our special business to ascertain the ruling rates of wages paid for labor, free and slave, in North Carolina. We found sober, energetic white men, between twenty and forty years of age, engaged in agricultural pursuits at a salary of $84 per annum—including board only; negro men, slaves, who performed little more than half the amount of labor, and who were exceedingly sluggish, awkward, and careless in all their movements, were hired out on adjoining farms at an average of about $115 per annum, including board, clothing, and medical attendance. Free white men and slaves were in the employ of the North Carolina Railroad Company; the former, whose services, in our opinion, were at least twice as valuable as the services of the latter, received only $12 per month each; the masters of the latter received $16 per month for every slave so employed. Industrious, tidy white girls, from sixteen to twenty years of age, had much difficulty in hiring themselves out as domestics in private families for $40 per annum—board only included; negro wenches, slaves, of corresponding ages, so ungraceful, stupid and filthy that no decent man would ever permit one of them to cross the threshold of his dwelling, were in brisk demand at from $65 to $70 per annum, including victuals, clothes, and medical attendance. These are facts, and in considering them, the students of political and social economy will not fail to arrive at conclusions of their own.

Notwithstanding the greater density of population in the free States, labor of every kind is, on an average, about one hundred per cent higher there than it is in the slave States. This is another important fact, and one that every non-slaveholding white should keep registered in his mind.

Poverty, ignorance, and superstition, are the three leading characteristics of the non-slaveholding whites of the South. Many of them grow up to the age of maturity, and pass through life without ever owning as much as five dollars at any one time. Thousands of them die at an advanced age, as ignorant of the common alphabet as if it had never been invented. All are more or less impressed with a belief in witches, ghosts, and supernatural signs. Few are exempt from habits of sensuality and intemperance. None have anything like adequate ideas of the duties which they owe either to their God, to themselves, or to their fellow-men. Pitiable, indeed, in the fullest sense of the term, is their condition.

It is the almost utter lack of an education that has reduced them to their present unenviable situation. In the whole South there is scarcely a publication of any kind devoted to their interests. They are now completely under the domination of the oligarchy, and it is madness to suppose that they will ever be able to rise to a position of true manhood, until after the slave power shall have been utterly overthrown.

13.5:   A Northerner Describes the Old South (1854)

Many northern visitors were charmed by the Old South and were happy to confirm its own self-evaluation. One observer who demurred was the New York gentleman farmer and landscape architect Frederick Law Olmstead.

Olmstead disliked slavery, but was unwilling to condemn the system or its beneficiaries outright. This attitude led to frequent arguments with his good friend Charles Loring Brace, a dedicated abolitionist, and in 1850 Olmstead decided to see the South for himself. Before Olmstead left, Brace contacted Henry J. Raymond, editor of the New York Times, *who agreed to appoint Olmstead as special correspondent and publish his letters as dispatchers in the* Times.

In all, from late 1852 to the summer of 1854, Olmstead spent fourteen months traveling through eleven slave states on three separate expeditions. He traveled by horseback along the dirt roads and back country trails that made up the rough communication system of the rural South. He spoke to everyone he could—planters, slaves, towns-people, yeoman, and poor whites—and relied on private hospitality rather than hotels for his meals and shelter. It was often tedious and grueling work, but he managed to send back a stream of descriptive letters that Raymond eagerly published. Collected in three books be-tween 1856 and 1860, these were praised by most critics and widely read in the North and in England. The three volumes were condensed into a single two-volume work, The Cotton Kingdom, *to meet the surge of demand after the Civil War broke out in 1861.*

Below are two excerpts from The Cotton Kingdom. *The first, written in 1854, tells of Olmstead's overnight stay at a white yeoman's farm in central Mississippi. The second is Olmstead's overview of the living arrangements of the planter class as he found them, and a contrast with their northern counterparts.*

Is either description complimentary? In the case of the yeoman fam-ily, what seems to have been the general level of physical comfort and education? What are Olmstead's conclusions about the comforts and "civilization" of the southern planters? As a northerner, can Olm-stead's views be considered reliable? Remember, although he was not an abolitionist and in fact at times defended slavery against its angrier detractors, one cannot dismiss the influence of his free state origins—and those of his readers. There is another factor to keep in mind in evaluating Olmstead's observations: They are anecdotal, based on a relatively few experiences rather than a scientific sampling. Can this spotty quality have affected the overall picture? There is an obvious contrast between the descriptions in The Cotton Kingdom *and in John Pendleton Kennedy's* Swallow Barn. *Aside from sectional bias, can the fact that Kennedy focuses on Virginia and Olmstead on the newer areas of the South help explain the differences in their depictions?*

(It might be interesting to contrast Olmstead's criticism of the Old South with George Fitzhugh's criticism, in Chapter 10, of the contem-porary North.)

A Northern Traveler Views Southern Slavery

FREDERICK LAW OLMSTEAD

The next house at which I arrived was one of the commonest sort of cabins. I had passed twenty like it during the day, and I thought I would take the opportunity to get an interior knowledge of them. The fact that a horse and waggon were kept, and

Frederick Law Olmstead, *The Cotton Kingdom: A Traveller's Observations on Cotton and Slavery in the American Slave States* (New York: Mason Brothers, 1861), vol. 2, pp. 78–82, 285–89.

that a considerable area of land in the rear of the cabin was planted with cotton, showed that the family were by no means of the lowest class, yet, as they were not able even to hire a slave, they may be considered to represent very favourably, I believe, the condition of the poor whites of the plantation districts. The whites of the country, I observe, by the census, are three to one of the slaves; in the nearest adjoining county, the proportion is reversed; and within a few miles the soil was richer, and large plantations occurred.

It was raining, and nearly nine o'clock. The door of the cabin was open, and I rode up and conversed with the occupant as he stood within. He said that he was not in the habit of taking in travellers, [sic] and his wife was about sick, but if I was a mind to put up with common fare, he didn't care. Grateful, I dismounted and took the seat he had vacated by the fire, while he led away my horse to an open shed in the rear—his own horse ranging at large, when not in use, during the summer.

The house was all comprised in a single room, twenty-eight by twenty-five feet in area, and open to the roof above. There was a large fireplace at one end and a door on each side—no windows at all. Two bedsteads, a spinning-wheel, a packing-case, which served as a bureau, a cupboard, made of rough hewn slabs, two or three deer-skin seated chairs, a Connecticut clock, and a large poster of Jayne's patent medicines, constituted all the visible furniture, either useful or ornamental in purpose. A little girl, immediately, without having had any directions to do so, got a frying-pan and a chunk of bacon from the cupboard, and cutting slices from the latter, set it frying for my supper. The woman of the house sat sulkily in a chair tilted back and leaning against the logs, spitting occasionally at the fire, but took no notice of me, barely nodding when I saluted her. A baby lay crying on the floor. I quieted it and amused it with my watch till the little girl, having made "coffee" and put a piece of corn-bread on the table with the bacon, took charge of it.

I hoped the woman was not very ill.

"Got the headache right bad," she answered. "Have the headache a heap, I do. Knew I should have it to-night. Been cuttin' brush in the cotton this afternoon. Knew't would bring on my headache. Told him so when I begun."

As soon as I had finished my supper and fed [my horse] Jude, the little girl put the fragments and the dishes in the cupboard, shoved the table into a corner, and dragged a quantity of quilts from one of the bedsteads, which she spread upon the floor, and presently crawled among them out of sight for the night. The woman picked up the child—which, though still a suckling, she said was twenty-two months old—and nursed it, retaking her old position. The man sat with me by the fire, his back towards her. The baby having fallen asleep was laid away somewhere, and the woman dragged off another lot of quilts from the beds, spreading them upon the floor. Then taking a deep tin pan, she filled it with alternate layers of corn-cobs and hot embers from the fire. This she placed upon a large block, which was evidently used habitually for the purpose, in the centre of the cabin. A furious smoke arose from it, and we soon began to cough. "Most *too* much smoke," observed the man. "Hope 'twill drive out all the gnats, then," replied the woman. (There is a very minute flying insect here, the bite of which is excessively sharp.)

The woman suddenly dropped off her outer garment and stepped from the midst of its folds, in her petticoat; then, taking the baby from the place where she had deposited it, lay down and covered herself with the quilts upon the floor. The man told me that I could take the bed which remained on one of the bedsteads, and kicking off his shoes only, rolled himself into a blanket by the side of his wife. I ventured to take off my cravat and stockings, as well as my boots, but almost immediately put my stockings on again, drawing their tops over my pantaloons. The advantage of this arrangement was that, although my face, eyes, ears, neck, and hands, were immediately attacked, the vermin did not reach my legs for two or three hours. Just after the clock struck two, I distinctly heard the man and the woman, and the girl and the dog scratching, and the horse out in the shed stamping and gnawing himself. Soon afterward the man exclaimed, "Good God Almighty—mighty! mighty! mighty!" and jumping up pulled off one of his stockings, shook it, scratched his foot vehemently, put on the stocking, and lay down again with a groan. The two doors were open, and through the logs and the openings in the roof, I saw the clouds divide and the moon and stars reveal themselves. The woman, after having been nearly smothered by the smoke from the pan which she had originally placed close to her own pillow, rose and placed it on the sill of the windward door, where it burned feebly and smoked lustily, like an altar to the Lares, all night. Fortunately the cabin was so open that it gave us little annoyance, while it seemed to answer the purpose of keeping all flying insects at a distance.

When, on rising in the morning, I said that I would like to wash my face, water was given me for the purpose in an earthen pie-dish. Just as breakfast, which was of exactly the same materials as my supper, was ready, rain began to fall, presently in such a smart shower as to put the fire out and compel us to move the table under the least leaky part of the roof. . . .

I think that the error which prevails in the South, with regard to the general condition of our working people, is much strengthened by the fact, that a different standard of comfort is used by most persons at the South from that known at the North, and that used by Northern writers. People at the South are content and happy with a condition which few accept at the North unless with great complaint, or with expressions of resignation such as are the peculiar property of slaves at the South. If, reader, you had been traveling all day through a country of the highest agricultural capability, settled more than twenty years ago, and toward nightfall should be advised by a considerate stranger to ride five miles further, in order to reach the residence of Mr. Brown, because Mr. Brown, being a well-to-do man, and a right good fellow, had built an uncommonly good house, and got it well furnished, had a score of servants, and being at a distance from neighbours, was always glad to entertain a respectable stranger—after hearing this, as you continued your ride somewhat impatiently in the evening chill, what consolations would your imagination find in the prospect before you? My New England and New York experience would not forbid the hope of a private room, where I could, in the first place, wash off the dust of the road, and make some change of clothing before being admitted to a family apartment. This family room would be curtained and carpeted, and glowing softly with the light of sperm candles or a shaded lamp. When I entered it, I could expect that a couch or an arm-chair, and a fragrant cup of tea, with refined sugar, and wholesome bread of wheaten flour, leavened, would be offered me. I should think it likely that I could then have the snatch of "Tannhaüser" or "Trovatore," which had been running faintly in my head all day, fingered clearly out to my entire satisfaction upon a pianoforte. I should then look with perfect confidence to being able to refer to Shakespeare, or Longfellow, or Dickens, if anything I had seen or thought during the day had haply led me to wish to do so. I should expect, as a matter of course, a clean, sweet bed, where I could sleep alone and undisturbed, until possibly in the morning a jug of hot water should be placed at my door, to aid the removal of a traveller's rigid beard. I should expect to draw a curtain from before a window, to lift the sash without effort, to look into a garden and fill my lungs with fragrant air; and I should be certain when I came down of a royal breakfast. A man of these circumstances in this rich country, he will be asking my opinion of his fruits. A man of his disposition cannot exist in the country without ladies, and ladies cannot exist in the country without flowers; and might I not hope for the refinement which decks even the table with them? and that the breakfast would be a meal as well as a feed—an institution of mental and moral sustenance as well as of palatable nourishment to the body? My horse I need hardly look after, if he be a sound brute;—good stables, litter, oats, hay, and water, grooming, and discretion in their use, will never be wanting in such a man's house in the country.

In what civilized region, after such advice, would such thoughts be preposterous, unless in the Slave States? Not but that such men and such houses, such family and home comforts may be found in the South. I have found them—a dozen of them, delightful homes. But then in a hundred cases where I received such advice, and heard houses and men so described, I did not find one of the things imagined above, nor anything ranging with them. In my last journey of nearly three months between the Mississippi and the Upper James River, I saw not only none of those things, received none of those attentions, but I saw and met nothing of the kind. Nine times out of ten, at least, after such a promise, I slept in a room with others, in a bed which stank, supplied with but one sheet, if with any; I washed with utensils common to the whole household; I found no garden, no flowers, no fruit, no tea, no cream, no sugar, no bread (for corn pone—let me assert, in parenthesis, though possibly as tastes differ, a very good thing of its kind for ostriches—is not bread: neither does even flour, salt, fat, and water, stirred together and warmed, constitute bread); no curtains, no lifting windows (three times out of four absolutely no windows), no couch—if one reclined in the family room it was on the bare floor—for there were no carpets or mats. For all that, the house swarmed with vermin. There was no hay, no straw, no oats (but mouldy corn and leaves of maize), no discretion, no care, no honesty, at the———there was no stable, but a log-pen; and besides this, no other outhouse but a smoke-house, a corn-house, and a range of nigger houses.

In nine-tenths of the houses south of Virginia, in which I was obliged, making all reasonable endeavour to find the best, to spend the night, there were none of these things. And most of these had been recommended to me by disinterested persons on the road as being better than ordinary—houses where they "sot up for travellers and had things." From the banks of the Mississippi to the banks of James, I did not (that I remember) see, except perhaps in one or two towns, a thermometer, nor a book of Shakespeare, nor a pianoforte or sheet of music; nor the light of a carcel or other good centretable or reading-lamp, nor an engraving or copy of any kind, of a work of art of the slightest merit. I am not speaking of what are commonly called "poor whites"; a large majority of all these houses were the residences of shareholders, a considerable proportion cotton-planters.

13.6   The World the Slaves Made (c. 1850)

Spiritual hymns reflected many facets of the inner world of slaves. African-American culture asserted its individuality to the extent that social parameters allowed. Do the hymns below emphasize particular aspects of Christianity? How does this theology compare to earlier Christian readings? Do the hymns suggest accommodation to, or triumph over, adversity?

Go Down, Moses

Go down, Moses,
'Way down in Egypt land,
Tell ole Pharaoh,
To let my people go.

Go down, Moses,
'Way down in Egypt land,
Tell ole Pharaoh,
To let my people go.

When Israel was in Egypt land,
Let my people go,
Oppressed so hard they could not stand,
Let my people go,

Thus spoke the Lord, bold Moses said,
Let my people go,
If not I'll smite your first-born dead,
Let my people go.

Go down, Moses,
'Way down in Egypt land,
Tell ole Pharaoh,
To let my people go.

Steal Away To Jesus

Steal away, steal away, steal away to Jesus!
Steal away, steal away home,
I ain't got long to stay here.

My Lord, He calls me, He calls me by the thunder,
The trumpet sounds within-a my soul,
I ain't got long to stay here.

Steal away, steal away, steal away to Jesus!
Steal away, steal away home,
I ain't got long to stay here.

Green trees a-bending, po' sinner stand a-trembling,
The trumpet sounds within-a my soul,
I ain't got long to stay here.

Steal away, steal away, steal away to Jesus!
Steal away, steal away home,
I ain't got long to stay here.

I Thank God I'm Free at Last

Free at last, free at last,
I thank God I'm free at last.
Free at last, free at last,
I thank God I'm free at last.

Way down yonder in the graveyard walk,
I thank God I'm free at last,
Me and my Jesus gonna meet an' talk,
I thank God I'm free at last.

On-a my knees when the light pass by,
I thank God I'm free at last.
Thought my soul would rise an' fly,
I thank God I'm free at last.

One o' these mornin's bright an' fair,
I thank God I'm free at last,
Gonna meet my Jesus in the middle o' the air,
I thank God I'm free at last.

13.7   Resistance and Rebellion (1849, 1831)

The ultimate forms of resistance to slavery were to run away individu-
ally or participate in a group uprising. The frequent accounts and ad-
vertisements in newspapers describing fugitives suggest that escape

attempts were fairly common. Less typical, but more terrifying to whites, was the prospect of a slave rebellion, which loomed as a constant fear. What forces discouraged Pennington from running away? Why did he go? Do his odds of success seem reasonable? What possibilities lay ahead if he succeeded? Would his life be better if free?

The Confessions of Nat Turner may tell us more about the fears of his inquisitors than about the true motivations of this leader of the largest slave revolt in North America during the nineteenth century. Nevertheless, what assessment of slavery can be deduced from the document? What does it imply about power and oppression in the Old South? How does the document explain the actions and intentions of Turner and his followers? To what extent did the revolt seem a product of conscious design, and what, if any, elements about it seemed spontaneous? Does this document force you to reassess any preconceived notions of slavery that you may have?

The Escape of a Fugitive Slave

JAMES W. C. PENNINGTON

The Flight

It was the Sabbath: the holy day which God in his infinite wisdom gave for the rest of both man and beast. In the state of Maryland, the slaves generally have the Sabbath, except in those districts where the evil weed, tobacco, is cultivated; and then, when it is the season for setting the plant, they are liable to be robbed of this only rest.

It was in the month of November, somewhat past the middle of the month. It was a bright day, and all was quiet. Most of the slaves were resting about their quarters; others had leave to visit friends on other plantations, and were absent. The evening previous I had arranged my little bundle of clothing, and had secreted it at some distance from the house. I had spent most of the forenoon in my workshop, engaged in deep and solemn thought.

It is impossible for me now to recollect all the perplexing thoughts that passed through my mind during that forenoon; it was a day of heartaching to me. But I distinctly remember the two great difficulties that stood in the way of my flight: I had a father and mother whom I dearly loved,—I had also six sisters and four brothers on the plantation. The question was, shall I hide my purpose from them? moreover, how will my flight affect them when I am gone? Will they not be suspected? Will not the whole family be sold off as a disaffected family, as is generally the case

FROM James W. C. Pennington, *The Fugitive Blacksmith; or, Events in the History of James W. C. Pennington, Pastor of a Presbyterian Church, New York, Formerly a Slave in the State of Maryland, United States* (London, 1849), pp. 12–29.

when one of its members flies? But a still more trying question was, how can I expect to succeed, I have no knowledge of distance or direction. I know that Pennsylvania is a free state, but I know not where its soil begins, or where that of Maryland ends? Indeed, at this time there was no safety in Pennsylvania, New Jersey, or New York, for a fugitive, except in lurking-places, or under the care of judicious friends, who could be entrusted not only with liberty, but also with life itself.

With such difficulties before my mind, the day had rapidly worn away; and it was just past noon. One of my perplexing questions I had settled—I had resolved to let no one into my secret; but the other difficulty was now to be met. It was to be met without the least knowledge of its magnitude, except by imagination. Yet of one thing there could be no mistake, that the consequences of a failure would be most serious. Within my recollection no one had attempted to escape from my master; but I had many cases in my mind's eye, of slaves of other planters who had failed, and who had been made examples of the most cruel treatment, by flogging and selling to the far South, where they were never to see their friends more. I was not without serious apprehension that such would be my fate. The bare possibility was impressively solemn; but the hour was now come, and the man must act and be free, or remain a slave for ever. How the impression came to be upon my mind I cannot tell; but there was a strange and horrifying belief, that if I did not meet the crisis that day, I should be self-doomed—that my ear would be nailed to the door-post for ever. The emotions of that moment I cannot fully depict. Hope, fear, dread, terror, love, sorrow, and deep melancholy were mingled in my mind together; my mental state was one of most painful distraction. When I looked at my numerous family—a beloved father and mother, eleven brothers and sisters, &c.; but when I looked at slavery as such; when I looked at it in its mildest form, with all its annoyances; and above all, when I remembered that one of the chief annoyances of slavery, in the most mild form, is the liability of being at any moment sold into the worst form; it seemed that no consideration, not even that of life itself, could tempt me to give up the thought of flight. And then when I considered the difficulties of the way—the reward that would be offered—the human blood-hounds that would be set upon my track—the weariness—the hunger—the gloomy thought, of not only losing all one's friends in one day, but of having to seek and to make new friends in a strange world. But, as I have said, the hour was come, and the man must act, or for ever be a slave.

It was now two o'clock. I stepped into the quarter; there was a strange and melancholy silence mingled with the destitution that was apparent in every part of the house. The only morsel I could see in the shape of food, was a piece of Indian flour bread, it might be half-a-pound in weight. This I placed in my pocket, and giving a last look at the aspect of the house, and at a few small children who were playing at the door, I sallied forth thoughtfully and melancholy, and after crossing the barn-yard, a few moments' walk brought me to a small cave, near the mouth of which lay a pile of stones, and into which I had deposited my clothes. From this, my course lay through thick and heavy woods and back lands to—town, where my brother lived. This town was six miles distance. It was now near three o'clock, but my object was neither to be seen on the road, or to approach the town by daylight, as I was well-known there, and as any intelligence of my having been seen there would at once put the pursuers on my track. This first six miles of my flight, I not only trav- elled very slowly, therefore, so as to avoid carrying any daylight to this town; but during this walk another very perplexing question was agitating my mind. Shall I call on my brother as I pass through, and shew him what I am about? My brother was older than I, we were much attached; I had been in the habit of looking to him for counsel.

I entered the town about dark, resolved, all things in view, *not* to shew myself to my brother. Having passed through the town without being recognised, I now found myself under cover of night, a solitary wanderer from home and friends; my only guide was the *north star,* by this I knew my general curse northward, but at what point I should strike Penn, or when and where I should find a friend, I knew not. Another feeling now occupied my mind,—I felt like a mariner who has gotten his ship outside of the harbour and has spread his sails to the breeze. The cargo is on board—the ship is cleared—and the voyage I must make; besides, this being my first night, almost every thing will depend upon my clearing the coast before the day dawns. In order to do this my flight must be rapid. I therefore set forth in sor- rowful earnest, only now and then I was cheered by the *wild* hope, that I should somewhere and at sometime be free.

The night was fine for the season, and passed on with little interruption for want of strength, until, about three o'clock in the morning, I began to feel the chilling ef- fects of the dew.

At this moment, gloom and melancholy again spread through my whole soul. The prospect of utter destitution which threatened me was more than I could bear, and my heart began to melt. What substance is there in a piece of dry Indian bread; what nourishment is there in it to warm the nerves of one already chilled to the heart? Will this afford a sufficient sustenance after the toil of the night? But while these thoughts were agitating my mind, the day dawned upon me, in the midst of an open extent of country, where the only shelter I could find, without risking my travel by daylight, was a corn shock, but a few hundred yards from the road, and here I must pass my first day out. The day was an unhappy one; my hiding-place was extremely precarious. I had to sit in a squatting position the whole day, without the least chance to rest. But, besides this, my scanty pittance did not afford me that nourish- ment which my hard night's travel needed. Night came again to my relief, and I sal- lied forth to pursue my journey. By this time, not a crumb of my crust remained, and I was hungry and began to feel the desperation of distress.

As I travelled I felt my strength failing and my spirits wavered; my mind was in a deep and melancholy dream. It was cloudy; I could not see my star, and had serious misgivings about my course.

In this way the night passed away, and just at the dawn of day I found a few sour apples, and took my shelter under the arch of a small bridge that crossed the road. Here I passed the second day in ambush.

This day would have been more pleasant than the previous, but the sour apples, and a draught of cold water, had produced anything but a favourable effect; indeed, I suffered most of the day with severe symptoms of cramp. The day passed away again without any further incident, and as I set out at nightfall, I felt quite satisfied that I could not pass another twenty-four hours without nourishment. I made but little progress during the night, and often sat down, and slept frequently fifteen or twenty minutes. At the dawn of the third day I continued my travel. As I had found my way to a public turnpike road during the night, I came very early in the morning to a tollgate, where the only person I saw, was a lad about twelve years of age. I inquired of him where the road led to. He informed me it led to Baltimore. I asked him the distance, he said it was eighteen miles.

This intelligence was perfectly astounding to me. My master lived eighty miles from Baltimore. I was now sixty-two miles from home. That distance in the right direction, would have placed me several miles across Mason and Dixon's line, but I was evidently yet in the state of Maryland.

I ventured to ask the lad at the gate another question—Which is the best way to Philadelphia? Said he, you can take a road which turns off about half-a-mile below this, and goes to Getsburgh, or you can go on to Baltimore and take the packet.

I made no reply, but my thought was, that I was as near Baltimore and Baltimore-packets as would answer my purpose.

In a few moments I came to the road to which the lad had referred, and felt some relief when I had gotten out of that great public highway, "The National Turnpike," which I found it to be.

When I had walked a mile on this road, and when it had now gotten to be about nine o'clock, I met a young man with a load of hay. He drew up his horses, and addressed me in a very kind tone, when the following dialogue took place between us.

"Are you travelling any distance, my friend?"

"I am on my way to Philadelphia."

"Are you free?"

"Yes, sir."

"I suppose, then, you are provided with free papers?"

"No, sir. I have no papers."

"Well, my friend, you should not travel on this road: you will be taken up before you have gone three miles. There are men living on this road who are constantly on the look-out for your people; and it is seldom that one escapes them who attempts to pass by day."

He then very kindly gave me advice where to turn off the road at a certain point, and how to find my way to a certain house, where I would meet with an old gentleman who would further advise me whether I had better remain till night, or go on.

I left this interesting young man; and such was my surprise and chagrin at the thought of having so widely missed my way, and my alarm at being in such a dangerous position, that in ten minutes I had so far forgotten his directions as to deem it unwise to attempt to follow them, lest I should miss my way, and get into evil hands.

I, however, left the road, and went into a small piece of wood, but not finding a sufficient hiding-place, and it being a busy part of the day, when persons were at work about the fields, I thought I should excite less suspicion by keeping in the road, so I returned to the road; but the events of the next few moments proved that I committed a serious mistake.

I went about a mile, making in all two miles from the spot where I met my young friend, and about five miles from the toll-gate to which I have referred, and I found myself at the twenty-four miles' stone from Baltimore. It was now about ten o'-clock in the forenoon; my strength was greatly exhausted by reason of the want of suitable food; but the excitement that was then going on in my mind, left me little time to think of my *need* of food. Under ordinary circumstances as a traveller, I should have been glad to see the "Tavern," which was near the mile-stone; but as the case stood with me, I deemed it a dangerous place to pass, much less to stop at. I was therefore passing it as quietly and as rapidly as possible, when from the lot just opposite the house, or sign-post, I heard a coarse stern voice cry, "Halloo!"

I turned my face to the left, the direction from which the voice came, and observed that it proceeded from a man who was digging potatoes. I answered him politely; when the following occurred:—

"Who do *you* belong to?"

"I am free, sir."

"Have you got papers?"

"No, sir."

"Well, you must stop here."

By this time he had got astride the fence, making his way into the road. I said,

"My business is onward, sir, and I do not wish to stop."

"I will see then if you don't stop, you black rascal."

He was now in the middle of the road, making after me in a brisk walk.

I saw that a crisis was at hand; I had no weapons of any kind, not even a pocket-knife; but I asked myself, shall I surrender without a struggle? The instinctive answer was "No." What will you do? continue to walk; if he runs after you, run; get him as far from the house as you can, then turn suddenly and smite him on the knee with a stone; that will render him, at least, unable to pursue you.

This was a desperate scheme, but I could think of no other, and my habits as a blacksmith had given my eye and hand such mechanical skill, that I felt quite sure that if I could only get a stone in my hand, and have time to wield it, I should not miss his knee-pan.

He began to breathe short. He was evidently vexed because I did not halt, and I felt more and more provoked at the idea of being thus pursued by a man to whom I had not done the least injury. I had just began to glance my eye about for a stone to grasp, when he made a tiger-like leap at me. This of course brought us to running. At this moment he yelled out "Jake Shouster!" and at the next moment the door of a small house standing to the left was opened, and out jumped a shoemaker girded up in his leather apron, with his knife in hand. He sprang forward and seized me by the collar, while the other seized my arms behind. I was now in the grasp of two men, either of whom were larger bodied than myself, and one of whom was armed with a dangerous weapon.

Standing in the door of the shoemaker's shop, was a third man; and in the potatoe lot I had passed, was still a fourth man. Thus surrounded by superior physical force, the fortune of the day it seemed to me was gone.

My heart melted away, I sunk resistlessly into the hands of my captors, who dragged me immediately into the tavern which was near. I ask my reader to go in with me, and see how the case goes.

Rebellion: The Confessions of Nat Turner (1831)

Agreeable to his own appointment, on the evening he was committed to prison, with permission of the jailor, I visited Nat on Tuesday the 1st November, when, without being questioned at all, he commenced his narrative in the following words:—

Sir,—You have asked me to give a history of the motives which induced me to undertake the late insurrection, as you call it—To do so I must go back to the days of my infancy, and even before I was born. I was thirty-one years of age the 2d of October last, and born the property of Benj. Turner, of this county. In my child-hood, a circumstance occurred which made an indelible impression on my mind, and laid the ground work of that enthusiasm, which has terminated so fatally to many, both white and black, and for which I am about to atone at the gallows. It is here necessary to relate this circumstance—trifling as it may seem, it was the com-mencement of that belief which has grown with time, and even now, sir, in this dun-geon, helpless and forsaken as I am, I cannot divest myself of. Being at play with other children, when three or four years old, I was telling them something, which my mother overhearing, said it had happened before I was born—I stuck to my story, however, and related some things which went, in her opinion, to confirm it—others being called on were greatly astonished, knowing that these things had hap-pened, and caused them to say in my hearing, I surely would be a prophet, as the Lord had shewn me things that had happened before my birth. And my father and mother strengthened me in this my first impression, saying in my presence, I was intended for some great purpose, which they had always thought from certain marks on my head and breast—[a parcel of excrescences which I believe are not at all un-common, particularly among negroes, as I have seen several with the same. In this case he has either cut them off or they have nearly disappeared]—My grand mother, who was very religious, and to whom I was much attached—my master, who be-longed to the church, and other religious persons who visited the house, and whom I often saw at prayers, noticing the singularity of my manners, I suppose, and my un-common intelligence for a child, remarked I had too much sense to be raised, and if I was, I would never be of any service to any one as a slave—To a mind like mine, restless, inquisitive and observant of every thing that was passing, it is easy to sup-pose that religion was the subject to which it would be directed, and although this subject principally occupied my thoughts—there was nothing that I saw or heard of to which my attention was not directed—The manner in which I learned to read and write, not only had great influence on my own mind, as I acquired it with the most perfect ease, so much so, that I have no recollection whatever of learning the alpha-bet—but to the astonishment of the family, one day, when a book was shewn me to keep me from crying, I began spelling the names of different objects—this was a source of wonder to all in the neighborhood, particularly the blacks—and this learn-ing was constantly improved at all opportunities—when I got large enough to go to work, while employed, I was reflecting on many things that would present them-

FROM *The Confessions of Nat Turner, the leader of the late insurrection in Southampton, Va. As fully and voluntarily made to Thomas R. Gray . . .* (Baltimore, 1831).

selves to my imagination, and whenever an opportunity occurred of looking at a book, when the school children were getting their lessons, I would find many things that the fertility of my own imagination had depicted to me before; all my time, not devoted to my master's service, was spent either in prayer, or in making experiments in casting different things in moulds made of earth, in attempting to make paper, gun-powder, and many other experiments, that although I could not perfect, yet convinced me of its practicability if I had the means.[1] I was not addicted to stealing in my youth, nor have ever been—Yet such was the confidence of the negroes in the neighborhood, even at this early period of my life, in my superior judgment, that they would often carry me with them when they were going on any roguery, to plan for them. Growing up among them, with this confidence in my superior judgment, and when this, in their opinions, was perfected by Divine inspiration, from the circumstances already alluded to in my infancy, and which belief was ever afterwards zealously inculcated by the austerity of my life and manners, which became the subject of remark by white and black.—Having soon discovered to be great, I must appear so, and therefore studiously avoided mixing in society, and wrapped myself in mystery, devoting my time to fasting and prayer—By this time, having arrived to man's estate, and hearing the scriptures commented on at meetings, I was struck with that particular passage which says: "Seek ye the kingdom of Heaven and all things shall be added unto you." I reflected much on this passage, and prayed daily for light on this subject—As I was praying one day at my plough, the spirit spoke to me, saying "Seek ye the kingdom of Heaven and all things shall be added unto you." *Question*—what do you mean by the Spirit. *Ans.* The Spirit that spoke to the prophets in former days—and I was greatly astonished, and for two years prayed continually, whenever my duty would permit—and then again I had the same revelation, which fully confirmed me in the impression that I was ordained for some great purpose in the hands of the Almighty. Several years rolled around, in which many events occurred to strengthen me in this my belief. At this time I reverted in my mind to the remarks made of me in my childhood, and the things that had been shewn me—and as it had been said of me in my childhood by those by whom I had been taught to pray, both white and black, and in whom I had the greatest confidence, that I had too much sense to be raised, and if I was, I would never be of any use to any one as a slave. Now finding I had arrived to man's estate, and was a slave, and these revelations being made known to me, I began to direct my attention to this great object, to fulfill the purpose for which, by this time, I felt assured I was intended. Knowing the influence I had obtained over the minds of my fellow servants, (not by the means of conjuring and such like tricks—for to them I always spoke of such things with contempt) but by the communion of the Spirit whose revelations I often communicated to them, and they believed and said my wisdom came from God. I now began to prepare them for my purpose, by telling them something was about to happen that would terminate in fulfilling the great promise

---

[1]When questioned as to the manner of manufacturing those different articles, he was found well informed on the subject.

that had been made to me—About this time I was placed under an overseer, from whom I ran away—and after remaining in the woods thirty days, I returned, to the astonishment of the negroes on the plantation, who thought I had made my escape to some other part of the country, as my father had done before. But the reason of my return was, that the Spirit appeared to me and said I had my wishes directed to the things of this world, and not to the kingdom of Heaven, and that I should return to the service of my earthly master—"For he who knoweth his Master's will, and doeth it not, shall be beaten with many stripes, and thus have I chastened you." And the negroes found fault, and murmured against me, saying that if they had my sense they would not serve any master in the world. And about this time I had a vision—and I saw white spirits and black spirits engaged in battle, and the sun was darkened—the thunder rolled in the Heavens, and blood flowed in streams—and I heard a voice saying, "Such is your luck, such you are called to see, and let it come rough or smooth, you must surely bear it." I now withdrew myself as much as my situation would permit, from the intercourse of my fellow servants, for the avowed purpose of serving the Spirit more fully—and it appeared to me, and reminded me of the things it had already shown me, and that it would then reveal to me the knowledge of the elements, the revolution of the planets, the operation of tides, and changes of the seasons. After this revelation in the year 1825, and the knowledge of the elements being made known to me, I sought more than ever to obtain true holiness before the great day of judgment should appear, and then I began to receive the true knowledge of faith. And from the first steps of righteousness until the last, was I made perfect; and the Holy Ghost was with me, and said, "Behold me as I stand in the Heavens"—and I looked and saw the forms of men in different attitudes—and there were lights in the sky to which the children of darkness gave other names than what they really were—for they were the lights of the Saviour's hands, stretched forth from east to west, even as they were extended on the cross on Calgary for the redemption of sinners. And I wondered greatly at these miracles, and prayed to be informed of a certainty of the meaning thereof—and shortly afterwards, while laboring in the field, I discovered drops of blood on the corn as though it were dew from heaven—and I communicated it to many, both white and black, in the neighborhood—and I then found on the leaves in the woods hieroglyphic characters, and numbers, with the forms of men in different attitudes, portrayed in blood, and representing the figures I had seen before in the heavens. And now the Holy Ghost had revealed itself to me, and made plain the miracles it had shown me—For as the blood of Christ had been shed on this earth, and had ascended to heaven for the salvation of sinners, and was now returning to earth again in the form of dew—and as the leaves on the trees bore the impression of the figures I had seen in the heavens, it was plain to me that the Saviour was about to lay down the yoke he had borne for the sins of men, and the great day of judgment was at hand. About this time I told these things to a white man, (Etheldred T. Brantley) on whom it had a wonderful effect—and he ceased from his wickedness, and was attacked immediately with a cutaneous eruption, and blood oozed from the pores of his skin, and after praying and fasting nine days, he was healed, and the Spirit appeared to me again, and said, as the Saviour had been baptised so should we be also—and when the white people would not let us be baptised by the church, we went down into the water together, in the sight of many who reviled us, and were baptised by the Spirit—After this I rejoiced greatly, and gave thanks to God. And on the 12th of May, 1828, I heard a loud noise in the heavens, and the Spirit instantly appeared to me and said the Serpent was loosened, and Christ had laid down the yoke he had borne for the sins of men, and that I should take it on and fight against the Serpent, for the time was fast approaching when the first should be last and the last should be first. *Ques.* Do you not find yourself mistaken now? *Ans.* Was not Christ crucified. And by signs in the heavens that it would make known to me when I should commence the great work—and until the first sign appeared, I should conceal it from the knowledge of men—And on the appearance of the sign, (the eclipse of the sun last February) I should arise and prepare myself, and slay my enemies with their own weapons. And immediately on the sign appearing in the heavens, the seal was removed from my lips, and I communicated the great work laid out for me to do, to four in whom I had the greatest confidence, (Henry, Hark, Nelson, and Sam)—It was intended by us to have begun the work of death on the 4th July last—Many were the plans formed and rejected by us, and it affected my mind to such a degree, that I fell sick, and the time passed without our coming to any determination how to commence—Still forming new schemes and rejecting them, when the sign appeared again, which determined me not to wait longer.

Since the commencement of 1830, I had been living with Mr. Joseph Travis, who was to me a kind master, and placed the greatest confidence in me; in fact, I had no cause to complain of his treatment to me. On Saturday evening, the 20th of August, it was agreed between Henry, Hark and myself, to prepare a dinner the next day for the men we expected, and then to concert a plan, as we had not yet determined on any. Hark, on the following morning, brought a pig, and Henry brandy, and being joined by Sam, Nelson, Will and Jack, they prepared in the woods a dinner, where, about three o'clock, I joined them.

Q. Why were you so backward in joining them.

A. The same reason that had caused me not to mix with them for years before.

I saluted them on coming up, and asked Will how came he there, he answered, his life was worth no more than others, and his liberty as dear to him. I asked him if he thought to obtain it? He said he would, or loose his life. This was enough to put him in full confidence. Jack, I knew, was only a tool in the hands of Hark, it was quickly agreed we should commence at home (Mr. J. Travis') on that night, and until we had armed and equipped ourselves, and gathered sufficient force, neither age nor sex was to be spared, (which was invariably adhered to.) We remained at the feast, until about two hours in the night, when we went to the house and found Austin; they all went to the cider press and drank, except myself. On returning to the house, Hark went to the door with an axe, for the purpose of breaking it open, as we knew we were strong enough to murder the family, if they were awakened by the noise; but reflecting that it might create an alarm in the neighborhood, we determined to enter the house secretly, and murder them whilst sleeping. Hark got a ladder and set it against the chimney, on which I ascended, and hoistering a window, entered and came down stairs, unbarred the door, and removed the guns from their places. It was then observed that I must spill the first blood. On which, armed with a hatchet, and accompanied by Will, I entered my master's chamber, it being dark, I could not give a death blow, the hatchet glanced from his head, he sprang from the bed and called his wife, it was his last word, Will laid him dead, with a blow of his axe, and Mrs. Travis shared the same fate, as she lay in bed. The murder of this family, five in number, was the work of a moment, not one of them awoke; there was a little infant sleeping in a cradle, that was forgotten, until we had left the house and gone some distance, when Henry and Will returned and killed it; we got here, four guns that would shoot, and several old muskets, with a pound or two of powder. We remained some time at the barn, where we paraded; I formed them in a line as soldiers, and after carrying them through all the manœuvres I was master of, marched them off to Mr. Salathul Francis', about six hundred yards distant. Sam and Will went to the door and knocked. Mr. Francis asked who was there, Sam replied it was him, and he had a letter for him, on which he got up and came to the door; they immediately seized him, and dragging him out a little from the door, he was dispatched by repeated blows on the head; there was no other white person in the family. We started from there for Mrs. Reese's, maintaining the most perfect silence on our march, where finding the door unlocked, we entered, and murdered Mrs. Reese in her bed, while sleeping; her son awoke, but it was only to sleep the sleep of death, he had only time to say who is that, and he was no more. From Mrs. Reese's we went to Mrs. Turner's, a mile distant, which we reached about sunrise, on Monday morning. Henry, Austin, and Sam, went to the still, where, finding Mr. Peebles, Austin shot him, and the rest of us went to the house; as we approached, the family discovered us, and shut the door. Vain hope! Will, with one stroke of his axe, opened it, and we entered and found Mrs. Turner and Mrs. Newsome in the middle of a room, almost frightened to death. Will immediately killed Mrs. Turner, with one blow of his axe. I took Mrs. Newsome by the hand, and with the sword I had when I was apprehended, I struck her several blows over the head, but not being able to kill her, as the sword was dull. Will turning around and discovering it, despatched her also. A general destruction of property and search for money and ammunition, always succeeded the murders. By this time my company amounted to fifteen, and nine men mounted, who started for Mrs. Whitehead's, (the other six were to go through a byway to Mr. Bryant's, and rejoin us at Mrs. Whitehead's), as we approached the house we discovered Mr. Richard Whitehead standing in the cotton patch, near the lane fence; we called him over into the lane, and Will, the executioner, was near at hand, with his fatal axe, to send him to an untimely grave. As we pushed on to the house, I discovered some one run round the garden, and thinking it was some of the white family, I pursued them, but finding it was a servant girl belonging to the house, I returned to commence the work of death, but they whom I left, had not been idle; all the family were already murdered, but Mrs. Whitehead and her daughter Margaret. As I came round to the door I saw Will pulling Mrs. Whitehead out of the house, and at the step he nearly severed her head from her body, with his broad axe. Miss Margaret, when I discovered her, had concealed herself in the corner, formed by the projection of the cellar cap from the house; on my approach she fled, but was soon overtaken, and after repeated blows with a sword, I killed her by a blow on the head, with a fence rail. By this time, the six who had gone by Mr. Bryant's, rejoined us, and informed me they had done the work of death assigned them. We again divided, part going to Mr. Richard Porter's, and from thence to Nathaniel Francis', the others to Mr. Howell Harris', and Mr. T. Doyles'. On my reaching Mr. Porter's, he had escaped with his family. I understood there, that the alarm had already spread, and I immediately returned to bring up those sent to Mr. Doyles', and Mr. Howell Harris'; the party I left going on to Mr. Francis', having told them I would join them in that neighborhood. I met these sent to Mr. Doyles' and Mr. Harris' returning, having met Mr. Doyle on the road and killed him; and learning from some who joined them, that Mr. Harris was from home, I immediately pursued the course taken by the party gone on before; but knowing they would complete the work of death and pillage, at Mr. Francis' before I could get there, I went to Mr. Peter Edwards', expecting to find them there, but they had been here also. I then went to Mr. John T. Barrow's, they had been here and murdered him. I pursued on their track to Capt. Newit Harris', where I found the greater part mounted, and ready to start; the men now amounting to about forty, shouted and hurraed as I rode up, some were in the yard, loading their guns, others drinking. They said Captain Harris and his family had escaped, the property in the house they destroyed, robbing him of money and other valuables. I ordered them to mount and march instantly, this was about nine or ten o'clock, Monday morning. I proceeded to Mr. Levi Waller's, two or three miles distant. I took my station in the rear, and as it 'twas my object to carry terror and devastation wherever we went, I placed fifteen or twenty of the best armed and most to be relief on, in front, who generally approached the house as fast as their horses could run; this was for two purposes, to prevent their escape and strike terror to the inhabitants—on this account I never got to the houses, after leaving Mrs. Whitehead's, until the murders were committed, except in one case. I sometimes got in sight in time to see the work of death completed, viewed the mangled bodies as they lay, in silent satisfaction, and immediately started in quest of other victims—Having murdered Mrs. Waller and ten children, we started for Mr. William Williams'—having killed him and two little boys that were there; while engaged in this, Mrs. Williams fled and got some distance from the house, but she was pursued, overtaken, and compelled to get up behind one of the company, who brought her back, and after showing her the mangled body of her lifeless husband, she was told to get down and lay by his side, where she was shot dead. I then started for Mr. Jacob Williams, where the family were murdered—Here we found a young man named Drury, who had come on business with Mr. Williams—he was pursued, overtaken and shot. Mrs. Vaughan was the next place we visited—and after murdering the family here, I determined on starting for Jerusalem—Our number amounted now to fifty or sixty, all mounted and armed with guns, axes, swords and clubs—On reaching Mr. James W. Parkers' gate, immediately on the road leading to Jerusalem, and about three miles distant, it was proposed to me to call there, but I objected, as I knew he was gone to Jerusalem, and my object was to reach there as soon as possible; but some of the men having relations at Mr. Parker's it was agreed that they might call and get his people. I remained at the gate on the road, with seven or eight; the others going across the field to the house, about half a mile off. After waiting some time for them, I became impatient, and started to the house for them, and on our return we were met by a party of white men, who had pursued our blood-stained track, and who had fired on those at the gate, and dispersed them, which I knew nothing of, not having been at that time rejoined by any of them—immediately on discovering the whites, I ordered my men to halt and form, as they appeared to be alarmed— The white men, eighteen in number, approached us in about one hundred yards, when one of them fired, (this was against the positive orders of Captain Alexander P. Peete, who commanded, and who had directed the men to reserve their fire until within thirty paces). And I discovered about half of them retreating, I then ordered my men to fire and rush on them; the few remaining stood their ground until we approached within fifty yards, when they fired and retreated. We pursued and overtook some of them who we thought we left dead; (they were not killed) after pursuing them about two hundred yards, and rising a little hill, I discovered they were met by another party, and had halted, and were re-loading their guns, (this was a small party from Jerusalem who knew the negroes were in the field, and had just tied their horses to await their return to the road, knowing that Mr. Parker and family were in Jerusalem, but knew nothing of the party that had gone in with Captain Peete; on hearing the firing they immediately rushed to the spot and arrived just in time to arrest the progress of these barbarous villains, and save the lives of their friends and fellow citizens.) Thinking that those who retreated first, and the party who fired on us at fifty or sixty yards distant, had all only fallen back to meet others with ammunition. As I saw them re-loading their guns, and more coming up than I saw at first, and several of my bravest men being wounded, the others became panick struck and squandered over the field; the white men pursued and fired on us several times. Hark had his horse shot under him, and I caught another for him as it was running by me; five or six of my men were wounded, but none left on the field; finding myself defeated here I instantly determined to go through a private way, and cross the Nottoway river at the Cypress Bridge, three miles below Jerusalem, and attack that place in the rear, as I expected they would look for me on the other road, and I had a great desire to get there to procure arms and ammunition. After going a short distance in this private way, accompanied by about twenty men, I overtook two or three who told me the others were dispersed in every direction. After trying in vain to collect a sufficient force to proceed to Jerusalem, I determined to return, as I was sure they would make back to their old neighborhood, where they would rejoin me, make new recruits, and come down again. On my way back, I called at Mrs. Thomas's, Mrs. Spencer's, and several other places, the white families having fled, we found no more victims to gratify our thirst for blood, we stopped at Maj. Ridley's quarter for the night, and being joined by four of his men, with the recruits made since my defeat, we mustered now about forty strong. After placing out sentinels, I laid down to sleep, but was quickly roused by a great racket; starting up, I found some mounted, and others in great confusion; one of the sentinels having given the alarm that we were about to be attacked, I ordered some to ride round and reconnoitre, and on their return the others being more alarmed, not knowing who they were, fled in different ways, so that I was reduced to about twenty again; with this I determined to attempt to recruit, and proceed on to rally in the neighborhood, I had left. Dr. Blunt's was the nearest house, which we reached just before day; on riding up the yard, Hark fired a gun. We expected Dr. Blunt and his family were at Maj. Ridley's, as I knew there was a company of men there; the gun was fired to ascertain if any of the family were at home; we were immediately fired upon and retreated, leaving several of my men. I do not know what became of them, as I never saw them afterwards. Pursuing our course back and coming in sight of Captain Harris', where we had been the day before, we discovered a party of white men at the house, on which all deserted me but two, (Jacob and Nat,) we concealed ourselves in the woods until near night, when I sent them in search of Henry, Sam, Nelson, and Hark, and directed them to rally all they could, at the place we had had our dinner the Sunday before, where they would find me, and I accordingly returned there as soon as it was dark and remained until Wednesday evening, when discovering white men riding around the place as though they were looking for some one, and none of my men joining me, I concluded Jacob and Nat had been taken, and compelled to betray me. On this I gave up all hope for the present; and on Thursday night after having supplied myself with provisions from Mr. Travis's, I scratched a hole under a pile of fence rails in a field, where I concealed myself for six weeks, never leaving my hiding place but for a few minutes in the dead of night to get water which was very near; thinking by this time I could venture out, I began to go about in the night and eaves drop the houses in the neighborhood; pursuing this course for about a fortnight and gathering little or no intelligence, afraid of speaking to any human being, and returning every morning to my cave before the dawn of day. I know not how long I might have led this life, if accident had not betrayed me, a dog in the neighborhood passing by my hiding place one night while I was out, was attracted by some meat I had in my cave, and crawled in and stole it, and was coming out just as I returned. A few nights after, two negroes having started to go hunting with the same dog, and passed that way, the dog came again to the place, and having just gone out to walk about, discovered me and barked, on which thinking myself discovered, I spoke to them to beg concealment. On making myself known they fled from me. Knowing then they would betray me, I immediately left my hiding place, and was pursued almost incessantly until I was taken a fortnight afterwards by Mr. Benjamin Phipps, in a little hole I had dug out with my sword, for the purpose of concealment, under the top of a fallen tree. On Mr. Phipps' discovering the place of my concealment, he cocked his gun and aimed at me. I requested him not to shoot and I would give up, upon which he demanded my sword. I delivered it to him, and he brought me to prison. During the time I was pursued, I had many hair breadth escapes, which your time will not permit you to relate. I am here loaded with chains, and willing to suffer the fate that awaits me.

I here proceeded to make some inquiries of him, after assuring him of the certain death that awaited him, and that concealment would only bring destruction on the innocent as well as guilty, of his own color, if he knew of any extensive or concerted plan. His answer was, I do not. When I questioned him as to the insurrection in North Carolina happening about the same time, he denied any knowledge of it;

and when I looked him in the face as though I would search his inmost thoughts, he replied, "I see sir, you doubt my word; but can you not think the same ideas, and strange appearances about this time in the heavens might prompt others, as well as myself, to this undertaking." I now had much conversation with and asked him many questions, having forborne to do so previously, except in the cases noted in parenthesis; but during his statement, I had, unnoticed by him, taken notes as to some particular circumstances, and having the advantage of his statement before me in writing, on the evening of the third day that I had been with him, I began a cross examination, and found his statement corroborated by every circumstance coming within my own knowledge or the confessions of others who had been either killed or executed, and whom he had not seen nor had any knowledge since 22d of August last, he expressed himself fully satisfied as to the impracticability of his attempt. It has been said he was ignorant and cowardly, and that his object was to murder and rob for the purpose of obtaining money to make his escape. It is notorious, that he was never known to have a dollar in his life; to swear an oath, or drink a drop of spirits. As to his ignorance, he certainly never had the advantages of education, but he can read and write, (it was taught him by his parents,) and for natural intelligence and quickness of apprehension, is surpassed by few men I have ever seen. As to his being a coward, his reason as given for not resisting Mr. Phipps, shews the decision of his character. When he saw Mr. Phipps present his gun, he said he knew it was impossible for him to escape as the woods were full of men; he therefore thought it was better to surrender, and trust to fortune for his escape. He is a complete fanatic, or plays his part most admirably. On other subjects he possesses an uncommon share of intelligence, with a mind capable of attaining any thing; but warped and perverted by the influence of early impressions. He is below the ordinary stature, though strong and active, having the true negro face, every feature of which is strongly marked. I shall not attempt to describe the effect of his narrative, as told and commented on by himself, in the condemned hole of the prison. The calm, deliberate composure with which he spoke of his late deeds and intentions, the expression of his fiend-like face when excited by enthusiasm, still bearing the stains of the blood of helpless innocence about him; clothed with rags and covered with chains; yet daring to raise his manacled hands to heaven, with a spirit soaring above the attributes of man; I looked on him and my blood curdled in my veins.

I will not shock the feelings of humanity, nor wound afresh the bosoms of the disconsolate sufferers in this unparalleled and inhuman massacre, by detailing the deeds of their fiend-like barbarity. There were two or three who were in the power of these wretches, had they known it, and who escaped in the most providential manner. There were two whom they thought they left dead on the field at Mr. Parker's, but who were only stunned by the blows of their guns, as they did not take time to re-load when they charged on them. The escape of a little girl who went to school at Mr. Waller's, and where the children were collecting for that purpose, excited general sympathy. As their teacher had not arrived, they were at play in the yard, and seeing the negroes approach, she ran up on a dirt chimney, (such as are common to log houses,) and remained there unnoticed during the massacre of the eleven that were killed at this place. She remained on her hiding place till just before the arrival of a party, who were in pursuit of the murderers, when she came down and fled to a swamp, where, a mere child as she was, with the horrors of the late scene before her, she lay concealed until the next day, when seeing a party go up to the house, she came up, and on being asked how she escaped, replied with the utmost simplicity, "The Lord helped her." She was taken up behind a gentleman of the party, and returned to the arms of her weeping mother. Miss Whitehead concealed herself between the bed and the mat that supported it, while they murdered her sister in the same room, without discovering her. She was afterwards carried off, and concealed for protection by a slave of the family, who gave evidence against several of them on their trial. Mrs. Nathaniel Francis, while concealed in a closet heard their blows, and the shrieks of the victims of these ruthless savages; they then entered the closet where she was concealed, and went out without discovering her. While in this hiding place, she heard two of her women in a quarrel about the division of her clothes. Mr. John T. Baron, discovering them approaching his house, told his wife to make her escape, and scorning to fly, fell fighting on his own threshold. After firing his rifle, he discharged his gun at them, and then broke it over the villain who first approached him, but he was overpowered, and slain. His bravery, however, saved from the hands of these monsters, his lovely and amiable wife, who will long lament a husband so deserving of her love. As directed by him, she attempted to escape through the garden, when she was caught and held by one of her servant girls, but another coming to her rescue, she fled to the woods, and concealed herself. Few indeed, were those who escaped their work of death. But fortunate for society, the hand of retributive justice has overtaken them; and not one that was known to be concerned has escaped.

❖ *14* ❖

The Clash of Sections

So long as the contention over slavery was primarily between abolitionists and militant slavery defenders, it did not seriously threaten national unity. Neither group had enough followers to tear the political fabric apart. But then, in the late 1840s, the issue of slavery *expansion* into the western territories brought North–South antagonisms to a boil. A much larger public in both sections was soon locked in an angry debate that jeopardized the nation's very survival.

Whether Congress had the right to determine if slavery should be excluded from the territories had stirred discord between North and South as far back as 1820, when Missouri, part of the Louisiana Purchase, had applied for admission to the Union as a slave state. The issue affected sectional balance, especially in the Senate, where each state was equally represented. It had been settled by the Missouri Compromise, which admitted one free and one slave state and divided the remainder of the Louisiana Purchase along the line 39° 30′ into free and slave territory. The Mexican War, which added an enormous slab of new territory to the United States, raised the slavery extension issue between the sections anew.

The first act of the new North–South showdown was the battle over the Wilmot Proviso, a motion introduced into Congress in August 1846 to exclude slavery from any region acquired as a result of the war with Mexico then underway. The Proviso set off a North–South confrontation that moved through successively belligerent stages that led to the South's secession in 1860–1861.

The documents below mark the progression of the sectional debate from the Proviso to the final crisis point. What are the essential principles of each side? Was the South right to feel besieged and oppressed? Were the North and "free society" victims of a southern conspiracy? Was there a moral dimension to the sectional dispute?

14.1: A Southern Champion Demands Equal Rights for the South (1850)

In 1850 the readiness of California for admission to the Union forced Congress to confront longstanding North–South grievances and consider how to balance competing sectional views and interests. The discussion that year coalesced around a set of proposals introduced by Henry Clay, which included the admission of California as a free state, a stronger federal fugitive slave law, the settlement of the boundary and debts of Texas, the prohibition of the slave trade in the District of Columbia, and the organization of the New Mexico and Utah territories without mention of slavery.[1] The debate in the Senate particularly became a clash of sectional champions, many of them aging titans of an earlier political era, others representing the new leadership that would govern the nation through the Civil War period.

The first selection below is an excerpt from the speech delivered by John C. Calhoun of South Carolina, the venerable defender of southern rights, in response to the Clay compromise proposals. Sixty-eight years old in 1850, Calhoun was deathly ill and too feeble to deliver his address himself. Wrapped in blankets to warm his wasted frame, he listened intently from his Senate seat as James Mason of Virginia read the speech to the members.

Calhoun does not speak specifically to the Clay proposals. Rather, he lays out the whole array of southern grievances as they had evolved since the days of Thomas Jefferson. Is Calhoun correct when he blames northern policies for the South's numerical inferiority? How could the North have imposed its policies if the two sections had been equal in power at the outset? Why, for example, did most immigrants go to the free rather than the slave states? How does Calhoun account, if at all, for the fact that slavery was excluded from most new territory added to the United States after 1800? How valid are his charges that the antislavery agitation was destroying the bonds that held the Union together? Even if Calhoun was right about the divisive nature of the antislavery movement, what could have been done, given Bill of Rights' protection for freedom of speech and the press, to stop the agitation? Calhoun depicts himself as a unionist. Was he?

---

[1]These items actually represent a revised set of proposals introduced by Stephen Douglas after the somewhat different original scheme, proposed by Clay, had been defeated.

The South Defended

JOHN C. CALHOUN

I have, Senators, believed from the first that the agitation of the subject of slavery would . . . end in disunion. Entertaining this opinion, I have . . . endeavored to call the attention of both the two great parties which divide the country to adopt some measure to prevent so great a disaster, but without success. The agitation has been permitted to proceed, with almost no attempt to resist it, until it has reached a point when it can no longer be disguised or denied that the Union is in danger. You have thus had forced upon you the greatest and the gravest question that can ever come under your consideration—How can the Union be preserved? . . .

. . . What is it that has endangered the Union?

To this question there can be but one answer,—that the immediate cause is the almost universal discontent which pervades all the States composing the Southern section of the Union. This widely-extended discontent is not of recent origin. It commenced with the agitation of the slavery question, and has been increasing ever since. The next question, going one step further back, is—What has caused this widely diffused and almost universal discontent?

It is a great mistake to suppose . . . that it originated with demagogues, who excited the discontent with the intention of aiding their personal advancement, or with the disappointed ambition of certain politicians, who resorted to it as a means of retrieving their fortunes. On the contrary, all the great political influences of the [Southern] section were arrayed against excitement, and exerted to the utmost to keep the people quiet. . . . The leaders and the presses of both parties [i.e., Whigs and Democrats] were very solicitous to prevent excitement and preserve quiet; because it was seen that the effects of the former would necessarily tend to weaken, if not destroy, the political ties which united them with their respective parties in other sections. . . . No; some cause, far deeper and more powerful than the one supposed, must exist, to account for the discontent so wide and deep. . . . What is the cause of this discontent? It will be found in the belief of the people of the Southern States . . . that they cannot remain, as things now are, consistently with honor and safety, in the Union. The next question to be considered is—What has caused this belief?

One of the causes is, undoubtedly, to be traced to the long-continued agitation of the slave question on the part of the North, and the many aggressions which they have made on the rights of the South. . . .

There is another lying back of it . . . that may be regarded as the great and primary cause. This is to be found in the fact that the equilibrium between the two sections . . . has been destroyed. At that time [i.e., at the beginning of the republic] there was nearly a perfect equilibrium between the two, which afforded ample means to each to protect itself against the aggression of the other; but, as it now

Congressional Globe, 31st Cong., 1st sess., 21, pt. 1, 1850, pp. 451–55.

stands, one section has the exclusive power of controlling the Government, which leaves the other without any adequate means of protecting itself against its encroachment and oppression. To place this subject distinctly before you, I have, Senators, prepared a brief statistical statement, to show the relative weight of the two sections in the Government under the first census of 1790 and the last census of 1840.

. . . .

[Here follows an analysis demonstrating the more rapid growth of population in the North than in the South and the consequent gap in favor of the North in representation in the electoral college and the House of Representatives. Calhoun also assumes that the census of 1850 will show a further increase in the power of the North over the federal government.]

The prospect is . . . that a great increase will be added to its [i.e., the North's] preponderance in the Senate, during the period of the decade, by the addition of two new States. Two territories, Oregon and Minnesota, are already in progress, and strenuous efforts are making to bring in three additional States from the territory recently acquired from Mexico; which, if successful, will add three other States in a short time to the Northern section, making five States; and increasing the present number of its States from fifteen to twenty, and of its Senators from thirty to forty. On the contrary, there is not a single territory in progress in the Southern section, and no certainty that any additional State will be added to it during the decade. The prospect then is, that the two sections in the Senate, should the efforts now made to exclude the South from the newly acquired territories succeed, will stand, before the end of the decade, twenty Northern States to fourteen Southern, . . . and forty Northern Senators to twenty-eight Southern. This great increase of Senators, added to the great increase of members of the House of Representatives and the electoral college on the part of the North, which must take place under the next decade, will effectually and irretrievably destroy the equilibrium which existed when the Government commenced.

Had this destruction been the operation of time, without the interference of Government, the South would have had no reason to complain; but such was not the fact. It was caused by the legislation of this Government, which was appointed, as the common agent of all, and charged with the protection of the interests and security of all. The legislation by which it has been effected, may be classed under three heads. The first is, that series of acts by which the South has been excluded from the common territory belonging to all the States as members of the Federal Union— which have had the effect of extending vastly the portion allotted to the Northern section, and restricting within narrow limits the portion left to the South. The next consists of adopting a system of revenue and disbursements, by which an undue proportion of the burden of taxation has been imposed upon the South, and an undue proportion of its proceeds appropriated to the North; and the last is the system of political measures, by which the original character of the Government has been radically changed. . . .

[I]f there was no question of vital importance to the South, in reference to which there was a diversity of views between the sections, this state of things might be endured. . . . But . . . there is a question of vital importance to the Southern section, in reference to which the views and feelings of the two sections are as opposite and hostile as they can possibly be.

I refer to the relation between the two races in the Southern section, which constitutes a vital portion of her social organization. Every portion of the North entertains views and feelings more or less hostile to it. Those most opposed and hostile, regard it as a sin, and consider themselves under the most sacred obligation to use every effort to destroy it. . . . Those less opposed and hostile, regard it as a crime—an offence against humanity, as they call it; and, although not so fanatical, feel themselves bound to use all efforts to effect the same object; while those who are least opposed and hostile, regard it as a blot and a stain on the character of what they call the Nation, and feel themselves accordingly bound to give it no countenance or support. On the contrary, the Southern section regards the relation as one which cannot be destroyed without subjecting the two races to the greatest calamity, and the section to poverty, desolation, and wretchedness; and accordingly they feel bound, by every consideration of interest and safety, to defend it.

.   .   .   .

[Calhoun recounts the history of the antislavery movement since the 1830s, including the dispersal of "incendiary" publications and the antislavery petition campaign against the internal slave trade and against slavery in the District of Columbia. He shows how the antislavery campaign grew increasingly loud and zealous.]

Such is a brief history of the agitation, as far as it has yet advanced. Now I ask, Senators, what is there to prevent its further progress, until it fulfills the ultimate end proposed; unless some decisive measure should be adopted to prevent it? . . . Is it . . . not certain, that if something is not done to arrest it, the South will be forced to choose between abolition and secession? Indeed, as events are now moving, it will not require the South to secede, in order to dissolve the Union. Agitation will of itself effect it. . . .

It is a great mistake to suppose that disunion can be effected by a single blow. The cords which bound these States together in one common Union, are far too numerous and powerful for that. Disunion must be the work of time. . . . It is only through a long process . . . that the cords can be snapped, until the whole fabric falls asunder. Already the agitation of the slavery question has snapped some of the most important and has greatly weakened all the others. . . .

.   .   .   .

If the agitation goes on, the same force, acting with increased intensity, . . . will finally snap every cord, when nothing will be left to hold the States together except force. But, surely, that can, with no propriety of language, be called a Union, when the only means by which the weaker is held connected with the stronger portion, is *force*. It may, indeed, keep them connected; but the connection will partake more of the character of subjugation, on the part of the weaker to the stronger, than the union of free, independent, and sovereign States, in one confederation, as they stood in the early stages of the Government, and which only is worthy of the sacred name of Union.

. . . How can the Union be saved? . . . —by adopting such measures as will satisfy the States belonging to the Southern section, that they can remain in the Union consistently with their honor and safety. There is, again, only one way by which this can be effected, and that is—by removing the causes by which this belief had been produced. Do *this*, and discontent will cease—harmony and kind feelings between the sections be restored—and every apprehension of danger to the Union removed.

14.2: A Northern Unionist Supports the Compromise of 1850 (1850)

The other giant of the past who spoke on the Clay proposals was Daniel Webster, the senator from Massachusetts. The "God-like Daniel" represented a state whose citizens were at the forefront of the movement to limit slavery expansion. He himself had voted for the slavery-restricting Wilmot Proviso. Many of his constituents were opposed to compromise with the South if it meant extending the area where the "peculiar institution" was legal. But Webster was a passionate unionist who had long denounced secession, a threat often used by the South to force concessions from the North. Here, in his famous speech of March 7, 1850, he once more deplores secession and yet seeks to satisfy southern grievances. Webster's address would help the passage of the measures called the Compromise of 1850, but he would be widely condemned in his home state as a betrayer of freedom, a man from whom "the soul has fled."

Webster clearly was responding in part to the charges leveled by John C. Calhoun. What are Webster's specific arguments against Calhoun's claims? To what "law of nature" is Webster referring? Is his argument convincing? Have later events confirmed or refuted that law of nature?

Webster's Seventh of March Speech Favoring the Compromise Measures

DANIEL WEBSTER

. . . And now let us consider, sir, for a moment what was the state of sentiment, North and South, in regard to slavery at the time this Constitution was adopted. A remarkable change has taken place since, but what did the wise and great men of all parts of the country think of slavery? In what estimation did they hold it in 1787,

Congressional Globe, 31st Cong., 1st sess., 21, pt. 1, 1850, pp. 476–83.

when the Constitution was adopted? No, it will be found, sir, that there was no great diversity of opinion between the North and the South upon the subject of slavery; and it will be found that both parts of the country held it equally an evil—a moral and political evil. It will not be found, that either at the North or at the South, there was much, though there was some, invective against slavery as inhuman and cruel. The great ground of objection to it was political; that it weakened the social fabric; that, taking the place of free labor, society was less strong, and labor was less productive; and, therefore, . . . that slavery was an evil. . . . The eminent men, the most eminent men, and nearly all the conspicuous men of the South, held the same sentiments, that slavery was an evil, a blight, a blast, a mildew, a scourge, and a curse. . . .

This was the state of things, sir, and this the state of opinion, under which those two very important matters were arranged, and those two important things done; that is, the establishment of the Constitution, with a recognition of slavery as it existed in the States, and the establishment of the ordinance [the Northwest Ordinance of 1787] prohibiting, to the full extent of all territory owned by the United States, the introduction of slavery into those territories. . . . But opinions, sir, have changed—greatly changed—changed North and changed South. . . .

The North [since that time has been] growing much more warm and strong against slavery, and the South [has been] growing much more warm and strong in its support. . . . What . . . have been the causes which have created so new a feeling in favor of slavery in the South . . . and from being thought of as described in the terms that I mentioned, . . . it has now become an institution, a cherished institution there; no evil, no scourge, but a great religious, social, and moral blessing, as I think I have heard it latterly described? I suppose this, sir, is owing to the sudden uprising and rapid growth of the cotton plantations of the South. So far as any motive of honor, justice, and general judgement could act, it was the cotton interest that gave a new desire to promote slavery, to spread it and to use its labor. . . .

Well, sir, we know what follows. The age of cotton became a golden age for our southern brethren. It gratified their desire for improvement and accumulation, at the same time that it excited it. The desire grew by what it fed upon, and there soon came to be an eagerness for other territory—a new area or areas for the cultivation of the cotton crop; and measures were brought about, somewhat rapidly, one after another, under the head of southern men at the head of Government—they having a majority in both branches of the Government—to accomplish their ends. The honorable member from Carolina [i.e., Calhoun] observed, that there has been a majority all along in favor of the North. If that be true, sir, the North acted either very liberally and kindly, or very weakly; for they never exercised that majority five times in the history of the Government. . . . [N]o man acquainted with the history of the country, can deny, that the general lead in the politics of the country, for three-fourths of the period that has lapsed since the adoption of the Constitution, has been a southern lead. . . .

Now, as to California and New Mexico, I hold slavery to be excluded from those territories by a law even superior to that which admits and sanctions it in Texas—I mean the law of nature—of physical geography—the law of the formation of the earth. That law settles forever, with a strength beyond all terms of human enactment, that slavery cannot exist in California or New Mexico. . . .

Mr. President, in the excited times in which we live, there is found to exist a state of crimination and recrimination between the North and the South. There are lists of grievances produced by each; and those grievances, real or supposed, alienate the minds of one portion of the country from the other, exasperate the feelings, subdue the sense of fraternal connection, and patriotic love, and mutual regard. I shall bestow a little attention, sir, upon these various grievances, produced on the one side or the other. I begin with the complaints of the South: I will now answer, farther than I have, the general statements of the Senator from South Carolina, that the North has grown upon the South in consequence of the manner of administrating this Government, in the collection of its revenues, and so forth. . . . I will state these complaints, especially one complaint of the South, which has in my opinion just foundation; and that is, that there has been found in the North, among individuals and among the Legislatures of the North, a disinclination to perform, fully, their constitutional duties in regard to the return of persons bound to service [i.e., slaves], who have escaped into the free States. In that respect, it is my judgement that the South is right, and the North is wrong. Every member of every northern Legislature is bound, by oath, like every other officer in the country, to support the Constitution of the United States; and this article of the Constitution, which says to these States, they shall deliver up fugitives from service, is binding in honor and conscience as any other article. . . .

Therefore, I repeat, sir, that there is ground of complaint against the North, well founded, which ought to be removed—which is now in the power of the different departments of this Government to remove—which calls for the enactment of proper laws, authorizing the judicature of this Government, in the several States, to do all that is necessary for the recapture of fugitive slaves, and for the restoration of them to those who claim them. Wherever I go, and whenever I speak on the subject . . . I say that the South has been injured in this respect and has a right to complain; and the North has been careless of what I think the Constitution peremptorily and emphatically enjoins upon it as a duty. . . .

There can be no such thing as peaceable secession. Peaceable secession is an utter impossibility. Is the great Constitution under which we live here . . . to be thawed and melted away by secession? . . . No sir! no sir! I will not say what might produce the disruption of the States; but, sir, I see it as plainly as I see the sun in heaven—I see that disruption must produce such a war as I will not describe. . . .

Peaceable secession! peaceable secession! . . . A voluntary separation, with alimony on one side and on the other. Why, what would be the result? Where is the line to be drawn? What States are to secede? What is to remain American? What am I to be?—an American no longer? Where is the flag of the republic to remain? Where is the eagle still to tower? Or is he to cower, and shrink, and fall to the ground? Why, sir, our ancestors—our fathers, and our grandfathers . . . —would rebuke and reproach us; and our children, and our grandchildren, would cry out, Shame upon us! if we, of this generation, should dishonor these ensigns of the power of the Government, and the harmony of the Union. . . . What is to become of the army? What is to become of the navy? What is to become of the public lands?

How is each of the thirty States to defend itself? . . . We could not separate the States by [a] . . . line, if we were to draw it. We could not sit here to-day, and draw a line of separation, that would satisfy any five men in the country. There are natural causes that would keep and tie us together, and there are domestic and social relations, which we could not break, if we would, and which we should not, if we could.

14.3: Antislavery Leaders Respond to the Kansas–Nebraska Act (1854)

The Compromise of 1850, based on the Clay proposals as revised and managed by Stephen Douglas, the Democratic senator from Illinois, ended talk of secession for a time. The Fugitive Slave Law, which made up part of the compromise package, would deeply offend the sensibilities of many northerners and lead to defiant resistance in several northern communities. Still, for a time the sectional agreement quieted North–South agitation.

Then, in 1854 Douglas reopened the issue of slavery expansion, this time as applied to the remaining unsettled portions of the Louisiana Purchase territory. His Kansas–Nebraska bill repealed the Missouri Compromise of 1820 and opened up the region from which Congress had excluded slavery to possible settlement by slaveholders and their property. Douglas was moved initially by a desire primarily to encourage settlement of the Nebraska country. His original bill had said nothing of slavery in the region. But the "Little Giant," who agreed with Webster that slavery could not take root in the plains, was pushed to support an explicit repeal of the Missouri Compromise by a group of southern senators who felt deeply that any act of Congress excluding them and their property from any part of the federal public domain was a heinous sectional affront. Strongly supported by the Democratic administration under President Franklin Pierce, Douglas's bill, including the explicit Missouri Compromise repeal, passed.

The result was a political explosion in the North. Even moderate northerners saw the new law as a deplorable concession to the slave South. Among the strong antislavery voters and politicians, the Kansas–Nebraska Act seemed to confirm the existence of a behind-the-scenes deal uniting the "slavocracy" and "northern men with southern principles." The following document is one expression of this view. Signed by group of antislavery leaders in Congress even before the Kansas–Nebraska Act had passed, it became a manifesto of an emerging political force focused on slavery limitation that would soon crystallize as the Republican Party.

Have you encountered in any previous document in this section another charge of the illegitimate use of power for sectional ends? How do you distinguish a wide-ranging political plot from the usual behind-the-scenes maneuvering by politicians in the course of passing routine legislation? Do the "Independent Democrats" who composed and signed this appeal betray any compassion for slaves? Or do they seem concerned only for the rights of white nonslaveholders?

The Kansas–Nebraska Act: A Plot Against the North

"INDEPENDENT DEMOCRATS"

As Senators and Representatives in the Congress of the United States it is our duty to warn our constituents, whenever imminent danger menaces the freedom of our institutions or the permanency of the Union.

Such danger, as we firmly believe, now impends, and we earnestly solicit your prompt attention to it.

At the last session of Congress a bill for the organization of the Territory of Nebraska passed the House of Representatives by an overwhelming majority. That bill was based on the principle of excluding slavery from the new Territory. It was not taken up for consideration in the Senate and consequently failed to become a law.

At the present session a new Nebraska bill has been reported by the Senate Committee on Territories, which, should it unhappily receive the sanction of Congress, will open all the unorganized Territories of the Union to the ingress of slavery.

We arraign this bill as a gross violation of a sacred pledge; as a criminal betrayal of precious rights; as part and parcel of an atrocious plot to exclude from a vast unoccupied region immigrants from the Old World and free laborers from our own States, and convert it into a dreary region of despotism, inhabited by masters and slaves.

Take your maps, fellow citizens, we entreat you, and see what country it is which this bill gratuitously and recklessly proposes to open to slavery. . . .

This immense region, occupying the very heart of the North American Continent, and larger, by thirty-three thousand square miles, than all the existing free States—including California . . . this immense region the bill now before the Senate, without reason and without excuse, but in flagrant disregard of sound policy and sacred faith, purposes to open to slavery.

We beg your attention, fellow-citizens, to a few historical facts:

The original settled policy of the United States, clearly indicated by the Jefferson proviso of 1784 and the Ordinance of 1787, was non-extension of slavery.

J. W. Schuckers, Appeal of the Independent Democrats, *Life and Public Services of Salmon P. Chase* (New York: D. Appleton and Company, 1874), pp. 140–44.

In 1803 Louisiana was acquired by purchase from France. . . .

In 1818, six years later, the inhabitants of the Territory of Missouri applied to Congress for authority to form a State constitution, and for admission into the Union. There were, at that time, in the whole territory acquired from France, outside of the State of Louisiana, not three thousand slaves.

There was no apology, in the circumstances of the country, for the continuance of slavery. The original national policy was against it, and not less the plain language of the treaty under which the territory had been acquired from France.

It was proposed, therefore, to incorporate in the bill authorizing the formation of a State government, a provision requiring that the constitution of the new State should contain an article providing for the abolition of existing slavery, and prohibiting the further introduction of slaves.

This provision was vehemently and pertinaciously opposed, but finally prevailed in the House of Representatives by a decided vote. In the Senate it was rejected, and—in consequence of the disagreement between the two Houses—the bill was lost.

At the next session of Congress, the controversy was renewed with increased violence. It was terminated at length by a compromise. Missouri was allowed to come into the Union with slavery; but a section was inserted in the act authorizing her admission, excluding slavery forever from all the territory acquired from France, not included in the new State, lying north of 36° 30'. . . .

Nothing is more certain in history than the fact that Missouri could not have been admitted as a slave State had not certain members from the free States been reconciled to the measure by the incorporation of this prohibition into the act of admission. Nothing is more certain than that this prohibition has been regarded and accepted by the whole country as a solemn compact against the extension of slavery into any part of the territory acquired from France lying north of 36° 30', and not included in the new State of Missouri. The same act—let it be ever remembered—which authorized the formation of a constitution by the State, without a clause forbidding slavery, consecrated, beyond question and beyond honest recall, the whole remainder of the Territory to freedom and free institutions forever. For more than thirty years—during more than half our national existence under our present Constitution—this compact has been universally regarded and acted upon as inviolable American law. In conformity with it, Iowa was admitted as a free State and Minnesota has been organized as a free Territory.

It is a strange and ominous fact, well calculated to awaken the worst apprehensions and the most fearful forebodings of future calamities, that it is now deliberately proposed to repeal this prohibition, by implication or directly—the latter certainly the manlier way—and thus to subvert the compact, and allow slavery in all the yet unorganized territory.

We cannot, in this address, review the various pretenses under which it is attempted to cloak this monstrous wrong, but we must not altogether omit to notice one.

It is said that Nebraska sustains the same relations to slavery as did the territory acquired from Mexico prior to 1850, and that the pro-slavery clauses of the bill are necessary to carry into effect the compromise of that year.

No assertion could be more groundless. . . .

The statesmen whose powerful support carried the Utah and New Mexico acts never dreamed that their provisions would be ever applied to Nebraska. . . .

Here is proof beyond controversy that the principle of the Missouri act prohibiting slavery north of 36° 30', far from being abrogated by the Compromise Acts, is expressly affirmed; and that the proposed repeal of this prohibition, instead of being an affirmation of the Compromise Acts, is a repeal of a very prominent provision of the most important act of the series. It is solemnly declared in the very Compromise Acts *"that nothing herein contained shall be construed to impair or qualify"* the prohibition of slavery north of 36° 30'; and yet in the face of this declaration, that sacred prohibition is said to be overthrown. Can presumption further go? To all who, in any way, lean upon these compromises, we commend this exposition.

The pretenses, therefore, that the territory covered by the positive prohibition of 1820, sustains a similar relation to slavery with that acquired from Mexico, covered by no prohibition except that of disputed constitutional or Mexican law, and that the Compromises of 1850 require the incorporation of the pro-slavery clauses of the Utah and New Mexico Bill in the Nebraska act, are mere inventions, designed to cover up from public reprehension meditated bad faith. Were he living now, no one would be more forward, more eloquent, or more indignant in his denunciation of that bad faith, than Henry Clay, the foremost champion of both compromises. . . .

We appeal to the people. We warn you that the dearest interests of freedom and the Union are in imminent peril. Demagogues may tell you that the Union can be maintained only by submitting to the demands of slavery. We tell you that the Union can only be maintained by the full recognition of the just claims of freedom and man. The Union was formed to establish justice and secure the blessings of liberty. When it fails to accomplish these ends it will be worthless, and when it becomes worthless it cannot long endure.

We entreat you to be mindful of that fundamental maxim of Democracy—EQUAL RIGHTS AND EXACT JUSTICE FOR ALL MEN. Do not submit to become agents in extending legalized oppression and systematized injustice over a vast territory yet exempt from these terrible evils.

We implore Christians and Christian ministers to interpose. Their divine religion requires them to behold in every man a brother, and to labor for the advancement and regeneration of the human race.

Whatever apologies may be offered for the toleration of slavery in the States, none can be offered for its extension into Territories where it does not exist, and where that extension involves the repeal of ancient law and the violation of solemn compact. Let all protest, earnestly and emphatically, by correspondence, through the press, by memorials, by resolutions of public meetings and legislative bodies, and in whatever other mode may seem expedient, against this enormous crime.

For ourselves, we shall resist it by speech and vote, and with all the abilities which God has given us. Even if overcome in the impending struggle, we shall not submit. We shall go home to our constituents, erect anew the standard of freedom, and call on the people to come to the rescue of the country from the domination of slavery. We will not despair; for the cause of human freedom is the cause of God.

S. P. Chase
Charles Sumner
J. R. Giddings
Edward Wade
Gerritt Smith
Alexander De Witt.

14.4:   John Brown and the Remission of Sins by Blood (1859)

The Kansas–Nebraska Act let loose a wave of violence in Kansas. Some of this derived from disputed land claims among settlers who poured into the region after its passage, but the primary cause was a contest to impose either free labor or slavery on the territory.

One participant in the struggle to decide the future of Kansas was John Brown, an antislavery zealot who believed that "without the shedding of blood there is no remission of sins." In May 1856, in retaliation for the sack of the free staters' settlement at Lawrence by proslavery guerrillas, Brown and his sons massacred several prosouthern farmers at Pottawatamie Creek.

Unpunished for this crime, Brown went east and hatched a scheme to stir up a slave insurrection in the upper South as the first step in dismantling the institution of slavery. Encouraged and supported by several prominent eastern abolitionists, he and his small band, including several of his sons, captured the federal arsenal at Harpers Ferry, Virginia, on the evening of October 16, 1859. The rebels hoped to arouse the local slaves and, apparently, expected to escape into the mountains with a small army equipped with their captured arms. The plan was bungled. The group's efforts to arouse the slaves were feeble and they failed to consider adequate plans for escape. State militia and U.S. marines besieged the arsenal and quickly killed or captured the rebels.

Brown and four others were captured alive, tried by a Virginia court for treason, and sentenced to be hanged. To many Americans Brown's scheme seemed an act of a murderous madman. To many southerners it confirmed their belief in the willingness of abolitionist fanatics to resort to any extreme to express hatred of Dixie. Even partisan Republican politicians condemned the resort to violence. But for a segment of the northern public, Brown seemed a righteous Old Testament prophet smiting sin and injustice regardless of consequences. During his in-

carceration before execution, his prison cell became a mecca for many fervent antislavery advocates. At his death he became a martyr to the cause of freedom for the slave.

In the selection below Brown explains his motives in simple, moving language that reinforced his martyr image. Was Brown being entirely candid about his motives? Do you think his brief speech was an attempt to avoid the death penalty? Or was it intended more for posterity than for the judge and his immediate audience?

John Brown's Last Speech

I have, may it please the Court, a few words to say.

In the first place, I deny everything but what I have all along admitted,—the design on my part to free the slaves. I intended certainly to have made a clean thing of that matter, as I did last winter, when I went into Missouri and there took slaves without the snapping of a gun on either side, moved them through the country, and finally left them in Canada. I designed to have done the same thing again, on a larger scale. That was all I intended. I never did intend murder, or treason, or the destruction of property, or to excite or incite slaves to rebellion, or to make insurrection.

I have another objection; and that is, it is unjust that I should suffer such a penalty. Had I interfered in the manner which I admit, and which I admit has been fairly proved (for I admire the truthfulness and candor of the greater portion of the witnesses who have testified in this case),—had I so interfered in behalf of the rich, the powerful, the intelligent, the so-called great, or in behalf of any of their friends,—either father, mother, brother, sister, wife, or children, or any of that class,—and suffered and sacrificed what I have in this interference, it would have been all right; and every man in this court would have deemed it an act worthy of reward rather than punishment.

This court acknowledges, as I suppose, the validity of the law of God. I see a book kissed here which I suppose to be the Bible, or at least the New Testament. That teaches me that all things whatsoever I would that men should do to me, I should do even so to them. It teaches me, further, to "remember them that are in bonds, as bound with them." I endeavored to act up to that instruction. I say, I am yet too young to understand that God is any respecter of persons. I believe that to have interfered as I have done—as I have always freely admitted I have done—in behalf of His despised poor, was not wrong, but right. Now, if it is deemed necessary that I should forfeit my life for the furtherance of the ends of justice, and mingle my blood further with the blood of my children and with the blood of millions in this slave country whose rights are disregarded by wicked, cruel, and unjust enactments,—I submit; so let it be done!

Franklin B. Sanborn, *The Life and Letters of John Brown, Liberator of Kansas and Martyr of Virginia* (Boston: Roberts Brothers, 1885), pp. 570–71.

Let me say one word further.

I feel entirely satisfied with the treatment I have received on my trial. Considering all the circumstances, it has been more generous than I expected. But I feel no consciousness of guilt. I have stated from the first what was my intention, and what was not. I never had any design against the life of any person, nor any disposition to commit treason, or excite slaves to rebel, or make any general insurrection. I never encouraged any man to do so, but always discouraged any idea of that kind.

Let me say, also, a word in regard to the statements made by some of those connected with me. I hear it has been stated by some of them that I have induced them to join me. But the contrary is true. I do not say this to injure them, but as regretting their weakness. There is not one of them but joined me of his own accord, and the greater part of them at their own expense. A number of them I never saw, and never had a word of conversation with, till the day they came to me; and that was for the purpose I have stated.

Now I have done.

14.5:   The Victory of the Republican Party (1860)

The electoral crisis of 1860 yielded a rare occurrence—the victory of a Presidential candidate nominated by a third party, the Republicans. Although Lincoln failed to obtain even close to a majority of the popular vote, he surely was the strongest overall candidate in the field of four, as the electoral vote reflected.

Not only had the Republican Party achieved success, it had done so in a relatively short period of time. What factors contributed to this success? In addition to challenging the extension of slavery into additional western territories, the Republicans proposed a number of initiatives that realigned sectional politics; the West, with ever-increasing political clout, was now brought into growing political empathy with the North.

Besides the matter of slavery, what other issues were important as expressed by the Republican Party platform? Can you connect specific resolutions in the platform to particular demands of the West or the North? How did the resolutions to pass a Homestead Act and approve internal improvements unite the West and North politically? Today, we pay relatively little attention to party platforms in presidential elections. Why would the Republican platform of 1860 have had a much more spectacular effect?

The Republican Party Platform of 1860

Resolved, That we, the delegated representatives of the Republican electors of the United States, in Convention assembled, in discharge of the duty we owe to our constituents and our country, unite in the following declarations:

1. That the history of the nation, during the last four years, has fully established the propriety and necessity of the organization and perpetuation of the Republican party, and that the causes which called it into existence are permanent in their nature, and now, more than ever before, demand its peaceful and constitutional triumph.

2. That the maintenance of the principles promulgated in the Declaration of Independence and embodied in the Federal Constitution. "That all men are created equal; that they are endowed by their Creator with certain inalienable rights; that among these are life, liberty and the pursuit of happiness; that, to secure these rights, governments are instituted among men, deriving their just powers from the consent of the governed," is essential to the preservation of our Republican institutions: and that the Federal Constitution, the Rights of the States, and the Union of the States, must and shall be preserved.

3. That to the Union of the States this nation owes its unprecedented increase in population, its surprising development of material resources, its rapid augmentation of wealth, its happiness at home and its honor abroad; and we hold in abhorrence all schemes for Disunion, come from whatever source they may; And we congratulate the country that no Republican member of Congress has uttered or countenanced the threats of Disunion so often made by Democratic members, without rebuke and with applause from their political associates; and we denounce those threats of Disunion, in case of a popular overthrow of their ascendency, as denying the vital principles of a free government, and as an avowal of contemplated treason, which it is the imperative duty of an indignant People sternly to rebuke and forever silence.

4. That the maintenance inviolate of the rights of the States, and especially the right of each State to order and control its own domestic institutions according to its own judgment exclusively, is essential to that balance of powers on which the perfection and endurance of our political fabric depends; and we denounce the lawless invasion by armed force of the soil of any State or Territory, no matter under what pretext, as among the gravest of crimes.

5. That the present Democratic Administration has far exceeded our worst apprehensions, in its measureless subserviency to the exactions of a sectional interest, as especially evinced in its desperate exertions to force the infamous Lecompton constitution upon the protesting people of Kansas; in construing the personal relation between master and servant to involve an unqualified property in persons; in its

Republican Party Platform. Chicago, Illinois, May 16, 1860. Printed in *A Political Text-book for 1860,* compiled by Horace Greeley and John F. Cleveland (New York: Tribune Association, 1860), p. 26ff.

attempted enforcement, everywhere, on land and sea, through the intervention of Congress and of the Federal Courts of the extreme pretensions of a purely local interest; and in its general and unvarying abuse of the power intrusted to it by a confiding people. . . .

7. That the new dogma that the Constitution, of its own force, carries Slavery into any or all of the Territories of the United States, is a dangerous political heresy, at variance with the explicit provisions of that instrument itself, with contemporaneous exposition, and with legislative and judicial precedent; is revolutionary in its tendency, and subversive of the peace and harmony of the country.

8. That the normal condition of all the territory of the United States is that of freedom; That as our Republican fathers, when they had abolished slavery, in all our national territory, ordained that "no person should be deprived of life, liberty, or property, without due process of law," it becomes our duty, by legislation, whenever such legislation is necessary, to maintain this provision of the Constitution against all attempts to violate it; and we deny the authority of Congress, of a territorial legislature, or of any individuals, to give legal existence to Slavery in any Territory of the United States.

9. That we brand the recent re-opening of the African slave-trade, under the cover of our national flag, aided by perversions of judicial power, as a crime against humanity and a burning shame to our country, and age; and we call upon Congress to take prompt and efficient measures for the total and final suppression of that execrable traffic.

10. That in the recent vetoes, by their Federal Governors, of the acts of the Legislatures of Kansas and Nebraska, prohibiting Slavery in those Territories, we find a practical illustration of the boasted Democratic principle of Non-Intervention and Popular Sovereignty embodied in the Kansas-Nebraska bill, and a demonstration of the deception and fraud involved therein.

11. That Kansas should, of right, be immediately admitted as a State under the Constitution recently formed and adopted by her people, and accepted by the House of Representatives.

12. That, while providing revenue for the support of the General Government by duties upon imports, sound policy requires such an adjustment of these imposts as to encourage the development of the industrial interests of the whole country; and we commend that policy of national exchanges which secures to the working men liberal wages, to agriculture remunerating prices, to mechanics and manufacturers and adequate reward for their skill, labor and enterprise, and to the nation commercial prosperity and independence.

13. That we protest against any sale or alienation to others of the Public Lands held by actual settlers, and against any view of the Homestead policy which regards the settlers as paupers or supplicants for public bounty; and we demand the passage by Congress of the complete and satisfactory Homestead measure which has already passed the house.

14. That the Republican Party is opposed to any change in our Naturalization Laws or any State legislation by which the rights of our citizenship hitherto

accorded to immigrants from foreign lands shall be abridged or impaired; and in favor of giving a full and efficient protection to the rights of all classes of citizens, whether native or naturalized, both at home and abroad.

15. That appropriations by Congress for River and Harbor improvements of a National character, required for the accommodation and security of an existing commerce, are authorized by the Constitution, and justified by the obligations of Government to protect the lives and property of its citizens.

16. That a Railroad to the Pacific Ocean is imperatively demanded by the interests of the whole country; that the Federal Government ought to render immediate and efficient aid in its construction; and that, as preliminary thereto, a daily Overland Mail should be promptly established. . . .

14.6: The South Secedes (1860)

The Harpers Ferry attack, continued violence in Kansas, and a host of real or imagined sectional slights and offenses encouraged the further sectionalizing of national politics. By the late 1850s the Whigs had collapsed as a party, with many of its northern members joining the new Republican organization. Dedicated to stopping the spread of slavery so as to "place it . . . in the course of ultimate extinction," the new party was almost purely northern in its support.

In 1860 the Republican candidate for president, Abraham Lincoln, won election in a field of four. Lincoln was not an abolitionist, but to the South his victory seemed an indescribable affront that could only be answered by the secession of the slave states from the Union. Within weeks of the election, the deep South states of South Carolina, Mississippi, Florida, Alabama, Georgia, Louisiana, and Texas all had passed ordinances of secession repudiating the compact known as the Constitution. In February 1861 representatives from these states met at Montgomery, Alabama, and established a provisional government for the Confederate States of America.

The following document is part of the "Declaration of Causes" that accompanied South Carolina's Ordinance of Secession of December 1860. What are the chief grievances of the secession convention delegates? How seriously do they take the constitutional arguments they advance, do you suppose? Why was the resistance by the free states to returning fugitive slaves so offensive to the South Carolinians? Why was Lincoln's election such an incitement to them?

Why South Carolina Is Leaving the Union

SOUTH CAROLINA SECESSION CONVENTION

DECLARATION OF CAUSES WHICH INDUCED THE SECESSION OF SOUTH CAROLINA.

The people of the State of South Carolina in Convention assembled, on the 2d day of April, A.D. 1832, declared that the frequent violations of the Constitution of the United States by the Federal Government, and its encroachments upon the reserved rights of the States, fully justified this State in their withdrawal from the Federal Union; but in deference to the opinions and wishes of the other Slaveholding States, she forbore at that time to exercise this right. Since that time these encroachments have continued to increase, and further forbearance ceases to be a virtue.

And now the State of South Carolina having resumed her separate and equal place among nations, deems it due to herself, to the remaining United States of America, and to the nations of the world, that she should declare the immediate causes which have led to this act. . . .

[Here follows a review of the history of the formation of the American union from the late colonial period, through the Revolution, and then to the adoption of the Constitution.]

By this Constitution, certain duties were imposed upon the several States, and the exercise of certain of their powers was restrained, which necessarily impelled their continued existence as sovereign states. But, to remove all doubt, an amendment was added, which declared that the powers not delegated to the United States by the Constitution, nor prohibited by it to the States, are reserved to the States respectively, or to the people. On the 23d May, 1788, South Carolina, by a Convention of her people, passed an ordinance assenting to this Constitution, and afterwards altered her own Constitution to conform herself to the obligations she had undertaken.

Thus was established, by compact between the States, a Government with defined objects and powers, limited to the express words of the grant. This limitation left the whole remaining mass of power subject to the clause reserving it to the States or the people, and rendered unnecessary any specification of reserved rights. We hold that the Government thus established is subject to the two great principles asserted in the Declaration of Independence; and we hold further, that the mode of its formation subjects it to a third fundamental principle, namely, the law of compact. We maintain that in every compact between two or more parties, the obligation is mutual; that the failure of one of the contracting parties to perform a material part of the agreement, entirely releases the obligation of the other; and that, where no arbiter is provided, each party is remitted to his own judgment to determine the fact of failure, with all its consequences.

"Declaration of Causes," ed. Frank Moore, *The Rebellion Record: A Diary of American Events with Documents, Narratives, Illustrative Incidents* . . . (New York: G. P. Putnam, 1862), vol. 1, pp. 3–4.

In the present case, that fact is established with certainty. We assert that fourteen of the States have deliberately refused for years past to fulfil their constitutional obligations, and we refer to their own statutes for the proof.

The Constitution of the United States, in its fourth Article, provides as follows:

> "No person held to service or labor in one State under the laws thereof, escaping into another, shall, in consequence of any law or regulation therein, be discharged from such service or labor, but shall be delivered up, on claim of the party to whom such service or labor may be due."

This stipulation was so material to the compact that without it that compact would not have been made. The greater number of the contracting parties held slaves, and they had previously evinced their estimate of the value of such a stipulation by making it a condition in the Ordinance for the government of the territory ceded by Virginia, which obligations, and the laws of the General Government, have ceased to effect the objects of the Constitution. The States of Maine, New Hampshire, Vermont, Massachusetts, Connecticut, Rhode Island, New York, Pennsylvania, Illinois, Indiana, Michigan, Wisconsin, and Iowa, have enacted laws which either nullify the acts of Congress, or render useless any attempt to execute them. In many of these States the fugitive is discharged from the service of labor claimed, and in none of them has the State Government complied with the stipulation made in the Constitution. The State of New Jersey, at an early day, passed a law in conformity with her constitutional obligation; but the current of Anti-Slavery feeling has led her more recently to enact laws which render inoperative the remedies provided by her own laws and by the laws of Congress. In the State of New York even the right of transit for a slave has been denied by her tribunals; and the States of Ohio and Iowa have refused to surrender to justice fugitives charged with murder, and with inciting servile insurrection in the State of Virginia. Thus the constitutional compact has been deliberately broken and disregarded by the non-slaveholding States; and the consequence follows that South Carolina is released from her obligation.

The ends for which this Constitution was framed are declared by itself to be "to form a more perfect union, to establish justice, insure domestic tranquillity, provide for the common defence, promote the general welfare, and secure the blessings of liberty to ourselves and our posterity."

These ends it endeavored to accomplish by a Federal Government, in which each State was recognized as an equal, and had separate control over its own institutions. The right of property in slaves was recognized by giving to free persons distinct political rights; by giving them the right to represent, and burdening them with direct taxes for, three-fifths of their slaves; by authorizing the importation of slaves for twenty years; and by stipulating for the rendition of fugitives from labor.

We affirm that these ends for which this Government was instituted have been defeated, and the Government itself has been destructive of them by the action of the non-slaveholding States. Those States have assumed the right of deciding upon the propriety of our domestic institutions; and have denied the rights of property established in fifteen of the States and recognized by the Constitution; they have denounced as sinful the institution of Slavery; they have permitted the open establishment among them of societies, whose avowed object is to disturb the peace of and eloin[1] the property of the citizens of other States. They have encouraged and assisted thousands of our slaves to leave their homes; and those who remain, have been incited by emissaries, books, and pictures, to servile insurrection.

For twenty-five years this agitation has been steadily increasing, until it has now secured to its aid the power of the common Government. Observing the *forms* of the Constitution, a sectional party has found within that article establishing the Executive Department, the means of subverting the Constitution itself. A geographical line has been drawn across the Union, and all the States north of that line have united in the election of a man to the high office of President of the United States whose opinions and purposes are hostile to Slavery. He is to be intrusted with the administration of the common Government, because he has declared that that "Government cannot endure permanently half slave, half free," and that the public mind must rest in the belief that Slavery is in the course of ultimate extinction.

This sectional combination for the subversion of the Constitution has been aided, in some of the States, by elevating to citizenship persons who, by the supreme law of the land, are incapable of becoming citizens,[2] and their votes have been used to inaugurate a new policy, hostile to the South, and destructive of its peace and safety.

On the 4th of March next this party will take possession of the Government. It has announced that the South shall be excluded from the common territory, that the Judicial tribunal shall be made sectional, and that a war must be waged against Slavery until it shall cease throughout the United States.

The guarantees of the Constitution will then no longer exist; the equal rights of the States will be lost. The Slaveholding States will no longer have the power of self-government, or self-protection, and the Federal Government will have become their enemy.

Sectional interest and animosity will deepen the irritation; and all hope of remedy is rendered vain, by the fact that the public opinion at the North has invested a great political error with the sanctions of a more erroneous religious belief.

We, therefore, the people of South Carolina, by our delegates in Convention assembled, appealing to the Supreme Judge of the world for the rectitude of our intentions, have solemnly declared that the Union heretofore existing between this State and the other States of North America is dissolved, and that the State of South Carolina has resumed her position among the nations of the world, as separate and independent state, with full power to levy war, conclude peace, contract alliances, establish commerce, and to do all other acts and things which independent States may of right do.

---

[1]That is, to alienate, or remove—ED.
[2]Refers to the grant of voting rights to free blacks by several northern states—ED.

❖ *15* ❖

The Civil War

From the very outset of the tragic sectional encounter we call the Civil War, Americans sought to discern its ultimate causes. We might assume that Unionists and Confederates inevitably reached different conclusions. But this would be an oversimplification. Americans as a whole differed over the causes of the North–South clash, but the divisions did not necessarily follow sectional lines. Rather, northerners and southerners often agreed on the war's causes but extracted different lessons and meanings from their conclusions. Contemporaries did differ on the origins and inner meaning of the war, but the arguments were as often *within* as *between* the sections.

In the selections below you will encounter a range of interpretations by contemporaries of the war's ultimate sources. From your general knowledge of the period, see if you can evaluate the respective views expressed. What do *you* think was the core issue over which Americans fought the Civil War, based on the evidence presented here?

15.1:   The War Is About Slavery (1861)

It is difficult to deny the role of slavery as the key to southern secession and the Civil War. And the claim of slavery's importance came from both sides, North and South. The first selection below is from an 1861 speech by Alexander H. Stephens, vice president of the Confederate States of America. Stephens here is describing the new Confederate constitution and comparing it with the one of 1787 under which the two sections had lived together for three-quarters of a century. In the excerpt he tells his cheering audience that the Confederate constitution, unlike its predecessor, makes a total and unequivocal af-firmation of slavery.

Nowhere in his speech does Stephens declare slavery the cause of the Civil War, yet clearly that is the implication. In what way does he imply that slavery lay behind southern secession? Was Stephens right?

Many northerners would have agreed with Stephens that slavery was the key issue of the war. The second piece, an excerpt from a Re-publican newspaper in Indiana, the Evansville Daily Journal, *provides a counterpoint to Stephens's emphasis on slavery. Although both state-ments make slavery a central issue, they obviously express different at-titudes toward its role in the expanding sectional conflict. How are the two views different?*

Slavery Is the Cornerstone of the Confederacy

ALEXANDER H. STEPHENS

But not to be tedious in enumerating the numerous changes for the better, allow me to allude to one other—though last, not least. The new constitution has put at rest, *forever,* all the agitating questions relating to our peculiar institution—African slav-ery as it exists amongst us—the proper *status* of the negro in our form of civiliza-tion. This was the immediate cause of the late rupture and present revolution. Jeffer-son in his forecast, had anticipated this, as the "rock upon which the old Union would split." He was right. What was conjecture with him, is now a realized fact. But whether he fully comprehended the great truth upon which that rock *stood* and *stands,* may be doubted. The prevailing ideas entertained by him and most of the leading statesmen at the time of the formation of the old constitution, were that the enslavement of the African was in violation of the laws of nature; that it was wrong in *principle,* socially, morally, and politically. It was an evil they knew not well how to deal with, but the general opinion of the men of that day was that, somehow or other in the order of Providence, the institution would be evanescent and pass away. This idea, though not incorporated in the constitution, was the prevailing idea at that time. The constitution, it is true, secured every essential guarantee to the in-stitution while it should last, and hence no argument can be justly urged against the constitutional guarantees thus secured, because of the common sentiment of the day. Those ideas, however, were fundamentally wrong. They rested upon the as-sumption of the equality of races. This was an error. It was a sandy foundation, and the government built upon it fell, when the "storm came and the wind blew."

Our new government is founded upon exactly the opposite idea; its foundations are laid, its cornerstone rests upon the great truth, that the negro is not equal to the

Henry Cleveland, *Alexander H. Stephens in Public and Private* (Philadelphia: National Publishing Com-pany, 1866), pp. 721–23.

white man; that slavery—subordination to the superior race—is his natural and normal condition.

This, our new government, is the first, in the history of the world, based upon this great physical, philosophical, and moral truth. This truth has been slow in the process of its development, like all other truths in the various departments of science. It has been so even amongst us. Many who hear me, perhaps, can recollect well, that this truth was not generally admitted, even within their day. The errors of the past generation still clung to many as late as twenty years ago. Those at the North, who still cling to these errors, with a zeal above knowledge, we justly denominate fanatics. All fanaticism springs from an aberration of the mind—from a defect in reasoning. It is a species of insanity. One of the most striking characteristics of insanity, in many instances, is forming correct conclusions from fancied or erroneous premises; so with the anti-slavery fanatics; their conclusions are right if their premises were. They assume that the negro is equal, and hence conclude that he is entitled to equal privileges and rights with the white man. If their premises were correct, their conclusions would be logical and just—but their premise being wrong, their whole argument fails. I recollect once of having heard a gentleman from one of the northern States, of great power and ability, announce in the House of Representatives, with imposing effect, that we of the South would be compelled, ultimately, to yield upon this subject of slavery, that it was as impossible to war successfully against a principle in politics, as it was in physics or mechanics. That the principle would ultimately prevail. That we, in maintaining slavery as it exists with us, were warring against a principle, a principle founded in nature, the principle of the equality of men. The reply I made to him was, that upon his own grounds, we should, ultimately, succeed, and that he and his associates, in this crusade against our institutions, would ultimately fail. The truth announced, that it was as impossible to war successfully against a principle in politics as it was in physics and mechanics, I admitted; but told him that it was he, and those acting with him, who were warring against a principle. They were attempting to make things equal which the Creator had made unequal.

In the conflict thus far, success has been on our side, complete throughout the length and breadth of the Confederate States. It is upon this, as I have stated, our social fabric is firmly planted; and I cannot permit myself to doubt the ultimate success of a full recognition of this principle throughout the civilized and enlightened world.

As I have stated, the truth of this principle may be slow in development, as all truths are and ever have been, in the various branches of science. It was so with the principles announced by Galileo—it was so with Adam Smith and his principles of political economy. It was so with [William] Harvey, and his theory of the circulation of the blood. It is stated that not a single one of the medical profession, living at the time of the announcement of the truths made by him, admitted them. Now, they are universally acknowledged. May we not, therefore, look with confidence to the ultimate universal acknowledgment of the truths upon which our system rests? It is the first government ever instituted upon the principles in strict conformity to nature, and the ordination of Providence, in furnishing the materials of human society.

Many governments have been founded upon the principle of the subordination and serfdom of certain classes of the same race; such were and are in violation of the laws of nature. Our system commits no such violation of nature's laws. With us, all of the white race, however high or low, rich or poor, are equal in the eye of the law. Not so with the negro. Subordination is his place. He, by nature, or by the curse against Canaan, is fitted for that condition which he occupies in our system. The architect, in the construction of buildings, lays the foundation with the proper material—the granite; then comes the brick or the marble. The substratum of our society is made of the material fitted by nature for it, and by experience we know that it is best, not only for the superior, but for the inferior race, that it should be so. It is, indeed, in conformity with the ordinance of the Creator. It is not for us to inquire into the wisdom of his ordinances, or to question them. For his own purposes, he has made one race to differ from another, as he has made "one star to differ from another star in glory."

The great objects of humanity are best attained when there is conformity to his laws and decrees, in the formation of governments as well as in all things else: Our confederacy is founded upon principles in strict conformity with these laws. This stone which was rejected by the first builders "is become the chief of the corner"— the real "cornerstone"—in our new edifice.

I have been asked, what of the future? It has been apprehended by some that we would have arrayed against us the civilized world. I care not who or how many they may be against us, when we stand upon the eternal principles of truth, *if we are true to ourselves and the principles for which we contend,* we are obliged to, and must triumph.

Thousands of people who begin to understand these truths are not yet completely out of the shell; they do not see them in their length and breadth. We hear much of the civilization and christianization of the barbarous tribes of Africa. In my judgment, those ends will never be attained, but by first teaching them the lesson taught to Adam, that "in the sweat of his brow he should eat his bread," and teaching them to work, and feed, and clothe themselves.

The War Will Destroy Slavery

The fearful commotion that is now shaking the country to its foundation, is incomprehensible to human understanding, except as interpreted in the light of Divine Providence. God uses man to carry out his mysterious purposes. In this instance, the believer in an overruling Providence can readily comprehend that God has some great end to accomplish, and makes use of the differences of this people, on the slavery question, to bring it about. Men on either side are carried in one direction or the other against their will, and forced to take sides, however much they may resist. A couple of weeks ago, or less, the people were divided into parties. Each man had his place, and each side opposed violently the opposing parties. Now, looking at the North, we find men almost unanimous for the Government. Party lines are obliterated, and whatever a man may have formerly been, almost all now are determined to stand by the lawful authorities and establish the fact that we have a government competent to perpetuate its own unequaled privileges and to punish traitors. This is the common feeling which actuates the people of the North, and, to their honor be it said, a host of gallant Union men in the South. We have in mind scores and scores of Democrats and Bell men[1] in this State and elsewhere who have opposed the Republican party violently, but who now lose sight of party considerations and stand by the constituted authorities for the preservation of law, order, and liberty. . . .

Surely when we see such a great change in the public mind in so short a time, we can but think that the hand of Providence has specially brought it about for a great purpose. What that purpose is, we can only imagine. Perhaps Providence wishes to punish the people of this country for their pride, arrogance, and corruption. Perhaps we do not appreciate the unnumbered blessings that he has literally showered down on us. Perhaps we do not sufficiently prize the glorious boon of freedom and good government that he has vouchsafed us. And—not to multiply the surmises that crowd on us—perhaps God has instituted the present troubles to rid the country of the predominance of slavery in its public affairs. The whole country, North as well as South, has been instrumental in the endeavor to spread it over the continent, and to force it on unwilling people. While the South has been actively propagating and perpetuating the institution, the North has winked at the wrongful business and encouraged it.—Therefore, in the coming troubles, the North must not expect to escape the penalty of her lack of principle. She must suffer, like the South.

It may even be possible that Providence designs by means of these troubles to put a summary end to slavery. The institution has gone on to spread until it interferes materially with the progress of the Nation. Our country can never reach its full stature and importance so long as this baleful influence extends over it. It is a paradoxical state of things to see a country, which boasts of its freedom, nursing and sustaining the most odious system of slavery known on earth. This is against nature, and our country cannot long endure it, as a permanent arrangement. There is truly an "irrepressible conflict" between free and slave labor, and eventually the country must be all slave or all free, or the two parts must separate; which, we shall soon know. The only question is, when this will come to pass, and whether the time has now come for the final issue. A few weeks will decide this point. The events transpiring throughout the country indicate that the end is not far off.

This quarrel has been brought about against the earnest efforts of the North, and forced on her after the most surprising forbearance. "Whom the gods would destroy they first make mad" is an old adage. So it seems in the case of the Southern madcaps who have forced the country into this deplorable war for their own villainous purposes. If slavery is crushed out between the "upper and nether mill-stones" of

---

[1]John Bell was a Whig Senator from Tennessee who ran in 1860 for President on the Constitutional Union Party ticket. The Bell candidacy represented an effort to avoid the divisive sectional issues of the day—ED.

the opposing forces, those who brought this difficulty on the country can console themselves with the reflection that they themselves were the cause of its death.

The people of the North as a body have been willing to let slavery alone—to have nothing to do with it one way or the other. They have no other desire now. But if the war goes on, God only knows what will come to pass. This much is certain—the institution of slavery must be affected for better or worse. The principle of eternal right forbids that it should in this Nineteenth century be benefited by such a movement. We must conclude, then—and we have asserted the same thing before—that the contest sound[s] the death-knell of slavery. Thomas Jefferson said, that, in such a contest as the present, God has no attribute that could cause him to take sides with the slave-owners.—No person can doubt the issue of the conflict between Freedom and Slavery—Order and Disorder—Law and Anarchy, which has commenced. It must result in favor of the *right*. To believe otherwise, we must believe history to be a lie, and that Satan rules on earth, instead of a benignant and just Providence. And, if the peculiar institution is doomed to come to an end by the acts of its friends, who will mourn its loss? It has kept the country in a ferment since its organization and hindered its progress and it would be truly a God's blessing to be rid of it. So every patriot feels in his heart of hearts.

15.2: The War Is Over Constitutional Issues (1861)

If for many Northerners and Southerners the Civil War was a confrontation over slavery, to others it seemed a struggle for political freedom. Northerners who held this view saw secession as a fundamental challenge to the American experiment in free, democratic government, and Lincoln himself, in his immortal Gettysburg Address, drew this conclusion explicitly. Paradoxically, Southerners, although living in a slave society, also saw the Confederacy as fighting for liberty. The South, they said—the white South—was asserting its rights against northern oppression.

The first selection below is the inaugural address of Jefferson Davis, the Confederacy's first and only president. In what way does Davis's speech illustrate the shared political values of both sections? Does the phrase "consent of the governed," as used by Davis, have the same meaning as it would have for us today? Who among the South's population might Davis exclude from the category of the "governed"?

Lincoln's Inaugural Address also brought up the constitutional issues raised by secession and obviously arrived at different conclusions. Lincoln did address the issue of slavery in his first public speech as president, but, surprisingly, what did he say about it? How do Lincoln's and Davis' perception of the constitution differ? How does each view minority rights? Furthermore, what seemed to be the actual importance of the slavery issue at this critical point in time, when the war was breaking out? Did Lincoln's speech leave alternatives to war, or was the tragedy that followed essentially inevitable?

Inaugural Address

JEFFERSON DAVIS

Gentlemen of the Congress of the Confederate States of America:

. . . Our present position has been achieved in a manner unprecedented in the history of nations. It illustrates the American idea that government rests upon the consent of the governed, and that it is the right of the people to alter or abolish a government whenever it becomes destructive of the ends for which it was established. The declared purposes of the compact of Union from which we have withdrawn were to establish justice, insure domestic tranquility, to provide for the common defence, to promote the general welfare, and to secure the blessings of liberty for ourselves and our posterity; and when in the judgment of the sovereign States now comprising this Confederacy it had been perverted from the purposes for which it was ordained, and had ceased to answer the ends for which it was established, an appeal to the ballot-box declared that so far as they were concerned the government created by that compact should cease to exist. In this they merely asserted a right which the Declaration of Independence of 1776 defined to be inalienable. Of the time and occasion for its exercise, they, as sovereign, were the final judges each for itself. The impartial and enlightened verdict of mankind will vindicate the rectitude of our conduct, and He who knows the hearts of men will judge the sincerity with which we have labored to preserve the government of our fathers, in its spirit and in those rights inherent in it, which were solemnly proclaimed at the birth of the States, and which have been affirmed and re-affirmed in the Bills of Rights of the several States. When they entered into the Union of 1789, it was with the undeniable recognition of the power of the people to resume the authority delegated for the purposes of that government, whenever, in their opinion, its functions were perverted and its ends defeated. By virtue of this authority, the time and occasion requiring them to exercise it having arrived, the sovereign States here represented have seceded from that Union, and it is a gross abuse of language to denominate the act rebellion or revolution. They have formed a new alliance, but in each State its government has remained as before. The rights of person and property have not been disturbed. The agency through which they have communicated with foreign powers has been changed, but this does not necessarily interrupt their international relations. . . .

It must follow, therefore, that mutual interest would invite good will and kindness between them and us. If, however, passion or lust of dominion should cloud the judgment and inflame the ambition of these States, we must prepare to meet the emergency, and maintain, by the final arbitrament of the sword, the position we have assumed among the nations of the earth. We have now entered upon our career of independence, and it must be inflexibly pursued.

Southern Historical Papers, vol. 1 (January–June 1876), pp. 19–23.

Through many years of controversy with our late associates, the Northern States, we have vainly endeavored to secure tranquility and obtain respect for the rights to which we were entitled. As a necessity, not a choice, we have resorted to separation, and henceforth our energies must be devoted to the conducting of our own affairs, and perpetuating the Confederacy we have formed. If a just perception of mutual interest shall permit us peaceably to pursue our separate political career, my most earnest desire will have been fulfilled. But if this be denied us, and the integrity and jurisdiction of our territory be assailed, it will but remain for us with a firm resolve to appeal to arms and invoke the blessings of Providence upon a just cause.

As a consequence of our new constitution, and with a view to meet our anticipated wants, it will be necessary to provide a speedy and efficient organization of the several branches of the executive departments having special charge of our foreign intercourse, financial and military affairs, and postal service. For purposes of defence, the Confederate States may, under ordinary circumstances, rely mainly upon their militia; but it is deemed advisable, in the present condition of affairs, that there should be a well instructed, disciplined army, more numerous than would be usually required for a peace establishment.

I also suggest that for the protection of our harbors and commerce on the high seas, a navy adapted to those objects be built up. These necessities have doubtless engaged the attention of Congress.

With a constitution differing only in form from that of our forefathers, in so far as it is explanatory of their well known intents, freed from sectional conflicts which have so much interfered with the pursuits of the general welfare, it is not unreasonable to expect that the States from which we have parted may seek to unite their fortunes with ours under the government we have instituted. For this your constitution has made adequate provision, but beyond this, if I mistake not the judgment and will of the people, our reunion with the States from which we have separated is neither practicable nor desirable. To increase power, develop the resources, and promote the happiness of this Confederacy, it is necessary that there should be so much homogeneity as that the welfare of every portion be the aim of the whole. When this homogeneity does not exist, antagonisms are engendered which must and should result in separation.

Actuated solely by a desire to protect and preserve our own rights and promote our own welfare, the secession of the Confederate States has been marked by no aggression upon others, and followed by no domestic convulsion. . . .

Inaugural Address

ABRAHAM LINCOLN

. . . Apprehension seems to exist among the people of the Southern States that by the accession of a Republican administration their property and their peace and personal security are to be endangered. There has never been any reasonable cause for

Abraham Lincoln, First Inaugural Address, March 4, 1861. In *Messages and Papers*, James D. Richardson, ed. (Washington, DC: United States Government Printing Office, 1897), vol. VI, p. 588.

such apprehension. Indeed, the most ample evidence to the contrary has all the while existed and been open to their inspection. It is found in nearly all the published speeches of him who now addresses you. I do but quote from one of those speeches when I declare that "I have no purpose, directly or indirectly, to interfere with the institution of slavery in the States where it exists. I believe I have no lawful right to do so, and I have no inclination to do so." . . .

A disruption of the Federal Union, heretofore only menaced, is now formidably attempted.

I hold that, in contemplation of universal law and of the Constitution, the Union of these States is perpetual. Perpetuity is implied, if not expressed, in the fundamental law of all national governments. It is safe to assert that no government proper ever had a provision in its organic law for its own termination. Continue to execute all the express provisions of our national Constitution, and the Union will endure forever—it being impossible to destroy it except by some action not provided for in the instrument itself.

Again, if the United States be not a government proper, but an association of States in the nature of contract merely, can it as a contract be peaceably unmade by less than all the parties who made it? One party to a contract may violate it—break it, so to speak; but does it not require all to lawfully rescind it?

Descending from these general principles, we find the proposition that in legal contemplation the Union is perpetual confirmed by the history of the Union itself. The Union is much older than the Constitution. It was formed, in fact, by the Articles of Association in 1774. It was matured and continued by the Declaration of Independence in 1776. It was further matured, and the faith of all the then thirteen States expressly plighted and engaged that it should be perpetual, by the Articles of Confederation in 1778. And, finally, in 1787 one of the declared objects for ordaining and establishing the Constitution was "to form a more perfect Union."

But if the destruction of the Union by one or by a part only of the States be lawfully possible, the Union is less perfect than before the Constitution, having lost the vital element of perpetuity.

It follows from these views that no State upon its own mere motion can lawfully get out of the Union; that resolves and ordinances to that effect are legally void; and that acts of violence, within any State or States, against the authority of the United States, are insurrectionary or revolutionary, according to circumstances.

I therefore consider that, in view of the Constitution and the laws, the Union is unbroken; and to the extent of my ability I shall take care, as the Constitution itself expressly enjoins upon me, that the laws of the Union be faithfully executed in all the States. Doing this I deem to be only a simple duty on my part; and I shall perform it so far as practicable, unless my rightful masters, the American people, shall withhold the requisite means, or in some authoritative manner direct the contrary. I trust this will not be regarded as a menace, but only as the declared purpose of the Union that it will constitutionally defend and maintain itself.

In doing this there needs to be no bloodshed or violence; and there shall be none, unless it be forced upon the national authority. The power confided to me will be used to hold, occupy, and possess the property and places belonging to the

Government, and to collect the duties and imposts; but beyond what may be neces-sary for these objects, there will be no invasion, no using of force against or among the people anywhere. Where hostility to the United States, in any interior locality, shall be so great and universal as to prevent competent resident citizens from hold-ing the Federal offices, there will be no attempt to force obnoxious strangers among the people for that object. While the strict legal right may exist in the government to enforce the exercise of these offices, the attempt to do so would be so irritating, and so nearly impracticable withal, that I deem it better to forego for the time the uses of such offices. . . .

From questions of this class spring all our constitutional controversies, and we di-vide upon them into majorities and minorities. If the minority will not acquiesce, the majority must, or the Government must cease. There is no other alternative; for continuing the Government is acquiescence on one side or the other.

If a minority in such case will secede rather than acquiesce, they make a prece-dent which in turn will divide and ruin them; for a minority of their own will secede from them whenever a majority refuses to be controlled by such minority. For in-stance, why may not any portion of a new confederacy a year or two hence arbitrar-ily secede again, precisely as portions of the present Union now claim to secede from it? All who cherish disunion sentiments are now being educated to the exact temper of doing this.

Is there such perfect identity of interests among the States to compose a new Union as to produce harmony only, and prevent renewed secession?

Plainly, the central idea of secession is the essence of anarchy. A majority held in restraint by constitutional checks and limitations, and always changing easily with deliberate changes of popular opinions and sentiments, is the only true sovereign of a free people. Whoever rejects it does, of necessity, fly to anarchy or to despotism. Unanimity is impossible; the rule of a minority, as a permanent arrangement, is wholly inadmissible; so that, rejecting the majority principle, anarchy or despotism in some form is all that is left. . . .

One section of our country believes slavery is right, and ought to be extended, while the other believes it is wrong, and ought not to be extended. This is the only substantial dispute. The fugitive slave clause of the Constitution and the law for the suppression of the foreign slave trade are each as well enforced, perhaps, as any law can ever be in a community where the moral sense of the people imperfectly sup-ports the law itself. The great body of the people abide by the dry legal obligation in both cases, and a few break over in each. This, I think, cannot be perfectly cured; and it would be worse in both cases after the separation of the sections than before. The foreign slave trade, now imperfectly suppressed, would be ultimately revived, without restriction, in one section, while fugitive slaves, now only partially surren-dered, would not be surrendered at all by the other. . . .

Why should there not be a patient confidence in the ultimate justice of the peo-ple? Is there any better or equal hope in the world? In our present differences is ei-ther party without faith of being in the right? If the Almighty Ruler of nations, with his eternal truth and justice, be on your side of the North, or on yours of the South, that truth and that justice will surely prevail by the judgment of this great tribunal of the American people.

By the frame of the government under which we live, this same people have wisely given their public servants but little power for mischief; and have, with equal wisdom, provided for the return of that little to their own hands at very short intervals. While the people retain their virtue and vigilance, no administration, by any extreme of wickedness or folly, can very seriously injure the government in the short space of four years.

My countrymen, one and all, think calmly and well upon this whole subject. Nothing valuable can be lost by taking time. If there be an object to hurry any of you in hot haste to a step which you would never take deliberately, that object will be frustrated by taking time; but no good object can be frustrated by it. Such of you as are now dissatisfied still have the old Constitution unimpaired, and, on the sensitive point, the laws of your own framing under it; while the new administration will have no immediate power, if it would, to change either. If it were admitted that you who are dissatisfied hold the right side in the dispute, there still is no single good reason for precipitate action. Intelligence, patriotism, Christianity, and a firm reliance on Him who has never yet forsaken this favored land, are still competent to adjust in the best way all our present difficulty.

In your hands, my dissatisfied fellow-countrymen, and not in mine, is the momentous issue of civil war. The government will not assail you. You can have no conflict without being yourselves the aggressors. You have no oath registered in heaven to destroy the government, while I shall have the most solemn one to "preserve, protect, and defend" it.

I am loath to close. We are not enemies, but friends. We must not be enemies. Though passion may have strained, it must not break, our bonds of affection. The mystic chords of memory, stretching from every battle-field and patriot grave to every living heart and hearthstone all over this broad land, will yet swell the chorus of the Union when again touched, as surely they will be, by the better angels of our nature.

15.3: The War Is a Clash of Economic Interests (1860, 1861)

Contemporaries, as well as later historians, argued that the Civil War was at heart a confrontation of two societies defined by distinctive and antagonistic economic interests. The South's slave system, directly or obliquely, committed it to plantation agriculture; the North's free labor system and capitalist values committed it to commerce and industry. The two sections, this view notes, had fought major battles in Congress over tariffs, a Pacific railroad, a federally chartered bank, and the use of the national government generally to advance business enterprise. These struggles, then, must be considered in any analysis of the escalating sectional contention that ended in secession.

The selections below consider the Civil War as a contest of rival economic interests and the triumph in the end of northern commercial-industrial policies and values over southern agrarian ones.

The first piece is an editorial from the Vicksburg Daily Whig *of January 18, 1860, a year before actual secession. The* Whig, *as its name implies, was a Mississippi paper affiliated with the more traditionally conservative and unionist of the two southern parties. Southern Whigs were also more commercially oriented than southern Democrats. How are these characteristics revealed by the editorial below? There was less disagreement between southern Whigs and northern Republicans than between southern Democrats and Republicans, but this editorial nonetheless catches the flavor of southern economic resentment of the North. What are these resentments? How does the author express them?*

The next selection is from a speech delivered by Edward Everett of Massachusetts in July 1861, after actual fighting between the two sections had broken out. A Unitarian clergyman, Everett had served as Whig congressman and governor of his state. In 1860 he ran for vice president on the Constitutional Union Party ticket, a moderate group representing conservative unionists unwilling to support either Democrats or Republicans, both of whom they considered sectionally divisive.

In this document Everett defends the Union cause by seeking to refute the southern charge that the tariff, supported by northern business leaders and politicians, had oppressed Dixie. What are Everett's essential arguments? Are they convincing? Do you know which policy— northern protectionism (protariff) or southern free-trade (antitariff)— had prevailed in the years immediately preceding 1860? Was the tariff a major issue during the 1860 presidential campaign?

The North Opposed the South Economically

Vicksburg Daily Whig

Whilst this journal would by no means advocate the commercial independence of the South, as a distinctive measure, intended as an initiatory step for dissolving the Union; still, we are free to declare that, in our opinion, the South ought,

Vicksburg Daily Whig, January 18, 1860, in Dwight L. Dumond, ed., *Southern Editorials on Secession* (New York: Appleton-Century-Crofts, 1931), pp. 13–16.

without further delay, to commence a system of measures for her own protection. The Southern Conventions, as they are called, which have from time to time assembled, were not only abortive, but positively injurious. Those assemblages, indeed, were conceived in a spirit of Disunion, and were hot beds for the speedy propagation of *fire-eating* sentiments. Such being their character, this journal, of course, had no sympathies with them; nor did we ever expect any substantial good to spring from their deliberations. However, it is manifest to even a casual observer of ordinary intelligence, that the policy in trade and commerce uniformly pursued by the South is not only blind and simple, but absolutely suicidal to our pecuniary prosperity.

By mere supineness, the people of the South have permitted the Yankees to monopolize the carrying trade, with its immense profits. We have yielded to them the manufacturing business, in all its departments, without an effort, until recently, to become manufacturers ourselves. We have acquiesced in the claims of the North to do all the importing, and most of the exporting business, for the whole Union. Thus, the North has been aggrandised, in a most astonishing degree, at the expense of the South. It is no wonder that their villages have grown into magnificent cities. It is not strange that they have "merchant princes," dwelling in gorgeous palaces and reveling in luxuries transcending the luxurious appliances of the East! How could it be otherwise? New York city, like a mighty queen of commerce, sits proudly upon her island throne, sparkling in jewels and waving an undisputed commercial scepter over the South. By means of her railways and navigable streams, she sends out her *long arms* to the extreme South; and, with an avidity rarely equaled, grasps our gains and transfers them to herself—taxing us at every step—and depleting us as extensively as possible without actually destroying us. Meantime, the South remains passive—in a state of torpiditiy—making cotton bales for the North to manufacture, and constantly exerting ourselves to increase the production as much as possible. We have no ships in the foreign carrying trade, or very few indeed. No vessels enter Southern harbors (comparatively speaking) laden with the rich "merchandise" of foreign climes directly imported from those distant countries. We extend but little encouragement to the various mechanical arts, but buy most of our farming implements from the Northern people. Although Mississippi has within her limits an extensive seaboard, affording capacious and secure harbors, capable almost of sheltering the shipping of the world, still the blue waters of our harbors are unbroken by a single keel, save the diminutive fishing smacks which frequent those waters. Although nature hath prepared for us most beautiful positions for commercial cities, and pointed, with her unerring finger, to the advantages spread before our *blind eyes;* still, we have no seaboard cities, except so far as they exist in imagination, or are delineated *on paper,* or are shadowed forth in pompous resolutions emanating from disunion conventions! Why is this? Why are we so far behind in the great march of improvement? Simply because we have *failed to act* in obedience to the dictates of sound policy. Simply because we have been almost criminally neglectful of our own pecuniary interests. What should we do? What remedy have we?

Why, in the first place, let us withdraw one-third, or even one-half of our capital from agricultural operations, and invest it in the establishment of manufactures of cotton. Thus, we will greatly reduce the production of the raw material; and, as a necessary consequence, greatly enhance the market price of our great staple. The business of manufacturing the common cotton fabrics can be as profitably conducted here in Mississippi as it can be in Massachusetts. This fact has been demonstrated by the humble history of the few manufactures already operating in our State. It has been proven that the business of making cotton goods in Mississippi pays from 10 to 12 per cent profit per annum on the investment. Now, suppose we had extensive establishments for producing common fabrics of cotton in every county of Mississippi, created by Southern capital, and owned and worked by our own people; we could clothe ourselves at a small expense, comparatively, and sell the Yankees our surplus cloth, and thus realize a profit, instead of buying for ourselves. Consider the enhanced price of cotton, consequent upon the reduced supply; calculate the profits of manufacturing at home; refer to the opportunity we would thus have of becoming stock raisers, and producers of the small grains and fruits which our climate and soil are capable of maturing; and who does not see, at a glance, how eminently advantageous and profitable such a system would be. Connected with this policy, let us encourage the mechanical arts. Let us fabricate here all of our carriages and wagons; all of our farming implements; every article of furniture required by our people; and thus secure to ourselves an accession of valuable citizens, those multiplied thousands of industrious, honorable, moral artisans, who are producers, instead of consumers, and who are valuable, indeed, to any community that can secure their presence. Let us sedulously cultivate the sentiment, so true in itself, *that labor is honorable and dignified.* Lastly, let us at once begin the business of direct importation and direct exportation, and thus keep at home the millions of dollars which we annually pay to the North. The business of direct importation and direct exportation would, of course, build up, as if by the wand of a magician, splendid Southern cities of commercial grandeur and opulence; and thus we might become the most happy, prosperous, wealthy and intelligent people upon whom the sun has ever smiled. All this we should do—not in spitefulness—not in a spirit of envy—not with a view of breaking the ties of national Union—not with a design of engendering sectional animosity, but in obedience merely to the dictates of enlightened sectional policy, and in obedience to that universal principle, so well understood and acted upon by our Yankee friends, of consulting our own pecuniary interests, and adding to our general and individual pecuniary emoluments.

This is a fruitful topic. It might be spoken of in *volumes.* We have but glanced at it in the foregoing observations. After all, what we have penned, so far from being original suggestions, is but the recapitulation of self-evident propositions, suggesting themselves to every intelligent mind. It remains to be seen whether the South will awake from her ignoble slumber, and act for herself, or whether she will indolently remain inactive, and continue to be mere "hewers of wood and drawers of water," for the merchant princes of the North.

The North's Economic Grievances Against the South

EDWARD EVERETT

But the tariff is, with one exception, the alleged monster wrong—for which South Carolina in 1832[1] drove the Union to the verge of a civil war, and which, next to the slavery question, the South has been taught to regard as the most grievous of the oppressions which she suffers at the hands of the North, and that by which she seeks to win the sympathy of the manufacturing States of Europe. It was so treated in the debate referred to. I am certainly not going so far to abuse your patience, as to enter into a discussion of the constitutionality or expediency of the protective policy, on which I am aware that opinions at the North differ, nor do I deem it necessary to expose the utter fallacy of the monstrous paradox, that duties, enhancing the price of imported articles, are paid, not by the consumer of the merchandise imported, but by the producer of the last article of export given in exchange. It is sufficient to say that for this maxim, (the forty-bale theory so called,) which has grown into an article of faith at the South, not the slightest authority ever has been, to my knowledge, adduced from any political economist of any school. Indeed, it can be shown to be a shallow sophism, inasmuch as the *consumer* must be, directly or indirectly, the *producer* of the equivalents given in exchange for the article he consumes. But without entering into this discussion, I shall make a few remarks to show the great injustice of representing the protective system as being in its origin an oppression, of which the South has to complain on the part of the North.

Every such suggestion is a complete inversion of the truth of history. Some attempts at manufactures by machinery were made at the North before the Revolution, but to an inconsiderable extent. The manufacturing system as a great Northern interest is the child of the restrictive policy of 1807–1812, and of the war [of 1812]. That policy was pursued against the earnest opposition of the North, and to the temporary prostration of their commerce, navigation, and fisheries. Their capital was driven in this way into manufactures, and on the return of peace, the foundations of the protective system were laid in the square yard duty on cotton fabrics, in the support of which Mr. [John C.] Calhoun, advised that the growth of the manufacture would open a new market for the staple of the South, took the lead. As late as 1821 the Legislature of South Carolina unanimously affirmed the constitutionality of protective duties, though denying their expediency,—and of all the States of the Union Louisiana has derived the greatest benefit from this policy; in fact, she owes the sugar culture to it, and has for that reason given it her steady support. In all the tariff battles while I was a member of Congress, few votes were surer for the policy than that of Louisiana. If the duty on an article imported is considered as added to its price in our market, (which, however, is far from being invariably the case,) the

Frank Moore, ed., *The Rebellion Record: A Diary of American Events* (New York: G. P. Putnam, 1862), vol. 1, pp. 27–30.

[1]The Tariff of 1832, passed by Northern votes, so offended South Carolina leaders that they sought to nullify the measure, thereby precipitating a Constitutional crisis—ED.

sugar duty, of late, has amounted to a tax of five millions of dollars annually paid by the consumer, for the benefit of the Louisiana planter.

As to its being an unconstitutional policy, it is perfectly well known that the protection of manufactures was a leading and avowed object for the formation of the Constitution. The second law, passed by Congress after its formation, was a revenue law. Its preamble is as follows: "Whereas it is necessary for the support of Government, for the discharge of the debts of the United States, and the encouragement and protection of manufactures, that duties be laid on goods, wares, and merchandise imported." That act was reported to the House of Representatives by Mr. [James] Madison, who is entitled as much as any one to be called the father of the Constitution. While it was pending before the House, and in the first week of the first session of the first Congress, two memorials were presented praying for protective duties; and it is a matter of some curiosity to inquire, from what part of the country this first call came for that policy, now put forward as one of the acts of Northern oppression, which justify the South in flying to arms. The first of these petitions was from Baltimore. It implored the new Government to lay a protecting duty on all articles imported from abroad, which can be manufactured at home. The second was from the shipwrights, not of New York, not of Boston, not of Portland, but of Charleston, South Carolina, praying for "such a general regulation of trade and the establishment of such A NAVIGATION ACT, as will relieve the particular distresses of the petitioners, in common with those of their fellow-shipwrights throughout the Union"! and if South Carolina had always been willing to make common cause with their fellow-citizens throughout the Union, it would not now be rent by civil war.

The Cotton Culture Introduced Under Protection

But the history of the great Southern staple is most curious and instructive. His Majesty "King Cotton," on his throne, does not seem to be aware of the influences which surrounded his cradle. The culture of cotton, on any considerable scale, is well known to be of recent date in America. The house-hold manufacture of cotton was coeval with the settlement of the country. A century before the piano-forte or the harp was seen on this continent, the music of the spinning-wheel was heard at every fireside in town and country. The raw materials were wool, flax, and cotton, the last imported from the West Indies. The colonial system of Great Britain before the Revolution forbade the establishment of any other than household manufactures. Soon after the Revolution, cotton mills were erected in Rhode Island and Massachusetts, and the infant manufacture was encouraged by State duties on the imported fabric. The raw material was still derived exclusively from the West Indies. Its culture in this country was so extremely limited and so little known, that a small parcel sent from the United States to Liverpool in 1784 was seized at the custom-house there, as an illicit importation of British colonial produce. Even as late as 1794, and by persons so intelligent as the negotiators of [John] Jay's treaty, it was not known that cotton was an article of growth and export from the United States. In the twelfth article of that treaty, as laid before the Senate, Cotton was included with Molasses, Sugar, Coffee, and Cocoa, as articles which American vessels should not be permitted to carry from the islands *or from the United States* to any foreign country.

In the Revenue law of 1789, as it passed through the House of Representatives, cotton, with other raw materials, was placed on the free list. When the bill reached the Senate a duty of 3 cents per pound was laid upon cotton, not to encourage, not to protect, but to *create* the domestic culture. On the discussion of this amendment in the House, a member from South Carolina declared that "Cotton was in contemplation" in South Carolina and Georgia, "and *if good seed could be procured he hoped it might succeed.*" On this hope the amendment of the Senate was concurred in, and the duty of three cents per pound was laid on cotton. In 1791, [Alexander] Hamilton, in his report on the manufactures, recommended the repeal of this duty, on the ground that it was "a very serious impediment to the manufacture of cotton," but his recommendation was disregarded.

Thus, in the infancy of the cotton manufacture of the North, at the moment when they were deprived of the protection extended to them before the Constitution by State laws, and while they were struggling against English competition under the rapidly improving machinery of [Richard] Arkwright,[2] which it was highly penal to export to foreign countries, a heavy burden was laid upon them by this protecting duty, to enable the planters of South Carolina and Georgia to explore the tropics for a variety of cotton seed adapted to their climate. For seven years at least, and probably more, this duty was in every sense of the word a protecting duty. There was not a pound of cotton spun, no not for candle-wicks to light the humble industry of the cottages of the North, which did not pay this tribute to the Southern planter. The growth of the native article, as we have seen, had not in 1794 reached a point to be known to Chief Justice Jay as one of actual or probable export. As late as 1796, the manufacturers of Brandywine in Delaware petitioned Congress for the repeal of this duty on imported cotton, and the petition was rejected on the Report of a Committee, consisting of a majority from the Southern States, on the ground, that "to repeal the duty on raw cotton imported would be to damp the growth of cotton in our own country." Radicle and plumule, root and stalk, blossom and boll, the culture of the cotton plant in the United States was in its infancy the foster-child of the Protective System.

When therefore the pedigree of King Cotton is traced, he is found to be the lineal child of the tariff; called into being by a specific duty; reared by a tax laid upon the manufacturing industry of the North, to create the culture of the raw material in the South. The Northern manufacturers of America were slightly protected in 1789 because they were too feeble to stand alone. Reared into magnitude under the restrictive system and the war of 1812, they were upheld in 1816 because they were too important to be sacrificed, and because the great staple of the South had a joint interest in their prosperity. King Cotton alone, not in his manhood, not in his adolescence, not in his infancy, but in his very embryo state, was pensioned upon the Treasury,—before the seed from which he sprung was cast "in the lowest parts of the earth." In the book of the tariff "his members were written, which in continuance were fashioned, when as yet there were none of them."

---

[2]Inventor of the spinning jenny—ED.

But it was not enough to create the culture of cotton at the South, by taxing the manufactures of the North with a duty on the raw material; the extension of that culture and the prosperity which it has conferred upon the South are due to the mechanical genius of the North. What says Mr. Justice Johnson of the Supreme Court of the United States, and a citizen of South Carolina? "With regard to the utility of this discovery" (the cotton gin of [Eli] Whitney) "the court would deem it a waste of time to dwell long upon this topic. Is there a man who hears us that has not experienced its utility? The whole interior of the Southern States was languishing, and its inhabitants emigrating, for want of some object to engage their attention and employ their industry, when the invention of this machine at once opened views to them which set the whole country in active motion. From childhood to age it has presented us a lucrative employment. Individuals who were depressed in poverty and sunk in idleness, have suddenly risen to wealth and respectability. Our debts have been paid off, our capitals increased, and our lands trebled in value. We cannot express the weight of obligation which the country owes to this invention; the extent of it cannot now be seen."—Yes, and when happier days shall return, and the South, awakening from her suicidal delusion, shall remember who it was that sowed her sunny fields with the seeds of those golden crops with which she thinks to rule the world, she will cast a veil of oblivion over the memory of the ambitious men who have goaded her to her present madness, and will rear a monument of her gratitude in the beautiful City of Elms, over the ashes of her greatest benefactor—ELI WHITNEY.

15.4:   The Union's Advance Undermines Slavery (1863, 1865)

Lincoln offered the Confederacy guarantees to protect slavery when he was inaugurated in 1861, but the progress of war swiftly undermined the possibility that a Northern victory would leave the peculiar institution intact. Both sides increased war aims as time dragged on and human and material costs mounted. If most Northerners were primarily determined to save the Union in 1861, by 1863 they were eager to punish the South, even if that meant ending slavery. As public opinion against slavery hardened in the North, Lincoln found himself forced to cautiously and incrementally initiate an end to it.

Contrary to popular misconception, the Emancipation Proclamation of 1863 did not simply end slavery by Presidential Order. It was, however, a carefully calculated political initiative that did in fact begin the institution's legal demise. Lincoln's greatest speech, the brief but famous Gettysburg Address, delivered on November 19, 1863, revealed how dramatically sentiment had shifted against Southern slavery by that time. In reading Lincoln's words, what emotions do you experience? Both documents exude the deep pain of civil war, but do you sense that Lincoln had reached the conviction that the war's suffering was for a worthwhile purpose? In what other ways had Lincoln's vision become more clear by the second document?

Few African Americans doubted that a Northern victory would hasten the end of slavery. Most hoped it would improve their status. For free African Americans living in the North, the war provided an opportunity for inclusion, and many enlisted in the Union Army, hoping to see combat. However, it was often a bitter experience for them; many realized that even if the end of slavery was at hand, the hope of racial equality seemed an elusive dream. One of these volunteers, James Henry Gooding, appealed to President Lincoln in 1863 on behalf of all African American soldiers. What do his remarks suggest about the state of racial equality in the Union Army?

Not all Northerners anticipated the end of slavery with enthusiasm. The notorious New York City draft riots of 1863 contained a definite racist motif, as Irish immigrants feared emancipated slaves would migrate north and provide harsh competition for jobs at the lower end of the urban labor market. The enclosed letters from The New York Times *reveal the complexity of opinion in the North regarding emancipation and racial equality. What do you find most striking in their remarks, and why is it hard to generalize about how Northerners viewed slavery?*

Finally, how did Southerners respond to the end of slavery? All activities in Washington aside, in the final analysis it was the Union Army that marched through the South, ending slavery in each local district that it occupied. How did white Southerners respond to military occupation and its dramatic social consequences? The account of Constance Cary Harrison, a member of the Southern aristocracy, describes the fall of Richmond in April 1865. What do her words suggest for subsequent race relations in the South at the conclusion of the war?

The Emancipation Proclamation, January 1, 1863

By the President of the United States of America:

A Proclamation.

Whereas on the 22d day of September, A.D. 1862, a proclamation was issued by the President of the United States, containing, among other things, the following, to wit:

Abraham Lincoln, The Emancipation Proclamation, January 1, 1863 (Reprinted from *U.S. Statutes at Large,* vol. XII, pp. 1268–1269).

"That on the 1st day of January, A.D. 1863, all persons held as slaves within any State or designated part of a State the people whereof shall then be in rebellion against the United States shall be then, thenceforward, and forever free; and the executive government of the United States, including the military and naval authority thereof, will recognize and maintain the freedom of such persons and will do no act or acts to repress such persons, or any of them, in any efforts they may make for their actual freedom.

"That the executive will on the 1st day of January aforesaid, by proclamation, designate the States and parts of States, if any, in which the people thereof, respectively, shall then be in rebellion against the United States; and the fact that any State or the people thereof shall on that day be in good faith represented in the Congress of the United States by members chosen thereto at elections wherein a majority of the qualified voters of such States shall have participated shall, in the absence of strong countervailing testimony, be deemed conclusive evidence that such State and the people thereof are not then in rebellion against the United States."

Now, therefore, I, Abraham Lincoln, President of the United States, by virtue of the power in me vested as Commander-in-Chief of the Army and Navy of the United States in time of actual armed rebellion against the authority and government of the United States, and as a fit and necessary war measure for suppressing said rebellion, do, on this 1st day of January. A.D. 1863, and in accordance with my purpose so to do, publicly proclaimed for the full period of one hundred days from the first day above mentioned, order and designate as the States and parts of States wherein the people thereof, respectively, are this day in rebellion against the United States the following, to wit:

Arkansas, Texas, Louisiana (except the parishes of St. Bernard, Plaquemines, Jefferson, St. John, St. Charles, St. James, Ascension, Assumption, Terrebonne, Lafourche, St. Mary, St. Martin, and Orleans, including the city of New Orleans), Mississippi, Alabama, Florida, Georgia, South Carolina, North Carolina, and Virginia (except the forty-eight counties designated as West Virginia, and also the counties of Berkeley, Accomac, Northhampton, Elizabeth City, York, Princess Anne, and Norfolk, including the cities of Norfolk and Portsmouth), and which excepted parts are for the present left precisely as if this proclamation were not issued.

And by virtue of the power and for the purpose aforesaid, I do order and declare that all persons held as slaves within said designated States and parts of States are, and henceforward shall be free: and that the Executive Government of the United States, including the military and naval authorities thereof, will recognize and maintain the freedom of said persons.

And I hereby enjoin upon the people so declared to be free to abstain from all violence, unless in necessary self-defense; and I recommend to them that, in all cases when allowed, they labor faithfully for reasonable wages.

And I further declare and make known that such persons of suitable condition will be received into the armed service of the United States to garrison forts, positions, stations, and other places, and to man vessels of all sorts in said service.

And upon this act, sincerely believed to be an act of justice, warranted by the Constitution upon military necessity, I invoke the considerate judgment of mankind and the gracious favor of Almighty God.

The Gettysburg Address, November 19, 1863

ABRAHAM LINCOLN

Four score and seven years ago our fathers brought forth on this continent, a new nation, conceived in Liberty, and dedicated to the proposition that all men are created equal.

Now we are engaged in a great civil war, testing whether that nation, or any nation so conceived and so dedicated, can long endure. We are met on a great battlefield of that war. We have come here to dedicate a portion of that field, as a final resting place for those who here gave their lives that that nation might live. It is altogether fitting and proper that we should do this.

But, in a larger sense, we can not dedicate—we can not consecrate—we can not hallow—this ground. The brave men, living and dead, who struggled here, have consecrated it, far above our poor power to add or detract. The world will little note, nor long remember what we say here, but it can never forget what they did here. It is for us the living, rather, to be dedicated here to the unfinished work which they who fought here have thus far so nobly advanced. It is rather for us to be here dedicated to the great task remaining before us—that from these honored dead we take increased devotion to that cause for which they gave the last full measure of devotion—that we here highly resolve that these dead shall not have died in vain—that this nation, under God, shall have a new birth of freedom—and that government of the people, by the people, for the people, shall not perish from the earth.

An African American Soldier Appeals for Equality (1863)

JAMES HENRY GOODING

Your Excellency, Abraham Lincoln:

Your Excellency will pardon the presumption of an humble individual like myself, in addressing you, but the earnest solicitation of my comrades in arms besides the genuine interest felt by myself in the matter is my excuse, for placing before the Executive head of the Nation our Common Grievance.

On the 6th of the last Month, the Paymaster of the Department informed us, that if we would decide to receive the sum of $10 (ten dollars) per month, he would come and pay us that sum, but that, on the sitting of Congress, the Regt. would, in his opinion, be allowed the other 3 dollars. He did not give us any guarantee that this would be, as he hoped; certainly he had no authority for making any such guarantee, and we cannot suppose him acting in any way interested.

Now the main question is, are we Soldiers, or are we Laborers? We are fully armed, and equipped, have done all the various duties pertaining to a Soldier's life, have conducted ourselves to the complete satisfaction of General Officers,

Abraham Lincoln, Address at Gettysburg, Pa., November 19, 1863. Quoted from *The Writings of Abraham Lincoln,* Constitutional edition (New York and London: G. P. Putnam's Sons, 1905), Vol VII, p. 20.

Herbert Aptheker, *A Documentary History of the Negro People in the United States* (New York: Citadel Press, 1990), pp. 482–484.

who were, if anything, prejudiced against us, but who now accord us all the encouragement and honors due us; have shared the perils and labor of reducing the first strong-hold that flaunted a Traitor Flag; and more, Mr. President, to-day the Anglo-Saxon Mother, Wife, or Sister are not alone in tears for departed Sons, Husbands and Brothers. The patient, trusting descendant of Afric's Clime have dyed the ground with blood, in defence of the Union, and Democracy. Men, too, your Excellency, who know in a measure the cruelties of the iron heel of oppression, which in years gone by, the very power their blood is now being spilled to maintain, ever ground them in the dust.

But when the war trumpet sounded o'er the land, when men knew not the Friend from the Traitor, the Black man laid his life at the altar of the Nation,—and he was refused. When the arms of the Union were beaten, in the first year of the war, and the Executive called for more food for its ravenous maw, again the black man begged the privilege of aiding his country in her need, to be again refused.

And now he is in the War, and how has he conducted himself? Let their dusky forms rise up, out of the mires of James Island, and give the answer. Let the rich mould around Wagher's parapets be upturned, and there will be found an eloquent answer. Obedient and patient and solid as a wall are they. All we lack is a paler hue and a better acquaintance with the alphabet.

Now your Excellency, we have done a Soldier's duty. Why can't we have a Soldier's pay? You caution the Rebel chieftain, that the United States knows no distinction in her soldiers. She insists on having all her soldiers of whatever creed or color, to be treated according to the usages of War. Now if the United States exacts uniformity of treatment of her soldiers from the insurgents, would it not be well and consistent to set the example herself by paying all her soldiers alike?

We of this Regt. were not enlisted under any "contraband" act. But we do not wish to be understood as rating our service of more value to the Government than the service of the ex-slave. Their service is undoubtedly worth much to the Nation, but Congress made express provision touching their case, as slaves freed by military necessity, and assuming the Government to be their temporary Guardian. Not so with us. Freemen by birth and consequently having the advantage of thinking and acting for ourselves so far as the Laws would allow us, we do not consider ourselves fit subjects for the Contraband act.

We appeal to you, Sir, as the Executive of the Nation, to have us justly dealt with. The Regt. do pray that they be assured their service will he fairly appreciated by paying them as American Soldiers, not as menial hirelings. Black men, you may well know, are poor; three dollars per month, for a year, will supply their needy wives and little ones with fuel. If you, as Chief Magistrate of the Nation, will assure us of our whole pay, we are content. Our Patriotism, our enthusiasm will have a new impetus, to exert our hearts more and more to aid our Country. Not that our hearts ever flagged in devotion, spite the evident apathy displayed in our behalf, but we feel as though our Country spurned us, now we are sworn to serve her. Please give this a moments attention.

James Henry Gooding

The New York City Draft Riots (1863)

MONDAY NIGHT—UP TOWN.

To the Editor of the New-York Times:

You will, no doubt, be hard on us rioters tomorrow morning, but that 300-dollar law has made us nobodies, vagabonds and cast-outs of society, for whom nobody cares when we must go to war and be shot down. We are the poor rabble, and the rich rabble is our enemy by this law. Therefore we will give our enemy battle right here, and ask no quarter. Although we got hard fists, and are dirty without, we have soft hearts, and have clean consciences within, and that's the reason we love our wives and children more than the rich, because we got not much besides them; and we will not go and leave them at home for to starve. . . . Why don't they let the nigger kill the slave-driving race and take possession of the South, as it belongs to them.

A Poor Man, But A Man For All That.

.   .   .   .

The mob in our City is still rampant. Though the increasing display of armed force has done something to check its more flagrant outrages, it is yet wild with fury, and panting for fresh havoc. The very fact of its being withstood seems only to give it, for the time, new malignity; just as the wild beast never heaves with darker rage than when he begins to see that his way is barred. The monster grows more dangerous as he grows desperate. . . .

It is too true that there are public journals who try to dignify this mob by some respectable appellation. The *Herald* characterizes it as the people, and the *World* as the laboring men of the City. These are libels that ought to have paralyzed the fingers that penned them. It is ineffably infamous to attribute to the people, or to the laboring men of this metropolis, such hideous barbarism as this horde has been displaying. The people of New-York and the laboring men of New-York are not incendiaries, nor robbers, nor assassins. They do not hunt down men whose only offence is the color God gave them; they do not chase, and insult, and beat women; they do not pillage an asylum for orphan children, and burn the very roof over those orphans' heads. They are civilized beings, valuing law and respecting decency; and they regard with unqualified abhorrence the doings of the tribe of savages that have sought to bear rule in their midst.

This mob is not the people, nor does it belong to the people. It is for the most part made up of the very vilest elements of the City. It has not even the poor merit of being what mobs usually are—he product of mere ignorance and passion. They talk, or rather did talk at first, of the oppressiveness of the Conscription law; but three-fourths of those who have been actively engaged in violence have been boys and young men under twenty years of age, and not at all subject to the Conscription. Were the Conscription law to be abrogated to-morrow, the controlling inspiration of the mob would remain all the same. It comes from sources quite independent of that law, or any other—from malignant hate toward those in better circumstances, from a craving for plunder, from a love of commotion, from a barbarous spite against a different race, from a disposition to bolster up the failing fortunes of the Southern rebels. All of these influences operate in greater or less measure upon any person engaged in this general defiance of law; and all concerned have generated a composite monster more hellish than the triple-headed Cerberus. . . .

You may as well reason with the wolves of the forest as with these men in their present mood. It is quixotic and suicidal to attempt it. The duties of the executive officers of this State and City are not to debate, or negotiate, or supplicate, but to *execute the laws.* To execute means to enforce *by authority.* This is their *only* official business. Let it be promptly and sternly entered upon with all the means now available, and it cannot fail of being carried through to an overwhelming triumph of public order. It may cost blood—much of it perhaps; but it will be a lesson to the public enemies, whom we always have and must have in our midst, that will last for a generation. Justice and mercy, this time, unite in the same behest—*Give them grape, and a plenty of it.* . . .

OBJECT OF THE MOB. If this mob was originated in a passionate spirit of resistance to the Conscription law, it very soon changed its purpose, and assumed the character merely of a mob for robbery, plunder and arson. This is shown in the rifling of houses, hotels and stores, and the assaults and felonies upon the persons of unoffending citizens. Some of the ringleaders are noted thieves, who have served out several terms in Sing Sing and other penitentiaries and prisons. Hundreds of the workmen who joined with the crowd on Monday were, of course, as honest as the average of us, but they were at once joined by all the knaves of the City, who saw in the occasion an opportunity for plunder such as had never before presented itself. They made good use of their opportunity, as hundreds of unfortunate citizens can testify. The whole thing, if it continues, bids fair to become a gigantic mob of plunderers, with no more reference to the Conscription than to the Koran. It is remarkable, and almost incredible, how infectious this spirit becomes. A man who joins in such a mob as this many never have stolen a pin's worth in his life before, but when a jewelry store like that up town, or a mansion like those in Fifth-avenue, is broken into, the temptation is almost irresistible to rush in, and obtain a share of things. If this affair is allowed to go on, if it be not promptly put down, it will quickly result in a state of things such as was never before known in a civilized city. It is now a question of the protection of firesides, property and persons against general plunder. It has nothing to do with the conscription.

LAW AND LIBERTY.—It has heretofore been the boast of this country that liberty regulated by law was the principle which governed its citizens. The most perfect freedom to every man in every relation of life—freedom of person, of speech and in the pursuit of happiness, has been our glory, while the universally upheld governance of law has been the safety both of ourselves and of our liberty. The dominance of the mob strikes at the root of this great and special American principle. It reverts us back to semi-barbarism, and throws us forward into despotism. A mob is un-American, anti-American. Every grievance can here be remedied, every wrong can here be righted by *law,* which has its power in the will of the people and "its fountain in the bosom of God." It will be a dark day for the liberties of America, for its honor, its greatness, its power, its glory, when this excrescence of European despotism fastens itself upon our free institutions and society. Every man who prides himself in the name of American must use his determined efforts to drive back this black and deadly tide of human depravity.

A Lady of the Old South Describes the Fall of Richmond (1865)

MRS. BURTON HARRISON

Grace Street, Richmond, April 4, 1865.

My Precious Mother and Brother:

I write you this jointly, because I can have no idea where Clarence is. Can't you imagine with what a heavy heart I begin it—? The last two days have added long years to my life. I have cried until no more tears will come, and my heart throbs to bursting night and day. When I bade you good-bye, dear, and walked home alone, I could not trust myself to give another look after you. All that evening the air was full of farewells as if to the dead. Hardly anybody went to bed. We walked through the streets like lost spirits till nearly daybreak. My dearest mother, it is a special Providence that has spared you this! Your going to nurse poor Bert at this crisis has saved you a shock I never can forget. With the din of the enemy's wagon trains, bands, trampling horses, fifes, hurrahs and cannon ever in my ears, I can hardly write coherently. As you desired, in case of trouble, l left our quarters and came over here to be under my uncle's wing. In Aunt M.'s serious illness the house is overflowing; there was not a room or a bed to give me, but that made no difference, they insisted on my staying all the same. Up under the roof there was a lumber-room with two windows and I paid an old darkey with some wrecks of food left from our housekeeping, to clear it out, and scrub floor and walls and windows, till all was absolutely clean. A cot was found and some old chairs and tables—our own bed linen was brought over, and here I write in comparative comfort, so don't bother about me! . . .

The ending of the first day of occupation was truly horrible. Some negroes of the lowest grade, their heads turned by the prospect of wealth and equality, together with a mob of miserable poor whites, drank themselves mad with liquor scooped from the gutters. Reinforced, it was said, by convicts escaped from the penitentiary, they tore through the streets, carrying loot from the burnt district. (For days after, even the kitchens and cabins of the better class of darkies displayed handsome oil paintings and mirrors, rolls of stuff, rare books, and barrels of sugar and whiskey.) One gang of drunken rioters dragged coffins sacked from undertakers, filled with spoils from the speculators' shops, howling so madly one expected to hear them break into the Carmagnole. Thanks to our trim Yankee guard in the basement, we felt safe enough, but the experience was not pleasant.

Mrs. Burton Harrison, *Recollection, Grave and Gay* (New York: Charles Scribner's Sons, 1911), pp. 210–215.

Through all this strain of anguish ran like a gleam of gold the mad vain hope that Lee would yet make a stand somewhere—that Lee's dear soldiers would give us back our liberty.

Dr. Minnegerode has been allowed to continue his daily services and I never knew anything more painful and touching than that of this morning when the Litany was *sobbed out* by the whole congregation.

❖ *16* ❖

Reconstruction

In April 1865 the nation faced colossal problems of readjustment and repair. The South was a devastated region, its railroads, its banking system, and many of its towns and cities reduced to ruins. The human cost in the former Confederacy had been enormous. Thousands of young southern men had died or been maimed. Most difficult of all, in some ways, 4 million former slaves had been wrenched from their accustomed place within the South's social and labor systems and left without clear roles and firm moorings.

The new circumstances also raised urgent constitutional problems for the nation as a whole. Having fought to leave the Union, the South was now out of constitutional alignment with the rest of the states. Should the North accept the logic of its own position—that secession was illegal—and simply allow the former Confederate states to return to full constitutional status without conditions? That response would go easy on the ex-rebels and at the same time allow the southern states a free hand in dealing with the newly freed men and women. Could white southerners be trusted to be fair to the former slaves? Should erstwhile Confederates be allowed to resume their place in the Union without punishment for committing atrocities against Union prisoners, for violating federal oaths of office, for creating the mountain of dead and wounded the American people had suffered?

For over a decade following Confederate defeat, the nation's politics would be roiled by the debate over how to manage the Reconstruction process. Americans would be deeply divided. Congress would battle the president, southerners would battle northerners, whites would battle blacks, Democrats would battle Republicans. On each issue there would often be a bewildering array of positions not easily categorized as pro or con.

The documents below express a range of views on important Reconstruction problems. They do not exhaust the full spectrum of either opinions or issues on this complex event in our history; they are only a sample of how Americans thought. As you read the selections that follow, try to determine the gist of each argument and try to understand why particular individuals felt the way they did.

16.1:   Harsh Versus Lenient Victors (1865)

Besides being influenced by differing ideologies or philosophies, northern leaders were swayed in their approaches to Reconstruction by differences of temperament and personality. Abraham Lincoln, a pragmatist and a compassionate man, was inclined to make the return of the southern states to full constitutional equality a relatively easy process. In several states that had been occupied by Union forces before the final Confederate surrender, he was able to put his lenient policies in effect.

The first selection below is an excerpt from Lincoln's last recorded address, remarks he made from the White House balcony to a group of citizens who had come to "serenade" him just four days before his death by an assassin's bullet. Lincoln discusses the issue of the constitutional status of the seceded states, a legalistic issue that had important implications for policy. If it was held that the southern states had never actually left the Union, then they remained sovereign entities like the other states, and Washington had only limited powers over them. But if it was decided that they had *left the Union and reverted to territorial status, as some believed, then Congress could constitutionally impose a wide range of conditions on them.*

What does Lincoln say about this issue? What is his overall tone? Was his estimate of the best thing for the nation to do valid in light of all that followed? How would you characterize Lincoln's views of the rights of the former slaves?

The second selection is a May 1865 proclamation by President Andrew Johnson establishing a provisional government for South Carolina. In the next two months Johnson issued six other proclamations establishing governments for other former Confederate states.

Johnson was himself a southerner (from Tennessee), but a strong unionist who had refused to disavow his government when his state seceded. Like Lincoln, he believed the southern states should be readmitted to the Union with as few preconditions as possible. What preconditions are imposed by the president's proclamation? Are they severe?

What obvious conditions that might have been imposed are omitted? Is there any mention of a role for Congress in the Reconstruction process? Should Johnson have assumed sole leadership in this all-important matter?

The third selection is from a speech by Representative Thaddeus Stevens of Pennsylvania. Stevens was a "Radical Republican." During the war he had, as other Radicals, pushed for the early emancipation of the slaves and aggressive policies against the Confederacy and its leaders. After the war he and his fellow Radicals would demand that the South be compelled to repudiate its prewar planter leadership and guarantee equal social and political rights for the freedmen.[1] Southerners and conservative northerners, mostly Democrats, would call Stevens and his colleagues mean-spirited "vindictives," who lacked Christian compassion toward their former enemies and were moved primarily by partisan political ends.

After Lincoln's assassination, Stevens rallied the congressional opposition to President Johnson's lenient Reconstruction policy. He and his supporters would seize from the president the management of the Reconstruction process. Ultimately they would break completely with Johnson, and in 1868 the Radical-controlled Congress would impeach the president—although not convict him—for defying the will and the laws of Congress.

From the excerpt below, would you say that Stevens deserves to be considered vindictive? Do his sympathies for the freed slaves seem sincere? Does his reference to "perpetual ascendency to the party of the Union" seem like a blatant grab for power by Republicans? Putting yourself in Stevens's shoes, how can such a partisan position be justified?

Reconstruction Must Be Gradual and Careful

ABRAHAM LINCOLN

I have been shown a letter . . . in which the writer expresses regret that my mind has not seemed to be definitely fixed upon the question whether the seceded States, so called, are in the Union or out of it. I would perhaps add astonishment to his regret were he to learn that since I have found professed Union men endeavoring to answer that question, I have purposely forborne any public expression upon it. As

Arthur B. Lapsley, *Writings of Abraham Lincoln* (New York: G. P. Putnam's Sons, 1906), vol. 7, pp. 362–68.
[1] Though the term might seem sexist today it was used to refer to *all* the freed slaves after 1865, and it is still so used—ED.

appears to me, that question has not been nor yet is a practically material one, and that any discussion of it, while it thus remains practically immaterial, could have no effect other than the mischievous one of dividing our friends. As yet, whatever it may become, that question is bad as the basis of a controversy, and good for nothing at all—a merely pernicious abstraction. We all agree that the seceded States, so called, are out of their proper practical relation with the Union, and that the sole object of the Government, civil and military, in regard to these States, is to again get them into their proper practical relation. I believe that is not only possible, but in fact [it is] easier to do this without deciding or even considering whether these States have ever been out of the Union, than with it. Finding themselves safely at home, it would be utterly immaterial whether they have been abroad. Let us all join in doing the act necessary to restore the proper practical relations between these States and the Union, and each forever after innocently indulge his own opinion whether, in doing the acts, he brought the States from without the Union, or only gave them proper assistance, they never having been out of it. The amount of constituency, so to speak, on which the Louisiana government rests, would be more satisfactory to all if it contained fifty thousand, or thirty thousand, or even twenty thousand, instead of twelve thousand, as it does. It is also unsatisfactory to some that the elective franchise is not given to the colored man. I would myself prefer that it were now conferred on the very intelligent, and on those who serve our cause as soldiers. Still, the question is not whether the Louisiana government, as it stands, is quite all that is desirable. The question is, Will it be wiser to take it as it is and help to improve it, or to reject and disperse [sic]? Can Louisiana be brought into proper practical relation with the Union sooner by sustaining or by discarding her new State government? Some twelve thousand voters in the heretofore Slave State of Louisiana have sworn allegiance to the Union, assumed to be the rightful political power of the State, held elections, organized a State government, adopted a Free State constitution, giving the benefit of public schools equally to black and white, and empowering the Legislature to confer the elective franchise upon the colored man. This Legislature has already voted to ratify the Constitutional Amendment recently passed by Congress, abolishing slavery throughout the nation. These twelve thousand persons are thus fully committed to the Union, and to perpetuate freedom in the State—committed to the very things, and nearly all things, the nation wants—and they ask the nation's recognition and its assistance to make good this committal. Now, if we reject and spurn them, we do our utmost to disorganize and disperse them. We, in fact, say to the white man: You are worthless or worse; we will neither help you nor be helped by you. To the blacks we say: This cup of liberty which these, your old masters, held to your lips, we will dash from you, and leave you to the chances of gathering the spilled and scattered contents in some vague and undefined when, where, and how. If this course, discouraging and paralyzing both white and black, has any tendency to bring Louisiana into proper practical relations with the Union, I have so far been unable to perceive it. If, on the contrary, we recognize and sustain the new government of Louisiana, the converse of all this is made true. We encourage the hearts and nerve the arms of twelve thousand to adhere to their work, and argue for it, and proselyte for it, and fight for it, and feed it, and grow it, and ripen it to a complete success. The colored man, too, in seeing all united for him, is inspired with vigilance, and energy, and daring to the same end. Grant that he desires the elective franchise, will he not attain it sooner by saving the already advanced steps towards it, than by running backward over them? Concede that the new government of Louisiana is only to what it should be as the egg is to the fowl, we shall sooner have the fowl by hatching the egg than by smashing it. Again, if we reject Louisiana, we also reject one vote in favor of the proposed amendment to the National Constitution. To meet this proposition, it has been argued that no more than three fourths of those States which have not attempted secession are necessary to validly ratify the amendment. I do not commit myself against this, further than to say that such a ratification would be questionable, and sure to be persistently questioned, while a ratification by three fourths of all the States would be unquestioned and unquestionable. I repeat the question, Can Louisiana be brought into proper practical relation with the Union sooner by sustaining or by discarding her new State government? What has been said of Louisiana will apply to other States. And yet so great peculiarities pertain to each State, and such important and sudden changes occur in the same State, and withal so new and unprecedented is the whole case, that no exclusive and inflexible plan can safely be prescribed as to details and collaterals. Such exclusive and inflexible plan would surely become a new entanglement. Important principles may and must be inflexible. In the present situation as the phrase goes, it may be my duty to make some new announcement to the people of the South. I am considering, and shall not fail to act, when satisfied that action will be proper.

Amnesty Proclamation

ANDREW JOHNSON

By the President of the United States of America. A Proclamation.

Whereas the fourth section of the fourth article of the Constitution of the United States declares that the United States shall guarantee to every State in the Union a republican form of government and shall protect each of them against invasion and domestic violence; and

Whereas the President of the United States is by the Constitution made Commander in Chief of the Army and Navy, as well as chief civil executive officer of the United States, and is bound by solemn oath faithfully to execute the office of President of the United States and to take care that the laws be faithfully executed; and

Whereas the rebellion which has been waged by a portion of the people of the United States against the properly constituted authorities of the Government thereof in the most violent and revolting form, but whose organized and armed forces have

James D. Richardson, ed., *A Compilation of the Messages and Papers of the Presidents* (New York: Bureau of National Literature, 1897), vol. 8, pp. 3508–10.

now been almost entirely overcome, has in its revolutionary progress deprived the people of the State of South Carolina of all civil government; and

Whereas it becomes necessary and proper to carry out and enforce the obligations of the United States to the people of South Carolina in securing them in the enjoyment of a republican form of government:

Now, therefore, in obedience to the high and solemn duties imposed upon me by the Constitution of the United States and for the purpose of enabling the loyal people of said State to organize a State government whereby justice may be established, domestic tranquillity insured, and loyal citizens protected in all their rights of life, liberty, and property, I, Andrew Johnson, President of the United States and Commander in Chief of the Army and Navy of the United States, do hereby appoint Benjamin F. Perry, of South Carolina, provisional governor of the State of South Carolina, whose duty it shall be, at the earliest practicable period, to prescribe such rules and regulations as may be necessary and proper for convening a convention composed of delegates to be chosen by that portion of the people of said State who are loyal to the United States, and no others, for the purpose of altering or amending the constitution thereof, and with authority to exercise within the limits of said State all the powers necessary and proper to enable such loyal people of the State of South Carolina to restore said State to its constitutional relations to the Federal Government and to present such a republican form of State government as will entitle the State to the guaranty of the United States therefor and its people to protection by the United States against invasion, insurrection, and domestic violence: *Provided,* That in any election that may be hereafter held for choosing delegates to any State convention as aforesaid no person shall be qualified as an elector or shall be eligible as a member of such convention unless he shall have previously taken and subscribed the oath of amnesty as set forth in the President's proclamation of May 29, A.D. 1865, and is a voter qualified as prescribed by the constitution and laws of the State of South Carolina in force immediately before the 17th day of November, A.D. 1860, the date of the so-called ordinance of secession; and the said convention, when convened, or the legislature that may be thereafter assembled, will prescribe the qualification of electors and the eligibility of persons to hold office under the constitution and laws of the State—a power the people of the several States composing the Federal Union have rightfully exercised from the origin of the Government to the present time.

And I do hereby direct—

First. That the military commander of the department and all officers and persons in the military and naval service aid and assist the said provisional governor in carrying into effect this proclamation; and they are enjoined to abstain from in any way hindering, impeding, or discouraging the loyal people from the organization of a State government as herein authorized.

Second. That the Secretary of State proceed to put in force all laws of the United States the administration whereof belongs to the State Department applicable to the geographical limits aforesaid.

Third. That the Secretary of the Treasury proceed to nominate for appointment assessors of taxes and collectors of customs and internal revenue and such other officers of the Treasury Department as are authorized by law and put in execution the revenue laws of the United States within the geographical limits aforesaid. In making appointments the preference shall be given to qualified loyal persons residing within the districts where their respective duties are to be performed; but if suitable residents of the districts shall not be found, then persons residing in other States or districts shall be appointed.

Fourth. That the Postmaster-General proceed to establish post-offices and post routes and put into execution the postal laws of the United States within the said State, giving to loyal residents the preference of appointment; but if suitable residents are not found, then to appoint agents, etc., from other States.

Fifth. That the district judge for the judicial district in which South Carolina is included proceed to hold courts within said State in accordance with the provisions of the act of Congress. The Attorney-General will instruct the proper officers to libel and bring to judgment, confiscation, and sale property subject to confiscation and enforce the administration of justice within said State in all matters within the cognizance and jurisdiction of the Federal courts.

Sixth. That the Secretary of the Navy take possession of all public property belonging to the Navy Department within said geographical limits and put in operation all acts of Congress in relation to naval affairs having application to the said State.

Seventh. That the Secretary of the Interior put in force the laws relating to the Interior Department applicable to the geographical limits aforesaid.

We Must Have a Radical Reconstruction

THADDEUS STEVENS

It is obvious . . . that the first duty of Congress is to pass a law declaring the condition of these outside or defunct States, and providing proper civil governments for them. Since the conquest they have been governed by martial law. Military rule is necessarily despotic, and ought not to exist longer than is absolutely necessary. As there are no symptoms that the people of these provinces will be prepared to participate in constitutional government for some years, I know of no arrangement so proper for them as territorial governments. There they can learn the principles of freedom and eat the fruit of foul rebellion. Under such governments, while electing members to the Territorial Legislatures, they will necessarily mingle with those to whom Congress shall extend the right of suffrage. In Territories Congress fixes the qualifications of electors; and I know of no better place nor better occasion for the conquered rebels and the conqueror to practice justice to all men, and accustom themselves to make and to obey equal laws.

As these fallen rebels cannot at their option reënter the heaven which they have disturbed, the garden of Eden which they have deserted, and flaming swords are set

Congressional Globe, 39th Cong., 1st sess., December 18, 1865, pp. 72–75.

at the gates to secure their exclusion, it becomes important to the welfare of the nation to inquire when the doors shall be reopened for their admission.

According to my judgment they ought never to be recognized as capable of acting in the Union, or of being counted as valid States, until the Constitution shall have been so amended as to make it what its framers intended; and so as to secure perpetual ascendency to the party of the Union; and so as to render our republican Government firm and stable forever. The first of those amendments is to change the basis of representation among the States from Federal numbers to actual voters. Now all the colored freemen in the slave States, and three fifths of the slaves, are represented, though none of them have votes. The States have nineteen representatives of colored slaves. If the slaves are now free then they can add, for the other two fifths, thirteen more, making the slave representation thirty-two. I suppose the free blacks in those States will give at least five more, making the representation of non-voting people of color about thirty-seven. The whole number of representatives now from the slave States is seventy. Add the other two fifths and it will be eighty-three.

If the amendment prevails, and those States withhold the right of suffrage from persons of color, it will deduct about thirty-seven, leaving them but forty-six. With the basis unchanged, the eighty-three southern members, with the Democrats that will in the best times be elected from the North, will always give them a majority in Congress and in the Electoral College. They will at the very first election take possession of the White House and the halls of Congress. I need not depict the ruin that would follow. Assumption of the rebel debt or repudiation of the Federal debt would be sure to follow. The oppression of the freedmen; the reamendment of their State constitutions, and the reëstablishment of slavery would be the inevitable result. That they would scorn and disregard their present constitutions, forced upon them in the midst of martial law, would be both natural and just. No one who has any regard for freedom of elections can look upon those governments, forced upon them in duress, with any favor. If they should grant the right of suffrage to persons of color, I think there would always be Union white men enough in the South, aided by the blacks, to divide the representation, and thus continue the Republican ascendency. If they should refuse to thus alter their election laws it would reduce the representatives of the late slave States to about forty-five and render them powerless for evil.

It is plain that this amendment must be consummated before the defunct States are admitted to be capable of State action, or it never can be. . . .

But this is not all that we ought to do before these inveterate rebels are invited to participate in our legislation. We have turned, or are about to turn, loose four million slaves without a hut to shelter them or a cent in their pockets. The infernal laws of slavery have prevented them from acquiring an education, understanding the commonest laws of contract, or of managing the ordinary business of life. This Congress is bound to provide for them until they can take care of themselves. If we do not furnish them with homesteads, and hedge them around with protective laws; if we leave them to the legislation of their late masters, we had better have left them in bondage. Their condition would be worse than that of our prisoners at Andersonville. If we fail in this great duty now, when we have the power, we shall deserve and receive the execration of history and of all future ages. . . .

This Congress owes it to its own character to set the seal of reprobation upon a doctrine which is becoming too fashionable, and unless rebuked will be the recognized principle of our Government. Governor Perry[1] and other provisional governors and orators proclaim that "this is the white man's Government." The whole copperhead party, pandering to the lowest prejudices of the ignorant, repeat the cuckoo cry, "This is the white man's Government." Demagogues of all parties, even some high in authority, gravely shout, "This is the white man's Government." What is implied by this? That one race of men are to have the exclusive right forever to rule this nation, and to exercise all acts of sovereignty, while all other races and nations and colors are to be their subjects, and have no voice in making the laws and choosing the rulers by whom they are to be governed. Wherein does this differ from slavery except in degree? Does not this contradict all the distinctive principles of the Declaration of Independence? When the great and good men promulgated that instrument, and pledged their lives and sacred honors to defend it, it was supposed to form an epoch in civil government. Before that time it was held that the right to rule was vested in families, dynasties, or races, not because of superior intelligence or virtue, but because of a divine right to enjoy exclusive privileges.

Our fathers repudiated the whole doctrine of the legal superiority of families or races, and proclaimed the equality of men before the law. Upon that they created a revolution and built the Republic. They were prevented by slavery from perfecting the superstructure whose foundation they had thus broadly laid. For the sake of the Union they consented to wait, but never relinquished the idea of its final completion. The time to which they looked forward with anxiety has come. It is our duty to complete their work. If this Republic is not now made to stand on their great principles, it has no honest foundation, and the Father of all men will still shake it to its center. If we have not yet been sufficiently scourged for our national sin to teach us to do justice to all God's creatures, without distinction of race or color, we must expect the still more heavy vengeance of an offended Father, still increasing his inflictions as he increased the severity of the plagues of Egypt until the tyrant consented to do justice. And when that tyrant repented of his reluctant consent, and attempted to re-enslave the people, as our southern tyrants are attempting to do now, he filled the Red sea with broken chariots and drowned horses, and strewed the shores with dead carcasses.

Mr. Chairman, I trust the Republican party will not be alarmed at what I am saying. I do not profess to speak their sentiments, nor must they be held responsible for them. I speak for myself, and take the responsibility, and will settle with my intelligent constituents.

This is not a "white man's Government," in the exclusive sense in which it is used. To say so is political blasphemy, for it violates the fundamental principles of our gospel of liberty. This is man's Government; the Government of all men alike;

---

[1]Benjamin F. Perry of South Carolina, a Unionist rewarded by Johnson with an appointment as provisional governor of the state—ED.

not that all men will have equal power and sway within it. Accidental circumstances, natural and acquired endowment and ability, will vary their fortunes. But equal rights to all the privileges of the Government is innate in every immortal being, no matter what the shape or color of the tabernacle which it inhabits.

If equal privileges were granted to all, I should not expect any but white men to be elected to office for long ages to come. The prejudice engendered by slavery would not soon permit merit to be preferred to color. But it would still be beneficial to the weaker races. In a country where political divisions will always exist, their power, joined with just white men, would greatly modify, if it did not entirely prevent, the injustice of majorities. Without the right of suffrage in the late slave States, (I do not speak of the free States.) I believe the slaves had far better been left in bondage. I see it stated that very distinguished advocates of the right of suffrage lately declared in this city that they do not expect to obtain it by congressional legislation, but only by administrative action, because, as one gallant gentleman said, the States had not been out of the Union. Then they will never get it. The President is far sounder than they. He sees that administrative action has nothing to do with it. If it ever is to come, it must be constitutional amendments or congressional action in the Territories, and in enabling acts.

How shameful that men of influence should mislead and miseducate the public mind! They proclaim, "This is the white man's Government," and the whole coil of copperheads echo the same sentiment, and upstart, jealous Republicans join the cry. Is it any wonder ignorant foreigners and illiterate natives should learn this doctrine, and be led to despise and maltreat a whole race of their fellow-men?

Sir, this doctrine of a white man's Government is as atrocious as the infamous sentiment that damned the late Chief Justice [Roger Taney] to everlasting fame; and, I fear, to everlasting fire.

16.2: The White South Responds (1865, 1866, 1868, 1874)

White southerners were themselves divided over Reconstruction. In the immediate aftermath of Confederate surrender, many were too stunned to resist the North's dictation. But that mood did not last very long. In a matter of months many southern leaders, including former Confederate officials, had regained their composure and were preparing to salvage what they could from the shambles of defeat. Under the state governments reestablished under President Johnson's auspices, they resisted major changes in relations between the races and refused to express contrition at their section's secessionist past. When Thaddeus Stevens and his Radical allies in Congress imposed more stringent conditions, they fought back even harder.

The first selection below is an example of the Black Codes passed by the conservative southern state governments established under Johnson's 1865 proclamations. These state laws were designed to regularize legal relations between blacks and the dominant white society now that slavery was gone. They accepted the end of slavery, but in most cases they cast blacks as inferior beings, not full citizens, and even placed them in jeopardy of quasi-reenslavement.

Among the harshest of the state Black Codes was that of Mississippi, a state, like South Carolina, with a black majority in its population. What elements of this code implied recognition of the end of the slave system? What provisions suggest that white Mississippians were not willing to accord the freed men and women full equality? Can you see from this document why black leaders and Radical Republicans considered Johnson's Reconstruction policy too lenient?

A substantial minority of native-born white southerners for a time came to terms with the Radical state administrations imposed by Congress when it seized control of Reconstruction policy. Called "scalawags," these Republican voters were particularly numerous in the former nonslaveholding parts of the South and among businessmen of Whig antecedents. To scalawags, the enemy was often the former planter elite that had pulled the South into a disastrous war, not the Republican politicians in Washington. Joining with blacks, newly enfranchised under the Fourteenth and Fifteenth Amendments to the Constitution, and with "carpetbaggers"—northern whites who came South to make their fortunes after 1865—they won control for a time over the state governments established under the Reconstruction Acts.

The second document is by a scalawag. James W. Hunnicutt was a South Carolina Baptist minister who had originally supported secession and then changed his mind. The selection is his testimony before the congressional Joint Committee on Reconstruction in early 1866. Why does Hunnicutt emphasize the treatment of white unionists in the South? Do you feel that the questioner, Radical Republican Senator Jacob Howard of Michigan, is leading the witness?

The third item in this section represents the position of the "redeemers," the ardent white conservatives who fought to wrest political supremacy from the Radical Republicans who controlled the state Reconstruction governments.

An editorial from the Atlanta News *of September 10, 1874, it charges the Republicans and blacks with barbarism. Were the charges valid? Do you know if the Radical regimes in the South were more corrupt, wasteful, and incompetent than state governments elsewhere during this era? Were the charges based more on race prejudice than on reality? How do you explain the vitriol of the conservative southern attack on the Radical regimes?*

Mississippi Black Code

MISSISSIPPI LEGISLATURE

1. Civil Rights of Freedmen in Mississippi

Sec. 1. *Be it enacted,* . . . That all freedmen, free negroes, and mulattoes may sue and be sued, implead and be impleaded, in all the courts of law and equity of this State, and may acquire personal property, and choses [sic] in action, by descent or purchase, and may dispose of the same in the same manner and to the same extent that white persons may: *Provided,* That the provisions of this section shall not be so construed as to allow any freedman, free negro, or mulatto to rent or lease any lands or tenements except in incorporated cities or towns, in which places the corporate authorities shall control the same. . . .

Sec. 3. . . . All freedmen, free negroes, or mulattoes who do now and have here-before lived and cohabited together as husband and wife shall be taken and held in law as legally married, and the issue shall be taken and held as legitimate for all purposes; that it shall not be lawful for any freedman, free negro, or mulatto to in-termarry with any white person; nor for any white person to intermarry with any freedman, free negro, or mulatto; and any person who shall so intermarry, shall be deemed guilty of felony, and on conviction thereof shall be confined in the State penitentiary for life; and those shall be deemed freedmen, free negroes, and mulat-toes who are of pure negro blood, and those descended from a negro to the third generation, inclusive, though one ancestor in each generation may have been a white person.

Sec. 4. . . . In addition to cases in which freedmen, free negroes, and mulattoes are now by law competent witnesses, freedmen, free negroes, or mulattoes shall be competent in civil cases, when a party or parties to the suit, either plaintiff or plain-tiffs, defendant or defendants, and a white person or white persons, is or are the op-posing party or parties, plaintiff or plaintiffs, defendant or defendants. They shall also be competent witnesses in all criminal prosecutions where the crime charged is alleged to have been committed by a white person upon or against the person or property of a freedman, free negro, or mulatto: *Provided,* that in all cases said wit-nesses shall be examined in open court, on the stand; except, however, they may be examined before the grand jury, and shall in all cases be subject to the rules and tests of the common law as to competency and credibility. . . .

Laws of the State of Mississippi Passed at the Regular Session of the Mississippi Legislature, Held in the City of Jackson, October–December, 1865 (Jackson: J. J. Shannon and Company, 1866), pp. 82–93.

Sec. 6. . . . All contracts for labor made with freedmen, free negroes, and mulattoes for a longer period than one month shall be in writing, and in duplicate, attested and read to said freedman, free negro, or mulatto by a beat, city or county officer, or two disinterested white persons of the county in which the labor is to be performed, of which each party shall have one; and said contracts shall be taken and held as entire contracts, and if the laborer shall quit the service of the employer before the expiration of his term of service, without good cause, he shall forfeit his wages for that year up to the time of quitting.

Sec. 7. . . . Every civil officer shall, and every person may, arrest and carry back to his or her legal employer any freedman, free negro, or mulatto who shall have quit the service of his or her employer before the expiration of his or her term of service without good cause; and said officer and person shall be entitled to receive for arresting and carrying back every deserting employe aforesaid the sum of five dollars, and ten cents per mile from the place of arrest to the place of delivery; and the same shall be paid by the employer, and held as a set-off for so much against the wages of said deserting employe: *Provided,* that said arrested party, after being so returned, may appeal to the justice of the peace or member of the board of police of the county, who, on notice to the alleged employer, shall try summarily whether said appellant is legally employed by the alleged employer, and has good cause to quit said employer; either party shall have the right of appeal to the county court, pending which the alleged deserter shall be remanded to the alleged employer or otherwise disposed of, as shall be right and just; and the decision of the county court shall be final. . . .

Sec. 9. . . . If any person shall persuade or attempt to persuade, entice, or cause any freedman, free negro, or mulatto to desert from the legal employment of any person before the expiration of his or her term of service, or shall knowingly employ any such deserting freedman, free negro, or mulatto, or shall knowingly give or sell to any such deserting freedman, free negro, or mulatto, any food, raiment, or other thing, he or she shall be guilty of a misdemeanor, and, upon conviction, shall be fined not less than twenty-five dollars and not more than two hundred dollars and the costs; and if said fine and costs shall not be immediately paid, the court shall sentence said convict to not exceeding two months' imprisonment in the county jail, and he or she shall moreover be liable to the party injured in damages: *Provided,* if any person shall, or shall attempt to, persuade, entice, or cause any freedman, free negro, or mulatto to desert from any legal employment of any person, with the view to employ said freedman, free negro, or mulatto without the limits of this State, such person, on conviction, shall be fined not less than fifty dollars, and not more than five hundred dollars and costs; and if said fine and costs shall not be immediately paid, the court shall sentence said convict to not exceeding six months imprisonment in the county jail. . . .

2. Mississippi Apprentice Law

Sec. 1. . . . It shall be the duty of all sheriffs, justices of the peace, and other civil officers of the several counties in this State, to report to the probate courts of their respective counties semi-annually, at the January and July terms of said courts, all freedmen, free negroes, and mulattoes, under the age of eighteen, in their respective counties, beats or districts, who are orphans, or whose parent or parents have not the means or who refuse to provide for and support said minors; and thereupon it shall be the duty of said probate court to order the clerk of said court to apprentice said minors to some competent and suitable person, on such terms as the court may direct, having a particular care to the interest of said minor: *Provided,* that the former owner of said minors shall have the preference when, in the opinion of the court, he or she shall be a suitable person for that purpose.

Sec. 2. . . . The said court shall be fully satisfied that the person or persons to whom said minor shall be apprenticed shall be a suitable person to have the charge and care of said minor, and fully to protect the interest of said minor. The said court shall require the said master or mistress to execute bond and security, payable to the State of Mississippi, conditioned that he or she shall furnish said minor with sufficient food and clothing; to treat said minor humanely; furnish medical attention in case of sickness; teach, or cause to be taught, him or her to read and write, if under fifteen years old, and will conform to any law that may be hereafter passed for the regulation of the duties and relation of master and apprentice. . . .

Sec. 3. . . . In the management and control of said apprentice, said master or mistress shall have the power to inflict such moderate corporal chastisement as a father or guardian is allowed to inflict on his or her child or ward at common law: *Provided,* that in no case shall cruel or inhuman punishment be inflicted.

Sec. 4. . . . If any apprentice shall leave the employment of his or her master or mistress, without his or her consent, said master or mistress may pursue and recapture said apprentice, and bring him or her before any justice of the peace of the county, whose duty it shall be to remand said apprentice to the service of his or her master or mistress; and in the event of a refusal on the part of said apprentice so to return, then said justice shall commit said apprentice to the jail of said county, on failure to give bond, to the next term of the county court; and it shall be the duty of said court at the first term thereafter to investigate said case, and if the court shall be of opinion that said apprentice left the employment of his or her master or mistress without good cause, to order him or her to be punished, as provided for the punishment of hired freedmen, as may be from time to time provided for by law for desertion, until he or she shall agree to return to the service of his or her master or mistress: . . . if the court shall believe that said apprentice had good cause to quit his said master or mistress, the court shall discharge said apprentice from said indenture, and also enter a judgment against the master or mistress for not more than one hundred dollars, for the use and benefit of said apprentice. . . .

3. Mississippi Vagrant Law

Sec. 1. *Be it enacted,* etc., . . . That all rogues and vagabonds, idle and dissipated persons, beggars, jugglers, or persons practicing unlawful games or plays, runaways, common drunkards, common night-walkers, pilferers, lewd, wanton, or lascivious persons, in speech or behavior, common railers and brawlers, persons who neglect their calling or employment, misspend what they earn, or do not provide for the support of themselves or their families, or dependents, and all other idle and disorderly persons, including all who neglect all lawful business, habitually misspend their time by frequenting houses of ill-fame, gaming-houses, or tippling shops, shall be deemed and considered vagrants, under the provisions of this act, and upon conviction thereof shall be fined not exceeding one hundred dollars, with all accruing costs, and be imprisoned at the discretion of the court, not exceeding ten days.

Sec. 2. . . . All freedmen, free negroes and mulattoes in this State, over the age of eighteen years, found on the second Monday in January, 1866, or thereafter, with no lawful employment or business, or found unlawfully assembling themselves together, either in the day or night time, and all white persons so assembling themselves with freedmen, free negroes or mulattoes, or usually associating with freedmen, free negroes or mulattoes, on terms of equality, or living in adultery or fornication with a freed woman, free negro or mulatto, shall be deemed vagrants, and on conviction thereof shall be fined in a sum not exceeding, in the case of a freedman, free negro or mulatto, fifty dollars, and a white man two hundred dollars, and imprisoned at the discretion of the court, the free negro not exceeding ten days, and the white man not exceeding six months. . . .

Sec. 7. . . . If any freedman, free negro, or mulatto shall fail or refuse to pay any tax levied according to the provisions of the sixth section of this act, it shall be *prima facie* evidence of vagrancy, and it shall be the duty of the sheriff to arrest such freedman, free negro, or mulatto or such person refusing or neglecting to pay such tax, and proceed at once to hire for the shortest time such delinquent tax-payer to any one who will pay the said tax, with accruing costs, giving preference to the employer, if there be one. . . .

4. Penal Laws of Mississippi

Sec. 1. *Be it enacted,* . . . That no freedman, free negro or mulatto, not in the military service of the United States government, and not licensed so to do by the board of police of his or her county, shall keep or carry fire-arms of any kind, or any ammunition, dirk or bowie knife, and on conviction thereof in the county court shall be punished by fine, not exceeding ten dollars, and pay the costs of such proceedings, and all such arms or ammunition shall be forfeited to the informer; and it shall be the duty of every civil and military officer to arrest any freedman, free negro, or mulatto found with any such arms or ammunition, and cause him or her to be committed to trial in default of bail.

[Sec.] 2. . . . Any freedman, free negro, or mulatto committing riots, routs, affrays, trespasses, malicious mischief, cruel treatment to animals, seditious speeches, insulting gestures, language, or acts, or assaults on any person, disturbance of the peace, exercising the function of a minister of the Gospel without a license from some regularly organized church, vending spirituous or intoxicating liquors, or committing any other misdemeanor, the punishment of which is not specifically provided for by law, shall, upon conviction thereof in the county court, be fined not less than ten dollars, and not more than one hundred dollars, and may be imprisoned at the discretion of the court, not exceeding thirty days.

Sec. 3. . . . If any white person shall sell, lend, or give to any freedman, free negro, or mulatto any fire-arms, dirk or bowie knife, or ammunition, or any spirituous or intoxicating liquors, such person or persons so offending, upon conviction thereof in the county court of his or her county, shall be fined not exceeding fifty dollars, and may be imprisoned, at the discretion of the court, not exceeding thirty days. . . .

Sec. 5. . . . If any freedman, free negro, or mulatto, convicted of any of the misdemeanors provided against in this act, shall fail or refuse for the space of five days, after conviction, to pay the fine and costs imposed, such person shall be hired out by the sheriff or other officer, at public outcry, to any white person who will pay said fine and all costs, and take said convict for the shortest time.

Johnson's Policies Criticized

JAMES W. HUNNICUTT

Mr. [Jacob] Howard: What is the effect of President Johnson's policy of reconstruction there? [South Carolina]—*A.:* . . . They are all in favor of President Johnson's policy of reconstruction. As soon as they get their ends served by him they would not touch him, but he is their man now. They say that in 1868 the South will be a unit, and that with the help of the copperhead party of the North they will elect a President. They do not care to have slavery back, but they will try and make the federal government pay them for their slaves. A man from Virginia told me today that they would be paid for their Negroes. This gentleman lost forty Negroes. This is their idea; they do not want slavery back, but they want to be paid for their slaves. They say that unless you accept their debt they will repudiate yours. They say they are not interested in this government.

Q.: They would be glad to have Uncle Sam assume the payment of the Confederate debt?—*A.:* Yes, sir, and to pay them for their Negroes and to indemnify them for their loss of property in the war. It is an impression of most of them, men, women, and children, that they are going to be paid for every rail burned, for every stick of timber destroyed, and for every Negro lost. One man told me in my house that as soon as they could get the reins of government in their hands they would undo everything that this administration has done, with an awful adjective prefixed to the word "administration." He said, "We have as much right to undo what the administration has done as they have to destroy the government of the Constitution"— as they claim the administration has done.

Q.: They propose to get back into the Union for the purpose of restoring the Constitution?—*A.:* Yes, sir; and the testimony of the Negroes will not be worth a snap of your finger, and all this is done for policy. A Negro can come and give his testimony, and it passes for what it is worth with the courts. They can do what they please with it; there are the judges, the lawyers, and the jury against the Negro, and

Report of the Joint Committee on Reconstruction (Washington, DC: Government Printing Office, 1866), pt. 2, pp. 150–51.

perhaps every one of them is sniggering and laughing while the Negro is giving his testimony.

Q.: Has not the liberal policy of President Johnson in granting pardons and amnesties rather tended to soothe and allay their feelings towards the government of the United States?—*A.:* No, sir, not towards the government of the United States nor towards the Union men.

Q.: What effect has it had in that respect?—*A.:* It has made them more impudent. They were once humble and felt that they had done wrong, but this policy has emboldened them, and they are more impudent today, more intolerant, and more proscriptive than they were in 1864. They say that we are the traitors and went over to the damned Yankees. Our present mayor [of Fredericksburg] Slaughter, had sixty men of Grant's army, who were wounded in the wilderness and sent to Fredericksburg, forwarded to General [Robert E.] Lee as prisoners-of-war. When Fredericksburg fell into our hands Slaughter made his escape. The federals arrested sixty citizens of Fredericksburg to be held as hostages for these sixty soldiers whom Slaughter had sent to the enemy, and among them was my wife's brother, who was living in Fredericksburg, and yet that same Slaughter was reelected mayor of Fredericksburg last summer after the collapse of the rebellion. Old Tom Barton, the commonwealth's attorney, said in 1861 (and I suppose his feelings are the same still) that all these Union shriekers ought to be hung as high as Haman, and this old man was reelected commonwealth attorney by the people of the county. Every member of the rebel common council was reelected. One of the men who were elected members of the common council from that district stated that none of the Union men who went over to the Yankees during the war should be allowed to return to Fredericksburg; he was also appointed director of a bank there. These are the men we have got over us, and what kind of justice can we expect in the courts?

Q.: You will probably get pretty summary justice?—*A.:* I think so; these are facts.

Q.: Where is Slaughter now?—*A.:* He is now mayor of Fredericksburg and will be reelected next month; we need not run a Union man there; we are disfranchised.

Q.: Is not Slaughter a good Union man?—*A.:* Oh! He has been notoriously Union all the time, as the papers say—notoriously Union! I saw that stated in a Fredericksburg paper; it stated that they had been persecuting Mayor Slaughter, who had been notoriously Union all the time.

Q.: You have not a great deal of confidence in the truthfulness of secession?—*A.:* No, sir; I have not.

Q.: Where their political standing is concerned?—*A.:* I used to have some confidence, not in secession, but in the people; but it seems to me that their whole nature and character has been changed, and that when treason enters a man's heart, every virtue he has departs.

Q.: Could Jefferson Davis be convicted of treason in that part of Virginia?—*A.:* As I went home last Sunday week in the boat, I was in company with a delegation from the Virginia legislature which waited upon President Johnson, and I heard one of them say that there could not be a jury obtained south of the Potomac who would convict Jeff Davis, and that the man who would write down there that Jeff Davis should be punished would be in danger. Jeff Davis cannot be punished down there, and they would elect Lee tomorrow, if there were no difficulty in the way, governor of Virginia. There is no question about that in my mind.

Q.: Do you think of anything that you wish to relate?—*A.:* No, sir; I simply wish to state that I make these remarks conscientiously. I was born and raised in the South; my interests of every kind, social, financial, religious and political, are in the South; my church is in the South, and I am going soon to Richmond to edit a paper. Nothing but the good of the country, my own safety, and the safety of my children, and of Union men and of freedmen, could have induced me to come before you and make this statement. I am a friend of the South. I have written for the South, and I shall write in behalf of the South, but the South is one thing, and traitors and treason in the South are different things.

White People Must Regain Control of Their States

EDITOR, *ATLANTA NEWS*

Let there be White Leagues formed in every town, village and hamlet of the South, and let us organize for the great struggle which seems inevitable. If the October elections which are to be held at the North are favorable to the radicals, the time will have arrived for us to prepare for the very worst. The radicalism of the republican party must be met by the radicalism of white men. We have no war to make against the United States Government, but against the republican party our hate must be unquenchable, our war interminable and merciless. Fast fleeting away is the day of wordy protests and idle appeals to the magnanimity of the republican party. By brute force they are endeavoring to force us into acquiescence to their hideous programme. We have submitted long enough to indignities, and it is time to meet brute-force with brute-force. Every Southern State should swarm with White Leagues, and we should stand ready to act the moment [President Ulysses S.] Grant signs the civil-rights bill.[1] It will not do to wait till radicalism has fettered us to the car of social equality before we make an effort to resist it. The signing of the bill will be a declaration of war against the southern whites. It is our duty to ourselves, it is our duty to our children, it is our duty to the white race whose prowess subdued the wilderness of this continent, whose civilization filled it with cities and towns and villages, whose mind gave it power and grandeur, and whose labor imparted to it prosperity, and whose love made peace and happiness dwell within its homes, to take the gage of battle the moment it is thrown down. If the white democrats of the

Walter L. Fleming, ed., *Documentary History of Reconstruction: Political, Military, and Industrial, 1865 to the Present Time* (Cleveland: The Arthur H. Clark Company, 1907), vol. 2, pp. 387–88.
[1]A bill proposed by Charles Sumner in 1870–71 that sought to guarantee blacks non-segregated, equal access to all public accommodations—ED.

North are men, they will not stand idly by and see us borne down by northern radicals and half-barbarous negroes. But no matter what they may do, it is time for us to organize. We have been temporizing long enough. Let northern radicals understand that military supervision of southern elections and the civil-rights bill mean war, that war means bloodshed, and that we are terribly in earnest, and even they, fanatical as they are, may retrace their steps before it is too late.

Organization and Principles of the Ku Klux Klan (1868)

Organization and Principles of the Ku Klux Klan

Appellation

This Organization shall be styled and denominated, the Order of the * * *

Creed

We, the Order of the * * * , reverentially acknowledge the majesty and supremacy of the Divine Being, and recognize the goodness and providence of the same. And we recognize our relation to the United States Government, the supremacy of the Constitution, the Constitutional Laws thereof, and the Union of States thereunder.

Character and Objects of the Order

This is an institution of Chivalry, Humanity, Mercy, and Patriotism; embodying in its genius and its principles all that is chivalric in conduct, noble in sentiment, generous in manhood, and patriotic in purpose; its peculiar objects being

First: To protect the weak, the innocent, and the defenseless, from the indignities, wrongs, and outrages of the lawless, the violent, and the brutal; to relieve the injured and oppressed; to succor the suffering and unfortunate, and especially the widows and orphans of Confederate soldiers.

Second: To protect and defend the Constitution of the United States, and all laws passed in conformity thereto, and to protect the States and the people thereof from all invasion from any source whatever.

Third: To aid and assist in the execution of all constitutional laws, and to protect the people from unlawful seizure, and from trial except by their peers in conformity to the laws of the land.

Titles

Sec. 1. The officers of this Order shall consist of a Grand Wizard of the Empire, and his ten Genii; a Grand Dragon of the Realm, and his eight Hydras: a Grand Titan of the Dominion, and his six Furies; a Grand Giant of the Province, and his four Goblins; a Grand Cyclops of the Den, and his two Night Hawks; a Grand Magi, a Grand Monk, a Grand Scribe, a Grand Exchequer, a Grand Turk, and a Grand Sentinel.

U.S. 42nd Congress, 2nd Session, Senate Report, No. 41 on the Ku Klux Klan, Washington, DC, 1871.

Sec. 2. The body politic of this Order shall be known and designated as "Ghouls."

Territory and its Divisions

Sec. 1. The territory embraced within the jurisdiction of this Order shall be coterminous with the States of Maryland, Virginia. North Carolina, South Carolina, Georgia, Florida, Alabama, Mississippi, Louisiana, Texas, Arkansas, Missouri, Kentucky, and Tennessee; all combined constituting the Empire.

Sec. 2. The Empire shall be divided into four departments, the first to be styled the Realm, and coterminous with the boundaries of the several States; the second to be styled the Dominion and to be coterminous with such counties as the Grand Dragons of the several Realms may assign to the charge of the Grand Titan. The third to be styled the Province, and to be coterminous with the several counties: *provided* the Grand Titan may, when he deems it necessary, assign two Grand Giants to one Province, prescribing, at the same time, the jurisdiction of each. The fourth department to be styled the Den, and shall embrace such part of a Province as the Grand Giant shall assign to the charge of a Grand Cyclops. . . .

Interrogations to be Asked

1st. Have you ever been rejected, upon application for membership in the * * * , or have you ever been expelled from the same?

2d. Are you now, or have you ever been, a member of the Radical Republican party, or either of the organizations known as the "Loyal League" and the "Grand Army of the Republic?"

3d. Are you opposed to the principles and policy of the Radical party, and to the Loyal League, and the Grand Army of the Republic, so far as you are informed of the character and purposes of those organizations?

4th. Did you belong to the Federal army during the late war, and fight against the South during the existence of the same?

5th. Are you opposed to negro equality, both social and political?

6th. Are you in favor of a white man's government in this country?

7th. Are you in favor of Constitutional liberty, and a Government of equitable laws instead of a Government of violence and oppression?

8th. Are you in favor of maintaining the Constitutional rights of the South?

9th. Are you in favor of the re-enfranchisement and emancipation of the white men of the South, and the restitution of the Southern people to all their rights, alike proprietary, civil, and political?

10th. Do you believe in the inalienable right of self-preservation of the people against the exercise of arbitrary and unlicensed power? . . .

. . . 9. The most profound and rigid secrecy concerning any and everything that relates to the Order, shall at all times be maintained.

10. Any member who shall reveal or betray the secrets of this Order, shall suffer the extreme penalty of the law.

16.3:   The Black Response (1865, 1868, 1866)

Emancipation and Union victory liberated almost 4 million black Americans from bondage. What role would they now play in the life of their region? Would they be citizens and voters? How would they earn a living? What claim did they have on their communities for education and other services? These and other questions confronted northern policy makers and voters after Confederate defeat.

To educated blacks, many of them former "free people of color," the most important right that the government could confer was that of suffrage, the right to vote. In the first selection below, Frederick Douglass, the prominent black abolitionist, argues for the necessity of giving the vote to the newly freed slaves. What are Douglass's arguments? This address was greeted with applause by his audience, but he was speaking to a Boston abolitionist convention. How do you think white southerners felt about suffrage for blacks? Do you know how most white northerners felt about giving black men the vote at this time—Douglass's Boston audience notwithstanding? Note Douglass's reference to woman suffrage. Why does he believe black males should be given the vote before white women?

The second selection is an excerpt from a debate at the 1868 South Carolina constitutional convention, which was called after Congress refused to accept the state's "Johnson government" and established stricter rules for southern readmission to the Union.

One of the many topics the convention delegates debated was land ownership. If conservative southern whites sought to reestablish a system of near slavery, blacks and some of their Radical defenders wanted what seemed to many contemporaries to be the other extreme: to create a black farm-owner class by redistributing white-owned land. The participants in the selection below are Richard H. Cain, a black minister originally from New York; Francis L. Cardozo, a South Carolinian of mixed race, also a minister; and N. G. Parker and C. P. Leslie, white carpetbaggers. Their debate focuses on a resolution asking the federal Congress to appropriate $1 million to be used to buy small homesteads for South Carolina freed men and women. What are the arguments pro and con? What is the reference to "confiscation"? Congress never made the appropriation.

Can you guess why from the evidence in this debate? What would have been the advantage to the nation at large if ideas such as Cardozo's and Cain's had been enacted?

The third selection adds education to the "wish list" of Southern blacks during Reconstruction. Why were they so eager for education? Did they have access to education in slave days? Was their faith in education as salvation part of the American tradition? Was it misguided or exaggerated?

What the Black Man Wants

FREDERICK DOUGLASS

MR. PRESIDENT,—I came here [to the annual meeting of the Massachusetts Anti-Slavery Society at Boston], as I come always to the meetings in New England, as a listener, and not as a speaker; and one of the reasons why I have not been more frequently to the meetings of this society, has been because of the disposition on the part of some of my friends to call me out upon the platform, even when they knew that there was some difference of opinion and of feeling between those who rightfully belong to this platform and myself; and for fear of being misconstrued, as desiring to interrupt or disturb the proceedings of these meetings, I have usually kept away, and have thus been deprived of that educating influence, which I am always free to confess is of the highest order, descending from this platform. I have felt, since I have lived out West, that in going there I parted from a great deal that was valuable; and I feel, every time I come to these meetings, that I have lost a great deal by making my home west of Boston, west of Massachusetts; for, if anywhere in the country there is to be found the highest sense of justice, or the truest demands for my race, I look for it in the East, I look for it here. The ablest discussions of the whole question of our rights occur here, and to be deprived of the privilege of listening to those discussions is a great deprivation.

I do not know, from what has been said, that there is any difference of opinion as to the duty of abolitionists, at the present moment. How can we get up any difference at this point, or at any point, where we are so united, so agreed? I went especially, however, with that word of Mr. [Wendell] Phillips, which is the criticism of Gen. Banks and Gen. Banks's policy. I hold that that policy is our chief danger at the present moment; that it practically enslaves the negro, and makes the [Emancipation] Proclamation of 1863 a mockery and delusion. What is freedom? It is the right to choose one's own employment. Certainly it means that, if it means any thing; and when any individual or combination of individuals, undertakes to decide for any man when he shall work, where he shall work, at what he shall work, and for what he shall work, he or they practically reduce him to slavery. (Applause.) He is a slave. That I understand Gen. Banks to do—to determine for the so-called freedman, when, and where, and at what, and for how much he shall work, when he shall be punished, and by whom punished. It is absolute slavery. It defeats the

William D. Kelley, Wendell Phillips, and Frederick Douglass, *The Equality of Men before the Law Claimed and Defended* (Boston: n.p., 1865), pp. 36–39.

beneficent intentions of the Government, if it has beneficent intentions, in regard to the freedom of our people.

I have had but one idea for the last three years, to present to the American people, and the phraseology in which I clothe it is the old abolition phraseology. I am for the "immediate, unconditional, and universal" enfranchisement of the black man, in every State in the Union. (Loud applause.) Without this, his liberty is a mockery; without this, you might as well almost retain the old name of slavery for his condition; for, in fact, if he is not the slave of the individual master, he is the slave of society, and holds his liberty as a privilege, not as a right. He is at the mercy of the mob, and has no means of protecting himself.

It may be objected, however, that this pressing of the negro's right to suffrage is premature. Let us have slavery abolished, it may be said, let us have labor organized, and then, in the natural course of events, the right of suffrage will be extended to the negro. I do not agree with this. The constitution of the human mind is such, that if it once disregards the conviction forced upon it by a revelation of truth, it requires the exercise of a higher power to produce the same conviction afterwards. The American people are now in tears. The Shenandoah has run blood—the best blood of the North. All around Richmond, the blood of New England and of the North has been shed—of your sons, your brothers and your fathers. We all feel, in the existence of this Rebellion, that judgments terrible, wide-spread, far-reaching, overwhelming, are abroad in the land; and we feel, in view of these judgments, just now, a disposition to learn righteousness. This is the hour. Our streets are in mourning, tears are falling at every fireside, and under the chastisement of this Rebellion we have almost come up to the point of conceding this great, this all-important right of suffrage. I fear that if we fail to do it now, if abolitionists fail to press it now, we may not see, for centuries to come, the same disposition that exists at this moment. (Applause.) Hence, I say, now is the time to press this right.

It may be asked, "Why do you want it? Some men have got along very well without it. Women have not this right." Shall we justify one wrong by another? That is a sufficient answer. Shall we at this moment justify the deprivation of the negro of the right to vote, because some one else is deprived of that privilege? I hold that women, as well as men, have the right to vote (applause), and my heart and my voice go with the movement to extend suffrage to woman; but that question rests upon another basis than that on which our right rests. We may be asked, I say, why we want it. I will tell you why we want it. We want it because it is our *right,* first of all. (Applause.) No class of men can, without insulting their own nature, be content with any deprivation of their rights. We want it, again, as a means for educating our race. Men are so constituted that they derive their conviction of their own possibilities largely from the estimate formed of them by others. If nothing is expected of a people, that people will find it difficult to contradict that expectation. By depriving us of suffrage, you affirm our incapacity to form an intelligent judgment respecting public men and public measures; you declare before the world that we are unfit to exercise the elective franchise, and by this means lead us to undervalue ourselves, to put a low estimate upon ourselves, and to feel that we have no possibilities like other men. Again, I want the elective franchise, for one, as a colored man, because ours is a peculiar government, based upon a peculiar idea, and that idea is universal suffrage. If I were in a monarchical government, or an autocratic or aristocratic government, where the few bore rule and the many were subject, there would be no special stigma resting upon me, because I did not exercise the elective franchise. It would do me no great violence. Mingling with the mass, I should partake of the strength of the mass; I should be supported by the mass, and I should have the same incentives to endeavor with the mass of my fellow-men; it would be no particular burden, no particular deprivation; but here, where universal suffrage is the rule, where that is the fundamental idea of the Government, to rule us out is to make us an exception, to brand us with the stigma of inferiority, and to invite to our heads the missiles of those about us; therefore, I want the franchise for the black man.

There are, however, other reasons, not derived from any consideration merely of our rights, but arising out of the condition of the South, and of the country—considerations which have already been referred to by Mr. Phillips—considerations which must arrest the attention of statesmen. I believe that when the tall heads of this Rebellion shall have been swept down, as they will be swept down, when the [Jefferson] Davises and [Robert] Toombses and [Alexander] Stephenses, and others who are leading in this Rebellion shall have been blotted out, there will be this rank undergrowth of treason, to which reference has been made, growing up there, and interfering with, and thwarting the quiet operation of the Federal Government in those States. You will see those traitors handing down, from sire to son, the same malignant spirit which they have manifested, and which they are now exhibiting, with malicious hearts, broad blades, and bloody hands in the field, against our sons and brothers. That spirit will still remain; and whoever sees the Federal Government extended over those Southern States will see that Government in a strange land, and not only in a strange land, but in an enemy's land. A post-master of the United States in the South will find himself surrounded by a hostile spirit; a collector in a Southern port will find himself surrounded by a hostile spirit; a United States marshal or United States judge will be surrounded there by a hostile element. That enmity will not die out in a year, will not die out in an age. The Federal Government will be looked upon in those States precisely as the Governments of Austria and France are looked upon in Italy at the present moment. They will endeavor to circumvent, they will endeavor to destroy, the peaceful operation of this Government. Now, where will you find the strength to counterbalance this spirit, if you do not find it in the negroes of the South? They are your friends, and have always been your friends. They were your friends even when the Government did not regard them as such. They comprehended the genius of this war before you did. It is a significant fact, it is a marvellous fact, it seems almost to imply a direct interposition of Providence, that this war, which began in the interest of slavery on both sides, bids fair to end in the interest of liberty on both sides. (Applause.) It was begun, I say, in the interest of slavery on both sides. The South was fighting to take slavery out of the Union, and the North fighting to keep it in the Union; the South fighting to get it beyond the limits of the United-States Constitution, and the North fighting to retain it within those limits; the South fighting for new guarantees, and the North fighting for the old guarantees;—both despising the negro, both insulting the negro.

Yet, the negro, apparently endowed with wisdom from on high, saw more clearly the end from the beginning than we did. When [William] Seward said the status of no man in the country would be changed by the war, the negro did not believe him. (Applause.) When our generals sent their underlings in shoulder-straps to hunt the flying negro back from our lines into the jaws of slavery, from which he had escaped, the negroes thought that a mistake had been made, and that the intentions of the Government had not been rightly understood by our officers in shoulder-straps, and they continued to come into our lines, threading their way through bogs and fens, over briers and thorns, fording streams, swimming rivers, bringing us tidings as to the safe path to march, and pointing out the dangers that threatened us. They are our only friends in the South, and we should be true to them in this their trial hour, and see to it that they have the elective franchise.

I know that we are inferior to you in some things—virtually inferior. We walk about among you like dwarfs among giants. Our heads are scarcely seen above the great sea of humanity. The Germans are superior to us; the Irish are superior to us; the Yankees are superior to us (laughter); they can do what we cannot, that is, what we have not hitherto been allowed to do. But while I make this admission, I utterly deny that we are originally, or naturally, or practically, or in any way, or in any important sense, inferior to anybody on this globe. (Loud applause.) This charge of inferiority is an old dodge. It has been made available for oppression on many occasions. It is only about six centuries since the blue-eyed and fair-haired Anglo-Saxons were considered inferior by the haughty Normans, who once trampled upon them. If you read the history of the Norman Conquest, you will find that this proud Anglo-Saxon was once looked upon as of coarser clay than his Norman master, and might be found in the highways and byways of old England laboring with a brass collar on his neck, and the name of his master marked upon it. *You* were down then! (Laughter and applause.) You are up now. I am glad you are up, and I want you to be glad to help us up also. (Applause.)

The story of our inferiority is an old dodge, as I have said; for wherever men oppress their fellows, wherever they enslave them, they will endeavor to find the needed apology for such enslavement and oppression in the character of the people oppressed and enslaved. When we wanted, a few years ago, a slice of Mexico, it was hinted that the Mexicans were an inferior race, that the old Castilian blood had become so weak that it would scarcely run down hill, and that Mexico needed the long, strong and beneficent arm of the Anglo-Saxon care extended over it. We said that it was necessary to its salvation, and a part of the "manifest destiny" of this Republic, to extend our arm over that dilapidated government. So, too, when Russia wanted to take possession of a part of the Ottoman Empire, the Turks were "an inferior race." So, too, when England wants to set the heel of her power more firmly in the quivering heart of old Ireland, the Celts are an "inferior race." So, too, the negro, when he is to be robbed of any right which is justly his, is an "inferior man." It is said that we are ignorant; I admit it. But if we know enough to be hung, we know enough to vote. If the negro knows enough to pay taxes to support the government, he knows enough to vote; taxation and representation should go together. If he knows enough to shoulder a musket and fight for the flag, fight for the government, he knows enough to vote. If he knows as much when he is sober as an Irishman knows when drunk, he knows enough to vote, on good American principles. (Laughter and applause.)

But I was saying that you needed a counterpoise in the persons of the slaves to the enmity that would exist at the South after the Rebellion is put down. I hold that the American people are bound, not only in self-defence, to extend this right to the freedmen of the South, but they are bound by their love of country, and by all their regard for the future safety of those Southern States, to do this—to do it as a measure essential to the preservation of peace there. But I will not dwell upon this. I put it to the American sense of honor. The honor of a nation is an important thing. It is said in the Scriptures, "What doth it profit a man if he gain the whole world and lose his own soul?" It may be said, also, What doth it profit a nation if it gain the whole world, but lose its honor? I hold that the American government has taken upon itself a solemn obligation of honor, to see that this war—let it be long or let it be short, let it cost much or let it cost little—that this war shall not cease until every freedman at the South has the right to vote. (Applause.) It has bound itself to it. What have you asked the black men of the South, the black men of the whole country, to do? Why, you have asked them to incur the deadly enmity of their masters, in order to befriend you and to befriend this Government. You have asked us to call down, not only upon ourselves, but upon our children's children, the deadly hate of the entire Southern people. You have called upon us to turn our backs upon our masters, to abandon their cause and espouse yours; to turn against the South and in favor of the North; to shoot down the Confederacy and uphold the flag—the American flag. You have called upon us to expose ourselves to all the subtle machinations of their malignity for all time. And now, what do you propose to do when you come to make peace? To reward your enemies, and trample in the dust your friends? Do you intend to sacrifice the very men who have come to the rescue of your banner in the South, and incurred the lasting displeasure of their masters thereby? Do you intend to sacrifice them and reward your enemies? Do you mean to give your enemies the right to vote, and take it away from your friends? Is that wise policy? Is that honorable? Could American honor withstand such a blow? I do not believe you will do it. I think you will see to it that we have the right to vote. There is something too mean in looking upon the negro, when you are in trouble, as a citizen, and when you are free from trouble, as an alien. When this nation was in trouble, in its early struggles, it looked upon the negro as a citizen. In 1776 he was a citizen. At the time of the formation of the Constitution the negro had the right to vote in eleven States out of the old thirteen. In your trouble you have made us citizens. In 1812 Gen. [Andrew] Jackson addressed us as citizens—"fellow-citizens." He wanted us to fight. We were citizens then! And now, when you come to frame a conscription bill, the negro is a citizen again. He has been a citizen just three times in the history of this government, and it has always been in time of trouble. In time of trouble we are citizens. Shall we be citizens in war, and aliens in peace? Would that be just?

I ask my friends who are apologizing for not insisting upon this right, where can the black man look, in this country, for the assertion of this right, if he may not look to the Massachusetts Anti-Slavery Society? Where under the whole heavens can he look for sympathy, in asserting this right, if he may not look to this platform? Have you lifted us up to a certain height to see that we are men, and then are any disposed to leave us there, without seeing that we are put in possession of all our rights? We look naturally to this platform for the assertion of all our rights, and for this one especially. I understand the anti-slavery societies of this country to be based on two principles,—first, the freedom of the blacks of this country; and, second, the elevation of them. Let me not be misunderstood here. I am not asking for sympathy at the hands of abolitionists, sympathy at the hands of any. I think the American people are disposed often to be generous rather than just. I look over this country at the present time, and I see Educational Societies, Sanitary Commissions, Freedmen's Associations, and the like,—all very good: but in regard to the colored people there is always more that is benevolent, I perceive, than just, manifested towards us. What I ask for the negro is not benevolence, not pity, not sympathy, but simply *justice*. (Applause.) The American people have always been anxious to know what they shall do with us. Gen. Banks was distressed with solicitude as to what he should do with the negro. Everybody has asked the question, and they learned to ask it early of the abolitionists, "What shall we do with the negro?" I have had but one answer from the beginning. Do nothing with us! Your doing with us has already played the mischief with us. Do nothing with us! If the apples will not remain on the tree of their own strength, if they are worm-eaten at the core, if they are early ripe and disposed to fall, let them fall! I am not for tying or fastening them on the tree in any way, except by nature's plan, and if they will not stay there, let them fall. And if the negro cannot stand on his own legs, let him fall also. All I ask is, give him a chance to stand on his own legs! Let him alone! If you see him on his way to school, let him alone,—don't disturb him! If you see him going to the dinner-table at a hotel, let him go! If you see him going to the ballot-box, let him alone,—don't disturb him! (Applause.) If you see him going into a work-shop, just let him alone,—your interference is doing him a positive injury. Gen. Banks's "preparation" is of a piece with this attempt to prop up the negro. Let him fall if he cannot stand alone! If the negro cannot live by the line of eternal justice, so beautifully pictured to you in the illustration used by Mr. Phillips, the fault will not be yours, it will be his who made the negro, and established that line for his government. (Applause.) Let him live or die by that. If you will only untie his hands, and give him a chance, I think he will live. He will work as readily for himself as the white man. A great many delusions have been swept away by this war. One was, that the negro would not work; he has proved his ability to work. Another was, that the negro would not fight; that he possessed only the most sheepish attributes of humanity; was a perfect lamb, or an "Uncle Tom"; disposed to take off his coat whenever required, fold his hands, and be whipped by anybody who wanted to whip him. But the war has proved that there is a great deal of human nature in the negro, and that "he will fight," as Mr. Quincy, our President, said, in earlier days than these, "when there is a reasonable probability of his whipping anybody." (Laughter and applause.)

The Ex-Slaves Should Have Land

Mr. [Richard H.] Cain: I offer this resolution with good intentions. I believe that there is need for immediate relief to the poor people of the State. I know from my experience among the people, there is a pressing need of some measures to meet the wants of the utterly destitute. The gentleman [C. P. Leslie] says that it will only take money out of the Treasury. Well, that is the intention. I do not expect to get it any-where else. I expect to get the money, if at all, through the Treasury of the United States, or some other department. It certainly must come out of the Government. I believe such an appropriation would remove a great many of the difficulties now in the State and do a vast amount of good to poor people. It may be that we will not get it, but that will not debar us from asking. It is our privilege and right. Other Conven-tions have asked from Congress appropriations. Georgia and other States have sent in their petitions. One has asked for $30,000,000 to be appropriated to the Southern States. I do not see any inconsistency in the proposition presented by myself.

Mr. C. P. Leslie: Suppose I should button up my coat and march up to your house and ask you for money or provisions, when you had none to give, what would you think of me.

Mr. Cain: You would do perfectly right to run the chance of getting something to eat. This is a measure of relief to those thousands of freed people who now have no lands of their own. I believe the possession of lands and homesteads is one of the best means by which a people is made industrious, honest and advantageous to the State. I believe it is a fact well known, that over three hundred thousand men, women and children are homeless, landless. The abolition of slavery has thrown these people upon their own resources. How are they to live. I know the philosopher of the New York Tribune says, "root hog or die"; but in the meantime we ought to have some place to root. My proposition is simply to give the hog some place to root. I believe if the proposition is sent to Congress, it will certainly receive the at-tention of our friends. I believe the whole country is desirous to see that this State shall return to the Union in peace and quiet, and that every inhabitant of the State shall be made industrious and profitable to the State. I am opposed to this Bureau system.[1] I want a system adopted that will do away with the Bureau, but I cannot see how it can be done unless the people have homes. As long as people are work-ing on shares and contracts, and at the end of every year are in debt, so long will they and the country suffer. But give them a chance to buy lands, and they become steady, industrious men. That is the reason I desire to bring this money here and to assist them to buy lands. . . .

I do not desire to have a foot of land in this State confiscated. I want every man to stand upon his own character. I want these lands purchased by the government, and

---

Proceedings of the Constitutional Convention of South Carolina, 1868 (New York: Arno Press, 1968), pp. 378–424.

[1]Cain probably means the work of the Freedmen's Bureau in negotiating labor contracts for the ex-slaves, contracts that were difficult to enforce—ED.

the people afforded an opportunity to buy from the government. I believe every man ought to carve out for himself a character and position in this life. I believe every man ought to be made to work by some means or other, and if he does not, he must go down. . . . I want to have the satisfaction of showing that the freedmen are as capable and willing to work as any men on the face of the earth. This measure will save the State untold expenses. I believe there are hundreds of persons in the jail and penitentiary cracking rock to-day who have all the instincts of honesty, and who, had they an opportunity of making a living, would never have been found in such a place. I think if Congress will accede to our request, we shall be benefited beyond measure, and save the State from taking charge of paupers, made such by not having the means to earn a living for themselves. . . .

Mr. C. P. Leslie: . . . I assert that time will prove that the petition offered, and the addresses made here to-day, were most inopportune. These addresses have been listened to by a large concourse of spectators, and have held out to them that within a very short time they are to get land. We all know that the colored people want land. Night and day they think and dream of it. It is their all in all. As these men retire from the hall and go home, the first thing they do is to announce to the people "joy on earth, and good will to all mankind." We are all going to have a home. . . . And when I know as they know, that without land a race of people, four millions in number, travelling up and down the earth without a home are suffering, I cannot but denounce those who would, for political purposes, add to their misery by raising expectations that could never be realized. . . .

Let us have a little more light upon the subject. Parson French, who, it is well known, has the welfare of the colored people at heart, did go to Washington and portrayed to leading Senators and members of Congress the terrible predicament of the colored people in the State. He said that cotton had sold so low that all the people were poverty stricken. The white people, he told them, were not able to plant, and there being no necessity to employ laborers, the colored people were turned out of house and home, and he begged them to loan the people, or the State, a million of dollars. Their answer was, "Mr. French, for God's sake, send up no petitions for money, for we cannot give one dollar." . . .

Mr. F[rancis] L. Cardozo: . . . The poor freedmen were induced, by many Congressmen even, to expect confiscation. They held out the hope of confiscation. [Union] General [William Tecumseh] Sherman did confiscate, gave the lands to the freedmen; and if it were not for President Johnson, they would have them now. The hopes of the freedmen have not been realized, and I do not think that asking for a loan of one million, to be paid by a mortgage upon the land, will be half as bad as has been supposed. I have been told by the Assistant Commissioner that he has been doing on a private scale what this petition proposes to do. I say every opportunity for helping the colored man should be seized upon. I think the adoption of this measure will do honor to the Convention. We should certainly vote for some measure of relief for the colored men, as we have to the white men, who mortgaged their property to perpetuate slavery, and whom they have liberated from their bonds.

Mr. N. G. Parker: I am glad that the gentleman who has just taken his seat has distinctly laid down the proposition that any member who votes against this petition votes against the colored man. I am a friend to the colored man, and he knows it. I have a record extending back for twenty years that shows it. . . .

I tell you, Mr. President, that the destitution that prevails this winter in those snow clad [Northern and Western] States is greater than it has ever been before. Thousands, yes millions, are out of employment, and what is the cause of it. I cannot stop now to elaborate the causes, but I will only briefly allude to them. War and its results are directly the cause of it. One of the results of the war, and the principal one, was the overthrow of slavery and tyranny in the Southern States; this was the good result of it; but the expense it caused the nation to do this, and the debt it incurred, and the overthrow of the labor system and consequent disturbance of trade and commerce, was the immediate evils. The burdensome taxation which followed is another principle cause of distress which now prevails in the Northern and Western States. The fact is patent that all the manufacturing States need aid; and let me tell you if the Congress of the United States grants additional aid to any of the unreconstructed States, for anything further than to perfect the reconstruction already half consummated, and the support of the Military and the Freedmen's Bureau, that in my opinion such a howl will go up as never was heard before, and I for one, would despair of success.

Our friends are trembling at Washington to-day, and all over the country, lest New Hampshire should cast a Democratic vote at her approaching election. I am of the opinion that if Congress should pass the appropriation called for just at this particular time, that every State from Maine to California would roll up such a Democrat vote in the coming election that was never heard of, or dreamt of, by the most ardent Democrat in this country. The result of the elections for the last year should not be unheeded.

Where would be our reconstruction if Andrew Johnson and the Democratic party had the handling of us? . . .

The Treasury of the United States has already as many drafts upon it as it can well bear. They have no money to purchase lands in South Carolina to sell on a credit—it is asking too much. Look at the almost overwhelming debt of the nation, and would you colored men, or white men, seek to increase it? For what was it contracted? and what keeps the expenses of Government to-day so large? It was contracted to make you free, and it is continually increased to preserve, protect and defend your freedom.

There never was a more liberal and humane government, nor never one that made such herculian [sic] efforts to retrieve the past as she has made and is making. We cannot ask her to do more than she is doing. There is such a thing as disgusting our friends. Do not let us weary them. If she will continue to afford us the protection she has afforded us in the past three years, if she will continue to the end in sustaining the reconstruction she commenced, if she will sustain the Freedmen's Bureau as long as it is a necessity, and give us the military necessary to protect and defend us, in God's name let us be satisfied. . . .

Mr. R. H. Cain: This measure, if carried out, therefore, will meet a want which the Bureau never can meet. A man may have rations to-day and not tomorrow, but when he gets land and a homestead, and is once fixed on that land, he never will want to go to the Commissary again. It is said that I depicted little farms by the roadside, chickens roosting on the fence, and all those poetical beauties. . . . I prefer this to seeing strong men working for the paltry sum of five or ten dollars a month, and some for even three dollars a month. How can a man live at that rate. I hate the contract system as I hate the being of whom my friend from Orangeburg (Mr. [Benjamin F.] Randolph) spoke last week (the devil). It has ruined the people. After fifty men have gone on a plantation, worked the whole year at raising twenty thousand bushels of rice, and then go to get their one-third, by the time they get through the division, after being charged by the landlord twenty-five or thirty cents a pound for bacon, two or three dollars for a pair of brogans that costs sixty cents, for living that costs a mere song, two dollars a bushel for corn that can be bought for one dollar; after I say, these people have worked the whole season, and at the end make up their accounts, they find themselves in debt. . . . I want to see a change in this country. Instead of the colored people being always penniless, I want to see them coming in with their mule teams and ox teams. I want to see them come with their corn and potatoes and exchange for silks and satins. I want to see school houses and churches in every parish and township. I want to see children coming forth to enjoy life as it ought to be enjoyed. This people know nothing of what is good and best for mankind until they get homesteads and enjoy them.

With these remarks, I close. I hope the Convention will vote for the proposition. Let us send up our petition. The right to petition is a jealous right. It was a right guaranteed to the Barons of England. The American people have always been jealous of that right, and regarded it as sacred and inviolate. That right we propose to maintain. It is said here that some high officers are opposed to it. I do not care who is opposed to it. It is none of their business. I do not care whether General [Robert K.] Scott, General [Ulysses S.] Grant or General anybody else is opposed to it, we will petition in spite of them. I appeal to the delegates to pass this resolution. It will do no harm if it does no good, and I am equally confident that some gentleman will catch what paddy gave the drum when they go back to their constituents.

The Ex-Slaves Crave Education

The Desire of the Blacks for Education

Senate Ex. Doc. no. 27, 39 Cong., 1 Sess. Report of J. W. Alvord, Superintendent of Schools for the Freedmen's Bureau

January 1, 1866

A general desire for education is everywhere manifested. In some instances, as in Halifax county [Virginia], very good schools were found taught and paid for by the colored people themselves. Said a gentleman to me, "I constantly see in the streets and on the door-steps opposite my dwelling groups of little negroes studying their spelling-books." . . .

Walter L. Fleming, ed., *Documentary History of Reconstruction: Political, Military, and Industrial, 1865 to the Present Time* (Cleveland: The Arthur H. Clark Company, 1907), vol. 2, pp. 182–83.

Not only are individuals seen at study, and under the most untoward circumstances, but in very many places I have found what I will call "native schools," often rude and very imperfect, but there they are, a group, perhaps, of all ages, trying to learn. Some young man, some woman, or old preacher, in cellar, or shed, or corner of a negro meeting-house, with the alphabet in hand, or a torn spelling-book, is their teacher. All are full of enthusiasm with the new knowledge the book is imparting to them.

Freedmen's Bureau Schools in North Carolina

Senate Ex. Doc. no. 6, 39 Cong., 2 Sess., p. 104. Report of Gen[eral] John C. Robinson of the Freedmen's Bureau

1866

It is no unfrequent occurrence to witness in the same rooms, and pursuing the same studies, the child and parent—youth and gray hairs—all eagerly grasping for that by which, obtained, they are intellectually regenerated. . . .

As an evidence of the great interest manifested for acquiring knowledge, an instance, probably never before equalled in the history of education, is to be found in one of the schools of this State, where side by side sat representatives of four generations in a direct line, viz.: a child six years old, her mother, grandmother, and great-grandmother, the latter over 75 years of age. All commenced their alphabet together, and each one can read the Bible fluently.

Night schools have met with gratifying success, and are eagerly sought for by those whose labors are of such a character as to prevent their attendance during the day. . . .

Sunday schools have been established at many points where teachers reside. . . . It is evident much good has been accomplished by their establishment, and no estimate can be made of the beneficial results of their full development.